Death by a Thousand Cuts

Islam, Fiscal Irresponsibility, and other Threats to Destroy America

RICHARD HOBBS

ColDoc Publishing, Sparks, Nevada

To Diane, Deanna, Christian, and Lily
With the hope that they will know a world in peace

Books by Richard Hobbs

La Grande Illusion, La Victoire Totale
Notebook and Readings for International Relations, "Operation Statesman," Co-Editor
Readings in International Relations, 2 Volumes, Editor
Operation Statesman, Focus on Southeast Asia, Editor
THE MYTH OF VICTORY What Is Victory In War?
THE NEW WORLD ORDER Tribalism, Nationalism, and Religious Fundamentalism
WORLD WAR IV China's Quest for Power in the 21st Century
YOU AND THE NEW WORLD ORDER How You Can Influence the Alarming and
        Growing International and Domestic Problems
WORLD WAR IV AND BEYOND Islamofascism, the Third Jihad, and other threats to the USA

Published by:

C   **ColDoc Publishing**
    D   Post Office Box 50682
        P   Sparks, Nevada 89435-0682 USA

Copyright © 2012 by Richard Hobbs

Library of Congress Cataloging-in-Publication Data
Hobbs, Richard 1931-
        Death by a Thousand Cuts: Islam, Fiscal Irresponsibility, and other Threats to Destroy America
        / by Richard Hobbs
        First Edition
                p.   cm.
        Includes glossary and index.
        ISBN-10: 0-9647788-8-2   ISBN-13: 978-0-9647788-8-7: $29.95
        1. World Politics -- 21st Century   I. Title.
        2. International Relations
        3. International Relations -- United States
        4. International Relations -- Middle East
        5. International Relations -- Europe
        6. International Relations -- Asia
        7. Islam
        8. US Economy
        9. Illegal Immigration
        9. China
        10. Population
        11. Oil – Water

CONTENTS

DISCLAIMER

The purpose of this book is to educate and to entertain. The author speaks for no organization, political party, or government, US or foreign. The author and ColDoc Publishing shall have neither liability nor responsibility to any person or entity with respect to any loss or damage caused, or alleged to be caused, directly or indirectly by the information contained in this book.

If you do not wish to be bound by the above, you may return this book to the publisher for a full refund.

PREFACE

Islam swept out of Arabia in the 7th Century and in the first great Jihad spread across North Africa to the Atlantic and east as far as Indonesia and north into Southwest Asia. The second Jihad, the Ottoman Empire, swept into Europe but it decayed and faltered and died after World War I. Little was heard about Islam in the early 20th Century, but a renaissance was underway. After World War II, the world was preoccupied with the Cold War, which, since it was extremely expensive, dangerous, and worldwide, was really World War III. Even before the end of World War III, two events reinvigorated the Muslim world: the *mujahedin* resistance against the Soviets in Afghanistan and the rise of a theocratic government in Iran after the fall of the Shah.

The rise of terrorism in the Middle East, some of which was aimed at Israel, alarmed us but we did not really react. It took the attack on 11 September 2001 to get our attention that there are people out there who really would like to destroy the United States and our way of life. Since then we have been in continuous conflict with various Islamic groups. As a country, we have been woefully ignorant about Islam and, unfortunately we still are. That is why Part I of this book is about Islam.

It is not that there is a big secret; the tenets and dogma of Islam, as pronounced by Muhammad and those who wrote of his words and deeds, have not changed in 1,400 years. True Islam is a totalitarian ideology with only a façade of religion and is more a cult of Muhammad, considered by the faithful as the perfect man.

This ideology is totally incompatible with liberty and democracy. We do ourselves a grave disservice when we refuse to recognize the true nature of Islam. Every where it has advanced, all other religions have been annihilated and the populace devolved into a form of mental slavery. This is the long range threat to America and human civilization and must be judged that way.

Part II deals with other threats. The most immediate threat is the terrible mess we have permitted our governments to make of our economy. Our fiscal irresponsibility can totally destroy the American dream. The political implications of immigration by groups which do not intend to assimilate have already been demonstrated in Europe which is well on its way to becoming Eurabia if they do not wake up. The multiculturalist disaster in the US is becoming more evident as we see this country deamericanized. The greedy politicians' quest for votes and the businessmen's quest for cheap labor add to the deterioration of the American dream. America's insatiable drug habit feeds the Mexican cartels and the criminal gangs in this country. Mexico teeters on the brink of becoming a narco-state, with dire implications for US security.

Our refusal to face our dependence on foreign oil exacerbates the destruction of our economy and we continue to send money overseas to governments, some of which support the same Islamic groups that want to change our civilization. Other threats include a rapidly growing world water shortage and population explosions, both of which can cause increased tensions and potential conflicts.

China continues to boom, but its economy may be fragile and instability is the nightmare for Chinese leaders. Russia is flush with oil money and striving to regain lost glory, but its internal politics are unstable. China and Russia are rivals for power, and along with India and Brazil, are destined to play key roles in this century.

The Jasmine Revolution which started in Tunisia has grown into the Arab World in Turmoil. The future of Egypt, Libya, and Syria are unclear as people face a new situation with no experience and the Muslim Brotherhood as the most organized group. Samuel P. Huntington wrote in his *The Clash of Civilizations,* "Decreasingly able to mobilize support and form coalitions on the basis of ideology, governments and groups will increasingly attempt to mobilize support by appealing to common religion and civilization identity." That does not portend well for the West. We should not expect democracy to take hold quickly in Muslim lands – we took 1,000 years to change the situation of man and to break the power of religion over government.

No one of these threats is enough to destroy America at this time but together they can. That is what prompted the title for this book. The "Death by a Thousand Cuts" torture technique was practiced in China as late as 1905. The victim was tortured by cutting/slicing him with the use of a very sharp knife. Torture usually started with the cutting out of the eyes. This was done to blind the victim for the rest of the act so as to increase mental agony. [That could be thought of as our ignorance and our refusal to face the facts.] Successive cuts would sever the victim's ears, nose, lips, fingers, toes and ultimately large parts of flesh. The entire process would take over 3 days. It was used from 900 until abolished in 1905.

Each one of these threats and concessions represents another cut into our body politic. If they are not addressed and stopped, the body can bleed to death.

A new world order is still evolving. With only a short respite after the demise of the Soviet Union, we were terribly slow in realizing that we were already in World War IV and that we have been for over 30 years. In this book, we will try to address these threats. We need to regain our government; we need to reinvigorate our economy; we need to wake up to the threats to our great country so that these seemingly small cuts do not end the noblest adventure in human history. We are in fight for our national survival and it is a global conflict for the very existence of Western civilization. Wake up America!

RICHARD HOBBS

Reno, Nevada
February 2012

Every man... should periodically be compelled to listen to opinions which are infuriating to him. To hear nothing but what is pleasing to one is to make a pillow of the mind.

- St. John Ervine

About the Author

Richard Hobbs graduated from the United States Military Academy at West Point in 1954 and entered the Infantry. As a paratrooper, Ranger, and Pathfinder, he had various troop assignments, including attending the British Jungle School in Malaya during the Emergency and in charge of Tropical Training for the 25th Division in Hawaii. He was selected as one of the original Olmsted Scholars and attended the University of Lyon in France receiving the degree of Docteur de l'Université in international law and international relations.

Two tours were spent in Viet-Nam (one year each) advising Vietnamese paratroopers, serving as Executive to the Deputy Commander in Viet-Nam, managing a large fire base, commanding the 2nd Battalion, 28th Infantry, and advising a Vietnamese regiment. Instead of attending the Army War College, he was an Army Research Associate at the Center for Strategic and International Studies in Washington. He had the pleasure of working with Admiral Arleigh Burke, the Founder of CSIS, and Dr. Alvin Cottrell. During that time he worked on a conference about the Western Mediterranean and reworked his thesis from Lyon which was later published by Westview Press as *THE MYTH OF VICTORY What Is Victory In War?* with a Foreword by Admiral Burke.

After serving in the Pentagon, his last assignment was as Politico-Military Advisor in the Bureau of Near Eastern and South Asian Affairs in the Department of State in Washington. He was responsible for politico-military activities in international relations and military assistance to the Middle East during the period after the 1973 War. He retired from the Army as a colonel after 27 years.

Entering the business world, he joined Teledyne serving in various positions for over 10 years including Vice President – International where he worked with the Departments of State, Commerce, and Defense and the embassies on international policy questions and export licenses. During those years, he continued to work with the Middle East, travelling in the area, particularly Egypt, every few months and extensively through Africa.

He established his own consulting firm, Service International Ltd., for international business development which he moved to Reno in 1991. There he ran an export-import company for a while, built a slot machine, and taught courses in international politics and international conflict for undergraduate and graduate students at the University of Nevada, Reno. In addition to the large amount of teaching in the military, he had served as Assistant Professor of International Relations on the faculty of the Department of Social Sciences at West Point.

He wrote several more books including *YOU AND THE NEW WORLD ORDER How You Can Influence the Alarming and Growing International and Domestic Problems* and *WORLD WAR IV AND BEYOND Islamofascism, the Third Jihad, and other threats to the USA.* He wrote a number of articles for *Pharaohs* magazine in Cairo. He hosted a call-in radio program, World In Conflict, for three years in Reno and recorded additional programs in 2011. Several presentations were made to the National Security Forum in Reno.

With an ongoing interest in national and international affairs, he wrote this book as a follow on to *World War IV and Beyond* to highlight the Islamic, economic, and other threats to our republic in an effort to emphasize that citizens need to be fully informed and they need to play a role in the momentous decisions of our times. His desire is to encourage people to take part in the political process and make their voices heard so that the active few cannot impose their views due to the apathy of the many.

Americans suffer from contagious apathy and
aggressive ignorance.

Isn't there an inoculation for this malady?

God looks after children, drunkards, and the United
States of America.
- Otto von Bismarck

Part I

The Islamic Threat

Islam's function is to change people's beliefs and actions as well as their outlook and way of thinking. Its method is Divinely-ordained and is entirely different from all the valueless methods of short-sighted human beings.
- Sayyid Qutb, *Milestones,* p. 40

Just because you do not take an interest in politics doesn't mean politics won't take an interest in you.

- Pericles (430 B.C.)

Chapter 1

World War IV

Slay the idolaters wherever you find them.

- Verse of the Sword, Qur'an IX:5

War is a divine blessing, a gift bestowed upon us by God.
The cannon's thunder rejuvenates the soul.

- Ayatollah Khomeini, September 1980[1]

The Jasmine Revolution in Tunisia followed by the tsunami of turmoil that swept across the Middle East in early 2011 clearly showed that the Islamic World is convulsed in internal struggles in addition to the efforts to expand Islamic ideology around the world. There is a civil war within Islam, not just between Sunnis and Shia but also the clash between tolerant and intolerant forms of Islam.[2] Rising costs for food and fuel exacerbate the widespread poverty, millions of young people who cannot find jobs, and a yearning for freedom all fire the protests. These young populations, many with college degrees, as in Tunisia, are linked worldwide by the new technology of the Internet, Facebook, and Twitter. Over 60% of the population of Yemen is under 24 years old. Jobless rates are 35% in Yemen and 30% in Libya while 45% in Yemen subsist below the poverty line and 30% in Libya.[3]

Young people make revolutions but old people some times steal them. Kerensky tried to establish a new free government in Russia in 1917 but by October, Lenin had taken over and imposed a communist dictatorship which endured for over 70 years. There are fears that the organizational skill of the Muslim Brotherhood, which is active in over 80 countries, may provide them the opportunity to seize these revolutions, impose sharia (Islamic law), and squelch the thirst for liberty and democracy.

World War III, the Cold War, ended with the fall of the Soviet Union and left the US as the only super power in a New World Order.

World War III, more popularly known as the Cold War, was one of the longest wars in recent history and it ended over two decades ago with the dismantling of the Union of Soviet Socialist Republics. We endured bloody wars in both Korea and Viet-Nam, but we were spared nuclear war, yet the passage of time and some revisionism resulted in a downplaying of the seriousness of World War III. The US was on a war footing for decades with strategic bombers in the air all the time with nuclear weapons on board and missiles in silos at the ready, all with pre-selected targets. Some crazy person, in the Dr. Strangelove mode, or a mistake could have sparked a nuclear holocaust. It was a very expensive, extremely tense, and dangerous period of history.

The Soviet collapse left the US as the only super power in a unipolar world while the other powers struggled to find their niches in the evolving New World Order. Expressions such as "clash of civilizations" (Professor Samuel Huntington's term), holy war, crusades, etc. have derived from the misleading religious tenor of this new world conflict. Money flowed from

Arab countries, particularly Saudi Arabia, and even from groups in the US, providing support to terrorist groups and for religious materials, print, radio, TV, and the explosive growth of the internet (There are hundreds of Islamist web sites dealing with bomb making to sermons.). One large spawning ground is the **madrassas**, or religious schools, mainly in Pakistan, where mostly poor youngsters study nothing but the Qur'an and are taught hatred of the **kafirs** (kafir is also spelled kaffir and kuffar) or infidels. If the Qur'an is all that a young person knows, he surely will not be ready for the modern world! A recent shocker is that there are over 250,000 Pakistani female high school and university graduates attending some 2,000 madrassas and they too are being radicalized.[4]

> **Pakistan produces holy warriors the way other nations produce microchips or MBAs.**
> **- London newspaper**[5]

We suffered bombings in Beirut, the embassies in Africa, the *USS Cole*, and the first World Trade Towers attack. We meekly responded by firing a few cruise missiles into Afghanistan and the Sudan with meager impact. It did not really dawn on America that we were in World War IV until the two World Trade Towers were reduced to rubble and the Pentagon was hit on 11 September 2001.[6]

However, a terrible mistake was made when this new war was mislabeled the War on Terror and later the Pentagon changed that to the Global War on Terror and even later took to calling it the Long War, which is at least more appropriate. Some called this evil Islamic radicalism; others militant jihadism. Even President George W. Bush took to calling it Islamic Fascism.[7] However, the administration of President Barrack Hussein Obama, some thought he was promoting Islam, watered down the title to "overseas contingency operations" while mention of Islam became taboo.[8] A letter found after Osama bin Laden was killed only reinforced the White House's politically correct "effort to eliminate religiously charged words from the government's language of terrorism," such as jihad.[9] I believe the label **"Islamofascism"** is more accurate.

After the collapse of the Soviet Communist Empire, three key events for America's future unfolded.

1979 – Muslim Reawakening

Unfortunately, many believe that World War IV began with the attacks of 11 September 2001. This **jihad** or "holy war" did not start then and it will not end in Iraq or Afghanistan, which will almost certainly be only footnotes in the larger history of this long war. This critical turning point in history occurred even before World War III ended when the Shah of Iran was ousted and the radical mullahs led by the fanatical Ayatollah Ruhollah Khomeini came to power followed by the Soviet invasion of Afghanistan and later the Israeli invasion of Lebanon.

The Shah tried to "westernize" Iran but he was fiercely opposed by the Communist Party, wealthy landowners, the former National Front, and religious leaders.[10] He instituted land reforms and reforms for the rights of women but the religious leaders exploited them to stir opposition to the Shah. His close ties with the US and Israel made him a target for radical religious elements led by Khomeini who had been in exile in Iraq and then Paris. Iranians unfortunately cheered his return but they soon regretted his fanatical regime marked by murder and rape.

The mullahs seized the world's attention when their minions invaded the American Embassy in Tehran in November 1979, 22 years before 9/11. The American prisoners were held hostage for some 444 days and life quickly became difficult for any Americans in the Middle East as they were being kidnapped and killed, airliners hijacked, our installations bombed, and there was little our government could do to protect them. In the 20 years between 1981 and 2001, there were reportedly 7,581 terrorist attacks worldwide including hijackings, murders, and kidnappings, and numerous other major attacks, yet America still failed to wake up.[11] According to one source, there have been 17,041 deadly Islamic terrorist attacks since 9/11.[12] America has been at war for over 30 years and still most refuse to admit it!

The Soviets became mired in Afghanistan and a new player appeared on the world military stage: the *mujahedin*, guerrillas who, with American help and equipment, particularly the STINGERs, finally forced the Soviets to withdraw from Afghanistan. We rationalized our role on the basis of weakening the Soviet Union, but in another example of unintended consequences, we created a new boogey man, the *mujahedin*, and the formation of a despicable government under the Taliban.[13]

It is critical to note that the *mujahedin* were not all native Afghans. An appeal spread throughout the Islamic world calling for Muslims to go to Afghanistan to join the *jihad* against the Soviets. Volunteers came from almost every Muslim country with particularly large contingents from Saudi Arabia, Egypt, Algeria, and Pakistan. With the Soviets expelled, these fighters returned home emboldened by their newly discovered power and pushed for changes, mostly unsuccessful, in the regimes in their countries. From the Afghan experience came forth an obscure rich boy from Saudi Arabia, Osama bin Laden and others like him.

In our religion, there is a special place in the hereafter for those who participate in jihad. One day in Afghanistan was like 1,000 days of praying in an ordinary mosque.
- Osama bin Laden[14]

Most of the *mujahedin* were extremely conservative, or fundamentalist, in their view of Islam, if they even held any views, but they were susceptible to those who held such views. The fundamentalists wanted a return to the fundamentals of the Qur'an and the teachings of Muhammad or those who had directly known him, referred to as the Companions of the Prophet Muhammad. These Muslims, known as *Salafis*, believe that the pure message of Islam has been corrupted by materialists or hypocrites over the centuries. They are extremely dogmatic and they make little effort to cooperate with other Islamist sects or groups.

In 1982 Israel invaded Lebanon ostensibly to push the Palestinian Liberation Organization (PLO) back from their frontier but Defense Minister Arik Sharon misled Prime Minister Menachem Begin and pushed all the way to Beirut and drove the PLO out of Lebanon. One of the bitter moments was the massacre of hundreds of civilians in the Sabra and Shatila refugee camps by the Christian militia while the Israel Defense Force (IDF) stood by and did not intervene. The result of this invasion was another new actor on the scene, *HezbAllah* (Party of Allah), created and supported by Iran. These three events combined to create a resurgence of pride in Muslims after their centuries of decline culminating with the end of the caliphate after World War I. They perceived that they could now influence world affairs and seek a return to their supposed greatness of centuries past.

A fatal mistake in war is to underestimate the strength, feeling and resources of an enemy.
- General W. T. Sherman, 1861

Islamofascism

Be clear, World War IV is not a War on Terror; terror is a method, a tactic, a means, not an enemy. The Crimean War is remembered for its charge of the Light Brigade made famous by Alfred, Lord Tennyson, but it is not called the Cavalry War; World War II is not called the Blitzkrieg War, the enemy is not aircraft or how they are employed; we fight against people. One of the key Principles of War is to know your enemy. We have fought various guerrilla wars and Communist-inspired insurgencies, but generally, wars in recent centuries have been between nation states. We face no Hitler or Stalin with a powerful army. Osama bin Laden, who had been in hiding for years, was a visionary leader and what guidance he was able to pronounce went to an amorphous group of fanatical jihadists who desire to drive the infidels out of Arab lands, then out of Muslim lands, and finally to take over the world. They rarely mention what government should look like (and probably don't think about it much either), but one has to presume it would be mullah theocracies with religious intolerance under sharia.

So the enemy is not Arabs, or Muslims (we also have Christian and Jewish fundamentalists but we do not have many of them going around killing in the name of religion), but those cult-like followers of Muhammad who rigorously follow the ideology of Muhammadism: the Qur'an, the Sira, and the Ahadith (plural of hadith, the traditions of Muhammad), the trilogy, under the religious façade of Islam. They believe that the precepts of Islam should be the only acceptable ones in the world and that sharia should be the only law. Even Sheikh **Abdul Ala Maududi**, the most prominent Muslim scholar of the 20th century, recognized the fascist nature: the Islamic state "seeks to mould every aspect of life and activity. In such a state no one can regard any field of his affairs as personal and private. Considered from this aspect the Islamic State bears a kind of resemblance to the Fascist and Communist states."[15] They appropriately should be called **Islamofascists**.[16]

> **Islamofascists believe that the precepts of Islam should be the only acceptable ones in the world and that sharia should be the only law.**

We are clearly in a world war because this conflict has no boundaries and it does not originate from any particular nation state. But calling it a War on Terror does not help. We need to focus on these fanatics and their motives and objectives. It is too simplistic to claim that they hate us just because we are Americans, that we are too open and licentious, or that they hate freedom. We need to listen to them. The Jasmine Revolution and the turmoil in the Middle East remind us that most of the Arab and Muslim governments are corrupt and oppressive to some extent and need reform. One positive from this war is that many of those governments, particularly Saudi Arabia, have taken this seriously and made efforts to implement reforms. The overthrow of the governments in Tunisia, Egypt, and Libya; the unrest in Bahrain; and the serious confrontations and fighting in Syria and Yemen show that the people are fed up with their governments. An excellent blueprint for urgent reform was the Alexandria Plan developed in Egypt under the direction of leading Egyptian businessmen.[17] Evidently, President Hosni Mubarak did not take it seriously.

Also, there is the constant complaint about US foreign policy, not just supporting the "corrupt" Arab governments, but the US Government's total support for Israel, its illegal occupation of Palestine, the apartheid wall, and refusing to support the ruling of the International Court of Justice that the wall is illegal. These policies make us look hypocritical to the rest of the world when we preach democracy and the right of self-determination and then ignore the plight of the Palestinians.

America is hated in the Arab world, some developing countries, and major states for various reasons including the perception of arrogance of its power. Some examples are the unilateral attack on Iraq and rejection of international agreements such as the International Criminal Court and the Kyoto Protocol. The main grudge, however, was the US Middle East policy and absolute, uncritical support for Israel to attack Palestinians and steal their land.

Senator Fritz Hollings stated it clearly on the Senate floor on 20 May 2004: the reason we invaded Iraq was because of a domino school of thought, led by Paul Wolfowitz, Richard Perle, and Charles Krauthammer, that to guarantee Israel's security we needed to spread democracy in the area. Referring directly to the other 99 senators, he said everybody knows we are in Iraq because we want to secure our friend, Israel.

Unfortunately, the attack on Iraq destroyed our excellent Two Pillar policy, which had served us well for decades, whereby Iraq and Iran balanced each other so that neither could dominate the Persian Gulf region. The imprudent attack turned into a tar baby that entangled America for years and cost about a trillion dollars. It also led to an increase in terrorism; left the US weaker to deal with the other two members of Bush's Axis of Evil, Iran and North Korea, which are much greater threats than was Iraq; and accelerated our devastating financial collapse. Many leaders, such as the king of Jordan, the prime minister of Kuwait, the president of France, have advised the US to settle the Israel-Palestine situation. The then President of Pakistan, Musharraf, told Senator Hollings and his colleagues, if you can settle the Israel-Palestine question, terrorism will disappear around the world. He may have overstated it, but it is certainly an element and provides great propaganda material for the Islamofascists.

The Third Jihad

It is impossible to understand World War IV without knowing history, what the Islamofascists or Jihadists or Islamic fanatics call the Third Great Jihad. They dream of the successes of the First Jihad from the time of Muhammad in the seventh century and the rapid expansion of Islam after his death in 632 AD. But context is critical: Europe was in the Dark Ages, the Roman Empire was faltering, and the Eastern Empire in Constantinople was struggling. Christianity had resulted in rising state taxes in addition to the forced tithes from the church.

So when Muslim warriors arrived and offered to stop your taxes and your tithe or you were dead, the choice was not too difficult.   Besides, initially Islam was not too hard to take since both Christians and Jews were recognized as "people of the book" – the Qur'an tried to establish a linkage with the Old and New Testaments. With this "convert or die" approach and firm conviction in their faith that Islam must rule the world, Islam raced out in all directions from the desert of Arabia, into Persia and Byzantium and swept across North Africa, up the Iberian Peninsula, and even into France until finally stopped at Tours by Charles Martel in 732. (We owe a great debt to Charles Martel, otherwise we might be speaking Arabic.) Meanwhile, they marched across Asia Minor, into South Asia, and finally into Southeast Asia to Indonesia.

Allah promises that anyone killed while fighting for His cause will be admitted without question into Paradise. If such a holy warrior survives the battles, he can return home with the captured property and possessions of the defeated.[18]

Those jihadis were simple fighting men who had come from a culture of living by pillage and exploiting settled populations. Loot and *jizya* (the tax imposed on those unbelievers permitted to live – the **dhimmi**) were the only means they knew for making a living.

Muhammad assured the jihadi warriors that Allah guaranteed them paradise if martyred (dying in battle) or the reward or booty (the spoils of war) they had earned. Thus to be a Muslim was profitable in this life and rewarding in the hereafter.[19] This was a win-win situation for the desert warriors. Unbelievers were killed or sold as slaves by the thousands.

The invasions were extremely harsh. The invasion of India, then one of the world's great civilizations, was particularly appalling because the Hindus and Buddhists were considered pagans and not even worth the "protection" of dhimmi status.[20] **Dhimmitude**, or the second-class non-Muslim citizens who were permitted to live, will be addressed in Chapter 3. Enormous numbers were slain: 50,000 Hindus were killed at Sonmath. Then there was the mass slaughter of Buddhists in 1193. By the end of the 12th Century, most of the Buddhists had been driven out of India – mostly to Nepal and Tibet.[21] After the destruction of the temples in a host of cities, Will Durant, in his *The Story of Civilization,*

> "lamented the results of what he termed 'probably the bloodiest story in history.' He called it 'a discouraging tale, for its evident moral is that civilization is a precious good, whose delicate complex order and freedom can at any moment be overthrown by barbarians invading from without and multiplying from within.' The bitter lesson, Durant concluded, was that 'eternal vigilance is the price of civilization. A nation must love peace, but keep its powder dry.'"[22]

"The massacres perpetrated by Muslims in India are unparalleled in history, bigger in sheer numbers than the Holocaust, or the massacre of the Armenians by the Turks."[23] A rough estimate of the kafirs killed by jihad is 270 million (120 million Africans [Islam ran the slave trade], 80 million Hindus, 60 million Christians, and 10 million Buddhists).[24] Massacres were not unknown to Muhammad who had created the dhimmi status and who had beheaded the Jews in Medina.

The Prophet said... jihad will be performed continuously since the day Allah sent me as a prophet until the day the last member of my community will fight with the *Dajjal* (Antichrist).

- Abu Dawud

The caliphs immediately after Muhammad ruled from Mecca, but within 30 years the Umayyad caliphate (661-749), which extended the empire with its great military conquests and developed the administrative structure of officials and taxation, moved the caliphate out of Arabia to Damascus. The Abbasids (named after Muhammad's uncle Abbas) then moved the capital to Baghdad and ruled for over 500 years (750-1258) where they came under Persian influence. After some good years in Baghdad and Spain, Islam began a history of decline. The violent creed from simple desert people simply ran out of gas. Except for the brief Turkish interlude, the narrow, fatalistic Islamic view of the world offered little. As with all totalitarian ideologies, Islam inevitably led to a closing of the mind.

The Crusades, starting in 1095, were an effort by the Christians of Europe to reclaim some of their lost lands, two thirds of the old Christian world had been captured, and to regain access to the Holy Land. Christianity had to defend itself as a culture and a faith to prevent being conquered and destroyed by Islam.

Baghdad was besieged by the Mongols led by Genghis Khan and later by his grandson Hulagu. Baghdad was completely destroyed in 1258 ending the primacy of Arabic civilization and it appeared it might be the end of Islam. The Mongolian assault was finally halted by Saladin and the Mamelukes[25] in Egypt. Egypt was a brilliant center of Muslim culture under the Fatamid Dynasty (968-1171).   After holding Spain for over seven hundred years, the Muslims (Moors) were expelled in 1492 and you still hear wistful mention of Andalusia (Al Andalus). The First Jihad was fading away.

The Second Jihad was the Ottoman Empire. The Islamic regime was continued by sturdy converted barbarians, the Ottomans, and their institution of slavery. Osman I [*Osmanli* (Ottoman) is derived from his name] announced the independence of his small area on the edge of the Byzantine Empire early in the 13th Century. Within a century, the Osman Dynasty extended from Mesopotamia to the Balkans. The Crusades, which had originally been an effort to regain lost Christian lands and reestablish contact with the Holy Land, were now a matter of survival as they tried to stop the advance of Islam into Europe.   Mehmet II conquered Constantinople on 29 May 1453 and after three days of murder, rape, and pillaging, the survivors were enslaved and the Ottoman Empire replaced the Byzantine Empire. It later replaced the Arab Caliphate after conquering Egypt in 1517.[26]

The Arabs were good at slavery but the Turkish *devshirme* was new even to the Arabs. It consisted of an annual "blood levy" or periodic taking of one fifth of all Christian boys in conquered lands. (Grand Admiral of the Fleet Mehmed Pasha Sokollu was an example. He was taken as a boy of 9 from his village in Bosnia.)   The "janissaries" were Christian boys captured and trained for the military. The "blood levy" was hated and left deep scars in Balkan Christians, particularly Serbs and Bulgarians who still hate all things Turkish (part of the brutal aspects of the Balkans wars of the 1990s).[27]

The Ottoman Empire was a successful Islamic expansion even though the religion was splitting into rivalries. It reached its zenith in the 16th Century and slid downhill thereafter due to corruption and degeneracy of the sultans. After a number of defeats at Belgrade, Rome, Malta, and in the Ukraine, the Turkish incursion into Europe was finally stopped at Vienna by the heroic charge by thirty thousand Polish hussars led by King Jan Sobieski on 11 September 1683 (ironic date! Maybe that was why it was chosen for 9/11.).[28]   That was the high point of Muslim expansion into Europe. No Islamic army has threatened the West since.

> The civilization of Europe, America, and Australia exists today at all only because of the victories of civilized man over the enemies of civilization…[including] those of Charles Martel in the 8th century [over Arab jihadists] and those of John Sobieski in the 17th century [over Ottoman Turkish jihadists]. During the thousand years that included the careers of the Frankish soldier [Martel] and the Polish king [Sobieski], the Christians of Asia and Africa proved unable to wage successful war with the Moslem conquerors; and in consequence Christianity practically vanished from the two continents; and today nobody can find in them any "social values" whatever, in the sense in which we use the words, so far as the sphere of Mohammedan influence [is]…concerned.
>
> **- Theodore Roosevelt**

Napoleon Bonaparte's invasion of Egypt in 1798 revealed that Islam could not overcome nationalism as a unifying power. On 14 November 1914, Sheikh ul-Ismail, the religious leader of the Ottoman Empire in Constantinople, declared an Islamic holy war calling for all Muslims to take up arms against Britain, France, Russia, Serbia, and Montenegro in World War I. He specifically mentioned jihad, martyrdom, and going to paradise.[29] The Turks chose the wrong side and the Ottoman Empire disappeared after World War I. Mustafa Kemal (Ataturk) abolished the caliphate in 1924, thus ending the Second Jihad.

The fall of the Shah in Iran provided a base for the Third Jihad along with oil wealth to support plans for the Great Caliphate. The goal is a world dominated by Islam and sharia. Initially they would like to replace all secular leadership in those countries with a Muslim majority.[30]

The Third Jihad, in addition to its basic goal of world domination, seems to have three shorter term strategic goals. It wants the US out of the Middle East, control of Muslim oil (which might be 75% of world reserves), and access to weapons of mass destruction. That makes Pakistan a special target because it already has nuclear weapons. The followers of Osama bin Laden considered him as the new caliph.

Know Your Enemy

World War III (the Cold War) ended leaving the United States with no obvious enemy, but we had already been in the opening skirmishes of what would become the first great war of the 21st Century, World War IV. Sun Tzu taught over two thousand years ago: assess yourself and your enemy, determine the circumstances that precipitated this war, and understand the enemy. Is this really a war against terrorism?[31]

> **Keep your friends close, and your enemies closer.**
>
> **- Sun Tzu**

Terrorism is not an enemy; it is criminal activity with no political legitimacy. Insurgency is armed political activity that may receive legitimacy if it gains authority within society. The Mau Mau "terrorists" became Kenya. The Jewish "terrorists" (including Menachem Begin, Yitzhak Shamir, and Ariel Sharon) became Israel, the FLN became Algeria. Knowledgeable people recognize that the Palestinian "terrorists" are fighting for their own state; even Presidents George W. Bush and Barrack Obama have called for it. Osama bin Laden's "terrorism" was an insurgency against what he considered the corrupt regimes of the *Umma*, the Muslim World. The terrorists have attacked the US but their immediate objective is political and religious domination of the Middle East.

The US has been involved with the Middle East since the birth of our country. After declaring our independence from England, our merchant ships lost the protection of the Royal Navy. The Turkish Ottoman Empire had lost control of North Africa and Barbary pirates seized our ships, enslaved the crews, and demanded tribute. Nearly a million white slaves had been taken over the years.

Our representatives in Europe at the time were John Adams, Benjamin Franklin, and Thomas Jefferson. The Barbary Pirates became a serious concern and Adams and Jefferson met with the ambassador from the Bey of Algiers. Ambassador Abdul al-Rahman told them that Allah directed in the Qur'an that all unbelievers were sinners and, if they did not convert, they should be made slaves. Ever the scholar, Jefferson obtained a Qur'an to better understand the foe.

> **The Muslims never called their naval raiders "Barbary pirates." They called them *ghazis*, sacred raiders....actually jihad by the army of Muhammad.[32]**

The navy we had established during the War for Independence had been disbanded so we had no force to take on the pirates. We were paying large sums in tribute, eventually exceeding 10 percent of the country's budget and increasing. At that time we were developing our constitution since the Articles of Confederation had proven inadequate. One of the arguments for a strong federal government was that we needed a federal navy. The US Navy was formed in 1794.

When Thomas Jefferson became president, one of his early acts was to send the navy to deal with the Barbary Pirates. Similar to modern day politics, he did not inform Congress until the fleet was too far away to be recalled. The *USS Philadelphia* ran aground and was captured in Tripoli. Stephen Decatur raided Tripoli, blew up the *Philadelphia,* and wreaked havoc in the port.

The American consul in Tunis, William Eaton, led a group of Marines and a motley crew of irregulars across the desert from Egypt and attacked Tripoli from the land. Thus, the Marine Hymn goes "From the halls of Montezuma to the shores of Tripoli." This was also the time of the Battle of Trafalgar and Lord Nelson. A young man by the name of Francis Scott Key wrote a song commemorating the battle. It was a flop, but in 1812 he rewrote the words, and with the same music it became famous as the Star Spangled Banner.

We had further problems with the Barbary Pirates in 1815, dealt with the Ottoman Empire in mid-19th Century, and again in the 20th Century until its demise after World War I. Islamic enmity was dormant until the 1979-1980 hostage seizure in Iran, which we now see, in hindsight, was the start of World War IV. Clashes with Muslim groups have appeared regularly since.

This is not a new form of war because it is a terrorist war; terror has been used for centuries by the weak against the strong as well as by many brutal conquerors. It is less a clash between civilizations but more a major struggle within Islamic civilization and we have been forced to take sides: first because they attacked us, and second because everything they stand for is anathema to our values and our definition of civilization.

We must understand our enemy. The US wants to fight a war against terrorism but they are fighting a war of politics manifested as religion, which are inseparable in Islam. These extremist Muslims are at war with the unbelievers, the *kafirs* (the West), those who have fallen away, and the half-believers (the countless Muslims the fundamentalists believe they can win over). There is no coexistence, only opposing views of life and civilization. Al Qaeda represents total rejection of our modern values. Some 11,000 men received training and inspiration in its Afghan camps. It is now a network of independent terrorist cells united in a struggle against the modern aspects of Arab governments and Western values, and is the diabolical opposite of the capitalist global economy, a global murder factory. Their Bible is the 11 volume, 6,000 page *Encyclopedia of Jihad* (even on CD-ROM!), with its instructions on all types of subversion including chemical, biological, and nuclear or radiation attacks.

To understand the enemy we face in World War IV, we must first understand Muhammadism.

It is far easier to kill people than it is to kill ideologies.[33]

Notes

1. Mohammed Mohaddessin, *Islamic Fundamentalism: The New Global Threat*, (Washington, DC, Seven Locks Press, 1993), p. 59.
2. See Richard Hobbs *WORLD WAR IV AND BEYOND Islamofascism, the Third Jihad and other threats to the USA*, (Sparks, Nevada, ColDoc Publishing, 2008), Chapter 3 Civil War within Islam, pp. 32-40.
3. Middle East social indicators, CIA World Factbook, 27 January 2011.
4. Rebecca Conway, "Pakistan's female madrassas breed radicalism," Reuters, 15 June 2011. One woman who was asked about the murder of the governor because he opposed the blasphemy law said "I am sorry to say this, but this is what he deserved."
5. Peter Popham, *Independent on Sunday*, London, 16 September 2001.
6. Nine months before 9/11, French intelligence warned the US that al Qaeda was planning a hijacking, possibly involving an American airline. "Everyone knew that something was cooking, that these people were preparing something big and spectacular," but they did not have the details. Angela Doland, AP, "Before 9/11, French Told U.S. Of A Plot," *Philadelphia Inquirer,* 17 April 2007.
7. President Bush's Speech at the National Endowment for Democracy, *The New York Times* on the Web, 6 October 2005. Bush was now using "war against Islamic Fascism." "War Turns to 'Islamic Fascism,'" *Washington Times,* 31 August 2006, p. 4.
8. "Possessing Freedom is Not Enough – We must Exercise Our Freedom to Preserve It," transcript of a speech by columnist Diana West at a free speech conference of the International Free Press Society held in Denmark's parliament in Copenhagen, posted 9 October 2010.
    The Bush Department of Homeland Security put out a memorandum "suggesting" that government officials stop using all such words as "jihad," "jihadist;" "Islamic terrorist," "Islamist," "Islamofascist," and the like… "we should not concede the terrorists' claim that they are legitimate adherents of Islam."
9. Matt Apuzzo, "Osama wanted new name for al-Qaida to repair image," Associated Press, 24 June 2011.
10. George Lenczowski, "Political Process and Institutions in Iran: the Second Pahlavi Kingship," in George Lenczowski, Editor, *Iran Under the Pahlavis*, (Stanford, California, Hoover Institution Press, 1978), pp. 458-459.
11. See Hobbs, *World War IV and Beyond*, p. 2, for a list of 15 of the major attacks.
12. TheReligionofPeace.com, 8 April 2011.
13. Aid went in through Pakistan and became particularly significant after we provided MANPADS (man portable air defense missiles), particularly the STINGER, which were quite effective against Soviet aircraft including the HIND gunship helicopters which wreaked havoc with the Afghans.
    "Few of the younger U.S. counter-intelligence agents remember that manpads literally brought down the Soviet empire. With U.S.-supplied Stinger missiles, the Afghan mujahideen, many of them fathers of today's al-Qaida terrorists, grounded Soviet fighter-bombers, gunships and troop transports. From the time the last Soviet troops withdrew from Afghanistan on Feb. 15, 1989, to the collapse of the Berlin wall and the liberation of Eastern Europe was only eight months." Arnaud de Borchgrave, UPI, 9 August 2004.
    For the story of this greatest CIA covert operation in history, see George Crile, *Charlie Wilson's War,* (New York, Atlantic Monthly Press, 2003).
14. Scott MacLeod, "The Paladin of Jihad," *Time,* 6 May 1996, p. 51, interview in Khartoum.
15. Quoted in "What Muslim Leaders Say About Islam Dispels the Myth that Jihadists are a 'Fringe' Element," Citizen Warrior, 1 October 2010.
16. Some of the characteristics of Fascism (according to Dr. Lawrence Britt from the Liberty Forum) that apply are: powerful and continuing nationalism (Islam), disdain for human rights, identification of enemies/scapegoats as a unifying cause (infidels, Crusaders, imperialists, Americans), supremacy of the military (terrorists for now, later Revolutionary Guards such as in Iran), rampant sexism (Islam), controlled mass media, obsession with national security (use of fear), religion and government intertwined (Islam and Sharia), disdain for intellectuals and the arts, obsession with crime and punishment (almost unlimited power to police), and rampant cronyism and corruption (groups of friends and associates who control power).
17. "The Alexandria March 2004 Document On Reform Issues in the Arab World," from the conference, "Arab Reform Issues – Vision and Implementation," held in Alexandria, Egypt 12-14 March 2004. They called for "a new social contract between the State and the citizens in the Arab societies." They saw the need to "eradicate sources of religious fanaticism, which is still present in the educational curricula, mosque sermons and the official and unofficial media." They "were convinced that reform is necessary and urgently needed, that it must stem from within our own societies, and that it must respond to the aspirations of its peoples in crystallizing a comprehensive reform project that encompasses the political, economic, social and cultural aspects."
    It is an excellent document and one that all Muslim governments should have adopted and implemented. Unfortunately, they ignored it and now they are paying the price.
18. Sahih Bukhari volume 4, book 54, number 46, quoted in Bill Warner, *The Political Traditions of Mohammed: The Hadith for the Unbelievers,* (CSPI Publishing, www.cspipublishing.com, 2006), p.16.
19. Serge Trifkovic, *The Sword of the Prophet: Islam, history, theology, impact on the world,* (Boston, MA, Regina Orthodox Press, Inc., 2002), pp. 87-88.
20. See Robert Spencer, *The Truth about Muhammad* (Washington DC, Regnery Publishing, 2006), p. 153.
21. Trifkovic, *The Sword of the Prophet*, p. 111.
22. Ibid.
23. Ibid., pp. 112-113.
24. Bill Warner, *Mohammed and the Unbelievers: The Sira, a Political Biography,* (CSPI Publishing, www.cspipublishing.com, 2006), pp. 160-161. "The Jews had no political control over any country and their deaths were limited to a few thousand killed in riots."

25. Mamelukes were a slave class developed to fight for Muslims to evade the prohibition in the Qur'an on Muslims fighting Muslims.

26. Trifkovic, *The Sword of the Prophet*, pp. 113-114.

27. Ibid., pp. 114-116.

28. Robert Spencer, *The Politically Incorrect Guide to Islam (and the Crusades)*, (Washington, DC, Regnery Publishing, Inc., 2005), p. 157.

29. The declaration read "Of those who go to Jihad for the sake of happiness and salvation of the believers in God's victory, the lot of those who remain alive is felicity, while the rank of those who depart to the next world is martyrdom. In accordance with God's beautiful promise, those who sacrifice their lives to give life to the truth will have honor in this world, and their latter end in paradise."

30. This includes Afghanistan, Algeria, Bangladesh, Egypt, the Emirates, Indonesia, Iran, Iraq, Jordan, Kuwait, Lebanon, Libya, Malaysia, Mauritania, Morocco, Pakistan, Sudan, Syria, Tunisia, Turkey, Yemen, the five former Soviet Union states, Kazakhstan, Kyrgyzstan, Tajikistan, Turkmenistan, and Uzbekistan; and of course what they refer to as the "occupied territory" of Israel.

31. See Ronald Spiers, "The Clear Thinking About 'Terrorists.'" *The International Herald Tribune,* 14 January 2003, reprinted in Other Voices, *Washington Report on Middle East Affairs* (*WRMEA*), April 2003, p. OV-1. "Americans are targets of terrorism for a variety of reason, most of them political or economic." But "al-Qaeda is fundamentally different: fluid, borderless, clandestine, undeterrable and without conventional forces or headquarters. Its aims are difficult to spell out with precision. It has to be countered primarily with persistence and craft, probably over a long period of time."

  See also Zbigniew Brzezinski, "Terrorized by 'War on Terror': How a Three-word Mantra Has Undermined America," *The Washington Post,* 25 March 2007, reprinted in Other Voices, *WRMEA,* May/June 2007, p. OV-14. Audrey Hudson, "House Panel Bans 'Terror War' Phrase," *Washington Times*, 5 April 2007. Robert Spencer, "Believing in the War on Terror," Human Events, 7 May 2007, p. 12.

32. Warner, *The Political Traditions of Mohammed: The Hadith for the Unbelievers*, p.167.

33. Fred Burton and Scott Stewart, "Al Qaeda in 2008: The Struggle for Relevance," Stratfor: Terrorism Intelligence Report, 19 December 2007.

The better rule is to judge our adversaries from their standpoint, not from our own.
- Robert E. Lee, 1865

Believing with you that religion is matter which lies solely between man and his God, that he owes account to none other for his faith or his worship, that the legislative powers of government reach actions only, and not opinion, I contemplate with sovereign reverence that the act of the whole American people which declared that their legislature should "make no law respecting an establishment of religion, or prohibiting the free exercise thereof," thus building a wall of separation between church and state."
                    - Thomas Jefferson in a letter to the Danbury (CT) Baptists, 1 January 1802

Chapter 2

Muhammadism – The Cult of Muhammad – Moism

Every Prophet was sent to his nation but
only I have been sent to all mankind.

- Muhammad[1]

Islam is a caustic blend of regurgitated paganism and twisted Bible stories.
Muhammad, its lone prophet, conceived his religion solely to satiate his lust
for power, sex, and money. He was a terrorist. And if you think these
conclusions are shocking, wait until you see the evidence.

- Craig Winn, *Prophet of Doom*[2]

America has been at war with Islamofascism for over 30 years; we are fighting two wars in Muslim countries, and involved in the turmoil which spread across the Middle East, particularly in Libya. Islam is proclaimed in all these countries and sharia is generally the law of the land. Throughout, the man called Muhammad is revered not only as the Prophet but as the perfect man. Since Muhammad has had such a major impact on history in much of the world, he is clearly a great historical figure; but, as with most cultures, there is an enormous amount of myth that has evolved so that it is nearly impossible to distinguish historical facts from Muslim beliefs. This excessive worship or admiration, even deification, for one man is more like a cult. The fanatical reaction to the Muhammad cartoons published in 2005 is incomprehensible to the Western mind. Muhammad and Islam are so totally intertwined as to be inseparable. Muhammad is Islam. There is no Islam without Muhammad.[3]

Islam, claimed to be the third monotheistic religion after Judaism and Christianity, arose in Arabia early in the 7th Century. Central to the beliefs is that the Qur'an, which is claimed to be the direct word of Allah (originally Illalla, the Moon God, one of the 360 gods worshipped in pre-Islamic Arabia)[4], was revealed to Muhammad by the angel Gabriel over a span of 23 years. But since there are really no reliable written Muslim sources on Islam, all the documents have to be viewed as coming from oral history and legend and written by people with various interests which likely made them apologists.

Islam or Muhammadism is a totalitarian ideology, a complete path of life dictating every minute aspect of personal and public life. It is impossible to try to understand Islam and the Qur'an without reviewing the life of Muhammad because Islam is Muhammad.[5]

Muhammad

Islam was created in the desolate desert of Arabia, where Muhammad ibn Abdallah ibn Abd al-Muttalib ibn Hashim, Abu al-Qasim was born around 570 AD (perhaps on 20 April) in the city of Mecca, then the principal commercial and religious center of Arabia. Mecca is located in the western edge of the Hejaz, an immense large plateau with high mountains (somewhat like parts of Nevada and Utah). He belonged to the Quraysh tribe which was in charge of the sacred **Kaaba** (cube)[6], which even then was visited in annual pilgrimages by various heathen Arab tribes.

Arabia was a region but not a nation. The term "Arab" was used in early writings to mean "desert" or "people of the desert" or "nomad." This harsh land made for rough people. Lack of central authority bred a somewhat Hobbesian mindset. The possession of arms and the scant regard for human life, especially if it infringed on one's honor, or claim to pastures, camels, women, or some other earthly good, was the mark of manhood. Robbery and murder outside the protective confines of one's clan were not deemed bad *per se*, they were judged by the results as a means to an end.[7] Pagan Arabia was a rough land. Blood feuds were frequent, and the people had grown to be as harsh and unyielding as their barren desert land. Women were treated as chattel; child marriage (of girls as young as seven or eight) and female infanticide were common, as women were regarded as a financial liability.[8]

Arabia of the late sixth century was a region, not a nation, with a harsh life in a violent culture of mostly pagan polytheists characterized by vendetta, infanticide, and banditry.

Arabia of the late sixth century was a violent culture of mostly pagan polytheists with vendetta, infanticide (mainly killing female infants), and banditry.[9] These desert people lived a harsh life, "certainly brutish and often short." The extended family and the tribe were basic to survival. Their social order was based on "Love your tribe" for they are your brothers. For people who lived and often left no trace in the sand, material items were subject to robbery, rape, and plunder; but that was a two-way street with revenge and loot always available. There were few earthly delights for these people so it is not surprising that they focused on sensual pleasures. This "truly barbarian society" was the milieu of the young Muhammad.[10]

Muhammad's father died before he was born and he lost his mother when he was six, then his grandfather, Abdel-Muttalib, cared for him. However, he died within three years and the young boy was passed to his uncle, Abu Taleb, a businessman and who made him a camel driver in his caravans. Those caravans took him to Syria and Palestine where he met many Jews and Christians and gained an imperfect understanding of their religions. By age 25, he was a shepherd, a lowly position, and then worked with a traveling cloth merchant. On one of his trips, he met a distant cousin, **Khadija** bint Khuwaylid, a wealthy widow 15 years his senior, and went to work for her. He did well managing her business and they eventually married and had six children, all of whom died early except for his daughter, **Fatima**.

Sources of Muhammad's biography are numerous but untrustworthy. None were written during his lifetime and the first was not written until a century and a half after his death.[11] Also, there are contradictions (Islam is rife with contradictions). One author stresses that Muhammad was a man of war who had fought in numerous battles, including two local wars between his tribe, the Quaraysh, and their rivals, Banu Hawazin.[12] Another author cites an event in 595 when Mecca was threatened by Ethiopians and Abu Taleb assembled a coalition to repel them. "It appears that Muhammad could not bear the sight of the battlefield and ran away, which exposed him to contempt and ostracism."[13] Evidently he was remote from his Quraysh tribe and the Meccan society and was contemplative and dreamy, supposedly addicted to prayer and fasting, and apparently had epileptic fits. He spent time in the hills in meditation and supposedly weeks at a time in the caves of Mount Hira. When he was 40, in the year 610, he told Khadija that he had been visited by a "majestic being" – the angel Gabriel – telling him "You are the Messenger of God."[14]

When Muhammad was 40, in the year 610, he told his wife that he had been visited by a "majestic being" – the angel Gabriel – telling him "You are the Messenger of God."

He had no more revelations for three years. Thereafter, for the rest of his life, Muhammad had frequent "revelations," – messages that he claimed came directly from Allah. Most were memorized and repeated by storytellers, some were supposedly written down (although it is not clear that he was literate).[15] These were oral communications, "delivered by the prophet in trance."[16] **Uthman**, the third caliph after Muhammad, supposedly ordered that they be collected and written down as the Qur'an in 650 AD (well after his death).

Muhammad started preaching his simple teachings: "focused on the submission to one transcendent Allah; on the end of the world and the Day of Judgment, when all will be brought to life; on the subsequent delights of paradise for the virtuous and of hell for the sinners; and on the practice of charity."[17] The Qur'an is replete with references to Paradise (the Garden) and Hell (the Fire). After his wife, his first two converts were his slave and adopted son, Zaid, and his cousin Ali. Only a few more joined him as he was not well received by the Meccans. His attack on idols was seen as a threat to their profitable business at the Kaaba. He even tried to compromise with them about idols,[18] but he later abrogated this section – thus they became known as the Satanic verses.

One has to be amazed at the confidence or arrogance of Muhammad. Here was a man claiming to be the last prophet, meaning there could be no other advances in religion after him, living in a very backward area which was not a civilization compared to any of the great civilizations such as Egypt, Rome, Greece, Persia, the Indus River, and China. Plus, all these revelations were in Arabic, a nondescript language in which there were no books. In the word of the people he tried to convert and then grew to hate, he had a lot of chutzpah.

Muhammad was not popular in Mecca (his uncle thought he was insane and tried to have the citizens pity him rather than persecute him) and by 619 his claims had grown wilder. That was when he claimed that Gabriel had taken him on his "journey into heaven" – **the Night Journey** - praying at the "Farthest Mosque" (Jerusalem - *Masjid al-Aqsa*) before visiting "the seven heavens" where he met "all the previous prophets, including Adam, Jesus, Moses, and Abraham, before being taken into the presence of God to be instructed in proper worship."[19] The Night Journey is one of the great stories, but as his wife Aisha said, he "never left the bed that night; however, his spirit soared."[20] That same year his uncle died followed by the death of Khadija. He was so furious when his uncle, Abu Lahab, withdrew the clan's protection that he reacted violently against both his uncle and his wife (his uncle to burn in fire and his wife to have a rope on her neck) which is in the Qur'an (the Qur'an can be quite personal!).[21] Muhammad was now an outcast in Mecca. During those first 13 years he had managed to gather only 150 followers.[22]

After 13 years of preaching, Muhammad had convinced only 150 followers and he had been driven out of Mecca – his "religion" was a failure.

In 621, some pilgrims from Yathrib, a town over 200 miles (a ten-day journey) north of Mecca, expressed their support for Muhammad. Yathrib was about half Jewish and half Arab with many Christians. There were quarrels there between nomads and farmers and they needed an arbiter. In June 622, another group of pilgrims from Yathrib promised to protect him.[23] IIe was probably anxious to flee Mecca because the tribal elders were preparing a council to try Muhammad as a traitor. He and his followers fled; this is known as the **Hejira** (Flight or night of migration – also *Hijra* and *Hegira*), and 24 September 622, when he arrived in Yathrib, is marked as the beginning of Islamic history.[24] Yathrib thereafter became known as the City of the Prophet, Medinnet el Nebi, shortened to **Medina**.

In addition to some eight Arab clans, there were several Jewish tribes and a Christian presence in Medina. He was soon the absolute ruler of Medina, combining both religious and political power. He was the legislator, administrator, judge, and general. These tribal warriors he now led were short of money and he wanted revenge against the hated Meccans so he planned raids against the Quraysh caravans.[25] In Medina, Muhammad had his first revelations permitting him to fight the Meccans. XXII:39-41, II:193.   The first several raids which Muhammad supposedly personally led failed. A successful raid at Nakla both kept the new movement solvent with the booty they took but also set a new precedent in their theology (ideology). The attack was during the month of *Rajab* (Ramadan) when fighting was traditionally suspended. Muhammad initially refused to share in the loot, but then he conveniently received a revelation justifying the raid: "persecution is worse than killing."[26]

> This was a momentous revelation, for it led to an Islamic principle that has had repercussions throughout the ages. Good became identified with anything that redounded to the benefit of Muslims, regardless of whether it violated moral or other laws. The moral absolutes enshrined in the Ten Commandments, and other teachings of the great religions that preceded Islam, were swept aside in favor of an overarching principle of expediency.[27]

The convenience and timeliness of revelations became routine. "From that point revelations suitable to the needs of the moment, helping Muhammad augment his political and legal authority (or even helping him keep his quarrelsome wives in check), had become frequent and surprisingly specific in the way Allah obliged in addressing the daily needs of his prophet."[28]

Only two months later, Muhammad led about 300 of his warriors against a rich Quraysh caravan returning from Syria. The Quraysh were ready for him this time with a large force (accurate numbers are difficult to verify historically, in this case ranging from 600 to 1,000). The battle of **Badr** on 15 March 624 was a surprising victory for Muhammad – a "miracle" with the help of Allah and an army of angels which was great personal revenge and added to his prestige. It was not accepted practice to attack one's own tribe and justification from Allah was required (and received) and Muhammad (Allah) grew even more bellicose:

I will cast terror into the hearts of those who disbelieve. Therefore strike off their heads and strike off every fingertip of them."

- Qur'an VIII:12.

There was a great amount of booty seized at Badr and that led to problems of how it was to be distributed. An entire chapter (Surah VIII) is devoted to "The Spoils of War." The booty belonged to Allah and Muhammad – "The windfalls are for Allah and the Apostle." (VIII:1) "And know that whatever thing you gain, a fifth of it is for Allah and for the Apostle and for the near of kin and the orphans and the needy and the wayfarer." (VIII:41) Perhaps most important was the legitimacy conferred by "Eat then of the lawful and good (things) which you have acquired in war." (VIII:69)

In the first note for this chapter, Muhammad had said in his usual modest way, "I have been given five things which were not given to anyone else before me." The first was: "Allah made me victorious by awe, by His frightening my enemies for a distance of one month's journey." "Mohammed was now a political force unlike any ever seen before in history. The fusion of religion and politics with a universal mandate created a permanent force. To this day, the mandate continues. There will be no peace until all the world is Islam. The treasure of war, the spoils, will provide the wealth of Islam. **The awe of Mohammed is the fear of Allah.**" [Emphasis added][29]

Muhammad in Medina – the Warlord

Muhammad fled Mecca as a preacher and a prophet with only 150 converts, and after a year in Medina, he had only some 250-300 who were Muslims and most were poor. The battle of Badr was the turning point; he was now a politician and a general. "Islam became an armed political force with a religious motivation, jihad."[30] The victory at Badr was a turning point in Muhammad's character. The Muslims were now a threat to their enemies and their leader showed a new personality when he expressed delight when the head of his old foe Abu Jahl ("which means 'Father of Ignorance,' a name given to him by Muslim chroniclers; his real name was 'Amr ibn Hisham.") was proudly presented to him and a number of the prisoners were beheaded.[31] The wimpish, reticent preacher was now a warlord bent on revenge. Muhammad was now the enemy of infidels (II:98) "Killing or, in the case of Jews and Christians, enslaving and robbing them, was not only divinely sanctioned but mandated."[32]

A victorious Muhammad returned to Medina and started settling scores, first with the Jews. He laid siege to the Banu Qaynuqa tribe until they surrendered, he was talked out of killing them so he took their property and they left Medina.[33] He did not like poets and had one killed who supposedly had insulted him.[34] The Quraysh sought revenge for their defeat at Badr and dispatched some 3,000 troops against perhaps 1,000 Muslims at the battle of Uhud. Muhammad led the fight but his force was routed and he was wounded. The taunts from the leader of the Quraysh, Abu Sufyan, drove Muhammad to even greater hatred of all infidels. His hatred intensified after discovery of the body of his uncle, Hamza, which had been mutilated by a woman who cut off his nose and ears and ate part of his liver. The fact that her father, brother, uncle, and eldest son had been slain at Badr brought no sympathy from Muhammad who proclaimed "we will mutilate them as no Arab has ever mutilated anyone."[35]

Kill any Jew who falls under your power.

- Muhammad

In addition to his hatred of the Quraysh, he again turned his wrath against the Jews. In Mecca, he had tried to win over the Jews but they had spurned him. Now, in Medina the Jews there remained loyal to their faith and refused to accept Muhammad as the prophet of Allah, so he set out to remove them. He arranged for the murder of a number of Jews and started what we have come to know as genocide or ethnic cleansing. The Banu Nadir tribe was forced into exile with only the property they could carry; what they could not carry with them became Muhammad's property.[36] Muhammad spelled it out with his order to "kill any Jew that falls into your power."[37]

Muhammad was now a wealthy man since he received one fifth of all booty. The clear benefits of the Muslims greatly assisted recruiting new members to Islam even if they were unsure about this self-proclaimed prophet.

After Muhammad fled to Medina, he never worked again. He made his living and for his people by stealing from caravans (highway robbery is punish by death in the Shafi'i law school) and by extortion from Christians and Jews, dhimmi. He was Don Muhammad, an early Mafia kingpin.

Muhammad's troops attacked the Banu al-Mustaliq tribe in 626 and slaughtered many and took thousands of camels and sheep and kidnapped some of their "excellent women."

There followed an orgy of rape by Muhammad and his men, however there was a problem: desiring ransom for the survivors, the Muslims had promised not to violate the captives.

> We... desired them, for we were suffering from the absence of our wives, but at the same time we also desired ransom for them. So we decided to have sexual intercourse with them but by observing 'azl [*coitus interruptus*]. But we said: We are doing an act whereas Allah's Messenger is amongst us; why not ask him? So we ask Allah's Messenger (may peace be upon him), and he said: It does not matter if you do not do it, for every soul that is to be born up to the Day of Resurrection will be born.[38]

The only issue was whether the value of the women for ransom might be diminished if they were returned to their husbands pregnant. The rape of captured women had already been resolved in Muhammad's revelations and the hadiths refer to Qur'an IV:24 – Forbidden to you are "all married women except those whom your right hands possess [meaning captives]."

Men never do evil so completely and cheerfully as when they do it from religious conviction.

- Blaise Pascal, *Pensées*, 1670

The people of Mecca were now fearful of this traitor who threatened their economy and determined they needed to stamp out Islam.[39] A quite large army for that time of perhaps 10,000 under Abu Sufyan marched on Medina and encountered a stalemate at what is known as the Battle of the Ditch (or the Trench which they dug around the city). Muhammad, following his own principle that "war is deceit," spread some false information and managed to divide the coalition and they withdrew.[40]

Muhammad now turned his attention to Banu Qurayzah, the last Jewish tribe in Medina, who he accused of having sided with the Meccans. Muhammad called Jews pigs and monkeys (Christians were swine).[41] Robbery and expulsion would no longer satisfy him. He laid siege to the tribe for 25 days until they finally surrendered. Muhammad put their fate into the hands of Sa'd bin Mu'adh who pronounced, "I give the judgment that their warriors should be killed and their children and women should be taken as captives."[42] "Muhammad offered the men conversion to Islam as an alternative to death; upon their refusal, up to 900 were decapitated at the ditch, in front of their women and children." The killing continued into the night under torchlight with his wife Aisha, then 12 years old, with him.[43] The women were raped and Muhammad supposedly took as his concubine Raihana bint Amr, who had just seen her husband and father slain hours before.[44] The Jews felt that Muhammad absolutely could not be the last prophet according to the Bible.[45] How many remember *judenrein* or *judenfrei* from the Nazis? This is one of the most embarrassing events in Islam and apologists have tried to downplay it and rationalize it. Muslims feel that denying that Muhammad was the prophet of Allah by the Jews was a crime against Islam appropriately punished by beheading. Kafirs consider it evidence of Islamic violence, evil, and ethnic cleansing. Dhimmis see it as an historic event, such as in all cultures, and it should not be judged. So it was either evil, a justifiable godly act, or just another historical event.[46] It depends on your viewpoint.

Muhammad had become an absolute ruler by mid 627 and there were reports of changes in his personality. One chief noted, "That man aspires to dominate the Arabs." His old foe, Abu Sufyan, noted "Prophetism is finished, the empire is beginning."[47] He is said to have reddened his hair and took to wearing a veil.[48]

"In the seventh century of the Christian era, a wandering Arab of the lineage of Hagar [i.e. Muhammad], the Egyptian, combining the powers of transcendent genius, with the preternatural energy of a fanatic, and the fraudulent spirit of an impostor, proclaimed himself as a messenger from Heaven, and spread desolation and delusion over an extensive portion of the earth. Adopting from the sublime conception of the Mosaic law, the doctrine of one omnipotent God; he connected indissolubly with it, the audacious falsehood, that he was himself his prophet and apostle. Adopting from the new Revelations of Jesus, the faith and hope of immortal life, and of future retribution, he humbled it to the dust by adapting all the rewards and sanctions of his religion to the gratification of the sexual passion. He poisoned the sources of human felicity at the fountain, by degrading the condition of the female sex, and the allowance of polygamy; and he declared undistinguishing and exterminating war, as a part of his religion, against all the rest of mankind. **THE ESSENCE OF HIS DOCTRINE WAS VIOLENCE AND LUST: TO EXALT THE BRUTAL OVER THE SPIRITUAL PART OF HUMAN NATURE**....Between these two religions, thus contrasted in their characters, a war of twelve hundred years has already raged. The war is yet flagrant...While the merciless and dissolute dogmas of the false prophet shall furnish motives to human action, there can never be peace upon earth, and good will towards men." (Emphasis in the original)
- **John Quincy Adams**[49]

Muhammad had a vision in 628 that he performed the old pagan pilgrimage to Mecca which he wanted to incorporate into his new religion and thus he marched on Mecca with 1,500 men. He was stopped outside the city by the Quraysh but was able to negotiate a ten-year truce (the **Treaty of Hudaybiyya**) which would permit a pilgrimage the next year and he agreed to temporarily drop his title of "prophet of Allah." The Companions were furious that Muhammad had accepted some bad terms, but, of course, he had another revelation pronouncing it as a victory (Qur'an XLVIII:1). Muhammad soon broke the treaty firmly establishing an Islamic principle "that nothing was good except what was advantageous to Islam, and nothing evil except what hindered Islam."[50] His ploy worked and he soon marched into Mecca and even Abu Sufyan saw the inevitable light and converted. The 360 idols in the Kaaba were destroyed and it was clear that this was an occupation not a liberation. The threat of beheading, as for Abu Sufyan, would play a major role in the future conquests of Islam.[51]

With or without religion, you would have good people doing good things and evil people doing evil things. But for good people to do evil things, that takes religion.
- Steven Weinberg, Nobel Prize Winner in Physics, 1979

The "crazy" preacher was now back as the master of Mecca. Other tribes converted and joined him and he was soon the king of Arabia. During nine years at Medina there were some 65 armed excursions with Muhammad participating in 27, averaging one every seven weeks. Jihad was Muhammad's way. In 632 AD, shortly after having led a large pilgrimage to Mecca and with his final words ordering that there should be no other religions in Arabia (no Christians or Jews – true to this day), Muhammad died at age 63 in Medina. His hatred of Christians and Jews has continued as evidenced by present-day Islamic intolerance of Christians and Jews worldwide.[52]

As noted above, after 13 years of preaching in Mecca, Muhammad had managed to gain only 150 followers and his religion was a failure. But now as the warlord of Medina and master of Arabia, his political force gained power reinforcing the premise that Islam is a political ideology with only a veneer of religion.

There is much confusion about religion and Islam. "For Muslims, the word 'religion' does not only refer to a collection of beliefs and rituals, it refers to a way of life which includes all values, behaviours, and details of living." Secularism is not acceptable to Muslims. "Islam cannot be separated from the state because it guides us through every detail of running the state and our lives. Muslims have no choice but to reject secularism for it excludes the law of Allah."

> **Separation of religion and state is not an option for Muslims because it requires us to abandon Allah's decree for that of a man.**
>
> **- Dr. Ja'far Sheikh Idris[53]**

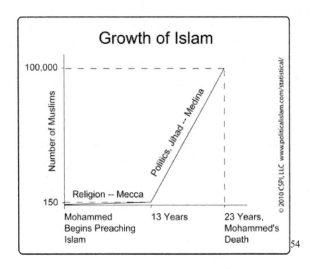

54

Muhammad and Women

Muhammad supposedly claimed that women and perfume were the two things which attracted him. His views on women are a bit strange, but were a reflection of his time. The critical point is that they were confirmed in his revelations and thus are part of Islamic dogma. This denigration of women did not start with the Taliban. Muhammad: "After I die, the biggest problem that I leave to man is woman."[55] Also, "A woman is like a rib; if you try to straighten her out, she will break. To get any benefit from her, you must leave her crooked."[56]

- It starts with sex. "The most important part of a woman is her vagina."[57] Muhammad said, "The marriage vow most rightly expected to be obeyed is the husband's right to enjoy his wife's vagina."[58] And they are to shave their pubic hair.[59]
- Women are to be used as wished. A "tilth" is a plowed field. "Your wives are a tilth for you, so go into your tilth when you like." Qur'an II: 223.
- If that is not enough, there are the slaves (what your right had possesses). Sex with another Muslim's wife is wrong, but sex with married slaves and captives is sanctioned. "And all married women except those whom your right hand possess (this is) Allah's ordinance to you." Qur'an IV:24.[60] Forced sex with captive women after a battle was sanctioned. This was

not rape because rape could only involve a Muslim woman; it was a method of war, part of jihad, supreme domination, and humiliation for the male relatives.[61]

● A woman's testimony is worth only half of that of a man. "Call in to witness from among your men two witnesses; but if there are not two men, then one man and two women from among those whom you choose to be witnesses, so that if one of the two errs, the second of the two may remind the other." Qur'an II:282. According to Muhammad, "That is because a woman's mind is deficient."[62]

● A woman's inheritance is only half that of a son. "Allah enjoins you concerning your children: The male shall have the equal of the portion of two females." Qur'an IV:11.

> **The rules regulating sex-slaves differ from those for free women [i.e. Muslim women]: the latter's body must be covered entirely, except for her face and hands, whereas the sex-slave is kept naked from the bellybutton up – she is different from the free woman; the free woman has to be married properly to her husband, but the sex-slave – he just buys her and that's that.**
> **- Salwa al-Mutairi, female political activist and former Kuwait parliament candidate[63]**

● Men can have up to four wives plus sex slaves; women can have only one husband. "And if you feel that you cannot act equitably towards orphans, then marry such women as seem good to you, two and three and four; but if you fear that you will not do justice (between them), then (marry) only one or what your right hands possess [slave girls]; this is more proper, that you may not deviate from the right course." Qur'an IV:3. Of course, Muhammad had a special revelation whereby he could have unlimited wives. Qur'an XXXIII:50.

The "Obedient Wives Club" in Malaysia "published a book urging men in polygamous Muslim marriages to have group sex with their wives" to prevent their men "from straying and pursuing divorce."[64]

> **When I want a sex-slave, I go to the market and pick whichever female I desire and buy her.**
> **- Muslim preacher Abn Ishaq al-Huwaini[65]**

● Muslim women cannot go out without a proper escort, a near relative who is not eligible to marry her.[66]

● Women have obligatory clothing for in the home, at prayer, and outside the home (fully covered).[67] There are variations in different parts of Islam as to covering the face from the veil all the way to the burqa. Iran even had a fashion show with what was acceptable dress and how the police were to control it.[68] Famous Salafi preacher Sheikh Abu Ishaq al-Huwainia told a group that women needed to wear the veil because a woman's face is like her vagina.[69]

● In addition to being inferior to men, wives should be ruled over by men and if disobedient, should be **beaten**. "Men are the maintainers of women because Allah has made some of them to excel others and because they spend out of their property; the good women are therefore obedient, guarding the unseen as Allah has guarded; and (as to) those on whose part you fear desertion, admonish them, and leave them alone in their sleeping-places and beat them." Qur'an IV:34. A woman went to Aisha complaining of her husband's brutality. Aisha took her to Muhammad and said "I have never witnessed women being mistreated as much as Muslim women. Look at her bruises. She has been beaten greener than the veil she wears."[70] Lebanon's highest Sunni authority rejected a bill against wife-beating and marital rape because it would have negative impact on children and lead to the demise "of the family as in the West."[71]

    ● Part of the dual ethics for men and women is **adultery**. A man gets one hundred lashes and exile while a woman is stoned to death, a sentence still imposed from Iran to Africa.[72] One of the most far reaching of Muhammad's convenient revelations is the requirement for four witnesses to rape. Muhammad usually took one of his wives along to battles. The veil had been imposed so no one could see his wives so they had a special enclosed box that went on a camel so she could not be seen. He took Aisha on one such mission and she went away to relieve herself. After she got back she discovered she was missing a necklace and went back to look for it. In the meantime, the men had broken camp and loaded the box on her camel not realizing she was not in it. She finally rejoined the group on a camel lead by young Muslim. There was much gossip and Muhammad finally resolved it with a revelation that is still part of sharia today. "Why did they not bring four witnesses of it? But as they have not brought witnesses they are liars before Allah." Qur'an XXIV:13[73] It is almost impossible to prove rape under sharia and to make it worse, if a woman makes an accusation of rape, she incriminates herself and is admitting to adultery. A result is that 75% of the women in Pakistani prisons are rape victims.[74] This is still the law: Pakistan's Supreme Court recently upheld the acquittal of 5 of 6 men in a high-profile village council-sanctioned rape case.[75]

Adultery and fornication are the same thing.

- Reliance of the Traveller

    ● **Circumcision** is obligatory for men and women in sharia law.[76] It is supposed to honor women, but "most authorities agree that female circumcision is designed to diminish a woman's sexual response, so that she will be less likely to commit adultery."[77]

    For females it is more properly called **female genital mutilation (FGM)**. This is widespread throughout the Muslim world even though it is supposedly not sanctioned. The schools of jurisprudence vary: it is obligatory in the Shafi'i school, not obligatory but sunna or commendable in the Hanabali school, while it is a courtesy to the husband to the Hanafis. Four categories of FGM are recognized by the World Health Organization. One is "clitoridectomy – the severing or excision of the clitoris – is standard practice as described in Umdat al-Salik, a Shafi'i jurisprudence manual certified as 'reliable' by al-Azhar University in Cairo." [Umdat al-Salik is *Reliance of the Traveller*.] In another, "Girls may have their outer genitals removed and stitched up to preserve their virginity, with an opening as small as a matchstick head, meaning it can take up to 20 minutes to urinate." This also happens in Muslim populations in other countries.

    Many Muslim girls are taken back to their home countries by their families for "cutting." Over 22,000 "British schoolgirls as young as eight face being taken abroad this summer to have their genitals mutilated and stitched up to preserve 'purity.'" It is estimated that "As many as 130 million women worldwide have suffered one form or another of FGM." It is really child abuse.[78] Education has not proved to be the solution. It "disguises the true nature of FGM as a form of systematic violence which intends to keep the subordination of girls and women in the concerned – predominantly Muslim – societies alive." It is not wealth either. After 70 years of "awareness-raising campaigns" in Sudan, "FGM did not decline a single percent and remains as high as 89%. The mutilation-rate in highly educated families is 3% higher than in uneducated ones. In the wealthiest class of population, the prevalence of

FGM is even 20% higher than in the poorest class."[79] This is a brutal and sadistic aspect of Muslim treatment of women.

Female Genital Mutilation is another example of the inhumane and brutal treatment of women by Muslims.

For a good review of the UN Human Rights Council meetings on FGM in which testimony was blocked by "point of order" 7 times by Egypt, twice by Pakistan, twice by Iran, and once by Cuba, see "FGM: 'traditional practice' in 32 countries, of which 29 are OIC States – 3 million girls mutilated worldwide each year, 95% of Egyptians."[80] The Muslim states hate to have this subject discussed in public.

Muslim men seem very insecure and are concerned about (or fear) women. Having been trained that females are just objects, perhaps they do not know how to make love to a woman as a partner. They seem to be the original "wham, bam, thank you ma'am" types, but it is doubtful they ever say thank you.

● The desert warriors evidently could not go long without sex but prostitution was banned. Muhammad came up with a solution, "**temporary marriage**," which was permitted for three nights. A Muslim can pay a woman for a temporary marriage, but that is not prostitution! Ali supposedly said that Muhammad later cancelled it, but it is still the custom in Shia Islam.[81]

As we saw with the uncivilized treatment of women by the Taliban in Afghanistan, the status of women under Islam is not likely to improve. They will continue to be treated as chattel, with polygamy, capricious divorce, false accusations, beatings, and loss of basic human rights as long as the Qur'an and sharia are dominant.[82]

As noted above, in another of Muhammad's convenient revelations, Allah allowed him to have as many wives as he wanted, and according to Islamic tradition, Gabriel gave him "the power of sexual intercourse equal to forty men."[83] He had at least fifteen wives, perhaps as many as twenty-five (none until after Khadija's death – his marriages included both a Jew and a Christian[84] and none of his marriages in Medina produced children who survived to adulthood[85] – in a different book it says "None of Mohammed's wives in Medina ever got pregnant."[86]).

Aisha, the daughter of Abu Bakr (who would become the first caliph), was the youngest at only six years old (consummated at age nine) and the only virgin he married; Muhammad was fifty-one by then. Aisha was his favorite wife and stayed with him until he died in her lap.[87] **Child marriages** were common at that time and still are in Saudi Arabia and other Muslim countries as well as selling females.[88] Ayatollah Khomeini married a girl of ten when he was 28.[89] Yusuf al-Qaradawi, the spiritual leader of the Muslim Brotherhood, married a girl of 14.

"**Muslim 'child-marriage'** – euphemism for pedophilia" as Raymond Ibrahim describes it is back in the headlines. A prominent cleric and member of Saud Arabia's highest religious council, Dr. Salih bin Fawzan, issued a **fatwa** stating "there is **no minimum age for marriage**, and that girls can be married '**even if they are in the cradle**.'" Stressing that there is "no age limit whatsoever; the only question open to consideration is whether the girl is physically capable of handling her husband/rapist." Fawzan documented his fatwa by quoting from Salih Bukhari: "The ulema [Islam's interpreters] have agreed that it is permissible for fathers to marry off their small daughters, even if they are in the cradle. But it is not permissible for their husbands to have sex with them unless they are capable of being placed beneath and bearing the weight of the men. And their capability in this regard varies based on their nature and capacity."[90] And who determines that capability?

Child marriages: **It is not permissible for their husbands to have sex with them [young girls] unless they are capable of being placed beneath and bearing the weight of the men.**
- Fatwa by Saudi cleric Dr. Salih bin Fawzan

A recent fiery example was when a notorious pro-Taliban Islamist clergy in Bangladesh, Mufti Fazlul Haque Amini, threatened to wage jihad in the country if the government dared pass any law banning child marriage. He said he had two hundred thousand jihadists who were ready to "sacrifice" lives if any such law, which goes against the Qur'an and Sunna, were passed by the government.[91] There are even child marriages and forced marriages in Europe.[92]

Political marriages are not unknown in Arabia as Ibn Saud did the same as he built Saudi Arabia. Muhammad also married Hafsah whose husband was killed in battle; she was the daughter of Umar (who would become the second caliph). His daughter Fatima married a cousin Ali (the fourth caliph) and Umm Kulthum married Uthman (who was to become the third caliph).[93] Thus, at least three of the four Rightly Guided Caliphs were related to Muhammad by marriages.

Muhammad was a "vain and jealous man," which gave rise to some extremely personal verses in the Qur'an specifically pertaining to him. He started having his wives wear the veil and declared his wives mother of the faithful and forbade them to remarry after his death.[94] His passion for a Christian, Egyptian slave woman, Maryah, (this was Mary the Copt who was "fair of skin with curly hair"[95]) stirred a rebellion in the harem.[96] Of course, a revelation was needed to support his position – that he did not need to "forbid (yourself) that which Allah has made lawful for you… to please your wives." (Qur'an LXVI:1) This is another example in the Qur'an where it is impossible to understand the verses without the hadiths to put them in context. After a month with Maryah, he finally permitted the rebellious wives to return but with the reminder that, "Maybe, his Lord, if he divorce you, will give him in your place wives better than you, submissive, faithful, obedient, penitent, adorers, fasters, widows and virgins." (Qur'an LXVI:5).[97]

The most astonishing and scandalous revelation at the time involved his adopted son, Zaid, and his only wife, **Zeinab**. Muhammad visited Zaid's house one day while he was away and became infatuated with Zeinab (she was evidently not fully clothed or wearing some flimsy garment). She reported it to Zaid and he conveniently divorced her probably sensing his father's feelings.[98] This was soon approved by another convenient revelation so that Muhammad could marry her: "But when Zaid had accomplished his want of her, We gave her to you as a wife, so that there should be no difficulty for the believers in respect of the wives of their adopted sons, when they have accomplished their want of them; and Allah's command shall be performed." [Qur'an XXXIII:37.] It was convenient to be able to write the rules.

The Legacy of Muhammad

Much of his legacy is referred to as **Muhammadism** (or Mohammedism) – perhaps, for short, we should just call it **Moism**.[99] There are a number of assumptions and attitudes that arose in the minds of those early Muslims, particularly after the Battle of Badr, which still ring true today.

- Allah will grant victory to his people against foes that are superior in numbers or firepower, so long as they remain faithful to his commands.
- Victories entitle the Muslims to appropriate the possessions of the vanquished as booty.
- Bloody vengeance against one's enemies belongs not solely to the Lord, but also to those who submit to him on earth. That is the meaning of the word Islam: submission.
- Prisoners taken in battle against the Muslims may be put to death at the discretion of Muslim leaders.
- Those who reject Islam are "the vilest of creatures" (Qur'an 98:6) and thus deserve no mercy.
- Anyone who insults or even opposes Muhammad or his people deserves a humiliating death – by beheading if possible. [This is in accordance with Allah's command to "smite the necks" of the "unbelievers" (Qur'an 47:4).][100]

Without Khadija to control his passions, the last twelve years of his life were exemplified by revelations that were not solely for his political requirements but often for his personal life, again why the Qur'an is about Muhammad. There are Surahs devoted to The Women (II), The Divorce (LXV), which go into great detail about menstruation, wives, and then in another about beating wives (IV:34) as well as all the problems he had with his women.

> **Islam, this theology of an immoral Arab, is a dead thing. Possibly it might have suited tribes of nomads in the desert. It was no good for a modern progressive state.**
> **- Kemal Ataturk**[101]

The actions he condoned, from murder to rape, would be grounds for war crimes now. Many of the things he did were immoral even in the culture of his time. As one author noted, which is not in the politically correct language of today, the problem "is not that he was a Bedouin, but that he was a morally degenerate Bedouin."[102] Geert Wilders, member of the Dutch parliament who had been in court for his comments about Islam, wrote in a Dutch magazine, that much about Islam that we "regard as abnormal, is perfectly normal for Islam." Although it is taboo to discuss Muhammad, much has been written about his sanity. He quoted Ali Sina, an Iranian ex-Muslim, who wrote that Muhammad was "a narcissist, a paedophile, a mass murderer, a terrorist, a misogynist, a lecher, a cult leader, a madman, a rapist, a torturer, an assassin and a looter." Sina has offered $50,000 to anyone who can disprove it and no one has claimed the reward. The historian Theophanes (752-817) claimed Muhammad was an epileptic; these "crises are sometimes accompanied by hallucinations, perspiration forms [on] the forehead and foaming at the mouth, the very symptoms which Muhammad displayed during his visions." Herman Somers wrote in his book "The other Muhammad" (1992) that he suffered "from acromegaly, a condition caused by a tumor in the pituitary gland," which he said could cause "organic hallucinatory affliction with paranoid characteristics." Two other medical historians wrote of "paranoid hallucinatory schizophrenia." Dr. Masud Ansari ("Psychology of Mohammed: Inside the Brain of a Prophet") saw "the perfect personification of a psychopath in power." He had an "unhinged paranoid personality with an inferiority complex and megalomaniac tendencies. In his forties he starts having visions that lead him to believe he has a cosmic mission, and there is no stopping him." Perhaps he was chewing "qat" the narcotic weed popular in Yemen. It may not be pleasant or politically correct, but it is important for the rest of the world because the Islamic creed obliges 1.5 billion people to follow his example, including death for apostates and anyone who criticizes Islam.[103]

> **"the perfect personification of a psychopath in power."**
> **Dr. Masud Ansari ("Psychology of Mohammed: Inside the Brain of a Prophet")**

"Kill the unbelievers wherever you find them" is powerful and is found some 21 times in the Qur'an (including II:191, IV:89, VIII:12, IX:5). His emphasis on bloodshed is quite different from other religious teachings. The conveyed word from Allah, "And when We wish to destroy a town, We send Our commandment to the people of it who lead easy lives, but they transgress therein; thus the word proves true against it, so We destroy it with utter destruction." (XVII:16) was before we even had the word genocide. "And how many a town which was iniquitous did We demolish, and We raised up after it another people!" (XXI:11)   But destruction and death did not bring in any loot, so he devised a tax for conquered Jews and Christians. "Fight those who do not believe in Allah... out of those who have been given the Book, until they pay the tax in acknowledgment of superiority and they are in a state of subjection." (IX:29) This tax is called the *jizya* or poll tax.

> "How dreadful are the curses which Mohammedanism lays on its votaries! Besides the fanatical frenzy, which is as dangerous in a man as hydrophobia in a dog, there is this fearful fatalistic apathy. Improvident habits, slovenly systems of agriculture, sluggish methods of commerce, and insecurity of property exist wherever the followers of the Prophet rule or live. A degraded sensualism deprives this life of its grace and refinement; the next of its dignity and sanctity. The fact that in Mohammedan law every woman must belong to some man as his absolute property – either as a child, a wife, or a concubine – must delay the final extinction of slavery until the faith of Islam has ceased to be a great power among men.
>
> "Individual Moslems may show splendid qualities. Thousands become the brave and loyal soldiers of the Queen: all know how to die. But the influence of the religion paralyzes the social development of those who follow it. No stronger retrograde force exists in the world. Far from being moribund, Mohammedanism is a militant and proselytizing faith. It has already spread throughout Central Africa, raising fearless warriors at every step; and were it not that Christianity is sheltered in the strong arms of science – the science against which it had vainly struggled – the civilization of modern Europe might fall, as fell the civilization of ancient Rome."
>
> **- Winston Churchill**[104]

The lasting legacy of Muhammad is that he left the world divided in an open-ended ideological conflict between the **Dar al-Islam** (Land of Submission [Peace by Islamic definition]) and the **Dar al-Harb** (Land of War). He declared only three choices: convert to Islam, pay the jizya (only available to Jews, Christians, and some Zoroastrians), or death which leaves a world with no chance for real peace. Whether he really believed what he preached is irrelevant. He was a great man in terms of his role in history; the problem is that his created totalitarian political system with a veneer of religion claims to be the only universal standard for governance and morality. In the cult, he is considered the perfect man, the model for all Muslims, the "greatest and most influential human being in the history of mankind."[105] His call for bloodshed and loot as well as the threat of torture in Hell and the promise of reward in Paradise if slain were powerful calls for simple desert warriors. Therefore, it is important to understand Paradise and Hell as Muhammad portrayed them and how he was able to brainwash simple Arabs to accept his views.

Fear and Obey – Hell and Paradise

Muhammad built a complete philosophic system which includes politics and ethics in which the only reality is Allah who has pre-determined everything in human life, and therefore all humanity must submit to Allah.   Death, Fear, Submission, Hell, and Paradise are key to Islam in that he stressed the coming of the judgment day when the virtuous would go to paradise and the sinners would go to hell.   He established the relationship with Allah as Master/slave and on fear; there are some 300 references to fear in the Qur'an.[106]   The problem with this is that Allah is the unknown and unknowable while Muhammad was the true reality and he was to be obeyed – "listen to Mohammed, the prophet of the only god, Allah, or you will suffer eternal torture in Hell."[107]   "When Mohammed spoke, a Muslim had only one choice: Listen and obey."[108]   Again **Muhamm/Allah** or **MoAllah**?

Obey Allah and the Apostle, that you may be shown mercy.

- Qur'an III:132

There are over 300 references to Disbelievers and similar mentions that they are going to Hell (or suffer a painful doom, a painful chastisement, or suffer in the Fire – depending upon translations and the use of different expressions for hell).   Such mentions seem to appear several times on almost every page of the Qur'an.   Muhammad used Hell mainly as a political threat, "a political prison for dissenters."   According to one count, there are 146 references to Hell in the Qur'an with only 9 for moral failings.   The other 137 (94%) call for eternal torture for not agreeing with Muhammad.[109]

Whoever disobeys Allah and His Apostle, surely he shall have the fire of Hell.

- Qur'an LXXII:23

The descriptions of Hell were graphic, brutal, and crude: "whoever disobeys Allah and His Apostle, surely he shall have the fire of Hell," (LXXII:23) "then put a chain on him, Then cast him into the burning fire." (LXIX:30-31) "He shall have an entertainment of boiling water, And burning in hell." (LVI:93-94) "When the fetters and the chains shall be on their necks; they shall be dragged into boiling water, then in the fire shall they be burned." (XL:71-72) "This is the hell with which you were threatened.   And if We please We would surely put out their eyes," (XXXVI:63,66) "And (as for) those who disbelieve, for them is the fire of hell; it shall not be finished with them entirely so that they should die, not shall the chastisement thereof be lightened to them: even thus do We retribute every ungrateful one." (XXXV:36) "These are two adversaries who dispute about their Lord; then (as to) those who disbelieve, for them are cut out garments of fire; boiling water shall be poured over their heads.   With it shall be melted what is in their bellies and (their) skins as well.   And for them are whips of iron.   Whenever they will desire to go forth from it, from grief, they shall be turned back into it, and taste the chastisement of burning," (XXII:19-22) [The next verse is about paradise!]   "We have made hell a prison for the unbelievers." (XVII:8) "The punishment of those who wage war against Allah and His apostle and strive to make mischief in the land is only this, that they should be murdered or crucified or their hands and their feet should be cut off on opposite sides or they should be imprisoned." (V:33).

> **Indeed it would be difficult to imagine a more primitive God. The bloodthirsty Allah delights in the tortures of his hell and rewards those who by slaying his "enemies" by bestowing upon them the sensual delights of a heavenly brothel.**
>
> **- Rebecca Bynum**[110]

To see the crudeness of some of Muhammad's observations, look at Warner, *An Abridged Koran*, p. 70. In addition to torture and beheading, the Muslims could be quite mean. Muhammad sent one of his commanders out on a raid to find two people and burn them, but then changed the order because only Allah can punish with fire, so "just kill them." This same commander lost a battle and sought revenge. He was successful the next time and captured an old woman who was one of the leader's wives – "her legs were tied to two camels, and she was torn apart. Her daughter was taken back to Medina as a pleasure slave."[111] On his Night Journey, Muhammad "saw men with lips like camels. In their hands were flaming hot coals. They would shove the coals into their mouths and the burning coals came out of their ass."…and "he saw women hanging from their breasts."[112]

Apostates are particularly hated in Islam and the penalty is death. Some men killed a shepherd and stole the herd. They were brought before Muhammad who "ordered that their hands and feet be cut off and their eyes gouged out with hot pokers. They were then thrown on jagged rocks, their pleas for water ignored and they died of thirst." According to the hadith, "They were thieves and murderers who abandoned Islam and reverted to paganism, thus attacking Allah and Mohammed."[113] Apostates are regularly attacked across the Muslim world, a current example being an Egyptian convert and his daughter who fled to Syria and then to France for asylum.[114]

> **Know that Paradise is under the shades of swords.**
>
> **- Muhammad**[115]

Muhammad said, "'Certainly, the gates of Paradise lie in the shade of swords.' A shabby man… then unsheathed his sword, broke and discarded his scabbard, advanced upon the enemy, and fought until he was killed."[116]

To balance the wrath of Allah and the threat of torture in Hell, was the promised delights of Paradise if one lived a good life and did what Muhammad ordered. The attraction for the simple Arab warriors was booty, but if they were killed in battle, Muhammad motivated them by guaranteeing a very material and sensual paradise in which to indulge their physical appetites – with everything a poor Arab of the desert could wish for: gold, jewels, fruit, water, wine, women, and boys. "The joys and glories of Paradise are as fantastic and sensual as the lascivious Arabian mind could possibly imagine."[117] The rewards of martyrdom are central to jihad. The word for martyr - shadid – has the same root as shahada – the declaration of faith, so it is the supreme expression of faith. It appears that everything that was prohibited or scarce in their miserable earthly lives was available in abundance in paradise. For people of the desert, water was a very precious commodity and it was promised as free flowing, as well as endless shade, comforts, and companionship. There are many references in the Qur'an to the "garden" which is paradise.

"Surely Allah has bought of the believers their persons and their property for this, that they shall have the garden; they fight in Allah's way, so they slay and are slain." (IX:111) "A likeness of the garden which the righteous are promised; there flow beneath it rivers, its food and shades are perpetual; this is the requital of those who guarded (against evil), and the requital of the unbelievers is the fire." (XIII:35) There is much repetition in the Qur'an often with identical expressions or with only minor variations. Referring again to those who guarded against evil and the garden they are promised, "Therein are rivers of water that does not alter, and rivers of milk the taste whereof does not change, and rivers of drink [wine] delicious to those who drink, and rivers of honey clarified; and for them therein are all the fruits and protection from their Lord." (XLVII:15) There are numerous other references to the garden: "gardens of pleasure" (XXXVII:43), "gardens and springs" (XLIV:52), "gardens and bliss" (LII:17 and LVI:12), "garden and silk" (LXXVI:12), "Gardens and vineyards" (LXXVIII:32), and "In a lofty garden." (LXXXVIII:10).

> **"Where do I go if I am killed in battle?" Mohammed said, "Paradise." The man then threw away the meal that he was carrying, joined the battle, and fought until he was killed.**[118]

For the fallen warrior, he could expect to wear "fine and thick silk" (XLIV:53), reclining on decorated and exalted thrones (LVI:15 & 34) or beds with "silk brocades" or "green cushions and beautiful carpets" (LV:54,76) with silver vessels and glass goblets (LXXVI:15) for whatever he wished to eat or drink. There would be "water running out of springs," (XXXVII:45), "fruits such as they choose, and the flesh of fowl such as they desire." (LVI:20-21), and of course all they wanted to drink. Interesting that the Muslims prohibit wine on earth but permit it in paradise! But that wine is special because it does not cause any hangover. "They shall not be affected with headache thereby, nor shall they get exhausted." (LVI:19)

Then there were the ravishing girls – the **houris**. Muhammad had a thing about beautiful eyes. "And with them shall be those who restrain the eyes, having beautiful eyes; As if they were eggs carefully protected." (XXXVII:48-49). "We will wed them with Houris pure, beautiful ones." (XLIV:54). "Reclining on thrones set in lines, and We will unite them to large-eyed beautiful ones." (LII:20) – "those who restrained their eyes; before them neither man nor jinni shall have touched them." - "As though they were rubies and pearls." – "Pure ones confined to the pavilions." - "Man has not touched them before them nor jinni." (LV:56,58,72,74) – "And pure, beautiful ones, The like of hidden pearls." "Then We have made them virgins. Loving, equals in age. For the sake of the companions of the right hand." (LVI:22-23,36-38). The descriptions of paradise can be extravagant. One refers to giving each man the "potentialities of a hundred individuals," a large mansion for each, 80,000 servants, 72 wives, 300 attendants serving 300 kinds of food on gold plates, "an inexhaustible supply of wine and liquor," etc.[119]

For those so inclined, boys are mentioned often. "And around them shall go boys of theirs as if they were hidden pearls." (LII:24) – "Round about them shall go youths never altering in age." (LVI:17, also LXXVI:19 and LXXXVIII:33)[120]

A Saudi diplomat sought asylum in the US, saying he feared for his life if he went home because of being gay and his friendship with a Jewish woman.[121] His request was denied.

In case you think this is all nonsense from the seventh century, remember that Muhammad Atta, the hijacker of 11 September, had a paradise wedding suit in his luggage and the letter he left mentioned his "'marriage' with the 'women of paradise… dressed in their most beautiful clothing.'"[122]

With the often reference to the 72 women in paradise for suicide bombers, Muhammad's paradise is still alive. But what does a female suicide bomber get?

Muhammad's paradise was for men – there is nothing for women![123] A man who died a martyr in jihad was guaranteed entrance to Paradise.[124] The only way for a woman to be guaranteed entrance to Paradise was if she pleased her husband, further subjugation![125]

Now we should look at what Muhammad created: a completely new ethos called Islam.

> **One ought never to allow a disorder to take place in order to avoid war, for war is not thereby avoided, but only deferred to your disadvantage…. Thus it comes about that all armed prophets have conquered and unarmed ones failed.**
>
> **- Machiavelli**[126]

Notes

1. Number 5 of The Prophet said, "I have been given five things which were not given to anyone else before me.
    1. Allah made me victorious by awe, by His frightening my enemies for a distance of one month's journey.
    2. The earth has been made for me and my followers a place for praying and to perform my rituals; therefore, anyone of my followers can pray whenever the time of a prayer is due.
    3. The spoils of war have been made lawful for me yet they were not lawful for anyone else before me.
    4. I have been given the right of intercession on the Day of Resurrection.
Sahih Bukhari, volume 1, book 7, number 331, quoted in Bill Warner, *Mohammed and the Unbelievers: The Sira a Political Biography,* (CSPI Publications, www.cspipublishing.com, 2006), p. 71, hereafter *Sira.*
2. Letter to the Reader. To Muslims May the Truth Set You Free, *Prophet of Doom, Islam's Terrorist Dogma In Muhammad's Own Words,* www.prophetofdoom.net.
3. Bill Warner, *The Political Traditions of Mohammed, The Hadith for the Unbelievers,* (CSPI, cspipublsihing.com, 2006) p. 165, hereafter *Hadith.*
4. Allah, a moon god, was one of many gods in Mecca and was the god of the Quraysh tribe of Muhammad's family. His father was named Abdullah, which means slave of Allah. Bill Warner, *An Abridged Koran, A Reconstructed Historical Koran,* (CSPI, cspipublishing.com, 2006), p. 10, hereafter *An Abridged Koran.*
5. There are various ways of spelling Muhammad such as Mohammed, Muhamad, Mohamed, and Mahomet. The variations on the spelling of words from Arabic depend on the transliteration from Arabic into English.
    Translating Arabic is difficult even for native speakers. "There are many Arabics. Classical Arabic is derived from Islam's holy book, the Koran, and Islamic studies. It is written but rarely spoken. Modern Standard Arabic, although not spoken by the masses, is the language of modern journalism, used in newspapers and news reports. Then there is colloquial Arabic, spoken differently in each of the 22 Middle Eastern countries. Meanwhile, within these nations there are dozens of regional dialects that add or subtract letters, words, and accents, with a sprinkling of other languages mixed in as well."
    There can be serious consequences: two Muslim men were arrested in Albany, New York after mistranslation of the word which prosecutors thought meant "commander" (of a terrorist group) when the word was "brother." Souheila Al-Jadda, "Lost in Arabic translation," *The Christian Science Monitor,* 16 September 2004.

6. The Kaaba is the large black cube-shaped building in Mecca which is the center of the Hajj or pilgrimage to Mecca. It contains a certain black stone, probably a meteorite, which supposedly was brought down from heaven. Pagan Arabs had long made the pilgrimage to the Kaaba where their ritual included running around it seven times, kissing the black stone, and then running a mile or so to the dry well of Wadi Mina "to throw stones at the devil." The black stone held special prominence but the Kaaba eventually housed hundreds of idols [about 360] each revered by a different Arabian tribe. These various tribes, when away from Mecca, faced toward it at their prayers. Serge Trifkovic, *The Sword of the Prophet: Islam, history, theology, impact on the world,* (Boston, MA, Regina Orthodox Press, Inc., 2002), p. 21.

Islam contends that the Kaaba was built by Abraham, the patriarch of the Jews, Warner, *An Abridged Koran,* p. 2.

7. Trifkovic, *The Sword of the Prophet,* pp. 14, 17.

8. Robert Spencer, *The Truth about Muhammad, Founder of the World's Most Intolerant Religion* (Washington, DC, Regnery Publishing, Inc., 2006), p. 34.

9. Thomas W. Lippman, *ISLAM Politics and Religion in the Muslim World,* (New York, Foreign Policy Association Headline Series, No., 258, March/April 1982), p. 18.

10. Trifkovic, *The Sword of the Prophet,* pp. 17-19.

11. Gabriel Oussani and Hilaire Belloc, *Moslems, Their beliefs, practices, and politics,* (Ridgefield, Connecticut, Roger A. McCaffrey Publishing, no date but published after 11 September 2001, originally published in the *Catholic Encyclopedia* about 1907), p. 13.

12. Robert Spencer, *The Politically Incorrect Guide to Islam (and the Crusades),* (Washington, DC, Regnery Publishing, Inc., 2005), pp. 4-5.

13. Trifkovic, *The Sword of the Prophet,* p. 26.

14. Ibid., p. 27.

15. "He had no formal education and apparently remained illiterate all his life." Lippman, *ISLAM,* p. 19. Yet the *Encyclopedia Britannica,* 1944, Vol. 15, p. 646, states he "probably could read and write." See Spencer, *The Truth about Muhammad,* p. 56, that he was evidently illiterate. Spencer wrote that Muhammad replied to Gabriel "I do not know how to read.", p. 41. Also the biography of Muhammad in Ahmad ibn Naqib al-Misri, *Reliance of the Traveller, A Classic Manual of Islamic Sacred Law,* (Beltsville, Maryland, Amana Publications, 2008), x245, p. 1072, refers to him as "unlettered." Book V "Allah and His Messenger" refers to the "unlettered prophet" v2.1, p. 822.

16. *Encyclopedia Britannica,* Vol. 15, p. 646.

17. Trifkovic, *The Sword of the Prophet,* p. 29.

18. Surah VI:108. The Qur'an was written in Arabic so we are forced to deal with translations. Each seems to be quite different much like the many versions of the Bible. The Qur'an I use was translated by M. H. Shakir for Tahrike Tarsile Qur'an, Inc. Publishers and Distributors of The Qur'an, P.O. Box 1115, Corona-Elmhurst Station, Elmhurst, New York 11373-1515, Fifth U.S. Edition, 1988. Quotations are with the Surah (or Chapter) first followed by the number of the verse. As with almost any word translated from Arabic, there can be different spellings. Surah is also spelled surrah, surra, and sura.

19. Trifkovic, *The Sword of the Prophet,* p. 32. Evidently Muhammad did not know that the first Jerusalem Temple had been destroyed in 587 BC and the Second in 70 AD. The *Masjid al-Aqsa* was built in 691AD.

At the seventh heaven, Allah gave him the duty of 50 prayers. When he returned past Moses, Moses inquired as to how many prayers Allah had directed. Moses said that was too many, go back to Allah and ask for a reduction. He did this several times until Allah reduced it to five. Moses urged him to go back again but Muhammad was embarrassed to ask again. Warner, *An Abridged Koran,* p. 71.

20. Ishaq's *Sira,* margin note 265, Warner, *Sira,* p. 31.

21. Qur'an CXI:1-5.

22. Warner, *Hadith,* p. 169.

23. *Encyclopedia Britannica,* Vol. 15, p. 647, states they offered him the "dictatorship of Yathrib." See also Warner, *An Abridged Koran,* p. 98.

24. *Encyclopedia Britannica,* Vol. 15, p. 647, uses the date 22 July 622 AD as the beginning of the Muhammad era.

25. Trifkovic, *The Sword of the Prophet,* pp. 34-35.

26. Qur'an II:217.

27. Robert Spencer, *The Politically Incorrect Guide to Islam,* p. 7.

28. Trifkovic, *The Sword of the Prophet,* p. 36.

29. Warner, *Sira,* p. 71.

30. Warner, *An Abridged Koran,* p. 135.

31. Spencer, *The Truth about Muhammad,* pp. 104, 106.

32. Trifkovic, *The Sword of the Prophet,* p. 38.

33. Spencer, *The Truth about Muhammad,* p. 113.

34. Trifkovic, *The Sword of the Prophet,* p. 39. Music was also in trouble. Mainstream Islam does not accept music. p. 40. He had the Jewish poet Ka'b bin Al-Ashraf killed for supposedly insulting Muslim women. Spencer, *The Truth about Muhammad,* p. 115. He later had two other poets, Abu 'Afak and 'Asama bint Marwan killed for mocking him and his prophetic pretensions, pp. 162-163.

35. Spencer, *The Politically Incorrect Guide to Islam,* pp. 12-14.

36. Spencer, *The Truth about Muhammad,* pp. 121-122.

37. Spencer, *The Politically Incorrect Guide to Islam,* p. 12. Also in Tabari 7:97 ("The History of the Messengers and the Kings," by Muslim historian Abu Ja'far Muhammad bin Jarir al-Tabari (839-923). Volume 7, number 97). The morning after the murder of Ashraf, the Prophet declared, "Kill any Jew who falls under your power."

38. Trifkovic, *The Sword of the Prophet,* p. 43. Also Spencer, *The Truth about Muhammad,* p. 133.

39. *Encyclopedia Britannica,* Vol. 15, p. 648.

40. Warner, *Sira,* pp. 94-97.

41. See Spencer, *The Truth about Muhammad,* p. 129. There are three references in the Qur'an: II:65, V:60, and VII:166.

42. Spencer, *The Truth about Muhammad,* pp. 128-133. See also Trifkovic, *The Sword of the Prophet,* pp. 40-42.

43. Warner, *Sira,* p. xi.

44. Trifkovic, *The Sword of the Prophet,* p. 44. As with most numbers, the figure 900 is sometimes less but the lowest was 600.

45. Rebecca Bynum, *Allah Is Dead: Why Islam is Not a Religion,* (Nashville, Tennessee, New England Review Press, 2011), p. 145.

46. Warner, *Sira,* p. xi.

47. Trifkovic, *The Sword of the Prophet,* p. 45.

48. Ibid., pp. 45-46.

49. Spencer, *The Politically Incorrect Guide to Islam,* p. 83.

50. Spencer, *The Truth about Muhammad,* pp. 136-139.

51. Trifkovic, *The Sword of the Prophet,* pp. 48-49.

52. Saudi police raided an evening prayer meet4ing in December 2011 at the home of an Ethiopian Christian and arrested 42. "42 Ethiopian Christians arrested in Saudi Arabia, Persecution, 17 December 2011, Jihad Watch, 18 December 2011.

53. Dr. Ja'far Sheikh Idris, "Separation Of Church And State," Islam.com, Jihad Watch, 4 September 2010.

54. "The Key to Jihad is Money," Citizen Warrior, 22 June 2011. This chart is in Bill Warner, *An Abridged Koran* ,p. 201, *Hadith,* p. 170, and *Sira,* p. 166.

55. *Sahih Bukhari,* volume 7, book 62, number 33, quoted in Warner, *Hadith,* p. 92.

56. *Sahih Bukhari,* volume 7, book 62, number 113, quoted in Warner, *Hadith,* p. 92.

57. Warner, *Hadith,* p. 93.

58. Sahih Bukhari volume7, book 62, number 81. According to the law, it is customary. *Reliance of the Traveller,* m10.12(3), p. 541.

59. See Warner, *Hadith,* p. 94. *Sahih Bukhari,* volume 7, book 62, numbers 16 and 173. *Reliance of the Traveller,* e4.1(3), p. 58.

60. White slaves were much preferred for sex and their price was three to ten times higher than black slaves. Warner, *Hadith,* p. 80.

61. Warner, *Sira,* pp. 169-170.

62. *Sahih Bukhari,* volume 3, book 48, number 826.

63. Raymond Ibrahim, "Muslim Woman Seeks to Revive Institution of Sex-Slavery," FrontPageMagazine.com, 6 June 2011.

"Muslim men who fear being seduced or tempted into immoral behavior by the beauty of their female servants, or even those servants 'casting spells' on them, would be better to purchase women from an 'enslaved maid' agency for sexual purposes....'We want our youth to be protected from adultery,' said al-Mutairi, suggesting that these maids could be brought as prisoners of war in war-stricken nations like Chechnya to be sold later to devout merchants."

Ibrahim translated excerpts from a video on Al Arabiya: "The Kuwaiti female activist begins by insisting that 'it's of course true' that 'the prophet of Islam legitimized sex-slavery.' She recounts how when she was in Mecca, Islam's holiest city, she asked various sheikhs and muftis about the legality of sex-slavery according to Sharia: they all confirmed it to be perfectly legal; Kuwaiti ulema further pointed out that extra 'virile' men – Western synonyms include 'sex-crazed,' 'lecherous,' 'perverted' – would do well to purchase sex-slaves to sate their appetites without sinning.

"A Muslim state must attack a Christian state – sorry, I mean any non-Muslim state – and they must be captives of the raid. Is this forbidden? Not at all; according to Islam, sex slaves are not forbidden. [The quote in the box followed.]

Her suggestion: "For example, in the Chechnyan war, surely there are female Russian captives. So go buy those and sell them here in Kuwait; better that than have our men engage in forbidden sexual relations. I don't see any problem in this, no problem at all."

She is considerate! "Mutairi suggest the enslaved girls be at least 15 years-old."

Perhaps this is part of the "Stockholm Syndrome." Muslim females have been brainwashed since birth that they are inferior and are expected to do the bidding of males.

64. "Malaysian polygamy club 'encourages group sex'," *Agence France-Presse,* 15 October 2011.

65. Ibid.

66. Warner, *Hadith,* p. 97.

67. *Reliance of the Traveller,* w23.1, p. 899.

68. Thomas Erdbrink, "Ahmadinejad steps into Iran's dress0code debate," *The Washington Post,* 26 December 2011.

69. "Face of woman like her vagina," Elaph (in Arabic), 13 December 2011, Jihad Watch, 14 December 2011.

70. *Sahih Bukhari,* volume 7, book, 72, number 715, quoted in Warner, *Hadith,* p. 92.

71. "Lebanon Sunni clergy reject domestic abuse law," AFP, 24 June 2011. "Islam is very aware of and concerned with… resolving problems of poor treatment… but this should not happen by cloning Western laws that encourage the breakdown of the family and do not suit our society." The marital rape clause was referred to as "heresy." It continued, "'This will have a negative impact on Muslim children… who will see their mother threatening their father with prison, in defiance of patriarchal authority, which will in turn undermine the moral authority' of fathers."

72. *Sahih Bukhari,* volume 3, book 49, number 860. Warner, *Hadith,* pp. 89-90.

73. Warner, *An Abridged Koran,* pp. 165-166.

74. Spencer, *The Truth about Muhammad,* p. 68. Spencer, *The Politically Incorrect Guide to Islam,* pp. 74-76. See *Reliance of the Traveller,* o12.0, p. 610, for "The Penalty for Fornication or Sodomy and o13.0, p. 611, "The Penalty for Accusing a Person of Adultery Without Proof."

75. "Pakistan: Acquittals in Mukhtaran Mai gang rape case," BBC News, April 21, 2011, Jihad Watch, 22 April 2011. It was the usual "lack of evidence" due to the lack of four male witnesses.

76. *Reliance of the Traveller,* e4.3, p. 59. It calls for the removal of the prepuce of the clitoris, not the clitoris itself. However, Muhammad never forbade removal of the clitoris, which was common in his day and is still practiced in parts of the Islamic world. Warner, *Hadith,* p. 99.

77. Spencer, *The Politically Incorrect Guide to Islam,* pp. 76-77.

78. Jessica Elgot, "UK Girls At Risk of Mutilation Abroad," *Independent,* 4 July 2011. It is interesting to note that Iraqi Kurdistan has banned female genital mutilation. Hemn Hady and Patrick Smith, "Ban on female genital mutilation passed," *AKNews,* 23 June 2011.
     However, a mullah objected that it was obligatory in the Shafi'i school and should not be outlawed. "Female Genital Mutilation 'Is an Obligation' Says Mullah in Iraqi-Kurdistan," by Thomas v. der Osten-Sacken for Stop FGM Kurdistan, 15 August 2011, via the Assyrian International News Agency, Jihad Watch, 16 August 2011.
     "Each year, 6,500 girls in central London undergo female genital mutilation." Sen. Harry Reid (D-NV) introduced legislation in November 2011 (to close a "vacation loophole" in his 1996 bill) "that would make it a crime under U.S. law to take young girls out of the U.S. for the purpose of genital mutilation." Bulletin of the Oppression of Women, 14 November-15 December 2011, politicalislam.com.

79. Jamie Glazov, "Our Complicity in Female Genital Mutilation," an interview with Ines Laufer, FrontPage, 19 July 2011, Jihad Watch.

80. Jihad Watch, 4 April 2010.

81. See Warner, *Hadith,* pp.94-95. *Sahih Bukhari,* volume 7, book 62, numbers 51, 52, and 130. *Sahih Muslim,* book 008, numbers 3248 and 3252. Qur'an V:87.

82. See Spencer, *The Politically Incorrect Guide to Islam,* p. 77.

83. Spencer, *The Truth about Muhammad,* p. 172.

84. Lippman, *ISLAM,* p. 19.

85. Warner, *Sira,* p. 78.

86. Warner, *Hadiths,* p. 126.

87. The details are related in several Hadiths by Bukhari and Muslim, for example, *Sahih Bukhari,* volume 7, book 62, number 65, quoted in Warner, *Hadith,* p. 124.

88. "80-year-old man married 11-year-old girl in Saudi Arabia," *Al-Arabiya,* 17 January 2010. Another Saudi man over 80 married a 14-year-old girl, *Emirate 24/7,* 3 November 2010. See Spencer, *The Truth about Muhammad,* p. 172, for the legal age for marriage in Iran is nine for girls and that many girls are married by age thirteen.
     "Turkey: 12-Year-Old Girl Sold By Father for 4 Cows," ANSAmed, quoted in Jihad Watch, 21 January 2010. A 20-year-old woman was auctioned in Pakistan and the "Auction money was distributed equally among all the brothers of the girl." Sikander Khoso, "Woman sold in public auction in Pakistan for $3,200," *The Nation,* 13 December 2009.

89. Spencer, *The Truth about Muhammad,* pp. 170-171.

90. In Saudi newspapers 13 July 2011, Raymond Ibrahim, "New Saudi Fatwa Defends Pedophilia as 'Marriage'," Jihad Watch, 21 July 2011.

91. "Islamist leader threatens of waging Jihad," Weekly Blitz, 20 April 2011, Jihad Watch, 22 April 2011. A similar fight arose after a pre-pubescent wife (11 years old) was tied to a bed and raped. "Islamists Fight Yemen Law Banning Child Marriage," *Fox News,* 16 April 2009.

92. "Several hundred cases of child marriages in Sweden," *Dagen* (newspaper), 20 April 2011, translated by Nicolai Sennels, "Immigrants in Sweden: 200 child marriages yearly; 8,500 fear forced marriages."

93. Trifkovic, *The Sword of the Prophet,* p. 46. There is confusion about Umm Kulthum: Trifkovic refers to her as Muhammad's daughter; Spencer refers to her as a woman from the Quraysh who left Mecca to join Muhammad and he would not force her to return, which violated a treaty he had agreed to (mentioned above). Spencer, *A Politically Incorrect Guide to Islam,* pp. 16-17.

94. Warner, *An Abridged Koran,* p. 171.

95. Warner, *Sira,* p. 133. She bore his only son but he died in infancy.

96. Trifkovic, *The Sword of the Prophet,* p. 46.

97. Muhammad's wives were quartered in separate houses or apartments next to his mosque and he visited each on a schedule. He had set Mary the Copt up in a separate location in Medina. The scandal was supposedly that Hafsah caught him in her bed with Mary. He promised not to do it again but she told Aisha. The wives banded together and he swore to stay away from them for a month. Muhammad stayed with Mary for 29 days until he received another revelation releasing him from his oath. Spencer, *The Truth about Muhammad,* pp. 21-24. Warner, *An Abridged Koran,* pp. 168-169.

98. Trifkovic, *The Sword of the Prophet,* pp. 46-47.

99. See for example, "The Great and Enduring Heresy of Mohammed" by Hilaire Belloc in Oussani and Belloc, *Moslems,* which was written in 1936. "Mohammedanism was a *heresy*: that is the essential point to grasp before going any further. It began as heresy, not as a new religion. It was not a pagan contrast with the Church; it was not an alien enemy. It was a perversion of Christian doctrine." p. 105.

100. Spencer, *The Politically Incorrect Guide to Islam,* p. 10.

101. Ataturk also said, " Islam is an absurd theology of an immoral Bedouin, a rotting corpse which poisons our lives."

102. Quoted in Trifkovic, *The Sword of the Prophet,* p. 50. See also Serge Trifkovic, "New Book Reveals the Truth About Islam's Founder," Human Events, 30 October 2006, in which he reviewed Robert Spencer's book, *The Truth about Muhammad: Founder of the World's Most Intolerant Religion,* Regnery, 2006. The quote is in the book review also.
     Muhammad never had to explain who Allah is because he was already well known to his Quraysh tribe as a moon god. The cult treatment of Muhammad leads to the conjecture that Allah is Muhammad, the idea of MuAllah. Some have said that Muhammad is Islam, not Allah, and that Allah is Muhammad's "sock puppet, his prop, his 'enabler,' his unverifiable excuse." And that he was "a sick, brutish, misogynistic, paedophilic, charlatan and murderer" and the Hadith does not hide these nasty details. See Elanor's reply to classicus in Jihad Watch, 19 October 2010.

103. Geert Wilders, "Time to Unmask Muhammad," English translation of an op-ed piece in the Dutch magazine *HP/De Tijd,* 30 March 2011, posted in Jihad Watch, 30 March 2011. See also "Raymond Ibrahim: New book on Muhammad omits 'images of Muhammad as war-monger, highway-bandit, misogynist and assassin," Jihad Watch, 20 December 2010, in which Ibrahim

reviewed a book, *Images of Muhammad: Narratives of the Prophet in Islam across the Centuries,* by Tarif Khalidi in the Fall 2010 Middle East Quarterly. He noted that it was not unsurprising for today's academic establishment that Khalidi "omits the more troubling images" of Muhammad.

104. Spencer, *The Politically Incorrect Guide to Islam*, p. 92 and *The River War,* 1st edition, Vol. II, pp. 248-250, London.
105. *Reliance of the Traveller,*x245, p. 1072.
106. Warner, *An Abridged Koran,* p. 194.
107. Ibid., p. 199.
108. Warner, *Sira,* p. 70. Qur'an VIII:20.
109. Warner, *An Abridged Koran,* p. 196.
110. Rebecca Bynum, *Allah Is Dea,* p. 100.
111. *Sahih Bukhari,* volume 4, book 52, number 259, and Ishaq's *Sira,* margin note 980, quoted in Warner, *Sira,* p. 148.
112. Warner, *An Abridged Koran,* p. 70, quoted Ibn Ishaq's *Sirat Rasul Allah (The Life of Muhammad),* margin note 269. Re the men, "These were those who had stolen the wealth of orphans. Then he saw the family of the Pharaoh with huge bellies. Then he saw women hanging from their breasts. These women had fathered bastards on their husbands. Mohammed said that Allah hates women who birth bastards. They deprive the true sons of their portion and learn the secrets of the harem."
113. *Sahih Bukhari,* volume 8, book 82, number 797, quoted in Warner, *Hadith,* p. 104.
114. "Egyptian Convert Flees Potential Dangers in Syria," Compass Direct News, April 21, 2011, Jihad Watch, 22 April 2011. They had been in hiding for two and one-half years.
115. *Sahih Bukhari,* volume 4, book 52, number 73, quoted in Warner, *Sira,* p. 146. Also translated as "Be aware that Paradise lies under the shadow of swords." *Hadith,* p. 44.
116. *Sahih Muslim* 020, 4694, Warner, *Hadith,* p. 22.
117. Oussani and Belloc, *Moslems,* p. 26.
118. *Sahih Bukhari,*volume 5, book 59, number 377, Warner, *Hadith,* p. 25. There are other similar references: *Sahih Muslim,* book 20, number 4681, Warner, *Hadith,* p. 22, and Ishaq's *Sira,* margin note 445 (The promise of Paradise was so strong a warrior would throw off his armor and charge into the fight.), Warner, *Sira,* p. 64.
119. Oussani and Belloc, *Moslems,* p. 27.
120. Some wrote that those in paradise would have a permanent erection. Trifkovic, *The Sword of the Prophet*, p. 64.
121. Michael Isikoff, "Saudi diplomat seeking asylum: 'My life is in danger'." NBC News, 11 September 2011.
122. Spencer. *The Politically Incorrect Guide to Islam,* p. 106.
123. Isn't it odd that Muslim men are kept apart from women on earth and can't drink, but when they kill people, they will go to Paradise where 72 virgins await them and they will live in luxury with rivers of wine and boys? What does a female bomber get – 72 studs?
    Men martyrs have been told by recruiters "that a bevy of 72 virgins awaits them in heaven. But some women suicide bombers believe that in paradise they will become queens, while others are told by recruiters that no matter how old or grotesque they may be in this life, they will become the fairest of the 72 virgins that await each jihad warrior."
    One such woman, a 22-year old burn victim from Gaza was convinced by militants "she would never get married and that she was better off becoming a martyr." She was caught when her bomb failed to go off. "Later, crying, she told journalists, 'Maybe I have been used' by the recruiter." Tim McGirk, "Moms and Martyrs," *Time,* 14 May 2007, p. 50.
124. Warner, *Hadith,* pp. 16-17.
125. See Warner, *Hadith,* pp.88-89 for Muhammad's comment that most of the people in Hell were women because they did not show gratitude to their husbands, quoting from *Sahih Bukhari*, volume 1, book 6, number 301 and volume 2, book 18, number 161.
126. Translated a bit differently in *Imperial Hubris,* p. 161. "You ought never to suffer for your designs to be crossed in order to avoid war, since war is not so to be avoided, but is only deferred to your disadvantage....Hence it comes that all armed Prophets have been victorious and all unarmed Prophets have been destroyed."

We don't have freedom of speech in Islam. We have the freedom to obey Allah.

Every Prophet was sent to his nation but only I have been sent to all mankind.
                                                                      - Muhammad

Chapter 3

Islam

Islam is the Arabic word meaning "submission" and is derived from a word meaning "peace."[2] Those who accepted Muhammad's message were called **Muslims** – "those who have submitted."[3] Islam is vastly different from other religions in that it is a complete ideology. It combines religion and politics in a totally complete fatalistic submissiveness. "Islam is not only a religious doctrine; it is also a self-contained world outlook, and a way of life that claims the primary allegiance of all those calling themselves 'Muslim.' Islam is also a detailed legal and political set of teachings and beliefs."[4] "Christianity spread by acquiring believers and then land; Islam spread by acquiring land then believers."[5]

Islam

Islam is purported to be the last of the divine messages delivered by prophets, such as Adam, Abraham, Jacob, Moses, and Jesus who are mentioned in the Qur'an. However, Islam denies the Christian doctrine of the trinity, which Muslims consider akin to polytheism. Islam is not a religion as we understand one; it is a complete way of life. Islam considers itself to be universal, applicable forever, for everyone, and worldwide. It is based on the belief there is only one God, Allah, and that Muhammad is his messenger and the last prophet; fear and obey Allah and Muhammad; and be accountable on Judgment Day and go to Hell or Paradise. Islam claims that both the Bible and the Talmud predicted the coming of Muhammad, but that the Christians and Jews falsified their books to exclude Muhammad, another part of his intense hatred of Jews and Christians.

There are five pillars of Islam. The first is the profession of faith (*shadada*) by declaring that "There is no God but Allah, and Muhammad is His Prophet." Allah is all knowing, unknowable, and beyond human description. He is referred to by some 99 different attributes such as merciful and compassionate in the Qur'an, but the only purpose of the universe and man is to serve (obey) Allah. There are over 300 references to **fear** Allah but only three verses that command love of Allah but not a single verse about compassion or love for a *kafir*.[6] **There is no love in Islam.**[7]

The second pillar is prayer (*salat*). Muhammad established that prayers should be said five times a day: at dawn, noon, afternoon, sunset, and night. The only required communal prayer is at Friday noon, Friday being the Muslim Sabbath. Muslims are required to conduct ablutions, washing the face, arms, and feet before prayers. They stand shoulder to shoulder, regardless of status to symbolize equality. They kneel twice for the morning prayer and four times for the late-night prayer. All prayers face toward Mecca; this *qibla* (direction) adds unity to all Muslims.[8] "**Allahu akbar**" (Allah is Great) starts the call to prayer and, as you have probably noticed, is used regularly by demonstrators and terrorists. "**Al-hamdu Lillah**" (thanks be to Allah) is a very common expression used in almost any context when one is grateful or thankful.[9]

The third pillar is fasting during Ramadan (*siyam*). Ramadan is the ninth month of the lunar year which is 11 days shorter than the Gregorian year, so it moves around the seasons. Total fasting and abstinence are required from dawn to sunset.

The religious tax (*zakat*) is the fourth pillar which is an alms tax similar to tithing. A percentage (2½%) of surplus income or agricultural production is provided to support the poor and the community.

The final pillar is the pilgrimage (*hajj*) to Mecca which all Muslims are to make at least once if they are physically and financially able to make the journey. This was a difficult trip in early days. It is now big business in Saudi Arabia which receives about 2 million pilgrims annually and has developed a very efficient system for handling this large number.

An unwritten additional pillar [it was nearly the sixth pillar] added later is the participation in *jihad*, fighting in the cause of Allah. Interestingly, all these pillars have roots in pre-Islamic times. In particular, the rituals at the Kaaba, as described in a note in Chapter 2, are basically the same as in the pagan days. Many of Muhammad's followers were surprised that he did not abolish this pagan practice.[10] There is little original thinking in the Qur'an: "Almost every aspect of religious ritual in Islam came from the native tribal customs."[11] What originality there is came in its totalitarian political innovations.

Allah and His Messenger

It is important to understand the concept of Allah and His Messenger. *Reliance of the Traveller,* the classic Muslim legal manual, devotes an entire chapter, Book V, to it. Allah "does as he wills,"[12] His Oneness is defined as "He is one in being without partner, unique without peer, ultimate without opposite, alone without equal. He is one, preeternal, beginninglessly uncreate, everlastingly abiding, unceasingly existent, eternally limitless,...He is the First and Last, the Outward and Inward, and He has knowledge of everything."[13] "He is not a body with a form,...He does not resemble anything that exists,...is witness to everything....The existence of His entity is know by human reason."[14] He has no weakness, is "possessed of absolute sovereignty and might, of irresistible power and force....all beings are powerless in His grasp. He alone creates, begins, gives existence, and originates....The number of things He can do is limitless, the amount He knows is infinite."[15] "He knows all things knowable, encompassing all that takes place from the depths of the earth to the highest heaven."[16] He "wills all that exists and directs all events. Nothing occurs in the physical or spiritual world,...save through His ordinance, apportionment, wisdom, and decision. What He wills is, and what He does not will is not."[17] He "is all-hearing and all-seeing."[18] "He is wise in His acts and just in His decrees....Our origination, beginning, and responsibility are of Allah's generosity,...He is not obliged to anyone to do anything, nor is injustice on His part conceivable, for He does not owe any rights to anyone." – only obedience.[19] "Allah Most High sent Muhammad (Allah bless him and give him peace), the **Qurayshite unlettered prophet**, to deliver His inspired message to the **entire world**, Arabs and non-Arabs, jinn and mankind, **superseding and abrogating all previous religious systems** with the **Prophet's Sacred Law, except** for the provisions of them that the **new revelation** explicitly reconfirmed. Allah has favored him above all the other prophets and made him the highest of mankind, rejecting anyone's attesting to the **divine oneness** by saying 'There is no god but Allah,' **unless** they

also attest to the Prophet by saying '**Muhammad is the Messenger of Allah.**'" [Emphasis added][20] The book concluded with "All of the foregoing has been conveyed by prophetic hadith and attested to by the words of the early Muslims."[21]

Belief alone was not considered enough to enter paradise. The good life as early defined in Mecca demanded virtuous action and dealing with any evil encountered. For modern day Muslims, the definition of problems is less clear. There is no main source to interpret doctrine or represent religious authority and Islam is a religion without a priesthood. Differences of opinion on the doctrine of the religion were guaranteed.[22]

Trouble started immediately upon Muhammad's death and continues to this day – the question of succession since he left no heir. Since he was the last prophet, no one could inherit his religious role, but he was also the political leader. The elders of Medina chose Abu Bakr as caliph (*khalifah*) or successor because he had been one of the earliest to accept Islam. They thereby went with election rather than hereditary as the basis, bypassing Ali ibn abu-Talib, Muhammad's cousin and son-in-law, the strongest in line by kinship. This proved to be a critical and very wise decision and probably saved Islam. Abu Bakr was the first adult male to accept Islam. After Muhammad's death, the desert Arabs rebelled against Islam and Abu Bakr put down the insurrection. Without that, there would be no Islam! During his caliphate, he added Syria and Palestine to the realm.[23]

The supporters of Ali, *shiat Ali* or Shiites, were not happy with the decision believing that Muhammad had actually designated Ali as his successor and that the office of caliph should be hereditary from the line of Ali. So the first great division starts with the Party of Ali, **Shi'ah**. The majority followed the way of the prophet or the **sunna** and became known as Sunnites or Sunnis.[24]

Ali did become the fourth caliph (656-661), but by then the Muslim empire was breaking apart. Ali was forced to fight supporters of Muhammad and even though he prevailed in battle, he was marked as the first caliph to fight other Muslims. The **Kharajites** (seceders) rebelled with the motto "there are no verdicts but Allah's" and were "the first to advocate a fundamentalist outlook of Islam and the Quran as their official ideology, opposing any dynamic interpretation of the Quran which Ali pioneered and symbolized." It was a Kharajite who assassinated Ali in 661.[25]

Abu Sufyan was Muhammad's main opponent in Mecca and he only converted when it was clear he had no choice. He was a reluctant Muslim and a supporter of Ali. In an effort to appease him Umar (the 2nd caliph – Abu Bakr had died after only two years) appointed Sufyan's son, Muawiya, governor of Syria. When Ali became caliph, Muawiya refused to recognize him. After Ali was assassinated (and his head was presented to him), Muawiya named himself caliph and moved the capital to Damascus. Ali's son, Hussein, led a force which was lured into Iraq by Muawiya in 680 and massacred at Karbala, still a famous city in the Iraq War and a holy city to Shiites. Shiites still believe that Ali and his descendants should be the rightful heirs of Muhammad's spiritual authority and they celebrate Hussein's "martyrdom" annually with public mourning and self-flagellation.

Islam is Politics.
- **Ayatollah Ruhollah Khomeini, Iran, 1979**[26]

There are several results of this early division. The unity of the faithful was broken and power struggles ensued for centuries. Even the office of caliph was unfilled for many years even though several tried to seize it and it was abolished in 1924 after the revolution of Mustafa Kemal in Turkey. That is what made the call for a new caliphate by Osama bin Laden so interesting. Since Muhammad did not designate a successor or any constitution as such, his brotherhood of Islam fell into political rivalry and intrigues among factions. As a practical matter, even though Muslims profess to follow the prophet's doctrine, it was abandoned over 1,300 years ago.[27]

The division between Sunnis and Shia became permanent with the followers of Ali believing that Ali and his descendants were Imams, divinely guided spiritual leaders; whereas, as we have noted, the Sunnis have no central authority for doctrine. Also, the Shia believe that the sayings of Ali and Fatima are as authoritative as the Sunna for Islamic law.[28] Shia are dominant in Iran and the majority in Iraq and present in almost all Muslim countries, including a large population in the eastern provinces of Saudi Arabia, being about 10-15% of all Muslims.

This division is still very much alive. In May 2009, Mecca Mufti Sheikh Adil al-Kalbani told BBC that "Shiite clerics are infidels." (Infidels can be killed according to Islam.) This irritated Iraqi Prime Minister Nuri al-Maliki who criticized Arab and Muslim countries for their silence on the Saudi's comments a day after a massive bomb in predominantly Shiite Sadr City in Baghdad killed 62 and wounded 150.[29]

The move to Damascus took the center of Islam out of Arabia. In the 13 centuries since the move to Damascus, the capital has moved to Baghdad, Cairo, and Constantinople. Since the end of the Ottoman Empire after World War I, there has been no city which can claim the seat of Islam, even though the King of Saudi Arabia calls himself the Protector of the Two Holy cities of Mecca and Medina. Thus, even though the faithful pray toward Mecca, Islam has no geographical base.[30]

The **Umayyad Caliphate**, founded by Muawiya in Damascus, ruled for less than 100 years but extended the empire through its great military conquests and also developed the administrative structure of officials and taxation. It was overthrown by a rival Iraqi dynasty, the Abbasids. Note that the rivalry between Syria and Iraq goes back over a thousand years. With Europe sidelined in the Dark Ages, the **Abbasid Empire** was the center of civilization, the land of *The Arabian Nights*.[31] At the peak of their power, this was a time when Islam could have built a great empire, but corruption won and the power faded. The **Fatamids**, named after Muhammad's daughter, Fatima, set up a new center of power and culture in Cairo.

These infamous people, hated by God and infamous, boast of having got the better of the Romans [i.e., Byzantines] by their love of God…They live by the bow, the sword, and debauchery, finding pleasure in taking slaves, devoting themselves to murder, pillage, spoil…and not only do they commit these crimes, but even – what an aberration – they believe that God approves of them.

- Gregory Palamas (1296-1359), Greek monk and theologian imprisoned by the Turks (today revered as a saint by the Orthodox Church)[32]

The weakened Abbasids were soon overwhelmed by the Mongols led by Genghis Khan and later by his grandson Hulagu. They laid siege to Baghdad in 1258. The destruction of Baghdad was complete: the great libraries and schools were burned, most Muslims killed, and the primacy of Arabic civilization also died. Saladin and the Mamelukes[33] stopped the Mongols in Egypt, but Islam ceased to be the intellectual leader of the world. Europe entered the Renaissance and Islam fell into decline and the Golden Age of Islam disappeared.

There is an argument that there "has never been a totally Islamic culture that was golden, brilliant or prosperous," but that "the glory of Islam came not from Islam but its dhimmis' wealth and knowledge." This "secular knowledge of Islam came from the Christians,

Persians, and Hindus." "The dhimmis were the scholars, since the Arabs of Mohammed's day were barely literate and their classical literature was oral poetry." Islam is supposedly given credit for saving Greek knowledge from extinction. This is odd since it was jihad which caused the collapse of Byzantine/Greek culture and it was "Syrian Christian dhimmis who translated all of the Greek philosophers into Arabic." The zero came from Hindu mathematicians yet we call our numbers Arabic numerals. "From carpets to architecture, the Muslims took the ideas of the dhimmis and obtained historical credit." "Today there have only been eight Nobel prizes given to Muslims in the sciences. All of these were given for work done with Kafirs in Kafir countries. There has never been a scientific Nobel prize given for work in a Muslim country. For that matter, roughly half of all Arabs are illiterate. Without the dhimmis, Islam is poor. The total economic output of all Arab countries (without the oil) is equal to that of Spain."[34]

1492 marked not only the expulsion of the Moors (Muslims) from Spain but the opening of the New World. But why was Columbus looking for a new route to the Far East? Because the trade routes to the East had been closed to trade from Europe with devastating results by the Muslim conquest of Constantinople in 1453.[35] With new routes to the Far East, the old caravan routes of the Middle East were no longer needed which pushed the heartland of Islam into poverty and cultural isolation.[36]

The Ottoman Empire, even at its peak under Suleiman the Magnificent (1520-1566), could not reunify the Muslim world as they were basically foreign occupiers. Napoleon Bonaparte invaded Egypt in 1798 exposing this Muslim weakness and ushering in the era of European colonialism. Islam was unable to prevail over nationalism and has shown that on a transnational basis, the unifying power of Islam is very limited. The Europeans betrayed the Arabs after World War I with the Sykes-Picot Agreement, carved up their lands, and announced the Balfour Declaration of 1917 which resulted in Israel. The collapse of the Ottoman Empire came with the end of World War I. A new nationalism arose as parts of the old Caliphate gained their independence from European colonial domination. With such a history, it is not surprising that there is fertile ground for Islamic extremism that could well call for drastic changes.[37] In such circumstances, there were calls for a return to the fundamentals of the Qur'an and to the ways of the prophet.

Americans are particularly ill-prepared to deal with Islam, but even the British and French, with their long record of dealing with Arabs and Muslims, have trouble with the resurgent Islam. "The modern Muslim mind is alien both to Christian and Enlightenment ways of thinking."[38]

Islam is 95% ideology, 5% religion.

- Geert Wilders[39]

There are several key people who added to the core texts of jihadist ideology. The first was an Egyptian, **Sayyid Qutb** (1906-1966), the intellectual father of modern Islamist terrorism, who wrote and was later executed during the presidency of Gamal Abdul Nasser. Qutb harked back to a Pakistani, Abdul Ala Mawdudi (we already met him in Chapter 1), the intellectual father of modern Islamism and considered by some the most prominent Muslim scholar of the 20th Century. Maudidi, in addition to identifying the totality of Islamic life, called for jihad (struggle) as an obligation to fight *jahiliyyah* (ignorance). Qutb thought that the West was sunk in jahiliyyah which means a state of pagan disbelief or a state of ignorance of Divine guidance.[40] We will encounter other of these authors and the founder of the Muslim Brotherhood later.

> **Islam is "ordained for the whole of mankind." It is the "last message for humanity. We must return to the clear spring, the source that is the Koran and the Hadith, unsullied by Roman, Greek, Persian concepts such as democracy."**
>
> **- Sayyid Qutb**

It is part of our American culture to respect all religions. Muslims understand that and exploit it against us, so that any criticism or questioning of Islam is immediately labeled Islamophobia. This squelches any discussion of the totalitarian aspects of this political ideology.

Islam starts with the revelations from Allah to Muhammad over a period of 23 years which were eventually compiled as the Qur'an.

The Qur'an

The Qur'an (which means recitation) is a most unusual book; in many ways it is more like a compilation than a book. Also, in a political/historical context, it is the biography of Muhammad himself.[41] It is basically a monologue by Allah with no continuity in the narrative, thus rendering it confusing and often incomprehensible. Allah is the only speaker but he is usually addressing Muhammad with guidance as to what to say. Surah XLVIII:27 is unusual in that it contains "if Allah wills [pleases]" - odd wording for Allah himself to be using. The **Sunna** (which means the "way" – usually the "way of Muhammad"), the **Hadith**, the sayings and stories which are the traditions of Muhammad, are key to making the Qur'an comprehensible.[42] Following the poetic tradition of the desert, the Qur'an is noted for its poetical and literary style[43] and is written in rhymed prose (which is not translatable) with the style varying significantly in various Surahs at different times.[44]

To Muslims, the Qur'an is the exact word of Allah and is not open to critical evaluation or analysis, which makes it difficult to have discussion between religions. An example of the dogmatic nature was when the UN called for a public debate in the Maldives about flogging women found guilty of extra-marital sex. The Foreign Minister Ahmed Naseem refused saying, "What's there to discuss about flogging? There is nothing to debate about a matter clearly stated in the religion of Islam. No one can argue with God."[45]

The debate as to whether the Qur'an was created or uncreated will be reviewed in the section on "The End of Reason" below. Muhammad did not write down his revelations but gave them orally to his followers who wrote them down or memorized them. "Later, those who could write traced them in ancient characters on palm leaves, tanned hides, or dry bones."[46] This was an early time for writing because at the time of Muhammad's childhood, there had never been a book written in Arabic.[47]

> **To Muslims, the Qur'an is the exact word of Allah and is not open to critical evaluation or analysis.**

After his death, since Allah's revelations were considered complete, it was necessary to compile his words into a book since many of the reciters had been killed in battle and there was fear that the words would be lost. But the book is written in code. A short prayer was placed as the first Surah (chapter) with the remaining Surahs placed with the longest first followed by the shortest, thus assuring no chronological or narrative continuity. The original Qur'an made sense because it was a great epic story about the fantastic life of Muhammad, but by rearranging the chapters by length, it destroyed the story. The resulting book is unreadable, makes no sense, is confusing and contradictory, and is violent and unpleasant. Context was lost and it is very repetitive – "The story of Moses is told 39 times" and "there are 290 verses about Hell."[48]

The new Qur'an was approved in the time of Caliph Uthman with 114 Surahs – 86 revealed in Mecca and 28 in Medina (mostly longer ones that cover a third of the book)[49] with some 6,235 verses. Uthman then had all the source material and the various previous versions destroyed.[50]

The Qur'an is not only written in code and unreadable, there are also really two Qur'ans – the religious Mecca Qur'an and the political Medina Qur'an.

The Mecca Surahs are generally religious and more tolerant since Muhammad was trying to attract the Meccans to Islam. The Medina Surahs are more violent, less tolerant, longer, and less poetic, dealing with more ritual, politics, and law. In Medina, Muhammad "developed a complete political ideology" and "the divine right of aggression and violence" and calling for jihad against the infidels.[51] This is important because of *naskh* (abrogation) which annulled most of the peaceful verses, discussed below.

Each Surah has a name, usually related to the chapter, but some are evidently unrecognizable. The book is so revered as the word of Allah that some caliphs even threatened death to anyone denying the Qur'an.   However, even at the early time there was confusion. Caliph Umar is quoted as saying, "Much of the Qur'an has been lost." According to Umar, the Qur'an originally contained a verse enjoining stoning for adultery, but it was inadvertently dropped."[52] And Aisha, Muhammad's favorite wife and widow, was unhappy that one Surah had been reduced from 200 verses to 73 in Uthman's version. And sounding like the schoolboy telling the teacher the dog ate my homework, she related that some verses were lost during preparations for Muhammad's funeral when a domestic animal got in and ate them. There was supposed to be a "verse of the stoning" but no two witnesses were found who had memorized it exactly the same. There was even the accusation that Uthman was assassinated because of his changes to the Qur'an (though evidently not the correct motive). Also, the book was read in seven dialects, further adding to ambiguity.[53]

The book supposedly cannot be translated and is supposed to be read only in Arabic at prayers, but that is a foreign language for a large percentage of Muslims.[54] So is Allah's word only for Arabs? – ask Muhammad, "Love the Arabs for three things: Because I am an Arab, the Koran is in Arabic, and the language of the people of paradise is Arabic." Allah evidently only spoke Arabic, much to the consternation of speakers of some of the world's great languages! In addition, there are grammatical mistakes in the book, but that is impossible because it is supposed to be in perfect Arabic. Also, diacritical points, which are necessary to understand the meaning of words, were not invented until years after Muhammad's death. There are contradictions concerning the day of resurrection and the creation of heaven and earth. The verse, "Which then of the bounties of your lord will you deny" is repeated 31 times in Surah LV which has only 78 verses. There are many other repetitions.[55]

The stories in the Qur'an are more valuable than any others –we don't need the Torah, or Gospels, or any other book.

- Grand Mufti of Saudi Arabia[56]

Muhammad would receive a revelation at night and forget it in the morning. There were problems with the memories of those who were tasked to memorize what he told them.[57] Then there is the convenience (or perhaps prophetic license) of the revelations when Muhammad needed them for political problems such as breaking the taboo of attacking his own tribe, the Quraysh in Mecca, or for his personal problems such as the number of wives he could have[58] or the authority to wed his daughter-in-law. Whenever he got into a difficulty, there always was a quick and convenient revelation whereby Allah directed a solution. It seems as if Muhammad stepped outside and rang up Allah on his cellphone with his latest problem. To which Allah responded with a solution, which was normally "obey Muhammad." So is Allah Muhammad's alter ego? Or is it really **MuhammAllah** or **MoAllah**?

> **I studied the Quran a great deal. I came away from that study with the conviction that by and large there have been few religions in the world as deadly to men as that of Muhammad. So far as I can see, it is the principal cause of the decadence so visible today in the Muslim world and, though less absurd than the polytheism of old, its social and political tendencies are in my opinion more to be feared, and I therefore regard it as a form of decadence rather than a form of progress in relation to paganism itself.**
>
> **- Alexis de Tocqueville[59]**

The Qur'an is not about love for Allah; it is always fear and obey, and it is also impossible to know Allah which is also very convenient so that Muhammad never had to go into any explanation. Since the Qur'an was written in code, it leaves most Muslims confused, with only the imams and the scholars knowing what is going on and they are the ones calling the shots.[60]

Buy a Qur'an and read it, but find a version that puts the surahs in chronological order. Note which (86) are from Mecca and which (28) are from Medina since they are completely different.[61] Note the abrogation. Note the repeated citations to obey Allah and his messenger. Note how convenient revelations were – any problem with wives, followers, or others – quickly a revelation arrived with the answer to the problem from Allah.

Muslims pride themselves if they can memorize the Qur'an even if they do not really understand it. Check the Biographic Notes at the end of the *RELIANCE OF THE TRAVELLER A Classic Manual of Islamic Sacred Law* for how many are cited.[62] I watched a TV show, "Reciting the Koran," which was about a big contest in Cairo. Young people from all over the Muslim world were competing in front of a group of old men judges each sitting in front of a computer screen. The young contestant was to touch their computer screen and it would tell him/her the first few lines and they were to continue the recitation from there. Most of them did not speak Arabic and do not understand it or what they were saying (singing). But it is poetic and melodious. A Tajik boy, about 10, was great, but he is illiterate in Tajik and can barely read and write his language. A young girl from the Maldives was very good; she does not speak Arabic but she is a very good student. It is a shame to waste their time this way. This is the madrassa approach and that of the Grand Mufti of Saudi Arabia – that we do not need anything but the Qur'an. That is great for hiding in the seventh century but you cannot build an airplane that way! The program showed some young Arabs on a bus discussing the prophet and his compassion for Jews! Where did they learn that?

To believe that words committed to the memories of numerous people, speaking different dialects, and that they were not written down for many years, could reflect the "perfect" words of Allah is truly the height of faith but not very realistic. But then there is a revelation that states that non-Muslims are not permitted to understand the Qur'an (XVII:46-47).

The Trilogy

The Qur'an by itself is totally inadequate to comprehend Islam. The Qur'an provides the divine authorization for political Islam and jihad. Two additional sources are required. The Sira (the biography of Muhammad) lays out the strategy of conquest. Finally, the Hadith is the tactical manual for jihad.[63] All of these are difficult to read and understand because of awkward translations, endless repetition, and length. "Islam substitutes complexity for profoundness. A simplified Hadith would make the imam less necessary and give him less power. The entire Trilogy is designed to be difficult to understand."[64] We tend to think of the Qur'an as the "bible" of Islam, but it is actually only about 14% of the total doctrinal texts with the Sira being about 26% and the Hadith 60%.[65]

Supplements to the Qur'an, known as the **Sunna**, are the traditions of Muhammad, claimed to be the first-hand accounts of the Prophet's words and actions as preserved in the Hadith.[66] The hadiths, like most writings about Muhammad, were written about 200 years after his death.[67] A hadith is a short story or action about Muhammad, usually about a paragraph long varying from very mundane descriptions of his life to his opinions or decisions on major subjects. The Hadith or Traditions are a collection of these stories. The Shia have different hadiths. Not all the hadiths are about Muhammad. A few are about Abu Bakr, Uthman, Umar, and Ali, his closest companions, who became caliphs. "They are called 'the rightly guided caliphs,' and their Sunna (words and actions) are also considered ideal Islamic behavior."[68] It is impossible to understand the Qur'an without the hadiths.[69]

The biography of Muhammad, the Sira, also was written many years after Muhammad's death. The best sources are the biographies by Ishaq and Al Tabari. Ishaq's was not translated until 1955 due to lack of interest in Islam. It is long (800 pages), difficult to read (much in poetry), full of extraneous material, convoluted, and clearly political – some 67% of the text is devoted to jihad.[70]

Islam is a political system, a culture, and a religion based upon the Koran, Sira, and Hadith. To understand Islam, know the Trilogy.

- The CSPI Maxim[71]

Muhammad sanctified murder and theft, established the distribution of the spoils of war, and set ransom for prisoners. To resist Islam was worse than murder and it became a sacred act to kill those who did.[72] As we have already seen, brutality is constant throughout Islam.

After battles, Muslims regularly had sex with captive women as reported in the Trilogy. It was not considered rape if the woman was a kafir captive or slave. Under their dual ethics, rape is only possible if the woman is Muslim. Forced sex is a method of war, to humiliate, and it is not a sin because it is sanctioned in the Trilogy. Likewise with slavery; Muhammad dealt extensively with slaves for all purposes and it is considered a blessing and hopefully will create more Muslims.[73]

Islam is replete with contradictions as we will see below with abrogation. We know Hitler's views about Jews from *Mein Kampf*, but he did not start with a section indicating how much he admired them. That contradiction is in how the Jews were treated in Mecca as opposed to their treatment in Medina.[74] That is the dualistic logic of the real Islam.

Contradictory statements can both be true if they come from Allah. Muhammad was involved in violent events about every six or seven weeks during his final nine years yet he is purported to be the prophet of a religion of peace. This is dual logic and both are true and since both violence and peace advance Islam, both are true and good. That is Islam and "That is the message of the Sira and the power of Islam."[75]

Dhimmitude

Muhammad established the relationship between Christians and Jews and Islam as **dhimmi** status, or dhimmitude, after he crushed the Jews at Khaybar. This second-class citizenship meant forfeiting all civil rights and paying a humiliating special tax, the **jizya.** In the case of the Jews of Khaybar, they were permitted to stay and farm their land on the condition they paid half their harvest to Muhammad and his band, thereby becoming dhimmis under Islamic protection. Killing all kafirs would have been satisfying to the warriors but it created a problem. If all the kafirs were killed, the warriors would have had to find some work. But Muhammad's "unique political invention," jizya, became the significant cash flow of the Islamic empire and made Islam rich.

Jizya has generally disappeared but we saw a recent example. Taliban in Orakzai, in the Federally Administered Tribal Areas of Pakistan, banished 50 Sikh families for not paying jizya. They occupied the houses and shops of the Sikhs and auctioned off their valuables.[76] Threat of dhimmi status still flourishes. The Baha'i faith is an old group persecuted in Iran with its headquarters now in Haifa, Israel. Some nine Baha'i-owned shops have been attacked in Rafsanjan, Iran. The latest was fire bombed with a threatening letter left at the shop calling for no "propagating and preaching the Baha'i faith even in cyber space," no non-business "relationships and friendships with Muslims," and no "hiring Muslim employees."[77]

> **Fight those who do not believe in Allah, nor in the latter day, nor do they prohibit what Allah and His Apostle have prohibited, nor follow the religion of truth, out of those who have been given the Book, until they pay the tax [jizya] in acknowledgment of superiority and they are in a state of subjection.**
>
> **Qur'an IX:29**

"Dhimmi, an Arabic word meaning 'protected,' [or "guilty"] was the name applied by the Arab-Muslim conquerors to indigenous non-Muslim populations who surrendered by a treaty (dhimma) to Muslim domination." Islamic conquests extended over vast areas in Africa, Europe and Asia, for over a thousand years (638-1683). This growing Muslim empire incorporated various peoples which had their own religions, cultures, languages, and civilizations. "For centuries, these indigenous, pre-Islamic peoples constituted the great majority of the population of the Islamic lands. Although these populations differed, they were ruled by the same type of laws," based on sharia. Dhimmitude is "the Islamic system of governing populations conquered by jihad wars, encompassing all of the demographic, ethnic, and religious aspects of the political system. The term 'dhimmitude' as a historical concept, was coined by Bat Ye'or in 1983 to describe the legal and social conditions of Jews and Christians subjected to Islamic rule."[78]

> **The Koran gives Muslims the right to judge Christians and kill them with Jihad.**
> **- Archbishop Raboula Beylouni, Lebanon's Catholic Patriarch of Antioch**[79]

Dhimmis were not to study Islam and we still see this deference today as Christians and Jews are generally ignorant about Islam and the Sunna.[80] The sadder part is when people or organizations kowtow to Islamic requests and do not understand the significance of their capitulation. For example, NPR fired Juan Williams, "a dyed-in-the-wool liberal" for telling the truth, and yet the media do not see "the loss of the freedom of speech to Islamic supremacism and domination."[81] Another example is the distinguished professor Serge Trifkovic, who was barred from entering Canada for a talk. In February 2011, he was asked by the American Foreign Policy Council to write an entry on Bosnia for their World Almanac of Islamism. He submitted the article and later was told that there were difficulties – they were not really about the article but about some of his writings about Islam (which are quite good). They finally decided not to publish it at all. As he wrote, "This whole affair is a paradigmatic case of dhimmitudinal self-censorship at its worst. Its implications are dire and eminently predictable."[82]

As noted above, the dhimmis saved Islam from its own backwardness and produced the wealth of Islam. Bukhari recorded Caliph Umar as saying "You should continue the arrangement made by Mohammed regarding the dhimmis because the taxes they pay fund your children's future."[83] Jihad cracked open the culture and dhimmitude replaced it with Islam.

More than half of Christianity disappeared; half of Hindu culture disappeared; half of Buddhism was annihilated; Zoroastrianism disappeared. Languages were replaced by Arabic. The laws, customs, names, and history became extinct. When Napoleon invaded Egypt, he found that the Egyptian Arabs did not know anything about the pyramids or temples. Islam had annihilated even the memory of the pharaohs' 5,000-year-old culture.[84]

This pattern of jihad, dhimmitude, and destruction of native culture became the model for the next 1,400 years. Christians and some Zoroastrians (Magians) were added to the groups offered dhimmi status but the rest had only the choice of convert or death. A treaty with dhimmis set the standards.

We shall not build, in our cities or in their neighborhood new monasteries, churches, convent, or monks' cells, nor shall we repair, by day or by night, such of them as fall in ruins or are situated in the quarters of the Muslims.

We shall keep our gates wide open for passersby and travelers. We shall give board and lodging to all Muslims who pass our way for three days.

We shall not give shelter in our churches or in our dwellings to any spy nor hide him from the Muslims.

We shall not manifest our religion publicly nor convert anyone to it. We shall not prevent any of our kin from entering Islam if they wish it.

We shall show respect toward Muslims, and we shall rise from our seats when they wish to sit.

We shall not seek to resemble the Muslims by imitating any of their garments.

We shall not mount on saddles, nor shall we gird swords nor bear any kind of arms nor carry them on our persons.

We shall not engrave Arabic inscriptions on our seals.

We shall not sell fermented drinks.

We shall clip the fronts of our head (keep a short forelock as a sign of humiliation).

We shall always dress in the same way wherever we may be, and we shall not wear the zunar round our waists.

We shall not display our crosses or our books in the roads or markets of the Muslims. We shall only use clappers in our churches very softly. We shall not raise our voices when following our dead. We shall not take slaves who have been allotted to Muslims.

We shall not build houses higher than the houses of the Muslims.

Whoever strikes a Muslim with deliberate intent shall forfeit the protection of this pact.[85]

The world of the dhimmi was even worse than this excerpt. Islam dominated everything: government, education, dress, literature, his word "could not be used against a Muslim in court and crimes against dhimmis were rarely prosecuted. The wealth of Islam came from the wealth and labor of the subjugated dhimmis.... Islam is a political system with a divine license to take what is wanted from the *dar al harb*, the land of war."[86]

> **Islam is a political system with a divine license to take what is wanted from the dar al harb, the land of war.**

Eventually most dhimmis converted or fled but the Islamic attitude of contempt for kafirs has endured. The status of Christians is tenuous or dangerous throughout the Muslim world. Dhimmi Jews and Christians have been pushed out of Arab lands (900,000 Jews in 1948, less than 5,000 now; less than 10 Jews in Iraq now from over 140,000 in 1948; under 250,000 Christians in Iraq now from 1.25 million 10 years ago).[87] Examples abound. A pastor and two other Christians were severely tortured by police in Bangladesh; the next day thousands of Muslim villagers demonstrated chanting, "We want a Christian-free society."[88] Nigeria has had repeated attacks highlighting its division between Muslim North and Christian South. There have been recurring massacres over the years. In a recent spree, three pastors were beheaded after refusing to convert to Islam.[89] A Pakistani Christian was burned alive and his wife raped by police for refusing to convert to Islam.[90] In Bangladesh, Muslim settlers burned down a village and drove out the ethnic minorities.[91] This persecution is not abating. A Bishop fears for survival of Christians in the biblically important city of Nazareth.[92] Representatives from the Jamiat Ulema-e-Islam party in Pakistan's parliament have called for the Bible to be banned as "pornographic" and "blasphemous."[93]

> **Insecurity, non-peace, non-justice, and non-equality among the people. For Non-Muslims, that's really life under Sharia in a nutshell.[94]**

The Copts in Egypt, even though a large minority, have historically suffered dhimmi status. Copts (the word simply means Egyptian) continue to be persecuted with false accusations in the media and overt government actions to marginalize or ostracize them.[95] A mob attacked a young man in a Cairo slum and beat him severely. He remembered their threat: "This is a Christian son of a bitch. We're going to kill him."[96] Another mob in Upper Egypt, where they have had a lot of trouble, marched on a church chanted "We will kill the priest, we will kill him and no one will prevent us," and we will "cut him to pieces."[97] The daughter of a Christian widow in northern Sudan was kidnapped in mid-2010. The police have not helped her and bluntly told her, "You must convert to Islam if you want your daughter back."[98]

In addition to the situation in Egypt, the same atmosphere exists in Pakistan. There is "a climate of impunity for people who abuse Christian women." It has been reported that "at least 700 Christian girls are kidnapped and forced to convert to Islam every year" and Hindu girls are also targeted. An "important businessman" wanted a particular girl so he kidnapped her, forced her to convert, and married her. The police did nothing. When the family was finally able to get an official to speak with the girl, she stated she had been abducted and forced to convert and she had "no intention of abandoning Christianity." However, the "important businessman," Muhammad Junaid, "issued threats, saying that if he did not get the young woman back, there would be 'terrible consequences' to pay."[99]   Of course, there is no compulsion in religion in Islam!

While our troops are dying in Afghanistan trying to bring that country into something remotely close to the modern world, imams attack us and our efforts. The State Department reported (7 November 2011) that there is not one Christian church or school left in Afghanistan.[100] An imam in Kabul's largest mosque, "pledged support for 'any plan that can defeat' foreign military forces." Another imam in Kabul said, "Let these jackals leave this country," and "Let these brothers of monkeys, gorillas and pigs leave this country. The people of Afghanistan should determine their own fate." I agree completely and we should not waste the lives of our great troops for such fools. Throughout the mosques, "American troops are derided as crusaders and occupiers." Many mosques are used by the Taliban and many are linked back to madrassas in Pakistan. In the bedroom of one imam in Kabul two dozen mines were found. According to another imam, "The Jews and Christians [meaning Americans] are our enemies."[101] The list of attacks on churches is endless. It is sad how little Christians do to help their fellow persecuted Christians in the Muslim world; they still seem to be under dhimmitude.

Wahhabism

This radical intolerance of Islam is best expressed in the puritanical theme of Wahhabism. Mohammed Ibn abd al-Wahhabi (1703-1792), the son of a religious judge, was born in the Nejd (in the center of the Arabian Peninsula). He disapproved of the deviation from Quranic teachings that he observed in Mecca and preached a puritanical form of Islam based on returning to the strict teachings of the Qur'an, which resulted in his expulsion from his town. Emir Mohammed Ibn Saud (founder of the Saud dynasty) liked Wahhabi's view that Muslims guilty of unorthodoxy could be killed since he was searching for ideological approval to wage war against the Ottomans as foreign occupiers. Ibn Saud took al-Wahhabi in and embraced his views, thus forming the linkage between the House of Saud and Wahhabism.[102]

The dynasty had its problems up to 1891 when Abd ar-Rahman fled to Kuwait in exile taking with him his 10-year old son, Abd al-Aziz Ibn Saud, who was destined to be the founder of modern Saudi Arabia. In 1902, Abd al-Aziz captured Riyadh in a daring attack. He brought his father back from Kuwait; however, he abdicated from his leadership role but remained as the *imam* or religious leader of the Wahhabis. Abd al-Aziz dispatched Wahhabi missionaries to settle the Bedouins and he consolidated his power by marrying daughters of various tribal chiefs and by judicious application of the carrot and the stick. The ultra-puritanical Wahhabi movement became know as the *Ikhwan* (brethren) movement and pushed its influence to the point where it threatened the King's power, so he seized direct control of the *Ikhwan* in 1916. You might recall this time during World War I when the British were active in that area, securing an agreement with Hussein in the Hejaz (northwest part of Saudi Arabia) and the exploits of T. E. Lawrence, famous as Lawrence of Arabia.

> **The elephant in the Middle East living room is Wahhabism.**
>
> **- James Woolsey**

According to James Woolsey, "The elephant in the Middle East living room is Wahhabism. Over the long run, this movement is in many ways the most dangerous of the ideological enemies we face." These are Salafis (more about them in Chapter 4) who believe in theocratic totalitarianism ruled by a unified mosque and state. Their "objective is to unify first the Arab world under theocratic rule, then the Muslim world, then those regions that were once Muslim (e.g. Spain), then the rest of the world."[103]

Abd al-Aziz continued to consolidate his power and was crowned King of the Hejaz in Mecca in 1926 and King of the Hejaz and Nejd and Its Dependencies in Riyadh in 1927. He used the fanatical Wahhabi fighters to establish hi new kingdom and he defeated those fighters when they, the Ikhwan, rebelled in 1929. By 1932 he was King of Saudi Arabia and he made a deal with the Wahhabis that has endured. The ultra-conservative clergy was granted considerable independence, control of key ministries, and a share in the kingdom's wealth. In return they have aided the royal family and provided fatwas at critical times. For the first Gulf War, they blessed the entrance of US troops into the kingdom. With 15 of the 19 hijackers of 9/11 being Saudis, they publicly repudiated al Qaeda, tempered down some of the intolerance in school books, and supported the restriction of Saudi money to radical groups. After the Jasmine Revolution in Tunisia and the ensuing turmoil in the Middle East, they instructed the faithful that it would be un-Islamic to protest against the rulers. Oil was discovered in 1933. The rest is modern history and the alliance of the Saudi royal family and Wahhabism theocracy has continued to this day much to our regret due to their support of ultra-conservative Islam.

Abrogation

The principle of *Naskh* (abrogation) is critical to understanding the Qur'an. This is why the chronology of the Qur'an is so critical. This means that verses that were written later abrogate, supersede, annul, repeal, or cancel earlier ones. "Whatever communication We abrogate or cause to be forgotten, We bring one better than it or like it." (II:106)   The result is that later, more violent verses from Medina replace or supersede the more moderate verses from Mecca.

> **Whatever communications We abrogate or cause to be forgotten, We bring one better than it or like it. Do you not know that Allah has power over all things?**
> **- Qur'an II:106**

Surah IX called Taubah (translated as "Ultimatum" or "Repentance") is the most important about abrogation and jihad. It is the only Surah that does not begin with "In the name of Allah, the Beneficent, the Merciful." It was the next to last Surah, revealed in 631 when Muhammad returned from Mecca and was at the height of his power. Thus, the violent verses of Surah IX, including "Slay the idolaters wherever you find them," (IX:5, the Verse of the Sword) abrogate the peaceful verses of other chapters because they were revealed later. According to some theologians then, IX:5 abrogated no less than 124 (or 225) more peaceful verses.[104]

Apologists for Islam like to quote II:256, "There is no compulsion in religion." But they conveniently ignore the rest of the verse: "; truly the right way has become clearly distinct from error; therefore, whoever disbelieves in the Shaitan and believes in Allah, he indeed has laid hold on the firmest handle, which shall not break off, and Allah is Hearing, Knowing." That means Islam is still the only way! Interestingly, it is in the same Surah as abrogation (II:106), which is the longest Surah and was the first Surah from Medina. It also has such peaceful verses as "And fight in the way of Allah," (190), "And kill them wherever you find them,...but if they do fight you, then slay them," (191), "And fight with them until there is no persecution, and religion should only be for Allah." (193).

The significance of abrogation is that only 43 Surahs are not affected, meaning that most of the Surahs of the Qur'an cannot be taken at face value.

Taqiyya

Taqiyya is the principle which permits a Muslim to lie, particularly to kafirs, or non-Muslims, to protect himself or to protect Islam. "Let not the believers take the unbelievers for friends rather than believers; and whoever does this, he shall have nothing of (the guardianship of) Allah, but you should guard yourselves against them, guarding carefully; [other translations have this as *"unless you indeed fear a danger from them."*] and Allah makes you cautious of (retribution from) Himself; and to Allah is the eventual coming." (III:28) - "'*Unless you indeed fear a danger from them*' meaning, except those believers who in some areas or times fear for their safety from the disbelievers. In this case, such believers are allowed to show friendship to the disbelievers outwardly, but never inwardly.... 'We smile in the face of some people although our hearts curse them.'"[105]

The major Islamic legal text has a long section on Lying. "He who settles disagreements between people to bring about good or says something commendable is not a liar." According to Sahih Muslim, "I did not hear him permit untruth in anything people say, except for three things: war, settling disagreements, and a man talking with his wife or she with him." According to Imam Abu Hamid al-Ghazali, "When it is possible to achieve such an aim by lying but not by telling the truth, it is permissible to lie if attaining the goal is permissible." "One should compare the bad consequences entailed by lying to those entailed by telling the truth, and if the consequences of telling the truth are more damaging, one is entitled to lie."[106]

> **When it is possible to achieve such an aim by lying but not by telling the truth, it is permissible to lie if attaining the goal is permissible.**
>
> **- Imam Ghazali**

One of the most comprehensive reviews of taqiyya is by Raymond Ibrahim in the Winter 2010 *Middle East Quarterly*.[107] He starts with the paradox of the religion of peace and terror attacks and the added paradox of "Islam's dual notions of truth and falsehood." Deception is a noble means to the glorious end of Islamic hegemony under sharia; therefore, "lying in the service of altruism is permissible."

Ibrahim states that according to sharia, "deception is not only permitted in certain situations but may be deemed obligatory in others." Taqiyya comes from a word meaning fear and is associated with the persecution of Shiites living among Sunnis who could dissemble to survive. He states that taqiyya is not exclusively for Shia but is fundamental in mainstream Islam and "is very prevalent in Islamic politics, especially in the modern era." He quotes Muhammad on deception: "God has commanded me to equivocate among the people just as he has commanded me to establish [religious] obligations." "I have been sent with obfuscation." And "whoever lives his life in dissimulation dies a martyr."

In accord with war is deceit, Ibrahim said that talk of justice and peace from people like Osama bin Laden [or Ayman al-Zawahiri] is clearly taqiyya. Such leaders are waging not only a physical jihad but a propaganda war of deceit. "If he can convince the West that the current conflict is entirely its fault, he garners greater sympathy for his cause. At the same time, he knows that if Americans were to realize that nothing short of their submission can ever bring peace, his propaganda campaign would be quickly compromised. Hence the constant need to dissemble and to cite grievances."

The implications for Ibrahim are that as long as people believe that Allah and his prophet encourage deception, they will have no qualms about lying. Since Islam is in a perpetual war with infidels and deeds can be justified by intentions, then many Muslims will conclude that they have a "divinely sanctioned right to deceive." Therefore, as long as Islam endures, discussions of Islam as "war and peace" in the Western context would be more accurate as "war and deceit."

Moslems are a puzzle folded inside a mystery cached into a conundrum hidden within a contradiction layered beneath a fascinating riddle standing in misty fog cloaked by a perplexing enigma.

- Alarmed Pig Farmer[108]

The *Washington Post* permitted a Muslim to write a guest column claiming that the Qur'an "unequivocally forbids lying or hiding the truth."[109] And one of the leading female journalists in Saudi Arabia was permitted to do her taqiyya in the *Huffington Post* about "the idiotic allegations that Sharia is creeping into American society." She wrote, "Western extremists are now the new hijackers of Islam" – "Newt Gingrich, Geert Wilders and their slavish sycophants Robert Spencer and Pamela Geller." She goes on to say that the principles of sharia are compatible with democratic societies and are found in our Constitution and Bill of Rights and that the Muslim Brotherhood is irrelevant in the US and "struggles for credibility in Muslim countries." She attacked taqiyya but admitted that "Taqiyya, according to Western extremists, means that Muslims can lie with impunity to hide their true agenda of global domination. I must admit that this is a very clever tactic because anyone believing in this nonsense can conveniently disregard as a lie any Muslim argument that is contrary the western extremist position." She downplayed stoning for adultery as unproven and ended with "Of course, non-Muslims may have reason not to believe a word I write. This may by my idea of taqiyya." Amen![110]

Muhammad explicitly stated that "War is deceit" and that "He who makes peace between the people by inventing good information or saying good things, is not a liar."[111] This is another aspect of the dual ethics of Islam: one set of ethics for Muslims and a completely different set toward kafirs, who are considered sub-human.

Textbooks in our schools about Islam and textbooks in Muslim schools are another form of taqiyya. An analysis of textbooks, grades 6 through 12, had "historical falsehoods, bias and other misrepresentations of Islam" that are "egregious and persistent." The report was being completed and "will document over 2245 errors." One claimed Muhammad was a great leader in Medina and that the Jews and Christians accepted him. Another is that sharia is tolerant of Christians and Jews and that Islam became popular in the India subcontinent in the 8th century (no mention of 80 million Hindus slaughtered).[112] Textbooks in Pakistan's public schools as well as madrassas teach violent religious extremism. They "portray Hindus as extremists and eternal enemies of Islam" plus negative references to Christians and Jews are "predatory money lenders." "In every madrassa textbook reviewed, the concept of jihad had been reduced from its wider meaning of personal development to violent conflict in the name of Islam, considered to be the duty of every Muslim." Apostates should be killed and infidels are enemies that Muslims should "fight against until they submit or convert to Islam."[113]

This is not about what is morally right or wrong. This is the old axiom that the end justifies the means. An example is the popular Egyptian Salafi, Muhammad Hassan, who explained in a video "why Islam prefers strong, immoral men over weak, righteous ones" to go into battle. He quoted both Ibn Taymiyya and Muhammad. "As for the strong, immoral man, his strength benefits the Muslims, while his immorality only hurts himself. But as for the weak, righteous man, his righteousness only benefits himself, while his weakness hurts the Muslims."[114] The basic premise of Islam is that anything that promotes Islam is acceptable and anything that is against Islam is illegal and unacceptable.

Sex and the Frustrated Muslim

You have probably noted the numerous references to sex in previous pages. The Qur'an, the Hadith, and the legal manual are replete with extreme details about sex which seems a bit odd since one of the oft heard complaints from Muslim fundamentalists is about Western sensuality. It is a bit bizarre but sex, or the obscuring of it, may be Islam's greatest weakness.

In a society where there is a cult of virginity[115], where female genital mutilation is condoned, where a brother can kill his sister in broad daylight because she refused to marry the person chosen for her, when a father can slit the throats of his four children in front of his wife as honor killings, when women are raped and then considered the guilty party, when women are stoned to death for adultery, and when they want to kill a teacher because her students named a teddy bear Muhammad, there is obviously something extremely wrong with that society. When life is so bleak that all pleasure comes only in paradise, it is no wonder that such a culture breeds suicide bombers hoping to greet those 72 virgins in Paradise.

Honor Killings

Honor killings are not tolerated in civilized society. Nazir Ahmed slit the throats of his three girls, ages 8, 7, and 4 (but not his 3-month old son!) and his 25-year old stepdaughter (his brother had died 14 years earlier and he married his widow, per Islamic tradition). His stepdaughter had fled her husband because he abused her, but Ahmed accused her of adultery. So he killed her and "his daughters because he didn't want them to do the same when they grew up."[116]

> **My daughter was a disgrace to the family. We can't tolerate our children disrespecting their elders' wishes so we killed her, why would I want my husband to be punished? He did the right thing.**
> **- Father killed 14-year-old for refusing to marry his cousin**

Honor killings, almost exclusively of females, continue in Muslim countries but are on the increase in non-Muslim countries, including Europe and the US. The UN estimates that there are some 5,000 each year with 91% by Muslims.[117] An article in the *Daily Mail* reported honor crime (murder, rape, and kidnap) up 40% due to rising fundamentalism, forced marriages up by 60%, plus increases in female genital mutilation and polygamy.[118]

The list is endless. Germany: Kurdish woman killed by her brother in "honor killing."[119] Jordanian teen stabs 22-year-old sister to death "to cleanse the family honor because she left the house too often."[120] Pakistan: Uncle guns down niece over honor.[121] Russia: Muslim father has daughter murdered for wearing a dress "that left her knees exposed."[122] Afghan Taliban kill young woman, man for eloping.[123] There were four honor killings in Gaza in one week.[124] Pakistani killed sister and niece for "honor."[125] Gaza Father kills daughter to "preserve family honor."[126] Israel: Muslim brothers, hired hit men, arrested over string of recent honor killings.[127] India: Muslim Father strangled daughter for insisting on marrying a Hindu.[128]   Pakistan: Muslim hacks wife, daughter to death on suspicion of infidelity.[129] Pakistan: 14-year-old killed for refusing to marry father's 52-year-old cousin.[130] Pakistan: Muslim son guns down mother in honor killing.[131]   Italy: Muslim father slits daughter's throat 28 times to "uphold family honor."[132] In Italy, Muslim murders his wife for being too "Western." Woman killed for "dressing in western clothes, working in a pizzeria.[133] Double honor killings in India: Muslim mothers murder daughters for marrying Hindus.[134]

We killed them because they had brought shame to our community. How could they elope with Hindus? They deserved to die. We have no remorse.
                              - Two Muslim mothers who killed their daughters.

It even appeared in the overthrow of Qaddafi in Libya. A father slit the throats of his three daughters, 15, 17, and 18, after they were raped by Qaddafi loyalists. "The assailants knew the girls and women's lives are over after they have been raped. They are essentially killing them twice."[135] A Jordanian man killed his 24-year-old widowed daughter after she gave birth to twins.[136] A Pakistani family was even harassed for not killing their daughter who had been raped.[137] The "tribal elders declared her kari (which literally means black female) for losing her virginity outside marriage." In 2009, "roughly 46 percent of all female murders in Pakistan that year were in the name of 'honor'."

The idiocy even went to the point of attacking women with acid. One student was attacked by fellow students for not covering her head – she "deserved for her face to be ruined because she had not covered her head." Another woman and five members of her family were attacked with acid after the woman, who had been beaten by her husband, refused to leave with him.[138]

This is also "tribal" where women are treated as commodities and possessions. Revenge is big in Islam as we saw with Muhammad. In April 2011, two men entered the home of a Pakistani woman, "cut off six of her fingers, slashed her arms and lips and then sliced off her nose." She "was mutilated because her husband was involved in a dispute with his relatives, and they wanted revenge." This is not unusual in that "women are often used as bargaining chips in family feuds." The Human Rights Commission of Pakistan reported that about 800 women were victims of "honor killings" in 2010 and "2,900 women reported raped – almost 8 a day." The numbers were rising and they "represent only a fraction of the attacks."

The problem is that for these macho Muslim males, "a man's honor is intrinsically linked to how his wife or daughter behave." Who is sick? "If a couple is not married and they are having a relationship, a jirga may rule that the woman should be shot." The "slightest transgression by a woman" (even talking to a man on the street) can bring "harsh punishment and social ostracism of the family."

The arrogance of these poor souls is well displayed in this quote: "Women are cherished here. Men protect them. If a woman is out of her house then what is she doing? That is what people think here."

The most high profile instance of a violent ruling by a tribal court against a woman is that of the gang rape of Mukhtaran Mai, which took place near Multan in 2002. "Mai was allegedly attacked to settle a matter of village honor, as decided by a panchayat. She was then paraded naked through her village. "Unlike most rape victims, who face stark recriminations for speaking our, and who are sometimes even expected to commit suicide, she filed a criminal case against 14 men. "Six were convicted and sentenced to death that year, but in 2005 the Lahore High Court commuted one sentence to life in prison and acquitted the rest. Pakistan's Supreme Court upheld that decision in April" [2011], and the men were released. Obviously "she is afraid they will return and kill her." "The verdict also lays bare the misogyny of Pakistan's' judicial system because it is a judiciary that is instinctively unsympathetic to women."[139]

We have even had these killings here in the US. Islamic honor killing in Kentucky: Muslim slits throats of his three children, rapes his wife and hits her with a hammer.[140] Honor killing in Michigan: Muslim kills his stepdaughter for leaving home, not following Islam.[141] An Iraqi immigrant in Arizona ran over his daughter with his Jeep. When the police interviewed the mother, she said, "that's what she needs." He was convicted of only second degree murder.[142]

Gender Segregation

Gender segregation is still alive in Islam. A prominent Saudi cleric, Abdul-Rahman al-Barrak issued a fatwa stating that mixing of genders at the workplace or in education "as advocated by modernizers" is prohibited because it allows "sight of what is forbidden, and forbidden talk between men and women." "All of this leads to whatever ensues." Whoever allows this is an infidel and must be killed because he does not observe sharia.[143] Again in Saudi, "Religious police arrest famous actors, because men and women were performing together."[144]

A 19-year old Saudi woman was sentenced to prison and 90 lashes for being with an unrelated man. She "met a high school friend in his car to retrieve a picture of herself, since she had recently married. Two men got into the vehicle and drove them to a secluded area where five others waited, and then the woman and her companion were both raped." Note the **both!** She appealed and was given 200 lashes and 6 months in jail. Another judge said he would have given her death. After an international outcry, the king pardoned her.[145]

A British teacher in Sudan was sentenced to 15 days in jail "for insulting Islam by letting her students name a teddy bear Muhammad." Thousands of Sudanese protested in Khartoum calling for her execution, reminiscent of the cartoon riots of 2006. Again there was an international outcry over such idiocy and the Sudanese president finally pardoned her and she left the country.[146]

Clerics in Islamabad's Red Mosque issued a fatwa calling for the Minister of Tourism, Nilofar Bakhtiar, to be fired and punished because of a photo showing her hugging a man. She made a parachute jump in France to raise money for victims of the October 2005 earthquake in Pakistan and photos showed the instructor helping her and in one apparently she hugged him after her successful jump. The clerics were all bent out of shape by this "illegitimate and forbidden act…Without any doubt, she has committed a great sin." The fatwa declared that women must stay at home and must not venture out uncovered."[147]

Other incidents have enraged Islamic authorities. They were seething after African-American professor of Islamic studies, Amima Wadud, led a mixed-gender prayer service in New York in March 2005 and some wanted her dead. Soad Saleh, head of the Islamic Department of the women's college at Al-Azhar University in Cairo called it an act of apostasy – punishable by death in Islam. "It is categorically forbidden for women to lead prayers (if they include men worshippers) and intentionally violates the basics of Islam." She said women should not lead prayers because "the woman's body, even if veiled, stirs desire." She also suggested it was a ploy to weaken Islam. "It's a foreign conspiracy, through secular (Muslim) organizations, to sow seeds of division between Muslims….But God will protect his religion." Another from Al-Azhar called it "a bad and deviant innovation," and said that separation "is not discrimination between women and men but is to safeguard men from being conflicted and torn by human desire while they are standing behind a woman while she's bowing and kneeling." These were not just fringe comments: Al-Azhar is considered by some to be the highest Sunni authority. The two major Arab TV satellite networks; Al-Jazeera and Al-Arabiya both covered the incident.[148]

Another example of this concern about **men becoming "excited" over women's attire** came out of Indonesia. The Indonesian Islamic Ulemas Council announced that it is wrong for young women to wear "improper" garments during aerobic exercises in gyms or in the open air because of their effect on men. Women should avoid provoking men with "unduly sexy gym suits or physical exercises and movements that excite men." Such "sexy attire" is "against the spirit of Islam" and sexy outfits "provoke lust in men" and "should be considered haram (morally illicit)". Women should wear more chaste clothing so as not to arouse men. Note it is entirely the responsibility of women not to excite men.[149] A crazy case is the 28-year-old Libyan in Australia for a master's degree who went on a sexual assault spree because "he was upset at the way local women dressed and behaved, leaving him both angry and **aroused**."[150]

Rape – Adultery

Most civilized societies consider **rape** a serious crime, but Taj al-Din al-Hilali, the Mufti of Australia, gained worldwide attention when he said that if women are raped, it is generally their fault. He said that it was "**90% the woman's responsibility**…If you take uncovered meat and put it on the street, on the pavement, in a garden, in a park, or in the backyard, without a cover and the cats eat it, then whose fault will be, the cats' or the uncovered meat's? The uncovered meat is the disaster… If the woman is in her boudoir, in her house and if she's wearing the veil and if she shows modesty, disasters don't happen." [Emphasis added] Of course, there was an uproar, but his comments were nothing new.[151]

In September 2004, Mufti Shadid Mehdi said on Danish TV that women who venture outside without wearing the hijab are "asking for rape." There is an enormous problem in Scandinavia with young Muslim men [mainly from North Africa] raping local women because of their low esteem of them, yet they insist on bringing a young virgin girl from "home" to marry.[152] "In 2010, in the city of Oslo, <u>every single sexual assault leading to rape in which the perpetrator was identified was committed by a person of 'non-western origin'</u>. [That is "political correct speak" for Muslim.] Every single one. All 83 cases." It was reported in May 2011 that "every rape assault in the city of Oslo in the last five years had been committed by a person with a non-Western' background." Also, by October 2011, "there have already been twice as many rape assaults in Oslo so far this year as there were in all of 2010."[153]

Excerpting from his book *The Face of the Tiger,* Mark Steyn continued about Lebanese-Australian Muslim gang-rapists, "the lucky lady would be told she was about to be 'fucked Leb style' and that she deserved it because she was an 'Australian pig'." France deliberately hides their rape statistics, but they have a word for it: "tournante" or "take your turn." A University of Oslo professor explained that "one reason for the disproportionate Muslim share of the rape market was that in their native lands 'rape is scarcely punished' because it is generally believed that 'it is women who are responsible for rape.'." Once again it is the woman's manner of dress and they should adapt to the animals![154]

The Qur'an permits the taking of slave women (IV:24) and requires four male witnesses to establish rape (IV:4 and IV:13), making it virtually impossible to prosecute. If the witnesses cannot be produced, a woman's charge of rape becomes an admission of **adultery**. "That accounts for the grim fact that as many as 75% of the women in prison in Pakistan are, in fact, behind bars for the crime of being a victim of rape." The penalty of stoning to death for adultery is still imposed in some Muslim countries such as Iran.[155]

> **If four male witnesses cannot be produced, a woman's charge of rape becomes an admission of adultery.**

This is still going on. "A 23-year-old woman was awarded one-year prison term and 100 lashes for committing adultery and trying to abort the resultant fetus." This verdict was announced in the District Court in Jeddah (Saudi Arabia) after the woman confessed she had accepted a ride with a man who took her to a rest house outside Jeddah where he and four of his friends assaulted her all night. The lashes were deferred until after the birth of the baby.[156]

There have been disturbing reports from Bangladesh. A widow was whipped 202 times and critically hurt.[157] A woman died after receiving 40 lashes in Sharia punishment.[158] A 14- year-old girl was abducted and raped. Villagers responded to her cries, but an imam and teachers from a madrassa also arrived. They locked her up in the madrassa and later held a Sharia Law Committee trial and sentenced her to 200 lashes (and the man to a $150 fine). She became unconscious during the lashing and died. These Committees are illegal but no action has been taken against them.[159]

> **My rapist has destroyed my future. No one will marry me after what he has done. So I must marry my rapist for my child's sake.**
>
> **- Gulnaz, 19-year-old Afghan woman**

This sick mentality is well demonstrated by the case of Gulnaz, a 19-year-old Afghan woman, who was imprisoned for adultery after being raped. She gave birth in prison. At her first trial, she was sentenced to 3 years, then at a second trial, it was increased to 12 years, but with a pardon on the condition that she marry the man who raped her. Gulnaz was rightly concerned he might kill her so she was demanding that if she were to marry her rapist, that he make one of his sisters marry one of her brothers – an "insurance policy" to protect her, known as "baad" – a tribal way of settling disputes.[160]

In Pakistan, a 12-year-old Christian girl was gang raped for eight months, forcibly converted to Islam, and then "married" to her Muslim rapist. The legal age for marrying in the Punjab is 16. No charges were filed![161]

Temporary Marriages

Temporary marriages are illegal in Islam and having intercourse with a prostitute is considered a sin,[162] but abuse of temporary marriages flourishes. These are marriages for one night, three days, or whatever. "Temporary marriage is one way in which sexual immorality is cloaked with respectability in the Islamic world by those who scoff at the West's alleged immorality." It is common in Shia communities, especially in Iran and is flourishing in post-Saddam Iraq. It is **mut'a**, Arabic for pleasure and also the word for temporary marriage. Religious institutions exploit particularly poor women and they claim it goes back to Muhammad, "who once told his traveling companions they could purchase a wife with a handful of dates if they were away from their regular wives."[163]

Perhaps following the example of Muhammad's strong sex drive, an Islamic sex guide claimed that wives only meet 10% of husbands' desires.[164] In Kuwait, Sheikh Yasir al-Habib, a Shia, explained and justified mut'a, which is in a sense Islamically-sanctioned prostitution."[165] In Iran, new legislation, the Family Protection Bill ("activists call it the Anti-Family Protection Bill") would "give men the right to take a second wife without the permission of the first and it would enshrine a man's right to have an unlimited number of temporary marriages, which can last from 10 minutes to 99 years." "Those arrangements came from Sharia law and have always existed in Iran, but the Family Protection Bill would make them official.[166]

A man only has to say "I divorce you" "*Talaq*" three times and it is final.

Temporary marriages fit in with polygamy and the ease of divorce. A man only has to say "I divorce you" "*Talaq*" three times and it is final. This applies even if he says it jokingly. It has gone to the ridiculous in that it can be done by cellphone, even if the wife did not hear it, according to a fatwa from a leading Deoband seminary and has also been extended to texting.[167]

Harassment/Abuse of Women

Harassment of women has gone out of control. It is a problem in Cairo where nearly every woman has experienced leering, whistles, groping or other sexual harassment. There was the rape of the woman correspondent at Tahrir Square during the unrest that led up to President Mubarak's departure and another rape attack that left the journalist with both arms broken in the late November 2011 protests. A survey in 2008 found that 83% of Egyptian women and 98% of foreign women had been harassed and even 62% of men. A new web site, Harrasmap, has been setup so that women can quickly report incidents via text or Twitter and they will be loaded on a digital map of Cairo to show the hotspots. There are various theories as to the cause. Some feel it is the retrograde to conservatism and putting down women. Others blame unemployment which leaves youths "bored, frustrated and unable to marry." Many see it as "a breakdown of courtesy and morals."

The posting drew many comments: most of the males (evidently Muslim) wrote that women should not wear tight clothing and that they should wear the hijab. Others (probably females) wrote such as "Wow! So, if a man can't control himself and behaves like an animal it's the woman's fault?" "Are they animals?" "The problem is that men in Arab countries are raised to think women are sex objects. They are made to think women aren't just normal human beings like them but some sort of toy that must be ogled." "If hijab is the solution to this problem then explain why harassment is less common in western countries? Why is it generally safer for women to be out and about in Western countries as opposed to Arab countries?" "Muslim men –GROW UP!" "We need to accept that something is wrong with men in our culture who do this." "Women should be able to wear exactly what they want, without being molested. You men have an obligation to (and only to) prevent other men from treating women like a piece of grab-meat!!" "Crawl out of the 14th century and start behaving like civilized human beings." " I have seen there is no hope of dragging these people into the 21st century."

Remembering that there is no love in Islam, one comment came evidently from New York: "Thank goodness us males don't have such self-control issues as Muslims. Over here, beautiful women with makeup in tight jeans, high heels have more chances of meeting men with a large smile on their faces and eager to get to know them in a gentle, friendly manner, instead of harassers. Most men actually appreciate that women have put in so much time and effort to look good for us." "Of course, keeping beautiful women separate from men leads to a lot of sexual frustration in Muslim men, who are immature and lack self-control – thus the notion that kindness and friendliness goes a long way when dealing with sexy women is totally alien to them."[168]

Rayhana, an Algerian actress and playwright, who fled Algeria in 2000 because of threats from Islamists, was attacked outside the theater in Paris where her play about treatment of women in Algeria was being performed. "Two men insulted her in Arabic and poured petrol over her. They then threw a cigarette at her, which failed to ignite."[169] Attacks on women are routine across the Muslim world, for any reason including murder for not wearing the veil.[170]

This abuse can start at a very early age. In Pakistan, a nine-year-old Muslim child bride, who was forcibly married off at age six, was "hanged upside down, cut with a knife, and doused with acid for being a bad housekeeper."[171] There are endless reports of these atrocities. In Bangladesh, a man cut off his wife's fingers because she pursued higher education without his permission. He even kept the fingers from her so they could not be reattached.[172] A Pakistani woman was beaten, slapped, and tied up by her husband who then cut off her nose and lips. The police refused to register a case. The Pakistan domestic violence bill lapsed in 2009.[173] A Pakistani Taliban cut a nursing mother's breast and then asked other women to eat the pieces. This was in the FATA and women complained that they were forced to have sex to obtain necessities for survival, such as cooking oil.[174] A French Muslim in Marseille punched a nurse who tried to remove his wife's burqa during childbirth. The French judge gave him six months in jail: "Your religious values are not superior to the laws of the republic."[175]

This inhumane treatment of women is not some rare occurrence in some backward country. It is policy! Women's lack of freedom and outright abuse is a **fundamental feature of sharia.** Shaykh Ghawhi, who is a well-known and well-respected teacher of Islamic studies and Islamic law, says according to sharia:

1. A woman must only leave her house if she has a real need to do so.
2. Her husband or guardian must authorize her leaving the house.
3. When she is out, she must be completely covered, including her face.
4. When she is out, she must not look left or right but keep her head bowed down as she walks.
5. She must not wear perfume in public.
6. She must never shake a man's hand.
7. Even if she is visiting a female friend and is inside her friend's house, she must not uncover herself in case a man is hiding somewhere in the house.[176]

That same website, inquiryintoislam.com opens with a disgusting example.

AHMEDI BEGUM, a 50 year-old [Pakistani] woman, was showing two young women a room she was renting out when police rushed in and arrested the two girls and Ahmedi's nephew, who happened to be standing nearby.

That afternoon, Ahmedi went to the police station to see what could be done to release her nephew and the two girls, when the police arrested Ahmedi too, confiscating her jewelry and throwing her into a room.

In a short time, the two girls, naked and bleeding were thrown into the room too. Then police officers raped the girls in front of Ahmedi. She tried to look away, but they forced her to watch.

Ahmedi herself was then stripped and raped by several officers, and then beaten, and worse. At some point she passed out, and when she woke up, she had been charged with illegal fornication. [which carries the same penalties as adultery]

John Laffin, in *The Arab Mind Considered,* wrote of the Arab's "sexual frustration and obsessions, his paralyzing sense of shame." According to Larry Schweikart, Islam "has brought humiliation, shame, and honor to the forefront of geopolitics, due in no small part to the fact that Islamic societies have, for the most part, excluded women and treated all sexual relations as statements of power."[177] This treatment of women as possessions and the complete separation of men from women have a devastating effect on the Muslim male. Pierre Rehov, a French filmmaker, who filmed documentaries on suicide bombers, was interviewed on MSNBC.

> I came to the conclusion that we are facing a neurosis at the level of an entire civilization. Most neuroses have in common a dramatic event, generally linked to an unacceptable sexual behavior. In this case, we are talking of kids living all their lives in pure frustration, with no opportunity to experience sex, love, tenderness or even understanding from the opposite sex. The separation between men and women in Islam is absolute. So is contempt toward women, who are totally dominated by men. This leads to a situation of pure anxiety, in which normal behavior is not possible. It is no coincidence that suicide killers are mostly young men dominated subconsciously by an overwhelming libido that they not only cannot satisfy but are afraid of, as if it is the work of the devil. Since Islam describes heaven as a place where everything on earth will finally be allowed, and promises 72 virgins to those frustrated kids, killing others and killing themselves to reach this redemption becomes their only solution.[178]

Islam direly needs a renaissance in parts of its ancient thinking if there is any hope of regaining any of the grandeur of the Muslim past and joining the modern world and satisfying the needs and aspirations of its citizens. This is no more evident than in its treatment of women. It squanders the brain power of half its population and leaves macho men frustrated with a very limited outlook.

Isn't it sad, or better yet pathetic, when a poor Muslim gets all frustrated and aroused and cannot control himself if he sees a bit of female flesh, but a big, macho, red-blooded American (or most any non-Muslim male) can look at a woman in a bikini and only admire her beauty without ever thinking of attacking her!

The End of Reason - The Closing of the Muslim Mind

There was little or no philosophical discussion of Islam in the simple desert minds of Muhammad's time. The four caliphs after Muhammad stayed in Arabia and they kept the warriors quarantined outside conquered cities to prevent contamination from alien beliefs and cultures. But when the caliphate moved to Damascus and then to Baghdad, that was no longer practical as they encountered societies in which philosophical discussion was normal including Christianity. Thus rose a need for philosophical tools for discussing Islam and the follow-on question of which tools would be acceptable.

> **A people that deprives itself of philosophy necessarily exposes itself to starvation in terms of fresh ideas – in fact, it commits intellectual suicide.**
>
> **- Fazlur Rahman**

Much of this centered around the Qur'an – whether it was created in time or had existed with Allah forever. The Qur'an itself is unclear on this question. The traditionalist school contended that it was not created in time, but had co-exited with Allah forever on a tablet in heaven in Arabic (so Allah spoke Arabic!), beyond the scope of history and is thus ahistorical. This position made the Qur'an another god and a group called the **Mu'tazilites** noted this made those advocates polytheists. They claimed it had to have been created or the historical events in the Qur'an would have had to have been predetermined. This concept opened the door for free choice and reason. The Mu'tazalites saw reason as primary and the way to know Allah – Allah Himself is Reason - and if the Qur'an appeared inconsistent with reason, it should not be considered literally but as analogy or metaphor. They held that what is good or bad, just or unjust could be determined by reason. This became doctrine under Caliph al-Ma'mun (813-833) who was a great supporter of Greek thought and free will.

The Mu'tazalite school was dismissed by al-Bukhari, the Hadith collector: "The Qur'an is the speech of God uncreated, the acts of men are created, and inquiry into the matter is heresy." Many Muslims objected to the Mu'tazalite view and another school of theology arose, the **Ash'arites**, founded by Abn Hassan al-Ash'ari. They denied each Mu'tazalilte point. Allah is not reason; he is pure will and **power**. Allah is not constrained by anything; he can do whatever he wants. Allah is not even bound by his own word (contradictions in the Qur'an – removed by abrogation). They refuted human free will and claimed that reason cannot establish what is good or evil, only revelation. Caliph al-Mutawalkil (847-861) reversed the doctrine and established that the Qur'an is eternal and this is still the general orthodox view.

> **Criticism may not be agreeable, but it is necessary. It fulfills the same function as pain in the human body. It calls attention to an unhealthy state of things.**
>
> **- Winston Churchill**

According to **Abu Hamid al-Ghazali**, a prominent Ash'arite theologian and considered by some the most influential thinker after Muhammad, "no obligations flow from reason, but from the Sharia." This leaves Islam with no moral philosophy. Allah does not forbid murder because it is bad, but because he forbids it. Allah does everything and does not act for reasons. **This made reality incomprehensible.** The result was catastrophic: the denial of natural law, the relationship between cause and effect. To say that gravity made a rock fall instead of Allah made it fall is blasphemous. Al-Ghazili's Islamic world (some of his books: *The Incoherence of the Philosophers* and *Deliverance from Error*) and his rejection of Greek thought won out over the Mu'tazalites, but he drifted into mysticism (Sufism) which is itself irrational.

As Mark Steyn wrote, in most of the Muslim world, "there is simply no culture of inquiry….by the eleventh century all four schools of Islamic law had concluded they were pretty much on top of things and there was no need for any further interpretation or investigation. And from that point on Islam coasted, and then declined." The consequences of this "extraordinarily closed world" were momentous. "No Islamic country could have flown to the moon or invented the Internet, simply because for a millennium the culture has suppressed the curiosity necessary for such a venture."[179]

> Until the fourteenth century, Islam was the most progressive intellectual force in the world west of China. Then in a regrettable step, the religious leaders of orthodox – Sunni – Islam decided that its interpretative development, taking account of discoveries in non-theological thought, should come to an end. This "closing of the gates" spelled an end to Muslim openness. Thereafter right down to our own day, mainstream Islam found itself confined within intellectual boundaries set by scholars several hundred years dead.[180]

Thereafter, the law of Sharia – "the path to the waterhole" – controlled all aspects of life, business, and social intercourse.

> The interpretation of the spiritual and the material was, in practical terms a disaster for Islam. It prevented separation of theological and pragmatic paths of thought which the Christian West had achieved, if not without a struggle, even before the Protestant Reformation. While, from the Renaissance onwards, Italy, France, Germany, Holland and Britain soared off into the

heady altitudes of intellectual freedom that would usher in the Scientific Revolution and the Enlightenment, Islam remained stuck on the path to the waterhole. Its intellectual life decayed, its political institutions, the universal Caliphate foremost, fossilized. In its heyday, from the fifteenth to the seventeenth century, the Caliphate had conquered wherever it turned its steps. By the nineteenth century, Turkey, meaning the Caliphate, which still ruled North Africa in name, the Arab lands, and the Balkans as colonies, was the Sick Man of Europe. France and Britain fought Russia to prop Turkey up on its deathbed for fear of its final collapse.[181]

Minds are like parachutes – they only function when open.

Islamic jurisprudence has a principle: "Reason is not a legislator." All laws come from Allah, which is from sharia.[182] Therefore, there is no place for reason in either creating or interpreting laws. The political consequence of this primacy of pure will and power rules out representative democracy in the Islamic world. This is spelled out in *Reliance of the Traveller*: "ACTS THAT ENTAIL LEAVING ISLAM o8.7 (17) to believe that things in themselves or by their own nature have any causal influence independent of the will of Allah." [This is apostasy punishable by death.] **"We hate democracy,"** stated a Taliban cleric in Pakistan, "We want the occupation of Islam in the entire world. Islam does not permit democracy or election." [Emphasis added][183]

If you want a date on which the Muslim mind closed, 1195 A. D. might serve as the marker. It was then that Averroes' books [including *The Incoherence of the Incoherence*] were burned in the city square [Cordoba], that he was sent into exile, and that the teaching of philosophy was banned.

- Robert R. Reilly

Natural law and cause and effect are key to science, so their removal drastically limited science in the Muslim mind. There were scientific achievements in Islam's so-called Golden Age (9th to 13th centuries), but as Pakistani physicist, Pervez Hoodbhoy, noted, "But with the end of that period, science in the Islamic world essentially collapsed. No major invention or discovery has emerged from the Muslim world for well over seven centuries now." The 2003 UN report showed that the Arab world is near the bottom of every measure of development, except for sub-Saharan Africa, from education and health care to science and literacy. Spain translates more books in one year than the entire Arab world has in nearly a millennium.[184]

It is fairly simple. Religions developed when humans understood little of the world, our planet, the universe, the oceans, weather, diseases, etc. Religion provided "answers" where knowledge was limited or non-existent. But then modern science diverged from religion showing how inaccurate the religious understanding is. This made science the enemy of religion because when people have facts, they have less need for faith, and therefore are harder to control. "The greatest threat to any religion is a populace of educated, independent minds. The greatest asset to any religion is a populace that is ignorant and afraid."[185]

What is the significance of this closing of the Muslim mind? First is the Islamic terrorism worldwide based on **power** alone to settle disputes and violence in spreading Islam. Endorsement of violence was clear in Osama bin Laden's November 2001 video after 9/11: "Terrorism is an obligation in Allah's religion." The end of reason caused Islam's loss of science and hinders any prospect for developing constitutional government. The denial of cause and effect was devastating and helps explain the dysfunctional nature of much of the Islamic world today. This is a struggle within Islam (we have mentioned the civil war within

Islam before) and the dreadful effects of this deformed ideology that has produced a dysfunctional culture and spiritual pathology that seeks its success in death. The problem is theological. It came about because of de-Hellenization, the rejection of Greek thought. What is needed is a re-Hellenization of the Muslim world. Unless they decide to interpret the creation of the Qur'an, reason, and the use of force, it is hard to see any kind of reform succeeding.

We should say that we respect Islam as a source of moral and spiritual order in the lives of millions of people but that to the extent Islam cannot respect peoples' freedom of conscience, it is not acceptable to us.

- Robert R. Reilly[186]

Islam is heaven for Muslim men, but a hell for the believing women.

- The Liberated One[187]

Notes

1. Ahmad ibn Naqib al-Misri, *Reliance of the Traveller, A Classic Manual of Islamic Sacred Law,* (Beltsville, Maryland, Amana Publications, 2008), X245, p. 1073.
2. *Understanding Islam and the Muslims,* (Washington, DC, prepared by The Islamic Affairs Department, The Embassy of Saudi Arabia, 1989), p. 3.
3. Bill Warner, *Mohamed and the Unbelievers: The Sira, a Political Biography,* (CSPI, cspipublishing.com, 2006), p. 10, hereafter *Sira.*
4. Serge Trifkovic, *The Sword of the Prophet: Islam, history, theology, impact on the world,* (Boston, Regina Orthodox Press, Inc., 2002), p. 7.
5. Mark Steyn, *America Alone,* (Washington, DC, Regnery Publishing, Inc., 2006), p. 164.
6. Bill Warner, *An Abridged Koran, A Reconstructed Historical Koran,* (CSPI, cspipublishing.com, 2006), pp. 196-197, hereafter *An Abridged Koran.*
7. "And is it any wonder the worship of man and materialism in the form of Islam has come to claim adherents? And is it not the purpose of this materialistic creed to deny the reality and substance of love? Witness Muslim brothers beating and killing their sisters. Muslim fathers murdering their own daughters. Everyone sacrificing their sons and brothers to jihad. An inner 'thought police' so powerful as to never allow deviation from the thought system, a system that must deny the existence of that which it cannot control, a system at war with human affection." Rebecca Bynum, *Allah Is Dead: Why Islam is Not a Religion,* (Nashville, Tennessee, New England Review Press, 2011), p. 37.

    I found one exception in *Reliance of the Traveller*: t3.12 "Keep the thought of Allah Mighty and Majestic ever before you with respect to what He takes from you and what He gives. He takes away nothing except that you may show patience and win His love, for He loves the patient, and when He loves you, He will treat you as a lover does his beloved. And so too, when He gives to you, He bestows blessings upon you that you may give thanks, for He loves the thankful."
8. Up until the Night Journey, Muhammad had directed that prayers be facing toward Jerusalem; however, he received a revelation telling him to pray toward Mecca. Robert Spencer, *The Truth about Muhammad, Founder of the World's Most Intolerant Religion* (Washington, DC, Regnery Publishing, Inc., 2006), p. 101.
9. M. Cherif Bassiouni, *Introduction to Islam,* (Washington, DC, American-Arab Affairs Council, 1985), pp. 17-19.
10. Trifkovic, *The Sword of the Prophet,* p. 55.
11. Warner, *Sira,* fn p. 73.
12. v1.1 "He of the noble Throne and overwhelming force, the Guide of His elect servants to the wisest path and straightest way, who has blessed them, after having had them attest to His oneness, by preserving the tenets of their religion from the darknesses of doubt and misgivings, bringing them through His providence and guidance to follow His chosen Messenger and the example of his noble and honored Companions."
13. v1.2.
14. His Transcendence, v1.3.
15. His Life and Almighty Power, v1.4.
16. His Knowledge, v1.5.
17. His Will, v1.6.
18. His Hearing and Sight, v1.7.
19. His Acts, v1.9, "The obligation of men and jinn to perform acts of obedience is established by His having informed them of it upon the tongues of the prophets (upon whom be peace), and **not by unaided human reason**. He sent the prophets and manifested the truth of their message by unmistakable, inimitable **miracles**." [Emphasis added]
20. His Messenger, v2.1, followed by The Trial of the Grave, v2.2, "questioning being the first ordeal after death. It is also obligatory to believe in the torment of the grave"; The Scale, v2.3, where the pages about one's good deeds will be balanced by the pages of one's bad deeds; The Bridge Over Hell, v2.4, The Watering Place, v2.5, "It is obligatory to believe in a watering place people will come to, the watering place of Muhammad..., which believers will drink from before entering paradise, after having crossed over hell. Whoever drinks from it will never thirst again."; The Final Reckoning, v2.6, "It is obligatory to believe in the Final Reckoning and the disparity in the way various people are dealt with therein;" Believers Shall Depart From Hell, v2.7, "It is obligatory to hold that true believers in the oneness of Allah will be taken out of hell after having paid for their sins;" The Intercession of the Prophets and Righteous, v2.8, "It is obligatory to believe in the intercession of first the prophets, then religious scholars, then martyrs, then other believers, the intercession of each one commensurate with his rank and position with Allah Most High." ; and The Excellence of the Prophetic Companions (Sahaba), v2.9, "It is obligatory to believe in the excellence of the prophetic companions."
21. Conclusion, v3.1.
22. Thomas W. Lippman, *ISLAM Politics and Religion in the Muslim World,* (New York, Foreign Policy Association Headline Series, No., 258, March/April 1982), p. 20.
23. *Reliance of the Traveller,* x31, p. 1026.
24. For a description of the sunna – the teachings and personal actions of the prophet, see "The Sunnah – the 'Way' of the Prophet Muhammad," Citizen Warrior, 21 October 2010.
25. Mohammed Mohaddessin, *Islamic Fundamentalism: The New Global Threat,* (Washington, DC, Seven Locks Press, 1993), p. 4.
26. Bill Powell, "Struggle for the Soul of Islam," *Time,* 13 September 2004, p. 60.
27. Lippman, *ISLAM,* p. 24.
28. Bassiouni, *Introduction to Islam,* p. 33.
29. "Iraq PM criticises Muslim 'silence' on cleric's death calls," *Agence France-Presse,* 25 June 2009. Similar attacks on other parts of Islam are common. A bomb hit a mosque in a Sufi shrine 15 km from Peshawar, Pakistan killing 10 and injuring 30. The Pakistani Taliban considers worshipping at Sufi shrines "un-Islamic." "Terror strikes mosque at Friday prayers; 10

worshippers killed," *Economic Times,* 4 March 2011, Jihad Watch, 6 March 2011. See also Huma Imtiaz and Charlotte Buchen, "The Islam That Hard-Liners hate," *New York Times,* 7 January 2011 and "Hard-line militants now targeting Pak's most popular brand of Islam – Sufism," ANI, 7 January 2011.

30. Lippman, *ISLAM*, pp. 24-26.

31. Tariq Ramadan rebuked Pope Benedict XVI about a quote he made from an ancient emperor and pointed out the role of Muslims in "the development of Western thought." He listed the "decisive contributions of rationalist Muslim thinkers like al-Farabi (10th century), Avicenna (11th century), Averroes (12th century), al-Ghazali (12th century), Ash-Shatibi (13th century) and Ibn Khaldun (14th century)." "…And Where He's Still in the Dark," *Time,* 27 November 2006, p. 49.

32. Robert Spencer, *The Politically Incorrect Guide to Islam (and the Crusades),* (Washington, DC, Regnery Publishing, Inc., 2005), p. 41.

33. The Mamelukes were a slave class developed to fight for Muslims to evade the prohibition in the Qur'an on Muslims fighting Muslims.

34. Bill Warner, *The Political Traditions of Mohammed, The Hadith for the Unbelievers,* (CSPI, cspipublsihing.com, 2006), pp. 51-52, hereafter *Hadith.*.

35. Spencer, *The Politically Incorrect Guide to Islam*, p.97. The fall of Constantinople also resulted in the emigration of Greek intellcctuals to Europe which aided the Renaissance.

36. Lippman, *ISLAM*, pp. 28-29.

37. Ibid., pp. 30-33.

38. John Keegan, *The Iraq War,* (New York, Alfred A. Knopf, 2004), p. 90.

39. Jonathan Kay, "Geert Wilders' problem with Islam," *National Post,* 8 May 2011. What Wilders said was, "I see Islam as 95% ideology, 5% religion – the 5% being the temples and the imams. If you strip the Koran of all the negative, hateful, anti-Semitic material, you would wind up with a tiny [booklet]."

40. See Dr. Sebastian Gorka, "Jihadist Ideology: The Core Texts," transcript of a briefing given by Dr. Gorka at the Westminster Institute, 5 October 2010; and Ibn Waraq, The Westminster Institute about a conference on 25 May 2011, covered in Jihad Watch in four parts 13-16 June 2011.

41. Warner, *An Abridged Koran*, p. 199.

42. Spencer, *The Politically Incorrect Guide to Islam*, p. 33. There are some noble points in the Hadiths: Exhort every one not to do evil. Do not wish death to yourself or to others. Be kind to women. Respect women. The problem seems to be the contradictions in the Qur'an which permit almost any interpretation to fit one's predilections. See abrogation later in this section which removed many verses.

43. Bassiouni, *Introduction to Islam,* p. 12.

44. Oussani and Belloc, *Moslems,* p. 55.

45. Bulletin of the Oppression of Women, 14 November-15 December 2011, politicalislam.com.

46. Oussani and Belloc, *Moslems,* p. 55.

47. Warner, *An Abridged Koran,* p. 3.

48. Warner, *An Abridged Koran,* pp. xii-xvii.

49. Trifkovic, *The Sword of the Prophet*, pp. 74-75. The footnote on p. 75 has all the Surahs broken down chronologically into periods: early Mecca, middle period in Mecca, latter Mecca, and then Medina.

50. Warner, *Hadith*, p.142, Bukhari, volume 6, book 61, number 510.

51. Warner, *Hadith,* p. 10.

52. Spencer, *The Truth about Muhammad*, p. 174.

53. Trifkovic, *The Sword of the Prophet*, p. 76. Some historians contend that it is not the work of Muhammad or Uthman's secretary, "but a precipitate of the social and cultural pressures of the first two Islamic centuries." Ibn Al-Rawandi, "Origins of Islam: A Critical Look at the Sources," in *The Quest of the Historical Muhammad,* Ibn Warraq, editor, Prometheus Books, 2000, 111, quoted in Spencer, *The Truth about Muhammad*, p. 30.

54. An example of the difference in translations was in the London *Times* of 31 March 2007. An American, Dr. Laleh Bakhtiar rejected the idea that IV:34 of the Qur'an granted a husband the divine right to beat his wife. The key word to her was "*daraba,*" which she said "has 25 meanings in Arabic and has variously been translated as hit, strike, scourge, chastise, pet, tap and spank. She says the correct meaning is 'to go away from.'

  "M.A.S. Abdel Haleem's 2004 translation of the Qur'an reads: 'If you fear high handedness from your wives, remind them [of the teachings of God], then ignore them when you go to bed, then hit them.'

  "Bakhtiar translates the same verse as follows: 'But those whose resistance you fear, then admonish them and abandon them in their sleeping place, then go away from them; and if they obey you, look not for any way against them.'" "Wife-Beating Rejected in 'New Qur'an,'" Reports London *Times*," *WRMEA*, July 2007, p. 29.

55. Trifkovic, *The Sword of the Prophet*, pp. 77-78.

56. "Grand Mufti of Saudi Arabia: Qur'an Is 'Dominant' Over the Bible; 'We Don't Need…Any Other Book," Translating Jihad, 7 December 2010. "Regarding the previous books, their role has ended, and there is no longer any place for them. Almighty God has gathered all of their meaning into the Qur'an. The Qur'an has become dominant over them, and a substitute for all of them. The Qur'an with its stories and knowledge are sufficient for us." Robert Spencer pondered, "Could this be an explanation for why relatively few non-Islamic books are published in the Arab world, and very few books are translated from other languages into Arabic? Does this partly explain why nothing like the Renaissance ever happened in the Muslim World? If the Qur'an is all you need, then why waste time reading anything else?" Jihad Watch, 7 December 2010.

57. Trifkovic, *The Sword of the Prophet*, pp. 80-81.

58. When Muhammad already had numerous wives and concubines, Allah gave him specific permission to have as many women as he desired: "O Prophet! Surely We have made lawful to you your wives whom you have given their dowries, and those whom your right hand possesses [slaves] out of those whom Allah has given to you as prisoners of war, and the daughters of your paternal uncles and the daughters of your paternal aunts, and the daughters of your maternal uncles and the daughters of

your maternal aunts who fled with you; and a believing woman if she gave herself to the Prophet, if the Prophet desired to marry her – specially for you, not for the (rest of) believers" XXXIII:50. This resulted in polygamy and consideration of women as only objects.

       This is even a current problem such that in 2004, there was so much polygamy in the Muslim community in England that the British were considering recognizing it for taxes. Trifkovic, *The Sword of the Prophet*, pp. 72-73. See Robert Spencer, "Islamic Polygamy's Human Cost," Human Events, 20 August 2007, p. 11, about Muslim polygamy in the US. "Still on the question of polygamy, as with all instances of Islamic oppression of women, feminist groups maintain a stony silence." We will see more of this "dominance of multiculturalism and political correctness" in later chapters.

59.   Spencer, *The Politically Incorrect Guide to Islam*, p. 25.
60.   "Why the Standard Versions of the Quran are so Difficult to Decipher," www.inquiryintoislam.com, September 2010.
61.   Look at the cited works by Bill Warner.
62.   Book X, pp. 1019-1115.
63.   Warner, *Hadith*, p. 12.
64.   Ibid., p. xiii.
65.   Warner, *Sira*, p. xii.
66.   The Arabic plural of hadith is ahadith, but we will use the English version.
67.   There are numerous compilations of hadiths of varying acceptance. The two most reliable are by Muhammad Ibn Ismail Al-Bukhari, or Sahih Bukhari, and Abu Al-Husayn Muslim, or Sahih Muslim. Warner, *Hadith*, p. xii. Spencer *The Truth about Muhammad*, pp. 25-26. Bukhari studied 600,000 hadiths and selected 6,720 (even within them there is much repetition and only about 1,000 unique entries). There was major difficulty in tracing back in time for accuracy and there were many forgeries and various leaders created hadiths to support their political needs. Of the many collections, Bukhari and Muslim plus four more are considered the "Six Musannaf." Warner, Ibid., p. xiii.
68.   Warner, Ibid., pp. xii-xiii.
69.   Try to understand Surah LXVI without reading the hadith to find out about the problem he was having with jealous wives because of his attention to his slave Mary the Copt. Spencer, *The Truth about Muhammad*, pp. 20-24.
70.   Warner, *Sira*, pp. xii-xiii, and p. 164. The amount of text devoted to jihad is 9% for the Qur'an, 21% for Hadith, and 31% for the Trilogy overall.

       Indicative of our ignorance of Islam is that it was five centuries before the Qur'an was translated into another language, Latin, and another five centuries before there was another translation. The first translation of a Sira to English was not until the 17th Century. The major hadith, Bukhari, was not translated until the 20th Century. Bill Warner, politicalislam.com, 5 January 2012.
71.   Warner, *Hadith,* p. vi.
72.   Warner, *Sira*, p. 59.
73.   Warner, *Sira*, pp. 169-170.
74.   The text that was anti-Jewish was: Qur'an (Mecca) 1%, (Medina) 17%; Sira 12%; Hadith 8.9%; total Trilogy 9.3%; *Mein Kampf* 7%. Warner, *Sira,* pp. 168-169.
75.   Warner, *Sira*, p. 170.
76.   "Taliban banish Sikhs from Orakzai for not paying Jizia," *Daily Times,* 1 May 2009. See also "History's Hostages: Held to a huge ransom by the Taliban, NWFP's Sikhs have nowhere to go," *Outlook India,* 4 May 2009.
77.   "Another Baha'i-owned Business Fire Bombed, Threatening Letter Left Behind," Iran Press Watch, 9 January 2011, Jihad Watch 11 January 2011.
78.   http://www.dhimmitude.org/ Jamie Glazov, "Eurabia" Interview with Bat Ye'or, FrontPageMagazine.com, 21 September 2004.
79.   "Vatican: Koran encourages 'killing Christians,'" AKI, 22 October 2010, Jihad Watch.
80.   Warner, *Sira*, p. 169 and *Hadith*, p. 51.
81.   Pamela Geller, "Media Capitulation: If Juan Williams Is Fair Game…." *Big Journalism,* 25 October 2010.
82.   Jihad Watch, 15 April 2011.
83.   Volume 4, Book 53, Number 388, quoted in Warner, *Hadith,* p. 52.
84.   Warner, *Hadith,* p. 53.
85.   Warner, *Hadith,* pp. 53-54 (from Al-Turtushi, *Siraq Al-Muluk*, pp. 229-230.)
86.   Ibid., p. 54.
87.   Letter from David G. Littman, Representative to UN-Geneva for The World Union for Progressive Judaism, to High Commissioner for Human Rights, Navi Pillay, 31 December 2010.
88.   "Bangladesh: Police Torture Pastor, Two Others: Local Muslim leaders prompt officers to arrest, abuse evangelistic team," *Compass Direct,* 4 August 2009.
89.   Timothy Ola, "Boko Haram: How 3 pastors were beheaded eyewitness," *Daily Sun* (Lagos, Nigeria), Jihad Watch, 6 August 2009.
90.   "News Alert: Pakistan Christian Burned", Wife "Raped", for Refusing Islam," *BosNewsLife,* 20 March 2010. Another example of "You infidels have to convert or die" was when 100 Taliban militants attacked a Christian colony in Karachi. One young boy was executed and three churches and dozens of Christian owned shops were burned down. Ethan Cole, "Taliban Attack, Kill Christians in Pakistan Town," *Christian Post,* 26 April 2009.
91.   "ASIA/BANGLADESH – A village burned down, tribal Christians forced out by Muslim settlers," *Agenzia Fides,* 21 February 2011.
92.   "Bishop Concerned Over Survival of Christian Community in Nazareth," Voice of America, 1 June 2011, Jihad Watch, 4 June 2011.
93.   Nina Shea, "Call to Ban Bible Under Pakistan's Elastic Blasphemy Laws," *National Review,* 6 June 2011.

94. "Bishop Concerned Over Survival of Christian Community in Nazareth," Voice of America, 1 June 2011, Jihad Watch, 4 June 2011.

95. Raymond Ibrahim, "Egypt Cuts a Deal: Christians Fed to Muslim 'Lions,'" Hudson New York, 18 October 2010.

96. Abigail Hauslohner, "Attacks on Christians: Can Egypt Deal With Extremist Mobs?" Time, 12 June 2011.

97. Mary Abdelmassih, "Muslims Surround Church in Upper Egypt, Threaten to Kill Priest," Assyrian International News Agency, 24 June 2011. There was an optimistic, and hopefully not naïve, account of Muslim-Coptic cooperation, Bruce Feiler, "The Crescent and the Cross," Time, 20 June 2011p. 30.

98. "Islamists Suspected in Abduction of Christian Girl in Sudan," Compass Direct News, 22 February 2011.

99. Jibran Khan, "Punjab: Christian woman forced to convert and marry her kidnapper," AsiaNews, 6 August 2011.

100. Bill Warner, Bulletin of Christian Persecution, 28 October-27 November 2011.

101. Joshua Partlow and Habib Zahori, "Afghan imams wage political battle against U.S.," Washington Post, 17 February 2011.

102. See "Wahhabism: Toxic Faith?" Time, 15 September 2003. p. 46.

103. R. James Woolsey, "The Elephant in the Middle East living room: Watching Wahhabis," The National Review Online, 14 December 2005.

104. Spencer, Islam, pp. 24-25. The peaceful verses are still considered abrogated. Widely respected Saudi Sheikh Muhammad Saalih al-Munajid (b. 1962) wrote about fighting until Islam was the only religion said, referring to the Verse of the Sword, "These and similar verses abrogate those saying that there is no compulsion to become Muslim." Warner, An Abridged Koran, says 225, p. 123.

  There was a big brouhaha at the University of North Carolina at Chapel Hill when shortly after 9/11 the incoming freshmen were required to read the book, Approaching the Qur'an, by Michael Sells. The problem was that he only covered the early verses thus omitting the Verse of the Sword, etc. which are less peaceful.

105. Tafsir Ibn Kathir, Vol 2, 141, quoted in Shariah: The Threat to America, (Washington, DC, The Center for Security Policy, 2010), p. 32.

106. Reliance of the Traveller, r8.0, pp. 744-747.

107. Raymond Ibrahim, "How Taqiyya Alters Islam's Rules of War: Defeating Jihadist Terrorism," Middle East Quarterly, Winter 2010, http://www.meforum.org/2538/taqiyya-islam-rules-of-war.

108. Comment on "Surprise: Saudi clerics resist even minor reforms proposed by king." Jihad Watch, 2 July 2011.

109. Qasim Rashid, "Will the real moderate Muslims please stand up," 2 February 2011, Jihad Watch. 2 February 2011.

110. Sabria Jawhar, "The Idiocy of the Anti-Sharia Crowd," Huffington Post, 19 October 2010.

TheReligionofPeace.com did a mimic cover "Taqiyya for Dummies" A Reference Guide for Turning Useful Idiots into Deferential Dhimmis, by Muhammad, Medina Edition.

Citizen Warrior posted "Twelve Tactics of Taqiyya" on 6 October 2010 from Trencherbone. They are briefly:

1. Taqiyya about taqiyya. Muslims deny that taqiyya exists.
2. Playing the race card and guilt by association.
3. Godwin's Law. Criticism of Islam=Racism=Nazism. Therefore, if you criticize Islam, you are a Nazi.
4. Circular reasoning. Qur'an is the word of God, so must be true. Therefore, Qur'an is word of God because it says so.
5. Infidels' quotes from Qur'an are taken out of context.
6. Infidels cannot understand original Arabic of the Qur'an.
7. Tu Quoque ((you also). Referring back to Bible, Crusades, Inquisition, you also do violent acts.
8. False kin argument. Islam is just a further development of Christianity.
9. Quoting abrogated verses from Qur'an to appear moderate.
10. You owe us a debt of gratitude because Islam is the basis of Western civilization.
11. A third of the world's population believe in Islam, so it deserves respect.
12. We are victims of Islamophobia.

See also "An Example of Taqiyya," Citizen Warrior, 11 November 2009, quoting from the book, Terrorist Hunter: The Extraordinary Story of a Woman Who Went Undercover to Infiltrate the Radical Islamic Groups Operating in America," by Rita Katz.

111. Bukhari, vol. 4: 267 and 269 and vol. 3:857, p. 533, quoted in Shariah, The Center for Security Policy, p. 32.

112. Act! For America Education, November 2011.

113. "Pakistani Textbooks Demonize Non-Muslims," Newsmax.com, 13 November 2011.

114. "Shaykh Muhammad Hassan: Islam Prefers a Strong, Immoral Warrior," Translating Islam, 28 June 2011, Jihad Watch, 30 June 2011.

115. A French court ruled that a marriage could be annulled because the wife was not a virgin as she had claimed. It was considered a breach of contract because "essential qualities were misrepresented." It caused a stir in France "because the government has fought to maintain strong secular traditions as demographics change" – the largest Muslim population in Europe. Elaine Ganley, AP, "Lack of virginity annuls marriage," Reno Gazette-Journal, 5 June 2008, p. 5C.

116. Khalid Tanveer, AP, "Pakistani admits killing his 4 daughters for family honor," Reno Gazette-Journal, 29 December 2005, p. 1C.

  A 21-year-old woman was murdered in Pakistan by her brother because she refused her family's demand to divorce her husband. Rashid Ameer, "Honour crime: Woman killed for refusing to divorce husband," The Express Tribune, 23 February 2011, Jihad Watch.

117. There were 675 in the first 9 months of 2011 in Pakistan.

118. Rebecca Camber, "Honour crime up by 40% due to rising fundamentalism," Daily Mail, 7 December 2009, www.dailymail.co.uk/news/article-1233918/Honour-crime-40-rising-fundamentalis.html.

119. "German police accuse Kurdish men of 'honour killing,'" Deutsche Presse Agentur, 2 April 2009.

120. "Jordanian man charged with killing sister in honor crime," AP, 6 April 2009, 8th that year; about 20 annually.

121. "Uncle kills eloping niece over 'honour,'" *Daily Times,* 9 April 2009.
122. "Muslim father orders daughter killed over short skirt," *MosNews,* 13 April 2009.
123. Amir Shah and Rahim Faiez, AP, 14 April 2009. The woman was a Pashtun Sunni and the man a Shiite.
124. *Israel National News,* 16 April 2009.
125. *The News International,* 21 April 2009. He said they were having relations with locals and ignored his admonishments.
126. Gaza woman found slain in most recent 'honor killing'" *Ma'an News Agency,* 11 June 2009.
127. Yaniv Kubovich and Noah Kosharek, *Haaretz,* 21 October 2010.
128. "Muslim girl killed for love affair with Hindu," *Indo-Asian News Service,* 25 November 2010.
129. "Killer of wife, daughter arrested," *The News International,* 19 January 2011.
130. Shahid Mirza, "14-year-old killed for refusing to marry father's cousin," *Express Tribune,* 4 February 2011.
131. "Karo-kari: Man kills 55-yr-old mother for 'affair.'" *Express Tribune,* 22 February 2011.
132. Jihad Watch 12 April 2011. Robert Spencer cited an Islamic law manual that someone who kills his child incurs no legal penalty under Islamic law.
133. "Italy: Moroccan immigrant murders wife for being 'too Western.'" AKI, 28 June 2011.
134. "Turned over to kin after elopement, Baghpat women killed by mothers," *Indian Express,* 14 May 2011.
135. Liz Hazelton, "Father slits throats of three daughters in 'honor killing' after they were raped by Gaddafi's troops," *Daily Mail,* 30 August 2011.
136. "Jordan woman killed in hospital over pregnancy," *Agence France Presse,* 4 September 2011.
137. "Refusing to Kill Daughter, Pakistani Family Defies Tradition, Draws Anger," *The Atlantic,* 28 September 2011.
138. Shamsul Islam, "Acid attacks: 7 women burned in two days," *Express Tribune,* 18 September 2011.
139. Rebecca Conway, "Rape, mutilation: Pakistan's tribal justice for women," Reuters, 12 August 2011.
140. Jason Riley, "Police describe grisly scene in Somali man's trial in deaths of his children," *Courier-Journal,* 18 April 2011.
141. "Coon Rapids man accused of killing stepdaughter for leaving home, not following Islam," Associated Press, 3 May 2011.
142. "Disturbing Details Emerge in 'Honor Killing' case," Fox10, 6 August 2011.
143. "Saudi cleric backs gender segregation with fatwa," Reuters, 23 February 2010.
144. *Asia News,* 2 April 2009. They were filming a TV series when the religious police or muttawa (Riyadh Commission for Promotion of Virtue and Prevention of Vice) arrested them.
145. Abdullah, AP, "Gang-rape victim pardoned by Saudi king after criticism," *Reno Gazette-Journal*, 18 December 2007, p. 3B.
146. Mohamed Osman, AP, "Sudanese protesters demand teacher's execution," *Reno Gazette-Journal*, 1 December 2007, p. 1B.
147. Sadaqat Jan, AP, "Islamic clerics demand firing of tourism minister over hug," *Reno Gazette-Journal,* 10 April 2007, p. 3C.
148. Not all women are held back; it varies with countries. Note the woman head of the department at Al-Azhar. Women have reached high positions in numerous governments, but there are hundreds of millions of Muslim women. There are some very well educated women in Saudi Arabia in important positions (but they still cannot drive). Georgia Anne Geyer wrote about the advances in women's rights in Bahrain under the Al-Khalifa family, in Qatar under Sheikh Hamad Bin Kahlifa Thani and his activist wife, and in Oman under Sultan Qaboos. "'Progressive Islam' takes hold in Gulf." *Reno Gazette-Journal,* 26 February 2000, p. 13A.
       The late King Hassan II of Morocco permitted a woman to recite poetry at the opening of the Hassan II Mosque (second in size only to the Grand Mosque in Mecca – space for 100,000 with a 650-foot minaret, the tallest in the world) in September 1993. "Modern Mosque," *Time,* 13 September 1993, p. 6.
149. Mathias Hariyadi, "Aerobic contrary to Islam, promotes lust, Sumatra Islamic leader says," *Asia News,* 15 February 2010.
150. Elissa Hunt, "Foreign student upset by the way women dressed jailed for sex attacks," *Herald Sun,* 31 May 2011. He got five years and three months.
151. Robert Spencer, "'Unveiled Women Are Like Uncovered Meat,'" Human Events, 6 November 2006, p. 12.
152. For a report on the problem in Sweden and other parts of Scandinavia, see Fjordman, "Immigrant Rape Wave in Sweden," http://www.frontpagemag.com/Articles /ReadArticle.asp?ID=20552, 15 December 2005. The number of rape charges had tripled in 20 years. Rape cases involving children under 15 were up 6 times. In Oslo, two out of three rape charges were against immigrants in 2001; the same in Denmark but three out of four in Copenhagen. In one court, "85 percent of the convicted rapists were born on foreign soil or by foreign parents." In one poll, "82% of the women expressed fear to go outside after dark."
153. Bulletin of Oppression of Women, 25 October-15 November 2011.
154. http://www.steynonline.com/, 30 June 2011.
155. See "Activists: 9 Iranians set to be stoned to death," *Reno Gazette-Journal,* 21 July 2008, p. 2B. "Under Iran's Islamic laws, adultery is the only capital offense punishable by stoning. A man usually is buried up to his waist, while a woman is buried up to her neck. Those carrying out the verdict then throw stones until the condemned dies."
       Apologists like to say that stoning is not authorized in the Qur'an. However, it is reported several times in Sahih Bukhari that Muhammad ordered stoning: Volume 8, Book 82, Numbers 805, 809, 813, 815, and 817.
156. Adnan Shabrawi, "Girl gets a year in jail, 100 lashes for adultery," *Saudi Gazette,* 7 January 2011, quoted in Jihad Watch, 8 January 2011.
157. *Indo-Asian News Service,* 29 April 2009. The crime was "anti-social activity." The man involved was whipped 101 times. Such fatwas have been illegal in Bangladesh since 2001.
158. Ethirajan Anbarasan, "Bangladeshi 'stepson affair' woman dies after caning," *BBC News,* 20 December 2010.
159. Salah Uddin Shoaib Choudhury, "Sharia Brutality on a Raped Girl in Bangladesh," 2 February 2011, http://www.hudson-ny.org/1856/bangladesh-sharia-brutality-raped-girl.
160. Aaliss J. Rubin, "For Afghan Woman, Justice Runs Into Unforgiving Wall, *The New York Times,* 2 December 2011.
161. "Pakistan: A 12 year-old Christian is gang raped for eight months, forcibly converted and then 'married' to her Muslim attacker," Asian Human Rights Commission, 10 October 2011.
162. *Reliance of the Traveller,* m6.12, p. 530 and w52.1(345), p. 986.

163. Kelly McEvers, "Abuse Of Temporary Marriages Flourishes In Iraq," NPR, 19 October, 2010, quoted in Jihad Watch, 22 October 2010. Advocates refer to Qur'an IV:24 as justification.

164. Lindsay Murdoch, "Islamic sex guide say wives meet only 10% of husbands' desires," *Sydney Morning Herald*, 14 October 2011, Jihad Watch, 13 October 2011.

165. Bulletin of the Oppression of Women, 14 November-15 December 2011, politicalislam.com.

166. Ibid.

167. "Talaq uttered by Muslim man on cellphone valid: Deoband," PTI, 15 November 2010. A young Saudi woman received a text from her husband in Iraq. "Shariah court approves SMS divorce," *Arab News,* 9 April 2009.

168. Maggie Hyde, "Harasmap: A counter to web of women's harassment," arabnews.com, 25 October 2010.

169. "Playwright petrol attack handed to terrorist police," *RFI,* 15 January 2010.

170. "Somalia: Islamic supremacists murder Christian woman for refusing to wear veil." Islamic Jihad, 29 October 2009.

171. Bulletin of the Oppression of Women, 25 October-15 November 2011.

172. Arbarasan Ethirojan, "Bangladesh man 'admits' cutting off wife's fingers," BBC News, 15 December 2011.

173. "Man chops off wife's nose and lips," *Agence France Presse,* 19 December 2011.

174. "Taliban cut nursing woman's breast, asked others to eat pieces: UN-backed report," Press Trust of India, 16 December 2011.

175. Ian Sparks, "French Muslim jailed for punching nurse who tried to remove wife's burqa during childbirth," *Daily Mail,* 22 December 2011.

176. "What Muslim Leaders Say About Islam Dispels the Myth that Jihadists are a 'Fringe' Element," Citizen Warrior, 1 October 2010. www.inquiryintoislam.com/2010/06/islam-and-womens-rights.html.

177. Larry Schweikart, *America's Victories,* (New York, Sentinel, 2006), p. 19. With reference to Abu Ghraib, he wrote the message was: "Don't screw with the Americans. They'll turn their women loose on you!" p. 23.

178. "What is the solution?" MSNBC's "Connected," 15 July 2005.

179. Mark Steyn, *America Alone,* (Washington, DC, Regnery Publishing, Inc., 2006), pp. 16-17.

180. John Keegan, *The Iraq, War,* (New York, Alfred A. Knopf, 2004), p. 91.

181. Ibid., p. 92.

182. See *Reliance of the Traveller*, a1.4, pp. 2-3.

183. Jihad Watch, 5 August 2009.

184. The "Arab world translates just 330 books every year, abut 20% of what Greece alone does. In the last 1,200 years of Islam, just 100,000 books have been translated into Arabic, about what Spain does in a single year. Seven out of 10 Turks have never even read a book." Bryan Fischer, "A huge Muslim problem: Inbreeding," Bryan Fischer-Focal Point, May 2011.

185. Thanks to the Comment by LEB in Andrew Carey, "UK cleric leaves mosque over evolution," CNN, 22 March 2011.

186. Comments and quotations come from three interviews with Robert R. Reilly about his book, *The Closing of the Muslim Mind: How Intellectual Suicide Created the Modern Islamist Crisis: The Daily Caller,* 8 August 2010, InsideCatholic.com, 14 August 2010, and with Jihad Watch, 23 January 2011. Reilly, a former director of Voice of America, serves as senior fellow at the The American Foreign Policy Council.

187. The liberated One is a woman who has left Islam. She is evidently Pakistani but living in another country. She credits the quote to Aisha, but in her blog http://liberatednow.blogspot.com/2012/01/women-in-islam.html, she gives a long list of Muhammad's "sexual escapades" quoting from the Qur'an and various Hadiths. She ended with "So you see, the so-called Holy Prophet of Islam is nothing but a sick, perverted sex maniac, a pedophiliac misogynist, and a heartless creature who had absolutely no sense of morals or ethics. He was a self-proclaimed prophet who wanted nothing but power and pussies. That is all he was interested in, and yes, a lot of booty as well.

"In a time of intensifying strains, of faltering ideologies, jaded loyalties, and crumbling institutions, an ideology expressed in Islamic terms offered several advantages: an emotionally familiar basis of group identity, solidarity, and exclusions; an acceptable basis of legitimacy and authority; an immediately intelligible formulation of principles for both a critique of the present and a program for the future. By means of these, Islam could provide the most effective symbols for mobilization, whether for or against a cause or regime."

– Bernard Lewis, 2002

Chapter 4

Sharia and Jihad

The good is not what reason considers good,
nor the bad what reason considers bad.
The measure of good and bad,
according to this school of law,
is the Sacred Law, not reason.

- *Reliance of the Traveller*[1]

The acme of this religion is jihad.

- Osama bin Laden

As we have seen, Islam is based on the Trilogy of the Qur'an, the Hadith, and the Sira. The development of Islam into an ideology, particularly in Medina, required a political system. Thus was grown the Islamic law or sharia.[2] The other part of the political system was how to implement it and that is jihad.

Sharia

Since one of the objectives of expansionist Islam is to impose sharia, we need to briefly review it. Sharia is Islamic law, the principal source of which is the Qur'an. Remembering that Islam is not a religion as we think, but a complete way of life, applicable to everything everywhere and forever, sharia provides the rules for governing the Muslim world. It provides the rules for organizing and governing a Muslim society and deals with resolving conflicts among people and between people and the state.[3] The provisions of the Qur'an are to be scrupulously followed, but the sunna are a secondary source, and together represent the basis of sharia. There are other sources for sharia such as consensus (*ijma'*), analogy (*qiyas*), reasoning (*ijtihad*), precedents (*istihsan*), special judgment required by public interest and public policy (*istislah*), and custom and usage (*'urf*).

Different schools of jurisprudence developed over the centuries. There are four major Sunni schools (Hanafi, Hanbali, Maliki, and Shafi'i) with various sub-schools of each.[4] Along with two Shiite schools, Ja'fari and Ismaili Fatimid, sharia was codified by the tenth century and the fiqh ("understanding") has changed little since.[5]

As an example of the subjects covered, here are some from the 1238 pages of *Reliance of the Traveller* (which is a classic manual of sharia): Sacred Knowledge, The Validity of Following Qualified Scholarship, The Nature of Legal Rulings, Purification, The Prayer, The Funeral Prayer, Zakat, Fasting, The Pilgrimage, Trade, Inheritance, Marriage, Divorce, Justice, Enormities, Commanding the Right and Forbidding the Wrong, Holding One's Tongue, Delusions, A Pure Heart, The Gabriel Hadith, Belief in Allah and His Messenger.

Just like the Qur'an, sharia can be extremely personal and quite detailed. Purification includes "The Body" e4.0 (shave the pubic hair[6], don't shave one's beard, don't dye your hair black, and circumcision is obligatory for both men and women [remove the prepuce not the clitoris – maybe!), "Ablution" e5.0 (even put some water in your nostrils), "Going to the Lavatory" e9.0 (how to urinate and how many times to wipe yourself – three with stones [or an odd number] and which hand, of course), Justice includes "Apostasy From Islam" o8.0 ("Leaving Islam is the ugliest form of unbelief (kufr) and the worst….[and the person] deserves to be killed."), "Jihad" o9.0 ("Jihad means to war against non-Muslims, etymologically derived from the word *mujahada*, signifying warfare to establish the religion."), "The Obligatory Character of Jihad" o9.1, "Who is Obliged to Fight in Jihad" o9.4, "The Objectives of Jihad" o9.8, "The Rules of Warfare" o9.10 ("When a child or woman is taken captive, they become slaves by the fact of capture, and the woman's previous marriage is immediately annulled." o9.13), "Truces" o9.16, "The Spoils of Battle" o10.0 (explaining how divided starting with first fifth to the Prophet o10.3), "Non-Muslim Subjects of the Islamic State (Ahl Al-Dhimma)" o11.0 (the restrictions are spelled out – not applicable to people without a Book), "The Penalty for Fornication or Sodomy" o12.0, "The Penalty for Accusing a Person of Adultery Without Proof) o.13.0 (with the requirement for four witnesses o13.1(b) which is why 75% of the women in Pakistan's prisons are women who were raped), "The penalty for Theft" o.14.0 (rules on amputation), "The Penalty for Highway Robbery) o.15.0 (may seem outdated but harsh – "If a highway man kills someone, he must be executed." "If the highway man robs and kills, he is killed and then left crucified for three days.), "The Penalty for Drinking" o.16.0, and a long section on "The Caliphate" o25.0 with a long historical review.

Book P has a very long list of "Enormities" (any sin entailing either a threat of punishment in the hereafter explicitly mentioned in the Qur'an or Hadith) ranging from "Killing a Human Being" to "Drinking" ("If he drinks it [wine] a fourth time, kill him." p14.2(1)) to "Making Pictures" p.44.0. Book W "Notes and Appendices" runs nearly 200 pages. It deals with "Sufism" w9.0, "In What Sense Philosophy Is Unlawful" w10.0, "The Unlawfulness of the Sciences of the Materialists" w11.0 ("refers to the conviction of materialists that things *in themselves* or *by their own nature* have a causal influence independent of the will of Allah. To believe this is unbelief that puts one beyond the pale of Islam. Muslims working in the sciences must remember that they are dealing with figurative causes, not real ones, for Allah alone is the real cause." w11.1), "Women's Obligatory Clothing" w23.0 (Shafi'I school – different circumstances: "In the privacy of the home, her nakedness is that which is between the navel and the knees. In the prayer it means everything besides the face and the hands. And when outside the home on the street, it refers to the entire body."), "The Prohibition of Depicting Animate Life" w50.0 (from p44.1 with more detail about "Portraits" w50.7, "Photographs" w50.9, and "Television" w50.10. Another long "List of Enormities" w52.0, 442 plus another 17, including "not accepting fate (24), disbelieving in destiny (52), "neglecting to say the blessings on the Prophet when one hears his name mentioned" (60), "eating or drinking from a gold or silver vessel" (67), "tattooing" (81), "plucking eyebrows or facial hair" (83).

> **Sharia is "also a part of that universal law which governs the entire universe, including the physical and biological aspects of man."**
>
> **- Sayyid Qutb**

Sayyid Qutb (1906-1966) wrote a book, *Milestones,* which is a key Islamic text and considered the inspiration for 9/11. His views on sharia are all encompassing: "In Islam the meaning of Shariah is **not limited** to mere legal injunctions, but includes the principles of administration, its system and its modes….By the Shariah of God [Allah] is meant everything legislated by God [Allah] for **ordering man's life**; it includes the **principles** of **belief**, principles of **administration** and **justice**, principles of **morality and human relationships**, and principles of **knowledge**….It includes **political, social and economic affairs** and their principles, with the intent that they reflect **complete submission** to God [Allah] alone….It deals with the **morals, manners, values and standards** of the society." [Emphasis added] As Ibn Warraq stated, **"You cannot get more totalitarian than that."**[7]

The significance of sharia in the modern context is the call for sharia by minority Muslims for themselves in a non-Muslim society and the jihadist (or Islamic extremist) call for the imposition of sharia everywhere.

M. Cherif Bassiouni summed it up well. With the diversity of the schools and various interpretations, it is difficult to develop a solid Islamic law. To do so, "enlightened scholars must combine a knowledge of the past with an understanding of the present and a vision of the future. That is an educational challenge that has yet to be met in the Muslim world." He said the Islamic fundamentalists are playing to the masses and they "advance simplistic views as panaceas for complex problems." He ended with, "gaining of power is the real objective. Islamic criminal justice reform thus becomes the victim of movements that have other goals, and which would eventually use and abuse the criminal justice system to strengthen their authority."[8]

With over 1.5 billion Muslims, there may be variations in their beliefs and we may not be able to define the "real Islam," but we can establish certain facts. Sharia is firmly rooted in the Qur'an and the sunna and is favored by leading Islamic supporters, including al-Azhar University in Cairo. It has been lavishly financed and supported by regimes such as Saudi Arabia and Iran and international organizations such as the Muslim Brotherhood for over 50 years. Since Islam has no central authority, it is extremely difficult for any Islamic moderates or reformers to delegitimize sharia. Since sharia is a totalitarian system, it is a threat to the United States.[9]

Even though sharia has been basically frozen for a thousand years, it is still the only law according to even "moderate" contemporary Islamic legal scholars. Abdur Rahman I. Doi (born in India, died in 1999) who taught Islamic law in Malaysia, Nigeria, and South Africa wrote in *Shariah: The Islamic Law*:

> In the shariah, there is an explicit emphasis on the fact that Allah is the Lawgiver and the whole ummah, the nation of Islam, is merely His trustee. It is because of this principle that the ummah enjoys a derivative rule-making power and not an absolute law-creating prerogative.

> The shariah was not revealed for limited application for a specific age. It will suit every age and time. It will remain valid and shall continue to be, till the end of life on earth. Its injunctions were coined in such a manner that they are not affected by the lapse of time. The do not become obsolete, nor do their general principles and basic theories need to be changed or renovated.

For Doi, sharia and democracy are incompatible. He quoted the Qur'an about those who fail to follow sharia: "And if any fail to judge by the light of what Allah has revealed, they are no better than unbelievers."[10]

Pakistani professor of Islamic law, Imran Ahsan Khan Nyazee, wrote in *Theories of Islamic Law: The Methodology of Ijtihad*:

> No other sovereign or authority is acceptable to the Muslim, unless it guarantees the application of these laws [shariah] in their entirety. Any other legal system, howsoever attractive it may appear on the surface, is alien for Muslims and is not likely to succeed in the solution of their problems; it would be doomed from the start….A comprehensive application of these laws, which flow directly or indirectly from the decrees (*ankam*) of Allah, would mean that they should regulate every area of life, from politics to private transactions, from criminal

justice to the laws of traffic, from ritual to international law, from the laws of taxation and finance to embezzlement and white collar crimes.[11]

To be completely current, we can turn to **Yusuf al-Qaradawi**, the spirtitual leader of the Muslim Brotherhood, who, unfortunately, was permitted by the military to return to Egypt from 50 years of exile after the overthrow of President Hosni Mubarak in 2011. (Qaradawi is probably one of the most dangerous people in the world and perhaps should be listed as World Enemy #1.) "The shariah cannot be amended to conform to changing human values and standards. Rather, it is the absolute norm to which all human values and conduct must conform."[12]

Sharia is the fusion of church and state. Since all Muslim countries implement sharia to varying degrees, let us examine jurisprudence, official *fatwas* (legal opinions), in Saudi Arabia, the home of Mecca. For some of them, I have noted the same or similar law from *Reliance of the Traveller* (RotT), the classic Islamic legal manual.

Shari'ah Law & Freedom of Speech:

- The punishment for apostasy (changing or discarding one's Islamic relgion) is death.
  Fatwa 4400, Part No. 1, Page 334 & 335   RotT o8.2
- Mocking anything in the Qur'an or the Sunnah of the prophet Muhammad is apostasy and therefore punishable by death.
  Fatwa 2196, Part No. 2, Page 42   RotT o8.7
- Criticizing Islam, shari'ah law or the Sunnah of the prophet Muhammad is apostasy and therefore punishable by death.
  Fatwa 21021, Part No. 1, Page 414   RotT o8.7
- Any Muslim who states a preference for democracy rather than shari'ah law or questions anything in the Qur'an or Sunnah is a kafir (disbeliever), considered an apostate, and therefore sentenced to death.
  Fatwa 19351, Part No. 22, Page 239-248   RotT o8.7

Shari'ah Law & Human Rights:

- The punishment for theft is amputation of the right hand up to the elbow.
  Fatwa 3339, Part No. 22, Page 218 & 219   RotT o14.1
- The penalty for premarital sexual intercourse is 100 lashes with a whip and one year of exile.
  Volume 3, Part No. 3, Page 359   RotT o12.2
- The penalty for adultery between a married man and a married woman is 100 lashes with a whip and death by stoning.   Volume 3, Part No. 3, Page 359   RotT o12.2
- The penalty for homosexuality is death.
  Fatwa 4324, Part No. 22, Page 53 & 54   RotT o12.2
- Non-Muslims living in lands ruled by Islamic law (shari'ah) must pay a poll tax (jizyah) in order to be subdued and feel subjugated to Muslims. Refusal to pay the tax grants Muslims the right to wage war against the non-Muslims.
  Fatwa 4461, Part No. 1, Page 215
  Volume 3, Part No. 3, Page 183-190   RotT o11.3
- Waging war against non-Muslims (jihad), even those who are peaceful, is encouraged so that other religions and atheism will be purged from the earth.
  Volume 2, Part No. 2, Page 437-440   RotT o9.0

- If a Muslim kills a Jew or Christian dhimmi (one who pays the poll tax), he must pay only half the amount of "blood money" he would have to pay for killing a Muslim.
Fatwa 5414, Part No. 21, Page 245   RotT o4.9
(but 1/3, 1/15 for a Zoroastrian)

Shari'ah Law & Women's Rights:

- Women are permitted an education in Islamic issues (religious education) and family duties, but academic study is not encouraged.
Fatwa 9019
- Women are not permitted to attend universities where both men and women are taught or all-female schools with male teachers.
Fatwa 13814, Part No. 12, Page 150
- Women over the age of puberty are not permitted to leave the house without covering the body (except face and hands).
Fatwa 667, Part No. 17, Page 142-150   RotT w23.0
- Women are not permitted to visit the graves of loved ones.
Fatwa 2501, Part No. 1, Page 429   RotT g5.9
- Women are not permitted to obtain passports (since their photographs in them may tempt men), unless for the purpose of making Hajj (pilgrimage to Mecca).
Fatwa 2595, Part No. 1, Page 719
- Women are not permitted to travel without a spouse or male relative.
Fatwa 12139, Part No. 11, Page 38   RotT m10.3
- Women are not permitted to be alone with men who are not relatives or spouses, and the punishment for such "indecency" is whipping or stoning.
Fatwa 9693, Part No. 12, Page 381 & 382   RotT m2.3
- Women are not permitted to speak softly to a man or otherwise provoke his desire with letters, phone calls or glances, the punishment of which is whipping or stoning.
Fatwa 9693, Part No. 12, Page 381 & 382

Shari'ah Law & Civil Matters:

- A man may divorce his wife by simply giving her a triple talaq (saying "I divorce you" three times simultaneously).
Fatwa 6542, 2nd question   RotT n3.0
- A woman whose husband divorces her three times by simply saying "I divorce you", even if divorced against her will, cannot seek alimony unless she is pregnant.
Fatwa 20918, Part No. 20, Page 227
- A man may not adopt any children, even if they are his step-children born to his wife from a prior marriage.
Fatwa 5124, Part No. 9, Page 10
- Men are entitled to twice the amount of inheritance a woman receives, regardless of what a person's wishes are as detailed in a will.
Fatwa 8778, Part No. 21, Page 234   RotT Book L
great detail

Shari'ah Law & Business Matters:

- Since usury (charging or paying interest) is a sin, working at banks with interest-bearing deposits, keeping money in interest-bearing deposits, or accepting loans that charge interest is prohibited.
Fatwa 4011, Part No. 12, Page 80

- It is illegal to work in certain industries, such as retailers selling musical instruments, wine, tobacco, or music CDs; a photography studio; or any company that requires its employees to be photographed.
  Fatwa 5436, Part No. 13, Page 42
- Muslims are encouraged not to enter into business partnerships with non-Muslims.
  Fatwa 5855, Part No. 2, Page 98 & 99

Shari'ah Law & Personal Hygiene:

- Women are required to pluck, depilate or otherwise remove all facial and body hair, with the exception of shaving the eyebrows or head.
  Fatwa 5007   RotT e4.0
- Men must let their beards grow without cutting but keep their mustache trimmed so as to appear different from non-Muslims.
  Fatwa 2196, Part No. 2, Page 41 & 42   RotT e4.1(2)
- Failure to take a ritual bath for the purpose of purifying oneself after sexual intercourse is a sin that must be repented from and will invalidate one's prayers to Allah.
  Fatwa 11188, Part No. 6, Page 198   RotT e10.1[13]

Fatwas are still being published. "Saudi Sheikh Rejects Equality Between Muslims and Infidels, Men and Women," from *Translating Jihad*, 12 January 2011. Saudi Sheikh 'Abd-al-Rahman bin Nasir al-Barrak explained that there is no equality in Islam.

Fatwa Title: What is the ruling on the saying uttered by some people: "Islam is a religion of equality"?
Fatwa no. 38610, 7 Oct 2010
Answer: Praise be to God. Many people have spoken the phrase, "Islam is a religion of equality." They should know that this statement is heinous and false. Some Muslims may say it out of good intentions, seeking to praise and glorify Islam. Perhaps they don't know the real truth behind this phrase. This phrase is spoken by some whimsical people, who thereby reach out for purposes that are contrary to the law of Islam, such as the equality of rights between Muslims and infidels, and between men and women. They do this for the infidels, running behind their ways and their calls. But God hath differentiated between men and women in terms of rights, duties, and judgments. He hath also differentiated between Muslims and infidels in terms of judgments and penalties. The universal, legitimate, and penal Sunnah of God recognizes the differences—this is common sense. The Qur'an is frank in rejecting equality among things that are different.

"Fatwa: 'Whoever Insults One of these Four Things, Whether in Jest or Sincerity, Has Become an Infidel and Must Be Killed,'" *Translating Jihad,* 26 January 2011. This is Fatwa No. 349, 29 November 2009 from the Islamic Fatwa Council of Jerusalem, presided over by Sheikh Khalid Ghanayim, answering the question about the ruling on one who insults the divine, the Prophet, the Qur'an, and Islam. Still frightened that their women might go out and have sex, another fatwa came from Saudi Grand Mufti Sheikh Abdul Aziz Al-Sheikh that "Women are not allowed to work with men....Women's work and education should be done without mingling with men. They should work in women-only workplaces, as Islamic teachings ban the mingling of sexes."[14] King Abdullah had to step in to stop the idiocy of men being the salesmen in lingerie shops. He announced that "from now on some jobs would be reserved for women only – including working in lingeries shops."[15]

The king was criticized for his decision to permit "male and female researchers to work together at the new multibillion pound science university built on the Red Sea coast." The king called the university a "beacon of tolerance." He fired Sheikh Saad Bin Naser al-Shethri from the high council of religious scholars for criticizing him: Shethri had called it "a great sin and a great evil….When men mix with women, their hearts burn and they will be diverted from their main goal [of] education." Unrepentant, Shethri contended that religious scholars should advise rulers, "to make governors fear God [Allah] if they err from the right path and to remind them of God's [Allah's] punishment if they continue to err."[16]

We saw the brutality in Medina during Muhammad's days that has been institutionalized under sharia. Executions, amputations, beheadings, whippings, stonings, and sharia-inspired vigilante actions continue.[17] A young woman was stoned to death in Ukraine for participating in a beauty contest. The three Muslim youths who murdered her had no regrets saying "her actions were tantamount to adultery" and "she had violated the laws of Sharia (Islam)."[18]

Islamophobia

As we will see, sharia and jihad go hand in hand. **Creeping sharia** is a part of **stealth jihad**. Islam/sharia political influence is challenging our Constitution, courts, values, and culture "under the radar" by using our own 1st Amendment rights (freedom of religion) against us claiming "political correctness" calling anyone who is concerned about their actions **"Islamophobic."** It appears that it was the Muslims who coined the word deliberately to deflect criticism, emulating "the homosexual activists who used the term 'homophobia' to silence critics."[19]

Islamophobia: this loathsome term is nothing more than a thought-terminating cliché conceived in the bowels of Muslim think tanks for the purpose of beating down critics.
- Abdur-Rahman Muhammad

A phobia is supposed to be an irrational condition, but there are many rational reasons to criticize Islam.[20] Typical of those trying to limit our free speech is a report issued by Hamas-linked CAIR (the Council on American-Islamic Relations) and the University of California, Berkeley's Center for Race and Gender. [It is not clear what race or gender Islam is.] It is titled, "Same Hate, New Target: Islamophobia and Its Impact in the United States 2009-2010." It defines Islamophobia as a "closed-minded prejudice against or hatred of Islam and Muslims." The real agenda slipped out: "to limit criticism of Islamic supremacism and jihad."[21]

Two similar "exposés are "Fear, Inc.: The Roots of the Islamophobia Network in America" from the Center for American Progress, and "jihad Against Islam" from the "far-left" Southern Poverty Law Center. See "The Islamic supremacist propaganda machine cranks out another 'Islamophobia' report, for an attack on Robert Spencer.[22] As Geert Wilders said, "In far too many Western countries, it is still impossible to have a debate about the nature of Islam."[23]

Bill Warner wrote "The Virtuous Bigot," an outstanding description of the attacks on anyone who exposes true Islam. "You can find a virtuous bigot by reading the writings of just about any apologist for Islam. It seems that it's almost impossible for an apologist to resist proving the point of the beauty of Islam, by saying that those who find fault in Islam are bigots, racists, haters, and Islamophobes." As he wrote, "Any criticism of Islam is treated as hate speech." And why are these people insulted this way? Because **"Name calling is the first resort to those who don't have a logical point to make."** The Qur'an and Muhammad are full of insults, with *kafir* being the worst. As Warner summed it up, "There is a moral battle going on to save our civilization. Being a bigot in the fight against Political Islam and Sharia is a badge of honor and courage. Be a virtuous bigot in the ranks of the anti-Political Islam fighters. Virtuous bigotry is the high moral position."[24]

One of the major players in the campaign against freedom of speech is the **Organization of the Islamic Conference (OIC)**, 56 Muslim nations plus the Palestinians, which is particularly active in the UN.   Hugh Fitzgerald called using a term like "Islamophobia" is "a tried and tested tactic, designed precisely to divert attention from Islamic jihad attacks and to shame and discredit those who would dare stand up to jihad (both violent and stealth) and Islamic supremacism in the West."[25]

Since Islam is the best community, "It is the 'historical role' of the ummah to 'civilize' the rest of the world – not the other way around." For the OIC, "Islam may not be critically examined, nor will the ummah abide any dissemination of 'information' that would 'violate sanctities and the dignity of Prophets, undermine moral and ethical values, or disintegrate, corrupt or harm society, or weaken its faith.'"[26]

Slander (ghiba) means to mention anything concerning a person that he would dislike, whether about his body, religion, everyday life, self, disposition, property, son, father, wife, servant, turban, garment, gait, movements, smiling, dissoluteness, frowning, cheerfulness, or anything else connected with him.

- Reliance of the Traveller, **r2.2, p. 730.**

The OIC campaign is "to criminalize speech that 'offends' Muslims." It "seeks to define **slander** according to Islamic Sharia law – making Islamic 'slander' a serious crime in every jurisdiction in the world including the United States."   Gloating over the Danish cartoons and the trial of Geert Wilders in the Netherlands, OIC General Secretary Ekmeleddin Ihsanoglu noted "their success in causing the West to deter "freedom of expression.'" According to the Dutch court, "It is irrelevant whether Wilders' witnesses might prove Wilders' observations [about Islam] to be correct, what's relevant is that his observations are illegal" "It doesn't matter what's true; the court says speaking the truth in regard to Islam is illegal in the Netherlands because it may incite violence. Just what the OIC ordered." Fortunately, the Dutch court wisely acquitted Wilders in June 2011.

In 2009, the UN Human Rights Council passed a resolution (without a vote), submitted by the Obama Administration, which would subordinate U.S. free speech rights to UN oversight standards. These standards mirror the OIC's Ten-Year Plan objectives.

The OIC seeks deterrent punishments for speaking against Islam to garner silence and submission to Sharia law."

"The subordination of 1st Amendment rights to Islamic law under threat of lethal jihadi attacks should be understood to be a declaration of hostility by those making the demands."[27]

Our erstwhile ally, Pakistan, has been instrumental in promoting Muslim causes around the world.[28] The UN Human Rights Council passed a resolution, authored by Pakistan, in March 2010 criminalizing so-called "defamation of religion" – the only religion mentioned was Islam. The 1948 Universal Declaration of Human Rights was rejected by the OIC in 1990 and replaced by the Cairo Declaration on Human Rights in Islam which states in article 24 "All the rights and freedoms stipulated in this Declaration are subject to the Islamic Sharia."[29] The OIC continued its efforts and "The UN Human Rights Council unanimously adopted a new resolution on the elimination of forms of discrimination and violence based on religious beliefs" on 24 March 2011.[30] It seems that the goal of the OIC is to restore the caliphate.[31]

At a foreign ministers' meeting of the OIC in Kazakhstan in June 2011, the OIC changed its name and logo. It is now the **Organization of Islamic Cooperation**. It remains focused on Palestine and religions "defamation." Ihsanoglu spoke mainly about getting the UN to recognize a Palestinian state and stressed that "Islamophobia" was still "a matter of extreme priority for the OIC." He noted that the OIC was pushing for the International Convention on the Elimination of All Forms of Racial Discrimination to be amended to include religion. No matter that Islam is not a race! The host, Kazakhstan President Nursultan Nazarbayev, described the OIC as "the UN of the Islamic world."[32]

Washington has joined with the OIC to criminalize telling the truth and planned to host a meeting with the OIC to "implement resolution no. 16/18 on combating defamation of religions... Secretary of State Hillary Clinton had announced the intention of the U.S. State Department to organize a coordination meeting during her participation in the meeting which she co-chaired with the OIC Secretary General, Professor Ekmeleddin Ihsanoglu in Istanbul on 15 July 2011. The meeting issued a joint statement emphasizing the dire need for the implementation of resolution 16/18." It was reported that "the upcoming meetings aim at developing a **legal basis** for the UN Human Rights Council's resolution which help in enacting domestic laws for the countries involved in the issue, as well as **formulating international laws** preventing inciting hatred resulting from the continued defamation of religions." [Emphasis added][33] Actions to restrict freedom of speech rights under the US Constitution border on treason. This is part of the stealth jihad to destroy America.

Barack Obama and Hillary Clinton have joined with the OIC to violate the US Constitution's right to freedom of speech by making it illegal to criticize Islam.

One must be careful of the words Muslims use for they tend to have them mean what they want them to mean – shades of "newspeak" and "doublethink" in George Orwell's *1984*. The International Islamic Fiqh (Law) Academy held a five-day conference on Islamic jurisprudence in Sharjah. Their communiqué "recommended Muslim countries enact laws allowing freedom of expression and not to exploit freedom to malign Islam." "Freedom of expression is a protected right in Islam to be practiced within certain legal restraints," defined as "not abusing the dignity of others, adherence to truth and objectivity, and not being irresponsible." It also noted that religious freedom is an important principle of sharia and quoted the Qur'an that there is no coercion in religion (conveniently ignoring the rest of the verse or that that verse had been abrogated!). It "urged Muslim countries to strive to persuade other countries to make laws to protect sacred religious symbols of Islam and stop distorting them in the name of freedom" and then "demanded that non-Muslims respect Islamic symbols and stop abusing the Prophet of Islam." **Translation**: be a good dhimmi, supine and mute in the face of advancing Islamic supremacism, and consent quietly to their subjugation under sharia.[34]

The OIC wants to render the West mute, and hence defenseless, against the advancing jihad threat.

- Robert Spencer

An article in an Israeli newspaper decrying the "campaign to sanitize and understate Islamic extremism" and a "concerted campaign claiming that Islamophobia represents the greatest threat to human rights in the world!" noted the controversy in the US over the Ground Zero mosque and the audacity of the Muslims "to promote legislation at the UN and elsewhere which would make any criticism of Islam a criminal offense." We have seen our gutless reaction to fear of Muslim violence with the cartoon jihad of 2006 and the burning of a Qur'an by a Florida preacher. It happened again when Molly Norris, a Seattle weekly newspaper cartoonist, "was forced to adopt a new identity at the urging of the FBI because she had become a prime target for assassination after having drawn a satirical cartoon of the Muslim prophet in her local newspaper. This resulted in a fatwa being issued against her, stating that 'bombings and acts of arson were appropriate responses to acts of blasphemy.'"[35]   There was no response from our government.

Nicolai Sennels, the Danish psychologist you will meet below in the section on Inbreeding, wrote that we should not use the Muslim's self-chosen word based on fear but use the term **"Islamonausea"** which "is a normal and natural reaction to something abnormal." "There is nothing phobic or racist in feeling nausea when hearing about the Islamic massacres performed by Muhammad and his many devout copycats through history and all over the world today. The same goes for Muhammad's sexual relationship with a nine-year old girl, and the cutting off of limbs and stonings in the name of Allah and his Sharia laws." (Read the entire piece in Jihad Watch, 30 January 2012.)

> **A better term is "Islamonausea" – a normal reaction to something that makes us sick.**
> **- Nicolai Sennels**

Islamophobia has given us leaders who are fearful of Islam. We are dealing with a primitive honor/shame culture wherein it is legitimate, even required, to shed blood to save face, to redeem dishonored face. Public criticism is therefore an assault and freedom of speech is impossible. However, modernity is based on free discussion which is necessary for a society to advance. But loud voices in Islam vehemently reject self-criticism and to them criticism constitutes an unbearable assault on the Muslim manhood. Poor babies! They really do need to grow up and become men![36]

Concessions

There are numerous examples of concessions to sharia here in the US plus in other countries as we will see later. New York's Metropolitan Museum of Art censored its own Islamic collection lest displaying images of Muhammad offend Muslims.[37] Random House, after buying the rights to publish an historical novel about Muhammad, was warned by Muslims that publishing the book might result in violence, so they chose not to publish it. They were silenced by intimidation. In Hamtramck, Michigan, the City Council waived the noise ordinance in deference to the mosque there to allow them to broadcast an amplified call to prayer throughout the neighborhood. The Swift Beef Company tried to accommodate Somali workers by adjusting its schedule for Ramadan and installing footbaths and bidets but they still filed complaints.[38] In Florida, a judge ordered Muslims to follow sharia in a dispute over who controlled funds a mosque received from an eminent domain decision even though the current mosque leaders wanted it settled under Florida civil law.[39] In another case in Florida, the FBI called a Muslim leader to explain the arrest of two imams on terrorism charges to reassure him that the sanctity of the mosque had not been violated and there had been no rudeness or discrimination. It is sad since the Muslims should have been rushing to reassure the FBI that they were loyal Americans and not terrorists.[40]

> **If some among you fear taking a stand because you are afraid of reprisals... recognize that you are just feeding the crocodile hoping he'll eat you last.**
>
> **- Ronald Reagan**

The Los Angeles Sheriff's Department has a Muslim Community Affairs Unit, costing taxpayers $128,400 annually, while there is no such unit for other religions while Muslims are only 1% of the citizens and are targets for only 3% of the hate crimes, lower than the 88% against Jews and 8% against Christians. The Unit also trains department members about Islam and Muslims.[41] Again we have a politically correct concession that ignores the concept of "government neutrality toward religion." The US Government is supporting these concessions. "The Equal Employment Opportunity Commission sued on behalf of Samantha Elauf, who alleged she was denied a job at an Abercrombie & Fitch store in Tulsa's Woodland Hills Mall because she wore a hijab." A federal court awarded her $20,000. The real question is why should she want to work in such a place unless she was trying to force a US company to submit to Islamic norms?[42]

In another case, a young teacher was awarded $75,000 after quitting because she wanted to go on the hajj during the school year.[43] The US DOJ has become a foreign entity. This woman is young and the hajj is only required once in a lifetime. She obviously saw no impact on leaving her position during the school year.

You are aware of some of the extreme religious limitations such as on food to eat, music, dress, dogs, what to drink, etc. An example was the case of a blind Muslim woman in Dearborn, Michigan who was forbidden to use a seeing-eye dog (Muslims consider dogs unclean) and has to rely on a mini-horse.[44] The parliament in Iran is even considering a bill to criminalize dog ownership.[45] In northwest Pakistan, four men were listening to music in their car when the Taliban stopped them, smashed their cassettes and the cassette player and shaved half their heads and moustaches.[46] The Muslim World League, based in Mecca, banned cinematic depictions of Muhammad or his companions.[47] Islamists in southern Somalia banned watching DVDs or movies on television. They had already shut down cinemas in 2006 and were "inspecting mobile phones to prevent them from being used for watching movies."[48]

One of the more ludicrous examples was the Spanish teacher who was investigated for saying "ham" to a Muslim boy. The teacher was talking about different climates and "used the Granada town of Trevélez as an example of a cold, dry climate. As an anecdote, the teacher recounted that just such a climate was conducive to the curing of hams. Then the student asked the teacher not to speak of hams since the subject offended him as a Muslim."[49] Another case of someone who is in the wrong country!

Iran announced dress codes at some universities banning bright clothes, tight or short jeans, long nails, caps or hats without scarves, and body piercing (except earrings).[50] The Iranian "chastity squads" went on their annual rampage in June 2011 "to uphold the Islamic dress code and raise 'moral security' in the streets of Tehran, leading to many arrests and fines." Fines were for sandals, nail polish, and insufficient veiling.[51] Malaysia came up with a new one: non-Muslims can only recite the Qur'an if it is to understand religion, otherwise they would be deemed to have insulted the book.[52]

We are familiar with the Saudi ban on women driving and the case of the woman who drove in May 2011. She is a 32-year-old IT expert who was arrested before in her efforts to have the ban lifted. But the Wahhabis, who dominate the religious life in Saudi Arabia, "insist the ban protects against the spread of vice and temptation because women drivers would be free to leave home alone and interact with male strangers."[53]   The woman was sentenced to 10 lashes on 27 September but King Abdullah overruled the sentence on 29 September.[54]   By December, the Majlis a;-Ifta' al-A'ala, Saudi Arabia's highest religious council, issued a "scientific" report claiming that "relaxing the ban would also see more Saudis – both men and women – turn to homosexuality and pornography." They also warned that "Repealing a ban on women drivers in Saudi Arabia would result in 'no more virgins'."[55]   There is that sexual paranoia again that some woman might go out and do something without the approval of a dominating man.

Muslims around the US have pushed for Muslim holidays in schools and work places. Public schools in Cambridge, Massachusetts will have a Muslim holiday in response to "anti-Muslim hysteria."[56]   An Islamic public school, Tarek ibn Ziyad Academy – a K-8 charter school with campuses in Inver Grove Heights and Blaine, Minnesota - has been involved in law suits about its theocratic nature (for violating constitutional prohibitions against government endorsement of religion) and its use of threats and intimidation against any who have challenged it.[57]   Minnesota has had numerous incidents, particularly in the Minneapolis area. Some years back, Muslim cab drivers tried to stop passengers with alcohol and Muslim cashiers in Target stores refused to handle pork products.   Heinz has made numerous concessions to Muslim workers but more concessions were demanded.[58]

In addition to Minnesota, Michigan has numerous incidents, particularly in Dearbornstan.   Terry Jones, the Florida preacher famous for his Qur'an burning, was arrested for planning a protest outside the largest mosque in the US because it was likely to provoke violence and he was ordered to stay away from the Islamic Center of America for three years. Obviously, the threat of violence works!   So much for free speech and freedom of assembly. Even the ACLU was against this nonsense.[59]

The Army surrendered to CAIR to allow hijabs in Junior ROTC.[60]   Typical Muslim outrage was again displayed when Muslim students at a Catholic university felt that "their human rights have been violated by not getting special digs on campus, minus Catholic imagery, to do their daily prayers on college grounds."   Such nonsense!   "In the latest installment of how Islam is enacting their not-so-stealthy-any-longer jihad on America via our schools, Muslims are now taking on Catholic University for their Catholic art and imagery that insults delicate Muslim sensibilities."[61]

There has been a concerted effort by the media, with the support of some of the radical Islamic groups particularly CAIR, to deny that there is any attempt to bring sharia to the US and that sharia is anything to be concerned about.[62]   A New Jersey judge declined to charge a Muslim with sexual assault on his wife because under sharia, a woman may not deny sex to her husband at any time under any circumstances. Muslim workers at meat packing plants in Nebraska and Colorado forced employers to give them special breaks for Islamic prayer, thereby discriminating against non-Muslims.   Footbaths have been constructed in airports and schools for ablutions before Islamic prayers.   Jehan S. Harney, an Egyptian-American filmmaker, wrote in the Huffington Post that sharia "is simply the rules that govern the lives of Muslims from daily prayers and fasting to inheritance.   Sharia does not – and never will – apply to non-Muslims."   She fails to mention the Christians who are intimidated and often killed in Egypt, Iraq, Pakistan, and other Muslim countries.[63]

There are numerous examples of sharia in Canada also.   A 23-year-old Muslim man killed his sister and her fiancé in an honor killing because she got engaged without the permission of their father.[64]   A 13-year-old girl was beaten to death by her father over disputes because she did not always wish to participate in prayers.[65]   There are examples of blocking speakers who do not toe the Islamic line.   Pressure from Islamic groups in London, Ontario prevented Mark Steyn from speaking at the London Convention Centre which is owned by the city.[66] Serbian-American professor Dr. Serge Trifkovic, author of the excellent book on Islam and jihad, *The Sword of the Prophet,* quoted often here, was barred from entering Canada for a speaking engagement because of false accusations and so-called "hate speech."[67]

It can become brazen as when a dozen Muslim families newly arrived in Winnipeg wanted "their children excused from compulsory elementary school music and coed physical education programs for religious and cultural reasons." This makes public schools a proxy for the enforcement of sharia.[68] Instead of accommodating them, it would be better to inform them they are free to return home.

> **Each of these concessions to sharia serves as another cut that bleeds our political and cultural body further weakening our society.**

So, these are small concessions – no big deal! So banks stop giving away piggy banks because they don't want to offend Muslims because they don't like pigs is no big deal. That's not true! Each small concession is part of a gradual process to displace our law with sharia. By moving slowly on seemingly insignificant subjects, enough demands can be met that eventually we could be unable to mount a defense against further advances. This is the frog-in-the-soup-pot allegory: If you put a frog in a pot of cold water and then warm it slowly, the frog won't try to jump out until it's too late. By the time it figures out how hot the water is, it is too cooked to jump. Each concession is isolated and seems innocent enough. This brainwashing is similar to what the Chinese did to our prisoners during the Korean War. For radical Muslims, they know if they move slowly enough, stay under the radar, they can reach their goal of removing free speech which they desperately want removed to prevent criticism of Islam and prevent non-Muslims from organizing an effective defense. They cleverly use one of the strengths of our free culture, our tolerance of differences and intolerance of bullying of minorities by majorities, against us. Muslims must feel persecuted so they deliberately portray Islam as a persecuted, bullied minority. Each small concession "is a small commitment to the principle that our way of life, our values, and our freedoms should yield to Islam. When we allow it, we are committing to the principle 'when Sharia conflicts with our freedoms, it is our freedoms that must give way.'" It is like a python squeezing its prey until it can no longer breathe. Few concessions are ever undone. "Islam is a ratchet. It only goes one way."[69]

Each concession takes freedoms from non-Muslims and grants power, privilege, or advantage to Muslims. This is an invasion from within. Each concession is the establishment of sharia and confirmation that Muslims do not intend to conform to American practices. Each concession is one more cut that permits a little more blood to drain out of our constitution and our way of life.

Some parts of America are waking up. South Carolina[70], North Carolina, Louisiana[71], Tennessee[72], and Missouri[73] initiated actions to ban sharia. A study found that sharia was involved in some 50 appellate court cases from 23 states.[74] Former speaker of the US House, Newt Gingrich, is pushing for a law that "clearly and unequivocally states that we're not going to tolerate any imported law."[75] In November 2010, 70% of Oklahomans voted for a constitutional amendment to ban sharia, but a judge (Vicki Miles-LaGrange) overturned it accepting the CAIR (Council on American Islamic Relations) position that sharia is just private religious law. The state has tried again with new wording for the proposed law:

SECTION 1 (C) Any court, arbitration, tribunal, or administrative agency ruling or decision shall violate the public policy of this state and be void and unenforceable if the court, arbitration, tribunal, or administrative agency bases its ruling or decisions in the matter at issue in whole or in part on any law, rule, legal code or system that would not grant the parties affected by the ruling or decision the same fundamental liberties, rights, and privileges granted under the United States and Oklahoma Constitutions.[76]

Leave it to our Aussie friends to show real gumption. Australian Attorney General Robert McClelland stomped on the request from the Australian Federation of Islamic Councils for Muslims to be granted "legal pluralism." He said: "There is no place for sharia law in Australian society and the government strongly rejects any proposal for its introduction."[77] Australian Senator Cory Bernardi said' "Islam itself is the problem – it's not Muslims," and that "Islam is a totalitarian, political and religious ideology." For that he received death threats.[78] Australia still has radical Muslim clerics for these politicians to deal with. Ibrahim Saddiq Conlan called for the overthrow of the Australian legal system in favor of sharia saying it "is the primary cause of the spiritual, economic and environmental crisis in Australia," and "Democracy is evil, the parliament is evil and legislation is evil."[79] A survey of a group of imams showed they want sharia, including interest-free loans and for family law.[80] They also have their fanatics: five were convicted on terrorist charges and showed "no contrition and no acceptance of responsibility whatsoever" and seemed to "wear their imprisonment like some kind of badge of honour."[81]

Like the banning of veils in public in France and Belgium, Australia has encountered the same problem. With a population of 23 million, and only about 400,000 Muslims, it was estimated that less than 2,000 women wear face veils, and probably even less drive. The government of New South Wales, which includes Sydney, proposed a law that "a woman who defies police by refusing to remove her face veil could her sentenced to a year in prison and fined 5,500 Australian dollars ($5,900)." The state premier Barry O'Farrell said, "I don't care whether a person is wearing a motorcycle helmet, a burqa, niqab, face veil or anything else – the police should be allowed to require these people to make their identification clear." An incident motivated the law when a woman (47-year old Carnita Mathews, mother of seven) was given a ticket for a traffic violation and later a complaint was filed in her name accusing the officer of racism and attempting to tear off her veil. Unfortunately for her, the incident had been recorded by a police camera and she was sentenced to six months in jail for making a false statement. The significance of the whole veil question came out when the case was reversed on appeal because "a judge was not convinced that it was Matthews who signed the false statutory declaration. The woman who signed the document had worn a burqa and a justice of the peace who witnessed the signing had not looked beneath the veil to confirm her identity."[82] Again, people living in the wrong country!

The brazenness of some hardline Muslims was shown when Anjem Choudary – the British extremist who has said "the flag of Islam will fly over the White House" - was invited to Washington by the Islamic Thinkers Society, an Islamic supremacist group in New York, to lead a demonstration calling on Muslims to establish sharia across America.[83] The "Shariah4America" rally was planned for 3 March 2011 because it was on that date in 1924 that Mustafa Kamal Ataturk abolished the caliphate. The "Shariah4America website proposes ditching the U.S. Constitution for Shariah law, replacing the U.N. – whose sovereignty would no longer be recognized – with an International Shariah Court of Justice, converting the White House into a mosque, and terminating all treaties or promises made by the previous governments to instead conduct foreign relations according to the demands of jihad." The event was postponed amid a wave of opposition.[84] This welfare bum, and others like him, needs to be kicked out of England.

Apostasy and Blasphemy

The penalty for **apostasy** (leaving Islam) and blasphemy (denigrating any aspect of Islam) is death. There are many acts that entail leaving Islam ranging from reviling Allah or his messenger to reviling the religion of Islam.[85] A video was released in Afghanistan showing four militants (claimed to be Taliban) beheading a man believed to be a Christian in Herat Province. The men were wearing suicide vests and kaffiya head scarves to hide their faces. They cited verses from the Qur'an and read a decree: "You who are joined with pagans…your sentence [is] to be beheaded." While the man fought with them while they held him down, "one of the militants thrust a medium-sized blade into the side of his neck. With blood flowing onto the ground the militants shouted 'Allahu Akhbar' or 'God [Allah] is great' over and over until Latif was fully beheaded and his head was placed on top of his chest."[86] There have been recurring reports of people being killed or hounded for leaving Islam. In the Sudan, a husband attacked and evicted his wife who had converted to Christianity. When she went to her brother, he beat her and tried to knife her.[87] The Iranian Supreme Court upheld and confirmed the conviction and death sentence of Youcef Nadarkhani who left Islam and has been a pastor. He was due to be hanged but the government kept postponing it.[88] **[He was hanged 3 March 2012.]**

In India's East Bengal, a Muslim woman who had recently converted to Christianity was stripped and beaten by Muslim women who claimed that converts "get Christian marks on their body." About 50 Muslims disrupted a prayer meeting in her home and threatened her that she had to leave or they would burn her house down. She was ostracized in her community, not allowed to buy goods from the store, sell her vegetables, or get water from the village well.[89]

> **Whoever insults Muhammad [but not Allah], even if he later repents, must be killed.**
> **-Egyptian Sheikh Abu-Ishaq al-Huwayni on Egyptian TV**[90]

The most famous case of **blasphemy** was the fatwa issued by Ayatollah Khomeini in 1989 calling for anyone to kill Salman Rushdie, author of *The Satanic Verses*. A recent case was in Pakistan when the Governor of Punjab, Salmaan Taseer, was murdered by his bodyguard in January 2011 for his efforts to have the blasphemy laws repealed. The laws were passed under Gen. Zia ul-Haq to promote Islam but have been misused to convict opponents, both Muslims and minority non-Muslims.[91] The law is quite explicit and harsh. That was deliberate in that anything at variance with Islamic teaching could easily be labeled "blasphemy." "The law is designed to keep non-Muslims (and dissenting Muslims) silent and living in fear."[92]

Pakistan Penal Code

> **295-C** Use of derogatory remarks, etc; in respect of the Holy Prophet. Whoever by words, either spoken or written or by visible representation, or by any imputation, innuendo, or insinuation, directly or indirectly, defiles the sacred name of the Holy Prophet Mohammed (PBUH) shall be punished with death, or imprisonment for life, and shall also be liable to fine.

The reactions to Taseer's murder were disturbing. For committing "blasphemy" against the blasphemy law, lawyers showered the killer with rose pedals and a rowdy crowd patted his back and kissed his cheek as he entered court.[93] Over 500 Pakistani scholars and clerics from the supposedly "moderate" Barelvi sect of Sunni Islam praised the murderer as a "Ghazi," an Islamic warrior, and warned people not to lead or offer prayers for Taseer.[94] Qadri, the bodyguard, was sentenced to death on 3 October 2011; there were large protests in support of the "hero."[95]

If you have a thing about lawyers, you will enjoy this: over 1,000 lawyers from Islamabad and Rawalpindi signed their support for the killer. These young lawyers called their forum the Movement to Protect the Dignity of the Prophet, said they were "interested only in ensuring the rule of law, and "insisted they were liberal, not religious conservatives." They were "miles apart from the older generation of lawyers" and showed a "class divide, between the more secular and wealthy upper classes and the more religious middle and lower classes."[96]

In February, Prime Minister Syed Yusuf Raza Gilani said he would not consider any attempt to overturn the blasphemy law.[97] Throughout late 2010, threats were announced against Shahbaz Bhatti, 42, Roman Catholic, Minister for Religious Minorities, and the only Christian in the government and a critic of the blasphemy law, culminating in a fatwa in December.[98] On 2 March 2011, he was murdered by Islamist gunmen on the streets of Islamabad. Pakistani Taliban and al Qaeda claimed responsibility and left pamphlets at the scene addressing anyone who challenged the blasphemy law: "With the blessing of Allah, the mujahedeen will send each of you to hell."[99] PM Gilani was the only senior government official who attended his funeral; the others were afraid of any suggestion that they oppose the blasphemy law.[100] The government was set to close the case for lack of evidence and it abolished the Federal Ministry of Minority Affairs, shifting that responsibility to the provinces.[101]

The story goes on. Sherry Rehman an ex-minister who tabled a bill in parliament to remove the death sentence for blasphemy has had several fatwas calling for her death and she has been pressured to leave Pakistan.[102] The Pope called for repeal of the blasphemy law (he also condemned anti-Christian attacks in Egypt and Iraq) which evoked harsh responses from politicians and Islamist leaders.[103] It was obviously a very hot issue in Pakistan and Islamist parties turned out their supporters in the streets. On 31 December 2010, a crippling strike brought Pakistan to a standstill with "fiery speeches across all major cities and town," warning the government not to alter the law. In Peshawar and Faisalabad, over 10,000 rallied in support of the law on 24 January 2011 and on 29 January young women students demonstrated in Karachi.[104]

It was not just politicians, nearly 1,000 people have been charged with insulting Muhammad or defiling the Qur'an in the last 25 years.[105] The case of Asia Bibi is one of the best known. She is a poor Christian woman, married with 5 children, who while working as a laborer on a farm in 2009 got into a discussion on religion and the Muslim women beat her and she was later charged with blasphemy and sentenced to death.[106] Governor Taseer had voiced support for her and his murder "in broad daylight has put her in a state of paranoia." Many have called for her to be killed and "She knows the Muslims have announced a prize on her head and would go to any lengths to kill her."[107]

Many have called for her [Asia Bibi] to be killed and "She knows the Muslims have announced a prize on her head and would go to any lengths to kill her."

She has reason to be afraid. Even though none of those sentenced to death has been executed, 35 have been killed by vigilantes outside the legal system. Pakistani intelligence reported planning for a possible suicide attack to kill her.[108] An example is Imran Latif, 22, who was accused of burning pages of the Qur'an but released after five months in jail when the accuser said he was not sure. Two gunmen came to his home and killed him.[109] This happened again in April 2011 when an exonerated man was murdered.[110]

Blasphemy charges even went hi-tech. A man was "sentenced to death for committing blasphemy via cellphone text messaging." The case was odd not only because the evidence was murky, but that "the police and court system showed uncharacteristic zeal in pursuing this case." Special permission had to be obtained to raid in Sindh, hundreds of miles from the court in Punjab and the sentence was handed down in just over a year rather than dragging on for years as has been normal.[111]

One of the most stupid and idiotic examples of the blasphemy nonsense is when a murderous mob murdered the owner of a business and two others for the ridiculous concern over "an outdated calendar – which had verses from the Holy Quran written on it" was taken down and put on a table. The workers gathered colleagues and they ended up murdering three people.[112]   A similar incident involved differences between Deobandi and Barelvi sects of Sunni Muslims. An imam and his son were jailed for life "for removing a poster outside their grocery shop advertising an Islamic event in a nearby village which allegedly contained Quranic verses."[113]

Idiocy reached a high when an Ismaili Muslim was jailed for throwing away the business card of a salesman named "Muhammad."

Idiocy reached a high when an Ismaili Muslim was jailed for throwing away the business card of a salesman named "Muhammad."[114] Faith Freedom was trying to raise money to help a man who had been imprisoned for three years already, despite lack of evidence, and he was sentenced to seven more years.[115] The idiocy has continued. A bank guard was killed and four injured after terrorists attacked the bank because the "floor tile design was too similar to the Arabic script for the name of Allah."[116] A British tourist was hauled into court in Dubai and fined for supposedly insulting Islam.[117] Hundreds (brought in by bus and trucks) attacked Christians in the Gojra massacre in which ten died, eight burned alive, four churches and various homes were set on fire. Police detained a number of the Christians for months and witnesses were threatened and the main complainant had to flee Pakistan. "A Pakistani anti-terrorism court acquitted 70 people who, in various roles, were involved in the Gojra massacre of August 2009." According to Maulana Kashmiri, a Muslim leader, "There are no witnesses because they [the Christians] know that they are wrong. We got justice. Even though none of us did it, Christians still deserve it [death], because they are blasphemers."[118] In another case, ten Christian families were forced to flee from their village after an 8-year-old boy was harassed by students from a local madrassa and tried to force him to convert and his uncle who came to his rescue was attacked for "blasphemy."[119] The world is in a sad state until we can eliminate such stupidity!

This is not only in Pakistan. An imam was shot during prayers and a school principal was also killed in Dagestan because he "opposed the wearing of the hijab in school."[120] Iran reacted with a threat of "serious action" about a Documentary on Muhammad being prepared by BBC. The BBC made concessions trying not to offend Muslims, including "making this the first biographical documentary not to feature visual images of the subject."[121] One must not state facts if they pertain to Muhammad. A professor in the Arabic Studies Department of a Polish university lost his job evidently due to a book he wrote about Islam where in the chapter on Muhammad, his supervisor who gave him a negative evaluation wrote "he offends the religious feelings of Muslims by calling the Prophet of Islam a murderer, an assassin, a paedophile and a robber." One cannot criticize anything in Islam and still must be very careful not to hurt Muslims' feelings, but it is difficult to state harsh facts diplomatically.[122]

Sharia-Compliant Finance

One of the most egregious examples of the invasion of sharia into our Western culture is sharia-compliant finance (SCF) or sharia banking. The enormous amounts of money accumulated by Muslim countries, particularly from oil, has attracted Western bankers to gain access to those funds. To do so has required many of them to follow Islamic banking procedures. So what is sharia banking?

Islamic banks are managed according to sharia, the main difference being that the Qur'an prohibits charging interest, instead charging fees (and donations) for services provided. Islamic banks are governed by a Sharia Advisory Board, Islamic scholars and clerics responsible to ensure the bank's activities are in strict compliance with sharia. Since Islam is superior to greedy capitalism, this will make for "a more equitable and fair society" and properly distribute wealth. However, many of the scholars and clerics on these Advisory Boards come from the more radical elements of Islam and educational centers that promote and encourage violence against the West. This is an "opportunity to spread Islamic ideology." One example is Yusuf al-Qaradawi, noted above, the spiritual leader of the Muslim Brotherhood and head of the fundamentalist European Council for Fatwa and Research, who said that "the introduction of Islamic banking into the West will be the vehicle through which Islam will establish a caliphate throughout the world."

The goal of the Muslim Brotherhood is to replace Western "institutions with a global Islamic order." The "first Islamic bankers were members of the Muslim Brotherhood" who wanted to use the power of banking to advance the fundamentalist movement. Islamic Bank USA created a web site (now evidently removed) to educate non-Muslims about sharia banking. "According to their web site, sharia-compliant banking must be:

1. Interest free
2. Trade-related with a genuine need for the fund in its purest form, so it is therefore equity-related.
3. Ethically directed. Certain areas of finance are permitted, while others are not. For example, funds cannot be provided for liquor, pork, gambling, pornography and anything that Islamic law deems unlawful.

"Products offered through Islamic banks include a profit (mark-up) rather than charging interest on the amount at risk. Islamic banking prohibits trading in debt, so Islamic banks do not issue conventional bonds. Islamic bonds are not interest based; but returns are based on a mathematical formula that links the cash flow (that will be generated by the asset to be purchased) to the cost of the asset itself."

Sharia banking requires that a portion of all fees (2 1/2 to 20%) be paid to Islamic charities, which are often fronts for terrorist organizations. This is a good way to redistribute wealth to the Middle East.

If sharia banking becomes the accepted form in the West, the clerics would have a powerful platform to push their ideology, which could have a major impact on life in the US. If financial control is wrested from the Western system, the Golden Rule of Finance takes control. The Golden Rule of Finance is "He who has the gold makes the rules."[123]

While Muslims like to claim that sharia banking eliminates risk, it also eliminates capitalism. It prohibits interest transactions such as ATM fees or mortgage fees, as well as speculation, such as futures trading. The "zakat," or donation to Muslim charity sounds good, but al Qaeda received $300-500 million from zakat donations from charities and front companies. We saw that here in the US with the conviction of the Holy Land Foundation for sending funds to Hamas. Also, sharia banks are working with "hawala" dealers. **Hawala** is a system of informal money exchanges with no paper trails, which can easily lead to illicit transfers and money laundering. The NY City Bar Association held a class on SCF telling attendees there is no risk involved.[124] For the liabilities and exposures of SCF and the dangers corporations are facing by embracing sharia financing, see David Yerushalmi.[125]

The introduction of Islamic banking into the West will be the vehicle through which Islam will establish a caliphate throughout the world."

- Yusuf al-Qaradawi

Sharia banking, which is growing, is a stalking horse for the introduction of Islam. Bankers salivating over the money opportunities they see overlook the dangers. Islamists who advise sharia finance have called for full sharia to be adopted in Western countries. Some members of Congress have announced alerts that charitable contributions from these organizations could end up financing terrorists. Some of these people who dominate the Advisory Boards, like Yusuf al-Qaradawi, are banned from entry into Britain and the US, while Mufti Taqi Usmani, who has advised the Wall Street Islamic index, has promoted extension of sharia into the West. Of major concern is that Bank Melli of Iran is at the top of the world's top 500 Islamic financial institutions. Bank Melli is under US and EU sanctions for support of Hamas and HezbAllah and funding Iran's uranium enrichment program. Iran has six of the 10 biggest SFC institutions and double the assets of any other country.[126] US banks, including Citibank and Goldman Sachs, are buying in.[127]

A lawsuit was filed by the Thomas Moore Law Center against the government claiming that the AIG bailout used taxpayer money to promote Islam and sharia. The government has a majority interest in AIG and at least two of AIG's subsidiary companies practice SCF. Also, the government sponsored a forum entitled "Islamic Finance 101." The AIG Sharia Supervisory Committee consists of Sheikh Nizam Yaquby from Bahrain, Dr. Mohamed Ali Elgari from Saudi Arabia, and Dr. Muhammed Imran Ashraf Usmani from Pakistan. "Dr. Usmani is the son, student, and dedicated disciple of Mufti Taqi Usmani, who is the leading authority for Shariah-compliant finance in the world and the author of a book translated into English in 1999 that includes an entire chapter dedicated to explaining why a Western Muslim must engage in violent jihad against his own country or government."[128]

In January 2011, Judge Lawrence P. Zatkoff, a federal judge in Michigan, dismissed the challenge. According to the Thomas More Law Center, "Judge Zatfoff's ruling allows for oil-rich Muslim countries to plant the flag of Islam on American soil. His ruling ignored the uncontested opinions of several Sharia experts and AIG's own website, which trumpeted Sharia-compliant financing as promoting the law of the Prophet Mohammed and as an 'ethical product,' and a 'new way of life.' His ruling ignored AIG's use of a foreign Islamic advisory board to control investing in accordance with Islamic law." "This astonishing decision allows the federal government as well as AIG and other Wall Street bankers to explicitly promote Sharia law – the 1200 year old body of Islamic canon law based on the Koran, which demands the destruction of Western Civilization and the United States." An immediate appeal was filed which will take at least a year.[129]

Jihad

Jihad means holy war (Saudis prefer to call it struggle) or "striving in the way of Allah." A person engaged in jihad is called a mujahed, the plural is **mujahedin**. The first problem with jihad is the definition. There are two types of jihad. "*Jihad* means to war against non-Muslims, and is etymologically derived from the word *mujahada*, signifying warfare to establish the religion. And it is the **lesser jihad**." The **greater jihad** is "spiritual warfare against the lower self (nafs)," which Muhammad expressed upon returning from jihad.[130] The concept of greater or "inner" jihad is one's personal fight against sinful desires and ego (the Saudis prefer "inner struggle which everyone wages against egotistic desires, for the sake of attaining inner peace"[131]). "The concept of spiritual struggle was never meant to replace, let alone abrogate, the original warlike meaning."[132]

The concept of jihad under Islam only provided ideological justification and motivation for wars of conquest by desert people who were already prone to fighting and pillaging and not inclined to introspection. Once Muhammad had a safe power base in Medina, he started calling for jihad. "O Prophet! Urge the believers to war; if there are twenty patient ones of you they shall overcome two hundred, and if there are a hundred of you they shall overcome a thousand of those who disbelieve." (VIII:65) "O you who believe! Fight those of the unbelievers who are near to you and let them find in you hardness." (IX:123) "And kill them wherever you find them." (II:191)

To battle Kafirs in jihad for even one day is greater than the entire earth and everything on it.

- Muhammad[133]

Jihad was central to Muhammad. To him the most important deed, after faith as a Muslim, was "To participate in Jihad (holy fighting) in Allah's Cause." and that was better than anything else in the world.[134] He also made it clear that jihadis would be rewarded on earth with loot, etc., but if they died they would be rewarded with a higher level of paradise than others – an "act which elevates the position of man in Paradise to a grade one hundred (higher),… What is that act?... Jihad in the way of Allah!"[135] "Those who believe fight in the way of Allah." (IV: 76) And for "those who fight in the way of Allah…We shall grant him a mighty reward." (IV: 74)

We reviewed the Trilogy (Qur'an, Hadith, and Sira) in Chapter 3 – 31% of the complete Trilogy, 9% of the Qur'an (0% of the Meccan Qur'an but 24% of the Medinan Qur'an[136]), 21% of the Hadith, and 67% of the Sira are devoted to jihad.[137] As a summary,

- the Qur'an provides the divine authorization for Political Islam and jihad,
- the Sira shows the strategy of conquest, and
- the Hadith is the tactical manual.[138]

There could be temporary ceasefires in the war against the unbelievers, but they are only deceptions which are acceptable under Islam since the end justifies the means and are a furtherance of taqiyya. But there can be no end until there is submission. Remember there are only three alternatives offered: accept Islam, pay the jizya, or war (death). Dhimmitude, or paying the jizya, was not offered to people not of the Book - just convert or die.[139] Peaceful coexistence is not an alternative. The four main schools of Sunni Muslim law: Hanafi, Hanbali, Maliki, and Shafi'i, all support jihad as a divine institution.[140]

Jihad juridically means warfare. The Hanafi school emphasizes that "jihad is religious war against non-believers." Taqi al-Din ibn Taimiyya (1263-1328), the great Hanbali jurist, wrote that "since warfare is essentially jihad and since its aim is that the religion is God's entirely and God's word is uppermost, therefore according to all Muslims, those who stand in the way of this aim must be fought."[141] Ibn Khaldun (1332-1406), a major Maliki legal theorist, wrote in his *Muqaddimah* that jihad "is a religious duty, because of the universalism of the Muslim mission and (the obligation to) convert everybody to Islam either by persuasion or by force" and that Islam is "under obligation to gain power over other nations." This is not just writings from the Middle Ages. The classic Shafi'i manual of Islamic law, 'Umdat al-Salik (in English as *Reliance of the Traveller*), certified in 1991 by al-Azhar University in Cairo, the highest authority in Sunni Islam, defined "greater jihad" as "spiritual warfare against the lower self," and then devoted eleven pages to "lesser jihad."[142]

> *Jihad as Saif*, **Jihad by the Sword, had been Allah's plan for Muhammad from the beginning.**
>
> **- Abdullah Azzam, *The Defense of the Muslim Lands***

Historian Paul Fregosi documented the history of Islamic attacks on the West in "Jihad in the West: Muslim Conquests from the 7th to the 21st Centuries." He noted the basic philosophical and ethical difference between Islam and Christianity: "'The sword is the key to heaven and hell,' Muhammad told his followers. Six hundred years earlier, Christ had said, 'He who lives by the sword shall perish by the sword.'" Ayatollah Khomeini explained Jihad: "It means the conquest of non-Muslim territory. The domination of Koranic Law from one end of the earth to the other is…the final goal…of this war of conquest." Fregosi, as well as many other historians, defined jihad as "essentially a permanent state of hostility that Islam maintains against the rest of the world." In "The Decline of Eastern Christianity Under Islam: From Jihad to Dhimmitude (1996)," Bat Ye'or called jihad "a religious obligation" similar to a Christian sacrament, a religious duty Muslims must perform if called upon.

> **Only about three percent of the Hadiths concerning jihad are about the greater jihad, spiritual struggle. The other ninety-seven percent are about jihad as supreme war.**[143]

Dr. Andrew Bostom edited a book *The Legacy of Jihad* which is a massive volume of documents pertaining to the history and doctrine of jihad. This vast material from Islamic texts and Muslim jurists recounts brutal jihad battles around the world, explains the core mandate in Islam to wage war against the unbelievers and to establish sharia. He addressed the murderous intolerance, the destruction of churches, the beheadings, and martyrs.[144]

Andrew McCarthy gave a clear description of the mindset of the jihadists who conducted the 1993 World Trade Center bombing. They trained for years before the attack and "saw themselves as a committed jihad army." Fully convinced that their religion required them to brutality, they had no queasiness and were absolutely clear who their enemy was. They were led by Omar Abdel Rahman, the blind Egyptian cleric, who led the "Islamic Group" which was responsible for the murder of President Anwar Sadat. Abdel Rahman's principles were quite clear: authority does not come from the governed, only from Allah – who is "not a God of mercy and forgiveness, but a God of wrath and vengeance." For these jihadists, "there would be no toleration for other religions or other views. There was militant Islam, and there was everybody else."[145]

As we have seen, the world, according to Islam, is divided into two spheres: **Dar al-Islam**, Land of Submission, and **Dar al-Harb**, the Land of War. Thus there is a perpetual state of war with all non-Muslims.

> **Jihad is a continuous and never ending struggle waged on all fronts including political, economic, social, psychological, domestic, moral, and spiritual.**
> **- Brigadier S.K. Malik, *The Quranic Concept of Power***

Also as we have noted, Jihad is a military concept from the seventh century. That is why it is inaccurate to say that the jihadists are mere hijackers of a peaceful religion. They are not a tiny minority of Islam; they follow the teachings and life of Muhammad. Abdel Rahman, who is still influential (Osama bin Laden kept calling for his release from his life sentence), has a doctorate from the important al-Azhar University in Cairo, so his views on jihad are important. "There is no such thing as commerce, industry, and science in jihad.... If Allah says: 'Do jihad,' it means jihad with the sword, with the cannon, with the grenades, and with the missile. This is jihad. Jihad against God's enemies for God's cause and his word."[146]

Jihadists are not a "fringe" element of Islam; they are mainstream. Ali Gomaa, the grand mufti of Egypt: "Muslims must kill non-believers wherever they are unless they convert to Islam." Muhammad Sayyid Al Tantawi, president of Al Azhar University also approves of killing Christians, Jews, and other infidels: "This is not my personal view. This is what the Shari'a Law says, the law of Allah, the only valid law on earth." The Chief Justice of Saudi Arabia, Sheikh Abdullah bin Muhammad bin Humaid: "at first fighting was forbidden, then it was permitted, and after that it was made obligatory." He identified the two groups they are obligated to fight: "(1) they who start fighting against Muslims, and (2) they who worship gods other than Allah." Sheikh Abdulaziz Bin Abdullah Bin Mohammed al Sheikh, Grand Mufti of Saudi Arabia said on TV: "Killing producers who show women unveiled is legal." Sheikh Abu Ala Maududi, considered the most prominent Muslim scholar of the 20th century: "Islam wishes to destroy all states and governments anywhere on the face of the earth which are opposed to the ideology and program of Islam."[147]

A great Shia cleric, Ayatollah Jafar Sabhani, told students at the Qom seminary, "Muslims are not war-mongers and Islam is the religion of peace" and that "Islam is not a pro-war religion and the only thing which can keep our lands and countries safe is the sprite [sic] of jihad and martyrdom."[148] He added "a soldier who fights for getting money cannot [be] a serious combatant but when a soldier knows he sells his soul to get Heaven instead, then he has no fear." Muhammad's great win/win warrior machine: booty to the victorious soldier (VIII:41) and sensual delight of Paradise if killed (IX:111)!

The hatred of Jews continues. Dr. Salah Sultan, a lecturer of Muslim jurisprudence at Cairo University, issued a religious decree that it is permissible to kill any Israeli on Egyptian land – "every Muslim who meets a Zionist is entitled to kill him." This was in response to the deaths of Egyptian soldiers near the Israel border.[149]

> **A man came to Muhammad and said, "Instruct me as to such a deed as equals Jihad in reward." Muhammad replied, "I do not find such a deed."[150]**

There are apologists and people who do not seem to want to understand. John Brennan, President Obama's counterterrorism adviser, said, "The technical, broadest definition of jihad is a 'struggle' in the name of Islam and the term does not connote 'holy war' for all Muslims. He went on to say that we should not describe terrorists in "religious terms" and we should not use the word "jihad." "Nor do we describe our enemy as 'jihadists' or 'Islamists' because jihad is a holy struggle, a legitimate tenet of Islam, meaning to purify oneself or one's community, and there is nothing holy or legitimate or Islamic about murdering innocent men, women and children."[151] What has he been smoking?

We constantly hear this "unquestioned dogma of American policymakers and the mainstream media that Islamic jihadists have twisted and hijacked the authentic, peaceful teachings of Islam," but such nonsense is rebutted by comments such as Muslims must work toward "the conquest of the capitals of the world by the message of Islam, in order to save and liberate humanity, by pulling people out of the darkness and tyranny of capitalism into the light and justice of Islam."[152] "The truth is, relentless violence against (and subjugation of) non-Muslims is mainstream Islam. The terrorists have not 'hijacked' a religion of peace. This kind of intolerance toward non-Muslims has been mainstream Islam for 1400 years."[153] Apologists concede that jihad uses force but try to explain it as only in defense. The problem with that is that for the jihadists, "jihad means killing the enemies of the militant – which is pretty much anyone who is not a militant." And if your forces are outnumbered, that means using terror.[154]

Money is the key and the power behind jihad. We have seen how that started with Muhammad's raids on caravans and, as the money from plunder increased, the success of Islam skyrocketed.[155] Look again at the chart in Chapter 2, page 22. The plunder and the jizya were wealth taken from non-Muslims. We are still financing the jihad against ourselves; non-Muslim countries paid OPEC three and a half trillion dollars in one year. Money comes from many sources: Saudi Arabia, Iran, Syria, (Iraq and Libya earlier), donations from some Muslim communities in the US and Europe, plus some of the money that goes into some UN organizations. Some of the leaders live quite comfortably on this loot.[156] It was estimated that $100 million a year from "missionary" and "Islamic charitable" organizations (ostensibly with government support) in Saudi Arabia and the UAE went "to a jihadist recruitment network in Pakistan's Punjab province." Much of that money goes to madrassas and mosques.[157] There is little prospect of stopping the third jihad without stopping the flow of money.[158]

> **The minarets are our bayonets, the domes our helmets, the mosques our barracks and the faithful our army.**
>
> **- Turkish nationalist poet Ziya Gokalp, "The Soldier's Prayer," 1912**
> **Read publicly by now Prime Minister Recep Tayyip Erdogan**

Jihad is still in vogue. In November 2002, Osama bin Laden, trying to sound like Muhammad, wrote a letter to the American people calling them to Islam. He added, "It is the religion of Jihad in the way of Allah so that Allah's Word and religion reign supreme." Modern jihadists strive to impose sharia on the non-Muslim world under the banner of jihad.[159] In July 2004, The Abu-Hafs al-Masri Brigades (Al-Qa'ida) sent a message to the Ulema: "This is a message to you from Shaykh Ibn-al-Juzi, may Allah have mercy on his soul: 'O people, the war has broken out, the **call for jihad** has been made, and the doors of heaven have opened.'"[160] An abridged version of the translation of the broadcast is at Appendix A.

Many "moderate" Muslims are sensitive to the word jihad and try to limit it to the spiritual or inner jihad. But the Qur'an calls for striving for peace, but that is Islamic peace, which would only be in the Dar a- Islam after Islam's enemies were conquered. Déja vu! This is the same "peace" that the Soviet Union used in its imperial expansion 1944-1979 whereby it could only come about with the proletariat defeat of imperialism which was the last stage of capitalism. What matters now is not the spin people try to put on the word, but their actions. Jihad of the seventh century had specific purposes. Modern Christians outlawed crusades, but they did not revise history to support it. If Muslims who believe that jihad or holy war is no longer legitimate, then they should outlaw it.[161]

"Bolshevism combines the characteristics of the French Revolution with those of the rise of Islam. Marx has taught that Communism is fatally predestined to come about; this produces a state of mind not unlike that of the early successors of Mahommet. Among religions, Bolshevism is to be reckoned with Mohammedanism rather than with Christianity and Buddhism. Christianity and Buddhism are primarily personal religions, with mystical doctrines and a love of contemplation. Mohammedanism and Bolshevism are practical, social, unspiritual, concerned to win the empire of this world."

- Bertrand Russell[162]

"Islam is and always has been a religion of intolerance, a jihad without end." Regardless of how apologists try to depict it, "Islam was spread by the sword and has been maintained by the sword throughout its history." According to William Muir, a great orientalist, "the sword of Muhammad and the Qur'an are the most fatal enemies of civilization, liberty, and truth which the world has yet known." He considered the Arab empire "an unmitigated cultural disaster parading as God's will," and parading as the creed of equality. This hatred of non-Muslims compares with Karl Marx's social conflict but is far more lethal.[163]

The Jihadi conquests across North Africa to Europe to Asia were defensive just like Stalin's attack on Finland, Hitler's "counterattack" on Poland, and Israel's "preemptive" attacks in the Six Day War; they were all aggression. The Final Solution and the Gulag have nothing on the Muslims. The slaughters of Hitler, Stalin, and Mao Tse-tung hardly rival the massacres of the jihadists. As Daniel Pipes wrote:

"While fundamentalist Islam differs in its details from other utopian ideologies, it closely resembles them in scope and ambition. Like Communism and Fascism, it offers a vanguard ideology; a complete program to improve man and create a new society; complete control over that society, and cadres, ready, even eager, to spill blood."[164]

There is much similarity with the Fascist-Marxist propaganda we endured for nearly three-quarters of a century and some of the utopian revolutionary Islamist line we are currently hearing. Muhammad established this totalitarian character of the Islamic state in Medina where the caliph was in total control and all other institutions were abolished. All three systems have a common desire to dominate their citizens completely and a lust for their property.

He [Muhammad] declared undistinguishing and exterminating war, as a part of his religion, against all the rest of mankind...The precept of the Koran is, perpetual war against all who deny, that Mahomet is the prophet of God.

- John Quincy Adams

So why do Muslims wage jihad? Or better yet, why are there Muslims who hate the West so much that they are ready to kill themselves and any number of Westerners? Is it really our crazy music, our wild television, Hollywood, our technology? Oriana Fallaci wrote that we are in a war of religion:

"A war that they call *Jihad*. Holy War. A war that might not seek to conquer our territory, but that certainly seeks to conquer our souls. That seeks the disappearance of our freedom and our civilization. That seeks to annihilate our way of living and dying, our way of praying or not praying, our way of eating and drinking and dressing and entertaining and informing ourselves. You don't understand or don't want to understand that if we don't oppose them, if we don't defend ourselves, if we don't fight, the Jihad will win. And it will destroy the world that, for better or worse, we've managed to build, to change, to improve, to render a little more intelligent, that is to say, less bigoted – or even not bigoted at all. And with that it will destroy our culture, our art, our science, our morals, our values, our pleasure."[165]

But it is more than religion; it is also a war of liberation as the altruistic, kind-hearted Muslims do their duty to free the poor dominated masses from the darkness of their misery into the great light of Islam even if they do not want to be liberated. "The jihad is for the liberation of all Muslims around the world. When we succeed in this part, we will move to other parts until we ensure only Allah is worshipped in this world."[166] As the Arab horde burst out of Arabia, a soon-to-be conquered Persian commander asked the invading Muslims what they wanted. The reply explains all:

> God has sent us and brought us here so that we may free those who desire from servitude to earthly rulers and make them servants of God, that we may change their poverty into wealth and free them from the tyranny and chaos of [false] religions and bring them to the justice of Islam. He has sent us to bring his religion to all his creatures and call them to Islam. Whoever accepts it from us will be safe, and we shall leave him alone; but whoever refuses, we shall fight until we fulfill the promise of God.

"Fourteen hundred years later – in March 2009 – Saudi legal expert Basem Alem publicly echoed this view:

> As a member of the true religion, I have a greater right to invade [others] in order to impose a certain way of life [according to sharia], which history has proven to be the best and most just of all civilizations. This is the true meaning of offensive jihad. When we wage jihad, it is not in order to convert people to Islam, but in order to liberate them from the dark slavery in which they live.[167]

Can anything be more arrogant?

> **Islam was conceived in the desert under the banner of jihad and grew into an ideology of political and cultural imperialism disguised behind a façade of religion.**

Jihad has no comparable "just war" theory as in Christian thinking which became basic in international law and the Geneva Conventions. Jihad is both religious and political, just like Islam itself. It sprang from the desert and wherever it triumphs, it causes new cultural deserts like the Taliban where women were hidden in burqas, girls could not go to school, ancient monuments were destroyed, and the society was set back a thousand years.

Dr. Sebastian Gorka presented the "Jihadist Ideology – The Core Texts" starting with *Milestones,* by Sayyid Qutb (1964), *The Defense of the Muslim Lands,* Abdullah Azzam (1979), and *Knights Under the Prophet's Banner,* by Ayman al-Zawahiri (2001). The fourth is *The Quranic Concept of Power,* by Brigadier S.K. Malik (1979). It is particularly important because the Foreword was written by Muhammad Zia ul-Haq, then-President of Pakistan and Army Chief of Staff, and the Preface by Allah Bukhsh K. Brodi, the Advocate-General of Pakistan. That is high level official sanction. Malik's thesis is that the Qur'an provides a "concept of total war" and jihad is the "concept of total strategy" and the use of terror. "Terror struck into the hearts of the enemies is not only a means, it is the end in itself." All four thinkers drew heavily from the Trilogy and were motivated to impose Islam and sharia. Dr. Gorka concluded that we must understand: "There are violent Jihadists and there are non-kinetic Soft Jihadists." Al Qaeda, the OIC, and the Muslim Brotherhood are "taking different pathways to the same destination." They are just "two faces of the same foe."[168]

> **Ever since the religion of Islam appeared in the world, the espousers of it…have been as wolves and tigers to all other nations, rending and tearing all that fell into their merciless paws, and grinding them with their iron teeth; that numberless cities are raised from the foundation, and only their name remaining; that many countries, which were once as the garden of God, are now a desolate wilderness; and that so many once numerous and powerful nations are vanished from the earth! Such was, and is at this day, the rage, the fury, the revenge, of these destroyers of human kind."**
>
> **- John Wesley[169]**

Salafis

It might be comforting to label radical Islamists, such as Osama bin Laden or others, as not "real Muslims" but then we would not understand the roots of radical ideologies. The people we are dealing with in this war against Islamofascism (or IslamoNazis or Islamic fanatics or just plain Islamic criminals) are part of the "Salafi movement."[170] *"Salaf"* is Arabic for "to precede" and refers to the Companions of the Prophet Muhammad, the three generations of Muslims who learned directly from the Prophet or from those who knew him. Therefore, the Salafis believe that only the Companions had a pure understanding of Islam.[171]

> **Salafis believe that over the centuries misguided Muslims introduced innovations and new practices (mainly from the West) that corrupted the pure message of Islam, thus, they advocate a return to the fundamentals of the religion, the writings of the Prophet and the Companions.**

Salafis believe that over the centuries misguided Muslims introduced innovations and new practices (mainly from the West) that corrupted the pure message of Islam. Thus, they advocate a return to the fundamentals of the religion, the writings of the Prophet and the Companions. Saudi Arabia and its Wahhabists are the major producers and exporters of Salafi publications, missionary operations, and humanitarian assistance. Salafi ideas have become widespread throughout the Muslim world and in important groups such as Gamiyya Islamiyya in Egypt, Armed Islamic Jihad in Algeria, Islamic Jihad, and the Muslim Brotherhood. Since they are dogmatic in the correctness of their views, they make little effort to reconcile differences with other Islamist sects or groups.[172]

Salafists, such as the attackers of 9/11, "deny the right of mortals to make policy or frame laws, insisting that all they need to know of public life can be found in the Koran. This *Salafist* new world order – little known in the West and even less understood – nevertheless indirectly provoked a Western response." That response was the neoconservatives' policy of preventive war.[173]

Before the Afghan war, there was little mention of violence and jihad in the Muslim world. The Saudis and other Gulf states provided the support which established the *madrassas* (religious schools - still so prevalent with 18,000 to 22,000 schools and 1.5 million students or more[174]) and training camps in Pakistan for the Arab volunteers. There are both violent and non-violent elements within Salafi. The end of the war against the Soviets led to a split in the Salafi movement about the use of jihad. Reformists wanted emphasis on Salafi teachings before proceeding with jihad. However, the radicalized *mujahedin* from the war wanted to export jihad to other enemies. Saudi Arabia and the Gulf states supported volunteer efforts in Bosnia, Chechnya, Western China, Dagestan, Kosovo, Macedonia, the Philippines, Tajikistan, and Uzbekistan.[175] This defensive jihad, war in defense of Islam, is considered a Muslim obligation, or obligatory "nomadic jihad."[176]

Many of the indigenous jihadists in Iraq practice Salafism, a stringent brand of Sunni Islam that was brutally repressed by Saddam's regime after it began gaining adherents in Iraq a decade ago…. the Salafists model themselves on the *mujahedin* who drove the Soviets out of Afghanistan in the 1980s and on other international jihad movements.[177]

One of the problems for Salafis is that Islam rejects rebellion against Muslim leaders. Therefore, they have to go to great lengths to show that an individual or a government is no longer Muslim. They had to delve far back in history to a medieval scholar, Taqi al-Din Ahmad ibn Taymiyya, for justification for jihad. He lived during the Crusades and the Mongol invasions and established that even if a person followed all the basic tenets of the faith, if he failed to uphold any aspect of sharia, that person would no longer be considered a Muslim since he had left the faith. The Salafis thus labeled the governments of Algeria, Egypt, Saudi Arabia, and Yemen as *kafirs* (unbelievers) and declared jihad against them.[178]

Another problem for the Salafis was that *fatwas* (religious decrees) are usually issued by senior Muslim clerics or sharia courts. Osama bin Laden had no official position in Islam, yet he issued *fatwas* against the US. But they were carefully worded to indicate "defense of Islam" in face of US "aggression."[179] Thus he stressed that Arab governments are "puppets" of the US and therefore not Muslim, that the Saudis permit heathen American soldiers in the land of the two holy places, and that the US military and the Department of Defense are "controlled by Jewish interests intent on destroying Islam."[180]

The jihadi Salafis decentralized the use of *takfir* (declaring someone an apostate) taking into their own hands the determination of who is a Muslim.[181] The jihadi Salafis in Algeria attacked the Algerianists and seized control of the Armed Islamic Group (GIA). The GIA then issued a *fatwa* that said they could kill villagers who did not support the GIA. It also included the media, schools, and foreigners resulting in many brutal massacres.[182] Osama bin Laden's 1998 *fatwa* including attacking Americans, civilian and military, resulted in 11 September. Almost all jihadist terrorism traces its roots to radicalization from Salafism. The state interior ministers of Germany noted that the Salafist threat both in Germany and worldwide, wanted "a return to a stone-age Islam and want to turn Germany into a theocracy."[183]

The difference between the reformist and jihadi factions of Salafi is disagreement not over jihad but only the timing of any war. There is much reformist support for bin Laden's legitimizing an attack on the US. The US needs to carefully weigh its actions in the war against Islamofascism in terms of their effects on the reformist and jihadi Salafis and other groups predisposed to exhortations (like bin Laden's) toward the US and autocratic Muslim regimes.[184]

Inbreeding and Culture

There are other aspects of Islam that need mention. The first is a taboo subject, almost untouchable – that is the marriage of first cousins. This practice from the time of Muhammad, 50 generations (1400 years), "may well have done virtually irreversible damage to the Muslim gene pool, including extensive damage to its intelligence, sanity, and health." Nicolai Sennels, a Danish psychologist, has done extensive research into this problem. He estimates that nearly half of all Muslims are inbred: nearly 70% in Pakistan, half of Pakistani immigrants in the UK, Saudi Arabia 67%, Jordan and Kuwait 64%, Sudan 63%, Iraq 60%, and United Arab Emirates and Qatar 54%.

There are disastrous results. British Pakistani families are "more than 13 times as likely to have children with recessive genetic disorders." These families account for 33% of children with birth defects even though they represent only three percent of the UK births. The risk of "recessive disorders such as cystic fibrosis and spinal muscular atrophy is 18 times higher and the risk of death due to malformations is 10 times higher." Inbreeding results in a 100% increase in the "risk of stillbirths and a 50% increase in the possibility that a child will die during labor." According to Sennels, there is a lowered intellectual capacity with "10-16 points off their IQ and that social abilities develop much slower in inbred babies." The risk of an IQ under 70 ("retarded") increases by 400%! This makes it more difficult to operate in high-tech societies. This impacts on schools where, for instance, special education consumes one-third of the Danish schools budget, and some 64% of Arabic school children are still illiterate after 10 years in the Danish system. It also appears in insanity with Denmark's largest ward for clinically insane criminals having some 40% immigrants.[185]

Massive inbreeding within the Muslim culture during the last 1,400 years may have done catastrophic damage to their gene pool.

- Nicolai Sennels

Sennels worked in a prison and discovered that about two thirds of Danish teenage criminals were Muslim. He noted that discrimination and money were not the causes: "the Muslim concept of honor transforms especially their men into fragile glass-like personalities that need to protect themselves by scaring their surroundings with their aggressive attitude." He continued: "The show of so-called narcissistic rage is very common among Muslims. The fear of criticism is in many cases not far from paranoia." Self-irony and self-criticism are completely absent in Muslim societies and, from a psychological perspective, "Muslim culture is in many ways psychologically unhealthy to grow up in."[186]

Another problem is the unchanging nature of Muslim culture. All cultures have to have some self preserving mechanisms to survive, but the Muslim culture has very strong ones, such as violence or death for some actions (apostasy), not allowed to marry non-Muslims, marrying within the family, characteristic clothing (veils, etc.), special food (halal), ties to the ummah, and not making friends with non-Muslims. Sennels pointed out the feeling of shame, the pressure when one breaks the social rules of their culture – "Shame is the antidote to cultural evolution." "The concept of shame is dominating the Muslim culture and makes Muslims prevent themselves from deviating from cultural norms and behaviours. Installing a strong concept of shame thus becomes a psychological armour protecting the Muslim culture from changing." What is the medicine against shame – laughter! "Except for consequence, humour is probably the most underestimated weapon against religious fanaticism and lack of integration among Muslims." He noted it was no wonder the Muslims reacted so aggressively against the Muhammad cartoons, but that humor is needed to break open "a culture mummified by shame and for pointing out weaknesses in its behaviour and religion....and this is what we never stop serving them. With a smile"[187]

The cartoon stupidity will not end. Three terrorists were arrested after they traveled from Sweden to Denmark planning to cut the throats of reporters at the Jyllands-Posten newspaper that had printed the Muhammad cartoons.[188] Is that the real Islam?

Notes

1. Ahmad ibn Naqib al-Misri, *Reliance of the Traveller,* A Classic Manual of Islamic Sacred Law, In Arabic with Facing Arabic Text, Commentary and Appendices Edited and Translated by Nuh Ha Min Keller (Beltsville, Maryland, Amana Publications, 2008), a1.4, pp. 2-3. "The basic premise of this school of thought is that the *good* of the acts of those morally responsible is what the Lawgiver (syn. Allah or His messenger (Allah bless him and give him peace)) has indicated is good by permitting it or asking it be done. And the *bad* is what the Lawgiver has indicated is bad by asking it not be done."
2. Also spelled Shariah, Shari'a, and Shari'ah. It means a "straight path."
3. M. Cherif Bassiouni, *Introduction to Islam*, (Washington, DC, American-Arab Affairs Council, 1985), p.27.
4. M. Cherif Bassiouni, "A Search for Islamic Criminal Justice: An Emerging Trend in Muslim States," *The Islamic Impulse*, Edited by Barbara Freyer Stowasser, Center for Contemporary Arab Studies, Georgetown University, (London, Croom Helm, 1987), pp. 247-248.
5. SHARIAH: THE THREAT TO AMERICA An Exercise in Competitive Analysis, Report of Team "B" II, (Washington, DC. The Center for Security Policy, 2010), p. 41. It was later issued as a book. This is an excellent coverage of sharia.
6. It is supposedly sunna for women to depilate everything from the neck down every 20 days and men every 40 days, Geraldine Brooks in her book *Nine Parts of Desire,* in her chapter on meeting with HezbAllah wives.
7. Ibn Warraq, "The Westminster Institute (Virginia): Educating the Public and Government About the Ideology of the Terrorists, and Ways to Counter It," referring to a lecture by Dr. Sebastian Gorka, "Jihadist Ideology – The Core Texts," 5 October 2010 and a conference "Fighting the Ideological War: Strategies For Defeating Al Qaeda," 25 May 2011. He used the English translation of Qutb's book Dar al-Ilm, Damascus, Syria, [N.D.] pp. 88 and 107.
8. Ibid., pp. 252-253.
9. *Shariah,* The Center for Security Policy, p. 7.
10. Ibid., pp. 42-43.
11. Ibid.
12. Ibid., p. 43. Qaradawi is an interesting person widely referred to as a "moderate. Robert Spencer wrote that he had been "praised by Saudi-funded dhimmi pseudo-academic John Esposito as a champion of a 'reformist interpretation of Islam and its relationship to democracy, pluralism and human rights.'" His writings and preaching on Al-Jazeera are something different. He has said "that suicide attacks against Israelis were not actually suicide at all, but 'martyrdom in the name of God.'" In one of his broadcasts, "he prayed that Allah would kill all the Jews." He is the head of the European Council for Fatwah and Research (ECFR) based in Dublin, where they were having a large conference of top Muslim clerics. He has been banned from Britain and the US. Cormac O'Keefe, "Controversial Muslim leader to hold conference in Ireland," *Irish Examiner,* 29 June 2011.
13. "Shari'ah Law: Fusion of Church & State," www.islamrevealed.com. Laws listed are directly from Alifta.com, a website for official "fatwas" issued by the General Presidency of Scholarly Research and Ifta (issuing fatwas) of the Kingdom of Saudi Arabia.
14. Muhammad al-Sulalmi, "Fatwa body bans mingling of sexes," *Arab News,* 7 June 2011. "Last year, the committee issued a similar edict banning women from working as cashiers at supermarkets."
15. Richard Spencer, "Saudi Arabian lingerie law ends," *Telegraph*, 14 June 2011.
16. Jason Burke, "Saudi Arabia's clerics challenge King Abdullah's reform agenda," *Guardian,* 1 July 2011.
17. Examples: "Extremists sentence Somalis to amputations," Associated Press, 22 June 2009. "Iranian chocolate thief 'to have hand chopped off,'" AFP, 16 October 2010. "Taliban cut off man's hand for theft," *Press Trust of India,* 4 January 2011. They beheaded a fellow militant the previous day. "Two sisters shot dead in Indian Kashmir," AFP, 1 February 2011, no explanation or claim for responsibility, but "Militant groups are known to kill people suspected of being police informers." Tom Parfitt, "Masked gunmen kill three as Islamist militants target $14 billion ski resort plan," *Guardian,* 20 February 2011, three tourists from Moscow going to the resort in Russia's North Caucasus. Also in Russia, jihadis murdered a moderate imam. "Prominent imam killed in Russia's Dagestan," AFP, 9 April 2011. In Egypt, Muslims including a policeman attacked a Christian, cut off his ear, cut the back of his neck, his other ear, his face and his arm. They tried to convert him to Islam and wanted to throw him off the fifth floor but the policeman objected since he might get in trouble. They called the police and told them to come get the Copt saying, "We have applied the law of Allah, now come and apply your civil law." Mary Abdelmassih, "Muslims Attack Christian in Egypt, Cut Off His Ear," AINA, 26 March 2011.
18. Will Stewart, "Muslim girl, 19, 'stoned to death after taking part in beauty contest'," *Daily Mail,* 30 May 2011.
19. Claire Berlinski, "Moderate Muslim Watch: How the Term 'Islamophobia' Got Shoved Down Your Throat," Ricochet.com, 24 November 2010. Berlinski wrote that "Islamophobia" was deliberately invented by the Muslim Brotherhood front, the International Institute of Islamic Thought, based in Northern Virginia. Abdur-Rahman Muhammad quit IIIT in disgust and said he was an eyewitness to the creation. They needed to silence critics and they felt they needed terminology that would portray them as victims. He said he was present when they coined the term "Islamophobia" using the idea of "homophobia" to "beat up their critics."
20. See Hugh Fitzgerald's reply on "Islamophobia" in Jihad Watch, 28 September 2010. He then lists 27 criticisms ranging from terror to murder, from taqiyya to dhimmi status, from treatment of infidels to treatment of women and asks why are they irrational? See also Robert Spencer, "The 'Islamophobia' Weapon," Jihad Watch, 28 September 2010.
21. "New CAIR, UC Berkeley Report Documents Islamophobia in U.S. By Council on American-Islamic Relations Published: Thursday, Jun. 23, 2011."
22. Jihad Watch, 26 August 2011.
23. Geert Wilders, "In Defense of 'Hurtful' Speech," *The Wall Street Journal,* 24 June 2011.
24. politicalislam.com, 17 August 2011.

25. Ibid. For an excellent review of freedom of speech and our appeasing of Islam, see Diana West, "Possessing Freedom is Not Enough – We Must Exercise Our Freedom to Preserve It," transcript of her speech at a free speech conference of the International Free Press Society held in Denmark's parliament in Copenhagen, posted 9 October 2010.

26. Andrew C. McCarthy, "The OIC and the Caliphate: The Islamic agenda is not coexistence, but dominion," http://www.nationalreview.com/articles/260786/oic-and-caliphate-andrew-c-mccarthy?page=1.

27. Connie Hair, "Sharia Law's Threat to Free Speech," *Human Events,* 11 October 2010.

28. "OIC Slams Islamophobia In West," Bernama, 12 January 2011.

29. Geert Wilders, "The Failure of Multiculturalism and How to Turn the Tide," speech at the Annual Lecture at the Magna Carta Foundation in Rome, 25 March 2011, Jihad Watch, 26 March 2011.

30. "OIC commends resolution on religious discrimination," *Arab News,* 26 March 2011.

31. See Bat Ye'or, "OIC and the Modern Caliphate," *American Thinker,* 28 September 2010.

32. Patrick Goodenough, "New Name, Same Old Focus for Islamic Bloc," CNS News, 30 June 2011. The logo was changed from a red crescent with "Allahu Akhbar," to a "green crescent, a globe, and a representation of the Ka'aba."

33. "OIC/Islamophobia: OIC Observatory warned since 2009 against the growth of the extreme right in Europe, Washington plans to host a meeting on resolution opposing defamation of religions," International Islamic News Agency, 1 August 2011.

34. Badea Abu Al-Naja, "Freedom of expression should not be misused," *Arab News,* 2 May 2009.

35. Isi Leibler, "Candidly Speaking: Islamophobia and the Jews," *Jerusalem Post,* 29 September 2010, Breaking_NewsJPost.com. Also "FBI sends 'Draw Mohammed' cartoonist into hiding," Associated Press, Seattle, 18 September 2010.

36. See Richard Landes, "Liberal intellectuals are frightened of confronting Islam's honour-shame culture," *Telegraph,* 17 August 2011.

37. Isabel Vincent, "Jihad jitters at Met," *New York Post,* 10 January 2010.

38. Bruce Finley, "Civil-rights complaints investigated," *Denver Post,* 29 June 2009.

39. "Florida Judge orders Muslim to follow sharia law!" Act for America, 18 March 2011.

40. Dina Temple-Raston, "Imam Arrests Show Shift in Muslim Outreach Effort," NPR, 19 July 2011.

41. Amy Alkon, "LA Sheriff's Department Has A Muslim Public Affairs Unit," Men's News Daily, 11 July 2011.

42. "US Muslim Woman Gets $20,000 in Lawsuit Against Discrimination," Ahlul Bayt News Agency, 21 July 2011, Jihad Watch.

43. A first year school teacher in a suburb of Chicago quit her job when she was refused three weeks off to go on the hajj during the school year. Obama's Justice Department sued on her behalf that her civil rights had been violated. Jerry Markon, "Justice Department sues on behalf of Muslim teacher, triggering debate," *The Washington Post,* 22 March 2011.
    The DOJ forced the school district to pay Safoorah Khan $75,000 in lost back pay, compensatory damages, and attorney's fees and it must develop a policy accommodating religions consistent with the Civil Rights Acts. Tina Sfondales, "Woman wins right to Mecca trip," *Chicago Sun-Tribune,* 13 October 2011, Jihad Watch, 15 October 2011.

44. Ben Leubsdorf, "Tiny horse trains as guide for blind Muslim woman," *Chicago Tribune,* 10 April 2009.

45. Azadeh Moaveni, "The Latest Enemies of Iran: dogs and Their Owners," *Time,* 19 April 2011.

46. "Taliban shave men for listening to music," *Agence France-Presse,* 26 April 2009. The Taliban banned men from shaving their beards and women from getting their national identity cards (ID) made or leaving their houses. Hasbanullah Khan, "Bajaur Taliban ban shaving of beards," *Daily Times,* 11 April 2009.

47. David E. Miller, "Islamic Group Declares War on Religious Films, *Media Line,* 5 January 2011. Interestingly, Shiites encourage artistic depiction of their revered figures.

48. "Somali Islamists issue blanket ban on movies," *Agence France-Presse,* 13 June 2009.

49. Jonathan M. Seidl, "Police Investigate Spanish Teacher for Saying 'Ham' to Muslim Boy," Jihad Watch, 23 December 2010.

50. "Iran: Tight jeans, bright clothes banned in universities," *Jerusalem Post,* 11 January 2011.

51. Dudi Cohen, "Morality police hit Tehran streets," YNet News, 17 July 2011.

52. "Reciting from Quran only allowed if it's to understand religion," *The Star,* 7 April 2011, Jihad Watch.

53. Maggie Michael, "Wary of wider defiance, Saudis arrest woman driver," Associated Press, 23 May 2011. Abdel-Rahman al-Barak, a prominent Saudi cleric, posted a fatwa on his website that women who violate the driving ban are "sinful and are opening (the doors) of evil." See also, Aryn Baker, "Road Warriors," *Time,* 4 July 2011, p.46. She covers the various positions on the subject and exposed the conservative position: "it means a loss of control over women's lives."

54. "Saudi woman driver to be whipped," *Reno Gazette-Journal,* 28 September 2011, p. 1C.

55. Bulletin of the Oppression of Women, 14 November-15 December 2011, politicalislam.com.

56. Brock Parker, "School system to get Muslim holiday," *Boston Globe,* 10 October 2010.

57. Katherine Kersten, "TiZA vs. the search for truth: The school – public, mind you – tries to intimidate all who would challenge it," *Star Tribune,* 16 October 2010.

58. Steve Alexander, "Heinz, Islamic workers headed to mediation," *Star Tribune,* 9 August 2011, Jihad Watch, 10 August 2011.

59. Bernie Woodall, "Detroit mosque protest barred by court," Reuters, 22 April 2011.

60. Caroline May, "Army to allow hijabs, turbans in Junior ROTC," Daily Caller, 22 December 2011.

61. Doug Giles, "Muslims Miffed That Catholic University H as Catholic Imagery," Townhall.com 30 October 2011.

62. CAIR, which is linked to Hamas, keeps pushing their propaganda line that sharia is not a threat. Nezar Hamze [executive director of the South Florida chapter of CAIR], "Sharia law is not a threat," *Miami Herald,* 17 June 2011.

63. Robert Spencer, "Sharia? What Sharia?" Jihad Watch, 19 October 2010.

64. Neco Cockburn, "Not a whodunit, so much as 'why did he do it?' defence say," *The Ottawa Citizen,* 8 May 2009.

65. Irwin Block, "Family rallies around accused father," *Postmedia News* (Montreal), 13 October 2010.

66. Andrew Lawton, "BREAKING: Conference facility caves to pressure from Islamic groups, bans Mark Steyn from speaking," *Strictly Right,* 21 October 2010.

67. "Srdja Trifkovic barred from Canada," SYL, 24 February 2011.

68. Nick Martin, "Muslims want children excused from music, mixed phys-ed classes," *Winnipeg Free Press,* 5 February 2011.

69. "A Small Concession is No Big Deal," Citizen Warrior, 17 October 2010.

70. W. Thomas Smith Jr., "Bill Aimed at Protecting S.C. From Foreign Law Introduced in Legislature," *Human Events,* 26 January 2011.

71. Michael Biesecker, "Bill would ban courts from using 'foreign law.'" *News & Observer,* 29 April 2011.

72. Chas Sisk, "Muslims rally at Tennessee Capitol to protest legislation," for *The Tennessean* via WBIR.com, 20 April 2011.

73. John H. Tucker, "U.S. Attorney: Feds Could Challenge Missouri Anti-Sharia Legislation," *Riverfront Times,* 29 April 2011.

74. "Shariah Law and American State Courts: Assessment of State Appellate Court Cases," The Center for Security Policy, 17 May 2011.

75. Donna Leinwand, "States enter debate on sharia law," *Reno Gazette-Journal,* 12 February 2010, p. 1B. See also, Raymond Ibrahim, ""Is Newt Gingrich Wrong to Talk About Sharia?" Pajamas Media, 24 August 2010.

76. "Oklahoma tries again to outlaw Sharia," Jihad Watch, 22 March 2011. See also Connie Hair, "Oklahoma Bans Sharia Law," HumanEvents.com, 4 November 2010; "CAIR to Announce Suit Challenging Oklahoma Anti-Islam Amendment," PR Newswire, 3 November 2010, Jihad Watch, 4 November 2010; Tim Talley, "Court order blocks Okla. Amendment on Islamic law," Associated Press, 8 November 2010; Bill Mears, "Judge issues permanent injunction on Oklahoma Sharia law ban," CNN, 29 November 2010; and David Yerushalmi, "Criticism of the Oklahoma Amendment banning Shariah from State Courts: Legitimate or ill-considered?" Center for Security Policy, 29 November 2010.

77. "Govt says no to sharia law," Australian Associated Press, 17 May 2011. The government made similar strong statements in September 2005 saying if you want sharia, get out of Australia.

78. Michael Harvey and Steve Lewis, ""Islam's the problem, not Muslims, says Senator Cory Bernardi," *Herald Sun,* 19 February 2011, Jihad Watch, 20 February 2011.

79. Clayton Hinds, "'Democracy is evil, Parliament is evil' says radical Muslim cleric in billboard debate," *Christians Today Australia,* 19 June 2011, Jihad Watch.

80. John Masanauskas, "Give us our own laws, say Islamic leaders," *Herald Sun,* 11 July 2011.

81. Sally Neighbour, "Anger, venom and hatred," *The Australian,* 16 February 2010 and James Madden, "Terrorists smile as they're jailed," *The Australian,* 16 February 2010.

82. Rod McGuirk, "New Australian law to make Muslims lift veils," *Washington Examiner,* 10 July 2011.

83. "Extremist cleric to lead White House protest calling for Muslims to 'rise up and establish Islamic state in America,'" *Daily Mail,* 20 February 2011.

84. Diane Macedo, "Pro-Shariah Rally in D.C. Postponed Amid Opposition," http://www.foxnews.com/us/2011/03/02/pro-shariah-rally-dc-postponed-amid-wave-opposition/?test=latestnews, 2 March 2011.
    Choudary, 47, who lives on welfare in England, regularly makes the news with his outbursts. In addition to his statement that it is "only a matter of time" before the flag of Islam flies over Downing Street, the White House and the Kremlin in Moscow, he said it is an "obligation" to free fellow Muslims from infidel prisons. Simon Hughes, "Jailbust rant by fanatic," *The Sun,* 14 April 2009.

85. *Reliance of the Traveller,* o8.7 lists 20 and says "the subject is nearly limitless."

86. Mindy Betz "Brutal Beheading," *World Magazine,* 22 June 2011, Jihad Watch 4 July 2011.

87. "Sudan: Converts from Islam struggle to survive," Compass Direct News, (Khartoum), 14 April 2009.

88. Michael Ireland, ""Pastor's Death Sentence Upheld By Iranian Supreme Court," *AssistNews,* 30 June 2011. Jihad Watch, 1 July 2011. The Supreme Court called for the lower court to re-examine the death sentence but did not overturn it since it is based on fatwas by Khomeini, Khamenei, and Makarem Shirazi. "A convert from Islam, Iranian pastor risks the death penalty," Asia News, 12 July 2011.

89. "Muslim Extremists in India Attack, Threaten Christian Women," Compass Direct News, 6 August 2011, Jihad Watch 8 August 2011. In another district, "Muslim extremists held three Christian women for an hour on July 21, threatening to beat and burn them alive if they continued worshipping Christ."

90. "Egyptian Shaykh: 'We still kill him, even if he repents!,'" Translating Jihad, 13 July 2011, on TV station al-Hikma on 7 July 2011, Jihad Watch, 16 July 2011. "He said that insulting Allah of course makes one an infidel...yet the one who insults Allah is not killed—he is merely called to repentance. This is because even if the whole world insults Allah, it does not matter to him—it does not hurt him." That makes Islam Muhammad-centric – Muhammadism or the cult of Muhammad!

91. Salman Masood and Carlotta Gall, "Killing of Governor Deepens Crisis in Pakistan," *New York Times,* 4 January 2011.

92. Nina Shea, "Call to Ban Bible Under Pakistan's Elastic Blasphemy Laws," *National Review,* 6 June 2011.

93. Sebastian Abbott, "Cheers and tears in Pakistan after assassination," Associated Press, 5 January 2011. See also, Zahid Husssain and Tom Wright, "Pakistan Killer Had Revealed Plans," *Asia News,* 5 January 2011 and "Chaos over Mumtaz Qadri's court appearance," AFP, 6 January 2011 in which supporters disrupted his court appearance and he was again feted with rose petals.

94. "Salman Taseer's killer an Islamic warrior: Pakistani clerics," PTI, 5 January 2011.
    See also, Karin Brulliard, "Salman Taseer assassination points to Pakistani extremists' mounting power," *Washington Post Foreign Service,* 5 January 2011, noting that Pakistan "has been ruled by the military for half its 63-year history and where an elected government has never completed its term." They also denounced Taseer as an "apostate." Shehrbano Taseer, "My Father Died for Pakistan," *New York Times,* 8 January 2011. Ashraf Khan, "Thousands rally in Pakistan for blasphemy laws," Associated Press, 9 January 2011, Jihad Watch. 50,000 rallied in Karachi and a cleric said Taseer was "responsible for his own murder" because he criticized the law. The leader of an Islamic party told Taseer's daughter to remember her father's fate and be quiet about blasphemy law. "Taseer's daughter warned to back off," *Telegraph,* 14 January 2011. Even former president Musharraf got into the act: Ben Framer, "Blasphemy law must not be scrapped, says Musharraf," *Telegraph,* 17 January 2011.

95. Jibran Khan, "Muslim extremists and others oppose death penalty of 'hero' Mumtaz Qadri," Asia News, 3 October 2011.

96. Carlotta Gall, "Pakistan Faces a Divide of Age on Muslim Law," *The New York Times,* 11 January 2011, p. A1.

97. "Laws to be reformed according to Islam: Gilani," APP, 28 February 2011.

98. "Pakistan: Islamist terrorists issue death sentence for Christian government official," *Spero News,* 4 December 2010.

99. John Hayward, Human Events Daily, 3 March 2011. See also, Zahid Hussain and Tom Wright, "Minister Is Gunned Down in Pakistan," *The Wall Street Journal*, 3 March 2011, p. A8.

100. Jane Perlez and Waqar Gillani, "Slain Cabinet Minister Is Buried in Pakistan," *The New York Times*, 4 March 2011.

101. Jibran Khan, "Islamabad abolishes Minority Affairs Ministry, as Bhatti murder could go unpunished," AsiaNews, 30 June 2011.

102. "Pak ex-minister Sherry Rehman fit to be killed, says cleric," *Press Trust of India*, 10 January 2011.

103. "Pope urges Pakistan to repeal blasphemy law," BBC News, 10 January 2011. "Pope insults Muslims, say MPs," *The Times*, 12 January 2011. A senior leader of Jamiat-e-Ulema Islam said "Pakistan is an Islamic ideological state and the Pope cannot tell us to change our laws, which are in conformity to our belief."

104. Salman Masood, "Pakistanis Rally in Support of Blasphemy Law," *New York Times*, 31 December 2010. "In pak, blasphemy law supporters on the streets, Associated Press, 24 January 2011. Jibran Khan, "Karachi, women on streets in support of the blasphemy law," *Asia News*, 29 January 2011.

105. "Punjab: Christian woman sentenced to death for 'blasphemy,'" *Asia News*, 9 November 2010. "In addition to the death sentence, Bibi was also fined the equivalent for an unskilled worker of two and a half years' wages."

106. See "Islamic Apartheid," Roland Shirk, Jihad Watch, 26 December 2010.

107. "Jailed Pakistani Mother Living in Constant Fear, Husband Says," *Compass Direct News*, 19 January 2011. See also Tariq Ali, "Salman Taseer Remembered," *London Review of Books*, Vol. 33 No. 2, 20 January 2011, pp. 11-12.

108. Jibran Khan, "Extremist group announces suicide attack to kill Asia Bibi," *Asia News*, 7 January 2011. She has been in prison since 2009. Jibran Khan, "Asia Bibi gravely ill, fears for her life, after three months in solitary isolation," *Asia News*, 7 April 2011.

109. "Man accused of blasphemy killed in Pakistan," *Indian Express*, 18 November 2010, Jihad Watch.

110. Nick Paton Walsh, "Pakistan's blasphemy vigilantes kill exonerated man," CNN, 14 April 2011.

111. "Blasphemy sentence," *Dawn*, 23 June 2011, also on Jihad Watch.

112. "'Blasphemy' claims three more victims," *Daily Times*, 5 August 2009.

113. "Court convicts imam and son for blasphemy," *Agence France-Presse*, 11 January 2011. "The judge sentenced them to life imprisonment on charges of blasphemy and ordered them to pay a fine of 200,000 rupees ($2,359) each."

114. Jibran Khan, "Pakistan's blasphemy law claims another innocent victim," *Asia News*, 13 December 2010.

115. Jihad Watch, 12 January 2011. "The judge found no evidence against him except the words of his accuser, a man with whom he had a dispute over a business transaction. During the hearing, the mob chanted slogans inside and outside the court demanding that he be found guilty."

116. "Pakistan bank attacked by terrorists over 'sacrilegious' floor tiles, *Asian News International*, 18 June 2011.

117. Awad Mustafa, "British tourist fined for insulting Islam in shop," *The National*, 10 June 2011. Surprise: the salesman was a 19-year-old from Pakistan! Jihad Watch, 9 June 2011.

118. Jibran Khan, "Punjab: acquittal for 70 Muslim extremists on trial for Gojra massacre," *Asia News*, 11 June 2011. Fareed Khan, "eight Christians burned alive in Punjab," *Asia News*, 2 August 2009.

119. Jibran Khan, "Punjab: Christian families flee false accusation of blasphemy," *Asia News*, 17 June 2011.

120. "Imam, school principal shot dead in Russia's Dagestan," AFP, 10 July 2011.

121. "Iran threatens 'serious action' over BBC plans to screen documentary series on Muslim prophet Muhammad," *Daily Mail*, 7 July 2011.

122. Natalia Mazur, "Are researchers allowed to call Muhammad a paedophile?" *Gazeta Wyborcza*, 2 July 2011, translated by Brzegorz Kushierz for Jihad Watch, 7 July 2011. According to the university's press spokesperson, "Words used by scholars ought to be free from invectives, positive and negative emotions, and an affective vocabulary."

123. Thanks to John L. Terry III, Russellville, Arkansas, www.revelationfiles.com. See also *Muslim Mafia*, pp. 296-297 including Qaradawi's statement on donations which he calls "jihad with money, because Allah has ordered us to fight enemies with our lives and our money."

124. Andy Polk, "What You Need to Know About Sharia-Compliant Finance," http://www.familysecuritymatters.org/publications /id.2131/pub_detail.asp.

125. David Yerushalmi, Esq., "*Shari'ah's* 'Black Box': Civil Liability and Criminal Exposure Surrounding *Shari'ah*-Compliant Finance." Utah Law Review, No. 3, 2008, pp. 1019-1106.

126. Simon Roughneen, "Shariah bankers: West ready for faith-based alternative," *Washington Times*, 13 April 2009.

127. "Tehran – US Banks to Set up Iran Branches," *Voz Is Neias*, 18 April 2009.

128. "Trouble Brewing for AIG and Federal Government: Constitutional Challenge of AIG Bailout Allowed to Proceed," Thomas Moore Law Center, 27 May 2009.

129. "Sharia Law Gains Foothold in US: Federal Judge Upholds Government Funding of Islam - Thomas More Law Center Files Appeal," 27 May 2009.

130. *Reliance of the Traveller*, o9.0, p. 599.

131. Understanding Islam and the Muslims," (Washington, DC, The Islamic Affairs Department, The Embassy of Saudi Arabia, 1989), p. 23.

132. Serge Trifkovic, *The Sword of the Prophet*, (Boston, Regina Orthodox Press, Inc., 2002), p. 89.

    Different opinion: "Beginning first with the assassination of Mr. Pearl, the secular term 'barbaric' should be changed to the Islamic religious term 'satanic' – *shaitaniyah* in Arabic. But in the broader context in which this brutal killing is but one small element, the linchpin label on which al Qaeda's campaign depends is its blatant misuse of the Islamic word 'Jihad.'

    "Basically, the word describes the inner 'struggle' to perfect one's moral and spiritual self in the eyes of Allah but has been perverted into a meaning of worldwide 'Holy War' – a militant struggle not only against America or Christianity or the West but against any part of Islam which does not share al Qaeda's extremist interpretation of Islamic Law." Jim Girard, President, TrueSpeak Institute, truespeak@aol.com, "The 'Lightning' Words – *Hirabah* and *Shaitaniyah*." Since all the key Islamic documents define jihad as war against non-Muslims, this appears to be another example of taqiyya!

Jihad is "Quite a flexible word! How slippery it proves in the hands of Islamic apologists, who when confronted with the bloody results of self-proclaimed jihadists to massacre subway travelers in New York can claim that their holy book was really referring to the 'effort' to think pure thoughts, or the 'struggle' to raise olive trees." The olive trees comment referred to a headline in the Iran Daily, "Modern Olive Farming Bears Fruit," attributed to Iran's Islamic Republic's "Agricultural Jihad Ministry." Roland Shirk, "The Fiber of Jihad," Jihad Watch, 13 January 2011.

133. Bukhari, Volume 4, Book 52, Number 142.
134. Robert Spencer, *The Politically Incorrect Guide to Islam (and the Crusades)*, (Washington, DC, Regnery Publishing, Inc., 2005), p. 34.
135. Spencer, *The Politically Incorrect Guide to Islam*, p. 35.
136. Bill Warner, *An Abridged Koran, A Reconstructed Historical Koran,* (CSPI, cspipublishing.com, 2006), Warner, *An Abridged Koran,* p. 200.
137. Bill Warner, *Mohamed and the Unbelievers: The Sira, a Political Biography,* (CSPI, cspipublishing.com, 2006), p. 164.
138. Bill Warner, *The Political Traditions of Mohammed, The Hadith for the Unbelievers,* (CSPI, cspipublsihing.com, 2006), p.12.
139. Robert Spencer, *The Truth about Muhammad, Founder of the World's Most Intolerant Religion* (Washington, DC, Regnery Publishing, Inc., 2006), p. 161.
140. Spencer, *The Politically Incorrect Guide to Islam*, pp. 38-40.
141. "Counterterror Adviser Defends Jihad as 'Legitimate Tenet of Islam,'" FOXNews.com, 27 May 2010. Also spelled out in "Obama's counterterror chief: jihad is 'legitimate tenet of Islam,'" Jihad Watch, 27 May 2010.
142. Again, this was defined as "war against non-Muslims," stating that the word is derived from the word *mujahada* – "war to establish the religion." Spencer, *The Politically Incorrect Guide to Islam*, p. 40.
143. Warner, *Hadith,* p.13.
144. Andrew G. Bostom, *The Legacy of Jihad: Islamic Holy War and the Fate of Non-Muslims*, Prometheus Books, 2005, 759 pp.
145. Andrew C. McCarthy, "The War that Dare Not Speak Its Name – The battle is against militant Islam, not 'Terror,'" National Review Online, 13 May 2004, adapted from a speech given the previous month at the annual conference of the University of Virginia School of Medicine's Critical Incident Analysis Group. Andrew McCarthy, a former chief assistant US attorney, led the 1995 terrorism prosecution against Sheik Omar Abdel Rahman and eleven others.
146. Ibid.
147. Quoted in "What Muslim Leaders Say About Islam Dispels the Myth that Jihadists are a 'Fringe' Element," Citizen Warrior, 1 October 2010.
148. "Grand Shia Cleric: Islam is the Religion of peace," Ahlul Bayt News Agency, 14 August 2011.
149. Roce Nahmias, "Islamic scholar: Every Muslim has right to kill Zionists," Ynet News, 23 august 2011.
150. Bukhari, volume 4, book 52, number 44.
151. "Counterterror Adviser Defends Jihad as 'Legitimate Tenet of Islam,'" FOXNews.com, 27 May 2010.
152. Robert Spencer, "Misunderstanding Islam," FrontPageMagazine.com, 6 August 2009.
153. "But Jihad is an Internal Struggle," Citizen Warrior, 1 August 2010.
154. McCarthy, op. cit.
155. We have naïve fools (or practitioners of taqiyya) like Yusuf Estes who try to fool poor souls in California that Muhammad did not steal from caravans. Eman M. Shurbaji, "Islam exposed to receptive audience: Some came from Bay Area to hear speaker's informative discussion," Bakersfield.com, 10 April 2009.
156. Section on money in "A View from the Eye of the Storm," a talk by Haim Harari, Chair, Davidson Institute of Science Education, at a meeting of the International Advisory Board of a large multi-national corporation, April 2004.
157. "Pakistani jihad networks funded by Saudi, UAE charities," Reuters, 22 May 2011.
158. "The Key to Jihad is Money," Citizen Warrior, 22 June 2011.
159. Spencer, *The Politically Incorrect Guide to Islam*, p. 36.
160. The Mujahidin's Roadmap 8 July 2004 The Abu-Hafs al-Masri Brigades (Al-Qa'ida) (Translated by FBIS), 1 July 2004. See Appendix A.

   Gilles Kepel, a French scholar of Islam wrote *Jihad: Expansion et Déclin de l'Islamisme*. His thesis was that Islam was falling apart, would undermine itself, and fail to draw a mass following. His newer book *The War for Muslim Minds: Islam and the West* maintained his theme but claimed that US policies were working against it. "The war for Muslim minds, Kepel suggests, will be won in Riyadh, Cairo, and the suburbs of Paris. In Washington it can't be won – only lost." According to Kepel, "the Bush administration has done al-Qaeda two enormous favors. The first was to scuttle the Israeli-Palestinian peace process….The neo-cons' second gift to al-Qaeda was the invasion of Iraq." He claimed Americans have little knowledge of Islam and that the world is much more complex than they understand. He still contended that if "left to themselves, Muslim societies may vanquish al-Qaeda on their own." Peter Beinart, "Backfire," *The Atlantic Monthly,* March 2005, p. 121.
161. Trifkovic, *The Sword of the Prophet,* p. 131.
162. Spencer, *The Politically Incorrect Guide to Islam*, p. 173.
163. Trifkovic, *The Sword of the Prophet,* p. 132.
164. Daniel Pipes, There Are No Moderates: Dealing With Fundamentalist Islam," *National Interest,* Fall 1995, quoted in Trifkovic, *The Sword of the Prophet,* p. 133.
165. Oriana Fallaci, "Anger and Pride," *Corrier della Serra,* 29 September 2001 (translated from Italian by Chris and Paola Newnan, quoted in Trifkovic, *The Sword of the Prophet,* pp. 140-141.
166. Abdulkadir Khalif, "Al Shabaab ask [sic] Kenya to keep off," *The Daily Nation* (Kenya), 21 May 2010. The al-Shabaab spokesman was Sheikh Ali Mohamoud Raghe alias Sheikh Ali Dhere.
167. Quoted in Raymond Ibrahim, "How Taqiyya Alters Islam's Rules of War," *Middle East Quarterly,* Winter 2010.
168. Ibn Warraq: The Westminster Institute (Part IV), Jihad Watch, 16 June 2011.

169. From "The Doctrine of Original Sin, "*Works* (1841), ix. 205, quoted in Spencer, *The Politically Incorrect Guide to Islam*, p. 188.
170. For a very thorough analysis of the Salafi movement, see Quintan Witztorowicz, "The New Global Threat: Transnational Salafis and Jihad," *Middle East Policy*, Vol. VIII, No. 4, December 2001, pp. 18-38.
171. Ibid., p. 20.
172. Ibid., pp. 20- 21. It is difficult to believe, but we have Salafi schools in the US. The Al-Huda School in College Park, Maryland, "run by Dar-us-Salaam, one of the Washington area's most conservative congregations," practices Salafism. They prefer to live apart: "it hopes one day to become a self-contained Islamic community." These efforts were supported by Saudi Arabia, but after 9/11 the Saudi government "suspended its missionary activities in this country." Carlyle Murphy, "For Conservative Muslims, Goal of Isolation a Challenge: 9/11 Put Strict Adherents on the Defensive," *The Washington Post,* 5 September 2006, p. A01.
173. John Keegan, *The Iraq War,* (New York, Alfred A. Knopf, 2004), p. 95.
174. Pervez Hoodbhoy, "The Roots of Extremism in Pakistan," *Journal of International Affairs* (BILIA, Bangladesh), Vol. 12, Nos. 1 & 2, Jun-Dec 2008, p. 6.
175. Witztorowicz, "The New Global Threat," p. 22.
176. Ibid., p. 24.
177. Romesh Ratnesar with Phil Zabriskie, "The Rise of the Jihadists," *Time*, 26 January 2004, p. 30. The mosques are generally off limits to the US military but that is where much support comes from. As one extremist leader explained, "he receives instructions to attack U.S. forces from fundamentalist imams in local mosques, who 'take their orders from the Holy Koran.'"
178. Witztorowicz, "The New Global Threat," p. 26.
179. Ibid., p. 34.
180. Ibid., p. 35.
181. Ibid., p. 27.
182. Ibid., p. 28. Salafi actions range from the extreme to the absurd. "In May, The Times of London, interviewing witnesses in Diyala province in Iraq, described scenes from the hard-core Salafist version of Islam being enforced (similar to what the Taliban imposed in Afghanistan), including breaking the fingers of those who repeatedly smoked cigarettes, prohibiting grocers from displaying bananas (as 'obscene'), and requiring them to screen cucumbers from tomatoes (as the latter are 'feminine vegetables'). One local man said he assumed that another restriction that farmers modestly cover their goats' 'nether regions' was just a rumor, until he saw a goat wearing boxer shorts." "Latest religious messages," Calendar, *Reno Gazette-Journal,* 15-22 June 2007, p. 19.
183. "Salafist threat growing, interior ministers say," *The Local,* 21 June 2011, Jihad Watch, 22 June 2011.
184. Witztorowicz, "The New Global Threat," p. 34.
185. Bryan Fischer, "A Huge Muslim problem: Inbreeding," Bryan Fischer-Focal Point, May 2011. See also Sue Reid, "It's time to confront this taboo: First cousin marriages in Muslim communities are putting hundreds of children at risk," *Daily Mail,* 3 June 2011. Lack of education, village culture, religious views ("Will of Allah"), and forced marriages were part of the reason. But one British-Pakistani put it bluntly: "A main reason why this corrupt practice is still followed in Britain is because the family wants to keep their property, land, jewellery and money in the family."
   See also comments about high illiteracy rates in Muslim majority countries due to inbreeding in "How Islam Protects Itself From Legitimate Criticism in Free Countries," Citizen Warrior, 11 January 2011. Mahendra wrote, "Truly Islam is a vicious mental virus/meme that distorts one's sense of reality and ability to rationalize." He later added a comment about importing Islamic immigrants and professionals. "However, a profession, education, three-piece suit and tie does not a rational person make." Example: Major Hassan killing our troops at Fort Hood.
   Sennels analyzed an OECD report on immigrant students in Denmark. It is not good and, in addition to discipline problems, "showed that 64 percent of students with an Arab background in Denmark are 'functionally illiterate' – meaning that their reading and writing capabilities are so poor that they will not be able to complete even a simple education." "Research on Muslims in Danish schools: Extremely low intellectual skills, undisciplined, disrespectful, unambitious parents," Jihad Watch, 6 July 2011.
186. Frontpage interview, http://frontpagemad.com/2010/05/05/among-criminal-muslims/'Among Criminal Muslims'.
187. Nicolai Sennels, "Shame: Muslim culture's armour, Weapon? Humour," Jihad Watch, 11 June 2011.
   In a reply in comments section, lilredbird wrote about cults – that for a born Muslim the Cult IS their family, the ummah, etc. and "Every step away from the Cult puts them at risk for a barrage of shame-inducing responses from all sides." He agreed that humor was important and to fight political correctness and multi-cultural fueled censorship.
188. "Danes say men plotted to cut throats," UPI, 31 January 2011.
189. Peter L. Bergen, *Holy War Inc.: Inside the Secret World of Osama bin Laden,* (New York, The Free Press, 2001), p. 41.

> **Death of the martyr for the unification of all the people in the cause of God and His word is the happiest, best, easiest, and most virtuous of deaths**.
>   **- Taqi al-Din ibn Taimiyya, medieval Muslim scholar**[189]

Chapter 5

What is the Real Islam?

*No political system of earthly power should hinder Islam.
If someone does hinder Islam's spread then it is Islam's duty to
fight that person until he is killed or until he declares his submission.*

- Sayyid Qutb

Islam: "a great religion and its commitment to justice and progress."

- Barack Hussein Obama[1]

The Arab empire that grew from the early conquests grew into a Muslim world in the Middle Ages. It was a world of warring states that were Muslim, not only Arab, and as the Arab power waned others rose to replace it. The Arabs had brought military power but their desert culture was simple and unsophisticated. Even the Arabic language at that time could not compete with those of the lands they conquered and was not yet capable of dealing with abstract concepts. The Arabs absorbed the culture of the peoples they conquered and slowly translated the great works into Arabic – classical literature, Greek thought, Byzantine institutions, the law of Rome, the scholarship of Syria, and the art of Persia.[2] This was their finest hour. But a glorious past can be a burden.

The Terrifying Brilliance of Islam

One of the most outstanding descriptions of Islam was written by Citizen Warrior. He asked why millions of Muslims were dedicated to killing Americans and others. He then went through the doctrine of Islam and developed 26 key components of the "idea-collection" known as Islam. Some of them are:

- ◆ War as an Approved Tactic
- ◆ Never Relinquish Lands Once Conquered
- ◆ Polygamy to Ensure a Never-Ending Supply of Soldiers
- ◆ Don't Criticize or Leave Islam
- ◆ The Way to Paradise in Arabic
- ◆ Praying & Praying
- ◆ A Woman's Plight
- ◆ Allah as Editor
- ◆ Violence Supersedes Tolerance
- ◆ No Right and Wrong, Just "Allowed and "Dis-Allowed"
- ◆ Subjugation of the "Infidel"
- ◆ Double Standards…One for me, None for you.

He ends with Islam's "Success" is a Threat to Global Freedom and Mutuality – The Missing Link.

This is such a brilliant exposé of Islam that I asked Citizen Warrior for permission to use it and he graciously authorized me to print it in full which is at Appendix B. I urge you to read it in its entirety.

Islamic Fundamentalism

Fundamentalism is not an Islamic monopoly. Fundamentalist groups have developed in most religions, including Christianity and Judaism as well as Islam, fearful that modern society intends to destroy their faith and their religious values. Fundamentalist movements see "the events of history as part of a divine drama." The Christian Right, "the first fundamentalist reform movement of the 20th century" sought to "drag religion back to center stage." Fundamentalist movements are rooted in fear and humiliation and share the belief that "secularism and liberalism are attacking them," and that the "modern world wants to wipe them out." They are an "expression of a great sickness of soul," a sign that "something is rotten" in the society that produced them, and they "are not peaceable."[3] When people think they are struggling for survival, they sometimes turn to violence in desperation.

Religion can help us be kind, sincere, and honest; but all too often its teachings are cherry-picked to support arguments against an opponent or antagonist. One could quote Deuteronomy 13, 7-11 for kill him who would have you worship other gods, but Christians are not out killing people. Most fundamentalists do not condone violence, but whether they are Christian, Jew, or Muslim, they de-emphasize the benevolent aspects of their faiths and stress the more militant or warlike. This leads them down the slippery slope to killing in the name of God and terrible distortion of their religion.[4]

Andrew Sullivan wrote about the importance of spiritual doubt in religion. "The alternative to the secular-fundamentalist death spiral is something called spiritual humility and sincere religious doubt. Fundamentalism is not the only valid form of faith, and to say it is, is the great lie of our time." He wrote, "True belief is not about blind submission. It is about open-eyed acceptance," and he referred to Michel de Montaigne, a writer in the 16th century, "that complete religious certainty is, in fact, the real blasphemy."[5]

> **True belief is not about blind submission. It is about open-eyed acceptance….complete religious certainty is, in fact, the real blasphemy.**
>   **- Andrew Sullivan**

In every religion, fundamentalism starts within the religion and only later blames some outside enemy as the cause of all their problems. The humiliating defeat after the Israeli attack in 1967 was a major blow to Arab nationalism, then Nasser's death in 1970, followed by Sadat's peace with Israel, led to an Islamic revolt against the West. But the West included "Westernization" of their own society, thus it is a Muslim civil war.

There is no word in Arabic for fundamentalism and there is no Arab group that refers to itself as fundamentalist or uses the term to refer to others.[6] As we have noted, it is a call to return to the teachings of the Prophet and his Companions in the seventh century. Fundamentalists are those who want to apply the more extreme verses of the Qur'an to the letter. It is anti-intellectual because it denies any discussion of or changes to the traditions, and it is anti-modernist because it denies any of the modern contributions in science, technology, or military affairs.[7] Muhammad's anger in the harsher verses, which abrogate the nicer verses in the Qur'an, is the root of the violence which captivates the minds of the fundamentalist Muslims.

What was initially called Islamic Fundamentalism was later, due to some political objections, "referred to as Islamism, integrism, or simply Islamic zealotry." Many came to see a need to distinguish between Islam the religion and Islamism as a "militant political ideology." Islamists were driven by "rejection of the pro-Western policies and hedonistic lifestyle of the Saudi royal family." They preached "moral revivalism through obedience to strict discipline." From this came Osama bin Laden with his opposition to the infidels and his "uprising against the West." "Islam is the solution" – the alternative to unjust democracy with its imperfections and human fallibility. It is a vision for those disappointed by nationalism: "If Muslims are not materially superior to the West, then they could at least be spiritually and morally superior to it."[8]

Bassam Tibi, political science professor at both Harvard and Göttingen, Germany, also distinguished between Islam and Islamism or Islamic Fundamentalism, the roots of which he traced back to the Egyptian Brotherhood in 1928.[9] He also saw it as a Muslim civil war against the Westernization of their own civilization. "The explicit goal is to spread Islamism across the entire Muslim world." He is quite specific about the "Islamic solution" – "The goal of the Islamic fundamentalists is to abolish the Western, secular world order and replace it with a new Islamist divine order... The goal of the Islamists is a new imperial, absolutist Islamic world power." After the 11 September attacks, he said, "Today, I must admit that the fundamentalists' war – up until now a war of values – has taken on a military dimension that has manifested itself in the jihad-soldier's terrorism."[10]

It is a quest for their place in the modern world. The fundamentalists want to return the economic, legal, and sociopolitical situation of the Muslim world to what they consider "pure Islam." They deny that Islam has been dynamic and adapted to changes over the centuries. They are anti-capitalist in that they are against materialism, greed, economic exploitation (no charging of interest), economic competition, monopolies, class privileges, and all other aspects of capitalism (which they equate to imperialism). They see pure Islam as the universal answer for equity and justice as the alternative to nationalism, socialism, and communism – which of course came from the West.

There is even a parallel with Marxism even though Muslims cannot accept the materialist aspects. "Marxism and fundamentalist Islam share a vision of 'holy war' of the exploited against the exploiters, or Islamically speaking, of the weak on earth against the corrupt and unjust. Eventually, the proletariat will win out over the capitalists, or, the faithful will triumph over those who have gone astray."[11] According to Ibn Warraq, "radical Islamists are dangerous because they are utopian and totalitarian: They seek to impose a worldwide theocracy. And this worldview derives from Islam itself."[12]

Even though they cloak their actions in religion, the fundamentalists are really addressing power, ideology rather than theology, which is more about philosophy.

Even though they cloak their actions in religion, the fundamentalists are really addressing power, ideology rather than theology, which is more about philosophy. It is also, to a lesser extent, a generational or class struggle, not by the poor people in the slums but by the urban youth who cannot find jobs in an uncertain world and have little voice in their governments.[13] They are frustrated as they watch the Muslim world drift or fall farther behind in the global economy. Thus the Muslim world, so full of potential wealth but with corruption and meager results, has become a breeding ground for fanatics who blame everyone from the US to Israel to Western civilization except themselves for their situation.

As Pakistani writer and businessman, Izzat Majeed, wrote in an open letter to Osama bin Laden:

"We Muslims cannot keep blaming the West for all our ills... The embarrassment of wretchedness among us is beyond repair. It is not just the poverty, the illiteracy and the absence of any commonly accepted social contract that define our sense of wretchedness; it is, rather, the increasing awareness among us that we have failed as a civil society by not confronting the historical, social and political demons within us ... Without a reformation in the practice of Islam that makes it move forward and not backward, there is no hope for us Muslims anywhere. We have reduced Islam to the organized hypocrisy of state-sponsored mullahism. For more than a thousand years Islam has stood still because the mullahs, who became de facto clergy instead of genuine scholars, close the door on *itijhad* [reinterpreting Islam in light of modernity] and no one came forward with an evolving application of the message of the Holy Quran. All the mullahs tell you today is how to go back a millennium. We have not been able to evolve a dynamic practice to bring Islam to the people in the language of their own specific era...Oxford and Cambridge were the "madrassas" of Christendom in the thirteenth century. Look where they are today – among the leading institutions of education in the world. Where are our institutions of learning?"[14]

We produce practically nothing on our own, we can do almost nothing for ourselves, we cannot even manage our wealth.
- Dr. Mahathir bin Mohammed, former Prime Minister of Malaysia[15]

Khomeinism

As in any religion, Islamic Fundamentalists come in various sects and groups. One which completely changed the scene and encouraged more was the revolution led by Ayatollah Ruhollah Khomeini in Iran. His brand is more accurately referred to as **Khomeinism** which is particularly fanatical. "But Khomeini was not a 'fundamentalist' who called for a return to the 'pure' Islam of the Prophet's time. What he preached and practiced was of his own making, far away from the Islam of Muhammad."[16] He called for the Velayat-e Faqih (Rule of the Jurisprudent or regime of Iran's mullahs), a theocratic government under senior Shiite clerics. Khomeiniism was a demagogic, medieval reign of terror of murder and rape. Rape and torture are still sanctioned according to an ayatollah and President Mahmoud Ahmadinejad.[17] Khomeini was an interesting tyrant in history. It is amazing that he can be idolized here in the US a quarter century after his revolution, yet Muslims in Dearborn, Michigan carried large photos of him at an anti-America rally (also anti-Israel) in November 2004. Shortly thereafter, a "Tribute to the Great Islamic Visionary" was held in Irving, Texas (outside Dallas) by the Metroplex Organization of Muslims in North Texas. How could Americans honor such a man? His rebuke to the concept that Islam is a religion of peace is quite explicit:

"Those who know nothing of Islam pretend that Islam counsels against war. Those [who say this] are witless. Islam says: Kill all the unbelievers just as they would kill you all! Does this mean that Muslims should sit back until they are devoured by [the unbelievers]? Islam says: Kill them, put them to the sword and scatter [their armies].... Islam says: Whatever good there is exists thanks to the sword and in the shadow of the sword! People cannot be made obedient except with the sword! The sword is the key to Paradise, which can be opened only for the Holy Warriors! There are hundreds of other [Qur'anic] psalms and Hadiths [sayings of the Prophet] urging Muslims to value war and to fight. Does all this mean that Islam is a religion that prevents men from waging war? I spit upon those foolish souls who make such a claim."[18]

Khomeini's views on law, or sharia, are not what we consider the rule of law. The Islamic Republic of Iran's delegate to the UN in 1985, Sa'id Raja'i-Khorassani, stated that "the very concept of human rights was a 'Judeo-Christian invention' and inadmissible in Islam.... According to Ayatollah Khomeini, one of the shah's 'most despicable sins' was the fact that Iran was one of the original group of nations that drafted and approved the Universal Declaration of Human Rights."[19] That does raise concerns about Muslims accepting other religions and the rule of law.

Religion and government will both exist in greater purity, the less they are mixed together.

- James Madison

Khomeini was the first to wield both religious and political power in a Muslim state since 1258 when the Mongols sacked Baghdad. He was a tyrant who brutally committed atrocities in the name of Islam. He executed thousands, sent children through the mine fields in the Iran-Iraq War, and permitted "the guards to drain the blood of the Mojahedin before execution," and sanctioned "the rape of Mojahedin women on the eve of their execution."[20]

After Khomeini's death, the leadership concluded that Islamic Iran "could not survive without the spread of the Islamic revolution beyond Iran's borders." and "the only way to preserve their Islamic revolution was to foment Islamic revolution in other countries."[21]

Below are **Nine Danger Signs of Militant Islam** from an expert.

1. Justification of any Islamic Terrorism, Palestinian or otherwise.
2. Supporting or refusing to condemn Osama bin Laden, al Qaeda, Hamas, or other terrorists and terrorist organizations by name.
3. Promoting Jihad for Muslims to fight against what they determine "injustice" or "aggression."
4. Demands for Sharia law in the USA, or denying that Sharia forbids equal rights for women and members of religions other than Islam.
5. Demanding that Americans accommodate the public expression of Islamic laws, customs, and practices that conflict with, or are harmful to American laws, customs, and practices.
6. Denying that Muslims were involved in the terrorist attacks of 9/11 and other attacks around the world.
7. Refusal to cooperate with or inciting others not to cooperate with authorities or standard security procedures.
8. Branding progressive Muslims or Muslims with different opinions as apostates.
9. Refusal to interact, converse, or socialize with non-Muslims.[22]

The Poverty of Islam

The great Muslim era faded and died. Sadly, none of the Islamic nations has since lived up to its potential. Despite great wealth in some of them, they wander along on the edge of the Third World. A renowned scholar plainly stated that the "entire Moslem region is totally dysfunctional" and not because of the existence of Israel. He said the 22 Arab League states which stretch from the Atlantic to the Persian Gulf have a population of over 300 million, which is larger than the US and almost as large as the European Union before it expanded. They cover an area larger than the US or Europe. But with all their oil and natural resources, the Gross Domestic Product of those 22 countries is less than that of the Netherlands plus Belgium and equals only about half of the GDP of California. He also pointed out the terrible gaps between rich and poor, where money was made by corruption rather than in business, the social status of women worse than the Western World some 150 years ago, and a sad state of human rights. He noted a study by Arab intellectuals published by the United Nations that listed "the number of books translated by the entire Arab world is much smaller than what little Greece alone translates. The total number of scientific publications of 300 million Arabs is less than that of 6 million Israelis." Also birth rates are very high adding to poverty and cultural decline.[23]

We treated the Arab World as a big dumb gas station. As long as it kept the oil flowing and was nice to Israel, we did not care what happened to the women and children. Bad governance, rising unemployment, and soaring birthrate were killing the Arab future.

Jihad Watch came up with seven traits that characterize the dysfunctional societies of Islam:

- Belief in magic
- Belief in conspiracies
- Lack of innovation
- Lack of devotion to non-family/non-tribal/non-clan organizations
- Lack of empowerment of women
- Lack of skilled labor
- Lack of meritocracy.[24]

The complete submission to Allah comes with a price – freedom is incompatible with this doctrine. The entire concept of democracy, equality, and human rights is totally unacceptable to the followers of Muhammad. Moism is based on inequality: the difference between believers and unbelievers; Muslims are supposedly to be treated with compassion (not always done), while non-Muslims (kafirs, infidels) are to be converted or killed. The mosque and state are not to be separate because man cannot make laws over other men, only Allah can do that, via sharia. The total mind control, submission, of Moism precludes freedom. The severe predestination of Islam does simplify the religion but it results in a cruel fatalism.[25]

Human beings cannot be sovereign. Sovereignty is Allah's alone, therefore democracy must be destroyed as it posits man's sovereignty over man. Democracy is nothing more than a pagan religion. It is a form of *jahiliyyah*.

- Ayman al-Zawahiri

The battle between believers and unbelievers dominates Islam. It has no moral code similar to the Ten Commandments. Anything is acceptable as long as it is good for Islam. Evil is defined as anything that obstructs the advance of Islam. Lying (*taqiyya*) is acceptable if it means deceiving unbelievers and advancing Islam. Theft is approved as we have seen with booty, but is harsh for believers – "cut off their hands" (V:38). For killing, it is "slay the idolaters" (IX:5, II:191), but there is a double standard for Muslims in that the Qur'an states "it does not behoove a believer to kill a believer except by mistake" and the punishment is very light. (IV:92) There is no charity for the unbelievers. **There is no Golden Rule in Islam!**

Skeptical thinking and contemplation are not part of Islam. "By controlling the minds of men, Islam gains control over their bodies and it does this in order to create the 'perfect' society. Human souls are left to languish in this prison of mental bars." This is all encompassing and leads to erosion of freedom of thought or expression which means conformity to Islam.[26] This mind control is clear in Iran where the man who heads the Shia Taliban said, **"Democracy, freedom, and human rights have no place in Islam."**[27]

The murderous reaction to the Danish cartoons in 2006 showed that Islam is not only completely intolerant, but that it also has no sense of humor. As Khomeini wrote: "Allah did not create man so that he could have fun. The aim of creation was for mankind to be put to the test through hardship and prayer. An Islamic regime must be serious in every field. There are no jokes in Islam. There is no humor in Islam. **There is no fun in Islam.** There can be no fun and joy in whatever is serious." [Emphasis added][28]

Total submission to Allah (Muhammad) results in a religious fatalism which may make one feel pious, but also can be an excuse for not taking responsibility for one's actions. While we would question the sanity of anyone who claimed "God made me do it," Muslims regularly explain their actions, or inactions, or events as **InshAllah** (also In Sha' Allah) – "Allah's will." This justification for everything, good or evil, that occurs demands obedience not thinking, thus becomes the "opiate of the masses."[29] If what is good is defined as what advances Islam and what is bad is anything that hinders the progress of Islam, then morality becomes distorted. Morality becomes conformity or obedience. We can kill because we have been told we are superior and it is our right to kill.

IBM Syndrome:	**InshAllah (Allah's will) - the opiate of the masses!**
	Bukra (tomorrow) **Mumkin (maybe)**

Religions try to define reality; they serve several functions in society. They should exalt value; however, when the will of one man is raised to the divine level, we leave religion and enter ideology. Thus the will of Allah, or Muhammadism or **Moism**, controls the minutest aspects of life, emphasizing the material over the spiritual, effectively excluding values. Morality should be advanced but Moism does not have a guiding moral structure. If culture can be defined as being between the two poles of sentimentality and brutality, then "There can be no culture without self-control." However, in Moism, morality becomes expediency and obedience. Religions should encourage righteousness and higher values, but Moism submerges the individual and emphasizes the afterlife. We like to think that religion preserves wisdom, but Moism considers everything before its arrival as *Jahiliyyah,* the time of ignorance or pagan disbelief, and destroys it. Remember the 360 idols in the Kaaba after Muhammad returned to Mecca and the Bamiyan Buddhas the Taliban destroyed. In addition to religious and cultural artifacts, this rejection and destruction has included art, music, and literature. Religions claim to support social harmony and peace, but Moism created perpetual war against kafirs and even against Muslims who suffer extensively at the hands of fellow Muslims. Moism appears superficially to be a religion but its purpose seems to be only the "perpetuation of Islam."[30]

Islamization

Those who grew up during the period after World War I and during World War II and World War III (the Cold War) were not particularly aware of any Islamist threat. However, soon after the dissolution of the Caliphate in 1924, as we will see, the Muslim Brotherhood was created. The Wahhabis in Saudi Arabia already had a share of power with the royal family, but they did not gain much international influence until the arrival of the oil billions. The Salafis grew and eventually the Khomeinists became active. While the democracies were busy fighting Nazism and Fascism, and then Communism, Islamism was being rejuvenated. Those distractions kept us from recognizing the growing threat from Islam. In psychological warfare terms, we are losing the jihadi ideological war and, even worse, we have made fools of ourselves.

In psychological warfare terms, we are losing the jihadi ideological war and, even worse, we have made fools of ourselves.

Let us study the writings of three who lived in the system and know whereof they write. Walid Phares has written about the War of Ideas and Jihad for years, first in Lebanon in Arabic and then in English after he moved to the US. As we have pointed out, he noted that "The public – let alone the Government did not know that the jihadists have been at war with America and other democracies for many years before the Twin Tower attacks." Dr. Phares pointed out the fallacy of the label of War on Terror and "established that one major reason why neither the American public was aware of basic realities in the region nor the U. S. government was acting to counter the rising threat was a full fledged campaign waged by the jihadi forces, both financial and militant, to disable American and western abilities from perceiving, understanding and eventually countering the expanding menace." We have been completely outsmarted by those desert warriors! While we debated incoherently about something nebulous called a war on terror, the democracies have been in a war of ideas "since the 1970s at the hands of a bloc of regimes and ideological circles, whose main characteristics were and continue to be sympathizing with the jihadist ideologies and practicing authoritarianism domestically."

Dr. Phares wrote, "we need to identify the 'ideology' and what constitutes a threat within the components of this ideology." He listed the campaigns by the jihadi forces as three "Wars of Ideas." The first was the 1950s-1990s, with their expansion during the late parts of the Cold War. Most of the efforts were internal to the Muslim world but with the Wahhabis were able to start exporting their ideology because of the oil revenues. With the capitalist-Marxist clash keeping them busy, the Muslims were able to make advances in their world with the slogan "No East, No West, one and unique Umma." Yusuf al-Qaradawi, who we have already encountered, used his al-Jazeera sermons, to assert "Islamist awareness" and encourage the "spread of Islamist ideology" while the great powers were destroying each other. There was rivalry, of course, between Salafis who are Sunni and Khomeinists who are Shiite, but they found a common goal "against all infidels, liberal and progressive Muslims, the West, Communism, Israel, India, Russia, as well as against any polytheist Asian and African cultures." This first war of ideas "was essentially ideological and educational." Dr. Phares considers the US alliance with the Salafis in Afghanistan against the Soviet Union "the first strategic failure of the United States to predict the future" because they abandoned "liberals, human rights activists, and minorities to the advantage of the Islamists." The "1973 oil shock sent a strong message to Western industrialized democracies: hands off domestic affairs of the region's regimes."

The second war of ideas was 1990-2001. With the demise of the Soviet Union and democracy breaking out worldwide, the "Khomeinists, Wahhabis, Baathists, and other dictatorships in the region felt compelled to preempt potential democratic copycats." The Wahhabis and the Muslim Brotherhood launched the "most powerful battle of ideas in modern history. Their aim was to block the rise of awareness in the West regarding the necessity of backing the spread of democracy in the Greater Middle East and beyond." They spent "hundreds of millions of petro dollars" in Europe and North America. This money was invested "in the educational, media, and intellectual institutions in the West specializing in foreign policy, national security, and other related academic fields." They used "religious legitimacy" to block any criticism of jihadism.

This "cultural imperialism" by the petro dollar regimes was very successful. They 'targeted departments of Middle East studies, international relations, history and other political entities of American, European, and other Western campuses seizing control of setting the curriculum, determining the issues to research and teach and in may cases selecting the instructors and scholars.   Oil funding practically eliminated the study of human rights, democratization, minorities, feminism, and jihadist ideologies from Western academia."   The result was that graduates from these programs moved into the Foreign Service, the media, and teaching greatly reducing independent knowledge of the region.   Public opinion in the West was neutralized and any investigation into Islam or jihad was "met by a campaign of demonization and guilt imposition via concepts such as 'Islamophobia,' 'Zionism', or 'legacy of colonialism'."

Al Qaeda and Osama bin Laden split the Salafi movement by going public rather than the "silent strategies" of the early Salafis.   This led to Dr. Phares' third war of ideas 2001-2009.   The jihadi attacks forced a collision between those who blamed them on US foreign policy and those who tried to link the violence to Islamic theology or ideology.   The oil regimes redoubled their efforts to block any discussion of jihadism causing terrorism and that radicals in the Middle East are the cause of democratic risings.   They used the classical jihadi lobbying tool of charging any discussion of Islamic ideology as anti-Islamic and "Islamophobia."   According to Phares, "The gist of this campaign is to deter the United States and its allies from backing the liberal forces in the region under the charge of 'unilateral intervention in the affairs of other countries' while simultaneously blocking democracy forces in the Muslim world from reaching out to the international community under the accusation of 'serving the interests of imperialism and colonialism.'"[31]   The jihadists are winning.

I left Islam when I understood Islam is a sick and evil religion.

- Abdul Rahman

Now for the comments from a former Muslim who wrote, "I left Islam when I understood Islam is a sick and evil religion."   One interesting comment was "the greatest strength of Muslims is that they do not read any site or books that talk against Islam."   He asked, "Who will tell you the truth about Islam?"   Muslims, No.   "Muslims cannot even see the evil in Islam.   The West?   The gullible West has no clue."   His answer – only ex-Muslims.   "Muslims believe Islam will rule the world, very soon."   He added, "The constitution for the new Islamic Republic of EU and USA is under construction.   Welcome to 21st Century Islamic Warfare."   He wrote a list of items "Muslims are able to say with complete confidence:

American laws will protect us.
Democrats and Leftist will support us.
The UNO will legitimize us.
CAIR and MAB will incubate us.
The ACLU will support us.
Western Universities will educate us.
Mosques in the West will shelter us.
OPEC will finance us.
Moderate Muslims will fertilize us.
Hollywood will love us.
Koffi Annan will publish the politically correct sympathetic statements for Jihadists.
We will use your (West) welfare system.
We will take advantage of American kindness, gullibility, and compassion. When time comes, we will stab America in the back as we did on 9/11 and 7/7, the Islamic way. We will

say one thing on the camera (Islam is the religion of peace) and teach another thing (Quran 8:12 Terrorize and behead the infidels wherever you find them) to our children at home.

We will teach our children Islamic supremacy from their earliest childhood. We will take over Europe first and then the U.S. will be the next. We already have a solid ground in the UK, Holland, Sweden, Spain, Italy, Germany, and now in the U.S."

Rahman wrote keep your nukes and tanks, Muslims will build their military "by producing more babies." "We will use your (Western) values of kindness against you." No major media reproduced the Muhammad cartoons because they were afraid. "We now have unwritten partial Sharia laws in practice in the USA." As for the current discussions about sharia, "Using the Western legal system we will assert our Sharia Laws, slowly but surely."

Message to the West: until the West identifies, names, and warns the public who the real enemy is, the West won't have a chance to win this war. The real enemy is "Islam."
                                                                              - Abdul Rahman

---

His message is that "until the West identifies, names, and warns the public who the real enemy is, the West won't have a chance to win this war. The real enemy is 'Islam.'" As long as people like Bush and Blair, etc. "keep saying in public the blatant lie that 'Islam is a religion of peace' – we run the risk of losing our freedom."[32]

Bosch Fawstin is a writer and cartoonist who calls himself "a recovering Muslim." He wrote an article about non-Muslim Muslims and stated most Muslims "truly don't care about Islam," and because of "their silence and inaction against jihad that they're not on our side either." To him, "our problem is Islam" and "Islam wasn't hijacked by a 'small minority of extremists' on 9/11, it was hijacked by a very small minority of moderates whose embarrassment in being associated with such an immoderate religion leads them to engage in moderate truth telling about it, proving their irrelevance as allies."

He made an important observation "that Western analysts of Islam who are the most informed about Islam are also most critical of it, while those least informed are least critical." Also, "While it's true that jihadists don't represent most Muslims, they do represent Islam." He claims that out problem is not "Islamophobia," but "Islamophilia" – a scandal of "uncritical, uninformed, absolute defense of Islam by Western elites."

He ended with "This is war." "We can't be both for Islam and for ourselves." "War is the answer to jihad."[33]

What we have found, but refuse to recognize, is that Muslims are the real "unmeltable ethnics" who will not assimilate. The fact is that "there is no society that has received large numbers of Muslims that has not soon been confronted by an Islamic defiance of existing societal norms." "Muslims will not be 'melted'."[34] "Remember that it was Teddy Kennedy who wrote and sponsored the 1965 immigration 'reform' which opened the gates to millions of Muslim immigrants, since his bill was skewed not toward accepting migrants with skills and talents beneficial to the nation, but rather toward taking in large extended families in the name of 'family reunification'."

The following study reflects how Islamization progresses as the Muslim community grows.

Islam: Historical Roots and Contemporary Threat
Adapted from the book by Dr Peter Hammond

Islam is not a religion, nor is it a cult. In its fullest form, it is a complete, total, 100% system of life. Islam has religious, legal, political, economic, social and military components. **The religious component is a beard for all of the other components.**

Islamization begins when there are sufficient Muslims in a country to agitate for their religious rights. When politically correct, tolerant, and culturally diverse societies agree to Muslim demands for their religious rights, some of the other components tend to creep in as well. Here's how it works.

As long as the **Muslim population** remains around or **under 2%** in any given country, they will be for the most part regarded as a peace-loving minority, and not as a threat to other citizens. This is the case in:

- United States -- Muslim 0.6%
- China -- Muslim 1.8%
- Australia -- Muslim 1.5%
- Italy -- Muslim 1.5%
- Canada -- Muslim 1.9%
- Norway -- Muslim 1.8%

At **2% to 5%,** they begin to proselytize from other ethnic minorities and disaffected groups, often with major recruiting from the **jails** and among street **gangs**. This is happening in:

- Denmark -- Muslim 2%
- Spain -- Muslim 4%
- Germany -- Muslim 3.7%
- Thailand -- Muslim 4.6%
- United Kingdom -- Muslim 2.7%

From **5% on**, they exercise an inordinate influence in proportion to their percentage of the population. For example, they will push for the introduction of **Halal** (clean by Islamic standards) food, thereby securing food preparation jobs for Muslims. They will increase pressure on supermarket chains to feature Halal on their shelves -- along with threats for failure to comply. This is occurring in:

- France -- Muslim 8%
- Switzerland -- Muslim 4.3%
- Philippines -- Muslim 5%
- The Netherlands -- Muslim 5.5%
- Sweden -- Muslim 5%
- Trinidad & Tobago -- Muslim 5.8%

At this point, they will work to get the ruling government to allow them to rule themselves (within their **ghettos**) under **Sharia**, the Islamic Law. The ultimate goal of Islamists is to establish Sharia law over the entire world.

When Muslims approach **10%** of the population, they tend to increase **lawlessness** as a means of complaint about their conditions. In Paris, we are already seeing car-burnings. Any non-Muslim action offends Islam, and results in uprisings and threats, such as in Amsterdam, with opposition to Mohammed cartoons and films about Islam. Such tensions are seen daily, particularly in Muslim sections, in:

- Guyana -- Muslim 10%
- Kenya -- Muslim 10%
- India -- Muslim 13.4%
- Russia -- Muslim 15%
- Israel -- Muslim 16%

After reaching **20%,** nations can expect hair-trigger rioting, jihad militia formations, sporadic killings, and the burnings of Christian churches and Jewish synagogues, such as in:

- Ethiopia -- Muslim 32.8%

At **40%,** nations experience widespread massacres, chronic terror attacks, and ongoing militia warfare, such as in:

- Bosnia -- Muslim 40%
- Lebanon -- Muslim 59.7%
- Chad -- Muslim 53.1%

From **60%,** nations experience unfettered persecution of non-believers of all other religions (including non-conforming Muslims), sporadic ethnic cleansing (genocide), use of Sharia Law as a weapon, and Jizya, the tax placed on infidels, such as in:

- Albania -- Muslim 70%
- Qatar -- Muslim 77.5%
- Malaysia -- Muslim 60.4%
- Sudan -- Muslim 70%

After **80%**, expect daily intimidation and violent jihad, some State-run ethnic cleansing and even some genocide, as these nations drive out the infidels and move toward 100% Muslim, such as has been experienced and in some ways is on-going in:

• Bangladesh -- Muslim 83%	• Morocco -- Muslim 98.7%
• Egypt -- Muslim 90%	• Judea & Samaria (Israel) -- Muslim 99%
• Gaza -- Muslim 98.7%	• Tajikistan -- Muslim 90%
• Indonesia -- Muslim 86.1 %	• Pakistan -- Muslim 97%
• Iran -- Muslim 98%	• Syria -- Muslim 90%
• Iraq -- Muslim 97%	• Turkey -- Muslim 99.8%
• Jordan -- Muslim 92%	• United Arab Emirates -- Muslim 96%

100% will usher in the peace of 'Dar-es-Salaam' -- the Islamic House of Peace. Here there's supposed to be peace, because everybody is a Muslim, the Madrassas are the only schools and the Koran is the only word, such as in:

• Afghanistan -- Muslim 100%	• Somalia -- Muslim 100%
• Saudi Arabia -- Muslim 100%	• Yemen -- Muslim 100%

Unfortunately, **peace is never achieved**, as in these 100% states the most radical Muslims intimidate and spew hatred and satisfy their blood lust by killing less radical Muslims, for a variety of reasons.

"Before I was nine I had learned the basic canon of Arab life. It was me against my brother; me and my brother against our father; my family against my cousins and the clan; the clan against the tribe; the tribe against the world, and all of us against the infidel.

-- Leon Uris, *The Haj"*

It is important to understand that in some countries, with well under 100% Muslim populations, such as France, the minority Muslim populations live in **ghettos**, within which they are **100% Muslim**, and within which they live by Sharia Law. The national police do not even enter these ghettos. There are no national courts nor schools nor non-Muslim religious facilities. In such situations, Muslims do not integrate into the community at large. The children attend madrassas. They learn only the Koran. To even associate with an infidel is a crime punishable with death.

Therefore, in some areas of certain nations, Muslim Imams and extremists exercise more power than the national average would indicate. Today's 1.5 billion Muslims make up 22% of the world's population. But their birth rates dwarf the birth rates of Christians, Hindus, Buddhists, and Jews, and all other believers. **Muslims will exceed 50% of the world's population by the end of this century.** [Emphasis added.][35]

Scientists at Rensselaer Polytechnic Institute developed computer models of various social networks. They "found that when just 10 percent of the population holds an unshakable belief, their belief will always be adopted by the majority of the society."[36]

When just 10 percent of the population holds an unshakable belief, their belief will always be adopted by the majority of the society.
- Scientists at RPI

In an article that expands on Dr. Hammond's analysis, Bill Warner did an excellent historical analysis which clearly shows how the sunna is the basis for destroying civilizations. Bill Warner kindly agreed to let me include his brilliant work.

The Annihilation of Civilizations
By Bill Warner

"By the time Mohammed died in 632 AD, Islam had used persuasion and jihad to subjugate Arabia. **The annihilation of native Arabic culture is Sunna**, the perfect example for all times and all Muslims. Said another way, the political theory of Islam is annihilation of Kafir civilization. How well did this political theory work out in history? Is this theory of annihilation at work today?

"We have records of **Mohammed's last jihad against the Christians north of Arabia**. After he died, Umar, the second caliph, took Mohammed's jihad against the Christians and developed it into a war that conquered half of the Christian world. But this conquest was only the beginning of the political transformation. Sharia law was put into place and the Christian Kafirs became dhimmis. But **Umar was not able to conquer Anatolia**, the site known today as **Turkey**. For **centuries, Islam attacked Anatolia** and finally took Constantinople, now known as Istanbul, Turkey.

"Take a look at the demographic history of the annihilation of the Greek Christian civilization:

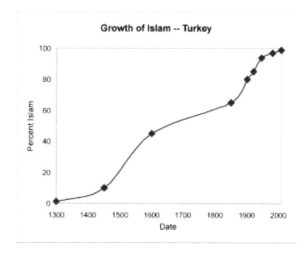

"This demographic growth chart of Islam has many things to teach us. The first is that the process **of annihilation took centuries**. Some people think that when Islam invaded, the Kafirs had the choice of conversion or death. No, absolutely not. Sharia law was put into place and the **Christian dhimmis** continued to have their "protected" status as People of the Book who lived under the Sharia law. The dhimmi paid heavy taxes, could not testify in court, hold a position of authority over Muslims and was humiliated by social rules. A dhimmi had to step aside for the Muslim, offer him his seat, could not carry a weapon and defer to a Muslim in every way. In all matters of society the dhimmi had to yield to the Muslim. **Over the centuries, the degradation, lack of rights and the dhimmi tax caused the Christian to convert. It is the Sharia that destroys the dhimmis.**

"Notice where the curve is headed — **100% Islam**, just **like Arabia. Today, Turkey is 99.7% Muslim. The Christian and Greek civilization of Anatolia is gone**. It is annihilated.

"What is tragic is that it seems that no one knows or cares. The **Fethullah Gülen Movement (Turkish Muslim Brotherhood)** of today pays for Christian ministers to go to Turkey and see an Islamic tolerant country where Christians live in beautiful harmony with Islam. And the ministers come back talking about what a wonderful society Turkey is and how well Christians are treated. After all, 0.3% of the Christians are still there in wonderful Turkey.

"Look at two more Christian lands—**Lebanon and Kosovo.** This data only covers modern times and we do not see the beginning as we did in Turkey. See where these areas are going. In short decades, **Lebanon and Kosovo will be 100%** Islamic and two more Kafir civilizations will be annihilated.

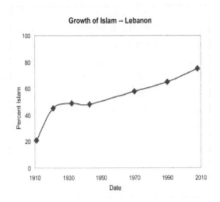
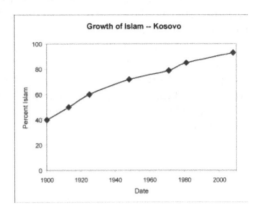

"It is a terrible irony that some Christians look at the destruction of Christianity and say that "those" were not real Christians. Indeed, that was the first reaction to the Islamic conquest of the first Christians, condemning those "other" Christians as heretics and saying that the jihad just pruned the garden of false doctrine.

"Now, look at the next two demographic growth charts:

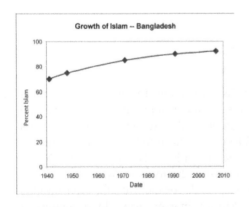
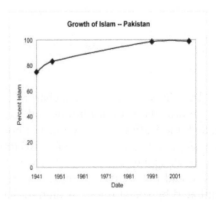

"**Pakistan and Bangladesh used to be Hindu cultures.** Now they are Islamic and the few Christians and Hindus left are persecuted every day. **While non-Muslims make great distinctions between religions, Islam sees them all as Kafirs.** Orthodox Christians are Kafirs, Evangelical Christians are Kafirs, Hindus are Kafirs and atheists are Kafirs. ALL KAFIR civilizations must be annihilated. It is Sunna.

"Let us look at one last feature of these curves. **Once it starts, it never reverses.** Islam never retreats. Slowly, year by year, century by century, the native Kafir civilization vanishes and is never able to fight back, never reverses Islam's gains.

"There is **one exception** to this law—**force and the acceptance of war. Twice in history Islam has been driven out in Spain and Eastern Europe.**

"Today we see another approach to dealing with the Islam of annihilation. We ignore the history of annihilation and say that **all we need to do is love Muslims** and we will live in harmony, a **wonderful multicultural civilization.** A history of **1400 years without a single exception** to the rule of annihilation and **we will repeal it with a smile and a hug.** All you need is love; love is all you need; **all you need is love;** love is all you need. Repeat that again and again, it will make a doctrine and history of annihilation go away. Actually, the way it works is that the history is never known. It is a cliché to say that **those who ignore history are doomed to repeat it.** It is a cliché but it is true. **We have our foot on the path to annihilation today because we refuse to know history.**

"What is the lesson? Islam, **peaceful Islam, is about destruction of all Kafir civilization.** Only if the Kafirs realize the **goal of Islam is annihilation of their culture**, can the destruction be stopped. **Islam is at war with Kafirs**, and Kafirs are trying to "nice" their way out of destruction. **Islam is at war, we are at nice.** Mohammed has a dream that is coming true while we sleep." [Emphasis added][37]

Allah is Not God

In the Chapter 4 we reviewed the concept of Allah and his Messenger. Allah created everything, knows all, and is unknowable; he must be feared and obeyed if you want to go to paradise or else you will go to hell. He is a bit bloodthirsty seeming to delight in the tortures of hell and there is only hate, no love. He provided the supernatural authority for legitimacy for Muhammad's commands. Dr. Wafa Sultan wrote in her book "A God Who Hates": "God, as described in the Koran…is highly strung, violent by temperament, lacking in foresight, capricious, fearful of being disobeyed or gainsaid. His fear is reflected in the nature of his commands, and he attacks without mercy and avenges himself evilly upon those who rebel against him." (p. 174)[38] Could this be a description of Muhammad?

> **Allah is "not a God of mercy and forgiveness, but a God of wrath and vengeance."**
> **- Omar Abdel Rahman**[39]

That is in sharp contrast to the beneficent god taught in other religions. The only source of information about Allah is the uncorroborated testimony of Muhammad. Jesus did not write the scriptures; the Bible was written by various authors, disciples who independently recorded his teachings.

The question came up in Malaysia in a fight over Christians using the word "Allah" for "God" in their Bibles which they had done for 400 years. Islamic scholars pushed their ire over Christians by pronouncing that the translation is incorrect and that the "use of 'Allah' for God must stop because it may cause Islamic anger." There is a severe divide between Muslims and non-Muslims with Malay-language Bibles blocked in ports for two years.[40]

Some think Jews are arrogant, many think Americans are arrogant, but the most arrogant is the cult of Muhammad – deification of an illiterate person from a backward corner of the world with no books and a poor language who proclaimed he was the last prophet and his was the last religion and that there could be no other prophet or religion. **"Every Prophet was sent to his nation but only I have been sent to all mankind."** On top of that, he proclaimed that everything before him – scriptures, prophets, history, and art – was irrelevant and of no consequence and worse, it should be destroyed. History starts with Muhammad but history stopped in the 7th century. All before was ignorance (*jahiliyyah*); all since has no thinking, only total obedience. The Muslim mind was closed and there is only one basic criterion; does an action advance Islam or not? InshAllah! Allah knows best; he decides everything, he is not to be questioned, and his decisions cannot be appealed. This fatalism basically wipes out knowledge. "Islam is a closed system of self-imposed isolation."[41] Allah does not resemble the merciful god of other religions.

Allah appears to be a figment of Muhammad's creative imagination. The Sacred Law is not the law of Allah; it is the **Sacred Law of Muhammad**. Throughout the Qur'an, it is "Allah and his Messenger," but sometimes, it is just the Messenger. It bears repeating: Allah sent Muhammad, "The Qurayshite unlettered prophet, to deliver His inspired message to the entire world, Arabs and non-Arabs, jinn and mankind, superseding and abrogating all previous religious systems with the **Prophet's Sacred Law**, except for the provisions of them that the **new revelation** explicitly reconfirmed. Allah has favored him above all the other prophets and made him the highest of mankind, **rejecting** anyone's attesting to the divine oneness by saying 'There is no god but Allah,' **unless they also attest** to the Prophet by saying '**Muhammad is the Messenger of Allah.**' He has obliged men and jinn to believe everything the Prophet has informed us concerning **this world** and **the next**, and does not accept anyone's faith **unless they believe** in what he has told us will happen **after death**." [Emphasis added][42]

Islam is concerned only with the bodies, not the souls of human beings.
- Rebecca Bynum[43]

Mo's Nos

Anyone who is not or refuses to be a Muslim (Moist) – make dhimmi or KILL.
Anyone who leaves Islam – KILL.
Mock Muhammad – KILL.
Write poetry against Muhammad – KILL.
Draw cartoons of Muhammad – KILL.
Make movies about Moism – KILL.
Criticize Muhammad or anything in Moism – KILL.
Get in the way or hinder the march of Moism – KILL.
Criticize Allah – KILL.
Anything before me, *jahiliyyah,* state of ignorance – destroy.
There can be no prophet after me.
There can be no other religion after me.
Do anything I don't like, you will go to hell.
Muhammad did not like drinking, music, art, gambling, pork, dogs, etc.
Result: uniformity and conformity – NO thinking.

Logic Fails

If Allah created dogs, why are they bad?
If Allah created pigs, why is it wrong to eat pork?
If Islam is the religion of peace, why do infidels have to be killed?
If cause and effect are key to science, why are they rejected in Islam?
If art, music, literature, poetry are considered culture, why are they taboo in Islam?

If humor and satire are considered normal to most, why is Islam afraid of them?
If homosexuality is prohibited in Islam, why are there young boys in paradise?
If fornication is prohibited on earth, why are there 72 virgins waiting in paradise?
If Allah created wine and it flows in paradise, why does Islam prohibit it on earth?
If Allah created men and women, why do they have to be circumcised?
If Allah created woman with a clitoris, why does it have to be cut off?
If Allah is merciful, why does he permit jihadists to send a child as a suicide bomber?
If jihad is good, why are innocent Muslim women and children murdered by it?
If women are mentally deficient, why was Madam Curie so successful?
If a woman can command the French Patrouille, fly F-15s, the F-35, and command a space shuttle, why is it that women are "mentally deficient"?
If women cannot go out, why were women heads of government in the UK, Germany, India, and even Pakistan and hold many key positions in business and governments?
If Islam is the perfect political system, why is it that no Muslim country could go to the moon or invent the Internet?
Jews and Christians are despised in Islam, but who made the great inventions and discoveries? Muhammad could not have accepted a great man like Albert Einstein, but Jews have made enormous numbers of great inventions and discoveries, including many of the great medical discoveries that save Muslim lives.

Problem: The Muslim mind has been closed. Without a sense of initiative, innovation, risk, responsibility, and reward, people are mental slaves. Muhammad designed it that way; all dictators want order and obedience. Moism is based on the likes and dislikes of one illiterate Arab. Actually, he is the **most brilliant illiterate in history**. He has 1.5 billion minds in the chains of his cult who slavishly follow his every utterance and consider him the model of the perfect man.

He has millions memorizing a book which in its original form was a great epic story, but when Uthman got finished with it, it was a discombobulated, incoherent collection of unrelated parts. It is considered the word of Allah and cannot be changed or critically examined and the book itself, the paper it is written on, is revered and demands very special handling. That is cultish.

Conclusion

Muhammad pursued preaching and persuasion for 13 years in Mecca trying to convince people to join his new religion but he ended up with only 150 Muslims. His "religion" was a failure. He was driven out of Mecca and fled to Medina where his dictatorial political force brought wealth to the Bedouins by stealing from the caravans and collecting jizya from the dhimmis he created. In his last 10 years, he drove the Jews out of Arabia, subdued the Christians, and brought all of Arabia under Moism by the time of his death. This was the product of his political ideology and force, not religion.

So is Islam a religion of peace as President George W. Bush[44] announced or an ideology of war and domination?[45] The answer is probably yes and no. Judging by the first century after the death of Muhammad, with its world wide expansion by the sword, by the comments of the famous people above, and the repeated exhortations to fight the unbelievers and impose sharia, Islam definitely has been based on the sword. But the religion constantly refers to peace (the word *Islam* is derived from the word *salaam*, peace), but an Islamic definition of peace (when the world submits to Islam) and Islam supposedly has a long tradition of tolerance, so which is the real Islam? Based on the dualistic logic of Islam, it is both. "Both peace and violence advance Islam; both are good and true. Both are Islam."[46] "If the vast majority of Muslims are peaceloving people, do non-Muslims really have anything to worry about? Yes we do."[47]

There are moderate Muslims, but there is no Moderate Islam.

- Ibn Warraq

The problem with "moderate" or peaceloving Muslims is that they are irrelevant. They may just want to get on with their lives, work, take care of their families, and survive. But if they speak out against Islam, they face the threat of attack and even death. Whether it is Jihad by the Sword or Stealth Jihad, the objective is the same, imposition of sharia locally and then worldwide. The problem is that "A Muslim has no obligations to any nation state; he does not owe any allegiance to a particular country."[48] "Hence Muslims living in the West, where jahiliyyah prevails, cannot possibly wish to assimilate to Western societies – they have no desire to integrate."[49] As Fouad Ajami noted, "Radical Islamism has come to mock the very principle of nationality and citizenship."[50] We see this in Europe which we will review later in Eurabia.

There are some who recognize that Islam is too rigid and should be reinterpreted, but moderates and reformers in the world of Moism are largely marginalized.   There is a monumental obstacle due to "the fact that there is no culture of dissent or freethought, or a tradition of uninhibited exchange of ideas as in the West." Add to that the "whole culture of honor and shame," and the prospects for reform are remote. Ibn Warraq made the following observations:

> We cannot hope to reform Islam without attacking the fundamental tenets of Islam adhered to by Muslims of all colors and stripes, not just Islamists. We shall never make progress until we subject the Koran to the kind of analysis and criticism that was applied to the Bible by Spinoza in the 17th Century, and the great German scholars of the Nineteenth Century, such as Julius Wellhausen and Albert Schweitzer. We must embark on a series of translations into Arabic of works of Koranic criticism, of skepticism, of the great books of Western civilization. We must support the separation of religion and state, and secularists in the Islamic world. We must defend the religious minorities in the Muslim world: by according non-Muslims their human rights, Muslims would already be on their way to secularism.[51]

One of the only real reformers was Mustafa Kemal Ataturk, who rebuilt Turkey after the end of the caliphate after World War I. He recognized that Islam, as we noted in Chapter 2, and sharia were not appropriate for a modern state. "We must liberate our concepts of justice, our laws and our legal institutions from the bonds which, even though they are incompatible with the needs of our century, still hold a tight grip on us."[52] Unfortunately, Turkey under Prime Minister Recep Tayyip Erdogan seems to be trending back to fundamentalist Islam. He rejected calling Turkey the representative of moderate Islam. "It is unacceptable for us to agree with such a definition….Islam cannot be classified as moderate or not."[53] One of his objectives is to change the constitution to reduce the power of the Army which has been the guarantor of the country since Ataturk.

President Obama has led the effort to improve US-Islamic relations and called Al-Azhar University a "beacon of learning" in his Cairo speech in June 2009, even though the university is far from a beacon of free thought. Moism is in direct opposition to our founding ideas in the Declaration of Independence, that "all men are created equal, that they are endowed by their Creator with certain unalienable rights, that among these are Life, Liberty and the pursuit of Happiness." Moism sanctions inferior status for kafirs, women are subordinated, children are taught to hate, and criticism of Moism is punishable by death. Religious tolerance for Moism is strictly a one way street.

> **"Western democracies must recognize that we are facing a global threat from a supremacist political-religious ideology that is at complete odds with self-government, human reason and individual liberties. We must challenge the ideas and methods of radical Islamists at every turn, not make excuses for them, accommodate them or pretend that a serious threat to our freedoms does not exist."**
>
> **- Joseph Klein**[54]

It is the height of naiveté and stupidity to refuse to consider the threats of those who announce they want to destroy us, our institutions, and our way of life. How do we tolerate a religion that is intolerant of us? We follow the Golden Rule, but it doesn't exist in Islam. How can there be democracy when they consider Muslims superior to all others and that men are superior to women, and those non-Muslim are dhimmis. If Islam is really at war with the rest of the world, does one have to be destroyed? How can they coexist? We believe in reason and questioning but one cannot question Islam. Where does this lead us?[55]

AMERICA – WAKE UP!

It is time to label Moism for what it is: a totalitarian ideology like communism or fascism. Remove the protection of religion which it exploits. It is time to consider banning it. Monitor all mosques and close the radical ones (currently about 80%). Slow immigration of Muslims. Stop proselytizing in prisons by radical imams.

MUSLIMS:

> Throw off the chains on your minds.
> Set your people, including women, free.
> Join the world.
> Use your minds for the progress of mankind.
> Get out of Qom and Al-Azhar and do some real creative thinking!

The real point is that it makes no difference whether Islam is the perfect religion, just another religion, or an imperialist, arrogant, aggressive ideology or whether Muhammad was the perfect man, a less than perfect person, or worse. If Islam cannot gain followers voluntarily by its message, it has no right to force it on those who do not want it. Its imposition by force is unacceptable – that is aggression and it must be fought.

Notes

1. Delinda C. Hanley, "President Obama Hosts *Iftar* Dinner, *The Washington Report on Middle East Affairs,* November 2009, p. 56.

2. John S. Badeau, "The Arab Role in Islamic Culture," in *The Genius of Arab Civilization, Source of Renaissance,* (London, Eurabia (Publishing) Ltd, 2nd Edition, 1983), pp. 6-12.

3. Carlton Cobb, CNI Staff, "Karen Armstrong: How Religious Movements Prolong the Arab-Israeli Conflict," 20 November 2006; a presentation by Armstrong on Capitol Hill, 16 November 2006.

    See Bernard Lewis for a review of religions and the meeting of civilizations. He wrote that Christianity and Islam are the only two religions that defined civilizations.

    "For those taking the relativist approach to religion (in effect, 'I have my god, you have your god, and others theirs'), there may be specific political or economic reasons for objecting to someone else's beliefs, but in principle there is no theological problem. For those taking the triumphalist approach (classically summed up in the formula 'I'm right, you're wrong, go to hell'), tolerance is a problem. Because the triumphalist's is the only true and complete religion, all other religions are at best incomplete and more probably false and evil; and since he is the privileged recipient of God's final message to humankind, it is surely his duty to bring it to others rather than keep it selfishly for himself."

    "When two religions met in the Mediterranean area, each claiming to be the recipient of God's final revelation, conflict was inevitable. The conflict, in fact, was almost continuous." Lewis referred to the Christian Reconquista in Spain. Bernard Lewis, "I'm Right, You're Wrong, Go to Hell," *The Atlantic Monthly,* May 2003, p. 36. (We will encounter Reconquista again in Chapter 10 as some Mexicans strive to take back part of the USA.)

4. Karen Armstrong, "GHOSTS OF OUR PAST To win the war on terrorism, we first need to understand its roots," *MM* (*Modern Maturity* magazine), January/February 2002, pp. 44-47, 66. She also wrote *The Battle for God: A History of Fundamentalism.*

5. Andrew Sullivan, "When Not Seeing Is Believing," *Time,* 9 October 2006, p. 58.

6. Bruce B. Lawrence, "Muslim Fundamentalist Movements: Reflections Toward A New Approach," Barbara Freyer Stowasser, Editor, *The Islamic Impulse,* (London & Sydney, Crom Helm, in association with the Center for Contemporary Arab Studies, Georgetown University, Washington, DC, 1987), pp. 18-19.

7. Ibid., p. 31.

8. Wolfgang Günter Lerch, "Islamism: Back on the Map," *Frankfurter Allgemeine Zeitung,* Frankfurt, Germany, 16 October 2001, reprinted in *World Press Review,* January 2002, pp. 7-8.

9. For some current views on the Egyptian Brotherhood, see Damien Pieretti, "Islamism and Democracy in Egypt: Converging Paths?" *WRMEA,* March 2008, p. 40.

    Life has changed in Cairo since I first visited in the early 1970s and regularly in the 1980s. The veil was rare then but has become much more prevalent. The article about Alexandria sums it up – a college student covered head to toe in the library. "It is the way most of Egypt has gone." The great cosmopolitan city of Alexandria is no more evidently. Hamza Hendawi, AP, "Alexandria: Former enlightened city turns militant," *Reno Gazette-Journal,* 10 June 2007, p. 14C.

10. Lisbeth Lindeborg, "Osama's Library," *Dagens Nyheter,* Stockholm, Sweden, 25 October 2001, reprinted in *World Press Review,* January 2002, pp. 9-10.

11. Barbara Freyer Stowasser, *The Islamic Impulse,* p. 8. "And for Western youths, taking up Islam can also serve as an outlet for rebellion. A majority of converts, especially in Western Europe, are in their late teens or 20s. 'Islam is a kind of refuge for those who are downtrodden and disenfranchised because it has become the religion of the oppressed,' says Farhad Khosrokhavar, a Paris professor and the author of several books on Muslim extremism. 'Previously – say 20 years ago – they may have chosen communism or gone to leftist ideologies. Now Islam is the religion of those who fight against imperialism, who are treated unjustly by the arrogant Western societies and so on.'" Jumana Farouky, "Allah's Recruits," *Time,* 28 August 2006, p. 37.

12. Grace Vuoto, "Warraq Book Counters Assaults on Western Civilization," *Human Events,* 7 January 2008, p. 19, a review of Ibn Warraq's *Defending the West: A Critique of Edward Said's Orientalism,* Prometheus Books, 2007.

13. "We haven't questioned in a serious manner the underlying causes of the spread of extremism among the ranks of our teen-agers and young adults.

    We haven't asked ourselves: Why is it that the youth of the world use their time in their studies and in universities, or at the very least adopt innocent pastimes and approach the world with tolerance and affection, whereas our sons are disfigured by extremist, murderous, and dissident ideals?

    What is the responsibility of religious sermons? How have we presented our religion to our young?... What is the source of this culture of extremism?

    Did it spread to us by chance or is it deeply embedded in the methods of religious sermons, schools, and other cultural sources?" Ahamd al-Ruba'i, "Our Lost Innocence," *Al-Sharq al-Awsat* (Saudi owned), London, 11 September 2002, reprinted in *World Press Review,* November 2002, p. 9.

    Professor Fawaz Gerges, Sarah Lawrence College in New York, called these radicalized young militants "the jihad generation." William J. Kole, AP, "Radical Islam gives rise to 'the jihad generation,'" *Reno Gazette-Journal,* 14 August 2006, p. 1C.

14. Printed in the popular Pakistani daily *The Nation* in November 2001, from Tom Friedman, *The New York Times,* 16 November 2001.

15. Mark Steyn, *America Alone,* (Washington, DC, Regnery Publishing, Inc., 2006), p.135.

16. Mohammad Mohaddessin, *Islamic Fundamentalism: The New Global Threat,* (Washington, D.C., Seven Locks Press, 1993), p. xxiii.

17. Nissan Ratzlav-Katz, "Ahmadinejad's Imam: Islam Allows Raping, Torturing Prisoners," IsraelNationalNews.com, 1 September 2009. Ayatollah Mohammad Taqi Mesbah-Yazdi spoke of raping men and women prisoners. If the female was to

be executed, raping by the executioner was equivalent to the hajj to Mecca; if she was not to be executed, it was only equivalent to a pilgrimage to Karbala.

18. Robert Spencer, *The Politically Incorrect Guide to Islam (and the Crusades)*, (Washington, DC, Regnery Publishing, Inc., 2005), pp. 190-191.

19. Spencer, *The Politically Incorrect Guide to Islam*, p. 191.

20. Mohaddessin, *Islamic Fundamentalism*, p. 3.

21. Ibid., p. 36.

22. Lawrence J. Martines is a retired law enforcement executive from the Los Angeles Sheriff's Department where he dealt with extremist groups. He was a member of the RAND Corporation "International Terrorism Thinktank," Chief of Security for Hughes Helicopters, worked with various US Government agencies, including the CIA, and served as Director of Homeland Security for the State of Nevada. He has taught and written extensively on terrorism.

23. From a talk delivered by Haim Harari, Chair, Davidson Institute of Science Education, Past President, Weizmann Institute of Science, at a meeting of the International Advisory Board of a large multi-national corporation, April 2004.

   A UN Development Program with Arab Fund for Economic and Social Development Report, June 2002 showed why the Arab World was falling off the globe. The GDP of Spain is greater than that of all the 22 Arab states combined. There was a shortage of freedom (lowest in the freedom index), women's rights, and quality education. The population was expected to well exceed 400 million by 2020. It was not because of a poverty of resources, but a "poverty of capabilities and of opportunities." The Arab-Israel conflict was both a cause and an excuse. The whole Arab World translated about 300 books each year, one fifth the number of Greece alone. Research and development investment was less than one seventh of the world average. Internet connectivity was worse than sub-Saharan Africa. 65 million adult Arabs were illiterate (2/3 women). Average per capita output was greater than the "Asian Tigers" in 1960 – now ½ of Korea's.

24. "Why Muslim cultures lag behind – a Muslim perspective" 31 May 2011.

25. Serge Trifkovic, *The Sword of the Prophet*, (Boston, Regina Orthodox Press, Inc., 2002), pp. 66-67.

26. Rebecca Bynum, *Allah Is Dead: Why Islam is Not a Religion,* (Nashville, Tennessee, New England Review Press, 2011), p. 15.

27. "Cleric in Iranian holy city of Qom: 'Democracy, freedom, and human rights have no place' in Islam," Mesbah Yazdi in a speech reprinted in Rooz, an online Iranian news website, Jihad Watch, 9 September 2010.

28. Quoted in "What Muslim Leaders Say About Islam Dispels the Myth that Jihadists are a 'Fringe' Element," Citizen Warrior, 1 October 2010.

29. Bynum, *Allah Is Dead*, pp. 22 and 41.

30. For a full discussion, see Rebecca Bynum, Chapter 11 "Why Islam is Not a Religion," *Allah Is Dead*, pp. 141-147.

31. Walid Phares, "Jihadism's War on Democracies, a chapter in *Debating the War of Ideas,* edited by Eric D. Patterson and John Gallagher, (Palgrave Macmillan, December 2009).

32. "Warning to the West," posted by Citizen Warrior, 4 July 2011. Abdul Rahman is an alias since the penalty for leaving Islam is death. The ex-Muslims web sites are FaithFreedom.org and ApostatesOfIslasm.com.

33. Bosch Fawstin, "Non-Muslim Muslims and the Jihad Against the West," http://frontpagemag.com/2011/12/02/non-muslim-muslims-and-the-jihad-against-the-west/, Bill Warner, politcalislam.com.

34. "Muslims will not be "Melted'," Jihad Watch, 7 January 2011.

35. From *Slavery, Terrorism and Islam: The Historical Roots and Contemporary Threat* by Dr. Peter Hammond, percentages from CIA: The World Fact Book., 2007.

36. Nicolai Sennels, "Research: 10 percent for sharia can change a country into sharia state," Jihad Watch, 25 August 2011.

37. Bill Warner, "The Annihilation of Civilizations" 8 August 2011 www.politicalislam.com. Bill Warner is the Director of the Center for the Study of Political Islam, Permalink /blog/the-annihilation-of-civilizations/copyright © CBSX, LLC, politicalislam.com.

38. Babs Barron, "The Show Trial of Geert Wilders – Part 1," Citizen Warrior, 9 June 2011.

39. Rahman is the blind sheikh who was behind the first Trade Center bombing and the Islamic Group that assassinated President Sadat.

40. "Malaysia: Christians can not use 'Allah' to define God," AsiaNews, 22 July 2011.

41. Bynum, *Allah Is Dead*, p.30.

42. *Reliance of the Traveller*, v2.0.

43. Bynum, *Allah is Dead*, p. 15.

44. Abu Qatada, the notorious al-Qaeda-linked imam in Britain said "I am astonished by President Bush when he claims there is nothing in the Koran that justifies jihad or violence in the name of Islam. Is he some kind of Islamic scholar? Has he ever actually read the Koran?" Quoted by Diana West, speech at free speech conference in Copenhagen, 9 October 2010.

45. See Don Feder, "Top 10 Reasons Why Islam Isn't Exactly a Religion of Peace," Human Events, 1 September 2006. Nadeem Haq, "True Islam is a religion of peace and tolerance," and Hugh C. Newton, "Al-Qaida reflects Islam's desire for world conquest," *Reno Gazette-Journal*, 15 December 2002, p. 15C. George Packer, "The Moderate Martyr: A radically peaceful vision of Islam," *The New Yorker*, 11 September 2006, p. 61, about Mahmoud Muhammad Taha, the unorthodox Sudanese mystic.

46. Bill Warner, *Mohammed and the Unbelievers: The Sira a Political Biography*, (CSPI Publications, www.cspipublishing.com, 2006),p. 170.

47. Citizen Warrior, 18 June 2011.

48. Sayyid Qutb, *Milestones*, p. 124.

49. Ibn Warraq: The Westminster Institute (Virginia): Educating the Public and Government About the Ideology of the Terrorists, and Ways to Counter It (Part I), Jihad Watch, 13 June 2011.

50. Quoted in Steyn, *America Alone*, p. 89.

51. Warraq, Westminster (Part 4), Jihad Watch, 23 June 2011.
52. Joseph Klein, "The Global Radical Islamic Threat To Freedom: Ignore Or Excuse At Our Peril," http://www.newsrealblog.com/2011/01/06/the-global-radical-islamic-threat-to-freedom-ignor-or-excuse-at-our-peril/, 6 January 2011.
53. "Prime Minister objects to 'moderate Islam' label," *Hurriyet,* 6 April 2009.
54. Joseph Klein, "The Global Radical Islamic Threat To Freedom," www.newsrealblog.com/2011/01/06/the-global-radical-islamic-threat-to-freedom-ignore-or-excuse-at-our-peril/2/.
55. Thanks to Frank Pastore, 18 February 2007.

> **There shall not cease from the midst of my people a party engaged in fighting for the truth until the Antichrist appears.**
>
> **- Muhammad, M448**

> **War is about thoughts and words.... It is especially difficult for Americans to consider the connection, for the country as a whole does not seem to believe words and thoughts are very important. But how the world's fundamentalists read their holy books during the next one hundred years will be a matter of life and death for millions.**
>
> **- Kent Gramm, 1999**

Chapter 6

Terrorism

It is the duty of every Muslim to kill Americans and their allies.

- Osama bin Laden

Yes, I am a terrorist.... being a terrorist makes me a good Muslim.

- Marwan, suicide bomber in Iraq

There is no terrorist threat.

- Filmmaker Michael Moore, 26 September 2003

We have seen gruesome terrorism in the bestial fighting among the cartels in the drug war in Mexico. However, we were trained by the media about the word "terrorism" through the Israeli massive propaganda coup which successfully labeled all Palestinians as terrorists, which they then were able to extend to all Arabs. With the introduction of HezbAllah, and by extension their former ally, Iran, they were further able to extend the terrorist label to all Muslims, since Iranians are not Arabs. Most of us were relatively remote from the Palestinian problem but the word terrorism began to garner our attention after the various incidents in the Middle East in the early years after Khomeini came to power in Iran. However, they seemed to be rather random acts and most did not really become aware until after 9/11. The American media and Hollywood picked up on it to the point where it is ingrained now, with Muslims and terrorists being almost synonymous.

The fallacy of the use of the term was evident when Iran, which the US State Department designated "as the world's most active state sponsor of terrorism," hosted the "First International Conference on the Global Fight against Terrorism" in late June 2011. According to Iran, the US and Israel are "satanic world powers" which have a "black record of terrorist activities." Leaders from some 60 countries attended, including Omar al-Bashir, the president of Sudan who has been indicted for genocide and war crimes. UN Secretary General Ban Ki-Moon sent a message of support. Most distressing for the US, the presidents of Afghanistan, Iraq, and Pakistan attended. The presidents of Afghanistan, Iran, and Pakistan issued a statement to "jointly combat terrorism" after a summit prior to the conference. Ayatollah Ali Khamenei sent a message to the conference which included, "The diabolical calculation of the dominating powers is to exploit terrorism as a tool to gain their illegitimate aims and they have used it in their plans. In their view, terrorism is whatever threatens their interests. They consider those who are fighting for their legitimate right against occupiers as terrorists but do not consider their mercenaries and malicious groups who harm innocent people as terrorists."[1] As you can tell, the psychological warfare goes on with its war of words – in that best *1984* tradition of "Doublespeak," words mean what someone wants them to mean.

> **We have expressed our rejection of the term "Islamic terror organization." Bringing together the words of "Islam" and of "terrorism" is the biggest injustice that can be made to Islam.**
>
> **- Turkish Premier Recep Tayyip Erdogan[2]**

We already noted that this is not a war on terror since terror is a tactic. It is used particularly by entities which do not have the resources or manpower required to fight conventional warfare. Most recent wars have been between or among nation states. Insurgencies are rebellions against an established government by a group or movement. Even though we like to think of irregular or guerrilla warfare as being limited, it too has often devolved into terror in some form. The Viet Cong killed local officials in Viet-Nam, the Irgun and the Stern Gang bombed the King David Hotel and assassinated the UN representative Count Folk Bernadotte in Israel, and there have been many other examples worldwide including in South America and Africa not to mention the Middle East.

Of course, one person's Freedom Fighter is another's Terrorist. "Terrorism" is a political term that can be used by the colonizer to discredit those who resist – as the Nazis and Afrikaaners named the French and Black freedom fighters. The term "terrorism" is psychological – both the word itself and its objective. When Jews smuggled arms into Palestine to fight the British and the Arabs, it was called the War of Independence. However, when Palestinians try to sneak arms into the West Bank or Gaza, it is called terrorism. When the Haganah, the Jewish terrorist organization, killed British soldiers, it was referred to as a revolt. If Palestinians kill Israelis, it is called terrorism.

Al Qaeda

The last decade of World War III saw the fall of the Shah, the Iran-Iraq War, the tanker war, and the Afghan war against the Soviet Union. Almost immediately after the end of World War III, Saddam Hussein invaded Kuwait in August 1990 resulting in a unified allied effort, including Arab states, to expel him. A key element was the Saudi-US cooperation (the Joint Force Commander was HRH General Khaled bin Sultan in "parallel command" with General Norman Schwarzkopf) which permitted many foreign troops, Arab such as Syrians and Egyptians but also infidels (non-believers such as French, British, and Americans), to stage in Saudi Arabia for the operation into Kuwait. This was unacceptable for Osama bin Laden and his followers for three main reasons. They considered the Saudi regime corrupt and that it supported infidel governments, mainly the US, which supported Israel against the Palestinians, their fellow Arabs. To them, Israel was the Western vanguard suppressing the Arab Palestinians. Probably worst of all, the Kuwait war allowed these infidels into the holy land of Mecca and Medina. Osama turned his hatred first on the Saudis and later turned his wrath against the Americans.

> **Al Qaeda thinks it's got America pegged – an effete fleshy Sultan sprawled languorously on overstuffed cushions, lost in sensual distractions.**
>
> **- Mark Steyn[3]**

The victorious *mujahedin* fighters who drove the Soviets out of Afghanistan had returned home fired up by their new found power. Now they wanted reforms in their own countries but usually hit a stone wall, so they turned their jihad against their governments. Those efforts were met by brutal suppression in Algeria, Egypt, and even the Sudan. Finally the *mujahedin* who could not find enough fights at home ventured off to the wars in Bosnia, Chechnya, Western China, Dagestan, Kosovo, Macedonia, the Philippines, Tajikistan, Uzbekistan, Iraq, and then back to Afghanistan.

Even though Osama bin Laden's father made his fortune from his connection with the royal family, his son had long been at odds with the Saudi government. Nevertheless, he had offered his services to the Saudi government to defend Saudi Arabia from Saddam Hussein after the invasion of Kuwait, but his offer was refused. He was stripped of his citizenship and exiled from Saudi Arabia ending up in the Sudan (which offered him to President Clinton who supposedly refused to take him.[4]

The Sudanese Government eventually expelled him and he returned to Afghanistan where he set up training camps in conjunction with the fanatical Taliban which by then controlled most of the country. Osama bin Laden was a self-appointed leader who had bought his influence in the *mujahedin* war in Afghanistan against the Soviets (which the US perhaps unwisely supported in that we let all our support go through Pakistani intelligence). It was there that he set up **al Qaeda al Jihad** (The Base of Holy War) to train operatives from around the world. The name has been shortened to al Qaeda and, in a letter the SEALs found, bin Laden wrote that lopping off "jihad" had allowed the West to "claim deceptively that they are not at war with Islam."[5]

Bin Laden and his followers directed their hatred at several regimes: the sheikhdoms on the Arabian Peninsula plus Egypt and Jordan all of which were considered corrupt successor colonialists; at Israel, backed by the US, for its theft of Palestinian land; and, worst of all, at Saudi Arabia, the keeper of the holy cities, which was "occupied" by non-believers, American soldiers. Osama bin Laden turned his wrath on the US and felt that the US cannot fight a war of attrition, so he saw the targets as the US economy and morale, "the media people and writers who have remarkable impact and a big role in directing the battle, and breaking the enemy's morale." A member of al Qaeda wrote "Fourth-Generation Wars" in February 2002. "The battle will not be limited to destroying military targets and regular forces, but will include societies, and will seek to destroy popular support for the fighters within the enemy's society. In these wars...'television news may become a more powerful operational weapon than armored divisions.'"[6]

The Clinton Administration was quite aware of the situation. During the transition to the George W. Bush Administration, Clinton's national security adviser, Sandy Berger, held a series of briefings and, in one, told Condoleezza Rice, his incoming replacement, "I believe that the Bush Administration will spend more time on terrorism generally, and on al-Qaeda specifically, than any other subject." The message was evidently not fully appreciated.[7]

Bin Laden spoke for a growing militancy that stems largely from the failure of Islamic leadership to adapt to a changing world.[8]

Shortly after the first air strikes in Afghanistan, Osama bin Laden referred to 80 years of Arab humiliation – that would have gone back to 1921. He was likely thinking of the 1920 Treaty of Sèvres after World War I which liberated the Arab provinces from Turkey and ended the Ottoman Empire. The 600 years of Ottoman rule had provided a degree of political harmony under the Sultanate and religious unity under the Caliphate. Evidently, to bin Laden and his ilk, the 1920 treaty was an original sin that created a political order in the Middle East controlled by Europeans, who then created Israel, just more Western interference. Is this a conflict between a nostalgic past and a mythical future?

Who are these "crazy" revolutionaries and where do they come from? The popular version was that "terrorists" were poor starving souls from the slums. However, bin Laden was the wealthy son of a very rich family who could easily have lived the playboy life in London or Paris. Instead he chose the life of the revolutionary, the heroic monk warrior in his camouflaged jacket with his AK-47 and living in a cave (even though there was no evidence that he was ever a warrior). At least for his last five years he lived in a large villa in Pakistan and may well have been in Iran before that. Although he was not necessarily cultured, he did represent two of the values of his culture: material wealth and religious fanaticism.

Ayman al-Zawahiri (born 1951), who was bin Laden's principal advisor and took over al Qaeda after his death, is another son of affluence. He comes from a prominent Egyptian family, his father was a medical professor at Cairo University and his mother is from a wealthy family. He trained as a doctor and earned a degree in surgery. He joined the Muslim Brotherhood when he was 14, evidently influenced by Sayyid Qutb. He led the Egyptian Islamic Jihad which was behind the assassination of President Anwar Sadat in October 1981. He was imprisoned but eventually got to Saudi Arabia, where he likely met Osama bin Laden. He merged his Islamic Jihad with bin Laden's al Qaeda organization in 1998. His failure against the Egyptian government (he had been sentenced to death in absentia) led him to refocus on America which he hated for supporting President Mubarak, the Saudi royal family, and Israel.

Zawahiri continued his terrorist participation and by 9/11 had his book, *Knights Under the Prophet's Banner* ready and had it smuggled out to London for publication. He "sees democracy as the chief enemy, and argues for jihad against the Near Enemy [Arab governments] and the Far Enemy [The United States]." He sees democracy as a pagan religion that must be destroyed. The "enemy is everywhere" and "the battle for Islam must go global." "Without a Caliphate or Muslim super-state, there cannot be victory." He ends his book, "In our means, methods, and resources we must combine patience with infliction of mass casualties and the best method to do this is suicide attacks."…. "This confrontation with Islam's enemies must be to the last drop of blood." By 2009, Zawahiri was al Qaeda's "operational and strategic commander."[9]

We are in a battle, and that more than half of this battle is taking place in the battlefield of the media.

- Ayman al-Zawahiri

As it turned out, most of the terrorists do not come from the slums, they tend to be educated with many college graduates. Those 19 kamikazes who attacked America on 9/11 were more at home in the cities of Europe than the desert. Many of the most diehard followers of Osama bin Laden and Ayman al-Zawahiri were not born and raised in Arab countries but in Muslim communities in Europe, where they travel with ease and many are "Takfiris."

Takfir wal Hijra (Anathema and Exile) is an extremist Islamic ideology which provides a religious justification for slaughtering infidels, not only unbelievers (the hated kafirs), but even those who consider themselves Muslims, sort of Islamic fascism. Takfiris attempt to blend into host communities to avoid suspicion. To do so, they drink, carouse, and ignore Ramadan. They are the core of the hardcore and are assigned the most difficult missions. It is like a sect with brainwashing and extreme discipline. Many of the 19 perpetrators of 9/11 were Takfiris.

Al Qaeda is not a hierarchical organization and never was; it is more a social movement. Al Qaeda should be viewed as an organization of organizations, a collective oversight of some 60 different terrorist groups – independent contractors - scattered over 100 nations under al Qaeda's aegis as the Islamic International Front under a unified central command and ideology. A comparison would be that bin Laden, now Zawahiri, is the chairman of the board (his Majlis Shura) of a multi-national corporation.[10]

The successful raid by SEALs that removed Osama bin Laden may have left al Qaeda bloodied and perhaps near its end as Admiral Eric T. Olson, commander of US special operations, said, "but he warned the next generation of militants could keep special operations fighting for a decade to come." With new leaders like Anwar al-Awlaki who he said "understands American better than Americans understand him," "It will morph, it will disperse, it will become in some ways more westernized (with) dual passport holders (and) fewer cave dwellers."[11]

Polarization is encouraged in this ideological, pseudo-religious war and terror is sacramental to emphasize the apocalyptic aspect of this relentless march of radical Islam against the modern, secular world. There are similarities with the war against Communism. Again we face an ideological mindset, this time with a religious façade, with a new version of wars of national liberation, preserve what it has (what's mine is mine; what's yours is negotiable), recoup lost lands, and which marches toward a Utopia where all the infidels are converted or killed.

Epitaph for Osama bin Laden "he destroyed much, he built nothing. His impact was like a footprint in the desert."

- Tom Friedman[12]

There are now several al Qaeda organizations. Al Qaeda in Iraq was fairly well decimated but remained active. The funding from overseas was evidently down so they were continuing their robberies and turning to extortion of businesses.[13] The efforts in Saudi Arabia were smashed by the Saudi government and moved to Yemen as **Al Qaeda in the Arabian Peninsula (AQAP).** This group has grown in strength and is in some ways the successor to al Qaeda. It put great pressure on the government of President Ali Abdullah Saleh, who was wounded and driven from the country and has specifically targeted the US. Saleh returned in September 2011 and agreed to step down and finally left the country in January 2012 for medical treatment in the US.

On 3 September 2010, a UPS cargo aircraft was downed outside Dubai. Later two packages were intercepted on UPS and FedEx aircraft from Sana to synagogues in the US. AQAP bragged about their work as having cost $4,200 and would cost the US billions in defensive measures in their glossy magazine *Inspire* (on line). In their very professional looking November 2010 special edition which showed a very distinct American flavor, they spelled out the details of their attacks. That probably was due to Samir Khan and Anwar al-Awlaki, the American Muslim cleric who left the US, settled in Yemen, was a leader in AQAP, and was the first US citizen to be put on the CIA kill list. Examples from *Inspire* magazine of 13 October 2010 include: "The Ultimate Mowing Machine" "mounting steel blades on the grill [of a pickup truck] then driving on crowded sidewalk." "Shoot up D.C. restaurants at lunchtime," and Samir Khan: "I am proud to a Traitor to America." In an odd move by the US State department, they contacted Khan's family and offered condolences for the death of this traitor.[14]

Yemen was falling into civil war with various factions rebelling against the government. In addition to fighting around the capital, Sana, foreign al Qaeda fighters were spotted in a town in the south held by jihadists.[15] Another concern for intelligence officials was information that AQAP was "trying to produce the lethal poison ricin, to be packed around small explosives for attacks against the United States." It was even discussed in *Inspire* in the fall of 2010.[16]

The same media group that publishes *Inspire* came out with a similar glossy magazine for women, *Al-Shamikha*, meaning The Majestic Woman. The "magazine's goal is to educate women and involve them in the war against the enemies of Islam." This jihadi version of Cosmopolitan magazine "mixes beauty and fashion tips with advice on suicide bombings" and told readers "it is their duty to raise children to be mujahideen ready for jihad."[17]

Another organization is **Al Qaeda in the Maghreb (AQIM)** which combined several groups in North Africa with emphasis in Algeria. With the growing pressure on al Qaeda in western Pakistan, some moved to Somalia, which has been without a government for over 20 years.[18] Bin Laden and Zawahiri had long supported **al-Shabaab al-Mujahedin** (Jihadist Youth) in its efforts against the various efforts attempting to bring stability to Somalia. It offered a new sanctuary and an opportunity to extend jihad into Africa. Al Qaeda's oldest training camp in Africa was in Ras Kamboni, surrounded by inaccessible swampy jungle at the very south next to Kenya. Militants from Somali were responsible for the attacks on the US embassies in Nairobi and Dar es Salaam as well as attacks on an Israeli hotel in Mombasa and an Israeli airliner.[19] In February 2010, Shabaab pledged allegiance to Osama bin Laden.[20] It came home to the US when we found Somalis living in the US: there are about 200,000 living in the US, mostly in Minnesota, were being recruited to go fight in Somalia.[21] In addition to the pirate attacks on international shipping in the waters off Somalia, the area has remained a hotbed with several US attacks and continued jihad activity.

The deteriorating image of AQAP and al-Shabaab led them to change their names. AQAP became **"Ansar al Sharia"** – translated as **"Army of Islamic Law"** but perhaps better translated as **"Sharia Helpers"** – since Helpers were those who aided Muhammad in Medina. Al-Shabaab became **"Imaarah Islamiya"** – **"The Islamic Authority."** There were reportedly over 1,000 foreign fighters in Yemen, four times the number in the tribal areas of Pakistan, and 750 in Somalia.[22]

Organizations

Al Qaeda is not the only terrorist group and was not the original ideological organization for waging jihad. There are many different jihadi organizations around the world, including in the US. We have become familiar with some of them: the Muslim Brotherhood, Hamas, HezbAllah, Islamic Jihad, Abu Sayyaf (Bearer of the Sword) in the Philippines, the Armed Islamic Group (GIA) in Algeria, and the Khomeinists from Iran.

Tablighi Jamaat

However, one, the very secretive **Tablighi Jamaat** (Proselytizing Group – also called Preaching Association), is largely unknown. This was deliberate with no details so that people would think they are apolitical. They are not allowed to discuss politics while proselytizing. They do their missionary work like the Mormons with personal appeals and door-to-door "invitations" to join them in spreading the word of Allah. Their annual conference at Raiwind, near Lahore, Pakistan, draws about a million members, making only the hajj larger. The annual conference in the US draws about ten thousand and the one in England attracts about eight thousand.[23]

It was formed in 1927 in Mewat, India, near Delhi, by a Deobandi cleric Maualan Muhammad Ilyas Kandhalawi and is close to the Wahhabi-Salafi jihadist ideology. The movement does not consider individual states to be legitimate and their ultimate objective is "planned conquest of the world" in the spirit of jihad. Members of the Tablighi Jamaat are trained missionaries who dedicate much of their lives to spreading Islam around the world. "They rejected modernity as antithetical to Islam, excluding women, and preached that Islam must subsume all other religions." It benefits from large-scale Saudi financing and al Qaeda has taken advantage of the group for recruiting.[24] Dozens of the detainees at Guantanamo had been involved with Tablighi Jamaat.

Muslim Brotherhood

The **Muslim Brotherhood** (Hizb al-Ikhwan al-Muslimum) – the **Ikhwan** – was founded in Egypt in 1928 by Hassan al-Banna. The MB is the mother of many other organizations, including al Qaeda, but "the Ikhwan is by far the strongest and most organized." It is active in some 80 countries, including the US. In each of those countries, the MB has "an Organizational Conference (planning group), a Shura Council (legal body), and a General Masul (Leader) or 'General Guide.' The 'Supreme Guide' is the individual leader of the International Muslim Brotherhood (IMB) and is based in Cairo, Egypt." "The MB is the root of the majority of Islamic terrorist groups in the world today." Hasan al-Banna wrote, "Islam is an all-embracing concept which regulates every aspect of life, adjudicating on every one of its concerns and prescribing for it a solid and religious order." He recognized different levels of jihad but considered "waging warfare against the infidels is the highest expression of fidelity."

It is a duty incumbent on every Muslim to struggle towards the aim of making every people Muslim and the whole world Islamic, so that the banner of Islam can flutter over the earth and the call of the Muezzin can resound in all the corners of the world.
                          - Hassan al-Banna, founder of the Muslim Brotherhood[25]

Their objective is to establish sharia worldwide and reestablish the caliphate. Their **creed** is: "Allah is our objective. The Prophet is our leader. The Qur'an is our law. Jihad is our way. Dying in the way of Allah is our highest hope." Al-Banna was assassinated in 1949. The MB worked with the officers who overthrew King Farouk in 1952, but they later turned against Gamal Abdel Nasser and tried to assassinate him. He cracked down on them in 1954, dissolved the Ikhwan, arrested some 15,000 members, and executed some including "Sayyid Qutb, the spiritual father of al Qaeda." Many fled the country establishing the Brotherhood in Europe and other countries. One of the most prominent was Yusuf al-Qaradawi who is known as the "spiritual guide" of the Brotherhood and a leading Islamic legal scholar[26] who spent 50 years in exile in Qatar but traveled all over the Middle East, Europe, and the US before returning to Egypt in 2011.

The Brotherhood learned from Nasser's harsh reaction "the great virtues of patience and perseverance." They now stress that "Gradual action does not impose Islam at once, but rather step by step." They learned to adapt, play the political game, and not move too quickly. Nasser recognized that it is impossible to negotiate or share power with Muslim organizations that are committed to theocratic rule.[27] Brotherhood leaders referred to their founder, Hassan al-Banna, and his guidance to impose sharia in phases.[28] Unfortunately for our future, Americans and the US Government have yet to learn this lesson.

We are hearing more about the Muslim Brotherhood now because of its potential role in Egypt after the overthrow of the government in 2011 and the return of Qaradawi.

Jemaah Islamiyah

Most Americans are unfamiliar with **Jemaah Islamiyah (JI)** the mysterious religious group in Indonesia that is an al Qaeda affiliate. Abu Bakar Bashir, a boarding school chief who is its leader, has been compared to Osama bin Laden.

The JI was founded in the 1990s with the objective of establishing a Daulah Islamiyah – an Islamic state including Brunei, Indonesia, Malaysia, the southern Philippines, and Thailand. The ideology of JI is that of Darul Islam, which was a violent movement that attempted to establish an Islamic state on Java but it was broken by the military in the early 1950s. The founders "conceptualized the group as a covert organization that would topple the secular state through a combination of political agitation and violence." It adopted its philosophical underpinnings from al Qaeda, its "inverse triangle model" whereby a "broad network of social services supports a smaller jihadist core" from Hamas and HezbAllah, and a model of charities and NGOs from Saudi Arabia and the Persian Gulf emirates.[29]

> **The democratic system is not the Islamic way. It is forbidden. Democracy is based on people, but the state must be based on God's law – I call it Allahcracy.**
>
> **- Abu Bakar Bashir**

Bashir set up the Rabitatul Mujahidin (RM) in 1999 as the military arm of the JI. It has been involved in many hijackings, bombings, and bank robberies. The RM cooperates with other militant Islamic groups in Southeast Asia: Laskar Jundullah and the Majelis Mujahid in Indonesia (MMI), the Kumpulan Militan Malaysia (KMM) in Malaysia, the Abu Sayyaf Group and the Moro Islamic Liberation Front in the Philippines, JI in Singapore, and other radical Islamic groups in Burma and Thailand. Bahsir heads the MMI which was established in 2000 to fight for establishing strict Sharia law in Indonesia.[30] These various terrorist groups are not centrally directed and there are many loosely affiliated groups but with similar objectives.

The Islamic Republic of Iran

Iran's constitution spells out its continued revolution to spread Islam "inside and outside the country." Khomeini was deeply hostile toward secularization and modernization, and he established his ideology of **Velayat-e Faqib** (or Rule of the Jurisprudent) which "calls for theocratic governance under a senior Shiite cleric." His policy calls for strict implementation of sharia along 7th century lines.[31]

The **Islamic Revolutionary Guard Corps (IRGC)** was created quickly after Khomeini seized power and is charged in the constitution with "jihad along the way of Allah, and the struggle to extend the supremacy of Allah's law in the world." It controls their chemical, biological, and nuclear programs and its leaders and affiliates now own 30% of the Iranian economy. In addition to its large scale supply of missiles and arms to HezbAllah which regularly go through Syria, Iran has sent arms to Hamas and rockets and missiles to the Taliban.[32]

The **Quds Force** – "the regime's international terror arm" - is the liaison with foreign terrorist groups and works with criminal groups and drug organizations. It provides support to "al Qaeda, Hamas, Hezbollah, the Iraqi Jaish al-Mahdi, Palestinian Jihad and the Taliban." The **Ministry of Intelligence and Security,** one of the largest in the Middle East with some 30,000 people, collaborates with terror organizations worldwide. It is not really a ministry since it reports directly to the Supreme Leader. Its mission is to keep the regime in power bay any and all means.[33]

HezbAllah

HezbAllah (Party of Allah) was created in Lebanon in the early 1980s by the IRGC to further Iran's agenda. It is powerful in Lebanon and now controls the government. It has conducted many attacks on Israel and fought them to a standstill in 2006. According to the Israelis, HezbAllah has nearly 1,000 underground military sites in Lebanon – "some 550 bunkers, 300 monitoring sites and 100 weapons storage facilities" in 270 villages.[34] It killed 241 US Marines in their barracks in 1983 and was involved in various attacks in Buenos Aires and has extensive activities in Africa and Latin America, including the Tri-Border area (Paraguay, Argentina, and Brazil). It is heavily involved in the world drug trade and has a strong relationship with Hugo Chavez in Venezuela.[35] For an extensive review of HezbAllah, see Casey L. Addis and Christopher M. Blanchard, "Hezbollah: Background and Issues for Congress," Congressional Research Service, 8 October 2010.

> **We are not fighting so that you will offer us something. We are fighting to eliminate you.**
> **- Hussein Massawi, former leader of HezbAllah[36]**

By late 2011, HezbAllah appeared to be "in dire financial straits" due to the uprising in Syria which reduced its cash flow and Iran had "cut its financial aid to Hezbollah by 25%" due to sanctions. Also, their investment manager had embezzled close to $1.6 billion."[37] The ferocious crackdown on protesters in Syria damaged HezbAllah's image to the point that they felt compelled to move to Qatar or Jordan.

Hamas

The **Islamic Resistance Movement (HAMAS)** was created out of the Palestinian Muslim Brotherhood in Gaza in 1988. Somewhat like the US support for the mujahedin which backfired, the Israelis initially supported the charitable aspects of Hamas. It was in competition with Fatah in the West Bank from the start and won the 2006 elections, which the US had insisted upon, and in 2007 took over Gaza completely. Hamas receives support from HezbAllah and Iran and has been linked with al Qaeda.[38]

Hizb ut-Tahrir

Hizb ut-Tahrir (HT) (The Party of Liberation) was founded by a Palestinian lawyer and member of the Muslim Brotherhood and alumnus of al-Azhar in Cairo, Taqiuddin Nabahani, in 1952 and is active in 45 countries. It wants to "liberate Islamic countries from Western thoughts, system and laws" and destroy Western civilization, democracy, and the capitalist system. It advocates "Islamic solutions" such as sharia-compliant finance in the West – the US. Even though it is purportedly non-violent, its manifestos stress violent jihad and violence.[39]

HT targets university students and professionals "to persuade people to overthrow their governments." "It has been described as both a peaceful movement to restore one-time Islamic glory and a breeding ground for future suicide bombers." It failed in coup attempts in Egypt, Jordan, and Syria and is now banned in most of the Middle East.

HT is expanding in Asia aiming to unite all Muslim countries in a bloc under sharia. It is active in China where it is estimated to have 20,000 members. Indonesia and China consider it a greater threat than violence form terrorists. HT "is built along Marxist-Leninist lines with secretive cells as key building blocks." "Students" face "up to five years of arduous training and indoctrination to prove their commitment" before becoming members.

HT has been banned in most countries, but not in the US, UK, Australia, and Indonesia. It calls for the annihilation of Israel and attacks on our forces in Iraq and Afghanistan. "One flyer shows a decapitated Statue of Liberty with New York City aflame in the background." The State Department won't name HT as a terrorist group but the NYPD called it a "tier one extremist group."[40]

> **Al-Qaeda is only a part of a much larger and older movement which has plans to destroy our Western systems by all means possible, including but not only violence. This conflict is more dangerous than the Cold War, because our enemy believes that God is on their side, and is not afraid to bring about mass destruction including its own.**
>
> **- Ibn Warraq**[41]

There are now hundreds of terrorist organizations around the world not necessarily responsive to al Qaeda. There are over 40 alone in Pakistan. A major one is **Lashkar-e-Taiba (LeT)**, which was originally created by the Interservice Intelligence Directorate (ISI) of the Pakistani military for operations against the Indians in Kashmir and was responsible for the 2008 Mumbai attacks and perhaps again for the 2011 attacks, which now operates in Pakistan and has expanded overseas. It appears to be expanding globally and now has networks in 21 countries. "LeT is part of the 'al Qaeda compact' and is a member of the 'International Islamic Front for the struggle against the Jews and the Crusaders' established by Osama bin Laden on February 23, 1998."[42] Many of these organizations, like Hamas and HezbAllah, provide social services as well as armed jihad. They receive funding from various sources including charities. For instance, the International Islamic Relief Organization is a Saudi government sponsored charity. From orphanages to thousands of mosques, Saudi funds have had widespread influence in Pakistan and other countries.[43]

> **Infidels develop technology to enhance life; jihadists appropriate it to end lives.**

There are "thousands of terrorist-related websites," and Zawahiri called in a video for "cyber-jihad." "Terrorists are increasingly using online technology to plan and disguise attacks and there will be more cyber-terrorism."[44] As part of the so-called "leaderless jihad," modern communications (Internet, Facebook, Twitter) allow any individual or group to send out information or call for specific acts. A new one was the publication on an al Qaeda-linked website of a hit list of 40 Americans and calling for readers to target these Americans in their homes. The list included 26 with photos attached and included "Wall Street firms, political leaders, leaders with think tanks and contractors who do business with the military." It has already been discussed on another al Qaeda-linked web forum. The posting called for readers to post home addresses and one suggestion was to send package bombs. This was only shortly after bin Laden's death and followed calls by Adam Gadahn (al Qaeda's American-born communications chief and the first US citizen to be charged with treason since the 1950s) for individual attacks. The only question is whether a lone stranger will be motivated to kill.[45]

We will review the organizations that operate in the US in Chapter 7 and those operating in Europe in Chapter 12. What then are the goals of these militant Islamic groups?

Goals

Almost all the organizations have the same long term goal of establishing Islam locally and then eventually worldwide with sharia as the only law. In the short term, they have various goals tied to local circumstances.

> **In Islam, our sources are the same. All these so-called differences – Wahabi, Salafi – all this is meaningless. All are superficial titles.**
> **- Abdel Moneim Abu El Fatttah, Muslim Brotherhood leader**[46]

Omar Abdel Rahman is the blind sheikh who led the 1993 attack on the World Trade Center. For him jihad means killing the enemies of militant Islam (which is almost everyone who is not a militant), and if one does not have enough resources or numbers, then one has to turn to terrorism. He was brazen in not fearing the word "terrorist." "If the terrorist is the person who defends his rights, so we are terrorists. And if the terrorist is one who struggles for the sake of God, then we are terrorists. We have been ordered to terrorism because we must prepare what power we can to terrorize the enemy of god." He stated that "to strike terror" comes from the Qur'an and they do not fear being called terrorists.[47]

Also, there is the thrill of killing, which we saw perhaps with Abu Mousab al-Zarqawi. Stanley Crouch wrote about the thrill of the action of a bank robber. He sees that as a problem with terrorists who "become addicted to the excitement and lose all sense of politics, which makes them even more bold and dangerous." They lose sight of the purpose of their political mission. "Love of action. Love of murder. The thrill that will not submit to reason because with reason comes limits."[48]

Ayatollah Ruhollah Khomeini's goals were absolute mullah control in Iran and then "setting up an Islamic republic in another country" which he did not live to see although his target was Iraq.[49] However, this tyrant saw sharia as superior and must be imposed by force. "Islam makes it incumbent on all adult males, provided they are not disabled or incapacitated, to prepare themselves for the conquest of countries so that the writ of Islam is obeyed in every country in the world....But those who study Islamic Holy War will understand why Islam wants to conquer the whole world."[50]

Osama bin Laden's original objectives had been the overthrow of the Saudi and Egyptian governments. He only shifted his focus toward the US after the Gulf War. He proclaimed the World Islamic Front for the Jihad Against Jews and Crusaders and in his 1998 *fatwa* against America, he announced that it was the "duty of every Muslim" to kill Americans and their allies. He said there would be no peace "until all infidel armies depart from the land of Mohammed." (That is the US out of Saudi Arabia – all American military forces were later withdrawn.) Zawahiri was the strategist and consistently influenced bin Laden's thinking, so now they had a worldwide jihad.

Even though the spiritual leader is gone, what were bin Laden's objectives, which are not likely to change under Zawahiri? His goals were to purge the Islamic World, especially Saudi Arabia, of Western influence, overturn established Arab governments, restore the clerical rule of the ancient caliphate, and purify Islam by returning to the idealized time of the prophet.

When bin Laden claimed that thousands of children had died in Iraq due to US sanctions and stressed the mistreatment of the Palestinians by Israel, he received sympathetic support, particularly in the Muslim world. Bin Laden hoped to draw the Americans into a war between Islam and Christianity. However, terrorism repels some and does not always win support.[51]

Only days after 9/11, bin Laden and Zawahiri appeared on Al Jazeera TV stating "We will not accept that the tragedy of Al Andalus will be repeated in Palestine," comparing the expulsion of the Moors from Spain and the war against the Palestinians. Al Andalus is the Arabic name for most of the Iberian Peninsula captured by Islam in 711 and held for nearly 800 years until the Inquisition and Ferdinand and Isabella forced the Jews and Muslims to convert or leave in 1492.

In February 2003, he identified Jordan, Morocco, Nigeria, Pakistan, Saudi Arabia, and Yemen as "the most qualified regions for liberation." (Note the absence of Iraq!) But he stated no political platform, no plan for those states if the present governments were overthrown. For the rest of the world, his aim seemed to be revenge (another key component of fanatical Muslim culture).

In January 2004, bin Laden broadcast a "Message to the Muslim People" on Al Jazeera lamenting the decline of the Islamic World: "It is enough to know that the economy of all Arab countries is weaker than the economy of one country that had once been part of our world when we used to truly adhere to Islam. That country is the lost Al Andalus." To some scholars, "in modern Arabic literature, Al Andalus is seen as the lost paradise."

The attacks on America were to draw retaliation which would overextend the US forces; and, if Muslim governments support the US, they can be portrayed as traitors to Islam, thus enhancing the insurgents' authority. In his message of 29 October 2004 to the American people, he estimated that it cost al Qaeda only $500,000 to carry out the 9/11 attacks which cost the US an estimated $500 billion. In business parlance, that would be considered an excellent ROI (return on investment). He noted that it was easy to "provoke and bait" the US, "So we are continuing this policy of bleeding America to the point of bankruptcy." He repeated this theme of **economic warfare** in subsequent messages indicating he believed he could win a war of attrition because the US does not have the stomach or attention span for a long fight.

It is easy to provoke and bait the US, so we are continuing this policy of bleeding America to the point of bankruptcy."

- Osama bin Laden

Michael Scheuer, former chief of the CIA bin Laden desk and author of *Imperial Hubris,* said, bin Laden had "become, for better or worse, the dominant Islamic leader in the world, the only, really, heroic figure in the Islamic world" and his potential for bin Ladenism, his potential for growth" was "virtually unlimited because he's focused on American policies and on Western policies, to some extent, that Muslims believe are an attack on their faith and on their God."[52]

After Osama bin Laden was driven from Afghanistan and the Taliban defeated, he moved across the border into Waziristan, part of the uncontrolled frontier provinces in Pakistan. The area became "one big terrorist-recruitment camp," with the new moniker Talibanistan. Not all the tribal leaders were happy with their "guests." "This is a jihad dictated by outsiders. It is not a holy war. They just want power and money."[53] Even though he was initially in a remote area, bin Laden's communications showed that he was aware of what was going on in US politics. He obviously moved on. Presciently, it did not seem likely that he was in a cave because he seemed to have access to satellite TV and perhaps the Internet. He focused on anti-war sentiment in the US and acted as if it were Viet-Nam again for the US.[54]

In July 2006, bin Laden called for Abu Hamza al-Kuhajer, the successor to Abu Musab al-Zarqawi, who was killed on 7 June to step up the struggle "to transform Iraq into the center of an Islamic Caliphate."[55] Bin Laden continued to call for attacks on Muslim leaders and, in

2008, vowed to fight Israel for the liberation of Palestine.[56] "The Palestinian cause is the major issue for my (Islamic) nation. It was an important element in fueling me from the beginning and the 19 others with a great motive to fight for those subjected to injustice and the oppressed."[57] Even women were speaking up, probably via the Internet. Zawahiri responded to a question from a female that a woman's role was "limited to caring for the homes and children of al-Qaida fighters." That brought an outcry from women who wanted to be terrorists.[58]

Some times the threat of violence can be as effective as the real thing. In Afghanistan, letters appear at night on walls threatening death to anyone defying them. Letters are sent to individuals stating they know all about what they are doing and when the government falls they will punish them. Terror is psychological warfare and fear is a powerful weapon. Many police officers have quit, medical clinics have closed and schools have been burned. In one area, two police officers were seized by the Taliban for supposedly helping the government. In two hours, they were publicly tried, sentenced, and beheaded. Peace and security are critical for government and terrorists continue to disrupt them.[59]

There have been a number of theorists for jihad who have influenced al Qaeda. Bin Laden himself said that "His goal, for at least five years, had been to goad America into invading Afghanistan." Abu Musab al-Suri (real name Mustafa Setmariam Nassar), was a member of the inner council, escaped, and travelled to several countries. In Iran, he wrote "Call for Worldwide Islamic Resistance," 1,600 pages long, published on the Internet in December 2004. He saw the jihad being individual terrorists or small autonomous groups (**"leaderless resistance"**) before moving on to open warfare for territory to establish a state.

My goal, for at least five years, had been to goad America into invading Afghanistan.
- Osama bin Laden

Another was a Pakistani, Abu Muhammad al-Maqdisi who wrote "The Evident Sacrileges of the Saudi State." He issued a fatwa excommunicating the royal family – "a license for any Muslim to murder them."

Abu Bakr Naji, identity unknown – Tunisian or possibly Jordanian - stressed that there were political actions in addition to military actions. "Alone among Al Qaeda theorists, Naji briefly addresses whether jihadis are prepared to run a state should they succeed in toppling one." He was not too successful: "The truth, as Naji essentially concedes, is that the radical Islamists have no interest in government; they are interested only in jihad."

Fouad Hussein, a radical Jordanian journalist, in 2005 wrote about an al Qaeda master plan in his book. "Al Zarqawi: The Second Generation of Al Qaeda." He claimed that a key strategy was to drag Iran into conflict with the US to overextend its forces. He wrote that al Qaeda drew up a 20-year plan starting with 9/11, a stage he called "The Awakening" up until the US entered Iraq in 2003.

The second stage, "Eye Opening," through 2006, was Iraq being the recruiting ground for people to attack the US. "Arising and Standing Up" from 2007-2010 was to focus on Syria and Turkey and also to confront Israel. The fourth stage, to 2013, was to bring down Arab governments with attacks on oil facilities and electronic attacks on the US. Then a caliphate could be announced in the fifth stage until 2016. The caliphate would form an Islamic Army and instigate a worldwide fight to achieve "definitive victory" by 2020.

"The ideology of the new generation, comprising a mixture of ethnic identities, is alarmingly vague. Their only political goal is to return to the ideals of the seventh-century Prophet and his early successors; they spout messianic slogans about the caliphate and imposing Sharia, without a clear idea of what those goals entail. They categorically reject the possibility of a peaceful path. They believe that the world is divided between 'sons of light' and 'sons of darkness,' and that a fight to the end is the will of God."[60]

> **They categorically reject the possibility of a peaceful path. They believe that the world is divided between "sons of light" and "sons of darkness," and that a fight to the end is the will of God.**

Yassin Musharbash called the plan "al-Qaida's strategy for the next two decades. It is both frightening and absurd, a lunatic plan conceived by fanatics who live in their own world, but who continually manage to break into the real world with their brutal acts of violence." He wrote that the idea that they could "set up a caliphate in the entire Islamic world is absurd. The 20-year plan is based on religious ideas. It hardly has anything to do with reality." He wrote, "What is interesting is that major attacks against the West are not even mentioned by Fouad Hussein." He wrote that these attacks seem to "simply supplement the larger aim of setting up an Islamic caliphate".[61]

Lawrence Wright wrote a long piece about Dr. Fadl, born Sayid Imam al-Sharif, an Egyptian doctor, former cohort of Ayman al-Zawahiri, and one of the first members of al Qaeda's top council. "Twenty years ago, he wrote two of the most important books in modern Islamist discourse; Al Qaeda used them to indoctrinate recruits and justify killing." In his new book, Fadl was rejecting violence. "We are prohibited from committing aggression, even if the enemies of Islam do that." It was in a fax from Tora Prison in Egypt where he is under a life sentence.[62] Having been sent from prison, there is no telling how much coercion may have been involved. Fadl was a major (and brutal) theorist of jihad, so his revisions are a major threat to the movement. Zawahiri issued a strong rebuttal but there was a rebellion in the organization.

Techniques

How can Muslims with all the good aspects of their religion, including prohibition of killing in general and harming innocents in particular, commit terrorist acts? As in all religions, one can find a verse in a holy book to support almost anything. They do not have to cherry-pick the Qur'an for supportive verses about killing unbelievers, beheadings, etc. because there are many such verses and those verses remain in force. A second way is to "take an idea to its logical extreme." A lady at a Muslim convention explained, "that the Muslim terrorists believed it was okay to kill innocent Americans because their tax money supports the U.S. government, which supports Israeli military might, which has oppressed Palestinians." That logic fails, of course, because it assumes "that American taxpayers have direct control over how the money is spent and a choice about whether to pay taxes or not."[63]

Terrorists

There has been considerable criticism of linking Islam with terrorism as noted above by the Turkish prime minister. It appears that most Muslims are good peaceful people; however, except for the Oklahoma City bombing, most attacks in the US have been by young Muslims. We have had a few eco-nuts burning houses, but they usually do not kill people; and we have had a few letter killers with bombs or some chemical. But the people who hit the Munich Olympics, hijacked US aircraft, kidnapped people in Lebanon, bombed our embassies, Marine barracks, the World Trade Center, and butchered people were all Muslims mostly between the ages of 17 and 40 who proudly announced they were acting in the name of Islam and usually quoted the Qur'an to justify their violence.[64]

So to label them Islamic terrorists is accurate and does not mean all Muslims are terrorists any more than using the term Italian fascists means all Italians are fascist or that Christian Zionists means all Christians are Zionists.

Labeling can be important. Calling these criminals terrorists indicates their method of operations not their intent. Using the term "jihad" links them to their ideology. However, they are proud to be jihadis and using that term may only reinforce their self-importance. Some have suggested using the term "Muharib" or the colloquial "hirabi" or "hirabist" coming from the base word "Harabah" meaning barbarism or piracy. This would be a term of condemnation. Using the term "Islamofascists" is an effort to describe their ideology and intent in addition to their barbarous actions.

> **Labeling them "Islamofascists" describes their ideology and intent in addition to their barbarous actions.**

There are differing degrees of terrorists. Some are fighting for a particular cause such as Palestinians who want to be free of the Israeli yoke. The ones who are a real threat are from a different millennium. We should recall the Old Man in the Mountain the Crusaders encountered in the 12th century. He had a base, similar to al Qaeda, in the castle of Alamut, on a mountain at the south end of the Caspian Sea and sent missionaries out from his secret society, the Ismailis, to preach his goal of Islamic fundamentalism. His terrorists were called **assassins**, the *Hashishiyyin*, because cannabis gave them courage. The Old Man, Hassan-I Sabbah, "would amuse and terrorize visitors by ordering a few of his young men to jump off a cliff to demonstrate that they would obey his slightest whim." That view of death is still evident with the Islamic terrorist view: that you choose life; we choose death. They take a long view of history. No concessions will appease them because as President George W. Bush said: "There is no mutual ground between civilization and terror, between good and evil, freedom and slavery, and life and death."[65]

How are these terrorist operations funded? The money did not all come from bin Laden, but large amounts come from various wealthy Saudis. In Afghanistan, which is in some ways a narco-state, a large source is from drugs. But there have been the usual criminal means of bank robberies, fraudulent use of bank cards, large amounts from Saudi Arabia via Syria, plus charities, businesses, and tribal relations.[66]

One of the despicable aspects of World War IV is the anti-Americanism of the US media and liberals who constantly berate US conduct on human rights and attack as if the US was as bad as al Qaeda. An example is the "torture" at Abu Ghraib and Guantanamo which was heavily publicized, yet when an al Qaeda torture manual was discovered, the mainstream media ignored it. The manual is quite explicit in comic book form and much harsher than loud music or lights. The techniques include: "eye removal," "victim's head in vice," "clothes iron on skin," "blowtorch to the skin," "drilling hands," and "suspending and whipping."[67] Torture is not uncommon in the Muslim world as we saw with Saddam Hussein in Iraq and Khomeini in Iran.[68] Captured American soldiers have suffered this barbaric treatment but it is little known in the US due to the fanatical self-hatred of some Americans.

We have already noted the massacres during the early Islamic conquests. Attacks on civilians and suicide missions continued. Nur ed-Din had all the Christians in Aleppo killed in 1148. We mentioned the Barbary Pirates; from the 17th to the 19th centuries, they kidnapped thousands (perhaps millions) of men, women, and children and sold them into slavery. The slave trade was big business under Islam. Suicide bombers are not new; Muslim Turks conducted suicide attacks against John Paul Jones in 1788.[69]

Fortunately we have not had another major attack in the US since 9/11, but that is primarily a result of outstanding intelligence work. A rather large number of plots have been foiled, including a plot to attack soldiers at Fort Dix and a plot to destroy JFK International Airport. A major attack on Heathrow Airport in London was foiled by the British. President Bush mentioned several hijackings, and attacks on Los Angeles, ships in international waters, and an overseas tourist site that were frustrated.[70] There have been numerous additional arrests of prospective terrorists before they could carry out their tasks.

However, bloody attacks have continued in Iraq, Afghanistan, Pakistan, India as well as London, Madrid, Casablanca, Bali, and in almost every country with a Muslim community. The weapons in the terrorist arsenal run the gamut from kidnappings and shootings to weapons of mass destruction. Kidnappings can be used for ransom to finance the struggle, hold hostages, intimidate the government, or drive particular elements of the society such as academics, doctors, or businessmen out of the country. Soldiers on a battlefield expect to get into a fight, but people sitting in a café or shopping in a market do not. Striking them with random gunfire, or bombs planted in cars, trains, bicycles, or backpacks generates fear and loss of confidence that the government can protect them. Bombs can be set to go off with timers or be detonated remotely by the ubiquitous cell phone which has been widely adapted to triggering bombs.

We are familiar with land mines and booby traps which can be detonated by trip wires or sensors. In the Iraq War, we encountered a new threat, the IED (Improvised Explosive Device), a combination of some kind of explosives, mostly old artillery shells from Iraq's enormous stocks which were dispersed all over the country, and a fusing system set off by wire or remotely by a cell phone, garage door opener, or other electronic device. A later innovation was added, EFP (Explosively Formed Penetrators) which are shaped charges to defeat even heavy armor. Most of these are remotely detonated for the most effect at the proper instant. There were repeated reports and evidence that those devices were being provided by Iran. Added to this are VIEDs (Vehicular Improvised Explosive Devices) which combine the explosives to a vehicle which can be parked or rammed into a target.

Since there are significant Muslim populations in almost every country, they can potentially provide support and cover for terrorists. This blending in makes for an enormous intelligence problem. With globalization there has been a vast increase of moving products and money around the world, but it has also resulted in a massive movement of people. Governments are now more concerned than ever about their borders. America has two very long borders with about 500 million (or many more) border crossings into the US annually, including well over 100 million passenger vehicles, over 800,000 planes, and over a quarter million ships. Congress called for better tracking of people entering the US on student visas, but it is an enormous problem with some 600,000 students and 22,000 institutions.[71]

All of the 19 terrorists flying in 9/11 were in the US on legal visas, but only one was on a student visa. It is almost impossible to defend against conspirators with an ideological grudge and a kamikaze mindset.[72]

Suicide Bombers

If terrorists have rockets, they often have to be homemade and they tend to be inaccurate and ineffective as we saw with HezbAllah and the Palestinians, however they are receiving much more accurate rockets from Iran. The answer for poor rockets is the terrorist guided missile, the suicide bomber. Now they control the time and location of the detonation for maximum effect.[73]

A nondescript looking person with explosives wrapped around his (or her) body under their outer garments can get on a bus, go into a disco or café, attend a wedding, get into a police station or government office, or go anyplace where they hopefully can find a gathering of people and set off the explosives.

To get more bang for the body, then the bomber can drive a car, a truck, or even an airplane into the target. We have seen the effects of car bombs nightly in Baghdad and trucks on our embassies in Beirut, Kuwait, Dar es Salaam and Nairobi plus the Marine barracks in Beirut plus Oklahoma City here at home. The attacks on the World Trade Center and the Pentagon show the devastating power of a large aircraft with a full load of fuel turned into a small weapon of mass destruction.

We should not forget the airplane as a weapon. There have been numerous reports of men of Middle Eastern appearance probing airport security measures, staking out airports, and running test drills on flights. Up to 14 Syrians in one case boarded separately and seemed to not know each other but then congregated around the lavatories during the flight. In another case, an air marshal forced his way into a lavatory after a Middle Eastern man had locked himself in for a long time. The mirror had been removed and he was attempting to break through the wall to the cockpit. They are still probing and testing our systems.[74]

Tank trucks are a vulnerable target. A tank truck was stolen in New Jersey and some 10,000 gallons of explosive chemicals were also stolen. We were lucky those were not terrorists. Every business day, there are something like 50,000 tanker loads of gasoline being delivered, plus another 50,000 trucks on the road carrying hazardous materials. There may have been a Plan B for 9/11 - at least seven of the 19 hijackers had US commercial driver licenses with endorsements to drive tank trucks with hazardous materials. US authorities captured a terrorist who admitted he had planned to ignite a fuel truck in a busy New York City tunnel. We have seen tank trucks used as bombs in Afghanistan, Ethiopia, Iraq, Israel, Saudi Arabia, and Tunisia and the British Army thwarted a fuel tanker attack at Heathrow Airport.[75]

The Department of Homeland Security (DHS) issued a memo on 7 July 2005 warning that al Qaeda wanted to duplicate the Madrid train bombing in the United Kingdom or the US. They had the UK right. But New York City has 7 million commuters daily on buses, trains, and subways – three times what London has. DHS also issued a warning that buildings could be targeted by al Qaeda. One scenario would be to rent some rooms in a building and fill them with natural gas with an explosion triggered by a timer in the ceiling.[76]

A 20-year old small, nondescript bomber from Abu Mousab al-Zarqawi's terrorist group, al Qaeda in Iraq, was interviewed by *Time* magazine. As he waited, he rehearsed his last prayer. "First I will ask Allah to bless my mission with a high rate of casualties among the Americans.... Then I will ask him to purify my soul so I am fit to see him and I will ask to see my *mujahedin* brothers who are already with him.... The most important thing is that he should let me kill many Americans." He was happy and said "I am ready to die now."

He was estranged from his family; his jihadi friends "are more religious people" always quoting the Qur'an. He had "embraced the jihadist worldview of one global Islamic state where there is "no alcohol, no music and no Western influences" although he conceded he had not thought much about what kind of life that would be. These volunteers undergo a training program "to discipline the mind and cleanse the soul.... supervised by field commanders and Sunni clerics." He had been reading about the history of jihad and of great martyrs. These volunteers are kept in isolation and have little say in the operation they will conduct.

This naïve young jihadi thought he was on the right path and did not beg off by calling himself a freedom fighter or anything. "Yes, I am a terrorist,... write that down: I admit I am a terrorist. [The Qur'an] says it is the duty of Muslims to bring terror to the enemy, so being a terrorist makes me a good Muslim."

> **Yes, I am a terrorist,... write that down: I admit I am a terrorist. [The Qur'an] says it is the duty of Muslims to bring terror to the enemy, so being a terrorist makes me a good Muslim.**

One difference from Palestine is that the Iraqi bombers are rarely identified and are not celebrated. This does not bother him. "It doesn't matter whether people know what I did... The only person who matters is Allah – and the only question he will ask me is 'How many infidels did you kill?'"[77]

There have been more female suicide bombers recently and their motivations were varied. Some were involved because of "honor." A Palestinian mother of two blew herself up at a Gaza border crossing – it appeared her husband discovered she was having an affair with a senior Hamas commander. Adultery is punishable by death according to some Muslims. As we saw earlier, some were promised paradise and others as the only alternative to a forced marriage or disfigurement which could mean no marriage. Revenge is another motive. Hanadi Tayseer Jaradat, "a glamorous, well-to-do 29-year-old lawyer" from Jenin blew herself up in a restaurant in Haifa after plain clothed Israeli soldiers had raided her home where she had witnessed the execution-style killing of her brother and her fiancé.[78] Another technique was a Russian Muslim woman who was kidnapped and her daughter taken from her after her husband had been arrested. They threatened to kill her daughter unless she became a suicide bomber.[79]

There was an increase in female suicide attacks in Iraq; it seemed that they were short of able-bodied men and were desperate. Also, it had become more difficult to penetrate some locations due to stiffened security measures. They even resorted to using mentally disabled women; two women with Down syndrome, they may not even have known they were on a suicide mission, struck killing over 90 people. Their bombs were detonated by remote control.[80]

The power of the internet was shown again in March 2006 with a posting on a jihadist message board advocating targeting American sporting venues and other public facilities. The posting, "How You Can Kill Thousands of Americans with a Few Hundred Dollars and Three Men," proposed that suicide bombers attack a sporting event at various locations throughout a stadium to incite panic and create a stampede. The author recommended an attack on a sporting venue using three to five "blond or black" American Muslim suicide bombers. The bombers would employ handmade explosive belts hidden under their clothing. In order to avoid detection, the author suggested the bombing take place in winter when bombers could wear heavy clothing to conceal the explosives without arousing suspicion. According to the posting, one suicide bomber would detonate explosives inside the stadium to create an initial panic. The other bombers would subsequently detonate their belts at the exit gates when spectators are fleeing. Citing past stampeding incidents, the author believed that the combined explosions would create a panic that would kill far more spectators that the bombing alone. Islamic extremists in previous operations have used secondary attacks to amplify the casualties, destruction, and disruption of an initial attack. The result was much heavier security at sporting events with long lines for security checks, another economic cost.

Leave it to the Iranians to hold a most unusual conference. A three-day conference was held in Tehran in June 2004 sponsored by the Iranian government and its state-financed "Committee for Commemoration of Martyrs of the Global Islamic Movement," which the mullahs with a straight face bill as a Non-Governmental Organization (NGO). We normally associate NGOs with humanitarian relief and peaceful advocacy work. So it is unusual that a NGO is involved with recruiting "suicide volunteers" to send overseas to strike at "world arrogance."

As always, it began following Friday prayers at mosques with calls to join the "Army of Martyrs." Tens of thousands of registration forms were distributed at local Islamic universities to attract prospective male and female suicide attackers. According to the Tehran-based daily *Sharq*, the conference provided a forum for volunteers to register their names for suicide attacks; supposedly more than 10,000 candidates from around the world signed up.

The conference was held in a government-owned hall where Brigadier General Sardar Salami, Director of Operations for the Revolutionary Guards, delivered the keynote speech, "Suicide Operations: A Security and Military Strategy Perspective." "Sometimes, creating a tactical incident brings about strategic results. As you see, the explosion of two World Trade Center towers divided history to before and after [11 September], and with this minor incident, policy of the United States and other world and regional powers changed."

In an indirect reference to Iran's nuclear weapons program, Salami added: "The Americans now know that the Muslims with tendencies for suicide missions have acquired new technology and have technological capabilities which have caused more fear for them."

Another high ranking Revolutionary Guards commander made an interesting comment about NGOs and where the power lies in Iran, when he stated: "Since the Committee for Commemoration of Martyrs is an NGO, it does not need to ask for permission of the country's military institutions if it decides to carry out an operation. Their operations would be similar to those by Palestinians and have nothing to do with the regime in Iran."

Hassan Abbassi, a top official of the Revolutionary Guards, the conference's closing speaker, attempted to rationalize Iran's support of terrorism in a speech, "Suicide Operations: The Last Resort." He called terrorism "asymmetric defense," and added: "If Muslims create fear in the heathen world, this fear is sacred; it is not terrorism or violence."

Abbassi made a fantastic statement at the Technical College of Tehran in May: "We have identified some 29 weak points for attacks in the U.S. and in the West. We intend to explode some 6,000 American atomic warheads. We have shared our intelligence with other guerilla groups and we shall utilize them as well. We have contacted the Mexicans and the Argentineans and will work with anyone who has an axe to grind with America."[81]

There was a split in the Muslim leadership over whether suicide attacks are forbidden by religious law. Some have come out with a strong "yes,' while others have said "not always." The exception according to some clerics is for strikes against an occupying power. That leaves it unclear and is perhaps why Muslim radicals can still recruit disaffected youths to be human bombs.[82]

Beheadings

Beheading is also not new in history in that it was common throughout the millennia from the Mongols to even the French guillotine, but it has been part of Islam from the earliest days of Muhammad. In the current context, the jihadists are extremely media savvy as we have seen with their use of the Internet, Facebook, Twitter, and al Jazeera television, and beheadings are the real shock and awe and their psychological impact is magnified.

For American television audiences, it started with the beheading of Daniel Pearl, the *Wall Street Journal* reporter, in Pakistan in 2002. The brutality peaked in Iraq with Abu Mousab al-Zarqawi himself pushing Nicholas Berg down on his side and putting a large knife to his neck and then cutting off his head as you could hear him scream and the killers shouted

"Allahu akbar!" – "Allah is Great!" These murderers proudly flaunted their barbaric act on the Internet around the world.

Paul Johnson Jr, an American engineer, was beheaded in Saudi Arabia a month later and more foreigners, including US soldiers, have been beheaded since, most grotesquely displayed on the Internet.

There had previously been decapitations in Algeria, Chechnya, Kashmir, and the Philippines, but the brutal beheadings in Iraq seem to have inspired radicals in other parts of the world who were attracted to the shock value of these horrifying attacks and the vast publicity they drew. There were what appeared to by copycat attacks with beheadings or throat slittings in Haiti, the Netherlands, and Thailand[83] plus the grotesque beheadings and dismemberments by the drug cartels in Mexico.

Iraqis have been regularly beheaded and we had the grisly example of a box of heads being left at a police station. Beheadings deliver a horrifying image with great shock value and provide spectacular media coverage. Therefore, since terrorism is part theater, it is an ideal terrorist tool.

These barbaric killings inspired some revulsion among Muslims with a debate as to whether Islam permits beheadings (however, it is in the Qur'an at VIII:12 "strike off their heads"). Many have spoken out claiming that it is damaging Islam. Mohamed Sayed Tantawi, Egypt's foremost religious leader said, "Beheadings (and the mutilation of bodies) stand against Islam."[84]

Terrorism at Sea

Most of the world's oil and natural gas passes through waters often infested with pirates. Since al Qaeda targets weak links in the global economy, terrorist groups have taken up piracy and pirate attacks have tripled. Al Qaeda is reported to own dozens of phantom ships which they have hijacked and registered with forged documentation.[85]

Pirates are part of our history as the US became involved with pirates in the early years of our country when the Barbary Pirates of North Africa preyed on US merchant ships after they lost the protection of the Royal Navy. When the constitutional convention met to replace the ineffective Articles of Confederation, one of the strong arguments for a federal government was the need for a federal navy to deal with pirates. Tired of having our sailors enslaved and paying huge sums in tribute (over 10 percent of our budget), the US Navy was established in 1794, and when Thomas Jefferson became president, he sent the fleet to deal with those pirates.

Oceans cover a large part of the world and some 50,000 large ships operate there carrying 80 percent of the world's cargo. The swashbuckling days have been replaced with modern fighters, many of whom are maritime terrorists, using speedboats, global positioning systems, satellite telephones, automatic weapons, grenades, and antitank missiles.

Piracy at sea has become big business (partly because ransoms keep growing larger) and is a worldwide phenomenon not only off the coasts of Africa, but also Indonesia, Malaysia, the Philippines, Yemen, and Venezuela. The major increase has been in attacks in the Gulf of Aden and the Arabian Sea, mainly off the coasts of Somalia, Yemen, and Oman with pirates operating hundreds of miles out into international waters. Some pirates are believed to have gone as far as 2,000 nautical miles from port. Exact statistics on piracy are difficult to obtain because the sea is an area of anarchy with little policing and because some shipping companies prefer not to report piracy in fear of their insurance rates being increased. There are two principal piracy watchdog groups which monitor pirate activity: the International Maritime Bureau (IMB) and the Regional Cooperation Agreement on Combating Piracy and Armed Robbery against Ships in Asia (ReCAAP). Several nations have deployed their naval forces and they have been successful in blocking some hijackings. These include the European Union Naval Force. The Russians liberated one of their ships and the US Navy SEALs freed a US vessel and the captain. ReCAAP noted a significant rise in piratical incidents in that region over previous years. There have been hundreds of attacks with many killed and kidnapped. These attacks are conducted with military precision and losses now exceed $16 billion per year.

From 2001 though 2004, successful hijackings ran from 2 to 8% of attempts. 2005 had 31 successful hijackings for a 33% success rate. Pirates were less successful in 2006 and 2007, but 2008 was a big year with 60 hijackings for a 45% success rate. There were 62 successful hijackings in 2009 but more attempts with a 27% success rate. There were 321 attempts in 2010 with 61 successful for a 19% success rate. There were 142 attacks in the first quarter of 2011 with 97 in the Somali region. That was a 177% increase from a year earlier and there were over 480 people being held hostage and about 50 ships in Somali waters waiting for ransom payment and release.[86]

Over 23,000 ships pass through the Gulf of Aden annually, including tankers which carry 40% of the world's crude oil. In April 2011, Intertanko, an independent tanker owners association, paid $13.5 million for the release of the Very Large Crude Carrier *Irene SL* which was carrying 1.8 million barrels of Kuwaiti crude worth $200 million. They held the crew for 58 days netting a 26,900% return on estimated expenses of $50,000. They even used the large tanker like a warship by pulling up alongside freighters as pirates fired down on the victims from the castle-like heights of the tanker's hull." It is estimated that the pirates have to raise about $300,000 for an operation to pursue a $4 million ransom, but the payoff is huge as packages of "new, sequential, Treasury-wrapped U.S. $100 bills" are parachuted in plastic floating containers to the ship. There are numerous fingers in the financial pie for these huge ransoms. The pirates get about 30%, 10% goes to the ground crew that watches the ship and hostages for weeks or months, 10% in bribes around the community and to politicians, 20% to the little backers, and 30% to one of the three big bosses who provide financing. This is big business.[87]

Crime syndicates have long supported piracy in Asian waters. Now Islamist terrorists operate in the Arabian Sea, the South China Sea, and off the coasts of Africa, in places out of control such as Somalia. Due to the efforts to freeze terrorist groups' finances, some of them have turned to piracy for funding. About 42 percent of the pirate attacks in 2003 took place in the relatively narrow 500-mile Strait of Malacca between Malaya and Indonesia. Its significance is shown by the fact that one fourth of world trade, including one half the oil going to eastern Asia by sea, and two-thirds of liquefied natural gas shipments world wide daily go through this strait. There have even been seizures by terrorists to practice steering but not docking much like the 9/11 hijackers who were interested in flying but not landing.[88] Both Jemaah Islamiyah and the Free Aceh Movement, radical Islamist groups from Indonesia, have been operating there. Increased maritime patrols and vessel security have greatly reduced the pirate attacks in the strait. Two more recent areas are off Malaysia and Venezuela.

We had a failed attack by al Qaeda in Yemen against the *USS The Sullivans* in January 2000 because the attacking boat sank from its own load, but they were successful in October when another boat hit the *USS Cole* killing 17 seamen. Just off Yemen, the French oil tanker, *Limburg*, was attacked. After that attack, Osama bin Laden warned of efforts to disrupt the global economy. Current world consumption is about 80 million barrels per day and there is very little extra capacity so oil has been a major target since 9/11 with attacks off Sri Lanka and in Nigeria, Iraq, and Saudi Arabia. The land areas can be protected to some extent, but the sea lanes are very vulnerable. Some 4,000 slow moving tankers transport about 60 percent of the oil for the world.

Opportunities for pirates are created because there are major choke points which these tankers have to transit. About 15 million barrels of oil pass each day through the Strait of Hormuz, which connects the Persian Gulf and the Arabian Sea, and it is only 1.5 miles wide at its narrowest area. Iranian President Mahmoud Ahmadinejad has threatened to sink ships in the strait to block it if Iran is attacked. Such an act would be a major blow to the world economy with oil prices shooting up. The Bab el Mandeb at the entrance to the Red Sea is similarly narrow and carries over 3 million barrels per day. The Bosporus is under a mile wide at some areas and about 5,000 tankers annually traverse from the Black Sea to the Mediterranean.[89]

Efforts to bypass the chokepoints have been studied. One would be to build a land bridge across the Isthmus of Kra in Thailand which would not only be 600 miles shorter to east Asia but would bypass the Strait of Malacca.

It is difficult to police the seas because of problems of sovereignty in national waters and international waters. Any type of security forces cannot be everywhere so only a ship can guarantee its own security. The two threats they face are hijacking and ramming. Ramming by a suicide boat is difficult to stop. Several actions have been taken to help against hijacking. Installation of high-voltage electric fences has been permitted since 2003 (of course not on oil and gas tankers). Since 2004 ships over 500 tons are required to have alarm systems which can silently transmit security alerts with tracking information and ships are now required to have their International Maritime Organization number embossed on their hulls. Arming of crews presents additional problems because crew members are often hired at various ports and there have been attacks with inside help by crew members.

Container ships present a serious concern since they deliver millions of containers annually to our ports. The threat of weapons of mass destruction from a ship includes dealing with containers to the possibility of ramming a large tanker into a port in a major city such as New York. Terrorists have gone to sea and it is a major threat.

Chemical and Biological Attacks

The world has already seen several chemical attacks. Letters with chemicals in them were mailed to members of Congress and we had a chemical incident in Florida. In 1995, five two-man teams from the Aum Shinrikyo religious cult rode on separate subway trains that converged on the Kasumigaseki station at the height of the morning rush hour in Tokyo and secretly released lethal sarin gas into the air. The terrorists took a sarin antidote and escaped. The toll was 12 dead and 5,500 treated in hospitals. A US review estimated that if the sarin gas had been disseminated more effectively, tens of thousands might have been killed.

That cult had a blind leader, Shoko Asahara, a self-styled Buddhist monk who thought he was the reincarnation of both Jesus Christ and Gautama Buddha. His group murdered more than a dozen political opponents and incinerated their bodies in specially built microwave ovens. They conducted their first sarin attack in 1994 using a car to release the gas in Matsumoto, west of Tokyo, against court judges killing seven and injuring 150.

The Islamic terrorists have not used gas yet, except for a couple artillery shells in IEDs which were probably leftovers from Saddam Hussein's regime and unmarked so that the terrorists may not have even known they were chemical shells. Nevertheless, it is a constant threat.

A man known to be linked to al Qaeda and evidently part of the Madrid train bombings was overheard in May 2004 describing for a woman a plot for a chemical or germ attack in America that would "wipe out an entire neighborhood." The Italians arrested the man, an Egyptian, in Milan and they had transcripts of bugged conversations and telephone calls which referred to the planned attack. According to Professor Paul Wilkinson, a terrorism expert at St

Andrews University, "Al-Qaeda is more advanced on weaponising chemicals rather than biological agents, so I should think we're talking about sarin gas, a cyanide-based weapon or a nerve gas."[90]

> **It is our right to fight them [Americans] with chemical and biological weapons.**
> **- Spokesman for Osama bin Laden**

The disturbing part about biological warfare is that now they can be custom built. In 2002, Eckard Wimmer, a German-born molecular geneticist created the first live, fully artificial virus (for polio but not like any from nature) in his lab from scratch. He made it completely from nonliving parts in his small laboratory at the State University of New York. He obtained the genetic code free off the internet and bought hundreds of small pieces of viral DNA online. The significance of this is, of course, enormous. Now almost anyone can build a virus, for good or for evil and there are no controls. As another geneticist said, "It's too cheap, it's too fast, there are too many people who know too much, and it's too late to stop it." Since 9/11, the government has spent about $8 billion each year for biodefense. Drugs have been stockpiled for each specific threat, such as anthrax. The potential to overwhelm the system presents an entirely new threat.[91]

Osama bin Laden's spokesman stated that, "it is our right to fight them [Americans] with chemical and biological weapons." Biological agents are not as spectacular as chemicals in that they take time to become effective due to incubation periods. However, an attack on the water supply of a major city or the spread of an epidemic for which we had no cure could do enormous damage even if it were slow to become evident.

Nuclear Weapons

Since our immoral terrorist enemies have shown they have no compunction about killing civilians, even their own countrymen, one of our biggest fears is that a terrorist group would obtain a nuclear device and detonate it in a city. They would not need to build the device but could steal or buy one. The enormous arsenal in the former Soviet Union has never been totally accounted for and several suitcase-size nukes were supposedly missing (there is considerable confusion and doubt about suitcase-size nukes). The Russians had some 8,600 warheads and material for another 80,000. The US has spent an enormous amount of money helping the Russians to improve the security of this vast arsenal. The good news is that since 10 years have passed, most of any rogue bombs are probably inoperable because these systems do require maintenance.

Pakistan is another possibility particularly if a radical Muslim regime came to power. It was Abdul Qadeer Khan, the father of their bomb, who was a kingpin in a black market for nuclear technology. The concern with Iran and North Korea having nuclear weapons is that they both have supported terrorist groups or might sell to anyone for cash. However, nuclear technology is such that the US could probably identify the source of any nuclear weapon which would leave the perpetrator vulnerable to retaliation.

Osama bin Laden long expressed interest in nuclear weapons and stated that production of one is "a religious duty." His spokesman, Suleiman Abu Gheith, made al Qaeda's objective very clear, "We have the right to kill 4 million Americans, 2 million of them children, and to exile twice as many and wound and cripple hundreds of thousands."[92]

> **We have the right to kill 4 million Americans, 2 million of them children, and to exile twice as many and wound and cripple hundreds of thousands.**
>
> **- Suleiman Abu Gheith**

It was belatedly revealed that a fatwa had granted permission to bin Laden and terrorists to use chemical, biological, and nuclear weapons against the US and its allies. It was issued on 21 May 2003 by Saudi cleric Nasir bin Hamid al Fahd, one of the "Three Takfir Sheiks" in Saudi Arabia. With his warped logic, he found that up to 10 million killed could be justified.[93]

Is it possible for terrorists to smuggle a nuke into our cities? One official half-jokingly said, Yes, all terrorists would have to do is wrap a bomb in one of the bales of marijuana regularly smuggled into New York and Los Angeles.[94]

We did have a scare in October 2001 when our intelligence believed a former Soviet Union nuclear weapon had been smuggled into New York City. A Nuclear Emergency Search Team was rushed to New York looking for a 10-kiloton bomb. That is about the Hiroshima bomb size and would have destroyed much of Manhattan. Vice President Dick Cheney spent weeks in the underground bunker outside Washington. The bomb was never found but the threat was credible.[95]

Depending on where it was detonated, a 10-kiloton bomb would be devastating in New York, particularly everything within a two-mile circle of ground zero which would probably have 75% mortality and total destruction. There would be heavy damage out to at least a seven-mile radius with light damage extending at least 10 miles. It would render parts of Manhattan uninhabitable for years as well as parts of the Bronx, Queens, and likely parts of New Jersey, and depending on the wind direction, the fallout would impact on a very large area. Remember that the Hiroshima blast was an air burst and even though the damage was extensive there was little fallout on the ground. A terrorist nuke would almost definitely be a surface burst which means enormous amounts of dirt and debris would be contaminated in the fireball and then spread downwind as fallout emitting alpha, beta, and gamma radiation.

The anti-nuclear terrorism strategy is based on securing all nuclear weapons, no new national capabilities to reprocess plutonium or enrich uranium, and no new nuclear weapons states.[96]

Radiation Attacks

An actual nuclear weapon is complicated and somewhat difficult to transport, maintain, assemble, and detonate. An alternative that has been talked about is **dirty bombs** - conventional explosives combined with some radioactive material. This would not be a nuclear explosion but a regular explosion to disperse radioactive material that might be stolen from hospitals or scientific research facilities or spent nuclear waste from nuclear power plants. There are over 1,000 irradiation machines which experts say "could shut down over 25 square kilometers, anywhere in the United States, for 40-plus years." Irradiators, used for radiation therapy and to sterilize food and blood, contain Cesium-137 which is one of the most dangerous and long-lasting radioactive materials. A government advisory panel recommended that the government should replace the Cesium with another material or swap them with X-ray machines.[97]

The nuclear material would not be explosive at all but would be packed around normal high explosives to be blown out over as large an area as possible. The radioactive material would cause casualties from radiation and it could make an area uninhabitable until it could be cleaned up.

The So-Called War on Terror

We are in a great clash: not a clash of civilizations, not a clash of religions, but a clash of political visions. "In the terrorist vision of the world, the Middle East must fall under the rule of radical governments, moderate Arab states must be overthrown, nonbelievers must be expelled from Muslim lands and the harshest practice of extremist rule must be universally enforced. In this vision, books are burned, terrorists are sheltered, women are whipped and children schooled in hatred and murder and suicide."[98]

We face a major problem in that democracy is toxic to Islamic extremism. Abu Mousab al-Zarqawi listed seven reasons to condemn democracy in a speech before the January 2006 elections in Iraq: Democracy calls for obedience to man, not Allah; democracy permits freedom of religion, even to convert to another religion; the people rather than Allah rule and pass judgment under democracy; freedom of expression under democracy would permit condemning Allah [the cartoon jihad]; separation of church and state permits secularism which is totally inconsistent with Islam; freedom of association would permit one to join an unacceptable party; and finally, the concept of majority rule is "totally wrong and void because truth according to Islam is that which is in accordance with the Koran and the Sunna, whether its supporters are few or many."[99]

> **America and the West are doomed to failure in this war unless they stand up and identify the real enemy. Islam.**
>
> **- Brigitte Gabriel**

Brigitte Gabriel blasted us for our apathy and political correctness. "America and the West are doomed to failure in this war unless they stand up and identify the real enemy. Islam." She stressed that the ridiculous reaction to the cartoons of Muhammad showed us the real enemy: various nationalities "who share one common ideology of hate, bigotry and intolerance derived from one source. Authentic Islam. An Islam that is awakening from centuries of slumber to re-ignite its wrath against the infidel and dominate the world. An Islam which has declared 'Intifada' on the West." To preserve our freedoms and way of life and for "the sake of our children and our country, we must wake up and take action."[100]

Efraim Halevy, former head of Mossad and former head of the National Security Council in Israel, says we are in a new world war where the terrorists' goal is not territorial gains or regime change but to dispatch western civilization into history. In this war, which is already one of the longest in modern times and with no end in sight, he said, "The aim of the enemy is not to defeat western civilization but to destroy its sources of power and existence, and to render it a relic of the past. It will show no mercy or compassion and no appreciation for these noble values when practiced by us."[101]

> *Nobody* **will state bluntly that we're in a fight for our lives.**
>
> **- Ralph Peters**

Ralph Peters decried our courage stating that "*Nobody* will state bluntly that we're in a fight for our lives." He said we will never win the hearts and minds of terrorists and therefore "Every terrorist mission should be a suicide mission." To win this war, "we must kill our enemies wherever we encounter them. He who commits an act of terror forfeits every right he once possessed."[102]

> **We are in a new world war where the terrorists' goal is not territorial gains or regime change but to dispatch western civilization into history.**
>
> **- Efraim Halevy**

We have often heard that terrorism is caused by poverty or despair. Several Arab columnists took exception with that view citing instead cultural and religious factors, particularly sheikhs who incite young people to terror.   Arab Columnists: Terrorists are Motivated by Cultural and Religious Factors, Not Poverty," The Middle East Media Research Institute Special Dispatch Series – No. 853, 26 January 2005. They make excellent points and show that there are intelligent and well meaning Muslims, but to really bring change they are going to have to radically modify Islam and, as we have seen, that will not be easy.

Muhammad Mahfouz wrote in the *Saudi Gazette* "The Only Way to End Violence and Terrorism Is to Fight a Cultural and Ideological Battle," (30 December 2004). He stated that the reason behind young people turning to terrorism is a "stereotyped understanding of religion." This explains how these youths can come from rich families or from good positions in the civil service. He stated that this is "religious violence carried out by a group of brainwashed youth influenced by glamorous slogans. This requires us to re-formulate the prevailing religious concepts and implant in their minds other religious values, such as the values of dialogue and religious tolerance, as well as recognizing pluralism. Thus… we need to formulate a new religious vision isolating and freeing it of all the facets of extremism and fundamentalism."

In his column in the United Arab Emirates daily *Al-Itihad*, Abdallah Rashid wrote, "The Reason for Arab Muslim Youth Involvement in Terrorism is Religious Brainwashing," (10 January 2005). Rashid gave as an example of a Kuwaiti from a well-off family who went off to fight in Iraq as not being poor. He was killed and left behind his widow, three orphan girls and grieving parents. He asked why are Arab youth involved in such criminal and despicable acts? "The simple reason is the terrifying brainwashing suffered by most of the Arab youth at the hands of 'religious clerics'… [who] nourish the Muslim youth with various kinds of racist views and destructive extremist principles, and nurse them with hostility, hatred, and resentment towards other people and towards members of other divine religions.

"Those who award themselves the title of 'religious clerics' incite Muslim youth to what they call 'Jihad,' while they do not know the meaning of Jihad. What is odd is that they incite others to cross seas and oceans in order to fight 'the atheist and Christian infidels,' as they put it, while not one of them volunteers to go himself and to serve as a model and an example to others."

Note that two of the columnists referred to brainwashing. This next columnist bravely points out that these valiant imams who send youth off to die to get to paradise never volunteer to go themselves. Perhaps they do not really believe the propaganda they espouse. Now who is hypocritical?

Saudi columnist Abdallah Nasser Al-Fawzan also asked "Why Don't the Sheikhs Who Encourage the Youth to Fight Jihad Do So Themselves" in his *Al-Watan* column (1 January 2005). He criticized sheikhs who incite youth to jihad but refuse to do so themselves. If a deed is so great that it guarantees going to paradise, why should only young people do it rather than older ones who might wish to end their lives with an honorable deed?

"These people who hold sway over the minds of the youth have deceived them into thinking that what they are doing is an act of Jihad that will bring them to paradise. These youth should ask themselves why is it that these people prefer them [i.e. the youth] to themselves, and give up for their sake [the merit of carrying it out] the 'honorable' deed that would bring them to paradise."

"Where are the adults and the elderly? Where are the adults who have been influenced by the organization's ideology? Is there not a single elderly person convinced that this is an act of Jihad? Is there not a single elderly person who would blow himself up or explode a booby-trapped car?"

> **"Oh youth, you who seek paradise, where are your sheikhs [when it comes to] this 'honorable deed'? ... Everybody wants paradise. Why then, oh youth, are your sheikhs shirking [Jihad], and not participating in your 'honorable mission?'"**

Marc Sageman, who served with the CIA in Afghanistan 1987 to 1989, is now a forensic psychiatrist and has researched terrorists. Rather than coming from poverty, "90 percent came from caring intact families. Sixty-three percent had gone to college... These are the best and brightest of their societies in many ways." About "73 percent were married and the vast majority had children." Most were not originally very religious. "They only became religious once they joined the jihad. Seventy percent of my sample [400] joined the jihad while they were living in another country from where they grew up."[103]

Lawrence Martines, our outstanding antiterrorism expert in Reno, provided five antiterrorism principles to be aware of:

1. Terrorism is like water: It seeks, finds and takes the path of least resistance.
2. Terrorists pick targets based on their belief in their capability to carry out the attack, and its ultimate success.
3. Terrorism is psychological warfare through the use of extreme violence! Of prime importance is creating in their enemy a real sense of omnipresent danger.
4. Prevention, not reaction, is the only truly successful strategy in fighting terrorism.
5. Intelligence collection is never perfect. However, in the Age of Terror, it is better to be safe than sorry!
   Stay alert![104]

Senator Ernest Hollings criticized Bush's war in Iraq ending with, "Acting militarily, we have created more terrorism than we have eliminated."[105]

Regardless, terrorism is a part of World War IV and will remain with us for a very long time. However, the tactics of Martin Luther King, Jr. and Mohandas Gandhi proved more successful with less hatred and unnecessary bloodshed.

> **We shall overcome.**
> **- Martin Luther King, Jr**
> **An eye for an eye and tooth for a tooth leaves the world blind and toothless.**
> **- Mahatma Gandhi**

The idea of terrorists' strength is an illusion. They can destroy but they do not build. Terrorists can fly an airplane but they cannot build one. They can blow down towers, but they cannot build them. The conflict between the West and radical Islam should be no contest. The system that delivers greater material wealth and greater personal freedom will triumph. Islamofascists, Islamonazis, jihadists, militant Islamists, criminals, or whatever you wish to call them, cannot be deterred and if they obtain the weapons of mass destruction they may well use them. They want to reestablish the caliphate and take over the world. They do not want to deal with us or change us; they want to remove us! There should be no doubt as to who should win when you are up against a 7th century mentality; however, we can lose if we are complacent and do not wake up and address this challenge. Don't ever think we can't lose; the average length of empires has been only 200 years.

We fell to the wrong path and created violence outside the rule of Islam, and we have learned that violence is a trap. How we feel about the government has not changed, but we have to coexist.

- Montasser Zayat[106]

If there is a single power the West underestimates, it is the power of collective hatred.
- Ralph Peters, 1999[107]

Notes

1. "Afghanistan, Iran, Pakistan to 'jointly combat terrorism'" AFP, 25 June 2011. Newt Gingrich, "A Diplomatic Defeat for President Obama and America," 6 July 2011, including quote from Cliff May, *National Review.*
2. "Turkish Premier Rejects Terminology Associating Islam with Terrorism, *Turkish Weekly,* 11 January 2011.
3. *America Alone,* (Washington, DC, Regnery Publishing, Inc., 2006), p. 175.
4. See Michael Scheuer, "Why I Resigned From the CIA," Commentary, *Los Angeles Times,* 5 December 2004. Scheuer was in charge of operations against al Qaeda from January 1996 to June 1999.

    Clinton was not completely unresponsive about bin Laden. See Bob Woodward, "The CIA's Eye on Bin Laden: Afghan agents were paid to track him and his network," p. 9, and Barbara Gellman, "Clinton's Covert War: The U.S. targeted bin Laden for years but shied away from a direct hit," p. 6, *The Washington Post National Weekly Edition,* 7-13 January 2002. However, Richard Clark wrote it was a myth, *Against All Enemies,* p. 142.)
5. Matt Apuzzo, "Osama wanted new name for al-Qaida to repair image," Associated Press, 24 June 2011.
6. Fred Burton, "Iraq: Jihadist Perspectives on a U.S. Withdrawal," Stratfor: Terrorism Intelligence Report, 21 February 2007.
7. Michael Elliott, "They Had A Plan," *Time,* 12 August 2002, p. 28.
8. Dennis Mullin, "The 21st-Century Crusade," *The Washington Post National Weekly Edition*, 13-19 January 2003, p. 22.
9. Ibn Warraq: The Westminster Institute (Part III), Jihad Watch, 15 June 2011.
10. See Jane Meyer, "Junior," *The New Yorker,* 11 September 2006, p. 35. Not all of these Islamic criminals were deeply religious, for some it was "a socially acceptable form of bad behavior. You get to blow stuff up and kill people, and your colleagues and peers think you're good. It's fun and you can be a hero." p. 37.

    The Majlis Shura has grown to some 20 members, the bosses of Arab groups, Chechens, Pakistanis, Bangladeshis, Filipinos, Indonesians, Central Asians, and Europeans – sort of a copy of the Mafia "Cupola." The Majlis Shura signs off on proposed terror attacks before money, logistics, and expertise are provided. Meetings need not be physical; modern technology permits them to communicate. In some ways, bin Laden was chief financial officer for al Qaeda with limited executive authority. Thanks to Lawrence Martines for background. However, documents found on site after his death indicate that he was a hands on CEO.

    Al Qaeda has been involved in over a dozen conflicts in Africa (from Algeria to Ethiopia and Sudan), Southeast, South, and Central Asia. Probably over 200,000 have died in those conflicts. One newer site for al Qaeda is Bangladesh where the jungle provides an optimal location for over 170 training camps and with some 2,000 suicide bombers ready for operations. Chris Blackburn, "Bangladesh: Osama's New Haven," FrontPageMagazine.com, 29 December 2005.
11. Kimberly Dozier, "Special ops chief warns of al-Qaida 2.0," Associated Press, 28 July 2011, Jihad Watch, 29 July 2011. Awlaki and Samir Khan, another American, were killed by a US drone attack in Yemen on 30 September 2011.
12. "Stalin and Mao killed a lot of their own people, but even those thugs had a plan for their societies. You, bin Laden are nothing but a hijacker – a hijacker of Islam, a hijacker of other people's technology, a hijacker of a vast Arab nation's anger at its own regimes. But you have no vision and no plan for your people. Which is why your epitaph will be easy to write: Osama bin Laden – he destroyed much, he built nothing. His impact was like a footprint in the desert." Tom Friedman, "Bush to Bin Laden," *The New York Times,* 12 October 2001.
13. Maamoun Youssef, "Al-Qaida in Iraq appeals for fundraising ideas," Associated Press, 26 July 2011.
14. Tim Funk, "U.S. State Dept. contacts Khan family: Official offers parents condolences on death of al-Qaida propagandist," *Charlotte Observer,* 7 October 2011.
15. Jeb Boone, "Militants said to gain ground in south Yemen," *Los Angeles Times,* 8 June 2011.
16. Eric Schmitt and Thom Shanker, "Qaeda Trying To Harness Toxin For Bombs, U.S. Officials Fear," *The New York Times,* 13 August, 2011.
17. "Glossy 'Jihad Cosmo' combines beauty tips with suicide bombing advice," *Daily Mail,* 14 March 2011.
18. "Jihadis leaving Af-Pak for Africa," *Times of India,* 29 April 2009.
19. Alex Perry, "Remember Somalia?" *Time,* 10 December 2007.
20. Alex Perry, "Somalia, Again," *Time,* 1 March 2010, p. 33. See also "Shabab leader admits links to al Qaeda," *The Long War Journal,* 22 March 2009.
21. "Somali Americans Recruited by Extremists: US Cites Case of Minnesotan Killed in Suicide Blast in Africa," *Washington Post,* 11 March 2009.
22. "Al Qaeda Rebranding Itself to Improve Image, Arab Diplomat Says," Fox News, 14 December 2011,
23. Malise Ruthven, *A Fury For God,* (London, Granta Books, 2004), pp. 192-193.
24. Alex Alexiev (Vice President for Research, Center for Security Polity, Washington, DC), "Tablighi Jamaat: Jihad's Stealthy Legions," *Middle East Quarterly,* Vol. XII, No. 1, Winter 2005.
25. "What Muslim Leaders Say About Islam Dispels the Myth that Jihadists are a 'Fringe' Element," Citizen Warrior, 1 October 2010.
26. "Shariah: The Threat to America," The Center for Security Policy, pp. 65-67.
27. Raymond Ibrahim, "Muslim Brotherhood: 'Impose Islam…Step by Step,'" Jihad Watch, 25 July 2011.
28. See his three phases: "learning," "forming," and "implementation," in "Muslim Brotherhood: We must implement Sharia in stages," Jihad Watch, 6 July 2011, from "Article on Muslim Brotherhood Website: Implement Shari'a in Phases," MEMRI, 5 July 2011 re an 11 June 2011 article.
29. Zachary Abuza, "Jemaah Islamiyah Adopts the Hezbollah Model: Assessing Hezbollah's Influence, *Middle East Quarterly* Winter 2009, pp. 15-26, http://www.meforum.org/2044/jemaah-islamiyah-adopts-the-hezbollah-model.
30. Tony Lopez, "What Is Jemaah Islamiyah?" *The Manila Times*, Manila, Philippines, 30 October 2002, *World Press Review*, January 2003, pp. 11-12.

    Australian Prime Minister, John Howard, placed JI on its list of terrorist organizations in late 2002 and said he was prepared to launch pre-emptive strikes on terrorists in other countries. Bashir, who was being held in a Jakarta hospital for a string of bombings, replied that Australia would be drawn into a war with Muslims if they went along with that "crazy idea." "Islamic leader warns Australia will be 'destroyed,'" *Reno Gazette-Journal*, 13 December 2002, p. 7A.

31. *Shariah: The Threat to America,* The Center for Security Policy, pp. 95-96.
32. Yaakov Katz, "Iran caught 10 times trying to send arms to terrorists," *Jerusalem Post,* 10 June 2011.
33. *Shariah: The Threat to America,* The Center for Security Policy, pp. 95-97.
34. "Israel releases army map showing nearly 1,000 purported Hezbollah underground military sites," *Washington Post,* 31 March 2011.
35. For a good review, see "Shariah: The Threat to America," The Center for Security Policy, pp. 98-104.
36. Mark Steyn, *America Alone,* p. 151.
37. "Report: Hezbollah in dire financial straits," UNet News, 18 December 2011.
38. See "Shariah: The Threat to America," The Center for Security Policy, pp. 104-108.
39. See "Shariah: The Threat to America," The Center for Security Policy, pp. 108-111.
40. Dennis D. Gray, "Global Islamic Group Rising In Asia," AP Enterprise, 2 October 2011.
41. "The Westminster Institute (Virginia): Educating the Public and Government About the Ideology of the Terrorists, and Ways to Counter It (Part IV), Jihad Watch, 16 June 2011.
42. Shrideep Biswas, "COMMENTARY – Lashkar-e-Toiba: Global Outreach," South Asia Intelligence Review/India Blooms News Service, 30 May 2011.
43. Declan Walsh, "Saudi Arabian charity to Pakistan offers education – is it extremism?" *Guardian,* 29 June 2011.
44. "The invasion of Facebook: Al Qaeda calls for 'cyber-jihad' to plan attacks on the West," *Daily Mail,* 13 July 2011, Jihad Watch, 14 July 2011.
45. Jonathan Dienst and Shimon Prokupecz, "Possible Al-Qaida Hit List Targets Specific Americans," NBC New York, 16 June 2011.
46. Betsy Hiel, "Islamist factions jockey for power, vow religious rule," *Pittsburgh Tribune-Review,* 31 July 2011, Jihad Watch, 1 August 2011.
47. Andrew C. McCarthy "The War that Dare Not Speak Its Name: The battle is against militant Islam, not 'Terror,'" National Review Online, 13 May 2004. McCarthy is a former chief assistant US attorney who led the 1995 terrorism prosecution against Abdel Rahman and eleven others.
48. Stanley Crouch "Terrorists kill for the thrill of it," *Reno Gazette-Journal,* 19 July 2006, p. 11A.
49. Mohammad Mohaddessin, *Islamic Fundamentalism: The New Global Threat,* (Washington, DC, Seven Locks Press, 1993), p. xxii.
50. Quoted in Robert Spencer, *The Politically Incorrect Guide to Islam (and the Crusades),* (Washington, DC, Regnery Publishing, Inc., 2005), pp. 109-191.
51. "George Habash, a Palestinian leader who participated in planning major international terror operations, told me in 1987 that his group had abandoned its campaigns only because it had not worked. Instead of winning U.S. sympathy or acquiescence, the attacks had turned Americans solidly against the Palestinian cause." Columnist Jim Hoagland, *Washington Post,* 4 August 1998, quoted in Richard H. Curtiss, "Osama bin Laden Repeating George Habash's Deadly Errors," *WRMEA,* October/November 1998, p. 13. "Bin Laden's methods can only weaken Islam's friends and strengthen its enemies."
    Most American Muslims rejected bin Laden. "As American Muslims, we join the vast majority of Muslims worldwide who reject the twisted teachings of Bin Laden. We deeply resent the fact that he has hijacked our faith and has attempted to justify his actions by hypocritically adopting many of the legitimate grievances of the Muslim and Arab worlds. Osama bin Laden has no more legitimacy in his claim to be the 'poster boy' for the Palestinian cause than did Saddam Hussein a decade ago." Riad Z. Abdelkarim, "American Muslims to Osama bin Laden and Co.: Don't Do Us Any Favors," *WRMEA,* December 2001, p. 72.
52. "Al Qaeda's New Front," produced and directed by Neil Docherty, Correspondent Lowell Bergman, PBS transcript, January 2005. "No one's going to listen to our diplomacy. No one will listen to our propaganda. We are just not heard in the Islamic world. It's not a matter of them not knowing what we're up to. The problem we have is they think they know what we're up to, and that's supporting tyrannies, we're after their oil, we're supporting the Israelis over the Palestinians at all times, we're supporting governments that suppress Muslims elsewhere, such as the Chinese, the Indians and the Russians. It's a matter of policy."
53. Aryn Baker, "The Truth About Talibanistan," Time, 2 April 2007, p. 28. Richard Willing, USA Today, "Study: Al-Qaeda regroups," Reno Gazette-Journal, 18 July 2007, p. 1B.
54. George Friedman, "Osama's Vietnam Syndrome," Stratfor, 24 January 2006.
55. Salah Nasrawi, AP, "Bin Laden endorses al-Zarqawi's successor," Reno Gazette-Journal, 2 July 2006, p. 2C.
56. Lee Keath, AP, "Bin Laden urges Pakistanis to wage jihad against leader," *Reno Gazette-Journal,* 21 September 2007, p. 8C. "Bin Laden lashes out at Arab leaders in message," *Reno Gazette-Journal,* 19 May 2008, p. 2B. He called Arab leaders "agents of the crusaders" and "wolves" for sacrificing the Palestinians.
57. Maggie Michael, AP, "Bin Laden vows to fight Israel," *Reno Gazette-Journal,* 17 May 2008, p. 4B.
58. Lauren Frayer, AP, "Al-Qaida women want larger part," *Reno Gazette-Journal,* 1 June 2008, p. 2B.
59. Aryn Baker, "Deadly Notes in the Night," *Time,* 10 July 06, pp. 38-39.
60. Lawrence Wright, "The Master Plan," *The New Yorker,* 11 September 2006, p. 48.
61. Yassin Musharbash, "The Future of Terrorism: What al-Qaida Really Wants," Spiegel Online, 12 August 2005.
62. Lawrence Wright, "The Rebellion Within: An Al Qaeda mastermind questions terrorism," http://www.newyorker.com/reporting/2008/06/02/080602fa_fact_wright, 2 June 2008.
63. Maureen Groppe, Gannett News Service, "Muslims ask: How does Islam create extremists?" *Reno Gazette-Journal,* 1 September 2002, p. 8A.
64. See Robert Spencer, "Candidates Criticized for 'Linking Islam with Terrorism,'" *Human Events,* 11 February 2008, p. 27.

65. James P. Lucier, "The Old Man in the Mountain," *Insight,* 13-26 April 2004, p. 14. This is a good article showing the roots of terrorism.

66. See AP, "Radical Islamics' ingenious ways to fund terror," *The Jerusalem Post,* 9 December 2004.

67. Mac Johnson, "Media Ignore Al Qaeda Torture Manual," *Human Events,* 4 June 2007, p. 15.

68. Brigitte Gabriel wrote in an OpEd "What the Arab World Thinks," 27 December 2005, that "Torture is accepted and even expected in the Arab world.... They prove their manhood by the way they treat their enemy.... Arab Muslim men gain honor by shaming, belittling, abusing and torturing their enemy in the most horrific ways. She said "Gitmo [Guantanamo] is a joke as far as the Arabs are concerned." They call it "Al muntazah al-dini lilmujaheden al Muslimin," The Religious Resort for Islamic Militants. She was angered with Illinois Democratic Senator Dick Durbin's criticism of the US at Gitmo and said he was "aiding and abetting the goals and strategy of Islamic jihadists." Gabriel is a Contributing Editor for FamilySecurityMatters.com.

69. Robert Spencer, "D'Souza Points Conservatives Toward Disaster," *Human Events,* 5 February 2007, p. 14.

70. See Peter Baker and Susan B. Glasser, "Bush Says 10 Plots By Al Qaeda Were Foiled," *Washington Post,* 7 October 2005, p.1. Wayne Parry, AP, "Attack Thwarted," *Reno Gazette-Journal,* 9 May 2007, p. 1B, for Fort Dix. Adam Goldman, AP. "'Chilling' terror plot halted; Officer: Thousand could have died at JFK," *Reno Gazette-Journal,* 3 June 2007, p. 1C. Robert Spencer, "Jihad at JFK," *Human Events,* 11 June 2007, p. 13. There were also some successful anti-terrorist operations; see Paul Alexander, PA, "American counterterror efforts bear fruit in Philippines," *Reno Gazette-Journal,* 13 May 2007, p. 9C.

71. 10 years ago, the numbers were 127 million passenger vehicles, 820,000 planes, and 250,000 ships, *Time,* 12 November 2001, p. 77. The numbers are likely higher now.

72. Japanese kamikaze pilots attacked US ships late in World War II. Kamikaze means "divine wind" after a legendary typhoon that foiled the invasion of Japan by Mongol Kublai Khan in 1281. "Shinto, an ancient Japanese religion somewhat akin to animism, was employed by Japanese militarists to arouse nationalism, much as today's jihadists dredge up primitive doctrines from Islam to inflame their shadowy armies against the West."

Even though 90 percent failed to reach US ships, conservatives in Japan are renewing the hero-worship of the kamikaze. "Idealistic young Japanese men went to their deaths in 1945 unaware that they were sacrificing not for a bright future that would soon materialize but for a dead past. Today, history is repeating itself in the Middle East. Both men and women are being employed by cynical reactionaries trying to preserve a political culture infamous for its cruelties." George Melloam, "Recalling The Kamikazes Of 60 Years," *The Wall Street Journal,* 16 August 2005, p. 17. Joseph Coleman, AP, "Japan's right sees kamikazes as model for youth," *Reno Gazette-Journal,* 15 July 2007, p. 4B.

73. For a good summary of suicide bombers, see Ralph Peters, "Living, And Dying, With Suicide Bombers," *USA Today,* 4 January 2006, p. 11. Peters called the suicide bombers the "ultimate precision weapons and genuine 'smart bomb,' the 'poor man's nuke.'"

74. Audrey Hudson "Terrorists testing jets, crews say," *The Washington Times,* 21 July 2004.

75. "Tank trucks seen as terrorist weapons" *Decatur Daily* (Alabama), 29 November 2004.

76. Peter Brookes (Townhall.com) "Complacency: Terror's Pal," *The Conservative Review,* 12 July 2005.

77. *Time,* 4 July 2005. pp. 21-26.

78. Tim McGirk, "Moms and Martyrs," *Time,* 14 May 2007, p. 48. Daoud Kuttab, "Mideast Violence Might Be Predictable, But Should Not Be Inevitable," *Jordan Times,* 29-30 August 2003, reprinted in *WRMEA,* November 2003, p. 14.

79. Will Stewart, "Terrorists threatened to kill my baby unless I became a Black Widow: Young mother on how she was groomed to be a Russian suicide bomber," *Daily Mail,* 31 January 2011.

80. They increased from eight in 2007 to at least 27 by mid-2008. Kim Gamel, AP, "57 killed in suicide blasts," and "Women bombers shifting insurgent tactics," *Reno Gazette-Journal,* 29 July 2008, p. 1B and 7 June 2008, p. 7B. Diaa Hadid, "Female bombers are more prevalent," *Reno Gazette-Journal,* 5 January 2008, p.1B. Robert H. Reid, AP, "Al-Qaida bomb kills 2 Marines, *Reno Gazette-Journal,* 23 April 2008, p.1B. Stewart R. Hurst, AP, "Disabled women used in bombings," *Reno Gazette-Journal,* 2 February 2008, p. 1B.

81. Nir Boms, "Iran's Suicide Registration Service," FrontPageMagazine, 6 July 2004.

82. "Moderate Muslims Split on Suicide bombings, ABCNews.com, 20 July 2005.

There were still mixed results. A Pew Research poll in 2007 indicated that more Muslims rejected violence and there was less support for Osama bin Laden. But support for suicide bombings remained high among Palestinians. Yet 13 percent of American Muslims thought such bombings could be justified: that would be over 300,000. Harry Dunphy, AP, "Global poll: More Muslims reject violence," *Reno Gazette-Journal,* 25 July 2007, p. 2B. Robert Spencer, "300,000 U.S. Muslims Approve Suicide Attacks," *Human Events,* 4 June 2007, p. 13.

A former Palestinian female bomber was released from jail and said she wanted to talk peace with Israelis. Karin Laub, "Former Palestinian suicide bomber wants peace," *Reno Gazette-Journal,* 5 March 2008, p. 2B. In Indonesia, where they practice a more moderate form of Islam, they find it difficult to comprehend how young people could be talked into suicide and the government started an education program against hard line Islam. Robin McDowell, AP, "Indonesians ask why Muslims turn to suicide bombings," *Reno Gazette-Journal,* 5 December 2005, p. 2C.

83. See Ambika Ahaja, AP, "Asia's Islamic Extremists use beheadings," *Reno Gazette-Journal,* 3 June 2007, p. 10C, about the young Thai who killed the owner of a rice mill on orders from a guerrilla commander.

84. Louis Meixler, "Militants Worldwide Copy Iraq Beheadings," Yahoo News, 6 November 2004.

85. See the excellent article by Anne Korin and Gal Luft, "Terrorism Goes to Sea," *Foreign Affairs,* November/December 2004. The *Washington Post* reported that US officials had identified about 15 cargo freighters believed to be controlled by al Qaeda, "Freighters believed linked to al-Qaida," *Reno Gazette-Journal,* 31 December 2002, p. 2A.

86. Robert Young Pelton, "Sea Dog Millionaires," *Bloomberg Businessweek,* 16-22 May 2011, p. 67.

87. Ibid., pp. 67-69.

88. See "Terror threats swell at sea: 'Piracy' attacks in maritime jihad increasing in number, violence," Worldnet Daily, 8 June 2004. They have targeted cruise ships and even the British aircraft carrier *Ark Royal* as it transited the Strait of Gibraltar. Other potential targets are civilian ports and oil rigs.

     In addition to learning how to drive large ships, terrorists are also learning about diving. Some were uninterested in learning about decompression, similar to wanting to learn to fly, but not land. US intelligence determined that as many as 28 acoustic sea mines were missing in North Korea – they could be on one of al Qaeda's ships.

89. Strategy Page of 19 May 2004 posted "The Mysterious al Qaeda Navy," about a freighter "The Baltic Sky" which was seized off Greece carrying 750 tons of TNT and 8,000 detonators. All the papers were forged and it is still a mystery. One problem was that it went to the Black Sea. If it had exploded under the Bosporus bridge, it would have "blocked the busiest shipping channel in the world (with 30 percent more traffic than the Strait of Malacca). It would have taken a year to clear the blockage, and that would have done hundreds of billions of dollars in economic damage."

90. John Follain, "US terror plot to 'wipe out a neighbourhood,'" *The Sunday Times*, 13 June 2004.

91. Joby Warrick "Custom-Built Pathogens Raise Bioterror Fears," washingtonpost.com, 31 July 2006.

92. Graham Allison, "Preventable Nightmare – Al Qaeda wants to nuke a U.S. city. There are simple ways to stop it," 21 September 2004. Graham Allison is director of the Belfer Center for Science and International Affairs at Harvard University's John F. Kennedy School of Government. His new book is "Nuclear Terrorism: The Ultimate Preventable."

93. "Osama bin Laden's Mandate for Nuclear Terror," JINSA Online, 10 December 2004. Al Fahd denied international law, since Islamic law overrides any man-made laws. He had been told that almost 10 million Muslims had been killed by American weapons so he justified an equal amount as permissible.

94. Allison, "Preventable Nightmare."

95. Ibid.

96. Ibid.

97. Pamela Hess, AP, "Panel: Accessible machines have bomb-making materials," *Reno Gazette-Journal*, 10 October 2007, p. 5B.

98. "Bush Casts War on Terrorism in Historic Terms" commencement address to the US Air Force Academy, 2 June 2004.

99. Larry Elder "What do the terrorists want?" *The Conservative Review*, 15 July 2005.

100. Brigitte Gabriel "Islam's March Against the West" from her speech delivered at the Intelligence Summit in Washington, DC, 18 February 2006.

101. Rupert Steiner "Terrorists' aim is to end western civilisation, says ex-Mossad head," Scotsman.com news, 10 July 2005.

102. Ralph Peters, "Kill, don't Capture: How to solve our prisoner problem," *New York Post*, 10 July 2006.

103. Marc Sageman, "Understanding Terror Networks," essay based on his FPRI BookTalk, 6 October 2004, 1 November 2004. He wrote another book, *Leaderless Jihad,* in 2008.

     See Aryn Baker, "The Jihadi Next Door," *Time,* 31 March 2008, p. 81. Referring to violent young terrorists, he wrote, "They view themselves as warriors willing to sacrifice themselves for the sake of building a better world, and this gives meaning to their lives.

     See also Amanda Ripley, "Reverse Radicalism," *Time,* 14 March 2008, p. 46, about re-education of detained terrorists because they really do not understand Islam.

104. Letter to the Editor, *Reno Gazette-Journal*, 16 June 2006, p. 11A.

105. Letter from Senator Ernest F. Hollings published in the *Charleston Post and Courier*, 6 May 2004.

106. Lawyer for Egyptian Islamists, 13 May 2002, quoted in *Pharaohs,* June 2002, p. 10.

107. Anonymous, *Imperial Hubris,* (Washington, D.C., Brassey's, Inc., 2004), p. 1.

All that is necessary for the forces of evil to win in the world is for enough good men to do nothing.

- Edmund Burke

Chapter 7

Islamic Extremists in America

*Treason against the United States,
shall consist only in levying War
against them, or in adhering to their
Enemies, giving them Aid and Comfort.*

- US Constitution, Article III, Section 3

*Muslims cannot accept the legitimacy of the existing American
order, since it is against the orders and ordainments of Allah.*

Imam Zaid Shakir, Former Muslim Chaplain, Yale University[1]

The 19 hijackers of 9/11 were in the US on legal visas. Khalid Sheikh Mohammed, the mastermind of 9/11, is being held at Guantanamo Bay as is Abu Zubaydah who once headed recruiting and operations for al Qaeda. Richard Reid, the shoe bomber is serving a life sentence in a Colorado prison as is Ramzi Yousef, who was convicted for his involvement in the 1993 World Trade Center attack. Also, the Blind Sheikh Omar Abdel Rahman, who was involved in the assassination of President Sadat in Egypt and the 1993 attack in New York, is also in a US prison. We have been warned repeatedly of possible new extremist attacks. The threat has increased as there are more radicalized American Muslims who obviously attract less attention from security personnel. There is also the threat of sleeper cells dormant here in the US, but none have surfaced yet.

Two characteristics that have shown up regularly in the backgrounds of suspected militants are high levels of education and an interest in technology.[2] We have already seen this in their interest in flight schools, bomb making, and weapons of mass destruction. We already have reports of suspects staking out airports and other sites and running dry runs for terrorist attacks by trying to draw out air marshals.

Adam Yahiye Gadahn was the first American to be charged with treason since the 1950s. He was born in California, converted to Islam, and became a video spokesman for al Qaeda threatening the US with attacks worse than 9/11 if every soldier was not removed from Muslim land and if the US did not stop all support "to the bastard state of Israel." Gadahn was believed to be in Pakistan.[3]

Anwar al-Awlaki was a cleric who influenced many young Muslims in mosques in the US. He fled to Yemen where he was a leader of Al Qaeda in the Arabian Peninsula and provided sermons on the Internet. One of his followers was Major Nidal Malik Hassan who was in contact with Awlaki before he killed 15 soldiers at Fort Hood, Texas. Hassan was not a soldier but was given military rank while working as a medical officer even though his radical views had already been observed. There is a problem with Muslims in the military unless they are thoroughly vetted.[4]

Syed Hashmi, an American citizen (born in Pakistan but came to the US as a child), was extradited from England for supposedly providing money and military gear to al Qaeda for use against US soldiers in Afghanistan.[5]

According to a National Intelligence Estimate, al Qaeda was still pursuing chemical, biological, and nuclear weapons, and was increasing its efforts to sneak terrorists into the US.

In early 2003, American officials uncovered an attempt to use hydrogen cyanide gas against New York City subways. What the intelligence had found was plans for the construction of a device called a *mubtakkar*, a means to deliver chemicals. Terrorists had long sought a means to combine sodium cyanide, widely available as rat poison, and hydrogen to make hydrogen cyanide, which is stable in water but, when turned into gas and inhaled, it is fatal. The *mubtakkar* (which means "invention" in Arabic or "the initiative" in Farsi) was a device to combine sodium cyanide and hydrochloric acid by a remote fuse creating the gas. Since this is a blood agent, a gas mask is needed for protection. It is quite effective in enclosed areas such as ventilation systems or subway cars. The CIA built a model about the size of a paint can and then took it to the President. This simple device was a real killer. The government was put on alert.

Intelligence determined that the *mubtakkar* was planned to be used on the New York subway system only six weeks away, but they also found another unexplained piece – Ayman al-Zawahiri, upon learning of the proposed attack, had called it off. The mystery of why Zawahiri called off the attack seemed best explained in that he did not want a second wave attack unless it was larger than 9/11 for psychological effect. The capability is still there and we do not know where these terrorists are.[6]

There are some 15,000 facilities across the US that produce or store deadly chemicals; a catastrophic accident or sabotage at over 100 plants could endanger more than one million people. There is one in New Jersey with 12 million people within a 14-mile radius which includes New York City (it contains chlorine which was the gas used in World War I); one in Chicago exposing three million people and one in California exposing eight million.

One of the concerns was the ease of entering the US from Europe because most Europeans can enter the US without visas. The NIE also expressed concern about extremists already inside the US.[7] HezbAllah has set up operations across the border in Mexico. They are raising money in the US and making money with illegal drug and immigration operations, but they are skilled terrorists, more advanced than al Qaeda, and could infiltrate and radicalize Muslim communities in the US. There are over 200,000 Lebanese and Syrian immigrants living in Mexico.[8]

Terrorists have joined with criminals to enter the US. A group in Colombia provided false Spanish passports that permit entry without a visa. To help them identify themselves as Spaniards, they also provided false Spanish driver's licenses, Spanish trade association cards, and Spanish identity documents.[9] Hugo Chavez has offered similar support in Venezuela.

Ultimately, we (Muslims) can never be full citizens of this country…because there is no way we can be fully committed to the institutions and ideologies of this country."
- Ihsan Bagby, Council on American-Islamic Relations[10]

A Christian Arab-American author, Anis Shorrosh, outlined a secret 20-year strategy for Islamic radicals to take over America. Shorrosh emigrated from Jerusalem in January 1967 and is the author of 10 books. This 20-point plan is abridged from his 10th book, *Islam: A Threat or a Challenge,* August 2004. "The following is my analysis of Islamic invasion of America, the agenda of Islamists and visible methods to take over America by the year 2020. Will Americans continue to sleep through this invasion as they did when we were attacked on 9/11?"

1. Terminate America's freedom of speech by replacing it with statewide and nationwide **hate-crime bills**.

2. Wage a war of words using black leaders like Louis Farrakhan, Rev. Jesse Jackson and other visible religious personalities who **promote Islam** as the religion of African-Americans while insisting Christianity is for whites only. What they fail to tell African-Americans is that it was Arab Muslims who captured them and sold them as slaves. In fact, the **Arabic word for black and slave is the same, "Abed."**

3. Engage the American public in dialogues, discussions, debates in colleges, universities, public libraries, radio, TV, churches and mosques on the **virtues of Islam**. Proclaim how it is historically another religion like Judaism and Christianity with the same monotheistic faith.

4. Nominate Muslim sympathizers to **political office** to bring about favorable legislation toward Islam and support potential sympathizers by **block voting**.

5. Take control of as much of **Hollywood**, the **press, TV, radio** and the **Internet** as possible by buying the related corporations or controlling stock.

6. Yield to the fear of the imminent shut-off of the lifeblood of America – black gold. America's economy depends on **oil** and 41 percent of it comes from the Middle East.

7. Yell "**foul**, out-of-context, personal interpretation, hate crime, Zionist, un-American, inaccurate interpretation of the Quran" **anytime Islam is criticized** or the Quran is analyzed in the public arena.

8. Encourage Muslims to **penetrate the White House**, specifically with Islamists who can articulate a marvelous and peaceful picture of Islam. Acquire **government positions** and get membership in local **school boards**. Train Muslims as **medical doctors** to dominate the medical field, research and pharmaceutical companies. (Ever notice how numerous Muslim doctors in America are, when their countries need them more desperately than America?) [Note that Pakistani origin doctors committed an attack in England.] Take over the computer industry. Establish Middle Eastern restaurants throughout the U.S. to connect planners of Islamization in a discreet way.

9. Accelerate Islamic **demographic growth** via:

  * Massive **immigration** (100,000 annually since 1961).

  * Use **no birth control** whatsoever – every baby of Muslim parents is automatically a Muslim and cannot choose another religion later.

  * Muslim men **must marry American women** and Islamize them (10,000 annually). Then divorce them and remarry every five years - since one can't legally marry four at one time. This is a legal solution in America.

  * Convert angry, alienated **black inmates** and turn them into militants (so far 2,000 released inmates have joined al-Qaida worldwide). Only a few "sleeper cells" have been captured in Afghanistan and on American soil.

10. Reading, writing, arithmetic and research through the **American educational system, mosques and student centers** (now **1,500**) should be sprinkled with dislike of Jews, evangelical Christians and democracy. There are currently **300** exclusively Muslim schools in the U.S. which **teach loyalty to the Quran**, not the U.S. Constitution. In January of 2002, Saudi Arabia's Embassy in Washington mailed 4,500 packets of the Quran and videos promoting Islam to America's high schools – free of charge. Saudi Arabia would not allow the U.S. to reciprocate.

11. Provide **very sizeable monetary Muslim grants to colleges and universities** in America to establish **"Centers for Islamic Studies"** with Muslim directors to promote Islam in higher-education institutions.

12. Let the entire world know through propaganda, speeches, seminars, local and national media that **terrorists have hijacked Islam**, when **in truth, Islam hijacked the terrorists**.

13. Appeal to the historically compassionate and sensitive Americans for **sympathy and tolerance towards Muslims** in America who are portrayed as mainly immigrants from oppressed countries. [The sociopathic goal of gaining **pity**!]

14. Nullify America's sense of security by **manipulating the intelligence community with misinformation**. Periodically terrorize Americans with reports of impending attacks on bridges, tunnels, water supplies, airports, apartment buildings and malls.

15. Form **riots and demonstrations in the prison system** demanding Islamic Sharia as the way of life, not America's justice system.

16. Open numerous **charities** throughout the U.S., but use the funds to support Islamic terrorism with American dollars.

17. Raise interest in Islam on **America's campuses** by **insisting freshmen take at least one course on Islam.**

18. **Unify** the numerous **Muslim lobbies** in Washington, mosques, Islamic student centers, educations organizations, magazines and papers by Internet and an annual convention to coordinate plans, propagate the faith and engender news in the media.

19. Send **intimidating messages and messengers** to the outspoken individuals who are **critical of Islam** and seek to eliminate them by hook or crook.

20. **Applaud Muslims as loyal citizens** of the U.S. by spotlighting their voting record as the highest percentage of all minority and ethnic groups in America. [Emphasis added]

A very large mosque was being built in Boston, but the people associated with it were either in prison or tied to radicals. One of the directors, an Egyptian Wahhabi cleric who had urged Iraqis to kill US soldiers, was banned from entering England, and said, "We will conquer Europe, we will conquer America!" As a local professor said, "This is a mosque that combines Wahhabi theology, Muslim Brotherhood politics and lots of money, and that's a very dangerous combination." Most of the money came from Saudi Arabia and the city of Boston sold them the land at way below market value.[11]

There are many vulnerable areas in any country such as subways, trains, airplanes, water systems, chemical plants, nuclear plants, etc. Some have been attacked. One of the papers found in the Osama bin Laden raid was a plan to derail a US train. This has been tried worldwide some 150 times, with about half being successful.[12]

Many would-be terrorists have been arrested due to good intelligence work thwarting their plans. The loner is the most difficult to locate and it is difficult to determine whether that person is a real threat or just a bit unbalanced. One Muslim woman stirred up the public on a D.C. Metro, wearing a hijab, ranting about Muslim Americans, and then saying "'Praise Allah. I'm going to kill the world,' before throwing a backpack onto the train and exiting." There was no explosive device, but she caused a panic.[13] Threats are sent to members of Congress and state legislatures and businessmen and they have to be investigated because we have had successful mail bombs in the past.

So where do American Muslims stand? Most are supposedly moderate, yet "7% say suicide bombing is sometimes justified," [that is almost 200,000 people] and "21% say there is a great deal or fair amount of support for extremism in their community." That would be almost 600,000 people so there is a problem here.[14] Still we have some who refuse. Two women in Minnesota who were in court for funneling money to al-Shabaab in Somalia were arrested after they refused to stand for the judge. They do not recognize the authority of US law, only sharia.[15] Again, people in the wrong country!

Tablighi Jamaat

We noted in the last chapter that many detainees at Guantanamo had been involved with **Tablighi Jamaat**, which has a significant presence in the US and al Qaeda has used TJ for recruiting. There are an estimated 50,000 US members and TJ runs mosques in at least ten states. Richard Reid attended a TJ mosque in Dewsbury, West Yorkshire, UK, which was the European headquarters for the group. The "American Taliban" John Walker Lindh went on a missionary tour after meeting TJ representatives at his California mosque. They placed him in a madrassa in Pakistan. Six Yemeni-Americans, who were arrested for traveling to Pakistan to train in al Qaeda camps, were recruited at a Lackawanna mosque in New York by a TJ cleric. Bryant Neal Vinas, a US-born al Qaeda member involved in the plot against the New York subway, learned his radical ways at the Al-Falah mosque in Corona, Queens, which is the US TJ headquarters.[16]

Jamaat ul Fuqra

After 9/11, we heard about militias operating in the US but little was written about Muslim training camps. The Pakistani terrorist group **Jamaat ul Fuqra** [community of the impoverished] was created in New York in 1980 by Pakistani cleric Mubarak Ali Gilani who calls himself "the sixth Sultan Ul Faqr" with the objective of purifying Islam through violence. The headquarters is located on 70 remote acres on "Moslem Road" in the Catskills near Hancock, New York, called "Islamberg," operating under the front **Muslims of the Americas, Inc.**, a tax-exempt organization formed by Gilani which "operates communes of primarily black, American-born Muslims throughout the U.S.," which also operates the International Quranic Open University. There is also a village in South Carolina called "Holy Islamville." The "group seeks to counter 'excessive Western influence on Islam' through any means necessary, publicly embracing the ideology that violence is a significant part of its quest to purify Islam." Their enemies are all non-Muslims and any Muslim who does not follow their fundamentalist ideas.[17]

> **Jamaat ul Fuqra may be the best positioned group to launch an attack on the United States, or more likely, help al-Qaeda to do so.**
>   **- The Center for Policing Terrorism**

There are more than 35 of these "Jamaats," or para-military training camps in 22 states and Canada with 3,000 or more members, many with criminal backgrounds. Military training is conducted at these camps to include small arms, IEDs, how to kill sentries (garrote), and kidnapping. These are closed communities with no outsiders allowed to enter these encampments which have armed guards at the entrances. Members who pass the training at camps such as Hancock "are then sent to Pakistan for training in paramilitary and survivalist training by Mr. Gilani." Fuqra recruits criminals and openly recruits "effectively among Afro-American prison inmates." JF members were involved in the 1993 World Trade Center attack and have been exposed in "vast criminal activities involving murder [12+], assassinations [10], weapons smuggling, counterfeiting, drug trafficking and terrorist exploits over nearly three decades" and at least 17 firebombings. Wall Street Journal investigator Daniel Pearl was on his way to interview Gilani in Pakistan when he was kidnapped and beheaded.[18]

> **I shall always hear and obey, and whenever given the command, I shall readily fight for Allah's sake.**
>   **- Pledge required of Jamaat ul Fuqra members**

Funding contributions go directly to Gilani "through a complex monetary transfer system....comprised of shell companies and charities....to fund terror operations, pay off members of Pakistan's ISI, and even distributed to other Islamic terror groups that include al Qaeda, HAMAS and Hezbollah." Members have been "observed wearing uniforms of the New York and New Jersey Port Authority." That is because they are employed in such places plus working "as school bus drivers, computer operations at credit card data centers, and public utilities." They have moved some of their military type training to remote parts of our national forests and for urban training, to "mosques and Islamic centers in New York City and upstate New York." The frequency of such operations is increasing and according to one Jamaat ul Fuqra member "participating in a paramilitary exercise at an Islamic center in New York, 'we are getting ready…the Day of Atonement is close at hand."[19]

These military training camps exist here in the US and we do little about them.

The Fethullah Gulen Movement

Another radical Islamist operating in the United States similar to Mubarak Gilani and his Jamaat ul Fuqra is **Fethullah Gulen** [referred to by some as the Turkish Khomeini] who fled Turkey in 1998 avoiding prosecution for trying to overthrow Turkey's secular government and establish an Islamic regime. "Gulen plots the overthrow of secular governments and oversees the spread of education jihad throughout Asia, Europe, and the United States." He has established some 700 madrassas around the world including some 120 Gulen charter schools in the US that are linked to his Gulen Movement and are funded with millions of taxpayer dollars. These madrassas indoctrinate children in Gulen's anti-Israel and anti-American worldview and the basic tenets of radical Islam. One of his US madrassas is the Tarek ibn Ziyad Academy in Minnesota mentioned earlier which is being shut down. The Clintons have been active in promoting Gulen and Bill Gates has supposedly donated money to one of Gulen's enterprises. He also has dozens of universities, "including the Faith University in Istanbul," which "train young men to become lawyers, accountants, and political leaders so that they can take an active part in the restoration of the Ottoman Empire and the Islamization of the Western World." He also trains jihadis in guerrilla warfare tactics. He has amassed over $30 billion with the goal of a universal caliphate.[20]

Gulen, known as Hodjaefendi (master lord), operates from a fortress headquarters on 28 acres at 1857 Mt. Eaton Road, Saylorsburg, Pennsylvania, which has a massive chalet, numerous other buildings, a helicopter pad, and firing ranges. He has a small army of over 100 Turkish armed militants guarding him (they wear coats and ties so they do not look like Islamists). A helicopter occasionally flies low around the area checking for intruders. Armed sentries guard the gates and monitor TV security cameras in the sentry hut. There is a sign in front of the hut: "Golden Generation Worship and Retreat Center."

The Justice and Democratic Party (AKP), which is supposedly under Gulen's control, now rules in Turkey and President Abdullah Gul, Prime Minister Recep Tayyip Erdogan, and Council of Higher Education head Yusuf Ziya Ozcan are all Gulen supporters. Turkey has been transforming into a much more Islamic country, reversing the secularization of Kemal Ataturk, with 85,000 mosques (1 per 350 persons the highest in the world), 90,000 imams (more than teachers and physicians), and thousands of state-run Islamic schools. Fethullahists "have gained control of the country's media outlets, its financial institutions and banks, and its business organizations.

Publicly, Gulen is quite liberal, condemning terrorism and promoting interfaith dialogue. Privately, he has stated, "in order to reach the ideal Muslim society 'every method and path is acceptable, [including] lying to people.'" That is our familiar *taqiyya*. He has preached that they must wait and not move too early. "You must move in the arteries of the system without anyone noticing your existence until you reach all the power centers…until the conditions are ripe."

Another organization operating freely in the US and the courts protect him as an individual with "extraordinary ability in the field of education" even though he has no formal education training and granted him permanent residence status. The question is: "Why has the federal government opted to turn a blind eye to Gulen and his mountain fortress?"[21]

US Prisons

We have repeatedly seen that the **US prisons** are a source for black Muslims. An Inspector General report from the Justice Department in May 2004 revealed our prisons as fertile breeding rounds for terrorists. Islamic extremists (imams) infiltrated prisons worldwide to gain converts. [It is also in Europe: Richard Reid, the "Shoe Bomber," converted to Islam under an extremist imam in a British prison.] Much of the funding has come from the Saudi National Islamic Prison Foundation, a "prison outreach' program with imams trained in Saudi Arabia. They are converting large numbers of African-American inmates with virulent anti-Americanism. According to *The New York Times*, 20 October 2003, some 200 African-American imams had been trained in Saudi Arabia by them, of course in Wahhabism.

Three converts who were radicalized while in Folsom prison [one founded Jam'iyyat Ul-Islam Is-Saheeh (JIS)] pled guilty to terrorism charges admitting plots to attack US "military operations, infidels, and Israeli and Jewish facilities in the Los Angeles area." *The New York Times* dismissed the JIS threat and generally downplayed the idea of US terrorism cells. The problem is radical prison chaplains, often imams with Wahhabist and radical links.[22] A senior former corrections official wrote, "Radical Islamic recruitment in the prison system is a reality. Years of sowing seeds among a captive audience are bearing fruit."[23]

> **The problem is radical prison chaplains, often imams with Wahhabist and radical links.**

There are nearly 2.5 million Americans in prisons, the largest in the world. Including those on probation, nearly one in 30 Americans is in the prison system.[24] and a very large percentage are non-white. Rick Mathes, who runs the Mission Gate Prison Ministries, wrote:

> The Muslim religion is the fastest growing religion per capita in the United States, especially in the minority races!!!
>
> Last month I attended my annual training session that's required for maintaining my state prison security clearance. During the training session there was presentation by three speakers representing the Roman Catholic, Protestant and Muslim faiths, who explained each of their beliefs.
>
> I was particularly interested in what the Islamic Imam had to say. The Imam gave a great presentation of the basics of Islam, complete with a video.
>
> After the presentation, time was provided for questions and answers.
>
> When it was my turn, I directed my question to the Imam and asked: "Please, correct me if I'm wrong, but I understand that most Imams and clerics of Islam have declared a holy jihad [Holy war] against the infidels of the world and, that by killing an infidel, (which is a command to all Muslims) they are assured of a place in heaven. If that's the case, can you give me the definition of an infidel?
>
> There was no disagreement with my statements and, without hesitation, he replied "Non-believers!"
>
> I responded, "So, let me make sure I have this straight. All followers of Allah have been commanded to kill everyone who is not of your faith so they can have a place in heaven. Is that correct?"
>
> The expression on his face changed from one of authority and command to that of a little boy who had just been caught with his hand in the cookie jar.
>
> He sheepishly replied, "Yes."

I then stated, "Well, sir, I have a real problem trying to imagine Pope John Paul commanding all Catholics to kill those of your faith or Dr. Stanley ordering all protestants to do the same in order to guarantee them a place in heave."

The Imam was speechless!

I continued, "I also have a problem with being your friend when you and your brother clerics are telling your followers to kill me!

Let me ask you a question: Would you rather have your Allah, who tells you to kill me in order for you to go to heaven, or my Jesus who tells me to love you because I am going to heaven and He wants you to be there with me?"

You could have heard a pin drop as the Imam hung his head in shame. Needless to say, the organizers and/or promoters of the/diversification training seminar were not happy with my way of dealing with the Islamic Imam, and exposing the truth about the Muslims' beliefs.

In twenty years there will be enough Muslim voters in the U.S. to elect the President![25]

The invasion of America by Islamic extremists is not recent but has been growing for years. There are numerous groups and councils but the major Islamic organization is the Muslim Brotherhood which has been operating in the United States for over half a century. For coverage of the MB, there are two key sources. First is "Shariah: The Threat to America" by the Center for Security Policy which provides a good historical review of the MB and its myriad front organizations plus coverage of the Holy Land Foundation trial. For an exposé of the inner workings of the Brotherhood and the Council for American-Islamic Relations (CAIR), see the *Muslim Mafia: Inside the Secret Underworld That's Conspiring to Islamize America* by P. David Gaubatz and Paul Sperry. Chris Gaubatz worked in CAIR as an intern and found out first hand what was really going on within this organization that wants to destroy American society and impose radical Islam. It must have been accurate because CAIR has pulled out the stops trying to stop it and filed a lawsuit trying to remove all copies of *Muslim Mafia*.[26]

Muslim Brotherhood

The **Muslim Brotherhood** has been mentioned several times already but little is ever said about it being in the US. Much of the development of the secretive Brotherhood in America was under the guidance of an Egyptian-born surgeon, Ahmed Elkadi (both his father and father-in-law were early leaders of the Muslim Brotherhood in Egypt), with its goal of "achieving Islamic rule in America." It is anti-American and supports violence in the Middle East. Elkadi's strategy was, "First you change the person, then the family, then the community, then the nation."

> **Allah is our goal; the Messenger is our guide; the Qur'an is our law; Jihad is our means; and martyrdom in the way of Allah is our highest aspiration.**
>
> **- Creed of the Muslim Brotherhood**

In 1953, Princeton arranged a meeting of "prominent Muslims" with President Dwight Eisenhower. The CIA noted that one, Saeed Ramahdan, seemed to be a Fascist and followed the Brotherhood line. The MB bylaws for the means to the Ikhwan's objectives in America had a mandate: "Make every effort for the establishment of educational, social, economic, and scientific institutions and the establishment of mosques, schools, clinics, shelter, clubs."[27] They have followed that mandate with zest. By their own documentation, there are now at least 32 known "organizations and organizations of our friends"[28] but there are many more. Those are the main organizations, but in the mid-1990s "the MB begins establishing between 80 and 120 new non-profit organizations annually.   Today, there are over 2,000 Islamic non-profit [501(c)(3)] organizations in the United States." Most are controlled by the MB.[29]

The MB established 5-year plans as they gradually developed their strategy for what is called the **"Civilization-Jihadist Process" for destroying our civilization from within.** They set goals as: "(1) Establishing an effective and stable Islamic Movement led by the Muslim Brotherhood; (2) Adopting Muslim causes domestically and globally; (3) Expanding the observant Muslim base; (4) Unifying and directing Muslim efforts; (5) Presenting Islam as a civilization alternative; (6) Supporting the establishment of the Islamic state wherever it is." This is a "massive Influence Operation" – or "massive counter-intelligence operations" – not terrorism (from the MB perspective).[30]

Muslim Students Association

During the 1960s, a wave (perhaps deliberately dispatched) of Arab immigrants flooded US campuses, particularly large Midwestern universities in Illinois, Indiana, and Michigan. Many belonged to the Brotherhood at home and in 1962, an Egyptian "Mother group" started a movement in the US helped by the Saudi-based Muslim World League.[31] They initially operated under the name of the Cultural Society, and then in 1962-1963, the Ikhwan created its first front organization in the US, the **Muslim Students Association (MSA)**, set up by three Iraqis at the University of Illinois, Urbana. From the MSA came almost every Muslim organization in the US. Chapters were established on most university and college campuses where initially "they presented Islam in public as an acceptable alternative to other religions, never mentioning its revolutionary aspects. In recent years, MSA members have become ever-more-aggressive in their demands for accommodations and silencing all who oppose them."[32]

The MSA has been intent on Islamizing campuses with what is known as **sharia creep**: hectoring college administrators to accommodate Muslim students with such as "Islamic prayer rooms; paid campus *imams*; special restroom facilities, such as footbaths, for ritual washing; separate food and housing for Muslim students; campus-wide observance of Islamic holidays; and separate athletic hours for Muslim women."[33]

MSA has the same ideology as the Muslim Brotherhood and al Qaeda, promotes sharia, and strives to spread Islam among American youth. It supports jihad, Hamas, HezbAllah, and MB leaders Hasan al-Banna and Sayyid Qutb. Its members attack Jews and Israel and try to control speech and frequently disrupt speakers who try to inform students about Islam, sharia, and jihad.

MSA has the same ideology as the Muslim Brotherhood and al Qaeda.

Offshoots from MSA include the Islamic Medical Association (IMA), the Muslim Arab Youth Association (MAYA), the Association of Muslim Social Scientists (AMSS), the Islamic Circle of North America (ICNA), and the Islamic Society of North America (ISNA). In the 1970s, the MB also established the Association of Muslim Scientists and Engineers (AMSE), the Muslim Communities Association (MCA), and the Muslim Youth of North America (MYNA).[34]

Even though it billed itself as a place where Muslim students could network, it "has been a virtual terror factory." Anwar al-Awlaki, who we have already met and went to Yemen, was president of MSA at Colorado State University in the mid-1990s. Ramy Zamzam, who was convicted in Pakistan for trying to join the Taliban and kill US troops, was president of the

Washington, DC council. Omar Hammami, now a leader of al-Shabaab in Somalia, was president of the chapter at the University of South Alabama. Abdurahman Alamoudi, who we will see more about below as al Qaeda's top fundraiser in the US and now serving a 23-year prison sentence, was national president of MSA during the 1980s. The MSA has served as "a recruitment tool to bring Muslims into the Brotherhood."[35]

North American Islamic Trust

The **North American Islamic Trust (NAIT),** often called the bank for the Muslim Brotherhood in the US and Canada, was created by the Saudis in 1973. According to the ISNA website, the NAIT is a *waqf*, endowment, serving Muslims in the US and is a tax-exempt 501(c)(3) organization.

> NAIT holds titles to mosques, Islamic centers, schools and other real estate to safeguard and pool the assets of the American Muslim community, develops financial vehicles and products that are compatible with both the shariah and the American law, publishes and distributes credible Islamic literature, and facilitates and coordinates community projects.

> **Islamic Centers Division:** Islamic Centers Division (ICD) manages Waqf program services of NAIT to Islamic centers, mosques and schools. NAIT's Waqf Program for the properties of Islamic centers, mosques and schools is based on NAIT holding titles to these assets. NAIT holds titles of approximately 300 properties. NAIT safeguards these community assets, and ensures conformity to the Islamic purpose(s) for which their founders established them. NAIT does not administer these institutions or interfere in their daily management, but is available to support and advise them regarding their operation in conformity with the shariah.[36]

NAIT was declared an "unindicted co-conspirator" along with 245 other entities and individuals in the Holy Land Foundation (HLF) trial. It appealed the ruling and in October 2010, the US Court of Appeals for the Fifth District (New Orleans) removed the "unindicted co-conspirator" and ruled that its association with Hamas be expunged.[37]

Islamic Society of North America

The **Islamic Society of North America (ISNA)** is the largest of the Muslim Brotherhood fronts and was created in Plainfield, Indiana in 1980 as an umbrella organization "to be a nucleus for the Islamic Movements in North America." Since religious institutions are considered off limits to the FBI and bank records are the domain of the Treasury Department, it is no surprise there was no investigation.

> A logical investigation will confront why four foreign students from Southern Illinois University came to Plainfield [Indiana] to buy a large land mass and build a multi-million dollar mosque where there were no Muslims within hundreds of miles.
> - Tim Pitchford, retired FBI agent, Indianapolis filed office[38]

These students "acquired 124 acres of farmland near the Indianapolis airport and moved the offices of the Muslim Students Association there, forming the roots of ISNA." The 42-acre campus includes "a $3.5 million mosque, along with classrooms, residences, a gym, and a recreational area" plus an 80,000 volume library and research facility.

Where did all this money come from? $21 million was raised by MB leaders such as our currently prominent Egyptian, **Yusuf al-Qaradawi** (he also co-founded the ISNA office in Boston), and another Egyptian tied with the Saudis, Youssef Nada, who founded Bank al-Taqwa ("Fear of Allah") which moved money to al Qaeda and Hamas. Also, the emir of Qatar, where Qaradawi was based in his exile, chipped in.[39]

We need to include more information on Qaradawi since, even though he is old, he is the spiritual leader of the MB and is back in Egypt at this critical time. He is considered one of the most influential scholars in Islam, including by Imam Feisel Abdul Rauf ["I do not believe in religious dialogue."] who was pushing for the Ground Zero Mosque and considers Qaradawi his guide. He is widely known in the Muslim world "whose weekly Al Jazeera program on the subject of sharia is viewed by millions and whose cyber-venture, Islam Online, is accessed by millions more, including Muslims in the United States." His "rabble-rousing was a prime cause of the deadly global rioting by Muslims" over the Danish cartoons of Muhammad. Andrew McCarthy continued, "Qaradawi regards the **United States as the enemy of Islam**. He has urged that Muslims **'fight the American military** if we can, and if we cannot, we should **fight the U.S. economically and politically.**' In 2004, he issued a **fatwa** (an edict based on sharia) calling for **Muslims to kill Americans in Iraq**. A leading champion of **Hamas**, he has issued similar approvals of **suicide bombings in Israel.**"[40] [Emphasis added]

With this new beachhead in America, immigrants poured in from the Middle East with ISNA sponsoring six-month visitor visas. As an FBI agent complained, "the visa frauds we presented were not prosecuted by Washington. These same visa visitors are still here illegally."[41]

The next 20 years were a period of massive growth as the MB "created hundreds of new organizations and built hundreds of mosques and Islamic schools" mostly with Saudi funding. ISNA has many chapters and "over 300 community and professional organizations in North America."[42] "ISNA was and is primarily a Dawah organization. Dawah is the "Call to Islam" and is a requirement under Islamic law before Jihad can be waged."[43]

The US government has given it considerable legitimacy and permits partnering with the White House, the FBI, the State, Defense and Homeland Security departments, plus the intelligence community. This is important because both ISNA and NAIT were named unindicted co-conspirators in the HLF trial. ISNA President Ingrid Mattson (ex-Catholic convert) was invited by Obama "to deliver a prayer at the inaugural National Prayer Service at the National Cathedral" and "spoke at a prayer service at the Democratic National Convention in Denver" and was invited to President Obama's 2010 Iftar dinner. [It is important to note that women have been used as "leaders' in several of these organizations "in order to project a softer image." This helps confuse non-Muslims to make it appear that these organizations do not adhere to the anti-female practices of sharia.[44]] This raises critical questions as to why ISNA is involved in certifying all Muslim chaplains for the military and the US Bureau of Prisons. Also ISNA provided training on Islam for US Army officers and men prior to deploying to Afghanistan and Iraq. ISNA is still the main government partner for "outreach" to Muslims, including the DHS and the FBI.[45]

> **We must implement Islam as a totality (in which) Allah controls every place…the home, the classroom, the science lab, the halls of Congress.**
> **- Imam Amir-Abdel Malik-Ali, Majid Al Islam mosque, Oakland, CA**

Valerie Jarrett, senior advisor and assistant to President Obama for intergovernmental affairs and public engagement, delivered a keynote address at ISNA's national convention in

Washington. Then-Deputy Secretary of Defense Gordon England spoke to the group in 2006, arranged by his special assistant, Hesham Islam, an immigrant from Egypt. Islam used his influence when he "convinced Pentagon brass not to renew the contract of Pentagon analyst Major Stephen Coughlin after Coughlin argued in briefings that the Defense Department should cease outreach programs with ISNA because of its radical Muslim Brotherhood ties."[46]

"Islamophobia" was mentioned in Chapter 4 including CAIR's teaming with UC Berkeley with an Islamophobia report. ISNA also has been very active and held its 48th Annual convention in Rosemont, Illinois in July 2011 with a focus on how Muslims should respond to Islamophobia. According to a news agency, "With the 10th anniversary of 9/11 looming, attendees at North America's largest Muslim gathering next month will be told that the best way to deal with Islamophobia is not to lay low, but get involved in politics, interfaith work and community affairs." The guest speaker was the Rev. Michael Kinnamon, general secretary of the National Council of Churches of Christ. The speaker at the 2009 conference with 8,000 Muslim Americans was Rick Warren of Saddleback Church.[47]

The October 2010 Appeals Court ruling for NAIT also included ISNA and CAIR.

Muslim Public Affairs Council

The **Muslim Public Affairs Council (MPAC)** was formed at one of the largest Wahhabi mosques in the US, the Islamic Center for Southern California, in 1986 as its Political Action Committee. It separated from the Islamic Center in 1988. The founders of the Center were two Egyptian brothers, Hassan and Maher Hathout who spent time in Egyptian prison and both are strong followers of MB founder, Hassan al-Banna. Maher in addition to being a founder of MPAC, he works with other Muslim Brotherhood organizations.

> **When we hear someone refer to the great mujahid Osama bin Laden as a "terrorist", we should defend our brother and refer to him as a freedom fighter."**
> **- Edina Lekovic, Muslim Public Affairs Council**[48]

MPAC is "a multi-faceted lobbying organization, which is involved in outreach to the religious, law enforcement, Hollywood, and political communities."[49] The current president of MPAC is Salam al-Marayati who claims that HezbAllah has the right to attack Israel and his wife, Dr. Laila al-Marayati was appointed by the White House to the US Commission on International Religious Freedom. MPAC provides an "aggressive propaganda arm" for the MB via *taqiyya* and disinformation. They won a major information battle by demanding that the descriptive words such as jihad, sharia, caliphate, and umma not be used when referring to terrorists and the government knuckled under.[50]

Muslim American Society

In June 1993, "three of the most prominent Muslim Brothers in the world" incorporated the **Muslim American Society (MAS)** in Chicago. One of those was Ahmed Elkadi, who was the General Masul, or General Guide, of the MB for 10 years. In 2000, MAS merged with the **Islamic Circle of North America (ICNA).**

MAS has "been more directly politically active than ISNA." It is now a national organization with some 50 chapters and works with far-left organizations including one affiliated with North Korea. It has a 501(c)(4) group, **MAS Freedom Foundation**, which gives the MB a lobbying vehicle to influence elections. The Executive Director of the

Foundation is Mahdi Bray, a convicted felon and Muslim convert, who has worked with numerous MB front groups and served on advisory boards of the American Muslim Council (Alamoudi) and MPAC and was president of the **Coordinating Council of Muslim Organizations (CCMO).**[51] On 31 August 2010, CCMO brought 25-30 Muslim leaders from 20 Muslim groups to a special workshop presented by the White House co-sponsored by the Department of Agriculture (with other departments like Education, Homeland Security, and Health and Human Services attending.) to provide "opportunities for funding, government assistance, and resources" to its members and their projects. The E-mail which went out from ISNA stated that they would be provided "direct access" and "cut through some of the red tape."[52] Evidently the CCMO has been renamed **DC's Council of Muslim Organizations (CMO)**.

> **You have learned the way, that you have known that the jihad way is the way to liberate your land.**
>
> **- Dr. Esam Omeish, Muslim American Society**[53]

MAS conducts a nine-months training course which includes study of Muslim Brotherhood heroes Hassan al-Banna and Sayyid Qutb. It also has a correspondence college in Detroit, Islamic American University. Its former chairman was the ubiquitous **Yusuf al-Qaradawi** who is barred from entering the US due to his terrorist statements including his fatwas authorizing attacks on US soldiers and his vow that the MB will conquer America.[54]

Council on American-Islamic Relations

"Senior leaders of Hamas, the Holy Land Foundation for Relief and Development and the Islamic Association for Palestine" met in Philadelphia in 1993. Less than a year later in 1994, **Omar Ahmad** and **Nihad Awad** formed the **Council on American-Islamic Relations (CAIR)** as "a new public relations arm for the organization not connected with the Brotherhood's other entities, to include the HLF." Both founders were senior members of the **Islamic Association of Palestine (IAP)** – Ahmad was the president. [Omar Ahmad was a computer engineer in Silicon Valley and Nihad Awad had been a MAS activist at the University of Minnesota.[55]] A recently surfaced video shows Awad saying "Who better can lead America than Muslims?"[56] The Department of Justice decided not to prosecute Ahmad over his Hamas link.[57] However, Awad continued his Hamas link by speaking on "a July 23 broadcast of Hamas-linked Al-Quds TV," stating that "American hostility towards Muslims was bound to turn into violence," and "his organization asked President Obama to stop U.S. intelligence agencies from allowing right-wing ideologues to 'train' political and military leaders about Islam."[58] The chairman of IAP was Hamas leader Mousa Mohammed Abu Marzook, also chairman of the United Association for Studies and Research (UASR) and the Occupied Land Fund (OLF), which later became the **Holy Land Foundation (HLF)**, [not the Christian charity]. Marzook was the Hamas leader in the US and was designated a terrorist by the US Treasury Department.[59]

> **Islam isn't in America to be equal to any other faith, but to become dominant. The Koran, the Muslim book of scripture, should be the highest authority in America, and Islam the only accepted religion on earth.**
>
> **- Omar Ahmad, founder of Council on American-Islamic Relations**[60]

The International Muslim Brotherhood created Hamas in 1987 and "ordered the Muslim Brotherhood chapters throughout the world to create Palestine Committees, whose job it was to support Hamas with 'media, money, and men.'" The US Palestine Committee consisted of the IAP, the UASR, and the OLF (HLF). "CAIR was later added to these organizations." Since it was clear that "CAIR is a Hamas entity," the findings of the HLF trial named both CAIR and Omar Ahmad as unindicted co-conspirators.[61]

According to its IRS records, CAIR's membership dropped from 29,000 at 9/11 to 1,700 and its annual income from $733,000 to $59,000. The bad part of that good news is that they still opened 25 new chapters and were spending $3 million a year! Who is funding them? – evidently "wealthy Persian Gulf governments" – including Saudi Arabia and the UAE.[62] Since CAIR refused to file required annual reports, it lost its tax-exempt status; however many of its chapters have their own non-profit designations which may remain active.[63]

Robert Spencer has been quoted often in this book. A fatwa was issued to kill him. "May Allah rip out his spine from his back and split his brains in two, and then put them both back, and then do it over and over." Spencer was invited to speak at a conference of the Young America's Foundation, but CAIR engaged a law firm to threaten him.[64] The response from YAF was most appropriate: "Jason Mattera, a spokesman for YAF said they would not be intimidated by Islamic thugs and followed up with: 'CAIR can go to Hell and they can take their 72 virgins with them.'"[65] We could use such courage in Washington.

There are some parts of US society that are not fully supportive of efforts to prevent terrorist attacks in this country. The Los Angeles Police Department wanted to map Muslim communities in an effort to identify people who might be involved in extremism. "The ACLU of Southern California, an association of Muslim lawyers called Muslim Advocates, the Islamic Shura Council of Southern California and" CAIR wrote to the LAPD that "singling out individuals for investigation, surveillance and data-gathering based on their religion constitutes religious profiling that is just as unlawful, ill-advised and deeply offensive as racial profiling...the mapping of Muslim communities... seems premised on the faulty notion that Muslims are more likely to commit violent acts than people of other faiths." The only problem with their logic is that there were some 9,000 attacks since 9/11 in the name of Islam. Being so politically correct leaves America vulnerable. American Muslims should want to work with law enforcement to remove these extremists from their communities.[66] But they have been most uncooperative.

CAIR and ISNA work closely as Brotherhood fronts; they "coordinate operations, share funding, and maintain interlocking boards of directors." Ihsan Bagby, who is an Associate Professor of Islamic Studies at the University of Kentucky and who told us Muslims can "never be full citizens of this country," sits on the boards of both ISNA and CAIR.[67]

I wouldn't want to create the impression that I wouldn't like the government of the United States to be Islamic sometime in the future.
                    - Ibrahim Hooper, Council on American-Islamic Relations[68]

"Despite ISNA's proven ties to terrorism and extremism, politicians in Washington continue to reach out to it, fooled as they are by the front group's carefully manicured facade of moderation."[69] The FBI finally cut off contacts with CAIR due to its relationship with Hamas, but the White House still praised it. Valerie Jarrett, senior advisor to Obama, "publicly applauded" CAIR for its work to counter bullying with other groups like the National Council of La Raza (a strong pro-immigration group we will meet again in Chapter 10).[70]

Muslim Brotherhood Documents and Holy Land Foundation Trial

Prior to that trial, there had been a major breakthrough in August 2004 when Ismail Elbarasse was stopped while casing the Chesapeake Bay Bridge in Maryland. The FBI discovered the archives of the MB in North America in a hidden sub-basement of his home in Annandale, Virginia. The documents confirmed the myriad Muslim groups in the US were mainly controlled by the Muslim Brotherhood with the goal of imposing sharia and "re-establishing the global caliphate."

The 2007 trial of HLF resulted in a mistrial since the jury could not reach a unanimous verdict. The second trial in 2008 "convicted HLF and five of its leaders on charges of providing material support to Hamas." The five received sentences from 65 to 15 years in prison.

I swear by Allah that war is deception... We are fighting our enemy with a kind heart... Deceive, camouflage, pretend you are leaving while walking away. Deceive your enemy.
- Shukri Abu Baker, (convicted of funding Islamic terrorism) Holy Land Foundation[71]

The 2004 raid produced one critical document that was used in the HLF trial: it was the Brotherhood's strategic plan for North America, *"An Explanatory Memorandum: On the General Strategic Goal for the Group."* It also has a list of 29 Muslim Brotherhood organizations.[72] It had been approved by the Shura Council in 1987 and was quite clear on their mission:

> The process of settlement [of Islam in the United States] is a **"Civilization-Jihadist Process"** with all the word means. The Ikhwan must understand that their work in America is a kind of **grand jihad** in eliminating and **destroying the Western civilization from within** and **"sabotaging"** its miserable house by their hands and the hands of the believers **so that it is eliminated** and God's [Allah's] religion is made victorious over all other religions. [Emphasis added][73]

The strategy is to wage "a cultural jihad now and a violent jihad later – once the proper 'infrastructure' is in place." While the Muslim Brotherhood is weak, the strategy is to accumulate power peacefully. When the Brotherhood becomes stronger in later stages, they would move to coercive power, including violence if necessary "to take over the government" and enforce sharia. The plan to Islamize America consists of five phases[74]:

Phase 1: "Establishment of an elite Muslim leadership, while raising *taqwa,* or Islamic consciousness, in the Muslim community." [The CSP Shariah study (p. 74) refers to a paper "Phases of the World Underground Movement Plan" with these five phases and added comments. It refers to this phase with "Phase of discreet and secret establishment of leadership."]

Phase 2: "Creation of Islamic institutions the leadership can control along with the formation of autonomous Muslim enclaves." [CSP Shariah – "Phase of gradual appearance on the public scene and exercising and utilizing various public activities (It greatly succeeded in implementing this stage). It also succeeded in achieving a great deal of its important goals, such as infiltrating various sectors of the Government. Gaining religious institutions and embracing senior scholars. Gaining public support and sympathy. Establishing a shadow government (secret) within the Government."]

Phase 3: "Infiltration and Islamization of America's political, social, economic, and educational systems, forming a shadow state within the state. Escalation of religious conversions to Islam. Manipulation of mass media, and sanitization of language offensive to Islam." ["Escalation phase, prior to conflict and confrontation with the rulers, through utilizing mass media. Currently in progress."][75]

Phase 4: "Openly hostile public confrontation over U.S. policies, including rioting, and militant demands for special rights and accommodations for Muslims." ["Open public confrontation with the Government through exercising the political pressure approach. It is aggressively implementing the above-mentioned approach. Training on the use of weapons domestically and overseas in anticipation of zero-hour. It has noticeable activities in this regard."]

Phase 5: Final conflict and overthrow (jihad)." ["Seizing power to establish their Islamic Nation under which all parties and Islamic groups are united."]

The Muslim Brotherhood is currently in Phase 3 but they are patient. Zaid Shakir advised Muslims to "think strategically" and "hold off on the violent phase until it can 'translate into political gains.'"

> For now, he says, wage informational and financial jihad, using words and money to defeat the infidels. When the Muslim community's numbers are large enough and its political 'infrastructure' is strong enough, then use bombs.
> First infiltrate and convert, then wage jihad, he reiterates. Use deception and propaganda – putting on a friendly face – until the time is right. Then drive the sword into the backs of the enemy.
> We have to start doing the real tough, nitty-gritty, unglamorous, boring work of developing our organizational and institutional strength in this country, Shakir said. If we put a nationwide infrastructure in place and marshaled our resources, we'd take over this country in a very short time.

America is the big prize. If Muslims can conquer the US, "they can conquer the world for Allah." Shakir gleefully noted that **"this is only made possible thanks to America's blind religious tolerance**: 'We're safe and free to practice and advance our religion here.'" [Emphasis added][76]

The documents and observations of Muslim Brotherhood activities show the techniques the MB is employing in its civilization jihad[77]:

- Expanding the Muslim presence by birth rate, immigration, and refusal to assimilate;
- Occupying and expanding domination of physical spaces;
- Ensuring the "Muslim Community" knows and follows MB doctrine;
- Controlling the language we use in describing the enemy;
- Ensuring we do not study their doctrine (sharia);
- Co-opting key leadership;
- Forcing compliance with sharia at local levels;
- Fighting all counterterrorism efforts;
- Subverting religious organizations;
- Employing lawfare – the offensive use of lawsuits and threats of lawsuits;
- Claiming victimization / demanding accommodations;
- Condemning "slander" against Islam;
- Subverting the U.S. education system, in particular, infiltrating and dominating U.S. Middle East studies programs;
- Demanding the right to practice sharia in segregated Muslim enclaves;
- Demanding the recognition of sharia in non-Muslims spheres;
- Confronting and denouncing Western society, laws, and traditions, and
- Demanding that sharia replace Western law.

Many of these techniques influence or neutralize the US government at all levels.

American Muslim Council

Abdurrahman Alamoudi has been mentioned several times already. He came to the US from Eritrea in 1979 and became a citizen in 1996. He founded the **American Muslim Council (AMC)** which was referred to by the FBI as "the most mainstream Muslim group in the United States" and what the Catholic Bishops called "the premier, mainstream Muslim group in Washington." The *Washington Post* called him "a pillar of the local Muslim community."[78] He was involved in over 20 other Muslim organizations and became a fixture in Washington which permitted him to gain access to the Clinton White House and even to George W. Bush.

In 1995, Alamoudi helped President Clinton and the ACLU develop a presidential guideline entitled "Religious Expression in Public Schools." In November of that year, Alamoudi and 23 other Muslim leaders met with President Clinton and Vice President Al Gore. On December 8, Clinton's National Security Adviser, Anthony Lake, met with Alamoudi and several other AMC Board members. ON February 8, 1996, Hillary Clinton penned a newspaper column based on talking points provided by Alamoudi. Later that month, Mrs. Clinton asked AMC to draw up a guest list for a reception marking the end of Ramadan that was to be held at the White House.[79]

His high level access enabled him to have a role in establishing the Muslim Chaplain Program for the Defense Department. He founded the **American Muslim Armed Forces and Veterans Affairs Council** (AMAFVAC) which was certified by DOD in 1993 as "one of two organizations (the other was the **Graduate School of Islamic and Social Sciences**) authorized to approve and endorse Muslim chaplains. His influence continued in the Bush Administration. His deputy, Khaled Saffuri, the Bush campaign's Muslim outreach coordinator, and another senior Muslim Brotherhood member was appointed to handle Muslim access in the White House Office of Public Liaison.

> If you don't give us justice. If you don' give us equality. If you don't give us our share of America. If you don't stay out of our way and leave us alone, we're gonna burn America down.
>
> **- Imam Abdul Alim Musa, Al Masjid mosque, Washington, DC**[80]

Unfortunately for Alamoudi, he admitted at a rally that he supported Hamas and HezbAllah. On his way back from Libya in 2003 with $340,000 that Muammar Qaddafi had given him in a plot to kill then Saudi Crown Prince (now King) Abdullah, he was arrested in the UK. He was extradited to the US and proved to be "a senior al Qaeda financier" with "his objective of making America a Muslim nation." He received a 23-year sentence to federal prison. Despite all his illegal financial transaction, false tax returns, and dealing with terrorists, the Federal prosecutors asked the court to reduce his sentence in 2011.[81]

There was speculation as to why Holder's Justice Department wanted his sentence reduced. The papers were sealed which usually means the criminal has provided "service" to the government. That could have been information on Qaddafi or on the Muslim Brotherhood.

We did not learn much from this reality check on the stealth jihad whereby such a person could control the placement of Muslim chaplains in the two most dangerous places: the military and the prisons.   The government did not learn though and transferred that responsibility for chaplains to ISNA.[82]

Fiqh Council of North America

Fiqh means "comprehension" or "understanding" in Arabic and refers to the comprehension of Islamic jurisprudence (sharia) by Muslim legal authorities. To ensure that Muslim Brotherhood activities were complying with sharia, a Fiqh Committee was established within the Muslim Students of America in 1963. It later became the **Fiqh Council of North America (FCNA)** in 1994.[83] The council's founding trustees were Jamal Barzinji, Taha al-Awani, and Abdurahman Alamoudi. Alamoudi is in Colorado prison. Awani is a leader of various MB entities, including the **Islamic Institute of Islamic Thought (IIIT)**, which is their own think tank. [It was created in 1985 as part of the Safa Group (a Virginia-based network of Saudi-funded fronts) with $25 million provided by the Saudi Islamic Development Bank.[84] **Yusuf al-Qaradawi**, banned from the US in late 1999 as a "terror-sympathizer," was a leader of the IIIT.[85]]

One of the council members was Salah Sultan who also founded and served as president of the Islamic American University in Southfield, Michigan; was national director of tarbiyah (Islamic instruction) for the Muslim American Society; and runs the American Council for Islamic Research in Hilliard, Ohio. The cleric warned on Egyptian TV of death and destruction for America. Sultan has permanent residency status and regularly travels on a US passport. After his latest rant, his named was removed from the Fiqh Council website.[86]

The council works closely with ISNA, each of its chapters being required to have sharia arbitration panels. This is a way to insinuate sharia as a parallel legal code into the US despite our Constitution which is the supreme Law of the Land (Article VI).[87]

American Muslim Task Force

The **American Muslim Task Force on Civil Rights and Elections (AMTF)** was created after 9/11 "to help elect more sympathetic politicians, including the president." About half of the AMTF groups are on the HLF list of co-conspirators or in Muslim Brotherhood manifestos and other secret documents.[88] Its website, the "About Us" tab now not functioning, revealed the coverage:

> The American Muslim Task Force on Civil Rights and Elections (AMT), an umbrella organization representing American Muslim Alliance (AMA), American Muslims for Palestine (AMP), Council on American Islamic Relations (CAIR), Islamic Circle of North America (ICNA), Islamic Society of North America (ISNA), Muslim Alliance in North America (MANA), Muslim American Society (MAS), Muslim Public Affairs Council (MPAC), Muslim Students Association – National (MSA), Project Islamic Hope (PIH), and United Muslims of America (UMA).

Other parts of the website clearly showed their "activism in the political arena" and their efforts "to focus on lawmakers and election campaigns at national and state levels."[89] After the HLF trial, the AMTF "vowed it would never allow CAIR to be marginalized." It threatened to suspend "all outreach activities with FBI offices, agents, and other personnel." That was a weak threat because they had never provided any assistance whatsoever to the FBI![90]

Some of these organizations printed books that were distributed at mosques and on college campuses. Books included Sayyid Qutb's *In the Shade of the Koran* and *Milestones,* "which urge jihad, martyrdom and the creation of Islamic states. Scholars came to view his writings as manifestos for Islamic militants." The Brotherhood has operated lately under the name **Muslim American Society** – a "charitable, religious, social, cultural and educational not-for profit organization," with about 10,000 members headquartered in Alexandria, Virginia, with 53 chapters nationwide.   Their spending is "aimed at schools, teachers and children." They set up Islamic American University in Detroit to train teachers and preachers. Realizing it will take time, "We may all feel emotionally attached to the goal of an Islamic state" in the US, but that would have to wait because of the modest Muslim population.[91]

Infiltration into US Society

There are many other organizations which are not necessarily directly associated with the Muslim Brotherhood but have some of the same goals: establishment of Islam, sharia, and restoration of the caliphate.   One group, **Hizb ut-Tahrir**, at a conference in Chicago made statements before a cheering crowd such as: "Islam will be made supreme in the land. Islam will be the ruling system in the land." "Under the Khalifah we will be unified. One state."[92]

Zakat is a major part of Islam and is not restricted to charitable activities as in the US. Pete Seda, also known as Pirouz Sedaghaty, was convicted of sending $150,000 to the Chechen mujahedin from his branch of **al Haramain Islamic Foundation (AHF)** in Ashland, Oregon. AHF has been banned by the US, Saudi Arabia, and the UN for its support of violent terrorist organizations.[93]   For an interesting memoir of a former employee, see Daveed Gartenstein-Ross, *My Year Inside Radical Islam.*   He passed out copies to true believers of the Qur'an which included an appendix, "A Call to Jihad: Holy Fighting in Allah's Cause" extolling violent jihad. He also distributed Mohammad bin Jamil Zino's book, 'Islamic Guidelines for Individual and Social Reform." It included, "Jihad is obligatory on every Muslim in two ways: by spending one's wealth or offering oneself for fighting in the cause of Allah."

The financial community has been penetrated with sharia-compliant finance, including AIG which the US government took over.[94]

Mosques

You have probably noted that many of the protests in Muslim countries take place after Friday prayers when Muslims leave the mosques. The imams fire up the crowd and they march off to do their bidding. The politically correct line in this country is "that mosques are benign houses of worship that are never used for any nefarious purposes."   The problem is that the reality is that "mosques are used to preach hatred, to spread exhortations to terrorist activity, to house a bomb factory, to store weapons, to disseminate messages from bin Laden [now al-Zawahiri], to demand (in the United States) that non-Muslims conform to Islamic dietary restrictions, to fire on American troops, to fire upon Indian troops, or to train jihadists, and much more."[95]

Mehrab (a mosque) means a place of war, a place of fighting. Out of the mosques, wars should proceed. Just as all the wars of Islam proceeded out of the mosques. The prophet had a sword to kill people. Our Holy Imams were quite militant. All of them were warriors. They used to wield swords. They used to kill people. We need a Caliph who would chop hands, cut throats, stone people. In the way that the messenger of Allah used to chop hands, cut throats, and stone people.

- Ayatollah Khomeini[96]

Reza Khalili, former member of Iran's Revolutionary Guards, stated, "they are used as a recruitment center, for backdoor meetings, transfer of arms and cash and putting together terrorist activities." From his experience, he said, "out of the mosques, there was a big effort within Afghan communities by the Iranian Revolutionary Guard members – and with Pakistanis, Turks and others…..And mosques provide a safe haven, and actually, in my view, were one of the centers of the operation." He was asked about the US? "It's absolutely the same. They recruit, they train, they sell the ideology of martyrdom, and many, many are guided and connected to terrorist groups. And you've seen this: many U.S. born citizens, Muslims, unfortunately, have been sold this idea and are sent to Al Qaeda camps or others. But the Iranians are very active in this country through the mosques and Islamic cultural centers to make those connections and run those operations."[97]

This is nothing new. We have known since at least 1999 when Sheikh Muhammad Hisham Kabban declared at the State Department that "Islamic supremacists controlled most mosques in America." He referred to the extremist ideology that took over the mosques and that of the 3,000 US mosques, they had taken over more than 80%. [Dr. Laurie Roth says there are 6,000 mosques now with $80 billion spent by Saudi Arabia to promote Wahhabism, and billions more spent by Iran to promote Shiism."[98]] In 2005, Yehudit Barsky came up with the same finding, 80% of the US mosques "have been radicalized by Saudi money and influence." In 2008, federal investigators found "that the Islamic Saudi Academy in Virginia, despite promises to stop teaching such material, was still using books that advocated that apostates from Islam be executed and that it was permissible for Muslims to kill and seize the property of 'polytheists.'" As a comparison, the Canadian Mounties "found that 85% of the imams in Canadian mosques were 'hardcore radical jihadists.'"[99] These statistics were verified by a very professional study in 2011 that found only 19% of mosques in the US don't teach jihad violence or Islamic supremacism.[100]

81% of the mosques in the United States teach jihad violence or Islamic supremacism.

An example of political correctness and naiveté occurred in Tulsa, Oklahoma when a police captain, Paul Fields, was stripped of his command after he "refused to order his officers to attend an Islamic propaganda event staged by a local mosque with ties to the Muslim Brotherhood." This was not "community outreach" and was "originally voluntary, but when not enough officers were willing to attend, it became mandatory." The Thomas More Law Center which is supporting Fields stated, "The City of Tulsa Police Department and its highest ranking officials are not only willfully blind to the threat that sharia poses in their own community,"… they, in effect, "are unwittingly complicit in the Muslim Brotherhood's 'civilization jihadist process.'"[101]

Again, one of the problems with allowing a totalitarian ideology to operate behind the front of religion!

Education system

We have already seen the problem of the Minnesota madrassa, the Tarek ibn Ziyad Academy, a charter school for Muslim students with an Arabic curriculum, which was finally being forced to shut down. [Tarek ibn Ziyad was the conqueror of Visigothic Hispania – or Christian Spain – in 711 A. D.][102] There are many of these schools around the country and they cover all levels from grammar school to universities. The Department of Education and school boards have been penetrated to try to impose sharia in textbooks and teaching. "The object is to control and soften the history of Islam and how it is taught to American students."[103]   As we noted above, one of the techniques of stealth jihad is "Subverting the U.S. education system, in particular, infiltrating and dominating U.S. Middle East studies programs."   This has happened in many of our major universities so that many students never receive a true picture of Islam in their studies.   One of the major donors has been Saudi Prince Alwaleed bin Talal who is one of the richest people in the world.   He gave $20 million in December 2005 to Georgetown University to establish the Prince Alwaleed bin Talal Center for Muslim-Christian Understanding (CMCU).   The center actively promotes the extremist Wahhabi agenda.   Georgetown is important because of its School of Foreign Service where many of our Foreign Service officers are trained.   Talal also gave $20 million for a similar center at Harvard.

One of the techniques of the stealth jihad is to subvert the U.S. education system, in particular, infiltrating and dominating U.S. Middle East studies programs.

Correspondence has been exposed which revealed a joint letter from CAIR Executive Director Nihad Awad and CMCU director John Esposito and a reply from OIC (Organization of the Islamic Conference) Secretary General Ekmeleddin Ihsanoglu which "offered $325,000 in cash from the OIC to finance an 'Islamophobia' symposium to be convened at Georgetown University."   We have already reviewed the OIC campaign about Islamophobia in Chapter 4. The money was to be funneled through CAIR to CMCU.

Other US universities have joined to "promote the OIC 'Islamophobia' agenda, most recently the University of California, Berkeley, which hosted the 'Islamophobia Production and Redefining the Global "Security" Agenda for the 21st Century,' just this past April."   That conference was "co-sponsored by the OIC's Islamic Educational, Scientific and Cultural Organization (IESCO) and CAIR, and featured IESCO representative Papa Toumane Ndiaey and CAIR Executive Director Nihad Awad as speakers."   This put to the lie CAIR's repeated claim that it does not receive foreign funding or support foreign agendas.   Particularly disturbing is that some of our top universities are working with Islamic foreign governments and groups like CAIR in direct opposition to the First Amendment right to free speech.

Robert Spencer's comments are particularly interesting about John Esposito and academic work on Islam: "Saudi-funded dhimmi pseudo-academic Islamic apologist John Esposito working with Hamas-linked CAIR to destroy the freedom of speech, cover up the truth about the global jihad and Islamic supremacism.

"It's ironic: Islamic supremacist critics sometimes point to my working outside of academia as if it were some indication that what I say isn't true.   But in reality, it's the universities that are bought and paid for by Islamic supremacist interests.   The only honest work on Islam and jihad is taking place almost completely outside of academia these days."[104]

This is not limited to the US, Saudi and other Middle East rulers gave £233.5 million to eight British universities, including Oxford, Cambridge, and the London School of Economics. Just as in the US universities, these students "were presented a world-view that was almost exclusively anti-Western."   As one study stated, our universities "are now effectively up for sale to the highest bidder."[105]

US Government

We have already seen that some of the radical US Muslims had access to the White House and that Muslims are on the staff that serves the president.   The radical Muslim groups also target that other great seat of power, the US Congress.   We have met Abdurahman

Alamoudi, "the most influential Islamic leader in Washington, D.C.," the "top al-Qaeda fundraiser in the US," now serving 23 years, who was a "regular fixture on Capitol Hill." One organization that has been trying to teach both Democrats and Republicans that "there is nothing inherently violent in Islamic law" is the **Congressional Muslim Staffers Association (CMSA)**. Unfortunately, they have a bad track record.

In time, this so-called democracy will crumble, and there will be nothing.   And the only thing left will be Islam.

- Imam Siraj Wahhaj, Masjid Al-Taqwa mosque, Brooklyn, NY

CMSA initiated Friday afternoon prayer services on Capitol Hill immediately after 9/11. Their first choice to lead the prayers was none other than **Anwar al-Awlaki**, killed in Yemen under a kill or capture order from President Obama. A video of that session shows CAIR leader Nihad Awad and then CAIR communications specialist Randall "Ismail" Royer (currently serving 20 years for terrorism) plus the CMSA founder Jameel Alim Johnson. Johnson got in trouble when as chief of staff to Rep. Gregory Meeks, he tried to set up a conference on Capitol Hill which "was to feature a long list of Islamic radicals."

The infiltration goes back even farther. The first Muslim cleric to deliver the opening prayer for Congress in 1991 was Siraj Wahhaj. Two years later, he "was named an unindicted co-conspirator in the 1993 World Trade Center bombing trial."   He has called for the establishment of an Islamic state in the US governed by sharia.

The King Hearings.   Rep. Peter King (R-NY), chairman of the House Homeland Security Committee, held hearings on Muslim extremism in America which prompted numerous members of congress and outsiders to display their ignorance and naiveté. The political pandering went wild. White House spokesman Jay Carney said America should not practice guilt by association. Democrats complained that all groups that foster terrorism should have been included (even though they are not going around killing people). Rep. Keith Ellison (D-Minn.), a convert to Islam aka Keith Hakim, stated that the hearings approach was "contrary to the best of American values and threatens our security." Rep. Sheila Jackson Lee (D-Texas) challenged that Muslims did not cooperate in the search for terrorists. She was oblivious to the difficulty of CAIR working with law enforcement or the California CAIR post, "Build a wall of resistance. Don't talk to the FBI." Nobody wanted to talk about this taboo topic, an elephant in the room.[106]

CNN's Ali Velshi claimed that King has a "seemingly strange obsession with Islam and Islamists."[107]   King received a stream of threatening phone calls and 54 Democrat congressmen wrote to him requesting cancellation of the hearing and to "broaden the scope to include white supremacist groups and environmental extremists. The Congressional Asian Pacific American Caucus, the Congressional Black Caucus, and the Congressional Hispanic Caucus denounced the hearing. Rep. Bennie Thompson (D-Miss.), the ranking Democrat on the committee, said, "I cannot help but wonder how propaganda about this hearing's focus on the American Muslim community will be used by those who seek to inspire a new generation of suicide bombers."[108]

The Muslim Brotherhood again displayed their resistance to any counter-jihad efforts. The Muslim Public Affairs Council provided talking points which several Democrats obediently parroted. Their points included: accuse King of "pure political posturing," these hearings appear little more than a political circus with Rep. King as the ringleader," the "hearings hurt our national security" because of their "narrow scope," and the hearings were not necessary since "active" partnerships with law enforcement already exist. Rep. Laura

Richardson (D-Calif.) picked up the "political posturing" by comparing it to the McCarthy era. Rep. Al Green (D-Texas) asked why King was not investigating the Ku Klux Klan. Keith Ellison regurgitated all the MPAC talking points at the beginning of the hearing.[109]

Keith Ellison regurgitated all the MPAC talking points at the beginning of the hearing.

Despite the propaganda outpouring from CAIR and their ilk, most Americans supported the hearings.[110] The circus continued. Rep. Jackie Speier (D-Calif.) called the hearing "grossly incomplete." Rep. Yvette Clarke (D-NY) called it "theater" and "reality TV." There were no law enforcement officials present except for Los Angeles Sheriff Leroy Baca, who was called by the Democrats, and had stressed "his strong collaboration with Muslim American organizations." Rep. Chip Cravaack (R-Minn.), after blasting CAIR, told Baca, "Basically, you're dealing with a terrorist organization. They might be using you, sir, to implement their goals."[111]

Steven Emerson, one of the true experts on terrorism in the US, blasted CAIR, ISNA, and the MAS for playing the "Islamophobia" card and manipulating the media to silence criticism of Islamic radicalism. He observed: The real underlying story here is how the self-anointed leadership of the Muslim community…are the ones responsible for instilling panic into the Muslim community by suggesting that these hearings will lead to 'hate crimes' against Muslims." He pointed out the "hype and scare tactics" of opponents and gave as an example a headline on MSNBC.com: "Inquiry by congressional committee looks like inquisition to many Muslims." He noted that over 80% of terrorist convictions involved radical Islamists. The small optimism he saw was that people are noticing how "paranoid and obnoxious" CAIR is.[112]

Patrick Poole addressed the question as to why the Islamic groups feared the hearings. He gave five reasons why the histrionics are attempting to silence the growing number of Americans who recognize the "growing homegrown terror threat." (1) These hearings challenge the Muslim Brotherhood's political monopoly. (They had that access to the White House and Congress, but revelations like the HLF trial had cut their ties.) (2) Their narrative is at war with reality. (Claim of "Islamophobia but in reality hate crimes against Muslims are down sharply since 9/11.) (3) Their agenda is increasingly in visible conflict with American values. (Efforts to criminalize "defamation of religion" [Islam], wife beating, and states trying to outlaw sharia.) (4) Their faux "de-radicalization efforts are increasingly irrelevant. (Plot to assassinate President Bush, and "experts" who worked with government agencies and later turned out to be extremists.) (5) These Islamic groups ARE the radicalization problem. (The problems with the mosques as terrorist factories, the NYPD called the MSA a "radicalization incubator", and the number of MSA leaders who are in prison on terror charges.[113])

Rep. Keith Ellison was mocked for his tearful presentation at the hearing. He said, "Look there is an organized anti-Muslim industry in the United States. It's Pam Geller, it's Robert Spencer, it's Steve Emerson…it's Frank Gaffney. They're well-known entities. They sell books doing this." He did not mention the $13,350 the MSA aka the Muslim Brotherhood gave him for his hajj to Mecca in 2008.[114]

Following the King hearings, Senate Majority Whip Dick Durbin called for Senate hearings on "Muslim rights."

Following the King hearings, Senate Majority Whip Dick Durbin called for Senate hearings on "Muslim rights." Even though anti-Muslim hate crimes are actually down, that did not stop Durbin who claimed, 'there has been a spike in anti-Muslim bigotry in the last year that demands closer attention."[115]

When Durbin held his hearing, Sen. Jon Kyl (R-Ariz.) stated, "I'm a bit perplexed by the focus," since most hate crimes are against Jews. "The point is, all bigotry is to be condemned; selective indignation is not helpful." Farhana Khera, executive director of Muslim Advocates, testified that "in the last several months, anti-Muslim rhetoric has reached a disturbing new level." She did not note Christians being brutalized and killed in Egypt, Pakistan, etc. Kyl defended the King hearings saying, "Political correctness cannot stand in the way of identifying those who would do us harm." He questioned whether Khera's organization "was committed to helping root out extremist elements of Islam, given that its website advises Muslims to consult a lawyer before speaking with the FBI about violent extremism." He added, "I would think Muslim Americans would feel a special obligation to help in such investigations."[116] Not likely!

CAIR showed its power again by getting the CIA to cancel a three-day conference the CIA was to host on "homegrown radicalization." On 18 July 2011, CAIR issued a press release: "CAIR Asks CIA to Drop Islamophobic Trainer." Nihad Awad had written a letter to CIA Director Leon Panetta.[117] This is clear evidence of the Muslim Brotherhood/CAIR objective to not permit any criticism of Islam.

A more disturbing situation is Secretary of State Hillary Clinton, who in addition to her support for Fethullah Gulen (above), has as her deputy chief of staff, **Huma Abedin-Weiner**. Huma Abedin had worked for Mrs. Clinton for years and then married Rep. Weiner who was forced to resign from Congress after a dalliance. Her marriage is odd in that she comes from a devout Muslim family and married a Jew. Huma was born in the US but her family moved back to Saudi Arabia around 1977. Her mother, Saleha Mahmoud Abedin, is co-founder and vice dean of Dar El-Kekma women's college in Saudi Arabia and is a member of the Muslim Sisterhood (aka International Women's Organization) which works with the Muslim Brotherhood. Her brother, Hassan, "is listed as a fellow and partner with a number of Muslim Brotherhood members." He works at Oxford University in the Centre for Islamic Studies, which has links with Al Azhar in Cairo. He has "worked with Saudi Prince Alwaleed bin Talal on a program of spreading Islam to the west." Working in the State Department and married to a congressman, has given her great access "to state secrets and access to the inner workings of Congress."[118]

Another case is the six year ban on letting Tariq Ramadan enter the US. The Swiss professor's mother was the eldest daughter of Hasan al-Banna, founder of the Muslim Brotherhood, and he follows the strategy of his grandfather in imposing sharia in the West. The ACLU sued to permit his entry. Hillary Clinton finally lifted the ban on him in 2010. He has a chair at Oxford but keeps his eye on the US. Speaking at a fundraiser organized by the Islamic Circle of North America (ICNA) (which is close to the Muslim American Society) in Dallas, he told his audience "not to be colonized" by this consumerist society, but "It should be us, with our understanding of Islam, our principles, colonizing positively the United States of America."[119]

Some people doubt Obama's Christian views, particularly due to his preacher in Chicago. Some call him a "closet Muslim" since he attended a Muslim school in Indonesia. Also, his statements are very supportive of Islam: "Islam has always been a part of the American family and Muslim Americans have long contributed to the strength and character of our country in all walks of life" and Islam is "a faith known for its diversity and a commitment to justice and the dignity of all human beings."[120] In his 2009 Cairo speech, he said, "I consider it part of my responsibility as president of the United States to fight against negative stereotypes of Islam wherever they appear." It would be better if he felt that way about America.

At the White House, Obama appointed Azizah al-Hibri to the US Commission on International Religious Freedom. "Al-Hibri believes that sharia law is superior to American law." One of Obama's earliest appointees was **Dalia Mogahed** to his faith advisiory council. Nonie Darwish has written that the "empowerment of Radical Islam under the Obama administration" is extremely disturbing. Mogahed is a supporter of sharia and denies any connection between radical Islam and terrorism. She is Obama's closest Muslim advisor, helps write Obama's speeches, and is a staunch defender of CAIR and ISNA.[121]

Mogahed worked with Imam Feisal Abdul Rauf, the controversial cleric behind the Ground Zero mosque. Besides her work in the White House, she is "on the advisory council of the Department of Homeland Security." She is also "a senior analyst and executive director of the Gallup Center for Muslim Studies." She led a survey which was the basis for a 2008 book she co-authored, 'Who Speaks for Islam? What a Billion Muslims Really Think'." Her "survey concluded only 7 percent of the world's Muslims are political radicals and that the majority support democracy."[122] How stupid does she think we are? 7% of 1.5 billion Muslims equal **105 million radicals!** It doesn't take that many to make revolutions. If her number is accurate, then she said there are **196,000 radical Muslims in the US**.

Mogahed made the headlines again when she blocked the meeting of the Maronite Patriarch of Lebanon and Obama. She was evidently "heeding a request by the higher leadership of the Muslim Brotherhood in Egypt, who consider that US Administration must support the Islamist Sunni current facing the Iranian current in the region."[123]

Obama's counterterrorism adviser, John Brennan, called jihad a "legitimate tenet of Islam" and argued that the term "jihadists" should not be used when describing violent extremists.[124] James Clapper, the Director of National Intelligence, told the Congress that the Egyptian Muslim Brotherhood was "a very heterogeneous group, largely secular, which has eschewed violence and has decried Al Qaeda as a perversion of Islam." His office had to issue a "clarification" that "He is well aware that the Muslim Brotherhood is not a secular organization."[125]

This "infiltration and willful blindness to the threat to America posed by Muslim Brotherhood front organizations…only leads us further into submission to the advocates of a global Islamic state and the imposition of shariah."[126]

Sleeper cells

Several incidents and the arrests of foreign workers in the US have raised the question of sleeper terrorist cells in the US. Maher "Mike" Mofeid Hawas, a lead engineer for Intel Corp. was sentenced to prison for seven years for aiding terrorists and trying to join the Taliban. Mohammed Atique, a Pakistani electrical engineer, received 10 years for being part of the "Virginia Jihad" (9 of 11 were convicted). Khwaja Hassan, a naturalized US citizen from Pakistan and also a member of the "Virginia Jihad" was sentenced to 11 years.

There are two background characteristics that appear in most of the suspects: high levels of education and an interest in technology. These people are able to hold legal jobs with US companies and since US companies are searching for highly trained people, they can usually stay and rise in these companies.[127]

We mentioned the global expansion of the Pakistani group **Lashkar-e-Taiba** in Chapter 6. Janet Napolitano, US Secretary of Homeland Security, has said that LeT ranks up high with al Qaeda as terrorist organizations. From its South Asia base, it has moved across Europe and into North America. "LeT has a network of sleeper cells in the US and Australia, has trained terrorists from other countries, and has entered new theatres of 'jihad', such as Iraq."[128]

A final audio message from Abu Musab al-Suri, an al Qaeda camp manager who was captured, mentioned that he had "trained American and British nationals at Al-Qaida camps in Afghanistan to carry out catastrophic terrorist strikes." He called for the mujahedin to strike "countries that have a military presence in Iraq, Afghanistan, or the Arabian Peninsula. They must either strike the territory of these countries or targets that are outside of their borders. **O' sleeper cells, wake up now!**" [Emphasis added][129]

People in sleeper cells likely receive little or no guidance from al Qaeda or other groups and can stay in place quietly for many years. They are very difficult to root out until they make a move.

Apologists

We have already encountered John Esposito above, who like most of the directors of Islamic Studies centers at universities funded by large Arab donations, become supporters of Islam and end up as apologists. Probably the major apologist is Karen Armstrong, the ex-nun, who has found her new calling in touting Islam as the religion of compassion. She has studied the Qur'an extensively (it is not clear she understands it!) and quotes it from memory and whenever she mentions the prophet, she spouts the normal Islamic ritual, Peace Be Upon Him (PBUH). In her view the Qur'an calls for good actions, compassion, and that "Islam came to spread compassion among the tribes, and consequently among the nations of the world." She thinks the "Qur'an strictly forbids any coercion in religion" (evidently she missed the part about abrogation) and that "Muslims did not impose their faith by the sword." In an interview, she stated, "Muslims should try to use the media; they have got to have a Muslim lobby. This is a jihad, an effort, a struggle, that is very important. If you want to change the media, then you have got to make people see that Islam is a force to be reckoned with politically and culturally." It is not clear yet whether she has finally converted to Islam, but the Muslims seem to have gotten her message.[130]

Another apologist is Lesley Hazleton, a British born Jew, who worked in the Middle East for years, and after 9/11 started reading the Qur'an. She has now become very supportive of Islam and writes and speaks on how Islam is misunderstood.

We regularly see Muslims try to post their propaganda views in the media such as when we noted Nezar Hamze, the executive director of he South Florida chapter of CAIR, write that sharia is not a threat. He claimed it as "absolutely baseless" that "Moozlims" were trying "to infiltrate our court systems and replace our Constitution."[131]   Aziz Huq, an assistant professor of law at the University of Chicago, wrote an Op-Ed piece for the *New York Times* (19 June 2011) "Defend Muslims, Defend America," in which he attacked the efforts by several states to ban sharia, which he called "discriminatory and pointless." To make it more startling, he claimed they were "a significant threat to national security." He wrote that "the bans would deprive Muslims of equal access to the law," make Muslims "second-class citizens." He claimed the bans would "chill cooperation by the Muslim-American community with counterterrorism efforts." Unfortunately, there is no cooperation now.

Then there is Janet Napolitano, the Secretary of Homeland Security, who thinks there is no logic in profiling Muslim men who are under 35.[132] And if you are tired of "Press 2 for Spanish," now it is "Press 3 for Arabic" in Michigan, which has the largest Muslim population in the US with Dearborn as the Muslim capital.[133]

Governor Christie of New Jersey appointed a Muslim to a Superior Court judgeship in Passaic County and when questioned about the wisdom of it responded that the "Sharia Law business is just crap."   Of course, the New Jersey politicians have been falling all over themselves on Muslim "outreach."   Perhaps it is because "Passaic County has the second largest Muslim population in the country.   And the Islamic Center of Passaic County is the state's largest mosque, and it's the only one run by an Imam who was a member of the Hamas terrorist organization."   When the US government tried to deport him, the politicians came to his aid, "despite his own guilty plea to being a member of Hamas."[134]

The Ground Zero Mosque controversy brought out all kinds of people.   Imam Feisal Abdul Rauf who strongly advocated it as a great example of "interfaith dialogue," has said in other places that "I do not believe in religious dialogue."[135]   He knows how to use taqiyya. With 70% of Americans opposing the mosque, New York City Mayor Michael Bloomberg repeatedly insisted it be built and those who oppose are "un-American."[136]

It is bad enough that we have Muslim honor killings here in the US, but it is disconcerting when officials are intimidated and cover them up due to "fear of violence from Muslims."   A Palestinian woman died in Tampa evidently from an honor killing, but the "Tampa Police Department claims that Fatima Abdallah killed herself by repeatedly beating her head against a coffee table."   One agent requested that her name be removed from the report because of "fear of Muslim reprisal."   "It appears that some officials feared Muslim reprisal, feared media attention if the case became public and therefore decided to promptly call this violent death an accident without any further investigation beyond the incident date."[137]   It is a sad day when we permit Muslims to intimidate our government agencies.

The initial objective is to create a state within the state.   It is already in existence – an "underworld – a parallel secret society:

> The Brothers have their own AFL-CIO; it's called ISNA.
> They have their own American Bar Association; it's called the Fiqh Council....
> They have their own VFW; it's called thee American Muslim Armed Forces and Veterans Affairs Council.
> They have their own NAACP; it's called CAIR.
> Their FCA, moreover, is the MSA, or Muslim Students Association.
> Their United Way is (or was) the Holy Land Foundation.
> Their NEA is the Council on Islamic Education, or CIE.
> And their YMCA is WAMY – except, instead of holding basketball camps, it holds jihad camps.
> They also have their own investment bank in the North American Islamic Trust...
> They have their own think tank – the International Institute of Islamic Thought – and their own colleges – the Islamic American University and the Graduate School of Islamic and Social Studies (aka Cordoba University), which has trained most of the U.S. military's Muslim chaplains.
> They also operate their own travel agency – Dar el-Eiman USA, Inc. – which enjoys an exclusive deal with the Saudi embassy to arrange travel for Muslim Americans to *hajj*...."
> They also have publications: *Islamic Horizons, The American Muslim*
> Printer – Amana Publishing
> Bridges TV and SoundVision – a Hollywood-style production company.[138]

The "Hard Jihad" is fought with violence.   There also is the "Soft Jihad" – an effort to destroy liberal democracies from within.   The most important organization promoting Soft Jihad is the Muslim Brotherhood and its many affiliates.

- Clifford D. May[139]

Notes

1. "D.C. Watson: Letter To Congress: Islamic Radicals? Or Fundamentalists?" Jihad Watch, 12 June 2011.
2. In May and June 2006, two bomb making sites were found in Iraq and terrorists arrested. In both cases, the head bomb makers had master's degrees (one in chemistry and one in physics) from American universities.
3. Inal Ersan, "In Video, Al Qaeda Militant Warns US Of Worse Attacks," *Boston Globe,* 30 May 2007.
4. A young Marine, Yonathan Melaku, was arrested for shooting at the Pentagon. A search of his home found radical literature including a book by Anwar al-Awlaki. Newt Gingrich, "A Diplomatic Defeat for President Obama and America," 6 July 2011.
5. Alan Feuer, "In First For Britain, U.S. Citizen Is Extradited On Terror Charges," *The New York Times,* 30 May 2007.
6. "The Untold Story of al-Qaeda's Plot to Attack the Subways," excerpt from Ron Suskind's book, *The One Percent Doctrine: Deep Inside America's Pursuit of Its Enemies Since 9/11, Time,* 26 June 2006, pp. 26-35.
7. Katherine Shrader, AP, "Al-Qaida renewing terrorism efforts, intel report says," *Reno Gazette-Journal*, 13 July 2007, p. 4B.
8. "Terrorist Group Setting Up Operations Near Border: Hezbollah Considered To Be More Advanced Than Al-Qaida," 10News.com, 4 May 2011. Reference a police bulletin from Doug Ross, "LulzSec doc drop: Arizona Officials Say Hezbollah Operating in Mexico," 7 July 2011, Jihad Watch.
9. "The Criminal-Terrorist Pipeline to the United States," http://www.douglasfarah.com/article/275/the-criminal-terrorist-pipeline-to-the-united-states.com, 16 November 1997.
10. http://www.discoverthe networks.org/individualProfile.asp?indid=2170.
11. "Boston Mosque: The Rise of Radical Islam," CBN, 16 November 2004.
12. Keith Johnson, "Terror Worries ride Rails," *The Wall Street Journal, 11 May 2011.*
13. Dana Hedgpeth and Amy Orndorff, "McLean woman committed in Red Line bomb threat," *Washington Post,* 13 June 2011.
14. Haya El Nasser USA TODAY "Poll shows U.S. Muslims are moderate," *Reno Gazette-Journal,* 30 August 2011, p. 1B.
15. Amy Forliti, "Minn. Woman facing Somali terror case arrested," Associate Press, 3 October 2011.
16. "Shariah: The Threat to America," The Center for Security Policy, 2010, pp. 111-113.
17. "Homeland Insecurity: Probe finds terrorists in U.S. 'training for war,'" WorldNetDaily.com 17 February 2006. For a complete review of this group, see Larry Martinez [sic]. "Jama'at al Fuqra," *Journal of Counterterrorism & Homeland Security Int'l*, Vol. 8, No. 3, p. 36.
18. Jamie Glazov, "Terrorist Camps in America," FrontPageMagazine.com 3 February 2009, interview with Ryan Mauro about "Homegrown Jihad: Terrorist Camps Around U.S.," documentary available at ChristianAction.org.
19. Douglas J. Hagman, "Jammat ul Fuqra," Canada Free Press and the Northeast Intelligence Network, 18 December 2009. "Today, the threat posed by these domestic terrorists is more severe than initially reported. Now more than ever is time to be very concerned. The operational tempo of Jamaat ul Fuqra is on the rise, and people need to be updated of this growing threat."
20. Paul L. Williams, Ph.D., "Islamic Armed Fortress Emerges From Pocono Mountains," Jihad Watch, 8 April 2010. Eileen F. Toplansky, "The Muslim Brotherhood and Weiner," *American Thinker,* 19 June 2011. Also see the website www.fethullahgulen.org.
21. Ibid.
22. Steven Emerson, "Terrorism and the Times: What's Not Fit To Print." IPT News, http://www.investigativeproject.org/article/576, 18 December 2007.
23. Patrick Dunleavy, "Converts to terror," *New York Post,* 2 September 2010.
24. Justice Policy Institute Report: The Punishing Decade, & U.S. Bureau of Justice Statistics Bulletin NCJ 219416 – Prisoners in 2006.
25. "Allah or Jesus," www.rickmathes.org.
26. WorldNetDaily, 14 June 2011.
27. "Shariah: The Threat to America," The Center for Security Policy, p. 70. For an extensive coverage of the Muslim Brotherhood, see Chapter 4, pp. 65-92.
28. Shariah, The Center for Security Policy, pp. 77-78.
29. John Guandolo, "The Muslim Brotherhood in America: Part II: MB History & Their Arrival in America," Guns & Patriots, 15 March 2011. This is a good series on the MB: Part I: Understanding the Threat, 8 March 2011 and Part III: "The Settlement Process," 29 March 2011.
30. Guandolo, op. cit., Part III.
31. P. David Gaubatz and Paul Sperry, *Muslim Mafia: Inside the Secret Underworld That's Conspiring to Islamize America,* (Los Angeles, California, WND Books, 2009), p. 248.
32. Shariah, The Center for Security Policy, p. 70. There are 150 campus chapters according to *Muslim Mafia*, p. 282. See also Erick Stakelbeck, "Muslim Student Group a Gateway to Jihad," CBN News, 21 March 2011.
33. *Muslim Mafia,* pp. 282-283.
34. Shariah, The Center for Security Policy, pp. 70 and 80.
35. Erick Stakelbeck, "Muslim Student Group a Gateway to Jihad," CBN News, 21 March 2011.
36. Shariah, The Center for Security Policy, p. 83. http://www.isna.net.
37. "Court removes 'coconspirator' tag from Muslim groups, Jewish Telegraph Agency, 22 October 2010, Jihad Watch.
38. *Muslim Mafia,* p.280.
39. *Muslim Mafia,* pp. 280-281 and 287. For a rogue's gallery of the founders, see pp. 286-287.
40. Quoted in "What Muslim Leaders Say About Islam Dispels the Myth that Jihadists are a 'Fringe' Element," Citizen Warrior, 1 October 2010.
41. *Muslim Mafia,* p. 283.
42. Shariah, The Center for Security Policy, pp. 71 and 80.

43. John Guandolo, "The Muslim Brotherhood in America: Part II: MB History & Their Arrival in America," Guns & Patriots, 15 March 2011.
44. Shariah, The Center for Security Policy, p. 79.
45. Shariah, The Center for Security Policy, pp. 81-82. *Muslim Mafia*, pp. 288-289; see p. 290 for details of planting Muslim chaplains.
46. *Muslim Mafia*, pp. 288-289.
47. Alex Murashko, "Largest U.S. Muslim Gathering to 'Deal With Islamophobia,'" *Christian Post*, 1 July 2011.
48. http://www.hyscience.com/archives/2007/05/video_steve_eme.php.
49. Guandolo, op. cit., Part II.
50. Shariah, The Center for Security Policy, pp. 89-90.
51. Ibid., pp. 87-88.
52. Christine Brim, "Coming August 31: 'Direct Access' Stimulus Grants for the Muslim Brotherhood," Big Peace, 29 August 2010. The full E-mail is posted at the end. She goes into detail about the CCMO's officers.
53. http://www.foxnews.com/story/0,2933,298278,00.html.
54. *Muslim Mafia*, p. 256. See "Who is Esam Omeish?" about the former MAS president.
55. *Muslim Mafia*, pp. 272 and 282.
56. "CAIR's chief's designs to 'run' U.S. revealed" 'Who better than Muslims,' Awad asks, to lead 'Christian-Judeo-Islamic' nation?," WorldNetDaily, 3 April 2011.
57. Josh Gerstein, "Holder: DOJ nixed CAIR leader's prosecution," Politico, 26 April 2011.
58. "CAIR Rep Speaks on Hamas TV," Investigative Project on Terrorism, 5 August 2011, Jihad Watch, 6 August 2011.
59. Shariah, The Center for Security Policy, pp. 83-84.
60. http://archive.frontpagemag.com/readArticle.aspx?ARTID=19439.
61. Shariah, The Center for Security Policy, p. 85.
62. Fred Thompson, "Good News about CAIR," *The Conservative Review*, 22 June 2007.
63. "CAIR Loses IRS Status," IPT News, 22 June 2011.
64. "An Urgent Message from the Desk of David Horowitz," HumanEventsonline, 28 August 2007.
65. Talk-show host Neal Boortz, Muth's News & Views, 4 August 2007.
66. Robert Spencer, "ACLU, Muslim Groups Again Resist Anti-terror Measures," Human Events, 19 November 2007, p. 15.
67. *Muslim Mafia*, p. 288.
68. http://archive.frontpagemag.com/readArticle.aspx?ARTID=19439.
69. *Muslim Mafia*, p. 288.
70. Neil Munro, "Hamas-associated CAIR applauded by White House," *The Daily Caller,* 18 March 2011.
71. http://www/anti-cair-net.org/FBItiesCAIRHamas.
72. Shariah, The Center for Security Policy, pp. 77-78; three more: CAIR, MPAC, and the Islamic Free Market Institute had not been established in 1991.
73. From court documents, quoted in Shariah, The Center for Security Policy, p. 73.
74. *Muslim Mafia*, pp. 259-260.
75. Experts believe the MB is working actively in Phase 3. An example is a protest at New York's Playland Amusement Park where women were denied access for wearing the hijab. It was deliberate because the organizer, the Muslim American Society of New York had been told ahead of time. "New York – Muslim Women Became Violent Over Amusement Park's Headgear Ban, Thomas Moore Law Center Alert, 8 September 2011.
76. *Muslim Mafia*, pp. 260-261. Zaid Shakir is a radical American black convert imam who is a favorite with the Muslim Brotherhood and CAIR.
77. Shariah, The Center for Security Policy, pp. 74-75.
78. From 2004 article by Daniel Pipes, quoted in "AP Exclusive: US seeks to cut prison term for man who worked assassination plot with Libyans," Associated Press, 8 July 2011.
79. Shariah, The Center for Security Policy, p. 75.
80. "D.C. Watson: Letter To Congress: Islamic Radicals? Or Fundamentalists?" Jihad Watch, 12 June 2011.
81. From 2004 article by Daniel Pipes, quoted in "AP Exclusive: US seeks to cut prison term for man who worked assassination plot with Libyans," Associated Press, 8 July 2011.
82. Shariah, The Center for Security Policy, p. 75.
83. The FCNA espoused a unique version of classical Islamic law drawn Yusuf al-Qaradawi's rulings. "Fiqh al aqalliyyat" is only for the interim encouraging Muslims to temporarily accept non-Muslim rule. It prefers to call the Dar al-Islam "dar-al ijaba," "land of response" and the Dar al-Harb "dar ad-dawah" where Islam "has to be spread." "Whether by conversion or war, the MB goal remains conquest of the West." Alyssa A. Lappen, "Yusuf Qaradawi's U.S. minions: The real aim of the Fiqh Council of North America," ACT for America, February 2011.
84. *Muslim Mafia*, pp. 202 and 248.
85. Ibid., p. 132.
86. Patrick Poole, "Top American Islamic Cleric Threatens U.S. on Egyptian TV," Pajamas Media, 7 January 2011.
87. Shariah, The Center for Security Policy, p. 89.
88. *Muslim Mafia*, pp. 61 and 84.
89. Shariah, The Center for Security Policy, pp. 90-91.
90. *Muslim Mafia*, p. 103.
91. Noreen S. Ahmed-Ullah, Sam Rose, and Laurie Cohen, "Underground U.S. chapter of the international Muslim Brotherhood: Struggle for the soul of Islam, A rare look at secretive Brotherhood in America," chicagotribune.com, 19 September 2004.
92. "USA: Hizb ut-Tahrir Leader Calls for Muslim Armies to Unite, Speaks of 'Sheikh Obama' ~ Video," Logan's Warning, 15 July 2011, Jihad Watch, 16 July 2011.

93. "Founder of Islamic Charity Convicted," Right Side News, 11 September 2010.
94. Shariah, The Center for Security Policy, p. 91.
95. "Iran Using Western Mosques to Plot Terrorism?," CBN, 16 December 2010. Also Robert Spencer, "The Use of Mosques," Closed for Business, 23 August 2010.
96. From a speech in commemoration of the birth of Muhammad in 1981, quoted in "What Muslim Leaders Say About Islam Dispels the Myth that Jihadists are a 'Fringe' Element," Citizen Warrior, 1 October 2010.
97. "Iran Using Western Mosques to Plot Terrorism?," CBN, 16 December 2010.
98. "Islam is a Government Dictatorship Housed in Religion," NewsWithViews.com, 3 September 2010.
99. Robert Spencer, "The Use of Mosques," Closed for Business, 23 August 2010.   Comment by Citizen Warrior, 25 August 2010.
100. Mordechai Kedar and David Yerushalmi, "Shari'a and Violence in American Mosques," *Middle East Quarterly,* Summer 2011, Vol. 18, No. 3, pp. 59-72.
101. "Thomas More Law Center Enters Oklahoma Mosque Controversy," 23 March 2011.
102. Sarah Lemagie, "TiZA kids seek new schools," *Star Tribune,* 1 July 2011.
103. Shariah, The Center for Security Policy, p. 91. There are now over 30 Muslim chaplains in private high schools and on college campuses, including Yale, Duke, Princeton, and Northwestern. Matthew Daneman, "Muslim chaplains fill a void," USA TODAY, *Reno Gazette-Journal,* 24 March 2011, p. 1B.
104. Patrick Poole, "PJM Exclusive: Georgetown U. Received $325,000 Funneled Through Terror Front Group," Pajamas Media, 14 June 2011, Jihad Watch, 15 June 2011. It should be noted that there is a similar control in think tanks and universities to support Israel. See Hobbs, *World War IV and Beyond,* pp. 172-175.
105. Stephen Pollard, "Libya and the LSE: Large Arab gifts to universities lead to 'hostile' teaching," *Telegraph,* 3 March 2011, Jihad Watch, 6 March 2011.
106. Laurie Kellman, "King: Next hearing is on radical Muslims in prison," Associated Press, 11 March 2011.
107. Matthew Balan, "CNN's Velshi: Rep. King Has 'Strange Obsession with Islam,'" Media Research Center, 12 March 2011.
108. Jordy Yager, "Surrender Alert: 'Tears, fears at hearings on Muslims,'" *The Hill,* 10 March 2011.
109. Matthew Boyle, "The DC Exclusive: Dems at radicalization hearings recite Muslim Brotherhood-affiliated group's talking points," *The Daily Caller,* 11 March 2011.
110. "King Draws Fire for Hearings on Radicalization of Muslims in U.S., But Most Americans Support Discussion," FoxNews.com, 10 March 2011.
111. Felicia Sinmez and Michelle Boorstein, "CAIR comes under fire during Peter King hearings on radical Islam," *Washington Post,* 10 March 2011.
112. Steven Emerson, "Muslim American groups, not Rep. Pete King, are the ones fomenting hysteria with hearings on tap," *New York Daily News,* 10 March 2011.
113. Patrick Poole, "Why Do Islamic Groups Fear Hearings on Islamic Radicalization?" pajamasmedia.com, 9 March 2011.
114. Evan McMorriss-Santoro, "Keith Ellison Shrugs Off Conservative Mockers," TPM, 17 March 2011.
115. Pamela Geller, "Durbin is wrong about Muslim rights," *Daily Caller,* 23 March 2011, Jihad Watch.
116. Stephanie Condon, "GOP senator turns table at Muslim rights hearing," CBS News, 29 March 2011.
117. Diana West, "Why can CAIR pull strings inside the CIA?" *The Examiner,* 13 August 2011.
118. Eileen F. Toplansky, "The Muslim Brotherhood and Weiner," *American Thinker,* 19 June 2011
119. "Tariq Ramadan openly calls for Muslim colonization of the U.S. -- Dallas, July 27, 2011," Jihad Watch, 5 August 2011.
120. "Islam has always been a part of our American family: Obama," *Indian Express,* 11 August 2011.
121. Nonie Darwish, "Appeasing the Muslim Brotherhood," *FrontPage,* 20 April 2010.
122. Aaron Klein, "Obama's faith adviser helped craft 'perfect Islamic state': Shariah project scrubbed from Internet, sought to 'implement' Muslim caliphate." WorldNetDaily, 17 April 2011.
123. "Obama's Muslim Advisers Block Middle Eastern Christian' Access to White House," Creeping Sharia, 26 October 2011.
124. "Counterterror Adviser Defends Jihad as 'Legitimate Tenet of Islam'," FoxNews.com. 27 May 2010.
125. "Obama Administration Corrects Clapper's Claim That Muslim Brotherhood Is 'Secular'," FoxNews, 10 February 2011.
126. Patrick Poole, "Al-Qaeda on Capitol Hill," Guns & Patriots, 28 September 2010.
127. "The Sleeper Cell Threat: A Search in Unlikely Places," Stratfor's Terrorism Intelligence Weekly, 23 June 2004.
128. Shrideep Biswas, "COMMENTARY – Lashkar-e-Toiba: Global Outreach," South Asia Intelligence Review/India Blooms News Service, 30 May 2011.
129. http//counterterror.typepad.com, 31 December 2005.
130. Siddeek Tawfeek, "Armstrong: Islam came to spread compassion among the nations of the world," Islam Online, 17 March 2011, Jihad Watch.
131. "Sharia law is not a threat," *Miami Herald,* 17 June 2011.
132. "Napolitano: No 'Logic' In Profiling Muslim Men Under The Age Of 35," Real Clear Politics, 9 June 2011, Jihad Watch, 10 June 2011.
133. http://www.michigan.gov/dhs/0,1607,7-124-5453_5527---,00.html.
134. Jonathan Seidl, "Chris Christie Blasts 'Crazies' After Appointing Muslim Judge: The 'Sharia Law Business Is Just Crap,'" The Blaze, 4 August 2011. Also Daniel Greenfield, "Governor Christie's Dirty Islamist Ties," Sultan Knish, 16 January 2011, Jihad Watch, 5 August 2011.
135. "D.C. Watson: Letter To Congress: Islamic Radicals? Or Fundamentalists?" 12 June 2011, Jihad Watch.
136. Shariah, The Center for Security Policy, p. 91.
137. "Tampa Police crime scene tech now admits 'fear of Muslim reprisal' in honor killing classified as accidental death," Jihad Watch, 8 August 2011.
138. *Muslim Mafia,* pp. 262-263.
139. "A Memo to New Members," Jihad Watch, 10 January 2011.

Summary

*In the Muslim community, the holy war is a religious duty,
because of the universalism of the (Muslim) mission and the
(obligation to) convert everybody to Islam either by persuasion
or by force...Islam is under obligation to gain power over nations.*

- Ibn Khaldun, 15th Century

*Most Muslims do not embrace this interpretation of Islam. But a
supremacist reading of the Koran caters to the pride and vanity of
a significant minority of the world's more than 1.3 billion Muslims.*

- Clifford D. May[1]

It is difficult to briefly summarize seven chapters on the threat of Islam to America. Is there something we should really be worried about? Let's start with **seven concerns** Citizen Warrior listed. First was actual **terrorism**, which we have seen plenty of and it continues. Second was Islamic **indoctrination** of our young people. We noted above the Muslim efforts to slant textbooks to hide some of the bad side of Islam and to distort US history such that our youth do not really know about their own country. Foreign money has been used to buy Middle East Studies centers at some of our top universities so that our students receive a biased view of Islam. Third is the biased influence the Muslim Brotherhood and its fronts have on the mainstream **media**. The theme is Islam is a religion of peace and most Muslims are just normal citizens who are unfairly criticized. He wrote of this infiltration, "Right under the noses of the brainwashed non-Muslims, and often with their help, Muslims with a political agenda are working their way into government positions, getting hired in national security positions, wielding influence over law-enforcement officials, and even advising presidents."

Fourth was their influence over **Hollywood** movies which adds to the indoctrination of the news media and textbooks. The Crusades are depicted as "unwarranted aggression" and "terrorists" must be depicted as anything but Islamic even though "most of the world's violence involves Muslims." Fifth is **Eurabia** or the Islamization of Europe. "What will happen to the world if Europe becomes a union of Muslim countries?" Sixth is the "great numbers of **non-Muslims** in the U.S., Canada, Australia, the UK, European countries, and India who are actually **helping orthodox Muslims** carry out their political plans, and fighting against those of us who know Islam's prime directive and wish to curtail it." It is not just ignorance, but the "Islam" they understand is "misleading and outright false information, deliberately planted there by orthodox Muslims."

Finally, seventh is **fear that we will not educate enough people before it is too late**. It is a race against time while we are still the majority in the world. Turkey is sliding back to orthodox Islam reversing the great improvements made by Kemal Ataturk. Lebanon, Malaysia, and Indonesia have all converted. With the Jasmine Revolution, we do not know how these countries are going but elections were won by Islamists in Morocco, Tunisia, Egypt, and will likely win in Libya. Only Spain and Eastern Europe escaped from the relentless march of Islam. Iraq and Afghanistan both have sharia written into their constitutions. **It is a race against time.**[2]

Christians are being oppressed and driven out of the Muslim countries, including Iraq. Yet Western Christians barely raise their voices to support their brethren. Part of this is the terrible ignorance of Islam by non-Muslims. It was five centuries before the Qur'an was translated into Latin and five more centuries before there was another translation. The first translation of a Sira into English was not until the 17th Century. The major hadith of Bukhari was not translated until the 20th Century.[3] This follows Islamic teaching that infidels are not to know about Islam. Such ignorance is dangerous. Never was Sun Tzu's advice more imperative: Know your enemy!

Dr. Laurie Roth wrote about the Ground zero mosque just being the tip of the iceberg. "Islam is in the process of taking over all of America and transforming her to an Islamic republic observing Sharia law." She calls it an insult to the 9/11 victims and an "arrogant and continued push of radical Islam behind the poisonous veil of peace and religious rights." She is concerned about the massive growth of Saudi and Iranian backed mosques in the US which has "nothing to do at all with Religious rights but is an arrogant and calculated plan to take over, capture and dominate America for Islam." She summed it up, "America, wake up! I want to know what is going on in the 6000 mosques, hiding behind 'freedom of speech.' I think it is high time American authorities stop waxing so polite and intimidated and start tracking what is being said and taught in US mosques and schools, then having the guts and clarity to shut more than a few down."[4]

> **Islam has continuously revealed that it is really a Government dictatorship package housed in the skeleton of a Religion.**
>
> **- Dr. Laurie Roth**

Citizen Warrior illustrated the "infuriating cleverness of orthodox Muslims" by comparing them to the psychiatric patient in the movie, *What About Bob?* They have to stress that they are oppressed and persecuted and of course must "defend" themselves. The stealth jihad tries to evoke pity portraying themselves "as innocent victims of wrongdoing." They use taqiyya masterfully as deceit. Leaders say one thing to Western media and the opposite to Muslims. "You see them speaking peace and tolerance to Westerners and two days later vigorously preaching jihad against the West to their fellow Muslims." They push for concessions for their "special requirements" or "their unique religion" or because they have been persecuted or whatever excuse and this "leads to Islamization of society." They appear to be nice but "Islamic countries are often very friendly to Western countries while at the same time whipping up national hatred against those same Western countries on Islamic television stations, and funding global jihad."

Another is using our enemies against us. "Iran sends soldiers into Iraq in order to kill U.S. soldiers, but Iran also supplies Russian and China with oil, so if the U.S. wants to do something about Iran, we will have our two biggest enemies to contend with. In essence, Iran uses our enemies against us." They exploit our weaknesses. "They immigrate into free countries and then use the democratic process and rights of free speech to agitate against those freedoms and seek to subvert democracy." They regularly exploit multicultural beliefs to gain concessions. We hope the problem will just go away but "Islamic supremacists are insinuating themselves more and more thoroughly into Western societies." They are very skillful and keep it concealed. Referring to CAIR, "They have successfully fooled most people in America that they represent moderate, peace-loving Muslim Americans." This is a long war. "Orthodox Muslims find every crack in the wall they can find and work their way in. And they twist every event and utterance to their purpose. They will not stop, they will not tire, and they have nothing else to live for. This is it. This is the meaning of their existence: Islam must win. Islam must dominate all other cultures, all other religions, all other governments. Allah wills it." Muslims "have created 'legitimate,' mainstream organizations that lobby Washington and 'represent the Muslim community' to governments and to the media, and yet have a secret agenda, revealed at the recent Holy Land Foundation Trial, of conquering America from within."[5]

Efforts have been made to try to find a "moderate Muslim," but that would have to be a Muslim who "rejects 97% of the references to jihad in the Hadith" and would have to reject the cult of Muhammad. He would also have to reject "the intolerance, hatred, and violence toward non-Muslims" in the Qur'an and "reject the subordinated position of women." We need to "stop coddling the so-called moderates. We need to be forthright and say, 'you either stridently reject jihad or we will assume you embrace it.'" Vague assurances are not acceptable. "Muslims need to be clear and explicit, and we need to demand that of them. Anything less will not do, and if they want to whine and complain about it, too bad." We understand Islam and the ideology and we "don't want you running the country or involved in law enforcement or teaching my children or writing textbooks or working in counterterrorism or joining the military, unless you can assure me of what parts of that ideology you reject." It is time for America to wake up. "Muslims must feel the heat. They must realize they have to come right out and say, 'Yes, there is a political agenda in Islam, and I completely reject it' or they will not be welcomed or trusted or invited to any 'interfaith dialogs for peace and understanding.'" Many Muslim leaders have been asked to sign the Freedom Pledge but few have. "We must make this clear to every Muslim: If you do not openly reject jihad in all its forms, we must assume you abide by it and believe in it, and we will have to treat you accordingly."[6]

The Freedom Pledge was sent out by Former Muslims United to 163 American Muslim leaders at 50 organizations, such as Nihad Awad of CAIR, and pointed out that according to Islamic law apostates are to be killed. By signing the pledge, a Muslim promises "to renounce, repudiate and oppose any physical intimidations, or worldly and corporal punishment, of apostates from Islam, in whatever way that punishment may be determined or carried out by myself or any other Muslim including the family of the apostate, community, Mosques leaders, Shariah court or judge, and Muslim government or regime." Less that 1.3% signed and are actually moderate.[7]

Dr. Tawfik Hamid circulated a similar document which he suggested be sent to mosque leaders, Muslim leaders, and Islamic organizations in the US and worldwide. It is a "Declaration of Beliefs of Muslim Moderates" which they must sign if they are to be considered moderates. It calls for repudiation of apostasy, violence against women, jihad to dominate the world, disrespect for Jews, slavery, and killing homosexuals. He ends his request with "Failure to publicly post and support these principles should be interpreted as clear evidence that a leader's mosque or Islamic organization must be considered radical."[8]

> **There may be moderate Muslims, but Islam itself is not moderate.**

Trying to identify "moderate" Muslims raises a very troubling truth. Even if the majority of Muslims just want to live in peace, like Germans under Hitler or Russians under Stalin, they are entirely irrelevant. The truth is that fanatics [true believers, followers of the teachings of Muhammad, the cult of Moism] rule Islam. It is the fanatics who are marching, killing, beheading, stoning, raping, honor killing, and teaching the young to kill and become suicide bombers. The "peaceful majority" or "silent majority" is cowed, extraneous, and therefore irrelevant. Russians may have just wanted to live in peace but the Communists killed 20 million people. Likewise with the Chinese, but their Communists killed 70 million people. Japanese killed 12 million. Muslims have killed 270 million. Many "peace-loving" people died because the peaceful majority failed to speak up until it was too late. As we have seen with American Muslims supporting Hamas, HezbAllah, attacking Jews, or protesting the cartoons, American Muslims are no different from the rest.

Various cases of American military men killing their fellow soldiers raised the ugly question of **Muslim disloyalty in America**. We had Hasan Akbar murdering US soldiers in Kuwait, Nidal Hassan murdering 13 soldiers at Fort Hood, and the latest Nasser Abdo who was captured before he killed more soldiers at Fort Hood and shouted "Nidal Hasan, Fort Hood, 2009" as he was led from a courtroom. Warren Richey, "Accused Fort Hood plotter got bombmaking recipe from Al Qaeda," *Christian Science Monitor,* 29 July 2011. The bomb making recipe was from *Inspire* magazine from Yemen – Anwar al-Awlaki. The problem comes from the Qur'an which directs that "Muslims shouldn't kill Muslims" and that "true Muslims do not befriend non-Muslims." This mandate to be loyal to Muslims and Islam and disloyal to non-Muslims results in these people considering themselves Muslim first and American second – totally unacceptable. This is loyalty in a tribal sense, from the Arab tribal loyalty to the *umma*, whereby Islam is a "super tribe" above race and language."

The Specter of Muslim Disloyalty in America

- Raymond Ibrahim

US Muslim jurists have announced that "It is forbidden to work for the FBI or for U.S. security services because these harm Muslims." The Assembly of Muslim Jurists of America issued a fatwa: it is "not permissible" for US Muslims to send aid, even food, to US troops in Muslim countries. But why are most examples limited to the military? Raymond Ibrahim answered it clearly: "Simple: Islam is primarily concerned with actual deeds; and the military is one of those rare institutions that requires people to demonstrate their loyalty through action." Similar to the saying in Muhammad's time, US terrorist Tarik Shah said, "I could be joking and smiling [with infields] and then cutting their throats in the next second." We have seen this repeatedly in Afghanistan where police or soldiers have murdered US and NATO soldiers. The ramification of this is not the 0.1% of US Muslims ever in the military, but Muslims in positions of authority in our government agencies, the Congress, or the White House. Remember Taqiyya![9]

Among the problems of our lack of understanding of Islam is our failure to comprehend jihad. We have been focused on terror – the bombings and killings – but the more insidious jihad, the **stealth jihad**, the gradual takeover of America and the slow imposition of sharia, is much more dangerous. We have already started down this slippery slope by banning the term "war on terror" and replacing it with ridiculous names like "global contingency operations" and "man-caused disasters." We accommodate and make concession to Muslims such that sharia gradually destroys our laws and our values and could lead to "the destruction of our Constitution, our form of government and our way of life. Islam is subverting our way of life without guns and bombs, and we seem to be totally unaware of what is transpiring. We are building our own gallows and putting the noose around our neck, without even knowing it."

The purpose of jihad is not to blow up buildings and kill infidels. Its purpose is to institute Shariah.

- Andrew C. McCarthy

The purpose of jihad is not violence but to impose sharia. If a battle can be won without firing a shot, so much the better. It is like extortion, mafia-style with resort to breaking knees only occasionally. Even Sayyid Qutb, a major proponent of violent jihad, saw its need only when the march of Islam was obstructed. Thus, like a bank robber, violence is only necessary if non-violence fails. We see with the Muslim Brotherhood that the work of the Ikhwan in the US is stated as a grand jihad to eliminate and destroy Western civilization from within. Violence helps because the idiotic, childish reaction to the cartoons of Muhammad and similar outbursts condition the infidels to be careful and not dare to excite the wild Muslims.

The list of those "little" concessions and accommodations is quite long. We have reached the point where the government has purged the terms "Islamofascism" and "jihad" from public use. Major efforts are underway to "criminalize and create civil liability for criticism of Islam." These concessions and accommodations are "undermining our own society and values." There is no right for these people to have such special treatment and our government should not be "partnering" with radical groups like the Muslim Brotherhood which "mean our society mortal harm, even if they're not blowing up buildings. The main challenge today is not protecting the buildings; it's protecting ourselves from what's going on inside the buildings."[10]

We have noted that Sun Tzu exhorted us to Know your Enemy, but we still refuse to name our enemy. The 9/11 Commission Report stated the perpetrators and their ideology and "used the word Islam 322 times, Muslim 145 times, jihad 126 times, and jihadist 32 times." This contrasts with the August 2009 National Intelligence Strategy which "uses the term Muslim 0 times, Islam 0, and jihad 0." Likewise, the FBI Counterterrorism Analytical Lexicon "uses the term Muslim 0 times, the term Islam 0 times, and the term jihad 0 times."[11] How can we possibly win a war when we refuse to name the enemy? It is the height of naiveté and stupidity not to identify those who announce they want to destroy us and our institutions and way of life.

It is harder to fight stupidity than it is to fight terrorists.

Diana West gave an interesting speech, "Possessing Freedom is Not Enough – We Must Exercise Our Freedom to Preserve it." She spoke of the "effect of Islam on speech in America" and how Americans have come to censor themselves. She gave the example of President Bush's use of the word "crusade" after 9/11, a word that has come to mean "any moral fight for right" in English. Yet it was quickly withdrawn and "regretted" because it might "alienate" Muslims. This psychological victory certainly encouraged "the Organization of the Islamic Conference's continuing efforts to outlaw all criticism of Islam" which has the full support of the Obama Administration. This is appeasing Islam. It has continued. The attack on the Taliban was originally called Operation Infinite Justice, but was changed to Operation Enduring Freedom because Muslims complained that only Allah dispenses infinite justice (obviously he does not dispense freedom!). Our media are so politically correct that they rarely mention Muslims, Islam, jihad or other appropriate words when reporting Muslim atrocities, refusing to recognize "the gross incompatibility of Islamic ideology with Western liberty." They are so scared of "giving offense" so as "not to criticize Islam" that we seem to be conducting a "war against alienating Islam" - "fighting for Islam. It calls us to self-censorship, self-abnegation, self-extinguishment. It depends on and encourages our submission. This is the behavior of the dhimmi and the culture of dhimmitude." As she said, "Honestly, I don't think Americans realize they're engaged in such a suicidal effort, which has even intensified under President Obama." She does not think Americans have lost their will and would rally to such nonsense, but "we have lost our language to mobilize that will. And very few Americans seem to realize it." She ended with "it's not enough to possess freedoms.

We must learn that it's vital to exercise our freedoms if we want to have any hope of preserving them."[12]

> **It's not enough to possess freedoms. We must learn that it's vital to exercise our freedoms if we want to have any hope of preserving them.**
>
> **- Diana West**

The president has said we need to be more tolerant, such as with the Ground Zero Mosque, even though 70% of Americans oppose it. Islamic countries have equal rights and vote in the UN but it is not right to say their form of government is as valid as ours. This "religion of peace" has killed 270,000,000 human beings. Islam and sharia enslave women, stone or kill them "to protect the male's honor;" worship virginity via female genital mutilation; and kill those who do not believe in Islam, criticize Islam, or leave it. The lady wrote, "Why should I tolerate a form of government, Sharia law, as it infiltrates us seeking to destroy our democracy? I say we should be extremely intolerant of the creeping Sharia influence." She continued, "This is a clash – not of civilizations, because stoning women to death is clearly not in any way a civilized thing to do – but a clash between our freedoms and Sharia law." She ended with "The free world needs to become completely intolerant of any religious intolerance."[13]

> **Tolerance becomes a crime when applied to evil.**
>
> **- Thomas Mann**

We have been tolerant of Islam for too long. There are rules of decency and human rights and we should not accept any violations. We need to stop being politically correct and permitting atrocities in the name of a phony "religion." Examples of Muslim intolerance appear daily around the world. Whether it is rioting and murdering over cartoons, burning cities, burning churches, murdering Christians, bombing and killing, or just complaining about some phony injustice, Muslim intolerance is unceasing. Ramadan is always a good excuse. In Indonesia, members of the Islamic Defenders Front destroyed a food stall operating during Ramadan and in another location arrested three men having lunch in a restaurant. Public Order Agency officers said, "We had to arrest them because they do not respect other Muslims who are fasting."[14]

Muslims want respect but they do not respect others, since everyone else is a kafir and useless. Obama adviser Dalia Mogahed, who is also the "Executive Director of the Abu Dhabi Gallup Center (ADGC) for Muslim Studies," [Is that a conflict of interest?] in a Gallup survey, evidently with John Esposito, called for respect for Islam. Supposedly 72% of Muslims meant by that: "not desecrating the Quran or Islam's religious symbols." Of course, that would mean curtailing freedom of speech and basically adopting sharia. As usual it is the "responsibility of the West to mend fences with Muslims. There is no hint of any possibility that Muslims might need to adjust their behavior in any way." It is all our fault![15]

Pamela Geller described it:

Islamic terror? Respect it, Islamophobes!
Clitorectomies? Respect them!
Honor Killings? Respect them!
Persecution of Christians, Jews, Hindus, non-Muslims? Respect it!
Desecration of non-Muslim holy sites? Respect it!

Islamic supremacism? Respect it!
Lack of candor and criticism of Islam? Respect it!
Homicide bombers? Respect them!
Jihad? Respect it!
Jew-hatred? Respect it!
Women as chattel? Respect it!
Burka? Respect it![16]

Muslims may want respect but they go into childish tantrums over the slightest action which bruises their fragile egos (or they feign it well for the effect they want!). Perhaps we should call this **The Cult of Perpetual Outrage!**[17]

Attorney General Eric Holder remarked that the threat of American citizens becoming radicalized and taking up arms against the US is real, and he had confidence in our counter-terrorism efforts, but the bad news is that "The terrorists only have to be successful once." To argue "that most American Muslims are moderate, and only a few are radical," does not help our security. It only took 19 for 9/11. "According to Holder, in the last two years, 50 of the 126 people charged with terrorism were U.S. citizens." If you understand Islam, you know that the ideology "allows for absolutely no national allegiance."

Radical Islamism has come to mock the very principle of nationality and citizenship."
- Fouad Ajami[18]

So we should ask, "if American Muslims, who enjoy Western benefits…are still being radicalized, why then do we insist that importing these same benefits to the Muslim world will eliminate its even more ingrained form of 'radicalization'?" Raymond Ibrahim ended with, "America needs to rethink its strategy for the war on terrorism – both at home and abroad. Domestically, this means cracking down without compunction on anything that smacks of Islamist activity, without fear of being 'politically incorrect;' it means better monitoring of jihadist websites which play a major role in radicalizing American Muslims, such as *Inspire* (which was started by a North Carolina Muslim); and it means exercising prudence when granting visas to people from dubious backgrounds. Internationally, it means understanding that the one solution to war promoted by most Western politicians – spreading Western values and ways of governance – is no solution at all."[19]

We constantly hear about "moderate" Muslims. As Ibn Warraq said, "There are moderate Muslims. Islam itself is not moderate." As Turkish Prime Minister Recep Tayyip Erdogan said in reply to a question about "moderate Islam," "These descriptions are very ugly, it is offensive and an insult to our religion. There is no moderate or immoderate Islam. Islam is Islam and that's it." Erdogan is leading the re-Islamization of Turkey overturning the secularization accomplished by Mustafa Kemal Ataturk. [Sadly (or naively), Secretary of State Hillary Clinton praised Turkey as "a democratic country with a secular constitution" during her visit to Ankara in March 2011.] What these people are saying is that "there is no difference between Islam and Islamism." As Hugh Fitzgerald wrote, "The point is this: Islam really is a dangerous ideology."[20]

The point is this: Islam really is a dangerous ideology.

- Hugh Fitzgerald

We see how Erdogan is reversing the secularization of Turkey with marginalization of the military and with the arrest of more generals.[21] This is in line with the pronouncements of Yusuf al-Qaradawi, "the leading Egyptian cleric," "the spiritual guide of the Muslim Brotherhood," "one of the most influential scholars in Islam," "the most well-known legal authority in the whole Muslim world today." In addition to urging "Muslims to kill the Jews" on Al Jazeera and saying "No peace can be made between us (Muslims) and the non-believers. This what our holy book says. This what Allah says," he wrote, "Secularism can never enjoy a general acceptance in an Islamic society."   According to Qaradawi, Islam and secularism cannot coexist.

As Islam is a comprehensive system of worship (Ibadah) and legislation (Shari'ah), the acceptance of secularism means abandonment of Shari'ah, a denial of the divine guidance and a rejection of Allah's injunctions. It is indeed a false claim that Shari'ah is not proper to the requirements of the present age. The acceptance of a legislation formulated by humans means a preference of the humans' limited knowledge and experiences to the divine guidance: "Say! Do you know better than Allah?" (Qur'an 2:140) For this reason, **the call for secularism among Muslims is atheism and a rejection of Islam. Its acceptance as a basis for rule in place of Shari'ah is downright apostasy.** [Emphasis added][22]

Muslims often criticize non-Muslims for cherry-picking harsh verses from the Qur'an. The sad part is that Muslims who want to be considered "moderate" do the real cherry-picking. They delude themselves by relying on the more moderate verses from the Mecca Qur'an conveniently ignoring the real Islam which Muhammad revealed in Medina. They like the parts where Muhammad was kind to Jews and Christians in Mecca as People of the Book, but forget his killing of Jews and Christians in Medina. They forget or overlook that as Muhammad lay dying in Aisha's lap, his final words were to rid Arabia of Jews and Christians. They like the verses about compassion, kindness, and doing good but overlook the subjugation of women, female genital mutilation, honor killing, jihad, sharia, and the objective to rule the world. These so-called "moderates" are not slaves to Allah, they are unthinking slaves to the cult of Muhammad, one of the greatest conmen in history.

It appears that a large percentage of Muslims are ignorant of the real tenets of their so-called religion, either innocently or through intimidation by the harsh treatment of any dissent within the cult. Their ignorance is exploited by imams, most of whom do understand the cult, and can lead the sheep. Average Muslims may or may not support the concept of Dar al-Harb and Dar al-Islam, the whole world divided between us and them, Muslims and infidels. But they dare speak out against it only at their own risk. The cult of Muhammad established double standards: one set of rules and ethics for Muslims and another set completely different and intolerant for all non-believers. A Muslim should treat a fellow Muslim well, but a Muslim should kill a non-Muslim.

The cult of Muhammad established double standards: one set of rules and ethics for Muslims and a completely different set for kafirs (non-believers).

The problem with the quixotic Dar al-Islam is that there are different Islams. The Sunni-Shiite divide is bitter at times with Saudis calling all Shiites "infidels" which is part of the centuries old Arab-Persian rivalry, very current in the leadership struggle for control of the Persian Gulf (and oil). Sunni Islam has always been a march toward Arab supremacism and that collides with the Persian supremacists. They are rivals, not enemies. They have the same goals but differ on who should be the leaders. That does not mean they cannot work together against a common enemy – the US – as Shiite Iran cooperates with Sunni al Qaeda in Afghanistan.[23] Islam is interpreted differently in Indonesia, Malaysia, and the Philippines, but they still kill Christians and drive to dominate. The large state of Nigeria is divided with a Muslim majority in the north where Boko Haram [roughly translated as "Western education is forbidden"] regularly attacks and kills Christians and burns their churches and is seeking to eliminate Christianity in northern Nigeria.[24] As we noted in earlier chapters, Islam has never been able to unify politically and any further world gains would almost assuredly be met with intra-Islamic competition for power. Thus the myth of the Land of Islam dominating the whole world and the Islamic definition of peace is a bad joke on millions of innocent people.

In World War III, the Cold War against expansionist Communism, the defeatists or cowards called for "Better Red than Dead." New age cowards would call for "Better Muslim than Dead." **NO!** There is a solution to stop this messianic cult that wants to dominate the world and all people in it. The English Defence League Forums issued an interesting paper "If we don't defeat Islam as an ideology it will exterminate us culturally and physically," edited by Bamiyan, 2 January 2011. It opens with "Islam is an utterly ruthless totalitarian political system disguised as a religion. Islam will literally stop at nothing to achieve its objective of world domination, with all non-Muslims exterminated or enslaved." It continued, "Consequently, the ideology of Islam MUST be defeated. It must be consigned to the dustbin of history along with those other vicious totalitarianisms – Nazism and Communism. The alternative is our extermination as a civilization, and the whole world being plunged into an endless theocratic Dark Age."

> **The only option for defeating Islam is to undermine it in the same way we undermined communism – by a slow process of ideological warfare.**

The paper lists a number of actions in this new cold war, this ideological war.

- **Altering the spiritual and material cost/benefits of being a Muslim**

Religions promise benefits such as avoiding hell and going to paradise, which in the cult of Muhammad is a "well-appointed brothel in the sky." The material benefits include immunity from normal law, superior status to dhimmis, and sanctioned rape and pillage. Faith and conformity are key to any belief system, so the spiritual benefits must be shown to be "bogus" – "Islam is confidence trick set up by a ruthless megalomaniac" - and the benefits of conformity, which is ruthless, need to be decreased as well as the benefits of being a Muslim.

- **Destroying and replacing Muslim beliefs**

Islam is fragile. The Qur'an is considered to be the literal word of Allah, dictated to but not written by Muhammad. It is "an all-or-nothing cult" all based on the truthfulness of Muhammad. Doubts could cause the system to disintegrate. "Muslims already subconsciously realise this, because they fly into tantrums whenever either Mohammed or the Koran is 'disrespected'" such criticism being blasphemy punishable by death. "This paranoid, hypersensitive defensiveness and outrage at criticism are not the reactions of a confident belief system, but of an information-control cult." We see this Achilles heel with the Satanic Verses, the cartoon riots, and the OIC effort to introduce global laws against any criticism of Islam. The effort should be to satirize and ridicule Muhammad. In contrast to Christianity and

Buddhism, "everything in Islam originates from the uncorroborated testimony" of one person. "If you destroy the credibility of Mohammed, you destroy Islam."

"The primary target of the propaganda counterjihad must be Mohammed.   If Mohammed is revealed as an imposter, a fraud and a conman then the Koran and Hadiths are worthless raving and ramblings, mere sound and fury signifying nothing." The problem is few Muslims know the truth about Muhammad. Anyone who exposes the truth using their own revered sources and asks Muslims to refute it is faced only with attempts to censor or to kill him.

- ● **Providing an alternative to Islam**

"The Muslims who have abandoned Islam will need somewhere else to go." Churches must help them, protect apostates, and perhaps set up covert online churches.

- ● **Destroying Mohammed's street cred among 'jihadi cool' youths**

"'Jihadi cool' Muslim youths in the west [particularly Europe] are a thuggish, predatory and parasitic criminal underclass of gangstsas." They do not have a sense of morality and rationality, are inbred leaving many with low intelligence, and have no loyalty to their country of residence. They do not obey "man-made laws" but have "an arrogant sense of unearned entitlement and the Allah-given right to rape and pillage at will." In that sense, Muhammad is an ideal role-model for them. The cult is tribal and is "maintained by physical threats and lynch-mobs rather than reason or spirituality." Therefore, "Appeals to normal human decency as an antidote to Islam are pointless" because the cult believes it is "their duty to kill, maim, rape, swindle and rob the kaffir (unbeliever)."

The way to get at them, is to damage their inflated and fragile egos." Since Muslims are "at a tribal state" of development, "they venerate the totems of their tribe, and will go into tantrums if these are 'disrespected'. Unstable adolescents are constantly seeking 'significance' and 'respect'." Of course, one of the main totems is Muhammad, "so one of the ways to discredit him is to turn him into a laughing stock. No cool teenager will follow a figure of ridicule, which is why the Muslims got so enraged when the Motoons came out. **Ridicule is one of the most effective weapons against Islam."** [Emphasis added]

- ● **Removing the benefits and increasing the costs of being Muslim**

Muslims are "pandered to and given special privileges just because they are Muslims. They believe that 'Islam must dominate and must not be dominated'." The paper then lists 19 examples of special privileges. "All pandering, appeasement, legal immunities and special privileges contribute to what Bin Laden calls the 'strong horse effect', which makes them confident of winning the Stealth Jihad." The paper lists 16 actions starting with "all special treatment should be withdrawn."   Others are: "Muslim immigration must be stopped." "Muslims must be regarded as enemy aliens."   "All illegal Muslim immigrants must be deported." "All Muslims guilty of serious crimes must be deported." "Translation at public expense must be banned." "Cousin marriage must be banned." "Remains of terrorists should be buried in pigskins, Russian style, to prevent them entering paradise." Of course, there is the requirement to "reduce our dependence on Muslim oil."

We are dealing with **ideologues** in a **war of ideas** that has gone on for decades already and likely will for decades more. The legitimacy of their aggressiveness comes from classical

Islam, from the Trilogy. The system needs to be brought into the modern world, but moderates and reformers in the Muslim world are largely marginalized. What makes the changing of beliefs of Muslims difficult or almost impossible is "the fact that there is no culture of dissent or freethought, or a tradition of uninhibited exchange of ideas as in the West." Compounding this potentially traumatic belief change is the "whole culture of honor and shame: a change in beliefs would bring shame on their family, tribe, and religion." Ibn Warraq concluded that "we cannot hope to reform Islam without attacking the fundamental tenets of Islam adhered to by Muslims of all colors and stripes, not just Islamists. We shall never make progress until we subject the Koran to the kind of analysis and criticism that was applied to the Bible."[25]

The additional problem for any potential reform of Islam is that there is no central authority; it is an ideology with no command center that can issue authoritative interpretations or changes. Various sheikhs, muftis, ayatollahs, and imams pronounce their own views plus there are the four major schools of Sunni jurisprudence plus several Shiite. Islam has been divided since the death of Muhammad and there is no likelihood it will ever be united.

Two final thoughts. Pamela Geller has a new book out, *STOP THE ISLAMIZATION OF AMERICA A Practical Guide to the Resistance*. It is a guide "to stopping the spread of Sharia and Islamic supremacism in America" (Dr. Wafa Sultan) and "a democratic defense to fight the stealth jihadist threat against civilization." (Bat Ye'or)

The other is a fascinating piece written by a reader of Citizen Warrior. The writer called it "An Unusual Birthday Party." It is set in Mecca in 2090 with a photo of the Kaaba with tourists around it in casual clothes and the narrator is 90 years old and is the historian and museum curator at the ancient sacred mosque which was now a museum. He tells the young kids about the odd things in the history like suicide bombings, sharia, and beheadings and the "children laughed uproariously." He pointed out a document in a locked case: "a piece of paper saved the world." "A brave move by the United States that officially reclassified Islam as a political organization, and no longer a religion, had a snowball effect. Europe followed suit, and within a space of five years all non-Muslim countries had reclassified Islam as a political organization, like the old communism. They arrested those same imams for sedition and stopped funding their organizations." Oil was unknown to the kids and it was now "Tourist Mecca" and "Noone followed Islam any more. In fact, the Koran had even gone out of print. It was such a boring thing to read!" They popped the champagne for the old man and asked him to make a wish. His secret wish was "that the world will never be pulled into any 'black-hole' of fascism, ever again. The End"

The key in that story is the reclassifying of Islam from a religion to a political ideology. We will not win the war against Islam until that is done. Recall that the relentless march of Islam has only been stopped twice: Spain and Eastern Europe. In Spain, it was "convert or leave." The West does not need to demand "convert or die" or "convert or leave." But since Islam is antithetical to democracy and incompatible with civilized life, the West needs to demand **"Renounce Islam or leave."**

With their refusal to assimilate or to be loyal to any country, their rejection of secularism, their overt, or silent acquiescence to, support of jihad and the imposition of sharia, their adherence to the principle of Islamic supremacy, their total refusal to accept the rights of non-believers, and their disregard for the rights of women, Islam is a **Fifth Column** in any country where it is located since their goal is to change the government and impose sharia.

Although we had a false sense of calm for a few years after World War I and then the distractions of World War II followed by the Communist War, World War III, we have been at war with Islam for over 30 years. There are 1.5 billion Muslims in the world now and the number is growing rapidly. But the numbers are irrelevant. It only takes one million, or 100 thousand, or 10 thousand or less to run a revolution. The rest either quietly support or are too intimidated to act.

The threat from Islam is very real because, despite all the nice words from apologists and so-called "moderate" Muslims, Islam is still a warlike, intolerant, expansionist, dictatorial, all-encompassing cult. We do ourselves a great disservice by permitting Islam to be considered a religion when it is truly an imperialistic, arrogant, aggressive, totalitarian ideology hiding behind the façade of religion with the intent to impose itself and sharia on the entire world.

As John Guandolo ended his articles on The Muslim Brotherhood in America, "The MB Settled in America to subordinate the Constitution to Shariah. The 'Process' by which they did it is a 'Civilization-Jihadist Process.' Their methodology is to subvert the primary/foundational institutions in our nation and co-opt our leadership. At a quick glance it appears the score at halftime of this football game is 200-0 in their favor. Time for us to take off the baseball uniforms and engage the MB on the football field."[26]

It is really irrelevant whether Muhammad was the greatest or not so great. It is also irrelevant whether Islam is the perfect religion or whatever. Muslims have no right to force it on those who do not want it; that is aggression and must be fought. We have no interest in submitting to a false religious cult and a seventh century totalitarian ideology. On the contrary, we should feel obligated to liberate Muslims from the chains that have imprisoned them mentally and physically.

Wake up America or you will lose this war and the America we know and love.

Every attempt to make war easy and safe will result in humiliation and disorder.
                                                                    - General W. T. Sherman, 1875

Notes

1. "A Memo to New Members," Jihad Watch, 10 January 2011.
2. "What Are You Worried About?" Citizen Warrior, 30 September 2010.
3. Thanks to Bill Warner, politicalislam.com, 5 January 2012.
4. "Islam is a Government Dictatorship Housed in Religion," NewsWithViews.com, 3 September 2010.
5. "Lessons on Jihad from the Movie, 'What About Bob,'" Citizen Warrior, 29 July 2011.
6. "A New Era in Muslim-Non-Muslim Relations," Citizen Warrior, 11 September 2010.
7. "Test for Defining 'Moderate:' What parts of Islamic doctrine should Muslim reject if they wish to live in free countries?" Defeat the Third Jihad, 15 July 2010.
8. "Is Your Local Mosque 'Moderate' or 'Radical'?" www.tawfikhamid.com.
9. Raymond Ibrahim, "The Specter of Muslim Disloyalty in America," Pajamas Media, 13 September 2010. Note that he mentioned Nasser Abdo in 2010 and that 24% of Americans think Obama is a clandestine Muslim!
10. Herb Denenberg, "US Sleeps While Society, Values Get Undermined By Stealth Jihad," The Bulletin, 10 April 2009.
11. Ibn Warraq: Westminster Institute Conference (Part 1), Jihad Watch, 20 June 2011.
12. Speech at the International Free Press Society held in Denmark's parliament in Copenhagen, 9 October 2010.
13. "We Need Less Tolerance, Not More," PinkNeck.com, quoted in "The Value and Limits of Tolerance," Citizen Warrior, 14 September 2010. We still have Muslim women trying to force employers to permit them to wear the hijab at work whether at Disney or an airline desk. The hijab is un-American and we do not need it!. See Laura Bly, "Muslim hostess and Disney still at odds over headscarf," USA Today, 13 September 2010. Disney offered her other positions but she refused them.
14. "Islamic Defenders Front Strike Again," and "Three Arrested for Failing to Fast in Aceh," Jakarta Globe, 8 August 2011, Jihad Watch, 9 August 2011.
15. Habib Toumi, "Obama adviser says politics roused Muslim anger towards US," Gulf News, 18 January 2011.
16. Megan Deterie, "Muslims tell West: 'respect Islam,'" The National, 28 November 2010, Jihad Watch, 30 November 2010.
17. Credit probably belongs to Brooks William Kelley, author of The Martyr's Prize, for the term "The Religion of Perpetual Outrage." "The fact that The Religion of Perpetual Outrage claimed immunity and minority status gave them immunity, at least as far as the major media and various government bodies were concerned." Quoted in Citizen Warrior, 27 May 2011. The book also described jihad as make life impossible for non-Muslims so that they are in constant fear for their lives unless they submit to Islam – "A jihad that could never be defeated because it would be all encompassing; everywhere at once. No focal point to attack with Western military might. Immune, because the West would never engage in genocide; would never outlaw a religion; would never take the steps necessary to defeat such an ideology."
18. Mark Steyn, America Alone, p. 89.
19. Raymond Ibrahim, "Radical Muslims in America: All the Benefits and Still Turning to Jihad," Hudson New York, 12 January 2011.
20. "Fitzgerald: Islam and Islamism, or 'Leaving the West With No Solutions,'" Jihad Watch, 15 March 2010. This is an interesting article about Islam. Also, see the article by Joanne Hill, "In defense of Wafa Sultan," 12 March 2010, in the comments.
21. "Istanbul court issues arrest warrant for propaganda website generals," Today's Zaman, 8 August 2011, Jihad Watch.
22. "What Muslim Leaders Say About Islam Dispels the Myth that Jihadists are a 'Fringe' Element," Citizen Warrior, 1 October 2010.
23. Stephen F. Hayes and Thomas Joscelyn, "The Hidden Hand: The Obama administration finally highlights Iran's key role in supporting al Qaeda," Weekly Standard, 15 August 2011.
24. "Muslim radicals kill ten Christians in Nigeria," International Christian Concern, 8 August 2011, Jihad Watch, 9 August 2011.
25. Ibn Warrraq: Westminster Institute Conference (Part 4), Jihad Watch, 23 June 2011. In Part 2, he wrote, "The West is still consumed with post-colonial guilt, is hampered by political correctness, and wishful thinking."
26. John Guandolo, "The Muslim Brotherhood in America: Part III: The Settlement Process," Guns & Patriots, 29 March 2011.
27. Treasury of Philosophy, Edited by Dagobert D. Runes, (New York, Philosophical Library, 1955), pp. 589-590.

THE DAMAGE RELIGION CAUSES

Religion makes enemies instead of friends. That one word, "religion," covers all the horizon of memory with visions of war, of outrage, of persecution, of tyranny, and death. That one word brings to the mind every instrument with which man has tortured man.

Whoever imagines himself a favorite with God, holds other people in contempt.

Whenever a man believes that he has the exact truth from God, there is in that man no spirit of compromise. He has not the modesty born of the imperfection of human nature; he has the arrogance of theological certainty and the tyranny born of ignorant assurance. Believing himself to be the slave of God, he imitates his master, and of all tyrants, the worst is a slave in power."

"When a man really believes that it is necessary to do a certain thing to be happy forever, or that a certain belief is necessary to ensure eternal joy, there is in that man no spirit of concession. He divides the whole world into saints and sinners, into believers and unbelievers, into God's sheep and Devil's goats, into people who will be glorified and people who will be damned."

- **Robert Green Ingersoll (1883-1889) "America's great agnostic"**[27]

Appendix A - The Mujahedin's Roadmap

The Abu-Hafs al-Masri Brigades (Al-Qa'ida)
(Translated by FBIS) 1 July 2004 (Abridged – Emphasis Added)

Our aims in the coming stage:

1. To enlarge the circle of the struggle by distributing the operations all over the world.
   To drag the United States into a **third quagmire** that is after Iraq and Afghanistan, and let it be **Yemen**,... We said this in our statement of ...11 March 2004.
   We tell the Abu-Ali al-Harithi Brigade: The leadership has decided that Yemen should be the third quagmire for the idol of the age, the United States.
2. Undermine the investor's confidence in the **US economy**.
3. Expose the **Crusader-Zionist scheme**.
4. Scatter and exhaust the enemy.
   After these steps comes the role of the **anticipated strike** that will make the United States yield or break its will and leave its agents so that we can settle accounts with them. The convoy will then move to **Jerusalem**,...

The **brothers** from the victorious community are **required**:

1. **To be sincere in your devotion to Allah** the Exalted and know that victory is at the doors, that Allah grants victory to those He helps, and that the massing of these forces, both non-Arab and Arab, is only what we have promised Allah and His Prophet. ...**Our dead are in paradise and their dead are in hell**. Know that victory is the **patience** of one hour and that the **enemy wants the world while we want the Hereafter** and he cannot be patient as we are patient. ...
2. **Form small organizations under different names**, like the **Monotheism** and **Jihad Group**, the **Abu-Hafs al-Masri Brigades**, etc. This will make it **difficult** for the enemy **to discover** and hunt them down and will scatter the security organs' efforts.
3. **Learn jihad** on the basis of the shari'ah as the creed & the allegiance & disavowal, & act according to this learning.
4. Physical and military **training**, and spreading this among the sons, relatives, and clans -- and then those who come next (because the battle might be long).
5. Learn modern skills like **computers**, the **Internet**, and anything that is of use for the mujahidin and Muslims.
6. Ignite a **psychological war** against the enemy.

The **nation is required**:

1. To learn the creed, especially the allegiance and disavowal.
2. To make good repentance for abandoning the jihad.
3. To pray for the mujahidin and support them morally and financially.
4. To establish **small cells** inside and outside cities.
5. To shelter the mujahidin and support them.
6. To defend their honor.
7. To join their ranks.
8. To advise them.
   We warn very strongly against defaming the **mujahedin's** honor, discussing and spreading what hurts them, searching and looking for their errors and stumbles, following their faults, mocking and ridiculing them. The duty at this stage and at this time is to **stand with them**, defend their honor, lift them from their stumbles, and treat as an enemy anyone who

wishes them harm or publishes anything that harms them. ...Of course, it is all the more reason to **boycott the secularist media**.

..."Jihad with the tongue means showing the truth and exposing this crusade and onslaught on Islam and defending the mujahidin and their honor. And this is done between man and his family and between the people in their forums, mosques, work, or schools. It is the **duty of every Muslim to fight jihad** with his tongue as much as he can. Jihad with the tongue does not have any condition but one must say every word that one learns and believes exposes the **Crusaders** or defends the mujahidin and tell it to the people...

A message to the **Muslim ulema**:

...The nation is expecting you to be in the first ranks with the mujahidin and not in the first ranks with the **apostate rulers**. The nation is expecting you to say the truth and not be afraid of anyone and not to distort the texts and deceive the people in the name of the call. ...

... "O people, the war has broken out, the **call for jihad** has been made, and the doors of heaven have opened. If you are not among the war knights, then open the way for the women to fight it...

The Messenger and the ancestor ulema had warned against entering the sultans' doors (for the sultans then were characterized by devotion and obedience to Allah alone, unlike **today's apostate sultans**).

...The more a slave gets closer to a sultan the further he is from Allah.

...That who seeks the company of kings goes astray. **The nearer a person is to a king the farther he is from God."**

...the Prophet, ...said: "**Beware of seeking the company of kings.** Seeking the company of kings is a **treacherous path** that brings about humiliation to the seeker."

...early ulema [religious scholars] warned ...**against frequenting the courts of kings.**

...**Beware of princes.** Do not get close to them or mix with them on any occasion....

A **message to Shaykh Usama Bin Ladin** and those with him:

...we are continuing, **determined to fight**,... It is **perseverance until death**,...

To our **martyrs**:

Among the believers are men who have been true to their covenant with Allah; of them some have completed their vow (to the extreme), and some (still) wait: But they have never changed ... in the least.

Our dead are in paradise and their dead are in hell.

To our **prisoners**:

We have not and will not forget you and we will not rest until we **get you out** of imprisonment,... leaders and soldiers without exception. The enemy will pay a heavy price until you return to us proud and noble.

Every Muslim has to work for your release and the best way for doing so is to **kidnap** the largest number of the enemy everywhere. This is the only way that the enemy understands.
***

We say briefly:

We do not accuse Muslims or Muslim societies of unbelief. It is for their sake that we came out to defend them and want them to have security and peace, but not at the expense of disobeying Allah. **We were ordered to fight jihad and make Allah's word above all so as to get the infidel out of our land**, release our prisoners, and rule with what He has revealed. We follow the Sunna and nation course, the course of the Companions whom the Prophet, ...died pleased with, the course of the **first three centuries**. No one can say no to jihad today, for as the Prophet, ... said: **Jihad continues until the Day of Judgment**. Let the people know that there are **two kinds** of **jihad**. **One** is the **quest jihad [jihad talab]** -- there are conditions for it and it is the one about whom the sultans' ulema and the sons of the submissive Islamic movements talk. The other jihad is the **thrust jihad [jihad al-daf]**, which has no condition apart from faith. One who becomes a Muslim now and fights an enemy before performing one prayer enters paradise…O Muslims, beware the enemy's lies as he tries to depict the mujahidin as criminals who understand nothing of Allah's religion….

What do we want from the Crusaders:

These operations will not cease until **[US President]**, his gangs, his Arab, non-Arab, and **Jewish lackeys** <u>review their policies</u> toward Islam and Muslims, which are summed up as follows:

To **release our prisoners** in US prisons, especially the **Guantanamo** prisoners, the mujahid Shaykh Umar Abd-al-Rahman, and those in the prisons of America's Arab, non-Arab, and Jewish lackeys.

To **cease their war on Islam** and Muslims all over the world in the name of fighting terrorism.

To **cleanse all Muslim lands** from the **desecration** by the **Jews, American, and Hindus, including Jerusalem and Kashmir.**

That the United States and its allies **do not interfere** in the Muslims' affairs politically, economically, socially, and culturally and do not prevent the establishment of **the state of Islam.**

That the Crusader West **does not intervene between the Muslims** and their **apostate rulers**.

Our <u>strategy</u> with the enemy is:

The enemy can be patient but cannot persevere. We, with our faith, creed, and love for meeting Allah, can persevere until the enemy collapses, even if this takes **decades or centuries. We are tasked to fight them until victory of [?or] martyrdom.**

An excuse and a <u>**warning**</u>:

To the European people. You have only few days left to accept the peace [sulh], otherwise you have only yourselves to blame.

To the **Muslims living in the West**, anyone among you who can **immigrate** to the lands of Muslims let him do so. Anyone who cannot do so, let him be on his guard by living in the Muslims' areas, have enough **food** for himself and his family for **one month**, have the means to defend himself and his family, leave in the house enough **money** for **one month** or more, and pray more and seek the help of Allah.

To the **dialogue of cultures** people: This is your day. Only a few days remain from Shaykh Usama's promise. The **race is now between you, time, and the European countries** that have refused to stop their attacks on Muslims. Do not blame us for what is going to happen. We apologize to you beforehand if you are to be among the dead.

<u>Short messages</u>:

To the **Arab and non-Arab agents of [US President]**: Who will stop the coming waves of death. **Let it be between us, America, and you and the Jews and will be saved.**

By Allah, **we fight** them a war that will make the child's hair turn gray before the old.

To [Israeli Prime Minister]: We are going **to cut off America's rope** that is giving you the strength and **then destroy the Arabs protecting you.** Then we will not find it difficult to **slaughter you like** sheep.

To **[CIA Director]:** You will need more than **five years** to confront us,…

To the **US Senate**: Sorry for disturbing you on 4-2-2004, but we needed to test the (Ricin) on some persons. We will need to return to you, but this time not for testing.

Summary:
The **Americans, Jews, and the Crusader West are our enemies** and they are combatants. They **must be killed wherever they are caught. Arabs and Muslims who support them are considered to be like them and must be killed because they are apostates.**

Palestine should not be partitioned no matter how things are. It is a Muslim waqf and no one has the right to dispose of it.

Combat is today the individual duty of every Muslim man and woman, ... If the enemy enters a single inch of the **Muslims' land**, then it becomes the Muslims' duty to fight until they get the **enemy out**. Let a million or more die in the battlefield and let those remaining live in dignity and freedom as this is **better than** having [words indistinct] die in the dialogue and humiliation field and the remaining ones live in humiliation and be the **slaves of the Christians and Jews**.

Muslims should support the mujahidin, pray for them, join their ranks, and not believe the news they get from the idols and infidels

Allah's victory is close and **America's collapse is coming** without any doubt, Allah...

The **United Nations is a crusader's establishment** that legislates for the humiliation of Muslims, the strikes on them, and their fragmentation....

The conclusion:
The **defense [al-ismah] is in the sword!**...

 Defense against evil: The evil of the **apostate ruler** who renounced Allah's shari'ah and resorted to the idol's international and local laws, stripped the nation of its religion, clothed it in the robe of **atheism**, such as **secularism, democracy**, and so on. He [word indistinct] the **enemies of Allah**, the **Jews, Christians, and pagans** and made the country a breeding ground for spreading their unbelief. He fought those preaching Allah's word and killed His mujahidin. The defense against that: **The sword**.

The defense against the evil, the evil of the **crusader, Jewish and pagan onslaught** on the Islamic world east and west: They are slaughtering the Muslim men, killing their children, raping their women, and looting their wealth. The defense against that: The sword...

The sword: To raise Allah's word so that **Allah's religion rules the world** and justice spreads all over it....The sword: To **terrorize** anyone tempted to harm even part of the **dignity of Islam and Muslims.** The sword: Or the certain death and the anticipated slaughter.

...**seek death and life will be given to you**. Do not be deceived by wishes and... by conceit.

 Beware of deceiving yourselves with books you read or things you do. Do not let preoccupation with comfortable things divert you ...

Let Muslims be assured that **the strike is coming to the United States** like the morning's dawn, but at the proper place and time for the mujahidin. We will obtain victory with peace and piety, Allah willing.

...we ask Allah [words indistinct] the **criminal tyrant Jews, Christians, hypocrites, and apostates** who want to sow corruption between Muslims:

Give victory to the Muslims and mujahidin over them. O Allah, give us victory over them everywhere....Amen, amen, amen. Allah Is Great, Allah Is Great. **Islam is coming**.

The Abu-Hafs al-Masri Brigades (Al-Qa'ida)

Thursday, [word indistinct] Jumada al-Awwal 1425 hegira, corresponding to 1 July 2004.

The Terrifying Brilliance of Islam

Citizen Warrior

In the War with Islamic Supremacism, Every Citizen in the Free World in on the Front Lines

2010

CITIZEN WARRIOR

Inside:

26 Keys to the Theo-Political Doctrine of Islam

- Submission to an Idea Set
- Unalterable "Divine" Law
- Forbidding of Criticism
- Superiority of "The Believers"
- Treatment of "The Non-Believers"
- Use of War, Violence & Terror
- Self-Perpetuation
- Uniformity & Repetition

Have you ever wondered...

...why millions of Muslim men are dedicated to killing Americans? Or why so many are willing to blow themselves up to kill Israelis? Or why they are so committed to blowing up random people in Bali, London, Madrid, etc.?

Islamic supremacists are doing this all over the world, attacking Westerners and their own fellow Muslims alike. Why?

Because of a doctrine. A **doctrine is a collection of ideas**. These could be customs, words, beliefs, etc. A religion is not a single idea; it is a collection of ideas. The collection of ideas that make up Islam makes Muslims behave and feel as they do.

Collections of ideas compete with each other in the same way that collections of cells (organisms) compete with each other. And because idea-collections compete, and because new ideas can often be added or subtracted from the collection, and because some collections gain more believers than others, collections of ideas can actually *evolve*.

Let's look at how religious idea-collections evolve and compete. To begin with, let's assume we already have a religion established. It already has a holy book and millions of people are already believers.

And then there is a *slight variation*

The original version had a **"live and let live"** attitude, and never tried to encourage its followers to get converts. But then someone comes up with the idea that if you can persuade a non-believer to become a believer, you **earn** some sort of **spiritual merit**. You are saving souls, and your chances of getting into heaven are better.

So now you have two variations on the same religion: One contains the idea that it doesn't really matter if you get anyone else to join the religion. The other **motivates** its believers to persuade others to join.

After 1,000 years, which has *More Believers*?

After a thousand years, which of the two variations will have **more believers**? I'm betting on the motivated-to-spread-it version.

Let's assume, for the moment, that the motivated version gets far more followers. Does that mean it makes people happier? Or more successful? Or do they have healthier children? No. Just

because a collection of ideas successfully gains followers does *not* mean it benefits any of the people believing those ideas.

The same is true in genetics. Contrary to common sense, a successful gene doesn't necessarily benefit the organism. It is "successful" in the sense that it has made lots of copies

The Terrifying
Brilliance of Islam

Islam has lasted 1400 years. Let's explore why this is so.

of itself and is found in many organisms. But it may actually be harmful for the organism.

For example, if there is a gene for alcoholism, and if drinking causes someone to start having children younger than someone who doesn't drink, over thousands of years, the alcoholism gene might be more successful (the gene makes its way into more offspring) than the non-alcoholism gene, even though it might be **bad for every individual person carrying the gene**.

A Doctrine is an "Idea-Collection"

In the same way, the success of doctrine or idea-collection (such as Islam) doesn't necessarily mean it's good for the people who believe it or follow it. This will be an important point to remember later.

If an idea-collection, or doctrine, says it is wrong to use contraception and wrong to masturbate, over time, that idea-collection would probably be followed by more people than the version that says these things are just fine (assuming people normally teach their children to believe as they do).

So the hapless believer of a particular idea-collection will try to follow the rules and be a good person by avoiding the evils of contraception and masturbation, and what will be the result for him personally? He may have more children than he might want or could afford, causing him to work overtime to support them — working two jobs if he must. This may send him to an early grave, but his effort creates more believers of that particular collection of ideas than someone who doesn't hold those ideas.

Is Man using the Doctrine, or *is the Doctrine using Man*?

So in a sense, the idea-collection has *used the man* for its own purposes, or at least that's one legitimate way to look at it. And it's a way that sheds new light on Islamic supremacism, which is why I've spent so much time explaining it.

If you were going to deliberately design a collection of ideas with the purpose of making it eventually dominate the world — one that would eventually **out-compete** every other religion, doctrine, or political system — you would be hard-pressed to do better than Islam.

Re-Enforcing an Idea-Collection

Let's look at some of the individual ideas within the collection of the doctrine that is Islam. Many of the ideas enhance or reinforce each other. In other words, adding one idea to the others can make the whole collection more effective because some ideas work **synergistically**.

Key components of the "idea-collection" known as Islam:

 # 1 A STANDARDIZED VERSION of the idea-collection is written down. This is something basic to (most doctrines and) several religions and isn't an Islamic invention, but it is an important factor in the success of Islam.

Something only transmitted orally can change over time, but something written will be *identical* a thousand years from now, and with modern printing presses, can be reproduced in the millions, giving it an enormous advantage in spreading *identical* copies of the idea-collection.

 # 2 The Qur'an includes INSTRUCTIONS for its own spread. It tells believers they must spread Islam. It is their *holy duty* to bring Mohammad's warnings and Islamic law to every corner of the world.

 # 3 The doctrinal idea-collection includes instructions for its own PRESERVATION, protection, and accuracy in reproduction. The Qur'an, the most important of the Islamic holy books, directly tells its followers that they can never change or modify or "modernize" any of the teachings within the idea-collection. It is **perfect as it is**. It is a capital sin to try to do so. This idea ensures the preservation of the whole collection.

CB   BO

The "Islamic Trilogy" consists of the Koran (the revealed word of Allah), the Sira (biography of Mohammed) and the Hadith (traditions of Mohammed).

These first three ideas are pretty standard for several successful religions. But now it gets interesting...

 # 4 Islam COMMANDS its followers to create a GOVERNMENT that supports it. This may be one of the most ingenious ideas in the whole collection. Islam is the only religion that uses it. Other groups of religious people have had political aspirations, but no other major religious group orders its followers — as a religious duty — to create a government that follows its own system of law. This government applied to its believers *and non-believers*. We must reconsider Islam's classification as a religion, but more on that later.

Islam has a **system of law, called Shari'a**, and all Muslims are obligated to continually strive to make their government — wherever they are — follow it. Because of some of the other ideas added to Islam, you will see that this political addition to the idea-collection has significant consequences. *Not only is this perhaps Islam's most brilliant innovation, it is also the most terrifying to non-Muslims.*

Islamic Shari'a Law
"The Path"

Shari'ah implements the Islamic Trilogy in law to reinforce culture, custom, and religion.

"War is Deceit"
—*Mohammed*

War as an Approved Tactic

#5 **Permission to SPREAD the religion BY WAR.** This is another brilliant innovation. Although some other religions have spread themselves using force, they had very little justification from their own religious doctrines to do so.

Not so with Islam. Expanding by conquest is very much accepted and encouraged by Islamic doctrine and reinforced in the idea-collection.

Islamic teachings present it this way:

> The poor non-Muslims not living in an Islamic state need to be saved from the sin of following laws other than Allah's. If they won't voluntarily change their laws to Shari'a, then it is the duty of Muslim warriors to insist. The world cannot be at peace until every government on earth follows the laws of Allah.

Mohammad's own experience showed *the* example — such an example, says the Qur'an, that every Muslim should follow. At first, Mohammad tried to spread Islam by peaceful means. After thirteen years he had a paltry 150 converts.

But then he changed tactics and started using **warfare, slaughter, executions and assassinations,** and within ten years he converted *tens of thousands.* After he died, they used the same aggressive, murderous tactics and converted *millions.* And by simple population increase and a few more converted Islamic states, it is now well over a billion.

The use of warfare combines synergistically and powerfully with the instruction to create an Islamic state. So Islam spread quickly as its armies got bigger. Muslim warriors con-

quered and set up Islamic states, most of which have lasted to this day. Huge areas of land, nations formerly Hindu, animist, Buddhist and Christian were conquered — and are being conquered today.

The laws within an Islamic state make Islam very difficult, nearly impossible, to dislodge. The laws also make it very advantageous to convert to Islam.

This is one of the most effective methods ever invented for getting an idea-collection into huge numbers of minds. It's a method of control and indoctrination similar to those used successfully by communist and other totalitarian rulers. But as you'll discover below, Islam makes unique use of the power of the law, Shari'a, to enforce complete conversion to the religion.

Never Relinquish Lands Once Conquered

#6 **Lands must be conquered.** And lands that Islam has lost must be **reconquered,** like Spain and Israel, for example. The Islamic empire must continually *expand.* Contraction is bad, expansion is good. So if a country was once Islamic but is no longer following Shari'a law, that's contraction, and must be remedied.

According to Islamic teachings, the earth is Allah's. If there are parts of the earth not following Islamic Shari'a law, it is the duty of the faithful to gain control of that land and establish Shari'a. It is a sin to let it be otherwise.

Polygamy to Ensure a Never-Ending Supply of Soldiers

 #7 **The idea-collection produces abundant new soldiers by allowing POLYGAMY.** A Muslim man can marry up to four wives, and he can have sex with as many slave girls as he wishes.

The Qur'an especially encourages men to marry widows. This is an important idea to add if you are going to be losing a lot of soldiers in war. You need some way of **replenishing** your army. Otherwise the idea-collection could die out from a lack of offspring.

Don't Criticize or Leave Islam

 #8 **It is a punishable OFFENSE TO CRITICIZE Islam.** You can see why this one is a good supporting idea for the collection. It helps suppress any ideas that would reduce the authority of Islamic ideas. This one, like many of the others, is good for the idea-collection, but bad for the followers — the actual people. This one **limits freedom of speech.**

 #9 **You CAN'T LEAVE Islam** once you're in. This is an interesting one. It is actually *illegal* in Islamic states to convert out of Islam. This is a critical part of Shari'a law. Someone who has rejected Islam who was once a Muslim is an "apostate." This is a **crime and a sin, and the punishment for it is death and eternal damnation** in hell thereafter.

Obviously, you can see why this idea has been included in the collection, but this one has actually caused Islam a problem because those who are following Islam to the letter consider more **"moderate"** Muslims (those who want to ignore or alter the more violent passages of the Qur'an) **to be apostates.** Since the punishment for apostates is death, **fundamentalist Muslims are fighting modernizing Muslims** all over the world, and keeping many rebellious, modernizing Muslims from speaking up for fear of death.

Every time a group of Muslims decides that maybe Islam should be updated for the 21st century and maybe women should have some rights or maybe the government should be more democratic, the devout Muslims call them apostates and try to kill them.

The idea-collection protects its own accuracy of reproduction by saying the original idea-collection cannot be altered. This is not good for the organisms, the Muslim human beings, but it's great for the perpetuation of the idea collection, the doctrine of Islam.

Another idea in Shari'a law says it's against the law for anyone to try to convert a Muslim to another religion.

 #10 **Islam must be your FIRST ALLEGIANCE.** This is a great idea to add to the collection if the goal is world domination. You are a Muslim first, before any allegiance you give to your family, your tribe, or your country.

This does two things: It causes a unity of people across borders, which allows the group to grow bigger than any other entity. In other words, the "Nation of Islam" can grow bigger than any country, no matter how large, which gives the group a massive numerical advantage.

Again, preserving the numbers of followers and preventing the potential influx of any new ideas.

The rejection of traditional borders bodes ill for sovereign nations the world over.

*'We Will Establish Islamic
Rule From Alaska and
Chile to South Africa,
Japan, Russia... To
Iceland... Be Warned, We
Are Coming'*
*Ibrahim Almaqdis,
Somali Jihad Fighters,
told Al Jazeera*

The Way to Paradise in Arabic

 # 11 **Dying while fighting for Islam is the ONLY way to guarantee a man's entrance into Paradise.** This is a great idea for **creating fearless, enthusiastic warriors**, especially given the Qur'an's vivid descriptions of the sensuous delights of Paradise.

A Muslim man has a *chance* of getting to Paradise if he is a good Muslim, but it is not guaranteed. However, if he dies while fighting for the advancement of Islam, he is *guaranteed* to get in, and that's the only thing he can do to guarantee it.

 # 12 **You must read the Qur'an in *ARABIC*.** This UNITES believers by language, and language is a very powerful unifying element. For added incentive to learn Arabic, another idea in the collection says you can't go to Paradise unless you pray in Arabic.

So all Muslims all over the world share a language. This makes it easier to coordinate far-reaching campaigns of protest, political pressure, and war. I doubt if Mohammad foresaw this possibility, but this idea is brilliant, even if it was an accident.

Praying & Praying...

 # 13 **You must pray five times a day.** This is one of the five "pillars" — that is, one of the five central practices — of Islam. Within an Islamic state, it is **enforced by law.** Every Muslim must pray five times a day. The practice helps the idea-collection dominate a Muslim's life, infusing his daily rhythm with Islam.

It would be impossible to forget anything you deliberately do so often. Five times a day, every day, a Muslim must bow down and pray to Allah.

Research has shown the more effort a person expends for a cause, the more he is likely to believe in it and value it. So this is a good way to eventually make believers out of people who became Muslims through coercion.

Islam completely takes over every aspect of Muslims' lives. Not only are they required to pray five times a day, they have to go through a washing ritual beforehand. Islam dictates the laws, and the laws cover many public and private behaviors. In an Islamic state, it is impossible to be a *casual* Muslim.

 # 14 **The prayers involve RHYTHMIC moving together in time.** When Muslims pray, they all face the same direction, they bow down, get on their hands and knees, and put their face on the mat, all in **unison**, and then rise back up. Again and again.

When people move together in time, whether dancing or marching or praying, it creates a physical and emotional bond between them.' That's why all military training involves close-order drill—marching in unison—even though it has been a long time since military groups have actually marched into combat. There is no longer a need for the skill, but military training retained the practice because it is so effective at creating a strong feeling of unity between soldiers.

The same is true of any physical movements people make in unison. So the method of prayer in Islam is a unifying idea added to the collection.

A Woman's Plight

#15 A WOMAN is in a thoroughly SUBORDINATE position. This idea really helps support other ideas in the collection, like five and six. If women had too much influence, they'd try to curb the warring. Women in general don't like to send their husbands and sons off to war. But if women have no say, then the rest of the ideas can express themselves without interference. By subordinating women, the idea-collection prevents their effective vote against war, violence, and conquest.

The rules and laws within Islam that keep women subordinate are numerous. For example, she is not allowed to leave her house unless she is accompanied by a male relative. Under Islamic law, a woman is forbidden to be a head of state or a judge. She can only inherit half of what a man can inherit. In court, her testimony is only worth half of a man's. She is not allowed to choose where she will live or who she will marry. She is not allowed to marry a non-Muslim or divorce her husband. He, however, can divorce her with a wave of his hand.

And according to Shari'a, he can (and should) beat her if she disobeys him.

All of these ideas keep her subordinate, which **helps keep the war machine going** unimpeded by domestic rebellion.

#16 The only way a woman can get into Paradise for sure is if her HUSBAND IS HAPPY with her when she dies. When I read about this one, I thought, "Mohammad, you are a crafty one."

This idea obviously helps with the **subjugation of women**. It **motivates her to subjugate herself**. It gives her a strong incentive to subordinate her wishes to her husband's, because while she might have a chance to get into Paradise if she's a good Muslim, the only way she can *guarantee* she will go to Paradise (and avoid eternal suffering in hell) is to make sure her husband is happy with her when she dies.

In the world of Islam, she can also can gain entry to Paradise by dying while advancing Islam, in jihad.

Allah as Editor

#17 Allah gives Himself permission to EDIT his own work. This is an interesting one. It says in the Qur'an that if a passage written later contradicts an earlier passage, then the later one is the better one. The Qur'an was written in sections (Mohammad's revelations, each written as a sura or chapter) over a period of 23 years. The circumstances of Mohammad's life and his religion changed quite a bit over those 23 years.

One of the ideas in the Qur'an is "this is the word of Allah." People had al-

ready memorized his earlier revelations, so Mohammad couldn't just change his revelations. It would look a little strange for the all-knowing, infinitely wise Allah to change something He had already said.

But with this new idea—that later revelations **abrogated** or overwrote any earlier revelations they contradicted—Allah's methods could change as Mohammad found more effective ideas.

"How can Islamic nations achieve greatness when they ignore half their potential talent?"
— *Bernard Lewis*

Much confusion about the content and meaning of the Qur'an lies in the concept and practice of "abrogation."

The Terrifying
Brilliance of Islam

"I HAVE BEEN MADE

VICTORIOUS

THROUGH TERROR."

- MOHAMMAD, FOUNDER OF ISLAM

*Tolerance becomes a
crime when applied to evil.*
Thomas Mann

FREEDOM
GO TO
HELL

Violence Supersedes Tolerance

As I pointed out earlier, in his first 13 years of peacefully preaching, Mohammad only managed to win 150 followers. But as a military leader and violent conqueror, he was able to subjugate all of Arabia to Islamic law in less than 10 years. The peaceful ways were too slow. Conversion by conquering and establishing Shari'a was much faster and more efficient. So this is the bad news for non-Muslims: The later, violent, intolerant verses abrogate, that is override, the earlier peaceful, tolerant passages.

No Right and Wrong, Just "Allowed" and "Dis-Allowed"

#18 **The Qur'an uses the CARROT AND STICK to reinforce behavior.** Throughout the book are vivid descriptions of hell, where sinners and non-Muslims will have to drink boiling, stinking water, will be thrown face down into a raging fire, and will be there for eternity, suffering endless torments in agony.

There are also vivid descriptions of **Paradise.** In Paradise, it says, believers will wear green silk robes and recline on plush couches. Trees will shade them, fruit will dangle nearby. They'll have tasty food and refreshing drinks served in silver goblets. And objects of sexual desire will be readily available. To have a chance of achieving this, they must be devout Muslims. To guarantee it, they must die in jihad (for men) or make sure their husbands are always happy with them (for women).

#19 **It provides a huge and inspiring GOAL.** Leaders of countries or companies or religions have all discovered that you can get the most motivation and enthusiasm from your followers if you provide them with an **expansive vision** — an enormous goal. In the Islamic idea-collection, the goal calls for a continuous effort to expand the domain of Islamic law until **all the world is subjugated** to it.

Many religions have the goal of converting everyone, but Islam has a method available nobody else has: To expand by seizing by war and converting through governments to Shari'a.

Once the whole world is Islamic, peace is said to will reign. That's why even terrorists can say with complete sincerity, **"Islam is a religion of peace"** however disingenuous we may view this assertion.

The Qur'an says it is best if nonbelievers accept Islam and become Muslims without force. But if they refuse, then devout Muslims must fight them and conquer them and save their poor souls by insisting they live by the laws of Allah.

Once all countries are conquered, the world will be at peace. It is an enormous and inspiring goal, and a strongly unifying purpose. It creates motivated, enthusiastic followers.

Subjugation of the "Infidel"

#20 **Non-Muslims must pay a large TAX.** Once Muslims conquer a country and convert the government to Islamic law, any non-Muslims have the choice between becoming Muslim or becoming a dhimmi. Dhimmis are allowed to practice their non-Muslim religion if they pay the jizya (a tax). If they convert to Islam, they no longer have to pay a tax, so there is a practical incentive to convert.

But another aspect of this makes it a brilliant idea to add to the collection. **The tax takes money away from the non-Muslims and their competing idea-collections and gives that money to support Islam.** This is pure genius! Once again Islam works to enlarge and strengthen itself and weakening everyone else.

The income from these taxes (usually a 25% income tax) helped fund the Islamic conquests during the first two major jihads. They conquered vast lands, most of them already filled with Christians and Jews, many of whom did not convert at first, and **their jizya poured huge sums of money into the Islamic war machine.**

Eventually, the numbers of previously majority Christians and Jews and others dwindled down as they converted or escaped, until now, in most Islamic countries, Jews and Christians are very small minorities.

The tax-the-non-Muslims idea helps the Islamic idea-collection make more copies of itself by suppressing competing religious idea-collections and financially supporting the spread of Islam.

Several ideas within Shari'a law extend this effect. For example, non-Muslims are not allowed to build any new houses of worship. They're not even allowed to *repair* already-existing churches or synagogues without permission, and requests are usually denied. This puts the houses of worship of any competing idea-collection in a state of permanent decline. Brilliant.

Also, non-Islamic prayers cannot be spoken within earshot of a Muslim — again, preventing Muslims from being infected by a competing religion. No public displays of any symbols of another faith may be shown either.

All of this **prevents the spread of any competing religion,** and makes **competing idea-collections die out** over time. That's why today there are so many "Muslim countries." Almost every other country in the world is made up of many different religions. But Islam not only spreads, it continually undermines and weakens all other forms of religion or government until it dominates.

One added idea makes it that much easier for Muslims to subjugate non-Muslims within an Islamic state: Non-Muslims are not allowed to own weapons of any kind. To force cooperation from people, all dictatorial rulers in the history of the world have done the same thing: **Disarm the subjugated people.** They are much easier to manage, less dangerous, and less capable of upending the status quo.

Emblem of the Bosnian Muslim 13th SS "Handschar" (خنجر) Division

The Islamic Trilogy says the Infidel can be mocked, tortured, punished, killed, beheaded, confused, plotted against, terrorized, destroyed, deceived, caused pain, insulted, enslaved, raped, made war on, subjugated and humiliated.

Deceit and the telling of half-truths (known as "taqiyya" and "kitman" respectively) further confuses the non-Muslim as to the content and meaning of the Qur'an.

What does it say in the Qur'an?

The unbelievers among the People of the Book and the pagans shall burn for ever in the fire of Hell. They are the vilest of all creatures.
Qur'an 98:1-8.

Those Pesky Infidels

#21 **A Muslim is forbidden to make friends with an infidel.** A Muslim is allowed to *pretend* to be a friend, but in his heart he must never actually be a friend to a non-Muslim. This is one of the best protections Islam has against Muslims **leaving the faith** because in every other religion conversions to the religion are usually made because a friend introduced it. Being forbidden to make friends with infidels effectively prevents that from happening.

#22 **The Qur'an counsels the use of deceit when dealing with infidels.** Mohammad instructed one of his followers to lie if he had to (in order to assassinate one of Mohammad's enemies). The principle was clear: If it helps Islam, **IT'S OKAY TO DECEIVE NON-MUSLIMS.**

This principle has served Islamic goals very well through history. **And it serves those goals today.** On the DVD, *Obsession: Radical Islam's War Against the West*, you can watch real-life examples of Islamic leaders saying one thing in English for the Western press, and saying something entirely different to their own followers in Arabic a few days later.

Deceiving the enemy is always useful in war, and Islam is perpetually at war with the non-Islamic world until the whole world follows Shari'a law. All non-Muslims living in non-Islamic states are **enemies**. So deceiving Westerners is totally acceptable. It is encouraged if it can forward the spread of Islam.

This leads to the strange phenomenon covered by Steven Emerson in *Terrorists Among Us*, where organizations in America were ostensibly raising money for orphans, but really giving the money to terrorists. They deceived good-hearted Western infidels into giving money to organizations that were actively killing Western infidels.

As it says in the Qur'an:

"War is deceit."

This idea gives Islam a tremendous advantage over idea-collections that encourage indiscriminate truthfulness.

Above Criticism

#23 **Islam must always be DEFENDED.** This idea is a primary linchpin that gives justification for war with almost anybody, as you'll see in the idea below. After the enemy is defeated, of course, Muslims are required to establish an Islamic state with Shari'a law.

Prelude to War

#24 Islamic writings teach the use of PRETEXT TO START WARS. The Qur'an devotes a lot of time complaining about people who did not support Mohammad when he first started his religion, with Allah often condemning them to torment in hell in the hereafter.

Mohammad was rather pushy and insistent with his religion, and when others felt intruded upon and protested, Mohammad took that to mean they were **trying to stop** Allah's holy prophet from bringing the revealed word of Allah to the world, so he was justified to fight them and destroy them as Allah's enemies. This is a demonstration of the principle of *pretext*.

Non-Muslims of the world need urgently to become aware of this principle. Of all the ideas in the Islamic collection, *this is the most dangerous to the West because it removes our natural self-preserving defenses*. Muslim propagandists spin Muslim violence as **self-defense**. Always. Check it out. No matter how blatantly they kill non-Muslims unprovoked, you will always hear Muslim apologists explain it as self-defense.

The use of pretext means you need only the barest excuse to begin hostilities. It means you're actually *looking* for an excuse, and even trying to provoke others into striking the first blow, thus "starting" the hostilities.

It is a natural outcome of the other ideas in the collection. If the only way to get to Paradise is dying while fighting for Islam, *you need war*. And if it is your holy duty to make all governments use Shari'a law, you need to conquer those governments. But you don't really want to *look* like the aggressor. So all throughout the Qur'an, Mohammad tries to justify his aggression as "defending Islam."

The Qur'an repeats over seventy times that followers of Islam should use Mohammad as a model and imitate him. So Muslims the world over try to find or **create grievances**, so they can get a holy war started, so they can fight and die in Allah's cause and help make the world ruled by Allah's laws.

And because of the rise of multiculturalism (respect for all other cultures) in the West, the use of pretext is very effective against people who are unfamiliar with Islam. Many people think al Qaeda is angry at the West for having troops in Saudi Arabia, for example. That's merely a pretext. They want all non-Muslims out of the Middle East. Then they say they will cease hostilities. It is a ridiculous and impossible goal, so they are **justified in permanent war** against the West to avenge the grievance.

It's surprising that so many Westerners accept this particular pretext because it flies in the face of a fundamental Western principle: **Equality**. What Osama bin Laden implies is that "infidels are so undeserving, their very presence defiles our holy places." Wow. What does that say about the non-Muslims?

Why doesn't this kind of **racism or prejudice or infidelphobia** (or whatever you want to call it) outrage more Westerners? Instead, many think we ought to pull out of the Middle East so these poor offended Islamic supremacists aren't so angry with us any more!

The principle of pretext means you try to provoke a hostile reaction and then use the hostile reaction as a reason to escalate hostilities. It's the same method schoolyard bullies have used for thousands of years: "What are you looking at? You wanna take it outside, punk?"

"I am with you: give firmness to the Believers: I will instill terror into the hearts of the Unbelievers: smite ye above their necks and smite all their fingertips off them."
Qur'an 8:12-15

*Most cultures have a
"Golden Rule" to do unto
others as you would have
them do unto you.
Not so with Islam.*

Double Standards...One for me, None for you

#25 **The explicit use of DOUBLE STANDARDS.** Islam has one standard for Muslims, and a different standard for non-Muslims, which always gives the **advantage to Muslims**, and within a Muslim country, it provides incentives to convert.

For example, Islam *must* be spread by its believers, wherever they are. But when other religions try to spread their *own* idea-collection, Muslims are supposed to see it as an aggression against Islam — an act of aggression that must be "defended." Remember, Islam must always be defended.

Another example of how the double standard idea gives Islam an advantage: When Islam is **defamed** in any way, **Muslims should violently defend it**. Even in a cartoon. But Muslims can and should defame Jews and Christians in Muslim newspapers and television (which they do), and **they should defame any infidel or enemy, as they defame the U.S. today.**

Here's another example: The Islamic supremacists of Saudi Arabia are pouring money into **building mosques** all over the free world. But according to Shari'a law, which is the basis of the legal code in Saudi Ara-

bia, no non-Muslim religious structures are allowed to be built. **It's a blatant double standard.**

Muslims all over the world protest loudly and violently when anyone in Europe or America resists the building of more mosques in their countries.

Islamic supremacists don't see the irony in it. They don't feel strange having such an *obvious* double standard. They are, after all, Allah's followers and everyone else is deluded. **Fairness and equality with such unworthy infidels would seem very out of place.** A double standard seems completely appropriate from that perspective.

The double standard principle is a key part of the idea-collection, and it has been a great advantage in the spread of Islam (and the suppression of competing religions).

#26 **It is forbidden to kill a Muslim (except for a just cause). IT IS NOT FORBIDDEN TO KILL AN INFIDEL.** This causes a bond between Muslims, **fear in non-Muslims,** and motivation to become Muslim. This is also another example of an explicit Islamic double standard.

In this Clash of Cultures, Just Who is being *Intolerant*?

Islam's "Success" is a Threat to Global Freedom

WE CAN ADMIRE or at least recognize the brilliance of the Islamic idea-collection in an abstract, intellectual sort of way, but it is terrifyingly real. The theo-political doctrine of Islam is a THREAT to all non-Muslims the world over. Millions of people try to follow these ideas to the letter. And their belief in the idea-collection is strongly supported by the side-effects of Shari'a law. By making the government and laws ruled by Islam, the idea-collection applies two powerful **principles of influence: social proof and authority.**

Social proof refers to the strong influence of "**what everyone knows.**" In an Islamic state, *everyone* practices the religion (or they are flogged, taxed, or killed) and no one can criticize it, not friend-to-friend, and not through any media. The psychological impact of this is enormous. Three generations later, it would be almost **impossible for any Muslim living in that state to think outside of Islam.** The authority and social proof would be overwhelming.

Of course, just because I recognize the genius of the idea-collection doesn't mean I'm in favor of it. As a non-Muslim, **I am wholeheartedly against** it. Remember, the success of an idea-collection has nothing to do with making people happy or healthy. "Success" only means it propagates well.

The same is true for genes. A successful gene is one that gets the most copies of itself into future generations. The genes making up a **deadly virus** may kill millions of people and cause untold misery, but from a genetic point of view, the virus is successful. Genes don't care about people. They don't try to make us happy. They are cold and indifferent to our plight.

Same with ideas. An idea-collection will use up and spit out human lives in the service of its propagation, indifferent to the pain, misery, or death it causes.

An idea-collection, well-drilled into someone's head and reinforced by the powerful authority and social proof of his whole society, **can cause him to blow himself up just to kill others** for the fulfillment of a fantasy goal of ultimately attaining world peace and the triumph of Allah (and a harem of 72 dark-eyed voluptuous beauties devoted to his every wish).

The Islamic idea-collection is **formidable.** It is a force to be reckoned with and *we ignore it at our peril.* It has already taken hold of the minds and lives of almost one and a half billion people, and it's the youngest of the major religions.

And yet, I don't think the situation is hopeless. Many Muslims now living in Islamic states are **trapped** and *would defect from Islam if it were safe to do so.*

The first thing we in the multicultural and tolerant West need to do is **help each other** become **aware** of the formidable idea-collection threatening to overtake us. We need to help our fellow citizens **awaken** to the fact that Islamic supremacists will deliberately take advantage of our tolerance and our freedom so as to ultimately eliminate it.

This is an **ideological war,** a war of doctrines – or idea-collections, so the ideas in the heads of your fellow Westerners makes all the difference. And you can help turn the tide. Find ways to introduce this information to your fellow non-Muslims. For ideas of how to do this, visit WhatYouCan-DoAboutIslam.com.

"I have been ordered by Allah to fight with people till they bear testimony to the fact that there is no God but Allah."
—*Hadith*

Citizen Warrior

In the War with Islamic Supremacism, Every Citizen in the Free World in on the Front Lines

2010

www.citizenwarrior.com

www.politicalislam.com

www.thereligionofpeace.com

www.jihadwatch.org

Mutuality——The Missing Link

TOLERANCE AND MUTUAL respect for different cultures and religions is great — as long as it is mutual. When it's not mutual, then tolerance becomes a self-destructive doctrine. When it is not mutual, one side gives and the other side takes. In normal parlance, it is called being a doormat.

Islamic fundamentalism is religiously-sanctioned intolerance, and many in the West tolerate the intolerance out of a blind multiculturalism. But multiculturalism (respect for other cultures) need not be blind. The addition of one simple distinction is all that is needed— mutuality.

But the multiculturalism doctrine is incomplete. It is a great strategy for most people and most cultures and most religions. But it is disastrous when you stick with it blindly.

All that's missing is the added distinction of mutuality. We can simply amend the doctrine to something like this: We respect all religions and cultures who do us the honor of respecting ours as well. All others will be treated with less generosity.

We would be fools to tolerate intolerance—even if that intolerance is hiding behind a cloak of religion.

Part II

Other Threats

> To wage war, three things are necessary: money, money, and yet more money.
>
> - Gian-Jacopo Trivulzio
> Marshal of France, 1499

People sleep peacefully in their beds at night only because rough men stand ready to do violence on their behalf.

- George Orwell

Chapter 8

US Foreign Policy in a World in Turmoil

To forestall or prevent such hostile acts by our adversaries,
The United States will, if necessary, act preemptively.

- The National Security Strategy of the USA, September 2002

The Middle East produces more history than it can consume locally.

After America finally entered World War I and helped bring it to an end, the US returned to its isolationist ways. World War II forced it back into the world arena. Barely returning to normal after that war, America found itself in a protracted war with Communism, the Cold War, World War III. That led to wars in Korea and Viet-Nam. Even before the demise of the Soviet Union, the US was in World War IV without recognizing it. Americans were attacked many times. In Iran our embassy was invaded, our diplomats were taken hostage, and we endured the idiocies of Ayatollah Khomeini. Our embassies were bombed in Beirut and Africa, our troops killed in Lebanon and Saudi Arabia, airplanes were hijacked or blown up, American hostages were killed, and US Navy ships attacked, but except for a few people killed in front of the CIA and the first World Trade Center attack, those events were far away and America continued to slumber.

The war soon became overt after Saddam Hussein invaded Kuwait in 1990 resulting in the first Gulf War in 1991. That war was mostly funded by the Arab oil countries in contrast to the terrible expenditures since, and President George H. W. Bush was wise enough not to pursue that war into Iraq. However, the neoconservatives were already calling for an attack on Iraq.

But 11 September 2001 changed everything with the terrible pictures of three large airliners being flown into the towers of the World Trade Center and the Pentagon, plus a fourth, which was intended to hit the Capitol, went down in Pennsylvania after a brave fight by passengers. We faced a fanatic enemy with values totally different from those of the civilized world. We were unable to comprehend that intelligent human beings could commit such atrocities.

The neocons had been fairly well exiled under Bill Clinton but came back in force under President George W. Bush. Having a strong bent toward supporting Israel, they believe in preventive war, imperialism, and redrawing the map of the Middle East – by force if necessary.[1] They had been calling for regime change in Iraq for years. The Bush Administration was already planning for an attack on Iraq long before 9/11 which finally gave them their opening. Only days after 9/11 at a National Security Council meeting while the discussion was about attacking al Qaeda in Afghanistan, Secretary of Defense Donald Rumsfeld and his Deputy, Paul Wolfowitz, were calling for an attack on Iraq, even though there was no known link between al Qaeda and Iraq.

It is good to review the authority the US Congress gave the President on 14 September 2001 in Senate Joint Resolution 23 and Public Law 107-40.

(The President is authorized to) use all necessary and appropriate force against those nations, organizations, or person he determines planned, authorized, committed, or aided the terrorist attacks that occurred on Sept. 11, 2001, or harbored such organizations or person, in order to prevent any future acts of international terrorism against the United States by such nation, organizations or persons.

The result has been a national policy of preventive war (wars of choice) and has kept us in war ever since 9/11 with disastrous effects on our economy and the loss of thousands of American lives. Two things have kept us in the Middle East for over 60 years: oil and Israel. The dependence on foreign oil transformed the US from a creditor nation to a debtor nation and the blind support of Israel only added fuel to the anti-American propaganda of Islam.

The Communist Threat

The euphoria of victory after World War II was short lived as our former ally, the Soviet Union, took over Eastern Europe and it soon became clear that the worldwide imposition of Communism was still on their agenda. Within only five years from the end of the war, we were back at war in Korea. World War III lasted some 40 years, was extremely expensive, grew hot in several proxy confrontations (Korea, Viet-Nam, and others), was extremely dangerous as the two nuclear powers faced each other with thousands of armed nuclear weapons ready for instant launch, and it was worldwide.

The world became divided into two blocs with a third non-aligned group trying to stay out of the fray. With the end of World War II, China continued its civil war between the Nationalists and the Communists, which ended in 1949 with the establishment of the People's Republic of China (PRC). The Korean War saw Russian pilots and advisors supporting the North Koreans as well as the large invasion of the Chinese Communist Army across the Yalu River. Both China and Russia supported the North Vietnamese in the Viet-Nam War, but the Sino-Soviet cooperation was never real close and eventually turned into rivalry as they tried to impose their different versions of Communism on other parts of the world.

Only the dead have seen the end of war

- Plato

We did not have direct contact with the Chinese until the Nixon opening in 1971, but we had maintained diplomatic relations with the Soviet Union which provided direct access during those precarious times, and after the Cuban Missile Crisis a direct hot line was established between Washington and Moscow. The Communist threat remained at the top of the US foreign policy agenda for years with the Korean War, the Cuban Missile Crisis, Viet-Nam, the 1967 Arab-Israel War, and then the Soviet invasion of Afghanistan. This almost total preoccupation with the Communist threat set the tone for our policies with other countries around the world, particularly our policies toward Arab/Muslim countries. We had established the Baghdad Pact in an effort to block Soviet encroachment to the south, but that collapsed with the overthrow of the Iraqi government. The Soviets had made serious arrangements with Iraq, Syria, and Egypt, which along with our support for Israel, set us on a confrontational path with these countries which complicated our interests.

We conducted a massive covert operation against the Soviets in Afghanistan, but unwisely were forced to conduct it through Pakistan, and unfortunately created the mujahedin, which led to al Qaeda. The PRC supported Pakistan as part of their rivalry with India as the world's two most populous countries began to square off for dominance in East Asia. During those years, we placed our support behind Iran and Israel. The US provided large amounts of arms and aid to Israel and to the Shah as a balance against Soviet influence.

President Anwar Sadat expelled the Soviets but Kissinger and Nixon did not grasp the significance of that major act and we faced another confrontation with the Soviets in the 1973 Arab-Israel War which led to the oil embargo and another hit to the US economy. Soon after the overthrow of the Shah and the coming to power of the mullahs under Ayatollah Ruhollah Khomeini, Iraq invaded and there was an eight-year Muslim war, partially the old Arab-Persian rivalry. The US supported each side at times trying to prevent either one from being able to dominate the Persian Gulf (oil).

The breakup of the Soviet Union removed much of the Muslim population in the republics in South Central Asia, but the Northern Caucasus were still a part of Russia. This is a predominantly Muslim region that includes Chechnya and Dagestan. Russia has faced a long war of insurgency in the area with attacks both in the area and in Moscow and Breslan. This is essentially a civil war. As one writer put it, Russia's "Afghanistan is inside Russia."[2]

With the demise of the Soviet Union, the US was hoping for a respite with a "peace dividend," but was soon caught up again in the Middle East with the 1990 Iraqi invasion of Kuwait over an oil dispute. The United States faces serious national security challenges from diverse countries: China, North Korea, Russia, and even Mexico but the true **Crucible of Crisis** is the threats and conflicts from the Mediterranean to South Asia.

The Crucible of Crisis

The area from the Mediterranean to India presents multiple national security problems. We are involved in a major ideological war with Islamofascism from this region, Israel-Palestine, oil, and we were mired in two wars there. At the left, center, and right we have artificial states – Israel, Iraq, and Pakistan. Even the Maghreb is partially artificial having been delineated by colonial rule with Libya probably the worst. The drive for a Jewish home arose in World War I in an effort to draw the US into that war. It reached fruition after the Holocaust in World War II. Actually, the entire area from Egypt to southern Turkey and from the Mediterranean to old Mesopotamia at one time known as Greater Syria is artificial. Syria, part of the Ottoman Empire, was carved up into Syria, Lebanon, Jordan, and Palestine (and eventually Israel). Iraq was created in the early Churchill days after the fall of the Ottoman Empire and England was particularly interested in the oil from Mosul. Pakistan was created as the British withdrew from their empire in India.

At the southwest corner, we have Yemen. where we have al Qaeda in the Arabian Peninsula and a civil war that drove out the president of 30 years. We have Egypt, currently in turmoil, which plays a major role in the area as does Turkey, which is a NATO member, a rising power, and growing more Islamic, plus Shia Iran, striving to be a nuclear power. This area has more history than it can handle. Mesopotamia and before that Babylonia go back to 3,500 BC, and is also considered to be the site of the Garden of Eden. The Persian Empire – from about 550 BC – the time of Cyrus the Great, Xerses, and Darius – dominated the area extending from the Mediterranean (as far west as Greece and parts of North Africa into what is now Libya) to the Indus and from the Caucasus to the Indian Ocean – surely Iranian children study this glory in school. This area has a long history of kingdoms, fiefdoms, etc. fighting, rising, and falling. This region from the Mediterranean to the Subcontinent is critical but few American vital interests are threatened at present and we need to keep it that way.

Israel – Outpost in the Arab World

With the Soviet Union gone, Mao Tse-tung dead, and China pursuing a new capitalism, the US finally could focus on the Middle East. Since World War II, its Middle East policy had been almost totally dominated by support for Israel. President Harry Truman, thanks to his Jewish former business partner and domestic politics, rejected the very strong objection of Secretary of State George Marshal and recognized Israel within minutes of its announcement of independence in 1948. Domestic politics have always played a dominant role in US relations with Israel due to the powerful Israel lobby and its enormous influence and money (particularly on Congress).

Israel is a dynamic, small, European – or American – style enclave in the Arab world and the only state without recognized boundaries. It has attacked all of its neighbors and has made peace with only two – Egypt and Jordan. It is a nuclear power and the most powerful country in the Middle East thanks to US arms, the US policy of guaranteeing them qualitative superiority, and yet it always claims to be besieged. It is a small country, in US terms it would extend from Harrisburg, Pennsylvania to the North Carolina line (about 225 miles) and it has a very narrow waist in the middle of the country which makes it quite vulnerable.

The only time the US has stood up to Israel was when President Eisenhower demanded the Israeli withdrawal from the Sinai after the British-French-Israeli invasion in the 1956 War. The difficulty with Nasser and the withdrawal of US support for the Aswan Dam led Nasser to turn to the Soviets for arms. This resulted in the foolish remarks by Nasser and a military buildup that the Israelis used as a pretense and invaded Egypt in 1967, destroying their military, reoccupying the Sinai, and then seizing the West Bank and East Jerusalem from Jordan, followed by seizing the Golan Heights from Syria – all in six days. They also tried to sink the US Navy ship the *USS Liberty* killing 34 Americans and wounding 171, which was totally covered up by Lyndon Johnson.

Israelis misread their great victories as evidence of divine support and their superiority, ignoring that they were surprise attacks. The 1967 War proved disastrous for Israel in that it transformed it into a colonial power in violation of international law.[3] The Palestinians, who had no say in the creation of Israel and *al Naqba* (the disaster and the ethnic cleansing of their area), have seen their land area increasingly diminish over time as the Israelis have built more and more settlements, more properly called colonies – the facts on the ground, with nearly 500,000 Israelis living in these colonies.

> **The 1967 War proved disastrous for Israel in that it transformed it into a colonial power in violation of international law.**

The world consensus for a Palestinian state, except for Israel, is the 1967 lines with some possible mutual modifications. Palestine would be the West Bank and Gaza with East Jerusalem as the capital. There are problems though: the Apartheid Wall has taken another 9.5% of the West Bank (to hold the major colonies, the best agricultural land, and the major aquifers). The colonies beyond the Wall occupy another 8%, plus the Jordan Valley 28.5%, leaving the Palestinian Authority with 54% of the 22% which equals only 12-13% of the original Palestine. Gaza is not connected to the West Bank and the Israeli government is moving as fast as possible to make sure the Palestinians cannot have any part of Jerusalem by building more houses/apartments. Also they have extended the city boundaries so that it is now 2½ times the size of Paris. Binyamin Netanyahu brusquely contradicted President Obama saying that "Jerusalem is not a settlement; Jerusalem is the capital of the State of Israel."[4]

Small problem: it is not so recognized by the international community. [There is a large part of the Israeli community that is embarrassed by the special treatment of and actions by the settlers and would like for the issue to be settled and over.]

The settlers, or colonists, have long been a problem in their actions in opposition to a Palestinian state since they claim their land was promised to the Jews in the Bible. They have frequently attacked Palestinians in the West Bank and even into Israel proper. According to the UN, "the number of incidents of settler violence resulting in Palestinian injuries or property damage has risen to 333 this year, compared with 217 in the same period last year."[5]

Up until the 1967 War, the US had maintained a fairly balanced policy toward the Middle East and provided little in the way of arms. France had been the major supplier, including helping develop the Israeli nuclear program, and they had cooperated on the 1956 attack on Egypt. President Charles de Gaulle was less supportive and strongly recommended to Israel not to attack. Just days before the Israelis attacked, "With great foresight, General de Gaulle said to Abba Eban... 'Don't go to war... you will create Palestinian nationalism and you will never again be rid of it.'"[6] Israel attacked anyway, France announced an arms embargo on the Middle East, and de Gaulle ended support for the Israeli nuclear program (which they did not need any longer as they had stolen or acquired adequate data and materiel from the US).

Lyndon Johnson changed US policy completely and opened the gates for massive military aid to Israel at US taxpayer expense. The humiliating loss in 1967 left the Arabs seeking revenge. With the Israelis sitting on the bank of the Suez Canal, there was a Phony War during the early 1970s with attacks back and forth and Israeli air strikes deep into Egypt. Sadat expelled the Russians but received no support from the West so he attacked in October 1973 in a brilliant limited attack across the canal in an effort to get Western attention. With the Israelis claiming they were about to be overrun, Nixon took equipment from US troops in Germany and airlifted it into the Sinai. The Soviets were threatening to intervene and the Arabs were threatening to embargo oil. The US frantically worked for a cease fire which the Israelis did not accept until they had seized all their objectives. The US failed to listen to the Arabs and they did cut off the oil. The US was now fully involved in trying to separate the two armies and restore peace.

The 1982 Israeli invasion of Lebanon to destroy the Palestine Liberation Organization (PLO) had the unintended consequence of creating HezbAllah (Party of Allah).

With the threat from Egypt neutralized by the Camp David Agreements, Israel was able to turn its attention to Iraq and the Palestine Liberation Organization (PLO). In 1981, they used America-provided aircraft (in violation of US law but ignored by Congress) to bomb the Osirak nuclear reactor. The 1982 Israeli invasion of Lebanon to destroy the PLO had the unintended consequence of creating HezbAllah which finally drove the Israelis out in 2000. Israel wanted to destroy HezbAllah and attacked in 2006 in a 34-day war that proved disastrous for Israel.[7] Washington viewed HezbAllah as the direct proxy of Iran and, with the concern over the Iranian nuclear program and with the neocons pushing for regime change in Iran to protect Israel, the US government did not try to restrain Israel; in fact, with the neocons leading, "the Bush administration enthusiastically endorsed Israel's plans for war in Lebanon."[8]

Israel was condemned by the international community for excessive brutality in its attacks on Lebanon.[9] Even though they lost a lot of equipment, HezbAllah was the big winner, for the guerrilla wins if he does not lose. The resistance by HezbAllah destroyed the myth of Israeli invincibility and greatly increased the prestige of HezbAllah. Hassan Nasrallah, already a hero for outlasting the Israelis and forcing them out of Lebanon in 2000, was now a major hero in the Arab world for being the only one who has ever fought Israel to a standstill or victory. The harsh Israeli response brought many Sunnis to support HezbAllah despite their general dislike for them as Shiites.[10] Now HezbAllah plays a major, almost dominating, role in Lebanese politics.

The myth of invincibility is a soufflé that cannot rise twice.

- George Galloway

A similar situation arose when Israel attacked Gaza over Christmas/New Year before Obama's inauguration causing terrible damage to the infrastructure, leaving Gaza under a total blockade, and enhancing the stature of Hamas. The dominant role of Israel in US foreign policy was evident again as Israel and its Israel First supporters in the US were the ardent proponents of the American invasion of Iraq.

The US has remained deeply involved in Israel-Palestine negotiations with only very limited success. The Oslo Accords were developed without a US role but they were never fully implemented. Ariel Sharon withdrew from Gaza, not as a signal of peace but to be rid of it and to strengthen the case for keeping the West Bank. The US pressured the Palestinians to hold elections but then was surprised and disappointed when Hamas won in Gaza and eventually drove Fatah out so that the Palestinian Authority is divided. Egypt does not want Gaza back and the split between Hamas in Gaza and Fatah in the West Bank complicates the Palestinian position and makes it easy for Israel to continue to delay saying they have no one to negotiate with. The issues involve the border, right to return, colonies, Jerusalem (originally to be an international city under the UN plan), Gaza, Golan Heights, and recognition.

Most of these issues have already been dealt with by the Saudi Initiative from King Abdullah and endorsed by the Arab League, reconfirmed in 2010, but Israel has refused to accept them and continues to build more colonies and raise new issues like recognition as a Jewish state and allegiance oaths for Palestinians in Israel. Prime Minister Ehud Olmert made an offer in September 2008 for "a Palestinian state on territory equivalent in size to the pre-1967 West Bank and Gaza Strip with mutually agreed-upon land swaps that take into account the new realities on the ground... Jerusalem would be shared ...the refugee problem would be addressed within the framework of the 2002 Arab Peace Initiative." It has never been formally rejected but the current Israeli government is less receptive.[11]

Obama made a strong speech in Israel's favor on 19 May 2011 but Netanyahu elected to lecture him. "Why on earth would Bibi Netanyahu choose to be so boorish and provocative? Because he can be. He has the U.S. Congress in his pocket, a fact made obvious by the applause tsunami that attended his speech to a joint session (and by the fact that an astonishing 68 Senators and 286 Representatives attended the American Israel Public Affairs Committee banquet the night before he spoke)."[12] Congressional support for Israel was clear with the "nearly three dozen standing ovations" and even amplified when Michael Grimm (R-NY) said referring to an explanation about US aid to train Palestinian police, that he "felt more comfortable receiving the explanation from the prime minister than from Obama administration officials"[13] This does not speak well for our so-called representatives in Washington.

Every Israeli action against Arabs feeds Arab anger against the U.S. and undermines its influence.

- Anthony Cordesman[14]

Israel is deeply divided internally and hardliners (such as Deputy Prime Minister and Foreign Minister Avigdor Lieberman) do not really want a Palestinian state and there is no contiguous entity that makes for a logical state. The Israeli government has elected to live with the status quo, a low level of violence, and ignore the Palestinians but it is a questionable policy for the long term survival of Israel. Israel is swimming against the tide of demographics and history. A little state of maybe only four million cannot dominate millions of Arabs for centuries. Israel must adapt to its environment or it will disappear.

We should remember that it is not only Muslims who may seem a bit eccentric. The ultra-Orthodox Jews with their beards and black suits demand segregation of men and women, that women cross the street and not walk in front of their synagogues, and that women should give up their seats to a man and move to the rear of the bus. They even harassed an 8-year-old girl spat on her, and called her a prostitute for the way she was dressed.[15]

The place in Israeli society of these ultra-Orthodox Jews, known as Haredim (those who tremble before God), "has erupted into a crisis. And it is centered on women." The ultra-Orthodox have always been ambivalent about the state of Israel and David Ben-Gurion, Israel's first prime minister "offered subsidies and army exemptions to the few in Israel then, he thought he was providing the group with a dignified funeral." However they multiplied and "now number a million, a mostly poor community" – they mostly do not work (just study the Torah – like the madrassas] and do not serve in the military. They have 20% of the children in the primary schools and what they learn in their school system leaves them "unsuited for the 21st century." The president of the Israel Democracy Institute said that the "coexistence between the two is breaking down," and "It is an extreme danger." He "compared the strictly religious Jews of Israel to the Islamists in the Arab world, saying there was a similar dynamic at play in Egypt."[16] This group only adds to the internal divisions within Israel.

The Israel-Palestine conflict is not in the US national interest because of the severe problems it causes in Arab/Muslim relations around the world as well as non-Muslims states that view the US policy as hypocritical. With the Middle East in turmoil from the Jasmine Revolution, "Israel's' illegal behavior in the occupied territories stands at odds with the values the U.S. is trying to promote in the region." The Israelis like to call it a "strategic alliance," but as Joe Klein wrote, "support for Israel is more a strategic liability than a strength."[17] The economic cost of that conflict is now estimated at about $12 trillion, with most of that borne by US taxpayers.[18] Any solution must have a major US role; however, that is severely hampered by domestic politics – the Israel Lobby and the US Jewish community. US total support for Israel is not the only cause of the war on terror but it is a contributing factor. For a full review of the history of the Israel-Palestine problem, I suggest the chapters in *World War IV and Beyond.*

Technology transfer – from the U.S. to Israel – is one of the favored activities of the Israeli intelligence services which conduct "the most aggressive espionage operations against the U.S. of any U.S. ally."

- General Accounting Office investigation[19]

Internally, Israel leads all countries [China is competitive for the title] in its active espionage directed against American companies, the US government, particularly the Defense Department but including the White House, and even law enforcement such as the Los Angeles Police Department. It also dominates two commercial sectors inside the US infrastructure: airline and telecommunications security. "Israel is believed to have the ability to monitor nearly all phone records originating in the United States, while numerous Israeli air-travel security companies are known to act as the local Mossad stations."[20] Verint, Inc. "handles most of American law enforcement's wiretaps" and Amdocs Ltd., working for US companies like AT&T and Verizon, has records of almost all telephone calls made in the US. Both companies are Israeli owned.[21] The Urim Base in the Negev, with "30 listening antennas, making Urim one of the largest signals intelligence bases in the world," is similar to the US National Security Agency. Among all these assets, Israel can probably monitor all telecommunications in the US, undersea cables to Europe, and from the Atlantic to the Indian Ocean.[22]

The Shah had initiated an ambitious nuclear power program but it was halted after the mullahs seized power.[23] With the rebirth of a nuclear program in Iran and the intense anti-Israel policy of their former ally Iran, Israel now called the Iranian nuclear program an "existential threat" and called for an attack on Iran. Any attack on Iran is a threat to the US because even if the US were not involved, it would be targeted for revenge as being complicit because of the close relationship with Israel.

Israel wanted to destroy the Iranian nuclear program but did not really have the capability due to distances and the wide dispersion of Iranian facilities. As in Iraq, they wanted the US to do it for them. They had the support of the Israel Firsters and AIPAC (American Israel Public Affairs Council) as well as most of the US negotiators working the "peace process." One of the most blatant was Dennis Ross, who spent years in the Clinton and Obama Administrations and was referred to by some as "Israel's lawyer." Longtime CIA member, Robert Grenier, wrote about Ross: "Like the Israelis, he is a brilliant strategist and a strategic ignoramus." As Ross left the White House, Grenier wrote, "Yes, Dennis Ross still has miles to go before he sleeps. And at the end of his personal journey, if he is successful, lies a US war with Iran."[24]

I gave up counting the times I heard the words "existential threat" to describe Ian's nuclear program capability.

- Philip Stephens, *Financial Times,* about Herzliya[25]

No one in the Western world likes the prospect of a nuclear Iran under the mullahs. However, pursuing the development of these weapons is a strong nationalistic urge. Finally possessing them brings a psychological maturation at the awesome power one has developed. Some of those who are alarmed by the prospect of a nuclear Iran, such as Senator Joe Lieberman, fear that it would result in chaos in the Middle East, send oil prices soaring, and end any hope for Israel-Palestine peace. But just the opposite might be possible. Instead of provoking chaos, Iranian nukes could stabilize the region and curb Israel's aggressive behavior toward its neighbors. Indeed, by creating a balance of power with Israel, thereby limiting its freedom of action, a nuclear Iran might actually encourage Israel to make peace with its neighbors, including the Palestinians. One development which would surely send oil prices soaring would be an Israeli attack on Iran.

Any attack on Iran could or will change the balance of power in the world and result in the end of the US reign as a great power. If the attack resulted in a very serious weakening of the US, the future of Israel would be dim. Israel's future is not good. If they do not make some serious decisions on Palestine soon, the likelihood of the continuation of the Jewish state will erode quickly. Demographics will overcome them and force them to choose between being democratic or being Jewish and an apartheid state.

The Jasmine Revolution has left Egypt in turmoil and there are already calls to cancel the treaty with Israel. The Egyptian security forces were withdrawn from the Sinai leaving the border with Israel open and there were incidents with Israelis killed. After three Egyptians were killed, the Israeli embassy in Cairo was attacked and ransacked. Israel withdrew its diplomats leaving only a deputy ambassador stationed in the US embassy. Turkey expelled the Israeli ambassador after Israel refused to apologize for the killing of nine Turks during an attempt to break the blockade of Gaza and Prime Minister Recep Tayyip Erdogan referred to Israel as "the West's spoiled child."[26] The Palestinians called on the UN Security Council to recognize Palestine and accept it as a member as the most viable of the only options they had: "Surrender, return to violence, or appeal to the international community."[27]

To show Israeli disapproval, just one day after the Palestinian presentation to the UN, Israel approved 1,100 new homes in East Jerusalem and "Netanyahu ruled out any freeze on settlement construction."[28] Netanyahu could count on US support since the US vetoed a UN Resolution on 18 February 2011 that called Israeli settlements illegal and called for an immediate halt to building. The other 14 members of the Security Council voted for it.[29]

Hamas and Iran had to add their fuel to the fire. Khaled Meshal, Hamas leader, said that "resistance" was the only option left for Palestinians, and Ayatollah Ali Khamenei attacked the two-state solution saying "all land belongs to the Palestinians" and "called Israel 'a cancerous tumor' that should be removed."[30] All of this added to the inflammatory nature of the Middle East and additional potential threats to the US.

Iran/Iraq

US relations were warm with Iran as we used it to transit supplies to Russia during World War II and then stood by Iran to force the Soviets out of the so-called People's Republic of Azerbaijan in Northern Iran after the war. The United States continued to support the Shah as a bulwark against Communism. The US had warm relations with Iraq during the time of the Baghdad Pact but they cooled after the change of government and it tilted toward the Soviets.

The Middle East had been generally under the sphere of influence of Great Britain which had been involved there for many years. But after World War II, the British Empire began to crumble. There was the growth of Mideast oil and a reordering of the world order. Raj India became independent in 1947 as India and Pakistan. Driven out of Egypt, Iraq, Palestine, and Yemen, Great Britain continued its withdrawal and in 1968 announced it would complete its withdrawal from East of Suez by 1971. The US picked up much of the slack and became more fully involved in the Middle East. The US developed a Two Pillar Policy in which neither Iran nor Iraq, the two most powerful states, should be permitted to dominate the Persian Gulf. That policy was tested during the Iraq-Iran War from 1980 to 1988 with the reflagging of Kuwait oil tankers and US support to both sides at different times. It was weakened by Saddam Hussein's invasion of Kuwait in 1990 and the ensuing years of sanctions and no-fly zones.

The US decided to invade Iraq under instigation from Israel and the neocons with unclear reasons except possible weapons of mass destruction, which Paul Wolfowitz said was the only one all could agree on. As we know, that turned out poorly, even the supposed biological weapons.[31] The US invasion of Iraq in 2003 ended the Two Pillar Policy and a new balance of power is evolving. The Iraqi military was destroyed in unwise decisions that disbanded the army and excluded all the Baathists party members from any positions in government. This provided hundreds of thousands of men without jobs as potential recruits for anti-American groups. The US never really had an exit strategy.[32]

After eight bloody years the US finally withdrew from Iraq but it is unclear what the future will be in this ancient region and there was already talk that Iraq was becoming the "forgotten war."[33] Iran is actively involved in influencing the government, now Shia after years of Sunni control under Saddam Hussein. The Shia-Sunni division remains bloody and the

Kurds still do not feel that they are included with the "Arabs." Christians were being hounded and driven out and the outlook for women's rights was bleak.[34] Prime Minister Nouri al-Maliki was consolidating and expanding his power; he wanted his Vice President arrested (he fled to the Kurdish area); and the outlook for democracy was not good as bombings continued. The US does not want Iraq to become a satellite of Iran and Iran does not want Iraq to become a threat again like the 1980-88 war and all want the oil to keep flowing. The division of the oil wealth among the three communities still has not been settled so unrest can be expected to continue.

The US invasion of Iraq in 2003 ended the Two Pillar Policy and a new balance of power is evolving.

The mullahs, although faced with unrest among the youth, still are firmly in control in Iran. One of their efforts was to close off the Internet and establish their own net which they can control. The regime still has its fanatics talking about sacrifice and martyrdom.[35] Their nuclear program, somewhat like North Korea's, is of great concern but no one knows exactly what to do about it. The sad truth is that there is really very little that any country can do about it short of aggression. The technology is widely known and available and any country that is willing to spend the time and money can build nuclear weapons. They can be delayed by various means (threats, sanctions, sabotage, attacks, killing scientists, etc.), but if they are willing to persist, they will. Remember Pakistan's Prime Minister Zulfikar Ali Bhutto, under threat from India, said they would eat grass if necessary but they had to have nukes.

But doesn't the US have the means to stop them? Yes, but only in the extreme. It would take an extensive air campaign to fully eliminate their nuclear capability and that is even doubtful. It is difficult to visualize the US government using nuclear weapons unless it was decided to destroy this ancient country. The US and/or Israel could bomb them (that terrible Victory through Airpower nonsense again!), but first that is aggression (a violation of international law) and second, unless we can totally remove the regime, it would only delay any program and have the disadvantage of uniting the country (and perhaps the entire Muslim world) behind their "sovereign right" to have nukes. The Iranian people do not particularly like the mullahs, but they love Iran. They would rally around Mother Iran like the Russians rallied around Mother Russia against the Germans despite their Communist masters. There are enough war hawks (including the neocons[36]) who would support a "surgical" strike on Iran, but it is very doubtful any US government would want to take on the opprobrium of destroying much of the infrastructure of Iran with the enormous civilian casualties it would entail. Finally, we do not have the ground troops which would be required to do anything useful in Iran.

America is not at war. The US military is at war. America is at the mall.

Israel is not capable of doing anything overtly except make the situation worse. They might have the political will, or political stupidity, but they do not have the capability. They know that if they attack, the US will be forced to bail them out. The US Congress and the media will scream for the US to aid our so-called "ally." Since we would be condemned as a co-conspirator, the US could be sucked into another major war which is why it must prevent Israel from attacking because it would almost absolutely cause a leap in oil prices which would place severe strain on an already reeling world economy resulting in a depression or a much more severe recession.

It is over 1,000 miles from Israel to Iran and all three of the possible flight routes violate the air space of other countries and increase the flight distances and requirements for aerial refueling aircraft in orbit somewhere, probably over the Persian Gulf. There are over 23 major nuclear sites plus hundreds of anti-aircraft sites, air bases, and command and control centers all hundreds of miles apart with Mashhad way to the East near the Afghan border at about 1,500 miles. One enrichment site has been placed adjacent to the religious center of Qom. Facilities might be destroyed or damaged, but most of the scientists and technicians would probably survive.

A direct military attack on Iran would be a disaster. It has no comparison to the attack on Osirak, because there are hundreds of targets, spread widely across the country, many of which have now been moved deep underground and others probably unknown. The most effective effort against the Iranian nuclear program so far has been in the new age of Cyber War with the cyber attack - the Stuxnet program – a computer virus(malware) which caused extensive damage to centrifuges by surreptiously reprogramming them to run too fast and exploding or being damaged and then brilliantly his its attack by sending "fake sensor signals to make the system believe everything is running smoothly," thus preventing a safety system from shutting down before it self-destructed. This is modern war: "It is about destroying its targets with utmost determination in military style." This was not the work of independent hackers.

It was a very sophisticated program that targeted specifically the Siemens industrial control computer – the P.C.S.-7 – by serial numbers at the enrichment plant at Natanz and perhaps the controllers of the steam turbines at Bushehr.[37] Some 984 centrifuges were shut down, but the Iranian program was delayed not stopped.[38] No one has claimed responsibility for the virus but due to the sophistication of the program it appears it had to come from a state, suspicions were on Israel and possibly the US.

Both the US and Israel did research on the P-1 centrifuges developed by Pakistan's A. Q. Khan which he later sold to Iran, Libya, and North Korea. The US obtained P-1s after Libya gave up its nuclear program in 2003, and Israel set up a P-1 centrifuge array at Dimona. A German computer security company tracked the worm and its precise targeting of centrifuge controllers. They found one section of code that targeted 984 centrifuges linked together. International inspectors reported in late 2009 "that the Iranians had taken out of service a total of exactly 984 machines."[39] The important point is that Israeli estimates of when Iran will have a nuclear weapon, which have been almost daily for the past 15 years, have been extended to 2015.

> **Any military attack on Iran by Israel and/or the US would be a disaster and would almost definitely result in a full-scale assault on Israel and US interests around the world.**

Any attack on Iran by the US and/or Israeli military forces would almost definitely result in a full-scale assault on Israel and US interests around the world and be disastrous for the fragile world economy. While the US might consider it a limited war, the Iranian Revolutionary Guards Corps (IRGC) and the leadership would likely consider it an attack on the integrity and the very existence of the Islamic Republic and would respond harshly. Their Quds Force is their international operations arm and has considerable experience supporting various groups such as al Qaeda, HezbAllah, and Hamas. There are many possible responses by Iran from direct action to the use of proxies. Iran has demonstrated through HezbAllah that it can strike almost anywhere in the world. HezbAllah would quite likely attack Israel – it fought Israel successfully in 2006 and has been fully rearmed by Iran including newer missiles with longer ranges. It announced in mid-November 2010 that it was ready for another war with

Israel, but it is present in other places as well, such as Iraq and South America and operates freely out of Iranian embassies.

There are many American targets – both individuals and installations – worldwide they could hit. The most critical target is the Strait of Hormuz through which flows some 20% of the world's oil daily (40% of the seaborne oil – about 16.5-17 million barrels per day), which Iran might try to close which would immediately affect the world economy. US Navy ships in the Persian Gulf would be vulnerable because the Iranians have developed their "swarming tactics" by which their small fast craft can attack large ships. Some could be suicide boats. George Friedman calls this "Iran's true 'nuclear' option."[40] They have Silkworm anti-ship missiles secreted in many locations along the Gulf and other missiles at sites inland. Aircraft carriers could be particularly vulnerable in the Persian Gulf.[41] Americans in Iraq and Afghanistan would be vulnerable to attacks as well as American embassies and civilians around the world. They have threatened the Arab leaders on the Gulf that if Iran is attacked, they will strike their oil installations. However, the oil weapon is a two-edged sword for them because they also need to sell their oil. Rather than attack Arabs, they could call on the entire Muslim world to join them in a Grand Jihad against Israel and the Great Satan.

There are additional points to consider. Sunni leadership and the Pan Arab movement have failed and Iran sees the opportunity to seize the leadership of the Muslim world. They have been pragmatic in dealing with Sunnis such as the Kurds in the PKK against Turkey and the Taliban. Iranian leaders have met with the presidents of Pakistan and Afghanistan to urge stronger ties. Khamenei reportedly told President Asif Ali Zardari: "The principal enemy of the Pakistani people and the unity of the country is the West, headed by the United States."[42] Iran is now less theocratic and ideological and more calculating and pragmatic pursuing its foreign policy interests. This indicates that Iran should now be dealt with as another power and, albeit not one we particularly like, should be seen as a significant player in power politics.

> **Sunni leadership and the Pan Arab movement have failed and Iran sees the opportunity to seize the leadership of the Muslim world.**

Iran does not really need nuclear weapons. They are strictly the trappings of a major power which Iran is and wants to be so recognized by the rest of the world. One nuclear warhead does not a nuclear power make, except that it elevates them as a member of the "club." It would take years to build a sizeable arsenal in face of hundreds of warheads in Israel and thousands in the US. "Any mention of an Iranian nuclear weapon is taboo in the Islamic Republic, which insists that its nuclear programme is entirely for peaceful, civil purposes." So it was quite unusual to see an article on the Revolutionary Guards' Gerdab website: "The day after Iran's first nuclear test is a normal day…but in the eyes of some of us there will be a new sparkle. A sparkle of national pride and strength."[43]

Nuclear weapons are primarily good for deterrence (against Israel) but of little value for actual war. Iranians have thoroughly developed their proxy war capability by their years of experience in Lebanon and Iraq and with the Kurds. They do not envision normal style conventional war; Lebanon taught them that you can defeat a conventional army (Israel) by sophisticated guerrilla warfare. They developed effective and accurate long and short range missiles, secure communications (fiber optics –no radios that can be monitored), cracked the Israeli codes, evasion by moving in small groups and hiding in the populace (negating reconnaissance by aircraft, drones, and satellites), use of car and truck bombs, developed Improvised Explosive Devices (IEDs) and later EFPs (Explosively Formed Penetrators) that took out Abrams tanks, etc.

One last point is that much can and has been accomplished by sabotage and special agents. The Israelis basically killed the Egyptian nuclear and missile program by killing German scientists. They also killed off many who were working on various programs in Iraq. Iran has killed off its own internal opponents overseas including Paris. Probably as much or longer delays could be attained in Iran with similar targeted programs against scientists and technicians and some facilities. [At least four significant Iranian nuclear scientists have been assassinated. The latest was Mostafa Ahmadi-Roshan, a chemical engineer who worked on procurement at Natanz who was killed by a car bomb on 11 January 2012.] We have already seen the effectiveness of Stuxnet. The advantage is deniability and the preclusion of reprisals and the terrible costs that overt attacks almost surely would invoke.

Iran is the center of the Crucible of Crisis. From their perspective, they are surrounded by US presence (Iraq, the Gulf, and Afghanistan) and of the nine nuclear powers, eight are nearby or threatening them (the ninth being North Korea which helps them with missile technology). There are major oil producing areas, pipelines, and proposed pipelines of interest to Iran, Afghanistan, Pakistan, and India. We have overlapping interests in that they want US troops out on their East and West and we want to bring our troops home, and we do not want the flow of oil restricted through Hormuz and they need oil flow for their economy. We should pursue those mutual interests but with a clear head.

> **The US and Iran have mutual interests in that Iran wants US troops out on its East and West and the US wants to bring its troops home, and the US does not want the flow of oil restricted through Hormuz and Iran needs oil flow for its economy.**

Belligerent threats in the region only exacerbate the situation. Bombastic threats from Iran only make the Israelis nervous and trigger-happy. Some were misleading. President Mahmoud Ahmadinejad's widely reported threat to "wipe Israel off the map" was misinterpreted by the media.[44] What he actually said was that *time alone* would remove Israel in its current form from the map. However, he has made enough other comments to keep the fire burning. Celebrating Quds Day (for Jerusalem [Quds is Jerusalem] and the Palestinians), he announced that when a Palestinian state is established, there will be no room for Israel in the region.[45] Interestingly, Ahmadinejad supposedly wants to "forge ahead openly with developing nuclear weapons but is opposed by the clerical leadership, which is worried about international reaction to such a move."[46] Supreme Leader Ayatollah Ali Khamenei added to the fray with his accusations at the US of terrorist attacks.[47] All the calls by Israelis and Israel Firsters in the US to attack Iran are also not very helpful and may be a self-fulfilling prophecy. Finally, the US is clearly in no position for another war.

It is not only Israel that is concerned by the prospect of a nuclear Iran, the Sunni Arabs are also nervous. Saudi Arabia and other members of the Gulf Cooperation Council (GCC) are buying more arms and the Saudis are possibly calling for a return of a Pakistani Army contingent to be based in Saudi Arabia. The Saudis and the UAE were quick to send troops in early 2011 to put down the protests in Bahrain which has a Shiite majority under the Sunni royal family. Iran long claimed that Bahrain was a part of Iran. In addition to its support of Syria and HezbAllah in Lebanon, Iran has reportedly been involved with Shia in eastern Saudi Arabia (where the oil is) and in two southwestern provinces where there are Ismailis (Shia sect) and with the Houthis in northern Yemen.

The US is concerned about Iran which calls it the Great Satan. Much of the justification for the Anti-Ballistic Missile Defense program is to defend against a nuclear missile attack from Iran. Unfortunately, the US has not had an embassy in Tehran since it was seized in 1979 and US diplomats were held for 444 days. Iran has provided arms to various foreign groups as we have noted earlier.[48] Iran is attacking the US directly and indirectly in Iraq by providing training and arms, including the Improvised Explosive Devices (IEDs) which have caused the majority of US casualties. In spite of the fact that the Taliban are Sunnis, Iran has provided them with missiles to fight their common enemy, the US. Iran was also providing cash to the Taliban and "paying bonuses of $1,000 for killing an American soldier and $6,000 for destroying a U.S. military vehicle."[49]

We fought another ideology, Communism, mostly by talking, for almost three-quarters of a century. It is not wise to refuse to deal with Iran as a major power. We kept an embassy in Moscow throughout World War II and the Cold War and invited Communist leaders to this country. Since it is really not in our interest to attack Iran, it is time to talk. The first law of International Relations is that states do not have friends, they only have interests. It is in the US national interest to determine how to mitigate the threat from Iran and to deter them from taking any action against American interests. Iran offered to permit "supervision" of its nuclear program for five years in return for lifting of the sanctions. It is not clear what they mean, but obviously the sanctions are having an effect and this offer should be explored.

When President Ahmadinejad was at the UN meeting in New York, he mentioned that they were talking with Russia about more nuclear power reactors. The Russians built the $1 billion Bushehr reactor which came on line 13 September 2011 (evidently delayed again). He then added, "And from here today I want to officially invite other firms and other entities to come and bid and propose their participation for building these power plants." He said Iran needs 20,000 megawatts.[50] This would be a great potential opportunity to transform confrontation into cooperation.

Ahmadinejad also again offered "to stop all nuclear enrichment if the West would supply nuclear fuel enriched to a 20 percent level. He insisted that Iran will happily give up its enrichment processing if it can get this enriched fuel for 'cancer treatment medication'."[51] The West should pursue these offers.

The rescue of 13 Iranian fishermen in January 2012 by the destroyer *USS Kidd* was a small incident that could have larger implications. Those fishermen who felt that the sailors were sent by God went home with *USS Kidd* baseball caps. The ultimate irony is that the destroyer was commanded by a woman, Cmdr Jennifer L. Ellinger!

There has been a great deal of pressure applied via UN sanctions and other international measures to try to reduce the threat from Iran; but, as it tries to expand its role in the Muslim world, it will remain a threat for years to come. Mullahs nowhere have shown any desire to be martyrs themselves; they reserve that for the cannon fodder. They can be deterred.

The Arabian Peninsula/Horn of Africa

The Arabian Peninsula is key for two things: oil and Islam. Oil from Kuwait, Saudi Arabia, and the United Arab Emirates (UAE) is vital to the world economy. Bahrain is the home port for the US Fifth Fleet, Qatar is the home of the US Central Command forward base and Al Jazeera TV, and Oman commands the southern side of the Strait of Hormuz. Yemen sits on the Bab el Mandeb across from Djibouti and Somalia, which has not had a government for 20 years, is across the Gulf of Aden.

Islam spread from Arabia, home of Mecca and Medina, west to the Atlantic and east to Indonesia. Osama bin Laden came from Saudi Arabia, though his family was originally from Yemen, and 15 of the 19 hijackers on 9/11 were Saudis. Much of the Islamic fundamentalist teaching around the world, particularly in the US, comes from Wahhabi sources in Saudi Arabia. The alliance between the House of Saud and the Wahhabis causes a conundrum for US policy. The US has maintained close relation with the Saudi family since World War II when President Roosevelt met with King Ibn Saud. The US has needed Saudi oil and the Saudis have needed the US to protect against any threats to their kingdom. The Wahhabi drive to impose Sharia and Islam on the world puts us at odds. The US and the family have finessed this for over 60 years but the situation is becoming more precarious.

Much of the Islamic fundamentalist teaching around the world, particularly in the US, comes from Wahhabi sources in Saudi Arabia.

Americans have been attacked and killed in Saudi Arabia as well as Saudis, including the attack on Mecca (evidently inspired by the Iranian revolution). The government cracked down hard on al Qaeda and drove it out of the country. It regrouped in Yemen as **Al Qaeda in the Arabian Peninsula (AQAP)**. It is now the most potent of the al Qaeda franchises and is, in some ways, the successor to al Qaeda itself. US intelligence officials warned Wall Street bank executives of possible attacks by package bombs or biological or chemical agents in the mail. AQAP's *Inspire* magazine mentioned targeting financial institutions and perhaps using anthrax.[52] In another case a Bangladeshi working for British Airways in the UK communicated with Anwar al-Awlaki about blowing up an airliner.[53]

With pressure on al Qaeda, mainly drone attacks on its bases in Pakistan, there were reports that some of the operatives had moved to Yemen or Somalia. After the death of Osama bin Laden, there was even a report that Ayman al-Zawahiri had left Pakistan.

The operations against AQAP and **al-Shabaab**, an al Qaeda affiliate in Somalia, raised legal questions between the State Department and the Pentagon as to what attacks were permissible under international law. The laws of war were written for conventional war and are unclear as to how to be applied against a worldwide non-state war. CIA and Pentagon lawyers announced that US citizens do not have immunity when they are at war with the US. Congress also became involved and planned to authorize a list of groups against which military action could be taken as well as a means to add new groups.[54]

The Horn of Africa continued to be unstable and two of the northern regions of Somalia broke away. Somaliland declared its independence in 1991 and has its own security forces and currency. Puntland announced itself as an autonomous state in 1998. The US decided to help both of them while still considering al Shabaab a significant threat to regional and international security.[55] The US also increased its drone capability, in addition to its bases in Djibouti and Socotra, by reopening a base in the Seychelles which would increase the capability to deal with pirates.[56]

As long as the world remains dependent on imported oil and as long as Islam continues on its ideological mission of world domination, the Arabian Peninsula and Eastern Africa will continue to play a dangerous role in world affairs.

Afghanistan/Pakistan

Afghanistan is an old country, but badly divided along tribal lines. The Durrani Empire in 1772, before the US Declaration of Independence, covered Afghanistan, all of what is now Pakistan, and parts of India and Iran. The British imposed the Durand Line in 1893 as the frontier between Afghanistan and Raj India as a barrier against invaders, but it divided Pashtunistan and left Pakistan with an almost ungovernable frontier area; the Pashtuns ignore the line and the Afghans have never explicitly recognized it. This area of the Federally Administered Tribal Areas (FATA) and Khyber-Paktunkhwa Province (KPP) [formerly known as the North West Frontier Province (NWFP)] is a large and rugged area which provides ideal sanctuary, which is key to an insurgency. The national boundaries in no way correspond to the tribal groupings. In addition to the Punjabis, Sindhs, and Baluchis in Pakistan, there are 11 major tribal groups in Afghanistan. Even the Wakhan Corridor to China between Pakistan and Tajikistan is divided with Tajiks and Kyrgyz.

After the attack on 9/11, it did not take long to remove the Taliban, but then started the slow and difficult task of trying to modernize this ancient land of tribal warlords. "But the Afghans are hardly a people, much less a nation. They are a nation of tribes constantly at war with each other. They are very heterogeneous, with an extreme ethnocentricity which makes them not only hate or suspect foreigners but Afghans living two valleys away."[57]

The Pashtun are not at peace unless they are at war.

- Pahstun Proverb

As noted earlier, Pakistan is an artificial country created by the British as they departed Raj India trying to form a Muslim state, Pakistan, separate from Hindu India. Pakistan is a state but not a nation. The name was created as an acronym by college boys at Cambridge in 1933.[58] Pakistan does not have a border agreement with India because of Kashmir which it believes should be a part of Pakistan. Kashmir is unique in that it had a Hindu raj who elected to join India even though it has a Muslim majority (67%). Kashmir has remained a major area of conflict between India and Pakistan. In addition, along the northern frontier, there is a disputed area with China.

Pakistan is to a large extent dominated by the Punjabis. The Baluchis in the West, divided with parts in Afghanistan and Iran, are in partial rebellion against the government in Islamabad. Pakistan is a nuclear power now with over 100 warheads with missiles and aircraft for delivery but has been unable to establish a stable democracy as no elected government has been able to complete a term due to military coups. General ul Haq pronounced it an Islamic state while he was president trying to gain wider support.

Pakistan is a nuclear power now with over 100 warheads with missiles and aircraft for delivery but has been unable to establish a stable democracy as no elected government has been able to complete a term due to military coups.

The security of Pakistan's nuclear sites is of concern because of either warheads falling into the hands of extremists or the country turning to a radical government. Al Qaeda in Afghanistan has made strong comments such as by leader Mustafa Abu al-Yazid on Al Jazeera, "God willing, the nuclear weapons will not fall into the hands of the Americans and the mujahideen would take them and use them against the Americans."[59] Now they have developed nuclear reactors to produce plutonium which could yield more efficient weapons than their uranium-fueled warheads.[60] In addition to the two new plutonium reactors, they have a new reprocessing facility which together, according to top US scientists, means that Pakistan could move from its present 90-110 nuclear warheads to 150-200 within a decade. They are also developing new delivery systems including a medium-range ballistic missile, two short-range ballistic missiles, and two cruise missiles.[61] The Pak military has imposed very strong security measures (The US has spent millions of dollars helping the Pakistanis with nuclear security.); however there is considerable unease among the Paks due to calls by some in the US for the US military to seize control of those sites and warheads.

The US-Pakistan relationship has been tenuous for years due to changing US support such as dropping them after the Soviet defeat in Afghanistan, embargoing them for their nuclear program, and then demanding they join the US in the war on terror. The US does not want to see Pakistan as a radical Islamic state and is dependent on it for its logistical routes into Afghanistan. Pakistan does not want the US as an enemy and needs it as a friend to counter India so that the US does not turn completely to India against Pakistan. The tense relationship, which intensified after the attack which killed Osama bin Laden[62], continues with some 84% of Pakistanis viewing the US presence in Asia as a greater threat than al Qaeda or the Taliban [that figure may be even higher now]. As we noted earlier about apostasy and blasphemy, this is consistent with the poll that 75% of Pakistanis favor the implementation of sharia.[63]

Tensions continued to mount. In September 2011, there was an assault on the US Embassy in Kabul and a truck bomb attack that wounded 77 US troops. ADM Mike Mullen, Chairman of the Joint Chiefs of Staff, told Congress, "With ISI support, Haqqani operatives plan and conducted that truck bomb attack, as well as the assault on our embassy."[64] After a US air attack which killed 24 Pakistani soldiers, supposedly Pak approval, there were more protests, both border crossings into Afghanistan were closed to supplies for NATO troops in Afghanistan, and the US was kicked out of an air base used for US drones. Then 30,000 Islamic supremacists rallied in Lahore on 18 December 2011 demanding Pakistan cut ties with the US, shouting "A friend of the USA and India is a traitor." The rally was led by Jamaat-ud-Dawa, "widely considered to be the front group for Laska-e-Taiba."[65] This incident reflected the lack of trust and mistakes on both sides.

In spite of the war on terror and the war in Afghanistan, Pakistan is always looking eastward toward India and does not want a government in Afghanistan that threatens what it considers its strategic depth against India. The capital Islamabad is only a short distance from the Indian frontier, open country very vulnerable to an armored force assault. Pakistan has lost three wars to India and developed its nuclear arsenal to deter another attack.

> **In spite of the war on terror and the war in Afghanistan, Pakistan is always looking eastward toward India and does not want a government in Afghanistan that threatens what it considers its strategic depth against India.**

Inter-Services Intelligence (ISI), almost an autonomous government agency, has supported (perhaps created) **Lashkar-e-Taiba (LeT)** [Army of the Pure] originally to fight the Soviets in Afghanistan but later shifted to Kashmir focused on attacking Indian interests. Evidently LeT is no longer satisfied with just the Kashmir conflict with India and "is committed to a campaign of jihad against the United States and Europe, and against American troops in Afghanistan." Adm. Mike Mullen, then Chairman of the Joint Chiefs of Staff, called LeT a "global threat" which is not surprising since Hafiz Muhammad Saeed, the leader, has regularly denounced "what he calls the imperialism of the United States, Israel and India." It was responsible for the 2008 Mumbai attack but also supports attacks in Afghanistan. The problem is that with the US getting out of Afghanistan, the Pakistanis feel they "should keep groups like Lashkar and the Haqqani network under their wing for future operations in Afghanistan and India." The government "believes too much is at stake to walk away from the groups it might need once the Americans leave Afghanistan."[66] Recently LeT's expanded range was demonstrated by using an American agent who was part of the Mumbai reconnaissance to check out the cartoon newspaper in Denmark.[67] The problem of ISI supporting groups that were killing US troops came to a head when then CIA chief Leon Panetta confronted the Paks with video showing "the militants evacuating two bomb factories in Waziristan" evidently alerted by ISI about a planned raid.[68] For a good review of Pakistan's role in Afghanistan, see "What Drives Pakistan's Interest in Afghanistan" by Lt Col Christopher L. Budihas.[69]

> **Lashkar-e-Taiba is no longer satisfied with just the conflict with India and "is committed to a campaign of jihad against the United States and Europe, and against American troops in Afghanistan."**

Bombs do not need to be smuggled into Afghanistan from Pakistan. The largest source of casualties to US troops in Afghanistan is the homemade bombs, IEDs (Improvised Explosive Devices), and 80% of those bombs are made from fertilizer from a single company in Pakistan, Pakarab Fertilizers Ltd. The calcium ammonium nitrate fertilizer when mixed with fuel oil makes a powerful explosive. There have been talks with the government and the company but there is still no regulation of distribution and sale of the fertilizer.[70]

India plays a large political and economic role in Afghanistan with a very large embassy and "reestablished its consulates in Afghan cities, including some near the Pakistani border." There are over 4,000 Hindus and Sikhs in country plus numerous military involved in major development and investment projects and commercial travel. They are building a dam and power lines. In cooperation with Iran, India completed a highway linking Afghanistan's ring road to Iranian ports on the Persian Gulf which could reduce Afghan dependence on Pakistan for access to the sea and marginalize Pakistan's Gwadar port on the Arabian Sea, which was financed by a $200 million Chinese investment. There were reports that India was arming and supplying Afghan foes of Pakistan.[71]

The Paks see India working with Israel to neutralize Pakistan's nuclear capability. India does not want a radical Islamistan in AfPak, but its actions may well lead, when NATO withdraws, to a confrontation with Pakistan which could be a nuclear showdown. Indian withdrawal could be boasted as a Muslim victory over polytheist India. The US-Indian nuclear agreement was seen in Pakistan as legitimizing India as a nuclear power, while Islamabad, with its proliferation record, was still a pariah.

China is poised to be the largest investor in Afghanistan – interested because of their problems with Muslim Quighurs in Xinjiang and access to raw materials. They have invested $3.5 billion in the Anyak Copper mine in Logar Province, south of Kabul, plus there are some of the world's largest untapped deposits of copper, iron, gold, uranium, and precious gems.

The Taliban grew out of the *madrassas* in Pakistan. The *madrassas* were created in the 11th century as centers of higher learning, but the current ones are basically boarding schools for very poor boys and young men. The government estimates there are 13,000 *madrassas* in Pakistan with 1.5 million students. However, "quoted figures range between 18,000 and 20,000 madrassas. The number of students could be correspondingly larger."[72] Radicalization began after the Soviet invasion of Afghanistan in 1979 which led to the flow of millions of Afghan refugees into northwestern Pakistan. The Pak government authorized many religious schools in an effort to support these refugees. These schools soon became recruiting grounds for fighters, and many of the Taliban (which can be translated as "student") came from the *madrassas*.[73]

These Islamic schools, *madrassas* where they study only the Qur'an, became a source of jihadis. Many students went into Afghanistan to join the Taliban and large numbers were killed. As a correspondent in Islamabad for a London paper wrote, "Pakistan produces holy warriors the way other nations produce microchips or MBAs." However, recruits for the terrorist groups have come from all over the Muslim world, and unbelievably even from the US.[74]

Pakistan produces holy warriors the way other nations produce microchips or MBAs.

A small boy spends six or more hours per day memorizing the Qur'an with breaks only for prayer and rest. There are no classes in math, geography, history, languages, or computers since his teachers tell him all he will ever need to understand is in the Qur'an. As one student recited, "Since the day of the Prophet, there are only two forces on earth, Muslims and infidels. And their fight will go on until Judgment Day." Such fanaticism is not taught in all Muslim schools, but the *madrassas* in Pakistan are different.[75]

After 9/11, there was pressure to rein in the *madrassas* with only limited success.[76] But behind the classroom doors, the anti-US rhetoric remains scorching with jihad still the legitimate weapon. Outside the schools, "jihad is everywhere, in graffiti, the Urdu newspapers, in tea-shop talk." Recruiters still work the *madrassas* and the ones that join are given only a little training and sent into Afghanistan to strike American targets and with so little training that they are usually the first killed.

The *madrassa* at the Red Mosque complex in Islamabad took on the Pakistani government in early 2007. In April, the deputy imam announced they were imposing Sharia and an Islamic court. Then thousands of students from the madrassa were sent into the city as morals police (Taliban style) smashing music and video shops, closing barbershops, and even kidnapping policemen. On 3 July students attacked police and ransacked ministries with 16 killed. It ended with the army attacking the mosque resulting in a battle for 36 hours and 106 dead. The Red Mosque proved to be a fortress with a stockpile of weapons and al Qaeda material. It was quite possible that other madrassas were also harboring weapons but the attack sent a strong message.[77]

The Red Mosque's imam, Maulana Abdul Aziz, who tried to escape in a burqa, was released by the Pakistani supreme court. He still wants to "talibanize" Pakistan and is now again calling for the "soldiers of Islam" to fight "to create an Islamic state" which of course would enforce sharia. Part of his complaint against the government for corruption was the drone attacks which he said killed Pakistanis. He claimed "I have over 5,000 students" and "we will use every means possible to make Pakistan an Islamic state." "The Red Mosque is located in the heart of the federal capital, and remains fertile grounds for extremism."[78]

The madrassas are like conveyor belts. If they are churning out more militants in waiting than we are capturing, killing, prosecuting, or otherwise neutralizing, then we are losing this war.

- Andrew McCarthy

Illiteracy and poverty drive these schools. Parents are reassured that their children will at least get a free meal. As one teacher noted, "It's poverty and hunger that drive these students to the madrasahs. If their stomachs weren't empty, they wouldn't come."[79] "The madrassas are like conveyor belts. If they are churning out more militants in waiting than we are capturing, killing, prosecuting, or otherwise neutralizing, then we are losing this war."[80]

However, it not only the poor young people in the madrassas, some of those with higher education are denouncing America and calling for an Islamic system. A university engineering student said, "In Pakistan, democracy and dictatorship have been tried and failed.

Now it is time to bring in an Islamic system." And a young man in advertising thought that "the Islamic system had been shown to work over the last 1,300 years."[81] [Perhaps that shows more his lack of knowledge.]

The Pak support for the Taliban was a hedge against US withdrawal and rising Indian influence in Afghanistan. They play both sides to assure pro-Pakistan forces will have the upper hand in Afghanistan after the US departs. The US is caught between the competing interests of Pakistan, India, and Iran. Osama bin Laden had been living in Abbottabad but Ayman al-Zawahiri was probably living in Momand in the FATA where he is protected by the tribal code of Pashtunwali.[82]

We need to find a way to cut our losses and get out expeditiously before our economy is destroyed. The Kashmir dispute and the India-Pakistan enmity are not in the US interest since they keep Pakistan focused against India so we should help Pakistan and India resolve their differences – offering our good offices if necessary.

The Jasmine Revolution – The Arab World Erupts

As we have seen, Islam left the Arab world poor and centuries behind. The "submissive" nature of Islam finally got to them. High unemployment/underemployment, inflation and shortages, lack of political participation, government corruption and cronyism, police state oppression, censorship, and social imbalances finally came to a head.[83] The Arab world missed out on globalization with "seething masses and the stultifying economy" – "the orphans of globalization." There are many "orphans" – 65% of people in the Arab League countries are under age 30. Youth unemployment rates run exorbitantly high – up to 75% in places like Algeria.[84] The numbers under age 30 run in the high 50% to mid 60% across most of the area to Iran with 70% in Somalia and 74% in Yemen.[85] Of young Arabs, 56% use the internet every day, 54% consider television the most trusted source of news, 67% are very concerned about the rising cost of living, and 30% (perhaps as high as 40%) would move permanently to another country if they could.[86] These young people are aware of the rest of the world and have aspirations which their governments cannot or will not fill.

The Arab world missed out on globalization with "seething masses and the stultifying economy" – "the orphans of globalization."

Yemen is an example of the impoverishment but growing population. Yemen now has 24 million, expected to be 40 million in 2030 and 50 million in 2045. While the rest of the world is aging, "in 2045 the average age in Yemen will be 18!" That is a disaster waiting to happen! Except for oil, the region has not integrated into the global economy. Egypt (80 million) exports less than 14% of what Thailand (68 million) exports. Viet-Nam (89 million), which only recently joined the global economy, has double the exports of Egypt. The UAE (6 million) has 50% of the "total Arab League exports, excluding fuel."[87] It is no wonder the Middle East is in turmoil; it only needed a spark.

Tunisia

That spark came on 17 December 2010 when Mohammed Bouazizi was slapped by a policewoman in Sidi Bouzid, Tunisia who humiliated him and confiscated his unlicensed produce cart and refused to accept his "10-dinar ($7, the equivalent of a good day's earnings) fine that Bouazizi tried to pay." He was the main breadwinner for his family of eight. Dejected he went to the provincial headquarters to complain to officials but they refused to see him. Within an hour of the confrontation, he set himself on fire in front of the headquarters. He did not die until 4 January 2011, but the revolt had started and President Zine el Abidine Ben Ali fled to Saudi Arabia on 14 January after 23 years in power.[88]

> **If one day, a people desires to live, then fate will answer their call,**
> **And the night will begin to fade, and their chains break and fall.**
>   **- Abdul-Qasim al-Shabi, Tunisian poet**

The previous president, Bourguiba, was a big supporter of women's rights and is so recognized in Tunisia. Ben Ali did well for his first few years in power. Tunisia has a high literacy rate with many well educated young people – but they cannot find work. Corruption expanded under Ben Ali and his wife and her Trabelsi family, which became known as the Family Mafia. The police were hated but the Army was respected. Large protests erupted and a new age began with Twitter and Facebook as the young could communicate all over Tunisia and actually around the world and the dictator was out.

All revolutions are messy as the political order is changing and it takes time for a new order to evolve. The protesters were unhappy that so many holdovers from Ben Ali stayed in power so the protests continued with more resignations. The interim government legalized Ennahda, an Islamist political party which had been banned and its controversial leader, Rachid Ghannouchi, returned to Tunis after 20 years in exile. There were already clashes over his return with protesters chanting "yes to Islam, no to Islamism."[89]

> **All revolutions are messy as the political order is changing and it takes time for a new order to evolve.**

The Hizb At-Tahrir party in Tunisia, an extremist branch of the **Muslim Brotherhood** founded in 1953, wants to impose sharia "by political means" but does not rule out "rebellion or civil disobedience in order to establish an Islamic state." The party's secretary general Abdelmajid Habibi said that sharia is "the only source of laws" and **"if the Islamists are successful in winning power they would ban other parties."**[90] That should be enough to make people wake up! While preparing for the new constitution, a pact was adopted that rejects "any normalisation with Israel."[91] All are not in agreement in revolutions. Most Tunisians support their secular character but the **Salafis** are threatening them. A gang of some 100 bearded men attacked a Tunis theater on 26 June smashing windows and harassing the audience. "Women wearing bikinis at the beach have been harassed, while extremists in southern Tunisia expelled musicians coming to entertain Libyan refugees in May on the grounds that music was against Islamic law."[92]

> **Sharia is "the only source of laws," and "if the Islamists are successful in winning power they would ban other parties."**
>   **- Abdelmajid Habibi, secretary general, Hizb At-Tahrir party**

The sparks flew to other countries as the Arabs found a collective voice, a common Arab identity, a shared resentment over economic woes; they watch TV and feel they have been deprived of a decent life and have been denied dignity and respect. There is "a broad sense of failure and frustration" across the Arab world where anything seems better than the status quo.

Tunisians protested in front of the Egyptian embassy chanting "Mubarak out." In Egypt, instead of the old Islamist chant of "Islam is the solution," it became "Tunisia is the solution." Yemenis chanted invoking Tunisia. In Lebanon, a newspaper "declared that all of the Middle East was watching Egypt." Tunisia had become the guiding light – the Jasmine Revolution. Al Jazeera TV joined Facebook and Twitter in spreading the message. Tunisian protesters were able to advise their Egyptian counterparts: "Protest at night, wear plastic bags to avoid electric shocks, wash your face with Coca-Cola to fend off the effects of tear gas and try to spray black paint on the windshields of police vehicles." A veteran dissident in Jordan, Laith Shbillat, said, "People want their freedom, people want their bread. People want to stop these lousy dictators from looting their countries. I'd follow anybody. I'd follow Vladimir Lenin if he came and led me." He mentioned North Africa's famous poet Shabi, who died young in 1934. "He's leading us from his grave."[93]

Egypt

A protest had already been scheduled in Egypt on Police Day, 25 January, but the revolution in Tunisia provided further inspiration. Massive protests in Tahrir Square resulted in the resignation of President Hosni Mubarak on 11 February as he turned power over to the military. Egypt is the founding place of the Muslim Brotherhood and the most disturbing event was the return from exile of Yusuf al-Qaradawi, the spiritual leader.

Events moved rapidly, not fast enough for some and too fast for others. The young, inexperienced protesters were eased aside by the various political factions. The new technology world came to reality when a young man was arrested for insulting the Qur'an and Muhammad on Facebook.[94] A quick referendum approved changes to the constitution leading one ultraconservative sheikh (Wahhabi influence) to say: "That's it. The country is ours." It soon became evident that "age-old religion, not the enthusiasm and slogans of the Facebook generation, is likely to be a crucial factor in choosing a new Egyptian government."[95] We have described earlier the sexual harassment and abuse of women on Egyptian streets. It did not take long for the Muslim Brotherhood to call for a Saudi-style modesty police to combat "immoral" behavior in public areas. Tombs of Sufis were attacked by Salafis, who particularly hate Sufis, and Salafis claimed Christians (Copts) should submit to Islam and they would be protected (that is become dhimmis).[96] The growing influence of the radical groups led the military to announce that "Egypt will not be ruled by another Khomeini."[97]

> It soon became evident that "age-old religion, not the enthusiasm and slogans of the Facebook generation, is likely to be a crucial factor in choosing a new Egyptian government.

Attacks on Copts continued with a suicide attack on a church killing 21 and an off-duty policeman killed an old man on a train.[98] The hardline Islamists continued their hatred of the Copts by blocking roads and railroads and taking over government buildings in the southern city of Qena over the appointment of a Coptic governor (the previous governor was also a Copt). They also stopped buses to separate women and men passengers.[99] A week later the prime minister suspended the governor for three months.[100] A Copt in Qena had his apartment set on fire. When he went to investigate, he was attacked by Salafis who beat him with the remains of his furniture and then cut off his right ear accusing him of renting his empty apartment to loose Muslim women. He reported that while they were beating him, they kept saying, "We won't leave any Christians in this country."[101]

State TV got into the anti-Copt attack by faking news. An army personnel carrier plowed through protesters and the state TV called for Muslims to "protect the army" from the Christian and mobs responded. However, it was all false.[102]

The Salafi attack on Christians continued. "The number of Christian girls abducted and coerced into conversion to Islam since the Egyptian "January 25 Revolution" has skyrocketed." An investigation exposed "a highly organized Muslim ring centered in the Fatah mosque in Alexandria." It found a "systematic 'religious call' plan, where young Muslim males in high school and university are urged to approach Coptic girls in the 9-15 age group and manipulate them through sexual exploitation and blackmail" to humiliate them and force them to flee their homes and convert Islam as a "solution." One of the architects is Salafi Sheikh Osama Borhammi.[103]

The role of women was very limited with no women involved in drafting the transitional constitution declaration and the repeal of the "Mubarak-era quota, which allocated 64 seats in parliament for women." Also, one of the presidential candidates talked of "an Islamic future for the country that would impose Saudi Arabia-style dress and behavior on the public." In addition, any woman wearing a bikini would be arrested.[104] There were numerous attacks on women. South African CBS correspondent Lara Logan was sexually assaulted on 11 February [2011] in Tahrir Square. French television reporter Caroline Sinz was violently sexually assaulted in November. That was only "shortly after Egyptian-American journalist Mona Eltahawy reported that she had been the victim of a grotesque sexual assault by police after she was arrested during the protests."[105]

Even before the Jasmine Revolution, the new leader of the Muslim Brotherhood threw down the gauntlet. The new supreme guide, Muhammad Badi, gave a sermon "How Islam Confronts the Oppression and Tyranny." He said Allah commanded jihad against the US and Israel "so that Allah's word will reign supreme" over all infidels. All Muslims are required by Islam to fight. This was a declaration of war against the US.[106] The deputy leader of the Muslim Brotherhood said the objective was "to take over the world" – interestingly it was mistranslated as "to establish an Islamic state and become world leaders."[107]

A government document declared that the military would be the guardian of "constitutional legitimacy." Tens of thousands of Islamists massed in Tahrir Square confronting the military. "Elsewhere, ultraconservative Salafis in long robes and bushy beards called for application of Islamic Sharia law."[108] The unpopularity of the 1979 peace treaty with Israel was shown by a poll in which 54% of Egyptians favored scrapping it.[109] There were calls for delaying elections to allow other parties to organize. The Muslim Brotherhood was angrily against this since they are already the best organized.[110] The Brotherhood could not stay out of the limelight; another leader called for the elimination of borders and the establishment of an Islamic state – the United States of Islam. He called out to the bearded radicals: "I say to our Salafi brothers: Why do you focus only on [external] appearance, on the beard, the miswak [tooth-cleaning stick noted in Islamic jurisprudence], and the jilhab [religious garment]?"[111]

The Muslim Brotherhood was approved to form the Freedom and Justice Party and the Salafis the Light (al-Nour) Party. The government committee banned the militant al-Gamaa al-Islamiyya from forming a party. Mubarak's National Democratic Party which was disbanded by court order in April formed a new Unity Party.[112] The Brotherhood announced that the treaty with Israel should be "reviewed" and the Salafist party called democracy "heresy."[113] The Islamist parties, including the Muslim Brotherhood and the Salafis, won nearly two-thirds of the votes and were clearly going to play a major role while the liberal parties did poorly. This put great pressure on the military as to how much power to relinquish.

There were enough radicals to keep the suspicions high with chants of "Islamist, Islamist" and calling for implementation of Sharia" from members of the Development and

Renaissance Party in Tahrir Square[114] to an interview with a senior official of Egyptian Islamic Jihad (EIJ) who was just released after 20 years in jail. The Egyptian daily *Roz Al-Yousef* published an interview on 13 August 2011 with Sheikh 'Adel Shehato. "The Term 'Democracy" is Not in the Arab or Islamic Lexicon; Once Allah's Law Reigns Supreme, the People's Role will End." The Qur'an "is our constitution" and "it is impossible for us to institute a Western democratic regime. I oppose democracy because it is not the faith of the Muslims." "The Christian is free to worship his god in his church, but if the Christians make problems for the Muslims, I will exterminate them. I am guided by the shari'a, and it stipulates that they must pay the jizya tax while in a state of humiliation." "Christian, convert to Islam or pay the jizya, otherwise we will fight you. The shari'a is not based on logic but on divine law." He talked of a world conquest and violence if necessary but "the shari'a does not call it 'violence' but jihad for the sake of Allah."[115]

Women had been active in the protests that led to Mubarak's departure, but they soon faced opposition. For International Woman's Day, a Million Woman March for women's rights was held in Tahrir Square, but it turned violent. There were many confrontations: "Egyptian women are too emotional. They are different from western ladies." "We rule by the Quran and the Quran does not allow a woman to rule men."

Male protesters disrupted the march and the "thugs" as the women's group called them, became "insulting and aggressive" and then "became violent and started pushing and harassing some women." The women fled to an area where the army was stationed. "The army fired in the air, and the thugs ran away."[116] "When the women argued back, some were verbally abused or groped. Others were beaten and had to be ripped away from the groups of men."[117]

Secretary of State Hillary Clinton seemed surprised that "women have been largely excluded from the transition process and even harassed in the street. There were few women candidates and the Supreme Council of the Armed Forces had abolished the "women's quota in parliament" in July.[118] On 17 December, protesters in Tahrir Square were beaten by soldiers and pictures spread of a woman half naked on the ground – actually she still had her bra on.[119]

One of the questions during the runup to a new constitution and elections was the role of the military. The military announced some "basic principles" that it planned to impose including keeping the defense budget secret and giving it a broad mandate to intercede to maintain the secular state and protect national unity.[120] Of course, the Muslim Brotherhood had to warn the military "not to interfere in the writing of a new constitution."[121] The Salafi boldness grew as they drove the moderates out of Tahrir Square chanting "Islamic, Islamic, we don't want secular," and with their banners of "Islamic law above the constitution."[122] The "pro-democracy activists are finding it increasingly hard to remain relevant" as the more radical elements take over.[123]

With the demise of Osama bin Laden, Ayman al-Zawahiri had to show that al Qaeda was relevant and to show support for his old country. He "called on Egyptians to make Islamic rule the basis of the country's future in an effort to 'foil Washington's efforts' in the country."[124]

> **It is difficult to attract foreign investment when the World Economic Forum "ranks Egypt, Syria and Libya behind Rwanda, Guatemala and Kazakhstan."**

Egypt faces many challenges: it needs to enter the globalization world but it lacks the engineering talent and institutions to compete. Its bureaucracy is stifling when it takes "more than two years for the license required to open a new store." It is difficult to attract foreign investment when the World Economic Forum "ranks Egypt, Syria and Libya behind Rwanda,

Guatemala and Kazakhstan."   Tourism, which accounts for 13% of GDP and 11% of employment, has been severely curtailed during the revolution.[125] It is going to take a major effort by Egyptian businessmen to move Egypt forward, but unfortunately the pro-democracy movement is anti-business.

Yemen

Yemen was already unstable with a revolt in the south and Houthi rebels in the north. Yemen is different from Egypt in that it is totally tribal. President Ali Abdullah Saleh had stacked the military and security apparatus with members of his family and those from his Sanhan tribal village. The Houthis in the northern province of Saada are from the Zaydi sect, a form of Shiite Islam. "The Saudis view Yemen as a subordinate power" and consider the Houthi rebellion, with Shiites anathema to Wahhabis, as a threat particularly to the Saudi southern provinces of Jizan and Najran, home to Ismailis, another offshoot of Shia. The Saudi fear is that unrest in the south could spread to their Shiite community in the east where the oil is concentrated. There had been Iranian support for the Houthis and that is considered a major threat by the Saudis. Saleh announced that he would not seek reelection, but then he was seriously injured in a bomb attack on 3 June 2011 and went to Saudi Arabia for treatment. He vowed to return to Sana'a and did on 23 September but finally turned the government over to his vice president of 17 years, Abdel Rabbo Mansour al-Hadi. Even so, he was slow to give up and did not leave the country until January 2012. With Al Qaeda in the Arabian Peninsula already very active in Yemen and with potential Iranian meddling, Saudi Arabia was facing a tough decision about Yemen.[126] The standoff continued as the country remained unstable and on the verge of civil war.

Bahrain

In Bahrain, the Shiite majority staged protests but the Sunni monarchy, the al-Khalifa family, requested support and Saudi Arabia and the UAE sent troops in to help put down the protests. The concern again was Iranian support for the Shiite population. "Iran has long cultivated a covert strategy in the Persian Gulf states, particularly in Bahrain, that has helped advance the recent Shiite unrest." Iran has considered this covert strategy as "a relatively low-risk and potentially high-reward method of realizing its strategic objectives." They have built relationships with Shiites over the years in the Gulf Cooperation Council (GCC) states and trained opposition groups and, as usual the Islamic Revolutionary Guard Corps' (IRGC) Quds Force has led the way, even infiltrated operatives from the IRGC disguised as laborers. Iran has been able to use its business, political, and militant connections to block negotiations between the al-Khalifa government and the Shiite opposition, and by escalating the protests and clashes to transform the unrest so that it could reshape the balance of power along the Arab side of the Gulf to favor the Shia. The Saudi-led intervention placed at least a temporary roadblock to the Iranian incursion.[127]

There were reprisals against the Shiites (including firings from jobs, humiliation, and torture) and protests continued. The US was concerned because Bahrain is the home port of the US Fifth Fleet, but its lack of strong reaction, such as in Syria and Libya, led the protesters to view the US as hypocritical with double standards. The economy was stagnant and the country was simmering. The Sunni-Shia animosity is only growing worse and if it is not mollified, more violence can be expected.[128]

Libya

In Libya, the people of Benghazi, who had long been at odds with Muammar Qaddafi, declared a new regime and were recognized by the US and others.[129] With Arab League and UN support, NATO conducted air strikes in Libya and the rebels entered Tripoli on 21 August 2011. Qaddafi was captured and executed. As noted earlier, Benghazi and Derna had been a hotbed of support for the mujahedin sending many volunteers to Afghanistan and Iraq (85% as suicide bombers). Almost 20% of the foreign fighters in Iraq were Libyans, nearly double those from Saudi Arabia on a per capita basis (52 from Derna and 21 from Benghazi).[130] Not surprisingly, the leader of the newly established Tripoli Military Council is Abdelhakim Belhadj, who led the terrorist Libyan Islamic Fighting Group (LIFG), which fought alongside al Qaeda and the Taliban in Afghanistan. He later went to Iran and was eventually arrested in Malaya and sent back to Libya where Qaddafi jailed him. He was released in 2010 after supposedly renouncing violence. The LIFG has been renamed the Islamic Movement for Change (IMC) and claims it would accept democracy in an Islamic state. There are other radical Islamic groups in Libya and many Salafis have been released from Qaddafi's jails and have joined the rebels.[131]

One of unknowns as the rebellion neared its end was the status of some 700 weapons experts (200 nuclear specialists and 500 others who worked on missile technology and chemical weapons). Libya gave up its weapons of mass destruction in 2003 and the US spent about $2 million yearly assisting these scientists and technicians move into other fields. The US was still trying to put the program back together.[132]

The transition to the post-Qaddafi era will be rough. In addition to Belhadj, a very influential politician is Ali Sallabi, an Islamic scholar and popular orator. Etilaf is "a well-organized Islamist umbrella group" with Muslim Brotherhood members dominating it. Some of the Muslim Brotherhood "wanted to ban theater, cinema and arts like sculpture of the human form," and "Etilaf began circulating a proposed fatwa, or decree, to bar women from driving."[133] Further adding to the threat to the role of women, Mustafa Abdel-Jalil, head of the interim government, indicated that Qaddafi's law restricting multiple marriages would be ended clearing the way for polygamy.[134]

A new party was formed in November 2011, the National Gathering for Freedom, Justice and Development, which was hoped to have broad support when they have elections. However, on should not be optimistic about elections with people who have no such experience.

Protests in **Syria** were met with harsh actions from the government of Bashar al-Assad with mover 3,500 killed. Protests continued but the government was relentless in subduing them. Turkey announced that its patience was wearing thin and urged a stop to the killing. Iranian President Ahmadinejad, in a surprising move, urged Assad to open talks with the opposition saying that a military crackdown was "never the right solution." The Arab League came up with a series of measures to try to stop the violence.[135] However, the economy was at a standstill with tourism (12% of GDP) almost zero and isolation from the world community bringing commerce to a halt.

The situation was so bad that the headquarters of HezbAllah announced it was planning to move from Damascus to Jordan. With all the harsh actions, "it is difficult to see how the regime can regain public trust."[136]

In **Lebanon**, Najib Miqati became the new prime minister and he was backed by HezbAllah meaning an enhanced role for Syria (however the Syrian situation was a major embarrassment for HezbAllah as well as the threat of loss of their Iranian access to the Bekaa via Syria) and a more difficult situation for the US. In **Jordan**, King Abdullah fired his prime minister and brought in a general, Marouf Bakhit, and called for elections but that may be dangerous as radicals would likely win. **Moroccan** King Mohammed VI announced reforms which were approved in a referendum with elections in November which the Islamists won, the Justice and Development Party. The new Prime Minister was Adelilah Benkirane. That seemed to be successful.[137] In **Algeria**, President Abdelaziz Bouteflika raised some pay and stabilized food prices, but promised reforms were slow to materialize. **Iraq** continued to have sporadic violence, mainly between Sunnis and Shiites, and Prime Minister al-Maliki announced he would not seek a third term, but he seemed to be tightening his grip on power.

Every place there were elections, Islamists won, so it is a new era with many challenges ahead.

Muslim Brotherhood

Lurking in the wings of all these countries is the Muslim Brotherhood (which is in 80 countries), poised to seize power and impose sharia. In Egypt, where the MB was created, it had been outlawed since 1954 but its Freedom and Justice Party was recognized on 7 June 2011 as a legitimate party and was allowed to participate in the elections and drew large support. After **Yusuf al-Qaradawi** returned from his 50 years of exile, he drew an enormous crowd of Egyptians to his sermon in Tahrir Square on 18 February. Three days later he issued a death fatwa against Muammar Qaddafi.[138] In April, Mahmoud Ezzat, deputy Supreme Guide, and leader Saad al-Husseiny said that the Brotherhood wants to establish an Islamic state.[139] In May, 50,000 at a Muslim Brotherhood and Salafi rally called for sharia and a Salafi preacher said, "The United Arab States and the United Islamic States are inevitably coming and soon we will have one caliph to rule us all."[140] Another MB leader said that they would apply sharia if they came to power.[141] The threat is very clear!

The **Salafis** are the most radical and have formed three political parties. Showing their medieval outlook, a medical doctor (Mustafa Abdu) said, "We want an Islamic state like the one that was in the Middle Ages." Mohammed Aly Farahat, a financial manager in the health ministry who preaches in a Cairo mosque "wants all women – including Christians, foreigners and tourists – to be veiled in public. A woman should show only 'the face and the palms of her hands,' he explains, and nothing 'that details the shape of the body is allowed. If her body appears, she will tempt the young men.'" Abdel Moneim Abu El Fattah, former MB leader and presidential candidate speculated that "Salafis outnumber the Brotherhood 20 to 1." Ramy Shaath, a leftish activist, called Salafis a "gang of hooligans with very narrow minds who can be easily led… protected by state security and funded by Saudi Arabia."[142]

The politics in Egypt were messy as some 30 new parties tried to get organized for elections. As the best organized group the Muslim Brotherhood was constantly at the forefront of discussions. The MB was caught between spouting their line and downplaying their line to gain support from doubters. In May, the Brotherhood announced it would not enter a candidate for the presidency but would enter candidates for half of the 508 parliament seats (earlier they had said one third) and tried to stress that it was "not a religious party, not a theocratic party."[143] The National Association for Change, anti-Mubarak groups, urged the Brotherhood to guarantee the secular nature of the state if there were elections before a new constitution was drafted.[144] It was not clear if they ever received much of a reply from the MB.

Statements by various Muslim Brotherhood members were not encouraging. One cleric repeated the basic tenet of Islam: convert, pay the jizya, or fight. He referred to the lowlifes (infidels): "The war of the Muslims is better than the peace of these dogs."[145] On the Muslim Brotherhood website, a veteran member wrote that sharia should be implemented gradually. He called for moving step by step in phases, "in order to facilitate understanding, studying, acceptance, and submission."[146] Another popular Brotherhood figure, Safwat Hegazy, who had television shows and stood directly behind Yusuf al-Qaradawi at Tahrir Square, threatened Jews referring to Qurayzah and Khaybar where Muhammad had dispatched the Jews. He said, "we will return and we will kill anyone who has polluted the al-Aqsa Mosque…. Al-Aqsa belongs to us. Jerusalem belongs to us, and the whole world belongs to us. Every land upon which Islam has set foot will return to us. The caliphate will return to us."[147]

> **We will return and we will kill anyone who has polluted the al-Aqsa Mosque…. Al-Aqsa belongs to us. Jerusalem belongs to us, and the whole world belongs to us.**
>
> **- Safwat Hegazy**

There were some who thought there was a possibility for the Muslims and Christians to live together in peace. The battle for them was for the hearts and minds of the young people who face two competing narratives: jihad, "orthodoxy, violence and terrorism, or the path, which the youth helped create this year, of coexistence, ballot boxes and job opportunities." So where is that "moderate" Islam?[148] In the midst of all this confusion about the Muslim Brotherhood, the US announced that it would resume formal contacts with the MB. Obviously, that has to be with great caution.[149]

The Non-Arabs – Iran and Turkey

Iran claimed credit for the awakening in the Middle East saying that it came from the Iranian revolution. However, the Arab calls for freedom have discredited Iran's position in the Arab street weakening its quest during the last decade for regional leadership. Its ties to its ally Syria have made it resemble the old Arab autocracies ("Khamenei is now one of the longest-serving dictators in the Middle East").[150]

Iran has learned from North Korea how to turn their nuclear program into a means of involving five members of the UN Security Council (the US, Britain, China, France, and Russia) plus Germany into treating Iran as their diplomatic equal and bringing in a seventh power, Turkey, as a facilitator and possible mediator. The US withdrawal from Iraq substantially increased Iranian power, regardless of nuclear weapons. While North Korea's goal was regime survival, Iran has ambitions for increasing its power in addition to survival and sees a great opportunity but wants to seize it without getting into a ground war.

With the US out of Iraq, the Saudi frontier with Iran is effectively the Iraq/Kuwait borders and this is very upsetting to Saudi Arabia. So, even if the Israelis say that an Iranian nuclear weapon capability is four or five years away, the Saudis are concerned now about the shift in conventional power. The future of the Arabian Peninsula is at stake due to the enormous pressure on the Saudis to reach an accommodation with Iran.[151]

One of the more weird aspects of the "mad mullahs" was a documentary film they produced which claims that "Iran is prophetically destined to lead the war against Islam's enemies, which is a prelude to the appearance of the **Hidden Imam**, also called the **Mahdi**, who brings the final victory for Islam and reigns over the whole world." It says his arrival is imminent and that Ayatollah Khamenei, President Ahmadinejad, and Hassan Nasrallah are the individuals called for in the prophecy to make this happen. Khamenei is claimed to be the Seyed Khorasani, which the Hadith mention as "the preparer" for the Mahdi's intervention. Khamenei claims that he privately meet with the Mahdi in July 2010 and was told he would arrive before the Supreme Leader ended his rule. Ahmadinejad is Shoeib-Ebne Saleh who is to be appointed commander-in-chief. The military commander who will march the Mahdi's army to recapture Mecca is called Yamani and is supposed to be HezbAllah chief Hassan Nasrallah. "These three prophesied Islamic leaders are to wage a war against the 'Antichrist' and 'the imposters,' which are said to be the United States, Israel and their allies, including Arab leaders. The current uprisings in the Arab world are viewed as the fulfillment of prophecy and confirmation that they are to wage war against the enemies of Islam." The rise of the Muslim Brotherhood is said to be "in accordance with the Hadith," and even though the Brotherhood is Sunni, "Iran is theologically-required to ally with it" as a "religious commandment." The Arab revolutions are to rid the Arab world of foreign influence to provide a united front to "reconquer Palestine." So is Ahmadinejad about to lead a coalition to destroy Israel?[152]

As Bernard Lewis said referring to Iran with nuclear weapons, the mullahs "are religious fanatics with an apocalyptic mindset. In Islam, as in Christianity and Judaism, there is an end-of-times scenario – and they think it's beginning or has already begun." With regard to the Arab awakening, he said "the tyrannies are doomed," but he added that elections "should be the culmination – not the beginning of a gradual political process."[153]

> **The tyrannies are doomed, but elections should be the culmination – not the beginning of a gradual political process.**
>
> **- Bernard Lewis**

This brings us to **Turkey** which has also been striving to be a leading power in the Muslim world. Turkey opposed the US invasion of Iraq because they correctly saw it would destroy the balance of power between Iran and Iraq. Their problem now is the relationship between Iran and Saudi Arabia – the old Persians versus Arabs. The Turks do not want to have to choose between Iran and the Saudis. They want to limit Iran's influence in Iraq and they do not want Iran to dominate the Gulf. Their dilemma, along with the US, is how to stabilize the region and maintain an Arab-Persian balance of power – a thankless job.

Turkish influence has grown and its seemingly "moderate" political Islamism combined with a liberal market-oriented economy is being seen as the most relevant model for the Arabs.[154] "Turkey has utterly eclipsed Iran as the leader of the Arab street." When Prime Minister Recep Tayyip Erdogan visited Cairo in September 2011, he faced mobs of people who treated him like a hero.[155] Erdogan is now one of the most popular figures in the region. His Justice and Development Party (AKP) won its third election by a landslide and he is changing Turkey. He did not win enough seats to rewrite the constitution to limit the role of the military which Ataturk established as the guardian of a secular order. He is weakening the military and all top generals resigned in July 2011 and Erdogan put the head of the military police in charge.[156]

Erdogan is "a pious Muslim with a head scarf-wearing wife," and if, during negotiations over rewriting the constitution, he tries "to push forward a religious agenda and consolidate his power base, he could end up alienating both Kurds [14 million of 78.8 million] and secular liberals and make it impossible for Turkey to serve as a model liberal Islamic democracy."[157] Erdogan had very successful visits to Egypt, Libya, and Tunisia. Foreign Minister Ahmet Bavatoglu boldly spoke of an axis between Turkey and Egypt and proposed an alliance.

There was debate in Turkey about the aims and officials in his party – "deeply pious, with roots in political Islam" – are sympathetic to the Muslim Brotherhood. Suspicion of Turkey, from the days of the Ottoman Empire, has faded helped by the appeal of Erdogan and "the soft power of popular Turkish television serials.[158]   Turkey continues to have good relations with the US and is poised to be a key player in the Middle East.

One should not be too optimistic about revolutions; not all turn out well. The Russian Revolution brought in Lenin. Thailand and the Philippines have not done well. France is on its fifth republic. Democracy is a very delicate system and requires institutions and a great amount of discipline, which are rarely available. "Democracy through revolution is heady stuff, but it's not always a template for building lasting freedom and justice." "Without the crucial check of a free press – or independent legislatures and courts – democracy exists in name only."[159] Peaceful transfers of power are very rare in the Arab world. The Muslim Brotherhood, al Qaeda, and other groups are confident these rebellions are not really about democratic change but who "will fill the vacuum left by dictators and consolidate power. These men also know that the answer to that question will ultimately come out of the barrel of a Kalashnikov."[160]

The governments that evolve from the Jasmine Revolution will not necessarily be democratic or free and they may well not be friendly to the US. It is safe to say the Middle East has changed forever, that the US position in the Middle East will be significantly different, and US foreign policy will have to be revised to deal with the new realities.

It should be clear why this area from the Mediterranean to the Subcontinent is a Crucible of Crisis and Conflict. The great challenge for any US president is to keep this cauldron from boiling over and threatening US vital national interests. These countries are definitely important but they are not the main players on the world stage. The US should strive for good relations with all of them and help them resolve their conflicts. India is more important than all of them with the strategic importance of the Indian Ocean and is a key to our future with China. The really important countries for our future are India, China, Russia, and Brazil. We need to concentrate on what is important and not unduly waste our national treasure on the marginal.

One should not be too optimistic about revolutions; not all turn out well. The Russian Revolution brought in Lenin. Thailand and the Philippines have not done well. France is on its fifth republic. Democracy is a very delicate system and requires institutions and a great amount of discipline, which are rarely available. "Democracy through revolution is heady stuff, but it's not always a template for building lasting freedom and justice." "Without the crucial check of a free press – or independent legislatures and courts – democracy exists in name only.

Notes

1. For background on the neocons, see Hobbs, Chapter 8, "The Neocons Take Over," *World War IV and Beyond.*
2. Nathan Thornburgh, "Russia's Long War," *Time,* 16 August 2010, p. 35.
3. Israel had initially announced that it would not take any new territory, but that quickly changed with the pressure of settlers and the desire to expand their borders.
4. Mark Landler and Ethan Bronner, "In Curt Exchange, U.S. Faults Israel on Housing," *The New York Times,* 9 November 2010.
5. Josef Federman, AP. "Israel copes with bout of violence," *Reno Gazette-Journal,* 10 October 2011, p. 3B.
6. Robert G. Neumann, "The Search for Peace in the Middle East: A Role for U.S. Policy," *American-Arab Affairs,* Summer 1982, No. 1, p. 9. De Gaulle's prophetic warning to Foreign Minister Abba Eban was: "Don't make war. You will be considered the aggressor by the world and by me. You will cause the Soviet Union to penetrate more deeply into the Middle East, and Israel will suffer the consequences. You will create a Palestinian nationalism, and you will never get rid of it." On 27 November 1967, de Gaulle described Jews as an "elite people, sure of themselves and domineering" and Israel as an expansionist state.

   David Ben-Gurion wrote him a letter complaining about his remarks with some of the usual fluff about "pioneering creativity," and turning "arid land into fertile soil and created townships, towns and villages on desert-like and abandoned terrain." (He did not mention how they became abandoned!) He blamed everything on the Arabs and accepted no responsibilities for the Palestinian refugees because he said they had fled during the Mandate. De Gaulle replied that he should have listened to him, that the "repression and expulsions were [in the occupied territories] – which are the unavoidable consequences of an occupation which has all the aspects of annexation – by affirming to the world that a settlement of the conflict could only be achieved on the basis of the conquests made and not on the condition that these be evacuated, Israel is overstepping the bounds of necessary moderation." Donald Neff, "De Gaulle Calls Jews Domineering, Israel an Expansionist State," *WRMEA,* October/November 1999, p. 81.
7. For details on the war, see Hobbs, *World War IV and Beyond,* pp.222-228.
8. See George Monbiot, "Israel Responded to an Unprovoked Attack by Hezbollah, Right? Wrong," *The Guardian,* 8 August 2006, reprinted in *WRMEA,* September/October 2006, p. 12. John J. Mearsheimer and Stephen M. Walt, *The Israel Lobby and U.S. Foreign Policy,* (New York, Farrar Strauss and Giraud, 2007), devote an entire chapter, #11 to "The Lobby and the Second Lebanon War." Also see "The Israel Lobby And the U.S. Response to the War in Lebanon," Transcript of John Mearsheimer and Stephen Walt at a panel 28 August 2006 Held by the Council on American-Islamic Relations at the National Press Club in Washington, DC, Other Voices, *WRMEA,* November 2006, p. OV-1. The "enthusiastically endorsed" quote is on p. OV-7.

   Seymour Hersh had reported that Israeli officials visited Washington to obtain the support of Cheney and the NSC, by that he had meant that Ehud "Olmert wanted the approval of [Elliott] Abrams and [David] Wurmser, which he surely got." Mearsheimer and Walt, *The Israel Lobby,* p. 310.
9. The IDF Chief of Staff, General Dan Halutz, said he was going "to turn back the clock in Lebanon by 20 years" and that "nothing is safe for Lebanon." And that is what he did. The Amnesty International report described the destruction. During more than four weeks of ground and aerial bombardment of Lebanon by the Israeli armed forces, the country's infrastructure suffered destruction on a catastrophic scale. The Israeli Air Force launched more than 7,000 air attacks on about 7,000 targets in Lebanon between 12 July and 14 August, while the Navy conducted an additional 2,500 bombardments.

   The ignoring of proportionality was clear at the highest levels. Ambassador Gillerman said "To those countries who claim that we are using disproportionate force, I have only this to say. You are damn right we are." Mearsheimer and Walt, Transcript, p. OV-9. Of course, the lobby tried to smear both Amnesty International and Human Rights Watch led by Alan Dershowitz. So the IDF put out press releases that "the IDF was conducting surgical strikes against terrorists and avoiding civilians." Mearsheimer and Walt, *The Israel Lobby,* p. 328.

   At the end of the war, "the Israeli Air Force dropped over a thousand cluster bombs over southern Lebanon," including some 540 villages, leaving a terrible legacy for the inhabitants. The US banned sales of cluster bombs to Israel after their use in Lebanon in 1982, so the State Department investigated whether Israel violated US agreements, which they did, but the Israel Firsters objected and "Shelley Berkley (D-NV) sent a letter to the State Department asking that the investigation by dropped." Terry Walz, "The U.S. and Israel: Lasting Legacies?" Council for the National Interest, 28 September 2006. The Senate proposed legislation to ban the use of cluster bombs in civilian areas and prohibit sale to countries that refused to accept that ban. AIPAC was able to kill it 70-30. Mearsheimer and Walt, *The Israel Lobby,* p. 329.
10. David Rising, AP, "Support Shifts to Hezbollah," *Reno Gazette-Journal,* 29 July 2006, p. 1C. Saudi Arabia and Egypt, for example, initially criticized HezbAllah, but shifted their animosity to "the common enemy: Israel." Nasrallah "has become a folk hero across the Muslim world, apparently uniting Sunnis and Shi'i." Richard H. Curtiss, "In Sixth Arab-Israeli War, Hezbollah Survives, Israel Loses, Bush Missing in Action," *WRMEA,* November 2006, p. 13.

    Support for HezbAllah had already been growing. It had become a state-within-a-state, with an army of about 6,000, a $100 million budget, charities, seats in the parliament and the cabinet, and its own TV and radio stations. Scheherezade Faramarzi, AP, "Hezbollah support grows since inception," *Reno Gazette-Journal,* 20 August 2006, p. 2C.
11. Ehud Olmert, "Peace Now, or Never," *The New York Times,* 21 September 2011.
12. Joe Klein, "Bibi Provokes Barack," *Time,* 6 June 2011, p. 25.
13. "How G.O.P. Tightens Its Bonds With Netanyahu," *The New York Times,* 20 September 2011.
14. Quoted in Mowahid Hussain Shah, "The spreading Rage," Pakistan's *The Nation,* 18 July 2006, reprinted in Other Voices, *WRMEA,* September/October 2006, p. OV-7.
15. Joshua Mitnick, "Israeli Women Rail Against Segregation," *The Wall Street Journal,* 6 January 2012.
16. Ethan Bronner and Isabel Kers;hner, "Israelis Facing a Seismic Rift Over Role of Women," *The New York Times,* 14 January 2012.
17. He continued, "The *moral* alliance between the U.S. and Israel is far more significant. It is an alliance undertaken, despite the disadvantages to the U.S., to support a democracy and redress a historic wrong. This is an argument that can be made,

profitably, to the young people in Tahrir Square – but only if Israel respects the territory and democratic rights of the Palestinians." Joe Klein, "Road Map for Reform," *Time,* 21 February 2011, p. 29.

18. Jordanian Ambassador Prince Zeid Ra'ad Zeid Al-Hussein citing a 2009 report by India's Strategic Foresight Group, *The Washington Report on Middle East Affairs,* July 2010, p. 65.

19. Justin Raimondo, "The Dark Side of the Special Relationship," *The Washington Report on Middle East Affairs,* December 2009, p. 22.

20. Philip Giraldi, "Israeli Mossad Spying in America," *American Conservative,* 24 August 2010. "FBI sources indicate that the increase in Mossad activity is a major problem, particularly when Israelis are posing as U.S. government officials, but they also note that there is little they can do to stop it as the Justice Department refuses to initiate any punitive action or prosecutions of the Mossad officers who have been identified as involved in the illegal activity." Stewart Nozette offered to sell classified material to an FBI agent posing as a Mossad officer but there was concern he would go free as did AIPAC spies Steve Rosen and Steven Weissman and Ben-Ami Kadish who gave defense secrets to Israel and walked free after only paying a fne. For information on Nozette, see Justin Raimondo, "The Dark Side of the Special Relationship," *The Washington Report on Middle East Affairs,* December 2009, p. 21. Nozette finally accepted a deal by pleading guilty to one count of attempted espionage and a sentence of 13 years. He could have received death if found guilty on all four counts. He had told an agent that "the secrets he was passing to Israel had cost the U.S. government anywhere from \$200 million to almost \$1 billion." "Scientist pleads guilty to attempted espionage," *Reno Gazette-Journal,* 8 September 2011, p. 2C

21. Christopher Ketcham, "An Israeli Trojan Horse, How Israeli Backdoor Technology Penetrated the U.S. Government's Telecom System and Compromised National Security," Other Voices, A Supplement to *The Washington Report on Middle East Affairs,* December 2008, p. OV-11.

22. Nicky Hager, "Israel's Omniscient Ears, Israel's Urim Base in the Negev Desert is among the most important and powerful intelligence-gathering sites in the world. Yet, until now, its eavesdropping has gone entirely unmentioned" *Le Monde diplomatique,* September 2010, also in Other Voices, A Supplement to *The Washington Report on Middle East Affairs,* December 2010 p. OV-7.

23. See Hobbs, *World War IV and Beyond,* p. 239.

24. Robert Grenier, "The incomplete legacy of Dennis Ross," AlJazeera.net, 23 November 2011.

25. Quoted in Patrick J. Buchanan, "Hysteria at Herzliya," Creators Syndicate, Inc., 31 January 2007.

26. Lee Smith, "Smoke Signals," http://www.tabletmag.com/news-and-politics/78349/smoke-signals/, 16 September 2011.

27. Ethan Bronner and Isabal Kershner, "Palestinians See U.N. Bid as their Most Viable Option," *The New York Times,* 17 September 2011.

28. Josef Federman, AP, "Israel approves 1,100 new homes in east Jerusalem," *Reno Gazette-Journal,* 28 September 2011, p. 3C.

29. See "The Debate on a Palestinian State," *Time,* 3 October 2011, p. 30. Republicans in the US House put a hold on \$200 million in economic assistance in late August during the runup to the UN sessions. By October, the impact was felt with cutbacks and layoffs. Mohammed Daraghmeh, AP, "Palestinians feeling US freeze," *Reno Gazette-Journal,* 4 October 2011, p. 2B.

30. "Hamas: 'Resistance' against Israel is only option left for Palestinians," *Haaretz,* 1 October 2011.

31. "Rafid Ahmed Alwan al-Janabi, the Iraqi defector code-named Curveball by the CIA, confirmed in an interview with the U.K.'s *Guardian* that he lied about the existence of a secret biological-weapons program in Iraq to instigate regime change." That was part of the information in Secretary of State Colin Powell's 5 February 2003 UN speech which buttressed the US case for invading Iraq in March. "Throwing a Curveball at The Iraq War," *Time,* 28 February 2011, p. 15.

32. If an "exit strategy" is key to the discussion, it might be wiser to rethink the reasons for entering before making that commitment. Mark Steyn wrote that an exit strategy equated to lack of will. "In war, there are usually only two exit strategies: victory or defeat." Steyn, *America Alone,* p. 169. Steyn asked "Is foreign policy just another one of those jobs Americans won't do?" p. 175.

33. Rick Hampson, USA TODAY, "Policy critic sees Iraq becoming 'forgotten war'." *Reno Gazette-Journal,* 11 December 2011, p. 1B.

34. Shashank Bengali and Sahar Issa, "2011 looks grim for progress on women's rights," McClatchy Newspapers, 31 December 2010, Jihad Watch.

35. "Disseminating the Culture of sacrifice and martyrdom makes us and our Islamic society secure against the conspiracies of enemies," Ahlut Bayt News Agency, 19 July 2011.

36. Uri Avnery wrote of the incredible arrogance of the neocons in their belief "That it is possible to overturn nations, change their regimes at will, and take control of their resources. For starters, they intended to put Iraq, Iran and Syria in their handkerchief. Iraq and Iran because of their oil, Syria because of its strategic location. Quite incidentally, these three countries were also considered a strategic threat by Israel, and the neo-cons, most of them themselves Jews, were glad to do the 'Jewish State' a favor." The only question was which country to conquer first; it fell to Iraq where the "army would be received there with flowers (how else?) and the war would be over in a jiffy... Today, in retrospect, one can wonder which was the greater: the ignorance of the neocons or their arrogance. They had no idea about Iraq, and it seems that this did not bother them." Uri Avnery, "The Giant's Daughter," *WRMEA,* January/February 2006, p. 10.

37. The Shah started his nuclear power program in 1957. Construction of Bushehr started in 1974 but was halted during the 1979 revolution and was moribund and damaged during the 1980-88 war. It took years to rebuild the facility and it finally was due to come on line on 8 May 2011 but it was delayed again.

38. Iran announced a target of 60,000 centrifuges.

39. William J. Broad, Johan Markoff and David E. Sanger, "Israel Tests on Worm Called Crucial in Iran Nuclear Delay," *The New York Times,* 15 January 2011.

      See also "Iran Admits That Stuxnet Bit Them," StrategyPage.com, 2 December 2010. John Markoff, "Malware Aimed at Iran Hit Five Sites, Report Says," *The New York Times,* 11 February 2011. There was evidently another one called Duga. John Markoff, "New Malicious Program by Creators of Stuxnet Suspected," *The New York Times,* 18 October 2011.

40. "The Turkish Role in Negotiations with Iran," Stratfor, 11 January 2011.

41. "A senior Revolutionary Guard commander threatened Saturday that U.S. aircraft carriers would be targeted if Iran came under attack amid a standoff with the West over Tehran's nuclear program." Ali Akbar Dareni, "Iranian commander: U.S. carriers target if attacked," Associated Press, 9 July 2011.
    Iran was expanding its naval reach by sending ships beyond the Gulf – two ships through the Suez Canal to the Mediterranean and others to challenge Somali pirates off the Horn of Africa. Brian Murphy, AP, "Iran looks to sea to project its power," Reno Gazette-Journal, 4 October 2011, p. 2B.

42. "Iran, Pakistan urge stronger ties," AFP, 16 July 2011. Ahmadinejad was quoted as saying about a multi-billion-dollar project, "Construction of the pipeline to export Iranian gas to Pakistan is underway, and we hope it will reach the frontier by the end of 2012."

43. Julian Borger, "The day after Iran's first nuclear test is a normal day," Guardian, 8 June 2011.

44. He was actually quoting Ayatollah Khomeini. Something akin to Reagan's famous remark that communism would be consigned "to the dustbin of history." Reagan did not call for an attack on the Soviet Union and Khomeini did not call for an attack on Israel.

45. International Quds Day was started by Khomeini in 1979 on the last Friday of Ramadan to express solidarity with the Palestinians and the importance of holy Quds to Muslims. "Iran's Ahmadinejad: No Place for Israel in Region," Fox News, 26 August 2011. Intelligence Minister Heidar Moslehi joined in: "Minister: Int'l Quds Day Rallies Echo Crush of Zionists' Bones," Fars News Agency, 26 August 2011. Jihad Watch 28 August 2011.

46. George Jahn, "AP Exclusive: Iran prez said pushing for nukes," Associated Press, 22 July 2011.

47. Ramin Mostaghim and Alexandra Sandels, "Iran slams U.S. at conference on fighting terrorism," Los Angeles Times, 26 June 2011, Jihad Watch.

48. Yaakov Katz, "Iran caught 10 times trying to send arms to terrorists," Jerusalem Post, 10 June 2011. "In March, Turkish authorities stopped an Iranian cargo plane bound for Syria." It was carrying AK-47s and about 2,000 mortar shells. "Hague fury as 'Iranian arms' bound for Taliban seized," BBC News, 9 March 2011. 48 rockets with much greater range were seized by British Special Force in Nimruz Province on 5 February.

49. "Report: Iran Paying Taliban to Kill U.S. Troops," Sunday Times via Fox News, 5 September 2010.

50. Edith M. Lederer, AP, "Iran asks Russia about more reactors," Reno Gazette-Journal, 24 September 2011, p. 3B. To put that in perspective, the Shah's program 50 years ago was for 20 nuclear power plants to produce 23,000 megawatts by the late 1990s. Hobbs, World War IV and Beyond, pp. 239-240.

51. Nicholas D. Kristof, "A Few Words With Iran's President," The New York Times, 21 September 2011.

52. "Report: U.S. Intel Officials Warn Wall Street Execs of Al Qaeda Plot," Reuters, 1 February 2011, Jihad Watch.

53. "BA worker 'plotted with terror preacher Anwar al-Awlaki'," Telegraph, 1 September 2011, Jihad Watch.

54. Charlie Savage "White House Weighs Limits Of Terror Fight," The New York Times, 16 September 2011, p. 1.

55. Matthew Lee, AP, "U.S. to strengthen ties with breakaway regions," Reno Gazette-Journal, 25 September 2010, p. 2B.

56. Julian E. Barnes, "U.S. Expands Drone Flights To Take Aim At East Africa, The Wall Street Journal, 21 September 2011, p. 1.

57. Howard Hart, CIA Station Chief, quoted in George Crile, Charlie Wilson's War, (New York, Atlantic Monthly Press, 2003), pp. 224-225.

58. "Stan" is usually a tribe or ethnic group – "country" in Hindi and Persian. The acronym is **P**unjab, **A**fghania (the old North West Frontier Province, now Khyber-Pakhtunkhwa Province), **K**ashmir, **I**ran, **S**indh, **T**ukharistan (ancient area, also called Bactria – N. Afghanistan, SE Uzbekistan, S. Tajikistan), **A**fghanistan, Baluchista**N** – Land of the Paks – spiritually pure and clean.

59. Inal Ersan, "Al Qaeda says would use Pakistani nuclear weapons," Reuters, 22 June 2009.

60. Jonathan S. Landay, "Pakistan's nuclear program grows as Islamists threat does, too," McClatchy Newspapers, 3 May 2009.

61. "'Pak will have 200 N-warheads in a decade'," Press Trust of India, 7 July 2011, Jihad Watch, 8 July 2011.

62. There was an uncorroborated report that "the Saudis were paying off the Pakistani military and intelligence (ISI) to essentially shelter and keep bin Laden under house arrest in Abbottabad." Rob Crilly, "Osama bin Laden 'protected by Pakistan in return for Saudi cash,'" Telegraph, 10 August 2011.

63. "84 percent Pakistanis consider US troops as bigger threat to country than Taliban, Al-Qaeda," New Kerala, 2 May 2009. That poll showed 62% considered al Qaeda the threat and 50% the Taliban. Hopefully those latter numbers have gone up with the increased attacks by al Qaeda and the Taliban in Pakistan which have killed many people. Over 50% believe that the major aim of the US forces was to weaken the Muslim world. "Some 59 per cent believe that the purpose of the US' 'war on terror' is to weaken the Muslim world and another 15 per cent believe it is to be specifically intended to ensure American domination over Pakistan."

64. Donna Cassata, AP, "Mullen: Intelligence agency from Pakistan to blame for attack," Reno Gazette-Journal, 23 September 2011, p. 3B.

65. Ashraf Khan, "Pakistani President Returns From Medical Treatment," Associate Press, 18 December 2011.

66. Mark Mazetti, "A Shooting in Pakistan Reveals Fraying Alliance," New York Times, 12 March 2011. Saeed, who also leads Jamaat-ud-Dawah (JuD), has called for jihad against India and the use of nuclear weapons if needed. "JuD leaders chant 'jihad', would not mind Indo-Pak N-war," PTI, 6 February 2011, Jihad Watch.

67. David Coleman Headley (Daood Gilani) born in Washington, DC to a Pakistani father and a wealthy Philadelphia mother. He was an informant for the DEA, worked for LeT, as a businessman with a US passport did a reconnaissance of Mumbai and later in Denmark.

68. "CIA chief confronts Pak over collusion with militants," Press Trust of India, 11 June 2011, Jihad Watch, 13 June 2011.

69. The Land Warfare Papers, No. 82, April 2011, The Institute of Land Warfare, Association of the US Army.

70. Chris Brummitt, "Pakistan fertilizer fuels Afghan bombs," *Reno Gazette-Journal,* 1 September 2011, p. 5C. An interesting side note was that a senior adviser to Afghan President Hamid Karzai said most Afghans want US troops to stay in country after the scheduled departure in 2014.

71. See Barnett R. Rubin and Ahmed Rashid, "From Great Game to Grand Bargain," *Foreign Affairs,* Volume 87 No. 6, November/December 2008, pp. 30-44.

72. Pervez Hoodbhoy, "The Roots of Extremism in Pakistan," *Journal of International Affairs* (BILIA, Bangladesh), Vol. 12, Nos. 1 & 2, Jun-Dec 2008, p. 6.

73. *Veja* (newsmagazine), São Paulo, Brazil, 25 October 2001, *World Press Review,* January 2002, p. 13.

74. Peter Popham, *Independent on Sunday,* London, 16 September 2001. "600 U.S. Taliban?" *Investor's Business Daily,* 18 July 2008. "All told, 600 American children are being indoctrinated into jihad in 22 madrassas across Pakistan…. One particularly radical school in Karachi freely displays a banner at its main gate urging Muslims to join the Taliban. At least 80 Americans are enrolled at Jamia Binoria, an international school. Many of its graduates joined the Taliban and became commanders.
     Another jihadist seminary in Pakistan connected to Jamia Binoria brainwashed John Walker Lindh, the American Taliban now serving time for attacking U.S. soldiers in Afghanistan. The mullahs who run these terrorist hatcheries come to America to recruit boys, many of them from Lindh's home state of California. Jamia Binoria's headmaster, Mufti Mohammad Naeem, travels to the U.S. each year during Ramadan to meet with Muslim parents - like a college football coach recruiting prospects." Why is this man allowed to enter the US and why is this allowed to continue? According to their mission statement, "The outgoing scholars of the Jamia are fighting a crusade against infidels and pagans."

75. *Time,* 15 September 2003, p. 56.

76. "Pakistan to rein in Islamic schools," *Reno Gazette-Journal,* 20 June 2002. "Pakistan announced new measures to strengthen control of the country's 8,000 Islamic religious schools….madrassas, would be shut down and fined if they fail to register with a government oversight board."
     However, under pressure from clerics, the government backed down. "5,000 of the 12,000 established schools have not registered." Salman Masood, "Pakistanis Back Off Vow To Control Madrassas," *The New York Times,* 2 January 2006.

77. Sadaqat Jam, AP, "At least 106 dead at Pakistan's Red Mosque, *Reno Gazette-Journal,* 13 July 2007, p. 4B. Daniel Pipes, "Islamists Learn New Tactics for Seizing National Control," Human Events, 23 July 2007, p. 16.

78. Jibran Khan, "Red Mosques imam ready for war to 'talebanise' Pakistan," Asia News, 10 August 2011.

79. *Time,* 15 September 2003, p. 57. But it is not only the poor areas; state run Islamic schools in Kuwait were breeding extremism. Many of the teachers in those schools came "from fundamentalist groups such as the Social Reform Society – Kuwait's branch of Egypt's Muslim Brotherhood" – or Salafis. These teachers taught their students "that Muslims are superior and unbelievers will go to hell." AP, "Kuwait's schools under fire for being planters of hatred," *Reno Gazette-Journal,* 24 November 2002, p. 24A.

80. Andrew McCarthy, "The War that Dare Not Speak Its Name," nationalreview.com, 13 May 2009.

81. Rameez Khan, "Youths protest against democracy," *The Express Tribune,* 21 February 2011, Jihad Watch, 23 February 2011.

82. Ayman al-Zawahiri is a son-in-law of Momands, one of the largest Pashtun tribes in Momand Agency. His wife is a Momand Pashtun living with her children on the border of Banjaur and Momand, the Agencies north of the Kyber Pass. Under Pashtunwali – the Pashtun tribal code – Zawahiri is part of the family and tribe and, therefore, must be protected with the lives of the tribesmen. About 40 percent of the Afghan population is Pashtun, but most Pashtuns live in Pakistan. The radical elements operate on both sides of the border, and have done so for thousands of years, long before any borders were drawn. The Pashtuns still pride themselves in standing up to Alexander the Great 2,500 years ago. Change does not come quickly in that part of the world. The Pashtuns were defeated by Alexander, but he left, and the tribes went back to their old ways. Timothy R. Greene, "Afghanistan: In Memory of Alexander the Great," Trends and Countering-Terrorism, 5 January 2006.

83. Part of the cause of political unrest was the sharp rise in food costs. In Tunisia, 36% of total household consumption expenditures goes to food. It is 38% in Egypt. *Time,* 28 February 2011, p. 19.

84. Jean-Pierre Lehmann, "The 21st Century Arab Awakening?" YaleGlobal Online, 28 January 2011.

85. Percentage of population under age 30 (percentage ages 15-29 not working and not going to school): Morocco 57% (34%), Mauritania 68% (25%), Algeria 58% (37%), Tunisia 52% (about 30%), Libya 58% (29%), Egypt 61% (37%), Sudan 67% (36%), Somalia 70% (36%), Yemen 74% (49%), Saudi Arabia 60% (25%), Jordan 64% (23%), Palestinian Territories 72% (37%), Lebanon 51% (16%), Syria 65% (32%), Iraq 68% (43%), Kuwait 49% (15%), Bahrain 54% (24%), Qatar 50% (13%), UAE 44% (16%), Oman 62%. *Time,* 28 February 2011, p. 37.

86. Ibid.

87. Lehmann, op. cit.

88. Rania Abouzeid, "Postcard: Sidi Bouzid," *Time,* 7 February 2011, p. 8.

89. See "Tunisia legalizes Islamist group Ennahda," BBC, 1 March 2011, Jihad Watch. David D. Kirk Patrick, "As Protests Mount, Tunisia Delays Cabinet Reshuffle," *New York Times,* 26 January 2011. "Thousands greet Tunisian Islamist leader's return," AFP, 30 January 2011, Jihad Watch. "Tunisia: Ghannouchi's Return, Opposers Attacked," ANSAmed, 31 January 2011, Jihad Watch.

90. "Islamist party wants to establish Shariah law in Tunisia," Agence France-Presse, 10 March 2011, Jihad Watch.

91. "Tunisia: Pact That Bans Normalisation With Israel Adopted," ANSAmed, 1 July 2011.

92. David E. Miller, "Tunisian Secularists Fight Back," The Media Line, 10 July 2011, Jihad Watch, 11 July 2011.

93. Anthony Shadid, "Yearning for Respect, Arabs Find a Voice," *The New York Times,* 29 January 2011.

94. "Egypt police arrest man for Facebook 'Islam insults,'" AFP, 21 August 2011, Jihad Watch.

95. Jeffrey Fleishman, "Islamists in Egypt seek change through politics," *Los Angeles Times,* 3 April 2011, Jihad Watch, 5 April 2011.

96. David E. Miller, "Muslim Brotherhood advocates Egyptian modesty police," The Media Line, 4 April 2011, Jihad Watch.

97. "We will not allow 'another Khomeini' to take control of Egypt, army says," DPA, 5 April 2011, Jihad Watch.

98. Hamza Hendawi, "Policeman shoots Christian dead in southern Egypt," Associated Press, 11 January 2011.

99. Sarah El Deeb, "Egypt Islamists defiant over Christian governor," Associated Press, 18 April 2011.

100. "Christian governor with Mubarak ties suspended," Middle East Online, 25 April 2011, Jihad Watch, 26 April 2011.

101. Yaroslav Trofimov, "As Islamists Flex Muscle, Egypt's Christians Despair," *The Wall Street Journal* via AINA, 12 June 2011, Jihad Watch.

102. Manar Ammar, "Egypt state television admits to making up news over soldiers 'deaths'," Bikya Masr, 15 October 2011, Jihad Watch.

103. Mary Abdelmassih, "Egyptian Muslim Ring Uses Sexual Coercion to Convert Christian Girls: Report," Assyrian International News Agency, 13 July 2011, Jihad Watch.

104. Bulletin of the Oppression of Women, 25 October-15 November 2011, poliltidaislam.com.

105. Bulletin of the Oppression of Women, 14 November-15 December 2011, politicalislam.com.

106. Barry Rubin, "Muslim Brotherhood Declares War on America; Will America Notice," www.rubinreports.blogspot.com, 7 October 2010.

107. "Brotherhood leader: Preparing for an Islamic government," Almasry Alyoum, 23 April 2011, Jihad Watch, 24 April 2011.

108. "Egyptian Islamists jam Tahrir Square," Associate Press, *Reno Gazette-Journal,* 19 November 2011, p. 1B.

109. Paul Schemm, "Poll: Over half of Egypt wants to end Israel peace," AP, 25 April 2011, Jihad Watch, 26 April 2011.

110. Hamza Hendawi and Maggie Michael, "Calls grow in Egypt to delay elections," Associated Press, 19 June 2011, Jihad Watch, 21 June 2011.

111. "Muslim Brotherhood Figure and Former Spokesman in the West: Establish a Global Islamic State," MEMRI, 24 June 2011, Jihad Watch, 29 June 2011.

112. "Egypt Bars Islamist Hard-Line Political Party," *The New York Times,* 19 September 2011.

113. "Muslim Brotherhood: Egypt-Israel peace treaty needs to be reviewed," Deutsche Press-Agentur, 9 December 2011, Jihad Watch, 10 December 2011.

114. "Protesters demand Sharia Law implementation, tourism that respects Islam," Al Masry Al Youm, 3 June 2011.

115. "Senior Official in Egyptian Islamic Jihad," MEMRI, 29 August 2011, Jihad Watch.

116. Ekram Ibrahim, "Egyptian million woman march ends with a gunshot," Ahram Online, 8 March 2011, Jihad Watch, 9 March 2011.

117. Hadeel Al-Shalchi, AP, "Egypt's women's rights protest disrupted by men," *Reno Gazette-Journal,* 9 March 2011, p. 3C.

118. "Clinton says women sidelined in Egypt transition," AFP, 16 December 2011.

119. AP, "Egyptian Military escalates Tahrir crackdown," *Reno Gazette-Journal,* 18 December 2011, p. 1B.

120. David D. Kirkpatrick, "Egypt Military Aims to Cement Muscular Role in Government," *The New York Times,* 16 July 2011.

121. "Egypt's Islamists challenge military rulers," Associated Press, 13 August 2011, Jihad Watch, 14 August 2011.

122. Edmund Blair and Marwa Awad, "Groups quit Egypt rally saying hijacked by Islamists," Reuters, 29 July 2011, Jihad Watch, 30 July 2011.

123. Yaroslav Trofimov, "Egyptians Turn Against Liberal Protesters," *The Wall Street Journal,* 2 August 2011, Jihad Watch.

124. Desmond Shepard, "Al-Qaeda: US hijacking Egyptian revolution," Bikya Masr, 10 August 2011, Jihad Watch.

125. Michael Schuman, "Seeking Growth After the Arab Spring," *Time,* 22 August 2011, p. Business 1-6.

126. "Yemen in Crisis: A Special Report," Stratfor, 21 March 2011.

127. "Iranian Covert Activity in Bahrain," STRATFOR, 14 March 2011.

128. Anthony Shadid,. "Bahrain Boils Under the Lid of Repression," *The New York Times,* 15 September 2011.

129. Souad Mekhennet and Eric Schmitt, "Exiled Islamists Watch Rebellion Unfold at Home," *The New York Times,* 18 July 2011.

130. Daya Gamage, "Libyan rebellion has radical Islamist fervor: Benghazi link to Islamic militancy: U.S. Military Document Reveals," *Asian Tribune,* 17 March 2011. Tim Dickinson, "U.S. Bombs Libya, Helps… Jihadists?!," *Rolling Stone,* 21 March 2011. The figures came from the Combating Terrorism Center at West Point.

131. "Libya Ex-Islamic terrorist leader heads Tripoli Military Council," posted 28 August 2011 by Stephen Morgan. For opposition to the war against Libya, see Andrew C. McCarthy, "Decoding Libya: Sharia can tell us how this story ends," nationalreview.com, 26 March 2011. He wrote that the MB and al Qaeda agree on imposing sharia and a global caliphate. The only disagreement "is strictly about tactics, especially in the West. In the United States and Europe, the Brothers think the best way to advance the sharia cause is stealth jihad, not violent jihad. They prefer having their sharia soul-mates (e.g., CAIR and the Islamic Society of North America) masquerade as civil-rights activists, the better to exploit Western freedoms and win the sympathies of the media and the academy." "The Muslims of the Middle East will gladly use us…The Libyan mujahideen will exploit us but never befriend us." He ended with "If we empower them, we will eventually rue the day."

132. Douglas Birch, "What will happen to Libyan scientists?" *Reno Gazette-Journal,* 10 March 2011, p. 2B.

133. Rod Nordland and David D. Kirkpatrick, "Islamists' Growing Sway Raises Questions for Libya," *The New York Times,* 14 September 2011.

134. Bulletin of the Oppression of Women, 25 October-15 November 2011, politicalislam.com.

135. Dominic Evans, "Syria, Arab League 'agree reforms' as killing go on," Reuters, 10 September 2011.

136. Aryn Baker, "Deeping Divide," *Time,* 13 June 2011, p. 27.

137. For "The King's Revolution," see Ahmed Charai, "Moroccan Democracy and the Future of the Sahara," FPRI, 11 March 2011. He called for a new constitution, separation of powers, individual liberties, an independent judiciary, an elected prime minister, regional governors would be elected instead of appointed, gender equality, and "the Berber mother tongue of Amazigh an official language alongside Arabic."

138. Aaron Rock, "Qaradawi's Return and Islamic Leadership in Egypt," Middle East Media Monitor, FPRI, 18 March 2011.

139. "Muslim Brotherhood Leaders: We Will Implement Sharia Law in Egypt," *AlMasry AlYoum* via AINA, 17 April 2011, Jihad Watch.

140. Hany ElWaziry, "Thousands attend joint Muslim Brotherhood-Salafi rally," *AlMasry AlYoum,* 8 May 2011, Jihad Watch, 9 May 2011.

141. Khalaf Ali Hassan, "Brotherhood leader: We shall apply Islamic sharia," *AlMasry AlYoum,* 25 May 2011, Jihad Watch, 26 May 2011.   For more on the Muslim Brotherhood, see Ayaan Hirsi Ali, "The Quran Is Our Law; Jihad Is Our Way," *The Wall Street Journal,* 18 February 2011.

142. Betsy Hiel, "Islamist factions jockey for power, vow religious rule," *Pittsburgh Tribune-Review,* 31 July 2011, Jihad Watch, 1 August 2011.

143. "Egypt's Muslim Brotherhood Outlines Political Ambitions," Radio Free Europe/Radio Liberty, 1 May 2011.

144. "NAC asks Muslim Brotherhood to guarantee secular state," AlMasry AlYoum, 1 June 2011, Jihad Watch, 12 June 2011.

145. "Egyptian Cleric Mazen Al-Sarsawi: We Ask a Person Nicely to Convert, But If He Refuses and Does Not Pay the Jizya Tax, We Fight Him," MEMRI, 2 June 2011, Jihad Watch, 4 June 2011.

146. "Article on Muslim Brotherhood Website: Implement Shari'a in Phases," MEMRI, 5 July 2011, Jihad Watch, 6 July 2011.

147. "Shaykh Safwat Hegazy: 'Jerusalem Belongs to Us, and the Whole World Belongs to Us,'" Translating Jihad, 8 July 2011, Jihad Watch, 11 July 2011.

148. Bruce Feiler, "The Crescent and the Cross," *Time,* 20 June 2011, p. 33.

149. Arshad Mohammed, "Exclusive: U.S. to resume formal Muslim Brotherhood contacts," Reuters, 29 June 2011, Jihad Watch.

150. Fareed Zakaria, "The Storm Before the Calm," *Time,* 3 October 2011, p. 19.

151. George Friedman, "The Turkish Role in Negotiations with Iran," Stratfor, 11 January 2011.

152. Ryan Mauro, "Radical Islam and Iran," FrontPageMag, 29 March 2011.

153. Bari Weiss, "The Tyrannies Are Doomed," *The Wall Street Journal,"* 2 April 2011.

154. Jean-Pierre Lehman, "The 21st Century Arab Awakening," YaleGlobal, 25 January 2011.

155. Fareed Zakaria, "The Storm Before the Calm," *Time,* 3 October 2011, p. 19.

156. Gul Tusuz and Sabrina Tavernise, "Top Generals Quit in Group, Stunning Turks," *The New York Times,* 29 July 2011.

157. Rana Foroohar, "Turkey's Man of the People," *Time,* 27 June 2011, p. 36.

158. Anthony Shadid, "In Riddle of Mideast Upheaval, Turkey Offers Itself as an Answer," *The New York Times,* 26 September 2011.

159. Hannah Beech "The Asian Experience," *Time,* 21 February 2011, p. 26.

160. Michael Scheuer, "Why the Mideast revolts will help al-Qaeda," *Washington Post,* 4 March 2011.

Democracy is the worst form of government -------- except all the rest!

- Winston Churchill

Old joke: A number of world leaders were talking to God. Each asks God if a particular problem in his country will ever by solved. To each, God replies, "Yes, but not in your time." Finally, God is asked if there will be peace in the Middle East. He replies, "Yes, but not in my time."

Chapter 9

Fiscal Irresponsibility –

Is America Committing Suicide?

With Americans reeling from home mortgages that are under water and with over 9% unemployment, 13.4% in Nevada, and true unemployment at over 20% when those who have given up searching or who work at less than sustaining jobs are counted, the public has finally awakened to an economic crisis, even though the government is slow to act. The crash of 2008 was created by government actions – "when Washington decides, in its infinite wisdom, that every living, breathing citizen should own a home." The Community Reinvestment Act of 1977 put pressure on banks to relax their lending standards and to provide more mortgages. The Federal Reserve Bank of Boston claimed in 1992 that racial discrimination was involved in the application of regular lending standards applied to those "whose incomes, assets, or abilities to pay fell far below the traditional homeowner spectrum."[1] According to one study, 18 percent of the loans in the subprime market went to black borrowers, compared to 5 percent of loans in the conventional loan market."

> **The most serious threat to the United States is not someone hiding in a cave in Afghanistan or Pakistan, but our own fiscal irresponsibility. The survivability of the republic is at stake – "catastrophic consequences" for the US if we don't do something now.**
>
> **- Comptroller General David Walker**

This was great liberal politics but it was widely understood that these people could not pay back these loans. However, Fannie Mae saw this as a great way to make more money and enthusiastically encouraged banks to provide home mortgages to individuals with credit that was not good enough to qualify for conventional loans. *The New York Times* noted in 1999 that "Fannie Mae, the nation's biggest underwriter of home mortgages, has been under increasing pressure from the Clinton Administration to expand mortgage loans among low and moderate income people and felt pressure from stock holders to maintain its phenomenal growth in profits." Franklin D. Raines, then chairman and chief executive officer, said, "Fannie Mae has expanded home ownership for millions of families in the 1990's by reducing down payment requirements." Presciently, the article observed, "Fannie Mae is taking on significantly more risk, which may not pose any difficulties during flush economic times. But the government-subsidized corporation may run into trouble in an economic downturn, prompting a government rescue similar to that of the savings and loan industry in the 1980's."[2]

These pseudo private-government corporations are another way for Washington insiders to rake off money. Raines walked off with million of dollars [one report was $240 million], and James A. Johnson, the chairman and CEO in the early 1990s made $100 million. Fannie Mae made $7 billion from these loans but kept $2.1 billion for Johnson and his crew. They gave large donations to groups they needed to protect them, including ACORN, the Congressional Black Caucus, the Congressional Hispanic Caucus, congressmen, etc. when experts testified to Congress that there was a very serious risk to taxpayers. These crooks cost the US $153 billion so far.[3] "Fannie Mae's political machine dispensed campaign contributions, gave jobs to friends and relatives of legislators, hired armies of lobbyists (even paying lobbyists not to lobby against it), paid academics who wrote papers validating the homeownership mania, and spread 'charitable' contributions across the congressional map." The government was involved in financing $3.4 trillion (about half) of the market for home loans. Not surprisingly, by mid-2005, "almost 40 percent of new subprime loans were for amounts larger than the value of the properties."[4] Crooks like Johnson and Raines [including Tim Howard, Chief Financial Officer of Fannie Mae] and others should be in prison (perhaps along with some of the Wall Street master thieves). [In China they would likely be executed.] Raines, Johnson, and Howard all served as financial advisers in the Obama campaign.

The numbers are mind boggling and incomprehensible. The Congress and the White House fought over the debt ceiling of $14.3 trillion, almost the size of our total GDP, and almost one third is held by foreign entities, about one third by China. But that debt pales compared to the **unfunded liabilities of $61.6 trillion** [Charles Koch wrote in the *Wall Street Journal* "The unfunded liabilities of Social Security, Medicare and Medicaid already exceed **$106 trillion**. That's well over $300,000 for every man, woman and child in America (and exceeds the combined value of every U.S. bank account, stock certificate, building and piece of personal or public property).] "The government added $5.3 trillion in new financial obligations in 2010, largely for retirement programs such as Medicare [$1.8 trillion] and Social Security [$1.4 trillion]." This amounts to $534,000 per household. Corporations are required to count liabilities when they are taken and report them as losses, but Congress does not follow standard accounting rules.[5]

Trillions are incomprehensible. Let's put it in perspective:

US tax revenue:	$2,170,000,000,000
Federal budget	$3,820,000,000,000
New debt	$1,650,000,000,000
National debt	$14,271,000,000,000
Recent budget cuts	38,500,000,000

Now let's remove 8 zeros and consider it is a household budget:

Annual family income	$21,700
Money the family spent	$38,200
New debt of credit card	$16,500
Outstanding balance on credit card	$142,710
Total budget cuts	$385

Make better sense now! Washington isn't doing much to alleviate the problem is it?[6]

The deficit and debt is like a cancer and it's going to destroy our country from within.
- Erskine Bowles[7]

It is not just the two wars in Iraq and Afghanistan which account for $3.7 trillion or perhaps as high as $4.4 trillion.[8] The US Congress constantly passes laws which require massive funding for which they do not provide any source. States, cities, and people can only spend money they actually have, but not the Congress; it just runs up the national debt. The money collected for Social Security was not kept apart and invested to grow with interest; instead our elected officials could not resist spending it with the result that the future of Social Security is in doubt. Likewise with Medicare. These programs were supposed to be self-financing. Then the prescription drug program was added with expected multi-trillion dollar costs with an enormous claim on taxpayers.

These unfunded liabilities which Congress incurred on our behalf now exceed by trillions the tax revenues projected to be available to pay for them. From days of surplus we have gone into great debt. For 2011, federal taxes are projected to bring in $2.567 trillion, 17% of GDP; however, spending is projected at $3.834 trillion, 25% of GDP, which means the government will have to borrow $1.267 trillion, 8% of GDP, to cover expenses. The welfare state Washington has created is estimated to burden us with immediate federal debt (the Washington way of accounting) of $20 trillion and we are on the road to paying **$1 trillion annually by 2020 for interest alone.**[9]

The most significant threat to our national security is our debt.
- Joint Chiefs of Staff Chairman Mike Mullen[10]

Is it possible to reduce this astronomical debt without resorting to hyperinflation and destroying the middle class? There are numerous examples of debt problems in various countries. It is worth looking at just the last century and a half and what happened in Egypt which was riding high. With the Civil War blocking cotton from the South, the price of cotton went up eightfold and Egypt built a massive railroad net and then the Suez Canal. The end of that war popped the bubble and Egypt resorted to heavy borrowing and its national debt went from £3 million to £100 million and as cotton prices continued to fall, its debt became unpayable. By 1875, Egypt was forced to sell its stake in the Suez company to Britain for a mere £4 million. Egypt defaulted on its debt the next year and by 1882, it was basically a British colony. But then Britain made unsustainable borrowing to fight two world wars, the US replaced the UK as the major world power, and by the time of the Suez War of 1956, the empire was gone. So is this the situation of the US with an unsustainable debt while still financing an ambitious foreign policy with foreign loans, particularly from a rising power like China? What happens if China sells its treasuries or quits buying them?

America not meeting its debt obligation is like allowing a child with matches in a room full of dynamite. I continue to find it close to inconceivable that elected policymakers would allow such a risk.
- Lawrence Summers, former chief economic adviser to Barack Obama

---

If investors fled treasuries, it would be ugly: "the government's borrowing cost would skyrocket. Some of the fleeing investors would take money abroad, so the dollar would plummet. And these first-round effects would be trivial compared with the larger psychological impact, for even more than the Lehman Brothers crash of September 2008, a Treasury meltdown would cause cardiac arrest in the heart of the economy." There are enormous political consequences of not fixing this debt. It will mark "the decline of the superpower that has guaranteed the safety of international sea lanes, provided the world's reserve currency and supported causes from free trade to the battle against global diseases." But it will require courage, something that elected leaders rarely possess.[11]

The Decline of the US Dollar

According to the Bureau of Labor Statistics, the purchasing power of $1 in 1914 was down to 5 cents as of 31 August 2010. The 2010 dollar is worth 18 cents in 1971 terms (in 1971 Nixon cancelled the right of dollar bearers to swap the notes for gold – in 20 years we had given away about 2/3 of our gold reserve, about 400 million ounces for $14 billion, worth about $620 billion now). That means that today you must spend $1 to get what would have cost you 18 cents in 1970 – a fall in purchasing power of 82%.[12] The US Government has had the benefit of being the world's reserve currency for the past 90 years permitting their profligate ways. However, "fiat currencies are nothing more than units of political promises." When the ability of the issuers to repay exceeds the units of debt, the system collapses. The debts and obligations of the US, Japan, Europe, and other countries are now unpayable, so it is "either overt default or a continuation of the currency debasement that has been a dominant theme of the last 50 years." The US acts as though its dollar will always be the reserve currency, but that is not true as historically "the typical reign of a reserve currency lasts just about 100 years."[13]

> **There is no surer means of overturning the existing basis of society than to debauch the currency.**
>
> **- Lord John Maynard Keynes (1883-1946)**

Portugal was quite wealthy and its currency was predominant in commerce from roughly 1450 to 1530, about 80 years. It was Spanish currency from 1530 to about 1640, 110 years. From 1640 to 1720, 80 years, it was the Dutch currency. It was the French franc from 1720 to 1815, 95 years. The English pound of the British Empire was the most widely used from 1815 to 1920, 105 years. The US dollar has been the global reserve currency since for over 90 years. When the currency is abused, a new reserve currency emerges. It has been a great run for the US but as noted above, the dollar has gone almost straight down since it took over from the British pound. Whether the dollar will make it to 100 years, "the dollar simply cannot come out of this crisis intact….the U.S. government is not just broke, it's the world's largest debtor – in history."[14]

"The greatest threat facing America today is not terrorism, or foreign economic competition, or illegal immigration. The greatest threat facing America today is the disastrous fiscal policies of our own government, marked by shameless deficit spending and Federal Reserve currency devaluation. It is this one-two punch – Congress spending more than it can tax or borrow, and the Fed printing money to make up the difference – that threatens to impoverish us by further destroying the value of our dollars."[15] The Chinese and some Europeans have been calling for a new reserve currency for some years.

Government Out of Control

The problem is that both Republicans and Democrats have not been able to quit spending even when there was not enough revenue coming in to cover their new expenditures. With no requirement (like the states and local governments) to have a balanced budget, they were free to promise more and more to gain votes. US Government spending as a percent of

GDP was almost back to World War II levels. Corruption and special favors reached new levels as we noted with the Fannie Mae thieves above. Once people arrive in Washington, they lose whatever moral objectivity they might have had and find no problem with spending other people's money. Being a politician has become a very rewarding profession instead of a civic duty as once envisioned. Politicians go to Washington poor and return as millionaires such as Harry Reid, Lyndon Johnson, and the Clintons. Barack Obama, who never held a serious job, became a millionaire by writing books (if not written by William Ayers, the Weather Underground terrorist and friend in Chicago) about how great he is and now rules and lives like a king.

Once in power, they develop royal tastes and feel they deserve royal treatment. Obama uses Air Force One as if it were the family car. In 2010, he flew 172 times, almost every other day; of course those were not political with the midterm elections! The Air Force estimated that it costs $181,757 per flight hour (not to mention the additional travel costs of Marine One, Secret Service, logistics, local police overtime, and they fly his limousine in a USAF C-17). It cost $1.75 million for his Hawaii vacation plus Michele's junkets to Africa and Spain with entourage. He has spent over $100 million on flying plus perhaps another $100 million on his entourage and he planned to do more in 2011[16] and even more for the 2012 election. Then there was the Queen, House Speaker Nancy Pelosi, who was already wealthy with her husband (helped by some special legislation that helped his overseas business). She demanded that she have her own US Air force aircraft for her use. Over a 16 month period (March 2009-June 2010), she made 85 trips or 1.25 trips per week at a cost of $2,100,744.59 (or $1,285,162.00 per year). The food and bar tab was $101,429.14. This is the same woman who said that "if the stimulus doesn't pass, five hundred million people might lose their jobs." (Maybe she drank too much on the plane.)[17]

A government big enough to give you everything you want, is big enough to take away everything you have.

- Thomas Jefferson

The Congress is pressured from every special interest group in the country resulting in some idiotic projects consuming taxpayers' money: $62 million for a tunnel to nowhere in Pittsburgh PA that even Governor Ed Rendell called 'a tragic mistake," $1.9 million for international ant research, $308 million for a joint clean energy venture with BP, $200,000 to help Siberian communities lobby Russian policy makers, $39.7 million to upgrade the statehouse and political offices in Topeka, Kansas, $760,000 to Georgia Tech to study improvised music, $193,956 to study voters perceptions of the economic stimulus, $363,760 to help NIH promote the positive impacts of stimulus projects, and $529,648 to study the effects of local population on the environment – in the Himalayas.[18] Pork is a staple food on Capitol Hill. According to The Heritage Foundation, "The amount spent in 2010 by Congress on frivolous 'pork' projects that use taxpayer funds to reward local special interests and pressure groups" was $16.5 billion.

The government went wild after 9/11 adding a giant new bureaucracy to our already massive security apparatus. The *Washington Post* ran a multi-part series "Top Secret America." They found that:

*   Some 1,271 government organizations and 1,931 private companies work on programs related to counterterrorism, homeland security, and intelligence in about 10,000 locations across the United States
*   An estimated 854,000 people hold top-secret security clearances. [about 250,000 are

contractors.]

* Just in Washington and the surrounding area, 33 building complexes for top-secret intelligence work are under construction or have been built since September 2001. Together they equal almost three Pentagons, about 17 million square feet of space.
* ...publishing 50,000 intelligence reports each year – a volume so large that many are routinely ignored.

Retired Army Lt. Gen. John R. Vines reviewed "how the Defense Department keeps track of its most sensitive programs.

He was shocked to find that there is no "agency with the authority, responsibility or a process in place to coordinate all these interagency and commercial activities. The complexity of this system defies description." He concluded that, "Because [the system] lacks a synchronizing process, it inevitably results in message dissonance, reduced effectiveness and waste. We consequently can't effectively assess whether it is making us more safe."[19]

I predict future happiness for Americans if they can prevent the government from wasting the labors of the people under the pretense of taking care of them.
                                                                      - Thomas Jefferson

---

With all the talk about creating jobs, the one sector that hired more people was the government bureaucracy. The government has large departments, such as Health and Human Services, Education, Homeland Security, as well as Defense, which spend enormous amounts of taxpayer money which is often of little value and some unaccounted for.

Government employees pay

There are two aspects concerning government employees: whether they are paid more than private workers and the power of their unions. *USA Today* reported that "At a time when workers' pay and benefits have stagnated, federal employees' average compensation has grown to more than double what private sector workers earn."[20] That was $123,049 versus $61,051 according to Bureau of Economic Analysis, a gap of $61,998, up from $30,415 in 2000. There are differences of opinion with some claiming that federal workers earn less than private workers for comparable jobs. However, the listing from the Bureau of Labor Statistics shows most federal position paying more.[21]

The number of federal workers earning over $150,000 a year jumped to 82,034 in 2010 up from 7,420 in 2005, a tenfold increase and double since Obama took office. "Top-paid staff has increased in every department and agency. The Defense Department had nine civilians earning $170,000 or more in 2005, 214 when Obama took office, and 995 in June [2010]." Federal pay and benefits have increased 3% annually above inflation since 2000 compared to 0.8% in the private sector.[22]

Just using Nevada as an example across the country, in the list of salaries of Nevada employees with about 50 names per page, you have to go to page 24 to get under $200,000 and page 88 to get under $150,000 for total pay and benefits. The top salary is about $1.4 million for a professor at the school of medicine. Then there are head coaches, more medicine professors, and many fire department personnel. Several, a marshal and fire captains, are listed with base pay of $70-80,000 plus benefits of $50,000+, but their total is listed between $600,000 and $800,000. An Assistant Fire Chief in North Las Vegas was paid $661,831. A Fire Battalion Chief in Henderson was paid $401,000. A Fire Captain in Las Vegas was paid $361,000.[23] This is one of the biggest problems across the country. A Fire Captain commands about three men in one station. A Fire Battalion Chief manages about three stations. They rip off the taxpayers by calling in "on short notice for vacation and sick days. When this happens, there is another fireman (usually a buddy) waiting to take the slot so they get the overtime. They take turns doing this for each other."[24] A battalion chief gets overtime even if he is at home watching TV if he is "on call."[25]

States are under great pressure, and they cannot print money out of thin air like the federal government. They have already cut their budgets $75 billion and raised taxes by $33 billion in the past two years and face $175 billion more in budget cuts in the next 2 ½ years.[26]

There are enormous commitments for government retirement obligations. "Private employers are legally required to put money into pension funds to match retirement promises. Private pensions have $2.3 trillion in stocks, bonds and other assets. States and local governments have $3 trillion in retirement funds. The federal government has nothing set aside."[27] Greed never stops as legislators passed laws including their reimbursements and per diem allowances in their salaries used to calculate pensions.[28]

The Reno, Nevada city budget is already approaching 90% for personnel. Nevada has some of the "most generous pension benefits in the country." There are many six-figure pensions, as in California which has seen their number quadruple. These problems are unsustainable across the country. Despite the "economic illiterates of the Occupy Wall Street movement" who want the public sector unions to help them against capitalism, "if there's going to be a revolution, it will be caused by the pension apocalypse."[29]

Government employee unions

There are 21.6 million government workers across the United States. There are 2.2 million federal civilian workers but there are 19.4 million at state and local governments. Of that 19 million, about "half work in education, which rivals health care for the most wasteful sector in America. The rest are mostly police officers, firefighters, social workers, nurses and prison guards." State and local governments have cut about 1% of employees but the federal government workforce is 12% larger than in November 2007.[30]

The more members coming in, the more dues coming in, the more money we have for politics.

- Larry Scanlon, AFSCME

Government employee unions have become so large that they brag about being the big dog and their influence on political campaigns has become a hindrance to good government creating severely underfunded pension plans that they want to dump on the backs of taxpayers. "Public employee unions are spending hundreds of millions of dollars on political campaigns while estimates of underfunded rank-and-file public employee pension plans reach a staggering $3 trillion dollars." That big dog is the American Federation of State, County and Municipal Employees (AFSCME) which spent almost $90 Million ($87.5 million by 25 October 2010) on the 2010 election and about "$360 million since the 1997-98 election cycle." Of the $160 billion that Congress sent to the states in bailouts, "$100 million went to union dues." As Brian McMahon, spokesman for the trade group, Associated Builders and Contractors, said, "We borrowed money from the Chinese again in order to give Democrats extra campaign help." He added that in the private sector, that would be considered bribery. Of the $3.04 trillion in underfunded pensions, it was not surprising that the worst debt obligation per capita was in Illinois, famous for its corrupt governments. "Every person drawing breath in Illinois owed a staggering $17,230 in unfunded debt to public pensions." There was an effort in Congress to bail out the unions by placing them under the government Pension Benefit Guaranty Corporation (PBGC) which was created in 1974.[31]

In addition to the large sums of money the unions spend in election campaigns, they donate millions of dollars directly to the parties, predominantly to Democrats. Not surprisingly, the AFSCME is at the top of the list with over $40 million to the Democrats and half a million to the Republicans. A list of some 24 "Leading Union Political Campaign Contributors 1990-2010" starting with the AFSCME plus National Education Association, Service Employees International Union, American Federation of Teachers, United Auto Workers, Teamsters, AFL-CIO, International Association of Firefighters, and American Postal Workers Union donated almost half a billion dollars ($486,440,870) to Democrats and only $27,886,800 to Republicans.[32]

> **Union members look at dues the same way they look at taxes: just something you got to pay the thieves who run things.**
>
> **- Al Capone**

The public watched the spectacle in Wisconsin in early 2011 where Governor Scott Walker, faced with a mounting deficit, wanted concessions from the unions plus an end to collective bargaining. It grew ludicrous when 14 Democrats left the state to prevent a vote on his proposal.[33] It is interesting that the liberal icon, Franklin Roosevelt, was strongly against collective bargaining and strikes by public employees. "All Government employees should realize that the process of collective bargaining, as usually understood, cannot be transplanted into the public service."[34]

Labor unions are declining in membership and public approval, but "Public-employee unions, with their lavish taxpayer-funded pensions, are driving governments to insolvency." The battle in Wisconsin has spread to other states. After the government bailed out the automakers, [the stock or bond holders were wiped out] the United Auto Workers union was given a major stake in the auto companies even though it was the health care plans the unions had negotiated which damaged the companies originally. The enormous campaign contributions were noted above. Some government pensions have gone crazy (almost as bad as the Congress!) with sweetheart deals: "New York policemen retiring at age 39 and earning a six-figure salary for the rest of their lives," "San Francisco city retirees getting an unexpected $170 million cost-of-living bonus on top on their regular COLA despite the retirement system having an unfunded liability of $1.6 billion," and "the school board superintendent in Wayne Township, Michigan, who retired in December after 15 years on the job and is already raking in more than $1 million in pension benefits."[35]

If ObamaCare is so great, why were one third of the first 222 waivers granted to union health plans? Three went to Chicago chapters of the Service Employees International Union in Chicago; the SEIU gave $28 million to Obama's 2008 campaign. Obama used a recess appointment to put Craig Becker, former SEIU and AFL-CIO counsel, on the National Labor Relations Board where he is the swing vote for the Democrats. And who can forget the New York snow storm when "Sanitation bosses told workers to slow down snow removal efforts because they were angry over budget cuts and layoffs among their union brethren in the agency."[36]

The teachers unions know that when they are negotiating, the schools will not be shut down. The US public schools are a disgrace as they rank low compared to other countries. Teachers have "become a reactionary force when it comes to school reform" opposing charter schools and merit pay sticking with seniority and last-hired, first-fired. "The strongest argument against public employees' unions lie there: in the power to block reform and strangle good governance." That drives talented professionals out of public service.[37]

Unions have generally been leftist and they showed their colors in California. At a May Day 2011 rally in Los Angeles, co-sponsored by the SEIU and various communist groups as well as other unions, they clearly identified themselves with communist and socialist ideologies. Not only did the SEIU help to organize the rally in conjunction with communists, they marched side-by-side with communists, while union members carried communist flags, communists carried union signs, and altogether there was no real way to tell the two apart. And, it wasn't just the SEIU at the march - other "normal" unions like the AFL-CIO were on hand as well. There were plenty of teachers' unions attending too, and they brought along many of their public school students for some good old-fashioned communist indoctrination. It appears that Communism is not yet dead in the US.[38]

As noted, the SEIU gave $28 million to Obama's campaign which made it the organization that gave the most and its President, Andy Stern, has been the most frequent visitor to the White House as his guest and confidant with 53 visits.[39]

> **I owe those unions. When their leaders call, I do my best to call them back right away.**
> **- Barack Obama, *The Audacity of Hope* (2006)**

Note the language on the signs.

The SEIU members wore purple T-shirts. This man had a red flag.

The banner and flags are red. Note the two languages.

Will America Face Up to Its Crisis?

Americans are accustomed to being number 1, but the world is changing and a new world order is evolving and they do not seem able to grasp the magnitude of the challenges they face. The great boom in the US economy was the result of developments and policies in the 1950s and 1960s: "the interstate-highway system, massive funding for science and technology, a public education system that was the envy of the world" plus good legal immigration policies. But look at us now: "our 15 year-olds rank 17th in the world in science and 25th in math. We rank 12th among developed countries in college graduation (down from No. 1 for decades). We come in 79th in elementary-school enrollment. Our infrastructure is ranked 23rd in the world, well behind that of every other major advanced economy." Our health numbers are bad: "27th in life expectancy, 18th in diabetes," but we are first in some things: obesity and the largest amount of debt in the world.[40]

> **America's success has made it sclerotic. We have sat on top of the world for almost a century, and our repeated economic, political and military victories have made us quite sure that we are destined to be No. 1 forever.**
>
> **- Fareed Zakaria**

But, we are not as great as we think we are; we have been resting on our past success. David Walker, the former Comptroller General, expressed the American dream quite well. Pointedly, he started with it was "not about owning a house." The first element was the opportunity to achieve one's full abilities based upon the individual's efforts. The second was "an obligation to leave the country better off and better positioned for the future" what he calls "stewardship." As values and principles that we have strayed from, he listed: "We were founded on opportunity, not entitlement. We were founded on thrift, not conspicuous consumption. We were founded on savings, not debt. We were founded on a limited role for the Federal government, with states having the power unless it was expressly reserved for the Federal government, and we recognize that the power ultimately belonged to the people, and that the first three words of the Constitution were the most important –'We the people.' Ultimately, we, the people, are responsible and accountable for what does or does not happen." He added one other principle: "limited involvement in foreign conflicts."[41]

Politicians do not want to touch the politically sensitive issues such as Social Security, Medicare, and Medicaid. "The American political system is actually quite efficient. It distributes the big bucks to popular programs and powerful special interests." It is not as if our democracy does not work, "it's that it works only too well. American politics is now hyperresponsive to constituents' interests. And all those interests are dedicated to preserving the past rather than investing in the future." It is similar to the paradox of World War II where Britain won the war, but fell into stagnation while Germany lost and yet grew more powerful. Britain became "complacent and rigid" with labor "unions, the welfare state, protectionist policies and massive borrowing" shielding it from international competition. Germany was devastated and had to rebuild almost from scratch so it was able to change its antiquated arrangements with a more modern approach. Americans are really quite insular and do not want to learn from other countries which may do some things better. "And it's not just politicians and business leaders. It's all of us. Americans simply don't care much, know much or want to learn much about the outside world."[42]

> **INEPTOCRACY – a system of government where the least capable to lead are elected by the least capable of producing, and where the members of society least likely to sustain themselves are rewarded with goods and services paid for by the confiscated wealth of a diminishing number of producers.**

We had a tradition that we would not run deficits unless we were in a declared war, which we have not had since World War II. But "economists" took over and said "we can run deficits equal to the growth of the economy" - thus the ratio of debt to GDP would not increase. But now we have a $1.4 trillion deficit which is 10% of GDP. We have lost our way. In 1789 the debt to GDP was 40% - all federal and state public debt – the government had taken over the state debt to get the Constitution ratified. The highest debt to GDP was 122% at the end of

World War II, but we had no foreign debt and the economy grew rapidly and we were down to about 30% by the 1970s. World War II was the only time we were over 60% but we are now at 61%, but that does not count the "so-called trust funds" for Social Security and Medicare because Washington uses a different language for them. As David Walker said, speaking from experience, "If you treated a private sector trust fund like the government treats the Social Security/Medicare trust funds, you'd be in jail." The crime is that "they're not funded. They are an accounting device....The government takes in the money. It spends every dime!" He argued that it is wrong. "It's an obligation. We ought to count it as a liability. If we did, debt to GDP would be 91 percent, not 61 percent." [That was in 2010, *Time* used 99% 23 May 2011, p. 17.][43]

He listed these unfunded liabilities at over $62 trillion, "$200,000 per person. No wonder newborn babies cry. They come into the world with an implicit obligation of $200,000. It's $500,000 per household." With median household income of $50,000, that means "the typical American household has an implicit second or third mortgage equal to ten times their annual household income and no house to back that mortgage." As for the trust funds, they are "a priority claim on future general revenues. Ain't no money there!"

With the US stock market falling over the problems in Europe, particularly Greece, Walker's comments are important: "we're already worse than Spain, Portugal, Ireland, and the United Kingdom. And we're within ten years of being where Greece is today [2010]. But they don't have this funny trust-fund debt. So if you added that, we're within three years of Greece." There are some points about Greece that are relevant and not applicable to the US. An article by Michael Lewis in *Vanity Fair* was quite harsh. He noted that Greece's banks did not load up on subprime US securities. "The cause for Greece's collapse is much simpler... It's socialism and good, old-fashioned government corruption. Greek banks took all the money and lent it to the government. And the government did what it does best... stole and squandered. In Greece, the banks didn't sink the country. The country sank the banks." "The average government job pays almost three times the average private-sector job." "The Greek people never learned to pay their taxes." "No self-employed citizens pay taxes." "During election years, politicians pull the tax collectors off the streets."[44] Rana Foroohar referred to a slow economic recovery and wrote that if "we grow at [only] 1.8% over the next 10 years, debt rises to 144% of GDP. That makes us Greece."[45]

If you put the federal government in charge of the Sahara Desert, in five years there'd be a shortage of sand.

- Milton Friedman

Part of the crisis is the continued growth of American government. US companies are quite efficient but the government is not. New departments like Homeland Security and Education and more agencies, more regulations, and more handouts are continually added. "Today, every government program and subsidy seems eternal."[46] We seem incapable of dropping ineffective programs. Teaching English as a Second Language has been a failure. Head Start is a program we spend $7 billion a year on and it has gone on for 45 years and is not even under the Department of Education since it was part of Lyndon Johnson's War on Poverty and has become "little more than patronage troughs for local Democratic party honchos." Like many government-run social programs, "Head Start simply does not work."[47] Homeland Security has sucked up billions of dollars and with the inefficiency of TSA, one could say that **Osama bin Laden won**.

The American Dream is dying. "We all believed that if you followed the basic compact, worked hard and played by the rules, that we'd have the highest standard of living in the world. And we were always on the front edge of the next new technology – but we're not anymore. We seem to be mired in mediocrity while China is steaming ahead."[48] The real estate and credit crises wiped out much of middle class wealth. "But the causes of inequality and any resulting decrease in social mobility are also very much about two megatrends that have been reshaping the global economy since the 1970s: the effects of technology and the rise of the emerging markets. Some 2 billion people have joined the global workforce since the 1970s. According to Goldman Sachs, the majority of them are middle class by global standards and can do many of the jobs that were once done by American workers, at lower costs. Goldman Sachs estimates that 70 million join that group every year."[49]

One of the feelings is that the financial industry "has drained our best young minds away from industry and into the creation of new financial products that, as Paul Volcker has said, haven't added anything to GDP." Volcker told a story about the 1980s. "A recent Ph.D. in aeronautical engineering from Princeton approached Volcker and asked him which Wall Street firm he should go to work for. 'Why don't you go to work for Boeing?' Volcker asked. The young man replied that he could start at $50,000 per year at Boeing, on a career track that might reach $90,000. 'I can make that overnight on Wall Street,' he said."[50]

"Amazingly, three years after the crisis, the percentage of the U.S. economy represented by the financial sector remains at historic highs of over 8%." The banking industry was considered the driving force of the economy providing the capital to create new businesses, but that argument has faded – "over the past several decades, the growth in size and importance of the financial sector has run in tandem with lower – not higher – rates of new-business formation." One of the factors is that "the financial sector is sucking talent and entrepreneurial energy from more socially beneficial sectors of the economy." Far more Harvard graduates go to financial jobs than in the 1970s and MIT graduates "who went to Wall Street rose from 18% in 2003 to 25% in 2006." These are the people needed to build new companies. "Some 40% of U.S. GDP this year will come from firms that didn't exist in the 1980s. And nearly all the new jobs in the U.S. are created by firms less than five years old."[51]

There are now more poor people in the US with over 15% below the poverty line. "The average real weekly earnings of a typical blue collar worker are lower today than in 1964." This is killing the American Dream – "specifically the dream of upward mobility." Some "8 out of 10 of the biggest occupations in America offer less than the mean hourly wage." [sales clerks and home health aides] "While Americans historically haven't been as inclined to riot over inequality (witness the protests that have taken place from London to Athens), it's hard to rule that out in a world in which the American Dream is increasingly a myth."[52]

Any system produces winners and losers. If the gap between them gets too great, the losers will organize themselves politically and seek to recast the existing system – within nations and between them.

- Henry Kissinger, in the *Economist*

Another sector where greed has spiraled out of control is executive pay which now even exceeds pre-crash levels. CEOs of the top 200 companies made over $11 million on average, a 23% increase, while workers, many of whom received no raise, made slightly under $40,000, only a slight increase, but with inflation, they actually made less. Philippe P. Dauman, Viacom, made $84.5 million in 2010 up 149%; Ray Irani, Occidental Petroleum, was paid $76.1 million, up 142%; Leslie Moonves, CBS, reaped $56.9 million, a 32% raise. We have reached the point where "the average wage was less than one-half of one percent of what the typical CEO made."[53]

The government says there is no inflation; of course when statistics do not support their desires, they change the rules so they do not count food and oil. Yet food prices soared 3.9% in February 2011, the largest gains since 1977. Crude oil was up 43%, sugar 63%, cotton 69%, corn 68% and cattle 45%. Thomas Hoenig, president of the Federal Reserve's 10th District, says, "Inflation is so unfair. It is the most regressive tax you can impose on the public. It erodes the buying power of the poor and people on fixed incomes." He feels that "government policy continues to smile on Wall Street but not on Main Street. Instead of breaking up the financial giants whose gambles crashed the economy, the government has let the biggest banks grow even bigger. [Too big to fail!] Now they are gorging on free money. Where is the penalty for failure?" Hoenig said, "We don't have a market economy now, I hate to use this term, but it's almost crony capitalism – who you know, how big your political donation is." To rein in the free wheeling financial industry, Hoenig would bring back the "Depression-era Glass-Steagall rule that barred commercial banks from taking excessive risk."[54] [The Glass-Steagall Act was passed in 1933 to keep banks out of the brokerage business hoping to prevent another crash like 1929. The banks and brokerages lobbied hard and it was repealed on 12 November 1999.]

"The problem is that while the banks are holding more capital, they still aren't lending." Bank profits were up 136% but bank lending was down 9%.[55]

Banking institutions are more dangerous to our liberties than standing armies. If the American people ever allow private banks to control the issue of their currency, first by inflation, then by deflation, the banks and corporations that will grow up around the banks will deprive the people of all property until their children wake-up homeless on the continent their fathers conquered.

- Thomas Jefferson

Government has become so complex that no one person can keep up with, much less understand, the myriad laws, rules, and regulations promulgated. The result has been continued growth in bureaucrats, staffs for Congress, and increased influence of lobbyists. Thousands of staffers have been hired to help the 535 members of Congress and these are the people who actually write the legislation. Many come from interest groups and many, after gaining experience, move to special interest groups. There are some 11,000 registered lobbyists in Washington being paid nearly $3.5 billion, largely for trying to understand the 17,000 pages of the US Tax Code.[56] Congressional bills have become so long and complicated, some running over 2,000 pages, such as on financial reform and health care, that members cannot possibly read and understand them leading to the idiocy where congressional leaders tell members to read it after we pass it! Demonstrating the reduced mental capacity of congressional leaders, we had Nancy Pelosi's brilliant statement, "We have to pass the bill so that you can find out what's in it." Additional amendments may be made in conference committee that neither house saw. But it does not stop there because regulations have to be written to implement the laws and that is where new interpretations can be entered to enact some of the nebulous language. Along with drastic reduction in the size of government, its programs, and tax reform, congressional reform also is needed.

> **The honest lawmakers of any country can be counted on your fingers. I could count Chicago's on one hand.**
>
> **- Al Capone**

The cost of political campaigns, particularly the enormous expenditures for media exposure, has risen to the point where congressmen are almost continually fundraising. Unfortunately, this has resulted in the Best Congress that Money can Buy. It is naïve to expect that interest groups that spend millions of dollars on the campaigns for particular congressmen will not expect their desires on legislation to be very seriously considered. This distorts both democracy and capitalism. Campaign finance reform is another issue that must be seriously addressed.

> **Someone once said that taxes are the price we pay for civilization. That may have been true when he said it, but today taxes are mostly the price we pay so that politicians can play Santa Claus and get reelected.**
>
> **- Thomas Sowell[57]**

Corporations are sitting on cash because of the uncertainty of what the government will do. Wealthy individuals are leaving the US. Taxes are set to go up. "Why would anyone take the risk of starting (or growing) a business when the government is going to take a total of 70% of the upside and leave you holding the bag if it doesn't work out?" [The 55% estate tax "makes it nearly impossible for most successful small businesses to be left in control of the founder's family."] Will Congress pass sensible policies when half of Americans no longer pay federal taxes? This is a problem for democracy. Is America "becoming a new type of fascist state, where government employees, unions, and everyone else on the dole constitutes the largest voting block?"[58]

> You cannot legislate the poor into prosperity by legislating the wealthy out of prosperity. What one person receives without working for, another person must work for without receiving. The government cannot give to anybody anything that the government does not first take from somebody else. When half of the people get the idea that they do not have to work because the other half is going to take care of them, and when the other half gets the idea that it does no good to work because somebody else is going to get what they work for, that my dear friend, is the beginning of the end of any nation,. You cannot multiply wealth by dividing it.[59]

A US Chamber of Commerce survey of small and medium business CEOs asked what "do you want out of Washington?" found 80% said "get out of the way." 89% said the economy is "on the wrong track" and only 1 in six planned to hire new workers in 2012. Concerns for not hiring were "uncertainty about what Washington will do next" and ObamaCare.[60]

> **The democracy will cease to exist when you take away from those who are willing to work and give to those who would not.**
>
> **- Thomas Jefferson**

Is the US Becoming a Socialist Nation?

The massive growth of government and its intrusion into almost every aspect of citizens' lives have brought many charges that the US has become a welfare state and is well on its way to being a socialist state. This country was founded on the basis of the pioneer spirit of individualism and the minimum of any form of governmental authority. The creation of the capital in Washington in a swamp with too many mosquitoes supported the idea to stay far from it and leave it alone. That worked fairly well as long as we were a predominantly agrarian society. Farmers really did not really need much from the outside world. They could grow their own food, dig a well for water, spin and weave if necessary or trade for the items they needed. They helped each other for harvests and in times of need and the family took care of itself. They could use horses for power and transportation until the gas engine came along and they had to buy gas. But that age is gone as only a miniscule percentage of the population now lives on farms meaning that almost all of us are totally dependent on others to survive. That raises the question of the sustainability of ever growing population which we will address in Chapter 15.

When we get piled upon one another in large cities, as in Europe, we shall become as corrupt as Europe.

- Thomas Jefferson

Labor on the farm provided enough for the family plus a surplus to sell or trade for needed items. Urban populations must have some form of income, usually from a job, to enable them to buy the necessities of life. So the key becomes employment, jobs, but there has to be a market of some sort to pay people for their skills offered. Modern technology has greatly reduced the requirement for labor raising the sensitive question of how many people can a society support. This is haunting the Third World as they keep producing babies but are having terrible problems with feeding, clothing, educating, and providing for them.

This brings us to the role of government. Governments do not produce anything so they have to take money from citizens to provide programs. This starts a vicious circle of providing for people by taxing others. If there are too many programs and too many needy, the government efforts eventually exceed the ability to raise the required funds by taxes. This leads to deficits and debt which eventually may become unrepayable. This is the problem now in Europe and ever more in the US.

It is incumbent on every generation to pay its own debts as it goes. A principle which if acted on would save one-half the wars of the world.

- Thomas Jefferson

Porter Stansberry wrote that the problem is not government or banks, but the very bad idea "that the state ought to sit in the center of society." He dates our problems from World War I in that before then the power of the federal government was quite limited including in revenues. Washington could not tax incomes until the XVIth Amendment. He wrote that "progressive" ideas emerged after the Civil War mainly from Germany – Karl Marx and Friedrich Engels – with the core idea being "that the state itself was superior to its citizens." The foundations of the modern state are based on the demands of Karl Marx's Communist

Manifesto. "In 1848, Marx threatened to organize a worker's revolution unless European governments:

1. Abolished property rights and applied all rents towards public purposes. [Modern corollary: Don't pay your property taxes, lose your house. So who really owns your house?]
2. Levied a heavy, progressive income tax to equalize wages. [Modern corollary: Combined federal and state marginal income and payroll taxes approach (or surpass) 50% in many U.S. states.]
3. Abolished all rights of inheritance [Modern corollary: The estate tax.]
4. Confiscated the property of all emigrants. [Modern corollary: The 2008 "Hero's Act," which forces people leaving the U.S. to pay the equivalent of their estate taxes on the global assets before they turn in their passports.]
5. Centralized access to credit in the hands of the State by means of a national bank and an exclusive monopoly. [Modern corollary: Fannie Mae and Freddie Mac, which make more than 90% of all of the mortgages in the U.S. and have dominated the market for mortgages for decades.]
6. Centralized the means of communication and transport in the hands of the State. [Modern corollary: AT&T was a legal monopoly for decades. Amtrak is a ward of the states. The government owns all the roads. And the State controls all air traffic.]
7. Provided free education for all children in public schools. [Note the emphasis on public schools. Paying for education isn't enough. What counts is indoctrinating the kids in glorifying the State.]
8. Produced a common agricultural policy to maximize the productivity of the land. [Modern corollary: Massive ethanol and agricultural subsidies.]"

> **The problem with socialism is that eventually you run out of other people's money.**
> **- Margaret Thatcher**

These ideas spread around the world because of "the allure of getting something for nothing." Of course, the problem arose, "How do you pay for them?" The answer was "A progressive income tax. Let the rich pay!" but "Tax revenues fail to meet projections. Deficits grow. Deficit spending soars. And debts mount." He ended with "The central truth of economics is scarcity. There can never be enough of anything to satisfy everyone. The central truth of politics is patronage: promising to give everything to everyone. Paper money is the bridge between economics and politics. The unpaid debts of an entire generation of people in Western countries are coming due. The so-called 'baby boomers' grew up in a world dominated by Marxian and Keynesian economics. These are bad ideas. They are destined to collapse. And the collapse is here."[61]

> **Socialism, in general, has a record of failure so blatant that only an intellectual could ignore or evade it.**
> **- Thomas Sowell[62]**

Two stories reflect the weakness of socialism and communism when you remove the fruits of one's labor and thus kill incentive.

An economics professor said that he had never failed a single student before, but had once failed an entire class. That class had insisted that Obama's socialism worked and that no one would be poor and no one would be rich, a great equalizer.

The professor then said, OK, we will have an experiment in this class on Obama's plan."

All grades would be averaged and everyone would receive the same grade so no one would fail and no one would receive an A.

After the first test, the grades were averaged and everyone got a B. The students who studied hard were upset and the students who studied little were happy. As the second test rolled around, the students who studied little had studied even less and the ones who studied hard decided they wanted a free ride so they studied little.

The second test average was a D! No one was happy.

When the 3rd test rolled around, the average was an F.

As the test proceeded, the scores never increased as bickering, blame, and name-calling all resulted in hard feelings and no one would study for the benefit of anyone else.

All failed, to their great surprise, and the professor told them that socialism would also ultimately fail because when the reward is great, the effort to succeed is great, but when government takes all the reward away, no one will try or want to succeed.

The American people will never knowingly adopt socialism. But, under the name of "liberalism," they will adopt every fragment of the socialist program, until one day America will be a socialist nation, without knowing how it happened….I no longer need to run as a Presidential Candidate for the Socialist Party. The Democrat Party has adopted our platform.

- Norman Thomas, 1944, six-time presidential candidate

At another college, a chemistry professor has some exchange students in his class. One day while the class was in the lab, the professor noticed one young man (exchange student) who kept rubbing his back and stretching as if his back hurt.

The professor asked the young man what was the matter. The student told him he had a bullet lodged in his back. He had been shot while fighting communists in his native country who were trying to overthrow his country's government and install a new communist government.

In the midst of his story he looked at the professor and asked a strange question. He asked "do you know how to catch wild pigs?"

The professor thought it was a joke and asked for the punch line. The young man said this was no joke. You catch wild pigs by finding a suitable place in the woods and putting corn on the ground. The pigs find it and begin to come every day to eat the free corn. When they are used to coming every day, you put a fence down one side of the place where they are used to coming. When they get used to the fence, they begin to eat the corn again and you put up another side of the fence. They get used to that and start to eat again. You continue until you have all four sides of the fence up with a gate in the last side. The pigs, who are used to the free corn, start to come through the gate to eat, you slam the gate on them and catch the whole herd.

Suddenly the wild pigs have lost their freedom. They run around and around inside the fence, but they are caught. Soon they go back to eating the free corn. They are so used to it that they have forgotten how to forage in the woods for themselves, so they accept their captivity.

The young man then told the professor that is exactly what he sees happening to America. The government keeps pushing us toward socialism and keeps spreading the free corn out in the form of programs such as supplemental income, tax credit for unearned income, tobacco subsidies, dairy subsidies, payments not to plant crops (CRP), welfare, medicine, drugs, etc. while we continually lose our freedoms – just a little at a time.

Remember: there is no such thing as a free lunch and a politician will never provide a service for you cheaper than you can do it yourself.

> **The inherent vice of capitalism is the unequal sharing of the blessings. The inherent blessing of socialism is the equal sharing of misery.**
>
> **- Winston Churchill[63]**

There have been a lot of questions about President Obama whether he is a hidden Muslim or a socialist, besides whether he was born in Hawaii or Kenya. Dinesh D'Souza wrote that "Obama is clueless about business" and that he is a "European-style socialist, with a penchant for leveling and government redistribution." D'Souza wrote that Obama is following his father's dream of anticolonialism to rid the world of the neocolonialists which "oppress not only Third World people but also citizens in their own countries. America is seen as the neocolonialist power now in the world and "He must work to wring the neocolonialism out of America and the West." D'Souza calls Obama "the last anticolonial," that "he candidly admits he is only living out his father's dream," and that "America today is governed by a ghost."[64]

What to Do?

We cannot continue with the circular logic of the politicians that spend a trillion or two more that they collected and then say that the citizens are not paying enough and that they must increase taxes because of the huge debt they had created. This is not only arrogant, but it is insane. If all the citizens were taxed at 100% of their income, it still would not pay for the reckless spending in Washington. Entire departments, agencies, commissions, laws, and regulations must be removed. We need honest accounting in Washington, not constantly cooking the books with phony numbers to make the situation look better than it really is. We need to quit printing phony money and live within our means. We need to stop trying to play the world's policeman and trying to impose our democratic values (which we are rapidly degrading) on other people who have long histories of their own.

> **We give you a Republic; now see if you can keep it.**
>
> **- Ben Franklin**

Our Constitution is truly a wonderful document written by really great men in the late 18th century, but they saw America as a work in progress. They were not afraid to recognize their mistakes; they saw the Articles of Confederation as a failure and junked them. The Constitution needs a review. Did we make a mistake with the XVIIth Amendment changing the election of senators from the state legislatures to popular vote? Now we have two chambers both elected the same way. Does it make sense for Rhode Island and Wyoming to have two senators like Texas and California?

The Congress is a mess. We have no statesmen any more. It used to be that domestic politics stopped at the waters' edge. Senate rules are such that any senator can stop any action without even an explanation. That leaves us with judicial positions vacant for years and important work delayed. "We have a crazy-quilt patchwork of towns, municipalities and states with overlapping authority, bureaucracies and resulting waste. We have a political system geared toward ceaseless fundraising and pandering to the interests of the present with no ability to plan, invest or build for the future."[65] Campaign finance reform is desperately needed to regain some moral ground in Congress. Likewise, the tax code needs to be totally revised to make it comprehensible rather than a mass of loopholes written in legalese that high priced lawyers can exploit.

Entitlement programs need to be brought up to date for the current world. Health (including Medicare and Medicaid) and Social Security alone are over 42% of the budget or over $6.6 trillion. They may be "the 'third rail' of American politics – touch it and you're electrocuted," because they involve seniors who are reliable voters[66], but they must be brought into the real world. Social Security is expected to run out of money in 2037 and the major strain coming is the 78 million baby boomers now reaching retirement age. Two actions that can be taken are a perhaps 1% increase in taxes for both workers and employers and, since people are living much longer, increasing the retirement age.[67]

> **If you think health care is expensive now, wait until you see what it costs when it's free.**
> **- P. J. Rourke**

Cutting the defense budget is also touchy, but "Our defense budget now equals that of the rest of the world's nations combined." When all the defense related costs are counted, it is almost 20% of the budget or over $6 trillion. The immediate threat to the security of America right now is not foreign enemies but the enormous debt which is destroying our economy. Given the state of our economy, we cannot afford "too much" defense or in view of our interests "too little," but we need to determine "prudent strategic risk." Spending must match requirements.[68] Richard Haas called for a doctrine of "restoration" – "a U.S. foreign policy based on restoring this country's strength and replenishing its resources – economic, human and physical." He wrote that the US could strengthen its "position abroad by focusing on nation building – our own."[69]

Defense will remain critical for threats from Islamofascism and potentially China, but it must be balanced against the immediate requirement to heal our economy. The defense budget has nearly doubled since 2000. Big weapons systems are terribly expensive; we will likely need some of them but others must be cancelled or postponed. We have to revisit our requirement for 11 carrier strike groups, troops in Europe 66 years after World War II, expensive submarines and airplanes and the high cost of personnel while our so-called allies spend only about one-fifth what we spend.[70] Most of the fighting we are doing now against jihadists is with relatively low cost systems.

There were over 46 million Americans living in poverty by 2010, the highest since the Great Depression, probably higher now. The middle class is getting poorer; the income of the average American household fell for the third straight year, to $49,455.[71]

> **Never in the history of the world has there been a situation so bad that the government can't make it worse.**
> **- Unknown**

We need serious political and policy reforms because our democracy has become dysfunctional. Along with campaign finance and redistricting reforms, we need term limits to stop the career politicians who lose their moral compasses when they become immersed in the heady life of Washington. We need statutory budget controls, a limit to the amount of debt that can be taken on as a percentage of GDP. Fiscal irresponsibility is the major cut politicians have struck to our young people. "We're mortgaging their future at record rates. We're reducing a lot of investments in their future because less of the budget is for investment, less is for basic research, or critical infrastructure innovation."[72] This "triple whammy" is destroying the American dream.

Let's try to recap this financial mess we are in. I strongly recommend you read Porter Stansberry's "End of America." "Most people still don't understand the risks we face as a nation because of our feckless leaders and their reckless ignorance of basic economics." He pointed out that if "we don't begin to solve these core financial problems, they will certainly destroy our country." The problem with the debt we owe is that it "continues to increase at a faster and faster pace." With the numbers compounding, "the result is geometric expansion." We are continuing to borrow money to pay interest. He explained it this way: "How big would your debts be today if you'd been using credit cards to pay your mortgage for the last several decades?"

Therefore, "our debts are compounding at an accelerating pace because we lack the political ability to limit the federal government's spending" and our economy is not growing. Adding to our debt are "the $15 trillion shortfall in Social Security," "the $20 trillion unfunded prescription drug benefit," and "the $115 trillion unfunded Medicare liability." These debts "obviously will never be paid. In fact, the federal government's total obligations today – including all future obligations – is more than $1 million per taxpayer. And that's if you assume all 112 million taxpayers really count. (They don't. Only about 50 million people in the U.S. pay any substantial amount of federal income taxes.)"

At the federal level, "we are spending $2.4 trillion per year on transfer payments and interest on our national debt." That does not include anything else in government. But "we are only collecting $2.3 trillion a year in income, payroll, and corporate taxes." If we cut all government programs – "including the entire military budget – the federal revenue collected still wouldn't be enough to merely cover the costs of our direct transfer payments."

Add in "$1 trillion in credit card debt," "nearly $1 trillion in student loans," and total personal debt in America ($15.9 trillion) which is larger than all of the federal debt. "In total – adding up all of our debts, public and private – Americans owe close to $700,000 per family. It is not possible to finance our federal government's spending via taxes because the American people are broke."[73]

Politics is the art of looking for trouble, finding it, misdiagnosing it, and then misapplying the wrong remedies.

- Groucho Marx

The things that will destroy America today are prosperity at any price, peace at any price, safety first instead of duty first, and love of soft living and the get rich quick theory of life.
- Theodore Roosevelt

Notes

1. Quoted from *Reckless Endangerment* by Gretchen Morgenson and Joshua Rosner in George Will, "Americans pick up cost of clueless compassion," *Reno Gazette-Journal,* 11 July 2011, p. 5A.
2. Stephen A. Holmes, "Fannie Mae Eases Credit To Aid Mortgage Lending, *New York Times,* 30 September 1999.
3. David Brooks, "Who is James Johnson?" *The New York Times,* 17 June 2011, p. A35.
4. George Will, op. cit.
5. Dennis Cauchon, USA Today, "U.S. owes $61.6 trillion," *Reno Gazette-Journal,* 7 June 2011, p. 1B.
      According to World Net Daily, 11 April 2011, the true negative net worth of the US Government is $76.3 trillion (5 times 2010 GDP - $14.681 trillion). The world GDP is $61.936 trillion. The real 2010 Federal budget deficit is $5.3 trillion not $1.3 trillion reported by the CBO. That is because the CBO uses "cash basis" instead of Generally Accepted Accounting Principles, which includes unfunded liabilities, such as Social Security and Medicare.
      Doug Hornig, Casey's Daily Dispatch, 18 August 2010, Boston University economics professor Laurence Kotlikoff in an article published on Bloomberg.com, wrote, "Let's get real. The U.S. is bankrupt. Neither spending more nor taxing less will help the country pay its bills." Kotlikoff took a hard look at the Congressional Budget Office's Long Term Budget Outlook, released in June. "Based on the CBO's data," he wrote, "I calculate a fiscal gap of **$202 trillion**."
6. The author of this perspective had a second food for thought. "Let's say, you come home form work and find there has been a sewer backup in your neighborhood – and your home has sewage all the way up to your ceilings. What do you think you should do? Raise the ceilings, or pump out the ____?"
7. Chairman, along with Alan Simpson, of the National Commission on Fiscal Responsibility and Reform, *Time,* 13 December 2010, p.56.
8. "Cost of war at least $3.7 trillion and counting," Reuters, 29 June 2011, from "Costs of War," Brown University's Watson Institute for International Studies.
9. Michael Crowley, "The Sacred Cows," *Time,* 13 December 2010, pp. 55- 56.
10. Michael Crowley, "The Sacred Cows," *Time,* 13 December 2010, p. 56.
11. Sebastian Mallaby, "You Are What You Owe, Why power built on debt is no power at all," *Time,* 9 May 2011, p. 34.
12. Daily Wealth, 22 June 2011. Porter Stansberry, "China's Secret Plan to Take Over the World's Gold Market," Stansberry's Investment Advisory, January 2012.
13. Casey Research, 17 December 2010.
14. Ibid.
15. Rep. Ron Paul (R-Texas), Texas Straight Talk, 22 August 2005.
16. "Air Force One/Mike Penketh," picklyman.wordpress.com, 7 June 2010. "Political Hot Sheet," cbsnews.com, 20 January 2010.
17. Judicial Watch Verdict, Volume 16, Issue 12, December 2010.
18. Senators Tom Coburn and John McCain, "Summertime Blues: 100 Stimulus Projects that Give Taxpayers the Blues," 3 August 2010.
19. Doug Hornig, "Out of Control," Casey Research, 20 July 2010.
20. From Mike Huckabee, 10 September 2010. Public employees earn more in pay and benefits than private workers in 41 states – mostly due to rising value of benefits. In California, public employee compensation rose 28% above the inflation rate in 2008-2009. In Nevada the gap was 35% higher for government employees. Dennis Cauchon, "In Wis., public workers earn more," *Reno Gazette-Journal,* 1 March 2011, p. 1B.
21. http://www.usatoday.com/news/nation/2010003-04-federal-pay_N.htm.
22. Dennis Cauchon, USA Today, "More fed workers' pay tops $150K," *Reno Gazette-Journal,* 10 November 2010, p. 1C. Congressional salary is now $174,000.
23. http://transparentnevada.com/salaries/all.
24. Tom Burkhart, "Scam is common with firefighters," *Reno Gazette-Journal,* 17 March 2011, p. 6A.
25. For Washoe County, you have to go to page 8 of 29 to get under $100,000 and to page 7 of 15 for Reno.
26. Liz Sidoti, AP, "Govs to feds: Avoid causing states any more pain," *Reno Gazette-Journal,* 29 February 2011, p. 2B.
27. Dennis Cauchon, AO, "Federal retirement benefits soar," *Reno Gazette-Journal,* 29 September 2011, p. 1C.
28. Thomas Frank, USA TODAY, "S.C. governor targets lawmakers' pension rule," *Reno Gazette-Journal,* 30 September 2011, p. 1B.
29. Glenn Cook, "Coming soon: Pension apocalypse," *Las Vegas Review-Journal,* 27 November 2011.
30. Amanda Ripley, "Meet Your Government Workers," *Time,* 7 March 2011, p. 40.
31. Connie Hair, "Public Union: The 'Big Dog,'" Human Events, 25 October 2010.
32. Center for Responsive Politics, Washington, D.C.
33. Scott Bauer and Patrick Condon, AP, "Facts overshadowed in union debate," *Reno Gazette-Journal,* 27 February 2011, p. 2B.
34. http://www.usmessageboard.com/politics/156088-fdr-opposed-collective-bargaining-for-government-employees.html.
35. "Top 10 Labor Union Outrages," Human Events, 25 February 2011.
36. Ibid.
37. *Time,* 7 March 2011, p. 39.
38. The mainstream media did not show any photos of the communist demonstrators but Ringo's pictures was there and took photos (www,rubgospictures.com) and they were also displayed on http://pajamasmedia.com/zombie/2011/05/06/seiu-drops-mask-goes-full-commie/. The blue and gold signs and the black and white "LA Labor Supports Immigration Reform" signs are in the media photos.
39. Timothy P. Carney, "Obama's top funder also leads the nation in White House visits," *Washington Examiner,* 23 February 2011.
40. Fareed Zakaria, "Are America's Best Days Behind Us?" *Time,* 14 March 2011, p. 28.

41. David M. Walker, "The Debt, The Deficit, and America's Role in the World," an address at the Foreign Policy Research Institute, 12 August 2010.
42. Fareed Zakaria, "Are America's Best Days Behind Us?" *Time,* 14 March 2011, p. 28.
43. David M. Walker, "The Debt, The Deficit, and America's Role in the World," an address at the Foreign Policy Research Institute, 12 August 2010.
44. *Vanity Fair,* 1 October 2010, in Stansberry & Associates Digest, 8 September 2010. "If the law was enforced," the tax collector said, "every doctor in Greece would be in jail."
45. "The 2% Economy," *Time,* 13 June 2011, p. 20. She ended with, "Whatever happens, there's no changing the bigger trend line. The U.S. and the world are in the middle of an economic rebalancing that hasn't been seen since the rise of the great European empires in the 1500s. Power is shifting from West to East, technology is rejiggering the relationship between growth and jobs, and both trends are intersecting in ways that have undercut the upward trajectory of our economy."
46. Fareed Zakaria, "Are America's Best Days Behind Us?" *Time,* 14 March 2011, p. 32.
47. Joe Klein. "Head Start Doesn't Work," *Time,* 18 July 2011, p. 27.
48. Joe Klein, "America from the Road," *Time,* 18 October 2010, p. 36.
49. Rana Foroohar, "Whatever Happened to Upward Mobility?" *Time,* 14 November 2011, p. 30.
50. Joe Klein, "America from the Road," *Time,* 18 October 2010, p. 36.
51. Rana Foroohar, "The Great Wall Street Sucking Sound,*" Time,* 4 April 2011, p. 28. She had another article, "Driven off the Road by M.B.A.s, The rise of business schools coincided with the fall of American industry," *Time,* 18 July 2011, p. 22. She noted that the only time Apple had problems was when it put MBAs in charge, but as long as the college dropout, Steve Jobs, was running the company, it soared. She ended with "There are, and will be for the foreseeable future, a lot more bean counters than engineers in this country."
52. Rana Foroohar, "The Truth About the Poverty Crisis," *Time,* 26 September 2011, p. 24.
53. Rachel Beck, AP, "Average CEO pay: $9 million," *Reno Gazette-Journal,* 7 May 2011, p. 5A. "The Great Divide, CEO pay is rising again, outpacing the rest of us," *Time,* 16 May 2011. Pradnya Joshi, "We Knew They Got Raises. But This?" *The New York Times,* 3 July 2011, p. BU1.
54. "Nation | Thomas Hoenig, *Time,* 14 February 2011, p. 45.
55. "After Three Years and Trillions of Dollars, Our Banks Still Don't Work," *Time,* 26 September 2011, p. 42.
56. For a review of lobbyists, see Steven Brill, "On Sale: Your Government," *Time,* 12 July 2010, p. 28.
57. Quoted in Muth's Truths, 13 April 2011.
58. Porter Stansbury, Stansbury & Associates, 20 August 2010.
59. Adrian Rogers, 1931.
60. "Jimmy Carter" The Sequel," from Stephen Moore of Political Diary, quoted in Muth's Truths, 18 October 2011.
61. Porter Stansberry with Braden Copeland, "How America Became a Communist Nation," Daily Wealth, 16 December 2010. See also "10 Signs The U.S. is Becoming a Third World Country," Activist Post, 16 August 2010. "1. Rising unemployment and poverty:" – an example was "30,000 people showed up to apply for public housing in East Point, GA for 455 available vouchers." "2. Economic dependence:" - The IMF uses 90% debt to GDP as its "make-or-break point" where "economic growth slows so much that growth is no longer a viable solution for reducing that debt, and the IMF insists on austerity measures." [The US is at 99%.] "3. Declining civil rights." "4. Increased political corruption" – with Congress at a record-low 11% confidence level, "It seems obvious to all observers that big corporations directly control the agenda in Washington." "5. Military patrolling the streets." "6. Failing infrastructure." "7. Disappearing middle class" – "The income gap between the rich and poor has increased at a staggering pace." "8. Devalued currency" – the 96% decline since 1914. "9. Controlling the media." "10. Capital controls."
62. "Occupy Wall Street," 28 December 2011.
63. Churchill had another slightly different quote: "Socialism is a philosophy of failure, the creed of ignorance, and the gospel of envy, its inherent virtue is the equal sharing of misery."
64. Dinesh D'Souza, "How He Thinks, The root of Obama's big problem with business," *Forbes,* 27 September 2010. p. 85.
65. Fareed Zakaria, "Are America's Best Days Behind Us?" *Time,* 14 March 2011, p. 33.
66. Michael Crowley, "The Sacred Cows," *Time,* 13 December 2010, p. 57.
67. Stephen Ohlemacher, AP, "Social Security," *Reno Gazette-Journal,* 15 August 2010, p. 3B.
68. LTG James M. Dubik, "The Strategic Challenge of the Decade," *Army,* April 2011, p. 22.
69. Haas is the president of the Council on Foreign Relations, Viewpoint, "Bringing Our Foreign Policy Home," *Time,* 8 August 2011, p. 42.
70. Mark Thompson, "How to Save a Trillion Dollars," *Time,* 15 April 2011, p. 24.
71. At Joe's Cigar Bar, The Palm Beach Letter, 20 September 2011.
72. David M. Walker, "The Debt, The Deficit, and America's Role in the World," an address at the Foreign Policy Research Institute, 12 August 2010.
73. "Porter Stansberry: These facts show the 'End of America' is coming," From Porter Stansberry in the S&A Digest, The Daily Crux, 7 February 2012.

A government big enough to give you everything you want is strong enough to take everything you have.

- Thomas Jefferson

When you see that trading is done, not by consent, but by compulsion – when you see that in order to produce, you need to obtain permission from men who produce nothing – when you see money flowing to those who deal, not in goods, but in favors – when you see that men get richer by graft and pull than by work, and your laws don't protect you against them, but protect them against you – when you see corruption being rewarded and honesty becoming a self-sacrifice – you may know that your society is doomed.

- Ayn Rand, *Atlas Shrugged* (1957)

Giving money and power to government is like giving whiskey and car keys to teenage boys.

- P. J. O'Rourke

So what have we learned in two millennia?

The budget should be balanced, the Treasury should be refilled, public debt should be reduced, the arrogance of officialdom should be tempered and controlled, and the assistance to foreign lands should be curtailed lest Rome become bankrupt. People must again learn to work, instead of living on public assistance.

- Cicero, 55 BC

Evidently, nothing…

Chapter 10

Illegal Immigration –

Deamericanization of the USA

*If there was a way for people across the world
to walk into the USA as Mexicans do, there
would be fully 4 billion people coming our way.*

- Dr. Todd. D. Stong, Leola, PA.

*The lesson from the 1986 experience is that
such an amnesty did not solve the problem.*

Edwin Meese III, Reagan's Attorney General

*Civilizations die by suicide, not murder, and liberalism is the Ideology
of Western suicide. If immigration and border controls aren't
reintroduced, it will be the end of America as we know it – and soon.*

- Patrick J. Buchanan

In 400 years (brief in comparison to some of the world's great cultures), what is now the United States of America grew from open spaces where a number of Indian tribes and 20,000,000 buffalo roamed, to the only superpower in the world. From the earliest settlers to the millions of immigrants who followed, their objective was to live in this new land and build it as their new home. For most of those who made the treacherous journey across the seas to the New World, it was a one-way trip as they had no plans to return from whence they came. This was to be their new destiny and their goal was to become citizens of this new country.

They came from many lands, spoke many different languages, followed many different religions, were different colors, some were poor, some rich, had different political views – half-jokingly some said they came from the best prisons in Europe, but with a commitment to their new land. From this melting pot of people, a new nation was forged. The first generations spoke the old languages, of course, but the following generations learned American (there is a difference from English) and most importantly, they thought of themselves as Americans. That was the basis of the nation.

Our philosophy was expressed in Emma Lazarus' words on the Statue of Liberty: "Give me your tired, your poor, your huddled masses yearning to breathe free." There were about 60 million people in the US when the statue was dedicated over 100 years ago. Our frontier was still open and immigration was useful.

Now our population is over five times larger, the frontier is gone, and population growth adds to the pressures on our society, economy, and the environment. Since 1950 some 30 million people have immigrated legally; more recently the Congress authorized about 1 million annually. The number of illegals is unknown but is said to be 11 million but evidently exceeded 20 million.

The US accepted during the past 50 years many more immigrants than any other advanced country. In 2010, an all-time high was reached of 40 million foreign-born residents with 14 million added between 2000 and 2010. The Census Bureau does not know but estimates that 10-12 million of those 40 million are illegal aliens. Although the average growth was 28%, it was over 60% in 11 states: Alabama (92%), South Carolina (88%), Tennessee (82%), Arkansas (79%), and Kentucky (75%). 27% of Californians are foreign-born, followed by New York (22%), New Jersey (21%), Florida 19%), and Nevada (18.8%). Mexico was the source of the most immigrants, 12 million, followed by China, Hong Kong, and Taiwan, 2.16 million; India, 1.78 million; Philippines, 1.77 million; Viet-Nam, 1.24 million; and El Salvador, 1.21 million. Montana has 58% of its foreign-born as citizens; Hawaii, 57%; and Maine, 56.6%. Only 27.7% of immigrants in Alabama are citizens. As one analyst concluded: "Absent a change in policy, new immigration will likely continue at very high levels."[1]

The original ingredients of the melting pot were predominantly European, with a sprinkling of Chinese, and a heavy dose of Africans from our unfortunate slave history. The more recent additions included many more Asians, Hispanics, and blacks who came as immigrants. The country has always been diverse with the Irish, the Swedes, the Germans, the Chinese; but diversity seems to have become more pronounced with less commitment to the nation. Even though there was some tradition of lawlessness in our romanticized "wild west" history, the current levels of violence and crime along with racial discord have brought the pot to a boil.

Anchor Babies

Added to that rapid growth, we have the ultimate idiocy in "Anchor Babies." Any pregnant woman who manages to make it across our border in time to pop out her baby on US soil, that baby is an American citizen with full rights and entitlements. This comes from a weird interpretation of the 14th Amendment to the US Constitution which was approved in 1868 to guarantee citizenship to the slaves who were freed in the Civil War, not to the children of illegal immigrants. It states: "All persons born or naturalized in the United States and **subject to the jurisdiction thereof**, are citizens of the United States and of the State wherein they reside..." A woman rushing across the border, or visiting as a tourist, or here illegally is not subject to the jurisdiction of the US; she is still subject to the jurisdiction of Mexico or whatever home country from whence she came. These babies who are automatically citizens thus "anchor" their parents to the US. The significance is shown by the name, because that baby becomes an anchor in America to bring in mother, father, brothers, sisters, uncles, aunts, grandparents, nieces, nephews, ad infinitum.

> **"All persons born or naturalized in the United States and *subject to the jurisdiction thereof*, are citizens of the United States and of the State wherein they reside..."**
> **- 14th Amendment to US Constitution**

A smaller group is "birth tourism" or "drop and leave." That is the term for a pregnant woman who takes a trip to the US so that her baby can be born here. This is an organized business with agencies operating in China and setting up maternity houses in the US. Wealthy Chinese, some paid about $35,000, use these agencies to provide their children with access to

US education. There were houses in California and at an upscale hotel in New York serving this business.[2]

The US is alone in this folly; every other modern developed country has ended birthright citizenship. Canada held out until 2009. Australia stopped it in 2007, New Zealand in 2006, Ireland in 2005, France in 1993, India in 1987, England in 1983, and Portugal in 1981. Only the US thinks so little of its citizenship that it wantonly distributes it to the babies of foreign tourists and to foreigners who violate their visitor, work, or student visas to stay illegally in the US, plus those who sneak across our borders.[3]

Statistics are always difficult, but it seems that about one out of 12 (8%) of the births in the US are by illegal aliens (closer to one out of six in California and Texas). There have been 4 million anchor babies born in the US by 2009 with 340,000 born in 2008.[4] There is a cost since the hospital bills are almost always paid by US taxpayers and these immigrant mothers are rarely deported. Columnist Bryanna Bevens wrote "Illegal Immigrants: Equal Medical Care Or Better Medical Care?" when she was pregnant and going to Parkland Memorial Hospital in Dallas, Texas, famous for where John F. Kennedy died in 1963. Parkland had the second busiest maternity ward in the country with almost 16,000 new babies each year (almost 44 a day), and 70 percent were to illegal immigrants – that's 11,200 anchor babies every year just in Dallas. The illegals got everything for free while the US citizens had to pay. The illegals complained about the staff not speaking Spanish so a Spanish program was instituted for these illegal people! Los Angeles Hospital is the number one in deliveries with about the same numbers or higher of illegals. She stated that the public medical care system treats illegal immigrants better than US citizens.

Then there was the complaint that there were not enough interpreters (paid for by taxpayers) for the illegals.[5] According to the Journal of American Physicians and Surgeons (Spring 2005), 84 hospitals in California alone were closing due to the high costs imposed on them by the rising number of illegal immigrants. Hospitals were driven into bankruptcy and many closed their emergency rooms because they had become the main medical facilities for illegals. The Civil Rights Act of 1964 bans denying medical care on the basis of national origin. So if "an ambulance pulls up to the border-crossing point near Bisbee [Arizona] and announces 'compassionate entry,' the border patrol waves it through, and the Copper Queen [Hospital] is compelled to treat the patient."[6]

Senator Harry Reid, who now leads the Obama charge for amnesty was not always so supportive. "If making it easy to be an illegal alien is not enough, how about offering a reward for being an illegal immigrant? No sane country would do that, right? Guess again. If you break our laws by entering this country without permission and give birth to a child, we reward that child with U.S. citizenship and guarantee full access to all public and social services this society provides. And that is a lot of services. Is it any wonder that two-thirds of the babies born at taxpayer expense in county-run hospitals in Los Angeles are born to illegal alien mothers?" (20 September 1993). "I believe that one of the reasons we have a continuing problem with illegal immigration is because we have an entitlement system that offers incentives to enter the country unlawfully. Whether it is undermanned border security or lax enforcement of laws prohibiting the distribution of funds to illegal immigrants, there just seems to be too many incentives." (5 August 1994)[7]

> **If you break our laws by entering this country without permission and give birth to a child, we reward that child with U.S. citizenship and guarantee full access to all public and social services this society provides. And that is a lot of services.**
>
> **- Sen. Harry Reid (1993)**

In 1993 when Reid was "just" a senator, he called illegal immigrants "freeloaders and scam artists" and actually introduced a bill in Congress to end birthright citizenship. It was TITLE X – CITIZENSHIP 4 SEC. 1001. BASIS OF CITIZENSHIP CLARIFIED, in which he referred to the 14th Amendment and stated that any person born to a person not a citizen or lawful permanent resident was "not subject to the jurisdiction of the United States" and therefore not a citizen. He told the *Los Angeles Times* that his bill would "accelerate the deportation process for criminals and illegal entrants." However, within six years he found his new role in Democrat party leadership and claimed he "didn't understand the issue" in 1993 and joined the Democrats in their efforts to open the borders and grant full amnesty to illegal immigrants.[8] Now he is a full member of the Obama team.

The anchor babies plus those born to racial minorities, many of whom were illegal and then gained citizenship in earlier amnesties, are changing the complexion of the US. "White infants are on the verge of being displaced as the majority of newborns now that nearly half of babies in the USA are ethnic and racial minorities." Between censuses, the   number of states where minority babies dominate has doubled to 14 with big changes in New York, Florida, New Jersey, and Georgia. "Minorities have been the majority in Texas and California nurseries for more than two decades.[9]

Study of the legal history of the 14th Amendment indicates that the authors clearly did not intend that everyone born here is a citizen. It is not required by the Constitution and would not require an amendment, as even Harry Reid noted. Experienced constitutional scholars have concluded that birthright citizenship could be eliminated by simply passing a Congressional Resolution.

Lack of Assimilation

The people who built this country learned the language and became "Americans." It is not clear that that is true for many of the newcomers, particularly the millions of Mexicans. There are many of Mexican heritage who have joined the nation and are and consider themselves Americans. But there are millions more who are here only for the benefits due to the poor conditions in Mexico and still consider themselves Mexicans, not Americans.

We have Spanish radio and TV stations, newspapers, magazines, books, and signs in many places and we have to "Press One" for English. Unfortunately, we have permitted the creation of an entire subculture in the US which watches Spanish TV, listens to Spanish radio, reads Spanish publications, and can even deal with the US Government in Spanish. There are lesser subcultures of Chinese, Vietnamese, Korean, and Japanese. The question is: Are they Americans?

Our ancestors, who gave up everything, cut their ties, and made a one-way trip across an ocean, made a commitment to become Americans. They had the desire and the community around them helped them to assimilate. Now we have people who go back and forth across the Mexican border like they were going to the mall. Most of them have no interest in or intention of becoming Americans.[10] Some keep coming back even if deported due to strong ties they have developed in the US.

As we will see with Eurabia, large unassimilated subcultures become a major threat to the survival of a society. "Guest Worker" programs can be a disaster in that, by definition, the "guests" are supposed to return home. In the meantime, the host country may be subsidizing another country, often for its inefficiency and corruption. Then if the "guests" don't go home, the host country is stuck with another unassimilated subculture.

> In the first place, we should insist that if the immigrant who comes here in good faith becomes an American and assimilates himself to us, he shall be treated on an exact equality with everyone else, for it is an outrage to discriminate against any such man because of creed, or birthplace, or origin. But this is predicated upon the person's becoming in every facet an American, and nothing but an American... There can be no divided allegiance here. Any man who says he is an American, but something else also, isn't an American at all. We have room for but one flag, the American flag...We have room for but one language here, and that is the English language, and we have room for but one sole loyalty and that is loyalty to the American people.
>
> **- Theodore Roosevelt 1907**

The encouragement of the use of any language other than English (American) is the gravest disservice we do to anyone who seriously desires to become an American. The do-gooders who are pushing such use are destroying the future of those people and hastening the decline of the US.[11] If a person wishes to have a real future in the US, that person will be severely handicapped if unable to speak English. If we create a country where one can grow up, go to school, and work all in a foreign language, then we will destroy the US, which will not last through the century.

There have been repeated efforts to declare English the national language but the Congress, as usual, has dithered and the government does not help. Democratic Senate leader Harry Reid thought it was racist. Thomas Perez, Assistant Attorney General for the Civil Rights Division of the Department of Justice is a staunch opponent of official English and a former executive of the radical CASA de Maryland. Perez, with the backing of anti-assimilation groups, demands that states provide court interpreters for non-English speakers, regardless of their legal status, at no cost to the individual, in every type of court proceeding, and every court function. But English is the national and common language. Anyone voting should be voting in English; they need to join the civic culture.[12] Ballots in other languages were mandated in 1992, but they "are incompatible with the American tradition of 'E Pluribus Unum.' A multitude of proud ethnic identities make up this country's vibrant cultural mosaic, but superseding them is a shared American identity indispensable to full-fledged citizenship. A crucial element of that identity is proficiency in English – an element we undercut when we provide foreign-language ballots to citizens who don't share the common tongue."[13]

> You've got to turn off the Spanish television set. It's that simple. You've got to learn English.
>
> **- California Governor Arnold Schwarzenegger**

The states pay tens of millions of dollars to print ballots in foreign languages and about 90 percent of the states give driver's license exams in foreign languages. In California, over 42 percent do not speak English at home (61 percent in Los Angeles – 85 percent in Santa Ana with 75 percent Spanish) – in Miami, 80 percent do not speak English at home, 70 percent Spanish. There are eight US metropolitan areas that have at least 1 million immigrants (Washington, DC, New York, Los Angeles, Miami, Chicago, San Francisco, Houston, and Dallas). The Chicago *Tribune* reported that, "With the influx of Spanish-language radio stations, cable channels and newspapers, marketers see a huge opportunity to tap into the fastest-growing segment of the population and one that accounts for virtually all of the area's population gains."[14]

"You've got to turn off the Spanish television set. It's that simple. You've got to learn English."[15] Governor Schwarzenegger had it right. **If we do not get rid of all the foreign language media, there will be no USA in just a few decades.**

We will address "Reconquista" below, but it is clear where the allegiance of very large numbers of Mexicans in the US really rests. When brats in high schools in California hoist the Mexican flag above an upside down US flag on the school's flag pole, it is time to take them to the border and kick them across. We had large protest marches with Mexican flags and repeated statements that they will take over.[16]

Miss USA was booed at the Miss Universe pageant in Mexico City in 2007; the US soccer team was booed in Mexico in 2004 and 2005 and the crowd booed the Star Spangled Banner and shouted "Osama! Osama!"[17] The US and Mexican soccer teams met in the Los Angeles Coliseum on 15 February 1998. The crowd was overwhelmingly pro-Mexican even though most lived in this country. They booed during the National Anthem and held US flags upside down. As the match progressed, US supporters were insulted, pelted with projectiles, punched, and spat upon. Beer and trash were thrown at the US players before and during the match. We do not have a friendly rivalry; we have antagonism. This happened again on 25 June 2011 as the US and Mexico met for World Cup soccer and there was the same disrespect for the Star Bangled Banner and the US team. It would appear we have too many Mexicans in Los Angeles who are not Americans. Many think they have some special right to be here and yet remain Mexican (see this note).[18]

Reconquista

Mention 1848 or the Mexican War to most Americans and you will get no reaction; they will not know what you are talking about. But every Mexican schoolboy "knows" that 1848 was when the "gringos" stole their land by annexing Texas, California, and New Mexico after the 1846 War and the Mexican government has kept this bitterness alive through constant reminders starting in every school.

First, a little background: on 13 May 1846, the US Congress overwhelmingly voted in favor of President James K. Polk's request to declare war on Mexico in a dispute over Texas. The US, under threat of war, had refrained from annexing Texas after the latter won independence from Mexico in 1836. But in 1844, President John Tyler restarted negotiations with the Republic of Texas, culminating with a Treaty of Annexation.

The treaty was defeated by a wide margin in the Senate because it would have upset the slave/free state balance between North and South and risked war with Mexico, which had broken off relations with the US. But shortly before leaving office and with the support of President-elect Polk, Tyler managed to get a joint resolution passed on 1 March 1845. Texas was admitted to the union on 29 December.

Mexico did not follow through with its threat to declare war, but relations between the two nations were tense over non-payment of debts and border disputes, and in July 1845, Polk ordered troops into disputed lands between the Neuces and Rio Grande Rivers. In November, Polk sent the diplomat John Slidell to Mexico to seek boundary adjustments in return for the US government's settlement of the claims of US citizens against Mexico and also to make an offer to purchase California and New Mexico. After the mission failed, the US Army under Gen. Zachary Taylor advanced to the mouth of the Rio Grande, the river that the state of Texas claimed as its southern boundary.

Mexico claimed the boundary was the Neuces River to the northeast of the Rio Grande and considered Taylor's advance an act of aggression and in April 1846 sent troops across the

Rio Grande. Polk, in turn, declared the Mexican advance an invasion of US soil and on 11 May 1846 asked Congress to declare war on Mexico, which it did two days later.

After nearly two years of fighting, peace was established by the Treaty of Guadalupe Hildalgo, signed on 2 February 1848. The Rio Grande was set as the southern boundary of Texas and California and New Mexico were ceded to the US. In return, the US paid Mexico $15 million and agreed to settle all claims of US citizens against Mexico. By the Gadsden Purchase of 30 December 1853, the US paid Mexico $10 million for a boundary adjustment for 30,000 square miles of the Gila River valley for construction of a railroad to the west by a southern route.

Naturally, the loser's memory tends to be much longer than the winner's. Thus the US expansion to the west was seen in Mexico as Yanqui imperialism and has never been forgotten. Relations have never been great; the Europeans invaded Mexico while the US was preoccupied with the Civil War and set up Maximilian as emperor for a brief time. According to the famous Zimmerman telegram, the Germans offered to help Mexico regain its "lost territories."

> **There are maps of *Aztlan* which covers the area north of Texas along the Rockies to the State of Washington as part of Mexico, that are taught in Mexico and in "Hispanic studies" programs in US schools.**

The goal of the *Reconquista* (Reconquest) movement is to "reconquer" those "lost" or "stolen" territories from the US returning them to Mexico for "La Raza" – the indigenous race of Mexico. With millions of illegal Mexican immigrants flooding into the US still swearing allegiance to Mexico, the Reconquista movement believes that eventually the large numbers will let them take political control of communities where there is a Hispanic majority. They hope to gain control of one or more of the southwestern states; then they could secede from the US and join Mexico.

This is not some joke; it is deadly serious. There are maps of *Aztlan* which cover the area north of Texas along the Rockies to the State of Washington as part of Mexico, that are taught in Mexico and in "Hispanic studies" programs in US schools. This is very much a Trojan Horse invasion. Taking advantage of American generosity while mocking us, illegal immigrants are to become citizens so they will be able to vote to return large areas of the southwest to Mexico.

> **We have got to eliminate the gringo, and what I mean by that is if the worst comes to the worst, we have got to kill him.**
>
> **We have an aging white America. They are not making babies. They are dying. The explosion is in our population... I love it. They are shitting in their pants with fear. I love it.**
>
> **- Professor Jose Angel Gutierrez, University of Texas, Arlington[19]**

These quotes below are not isolated; there are many and you probably saw some of the banners during the demonstrations in 2006 and even more recently such as in 2011.

Todos los Europeos son Illegals desde 1492 (All Europeans Illegal since 1492)
- Handwritten sign carried by a street demonstrator, New York City, *La Marcha,* 10 April 2006

Go back to Germany where you belong! Stay in Germany! Get out of here! This is Mexico! This is our land! Get out of here, racist pigs! *Viva* Saddam Hussein! *Viva* Cuba!
                          - Videotape of day labor site in Rancho Cucamonga, 7 January 2006

If you think I'm 'illegal' because I'm a Mexican, learn the true history, because I am in my Homeland.[20]

We are Indigenous! The ONLY owners of this continent.
                          - Banners and placards in protests plus waving Mexican flags and images of Che Guevara.[21]

This land belongs to God and not to the United States
                          - Gilbert Cortez, President of Casa Latina Centro de Informacion[22]

Go back to Boston! Go back to Plymouth Rock. Pilgrims! Get out! We are the future. You are old and tired. Go on. We have beaten you. Leave like beaten rats. You old white people. It is your duty to die... Through love of having children, we are going to take over.
                          - Augustin Cebada, Brown Berets

They're afraid we're going to take over the governmental institutions and other institutions. They're right. We will take them over. We are here to stay.
                          - Richard Alatorre, Los Angeles City Council

The American Southwest seems to be slowly returning to the jurisdiction of Mexico without firing a single shot.
                          - Excelsior, the national newspaper of Mexico

Remember 187-proposition to deny taxpayer funds for services to non-citizens was the last gasp of white America in California.
                          - Art Torres, Chairman of the California Democratic Party

We are politicizing every single one of these new citizens that are becoming citizens of this country... I gotta tell you that a lot of people are saying, "I'm going to go out there and vote because I want to pay them back."
                          - Gloria Molina, Los Angeles County Supervisor

California is going to be a Hispanic state. Anyone who doesn't like it should leave.
                          -Mario Obledo, California Coalition of Hispanic Organizations and
                          California State Secretary of Health, Education and Welfare
                          under Governor Jerry Brown (1st term), also awarded the
                          Presidential Medal of Freedom by President Bill Clinton

We are practicing "La Reconquista" in California.
                          - Jose Pescador Osuna, Mexican Consul General

We need to avoid a white backlash by using codes understood by Latinos.
                          - Professor Fernando Guerra, Loyola Marymount University

        You might have noticed some similarity with quotes by Muslims in London and Jews in Palestine. There is an Aztlan video at www.immigrationwatchdog.com which, in addition to showing Jose Gutierrez and others spouting their Reconquista line, shows Joe Baca, a California State Senator, saying "we" have to increase our numbers, we are in a civil war, and referring to Paul Revere crying out "The Latinos are coming! The Latinos are coming!"

> **Mexico does not end at its borders…. Where there is a Mexican, there is Mexico.**
> **- Mexican President Felipe Calderon**[23]

The "Mexica Movement" identifies with the ancient Aztec roots and stresses that current US citizens are colonialists and European imperialists who stole the land from the Mexican races going back untold centuries. Some of the rhetoric from their website: www.mexica-movement.org follows:

> Mexica Movement is a *Nican Tlaca* (Indigenous) rights and educational organization for the people of Mexican, "Central American," "Native American," and First Nation descend [sic] of *Anahuac,* in what is now called "North America." Occupied *Anahuac* includes the colonial nations of Canada, U.S., Mexico (also controlled by Europeans), and "Central America" (down to include "Costa Rica," which are also controlled by Europeans). North America is the geographical area of the culture of *Anahuac,* which is the culture of corn, which brought about our civilization. We, the *Nican Tlaca* people of *Anahuac,* are one people. We are one race. We have origins in one culture. We include all Full-bloods and Mixed-bloods as *Nican Tlaca.* We include ourselves with all similar movements in the Western Hemisphere (including those now starting in "South America."[24]

Note the stress on race, but one must not use the term racist. Photos from their website also show demonstrators on 25 March 2006 with signs claiming ownership of this continent and depicting Gov. Arnold Schwarzenegger and Rep. James Sensenbrenner in Nazi uniforms.[25]

Maps of Aztlan, the mythical place of origin for the Aztecs, usually include Texas, New Mexico, Arizona, and California. Another radical organization with the goal of liberating those states is the *Moviemento Estudiantil Chicano de Aztlán,* (Chicano Student Movement of Aztlan), abbreviated as **MEChA**. "The symbol of MEChA is a black eagle against a red background. The eagle holds in its right claw a weapon similar to a machete, and in its left hand a stick of dynamite. In the beak of the eagle is the lighted fuse needed to blast the dynamite." The MEChA constitution is quite clear:

> The Chicano and Chicana students of Aztlán must take upon themselves the responsibilities to promote Chicanismo within the community, politicizing our Raza with an emphasis on indigenous consciousness to continue the struggle for the self-determination of the Chicano people for the purpose of liberating *Aztlán.*

That would normally be called sedition and any acts would be treason.

MEChA has already crossed that legal border by starting a race war by claiming responsibility for starting wildfires in California to burn white people out. This was confirmed by Governor Schwarzenegger after officials received a letter with photos of individuals throwing Molotov cocktails into dry brush. Included was a rambling manifesto justifying the act of arson because "Aztlán belongs to indigenous people, the Chicanas and Chicanos of Aztlán. We are sovereign and not subject to a foreign culture."[26] [Sen. John McCain was criticized for saying there was "substantial evidence" that illegal immigrants were responsible for the enormous fires that raged in eastern Arizona "because they wanted to signal others" and "they wanted to divert law enforcement agencies."[27]]

MEChA is a version of Marxism with a racist tilt that fits in with the radical leftists who want to destroy the US. This radical organization has some 300 chapters in high schools and colleges in the US (see Azteca.net). We have been and are invaded! It should be banned.[28]

Another group which works against US interests is the National Council of La Raza, a

Latino supremacist group, which advocates open borders and amnesty for illegal immigrants. La Raza denounced a proposal to cut WIC, the welfare program of women and children, saying "Latinos make up two-fifths (42 percent) of all program participants....nearly nine out of ten Latino infants born in the United States participated in WIC in 2008." La Raza did not mention how many of those were illegal or "how illegal immigration worsens the condition of poor Latino citizens with added job competition and lower wages."[29] According to its tax returns for 2006-2008, it received grants from the US government of $11,948,205. The president and CEO, Janet Murguia, was paid $378,446 and they spent $550,787 lobbying legislative bodies and $250,000 for grassroots nontaxable lobbying. It appears that the US government pays La Raza to lobby the US government for money.[30]

The massive protest demonstrations of 25 March and 10 April 2006 required elaborate planning and coordination. There is an extensive and well-funded lobby that is fighting for illegal immigrants to gain citizenship. There were some 150 groups working on this radical left effort.[31] There was a good side to the protest marches. According to the Los Angeles County Sheriff, during the March 2006 march, LA had reductions of 82% in auto theft, 28% in murders/violent crimes/rapes, 73% in vandalism/tagging, 54% in drug related offenses (not including the area surrounding the march), 31% in domestic violence cases, 64% in misdemeanor cases (shop lifting, etc.), and CHP reported a record low in the least amount of traffic accidents on South California freeways.

And with the house ablaze, the Senate will debate the installation of smoke detectors – Our guests have become our conquerors.

- Bob Lonsberry[32]

The protestors got a little too much notice, particularly the high school kids with their Mexican flag above the upside down US flag, and were projecting the wrong image. "After all, the plan of the radical left is to launch an invasion that would only become obvious to Middle America when it was too late. The plan would fail if the American public saw too clearly the invading army instead of the cheap labor gift horse in which they were hidden. So, into the backpacks went the Mexican flags, replaced by the American flags that the protest organizers brought with them."[33] **WAKE UP AMERICA!**

Amnesty

As we noted, immigration was not a major problem up through 1964, but another part of Lyndon Johnson's legacy is the immigration act of 1965 pioneered by Teddy Kennedy. That changed the emphasis of our immigration from Europe to other parts of the world, particularly Hispanic.[34] The US was about 90 percent white with a Hispanic population growing to only about 4 percent by 1970. Then the Congress gave us the disastrous Immigration Reform and Control Act of 1986 which President Reagan reluctantly signed with strong restrictions because it included amnesty. That law gave us the 20 or 30 million illegal immigrants we have now.

Edwin Meese III, Reagan's Attorney General, wrote in a letter from the Heritage Foundation, "In exchange for amnesty, he [Reagan] required that border security and enforcement of immigration laws be greatly strengthened, particularly through sanctions against employers who hired illegal immigrants. And a path to citizenship was provided with certain conditions: immigrants had to pay application fees, learn to speak English, understand American civics, pass a medical exam and register for military selective services. Those with convictions for a felony or three misdemeanors were ineligible." Meese added, referring to the proposed amnesty bill in 2006, "Remarkable! These provisions are almost exactly what amnesty supporters are proposing today, except that they're usually afraid to use the word 'amnesty' so they call it something else." Meese stressed "**we cannot afford to repeat our mistake.**"

> **All these people say they are coming for the amnesty program. [They] have been told if they get 10 miles off the border, they are home free.**
>
> **- George Morin, Arizona rancher**[35]

Meese also wrote, "The lesson from the 1986 experience is that such an amnesty did not solve the problem. There was extensive document fraud and the number of people applying for amnesty far exceeded projections. And there was a failure of political will to enforce new laws against employers. After a brief slowdown, illegal immigration returned to high levels and continued unabated, forming the nucleus of today's large population of illegal aliens."[36] The law served as an enormous magnet attracting millions to cross our border such that the Hispanic population was about 14 percent by 2000 and growing rapidly. The worst part of it was the connivance of vote hungry politicians and their valueless business supporters to totally ignore the law. Even some cities declared themselves "sanctuaries" prohibiting police from arresting anyone solely on the basis of immigration status – examples were Takoma Park, MD, Houston, Los Angeles, San Francisco, Denver, Chicago, Salt Lake City, Arcata CA, and the entire state of Maine.[37]

Adequate laws were already on the books; it was the US government which refused to use them. Prosecutions against employers using illegal workers dropped to almost zero. Illegals who were caught were either sent back or told to report to the courthouse for a hearing and set free! Who would ever show up? The IRS and the Social Security Administration did not talk to each other about ridiculously obvious violations, such as seeing the same Social Security number thousands of times. "The potential crimes are so obvious that the failure to provide such information to investigators raises questions about Washington's determination to end the widespread hiring of illegal immigrants at cut-rate pay." One company "submitted 4,100 duplicate Social Security numbers for workers." The numbers of 2,000 children were being used and "One child's Social Security number was used 742 times by workers in 42 states."[38] This became really ridiculous when 2 illegal immigrants were given an Arizona ranch after a suit by do-gooder lawyers.[39]

This was a sad testimony for a country that supposedly was based on the rule of law. This sanctuary stupidity can be costly: San Francisco protected a MS-13 repeat offender who later killed a father and his two sons in their car. It does not require much effort: just a little border crackdown significantly reduced illegal crossings.[40]

In 2006, Bush and the Congress tried to foist another amnesty bill on the American people. Once again Bush and the US Congress were out of step with the citizens since fully 81 percent said illegal immigration was "out of control."[41] That did not deter Bush and Teddy Kennedy and the liberal crowd. Bush shifted to "comprehensive" immigration reform as his code word for amnesty after his buddy President Vincente Fox called Bush to complain about his deployment of the National Guard to the border. Just to show that they are in charge in this country, Fox's Foreign Secretary Luis Ernesto Derbez immediately threatened the US with, "If we see National Guard troops starting to directly participate in detaining people,… we would immediately start filing lawsuits through our consulates." (There were an unbelievable 56 Mexican consulates in US cities.) Then Fox issued his own threat, "President Bush knows it and knows it well – President Fox and Mexicans will neither accept more humiliations, nor more abuses of human rights and workers rights."[42]

> **Through family reunification and what demographers call 'chain migration,' every legalized immigrant eventually brings with him three to five of his own immediate family, who in turn bring more relatives.**

It was clear that any talk of amnesty fueled additional illegal immigration. After Bush announced his guest worker program, US Customs and Border Protection officials were ordered not to discuss any surge in apprehension of illegal immigrants trying to enter the US. "Do not talk about amnesty, increase in apprehensions, or give comparisons of past immigration reform proposals," according to the public affairs guidance from Customs and Border Protection, "White House Approved Talking Points Temporary Worker Program."[43] A Mexican official stated that more people would probably try to get into the US in the hope that they could benefit from any amnesty program.[44] The numbers kept increasing and there was little threat if caught since 98 percent who crossed the border illegally were never prosecuted. They were just escorted back to Mexico. Over 1 million were being arrested but another 2 or 3 or more likely 4 million were not caught.[45]

> **Thought for the Day: Calling an illegal alien an "undocumented immigrant" is like calling a drug dealer an "unlicensed pharmacist."**

There were many things wrong with the proposed legislation. Sen. Jim DeMint (R-SC) listed ten: (1) it rewarded illegal behavior with a path to citizenship and voting (while law-abiding people wait for years to enter legally), (2) the temporary worker program was neither temporary nor work-based and would permit millions to obtain green cards, (3) instead of the current level of 19 million immigrants over 20 years, it would permit 66 million over 20 years, (4) insufficient border security by not requiring the border security part to be implemented before a guest worker program could start, (5) it left a terrorist loophole that would disarm law enforcement, (6) it permitted social security benefits for illegal work, (7) it would cost the federal government $50 billion a year and the states would have to foot the health care and education costs, (8) it would hurt small business because it dictated "prevailing wage" which was often higher than that paid to citizens, (9) it gave immigrant workers greater job protection than US workers, and (10) it was quite weak in assimilation and English requirements.[46]

Sen. Jeff Sessions (R-AL) released a statement on 15 May 2006 stating that the Senate bill "would permit up to 217 million new legal immigrants into the United States over the next 20 years, a number equal to 66 percent of the total current population of the United States." Sessions referred to a study by Dr. Robert Rector of the Heritage Foundation who came up with a similar number of about 200 million.[47]

They tried again in 2007 and in some ways it was even worse. It was drafted in secret and no hearings were held; it was a complete "package," and anyone who opposed it was a "bigot or not interested in doing what was right for America (Bush).[48] Title VI of the Senate's Secure Borders, Economic Opportunity and Immigration Reform Act of 2007 had a great title, "Non-immigrants in the United States Previously in Unlawful Status." That takes a sense of humor! They would create a new "Z" visa exclusively for illegal aliens making them legal – no amnesty of course! – and bestow massive benefits on people who intentionally broke US laws. The Z visa would not be temporary because it could be renewed every four years forever. The bill allowed the government only one day for a background check to determine if applicants were criminals or terrorists and also provided amnesty for the 636,000 absconders who had been deported but defied the law. It even provided amnesty for gang members, tuition subsidies, and taxpayer funded lawyers for illegal aliens. Of course, it granted amnesty before the law enforcement goals needed to be met.[49]

"The belief that all 12 million illegal immigrants will show up at a federal courthouse to sign up for a special visa and pay a fine is silly.... Does anyone really believe that immigrants will work here for two years, go home for a year, return for two years and then go home again as the legislation proposes? Only someone inside the 17 square miles of logic free environment called Washington D.C. could seriously believe that is a solution."[50]

"Of all the people in the world who wish to come to America, why should we feel compelled to grant citizenship to a group whose sole qualification is that they broke our laws?" President Bush ceaselessly protested that the Senate bill was not amnesty. "In a certain sense, he is right: The bill goes way beyond amnesty. The root of the word 'amnesty' is to forget. In a normal amnesty the crime is 'forgotten' and penalties are waived. S. 1348 goes far beyond waiving penalties for all those who broke U.S. immigration laws; it rewards them with access to government benefits and citizenship."[51]

> There is yet another lesson of the amnesty phenomenon in Europe that is of key relevance to our own immigration debate, even if it's seldom discussed. Figures usually bandied about in amnesty discussions are highly misleading; in practice, legalizing one illegal alien means eventually providing legal entry documents to several times as many. Through family reunification and what demographers call 'chain migration,' every legalized immigrant in Europe eventually brings with him three to five of his own immediate family, who in turn bring more relatives. Throw in arranged and fictitious marriages and the migration chain becomes very long indeed. The vast majority of the 1.7 million immigrants who entered the European Union legally last year were just such chain migrants. In the United States itself, chain migration already makes up close to 70 percent of all legal immigration.
>
> Keep that in mind when politicians tell you that what's needed is just one more amnesty of ten million illegal aliens. At the very least, the American people deserve to know that the real figure is anywhere between 30 and 50 million.[52]

Stanley Crouch urged the legislators to limit the burden of the taxes the bill would incur. Referring to the cheap Mexican labor for Republican employers, he wrote, "Republicans have largely ignored the monumental cost of sudden citizenship... Democrats, meanwhile, apparently are ignoring the cost to the taxpayer because the cause seems like a good liberal one, so damn the taxes, full speed ahead. That is why elephants and donkeys are looking for a large-enough dunce cap to fit both parties. Give us a break!"[53] Fred Thompson put it bluntly, "No matter how much lipstick Washington tries to slap onto this legislative pig, it's not going to win any beauty contests."[54] The public outrage was able to stop the 2006 and 2007 efforts, but as we know when Obama and politicians smell a vote or pork, nothing can deter them.

Amnesty: It rewards illegal behavior, it shows contempt for the rule of law, and it is a slap in the face to the thousands of people around the world who line up, fill out the paperwork, and play by the rules to enter America legally.

Since the Obama Administration was unable to get amnesty through the Congress, they tried new tactics. Rep. Howard Berman (D-CA) reintroduced the DREAM Act, sponsored by Majority Whip Sen. Dick Durbin (D-IL) which would give "legal status to those under age 35 who arrived in the United States before age 16, provided they complete two years of college or ue two years in the military." Some 300 of these illegals were present at Durbin's hearing in

296   Death by a Thousand Cuts

serve two years in the military." Some 300 of these illegals were present at Durbin's hearing in addition to Homeland Security Secretary Janet Napolitano. Bob Dane, spokesman for the Federation for American Immigration Reform, denounced the presence of Napolitano as "ignoring the rule of law" and he called the bill "a massive amnesty bill designed as an education initiative."[55] The Congressional pro-amnesty supporters hoped to ram it through by holding the E-Verify bill hostage. E-Verify, The Legal Workforce Act, would require businesses to verify that employees are in our country legally.[56]

The American public has constantly been against the DREAM Act and amnesty, so the Obama Administration developed a way to bypass Congress and grant backdoor amnesty by administrative measures. Memoranda were prepared in Homeland Security including one, "Administrative Alternatives to Comprehensive Immigration Reform." The Memorandum to Alejandro N. Mayorkas, Director, included various ways by "issuing new guidance and regulations" and other actions to circumvent the laws.[57]

"The *Houston Chronicle* reported that the government is routinely dismissing cases against illegal aliens and permitting them to stay in the United States!" *The Washington Post* reported on the Obama Administration's "non-enforcement" of immigration law and that there was revolt in the Immigration and Customs Enforcement staff where its union voted "no confidence" for the agency's director and assistant director.[58]

> **The American public has constantly been against the DREAM Act and amnesty, so the Obama Administration developed a way to bypass Congress and grant backdoor amnesty by administrative measures.**

The Obama administration hired a supporter of sanctuary cities as coordinator of state and local activities for U.S. Immigration and Customs Enforcement (ICE). His support for cities that refuse to enforce immigration laws puts him in direct opposition to the agency's mission, and is a clear signal that his agency does not intend to enforce the law."

The Director of ICE, an Obama appointee, sent a memo declaring that the agency would essentially ignore "non-violent' illegal immigrant criminals and focus on certain violent criminals.

And then a second memo from the Director announced that thousands of pending deportations will be dismissed because the defendants don't face serious charges. (He obviously doesn't consider violating our immigration laws a serious charge.)[59]

Cecilia Munoz, director of intergovernmental affairs at the White House, was named head of the Domestic Policy Council, which would include immigration policy. Despite Obama's claim that he would have no lobbyists in his administration, Munoz spent 20 years as the chief registered lobbyist for the National Council of La Raza ("The Race'). She provided support for illegal aliens, pushed for the DREAM ACT, and advised the Mexican government on how to lobby for amnesty. Mexico's Institute for Mexicans Residing Abroad gave her their "Ohtli Prize" for her service to Mexico! La Raza received $1.4 million in federal subsidies in 2009, increased to $11 million in 2010, much from the Obama stimulus package. She worked with banks to water down mortgage standards. Democrats earmarked $1 million for "community development" projects and the US Department of Health and Human Services provided $25,000 to co-sponsor La Raza's annual conference in 2010. There are nearly 100 lobbyists, ex-lobbyists on the Obama payroll. Business as usual!

Arizona, which is on the frontlines of border crossings, passed a strong anti-illegal immigration law, but Washington sued Arizona in a critical test of states' rights, particularly since the federal government refuses to enforce the laws on the books. [The Administration was also having the law "reviewed" by the United Nations Human Rights Council (whose members include Cuba and China)!]   Alabama passed an even tougher law and a federal judge refused to block key parts of it.   It was certain to be appealed.[60]

Even talk of "amnesty" acts a magnet for ever more illegal immigration, causing yet more financial stress on already-strained state and local budgets. Amnesty is a touchy political issue with the public strongly against it but the politicians fighting for it for potential voters and business looking for cheap labor.

Greed – Politicians and Businesses

The line spouted by the vote-hungry politicians and Barack Obama is that these illegal immigrants are "doing jobs American won't do." As Thomas Sowell clearly pointed out, "There are no such jobs." This is the supreme **fraud** put out by people who want to pay people less, including Sen. Dianne Feinstein trying to sneak an amendment into the War Supplement Act to provide legal status for 1.35 million illegal aliens working in agriculture (in California no doubt!).   But in agriculture, which has the highest representation of illegal immigrants, "they are just 24 percent of the workers. Where did the other 76 percent come from, if these are jobs that Americans won't do?"[61] It is not jobs Americans won't do but jobs that Americans won't do at substandard wages with no benefits.

> **None of the rhetoric and sophistry that we hear about immigration deals with this plain and ugly reality: Politicians are afraid of losing the Hispanic vote and businesses want cheap labor.**
>
> **- Thomas Sowell[62]**

The authors of a recent book labeled this exploitation of foreign workers as the "21st Century slave trade," since it "involves an organized effort to bring into the United States an underclass of uneducated, impoverished illegal immigrants who will work for below-market wages for companies that plan to commit employment tax fraud and violations of labor and immigrations laws." We should add, with quiet government consent since they do not enforce the laws already on the books.   These slave traders cannot actually go to Mexico or other countries to capture workers in chains, but they still call it slave trade "because the practice of brokering workers into these jobs involves a determination to exploit them."

They claim the president's [Bush] core assumption is false, "that there is no job an American won't do. Moreover, there is no job classification in which foreign-born workers are the majority."   Going through the three job areas which have the most immigrants, they showed that there is substantial native-born unemployment in each.   Farming, fishing, and forestry: immigrants hold 44.7 percent of the jobs; the native unemployment rate is 12.8 percent.   Construction and extraction: immigrants hold 26.1 percent of the jobs; the unemployment rate is 11.3 percent. Building cleaning and maintenance: immigrants hold 34.8 percent of the jobs; the unemployment rate is 10.5 percent. [The book dates from about 2006 so the unemployment figures are likely much higher after the 2008 crash.]

A Bear Stearns report on the "underground labor force" noted that the labor market was being undercut by hiring illegal aliens at below-market wages. "This large infusion of the imported labor supply has reduced average annual earnings by approximately 4 to 6 percent." The report also expressed concern about the enormous social costs as well as lost tax revenues from jobs that are off the books due to the great influx of impoverished, poorly educated immigrants. This squeezes low-skilled US workers at increased social cost to US taxpayers.

The US has had "guest worker" programs before, The Bracero program brought in Mexican farm workers from 1917 to 1921 and again in 1942 during World War II until 1964. The same argument was used then. "In reality, what the farmers wanted was immigrant Mexicans who would work at wages so low that Americans wouldn't accept the jobs." This special treatment "will produce farm labor problems today and urban poverty tomorrow." There was a major impact in that "U.S. farm jobs have played an important role in moving about 10 percent of the persons born in Mexico to the United States, half in the 1990s."

The Left encourages illegal immigration and wants amnesty looking for votes. Ever since Lyndon Johnson, the Democrats have "cultivated a large clientele of inner-city voters living on welfare." Politicians and their special-interest friends see a large, uneducated, and easily manipulated voting bloc to keep them in office. Then unions joined the march with their eyes on more members. Employers gain by hiring labor off the books while the taxpayers get stuck with the bill. Greed drives this slave trade just like the original one. The old slave traders would have moved the entire population of Africa to the US if they could have. The 21st Century slave traders will move a large part of the Mexican population to the US if they can. "Slave traders of all centuries are morally cheap, with little or no regard for laws or human beings."[63]

> **The 21st Century slave traders will move a large part of the Mexican population to the US if they can.**

Unfortunately, the Republicans are just as vote hungry and think they can lure some of those votes even though "Hispanics vote Democratic over Republican by about a 7 to 3 margin."[64] The Republicans let illegal immigration roll forward unrestrained because it helped their friends who have tainted capitalism with their immoral greed. The Democrats let illegal immigration roll forward unrestrained because they believed they could claim ownership of the Latino vote as they have the black vote. And the American mainstream was ignored by both parties. Duped by both parties.[65]

The following comments are particularly important because they were written by an American of Mexican Heritage who used to have a column in the *Fort Worth Star Telegram*.

> This display of Mexican flags should give you a heads up on where these protesters allegiance lies: their hearts are in Mexico and their bellies are in the United Sates.... American Hispanics are not all thrilled with illegal immigration....Never in my life (I'm 68) had I witnessed the lawlessness, the deterioration of my community, and the black market criminal underground activities attributed to the influx of illegal immigrants.
>
> To add injury to insult, politicians soon caved in to the many demands of illegal immigrants. Notably: bilingual education, bilingual ballots, welfare aid, free medical care, etc. Through all this national disgrace allowed by our politicians, have you all noticed that no one ever blames the useless, corrupt, and disgraceful government of Mexico? In contrast, they lambaste and criticize our country. How does that grab you?[66]

During the 2008 campaign both John McCain and Barack Obama supported legal status for illegal immigrants trying to win Hispanic votes, but both tried to keep the sensitive issue out of the campaign debate.[67] Sure, this is all about cheap labor – but there is no such thing as "cheap labor." Illegal immigrants may work for $5 or $6 an hour but they receive benefits equaling $20 to $30 an hour and you pay for them.[68] All the parties to this greed are working against the long term national interests of the US and hasten the demise of this great nation.

Patrick J. Buchanan came out with a book in 2006, *State of Emergency: The Third World Invasion and Conquest of America* (St. Martin's Press) in which he claimed that the US is committing suicide led by the liberalism and the idea of open borders. He wrote that anchor babies should not be allowed, that immigrant children accounted for 100 percent of the increase in public school enrollment in the last 20 years, poor scores on math and reading were due to millions of uneducated immigrants, and that California is going Hispanic and that 100,000 native-born white Americans are leaving "Mexifornia" each year. He predicted that "America will no longer be one nation but more like the Roman Empire – a conglomerate of races and cultures held together by a regime."[69]

> **America will no longer be one nation but more like the Roman Empire – a conglomerate of races and cultures held together by a regime.**
>
> **- Patrick J. Buchanan**

Buchanan wrote that the massive flow of illegal immigrants into the US is really an invasion and yet the White House and the Congress do not do anything about it. The policies of open borders and almost unrestricted immigration have brought an influx of criminals and thugs into our country for the "benefit only of an entrenched political establishment that couldn't care less about the good of the American people." The political problem will only grow because, "any presidential candidate who speaks out against the Hispanic onslaught in the American Southwest will now lose the electoral votes of California, Arizona, New Mexico, and Texas." To stave off national suicide, "we must recapture control of immigration policy from politicians paralyzed by fear of ethnic lobbies and cultural contributors, or immobilized by ideology."[70]

The figures for Mexifornia are particularly dire. Whites are already a minority in California. "Hispanics are projected to become a majority of the population by 2042." According to the Department of Finance in Sacramento, the Hispanic population is projected to increase by 22 million to 59.5 million in 2050, to 52 percent from 36 percent. Whites will be only 26 percent down from 43 percent. Asians will be 13 percent up from 12 percent, and Blacks will drop to 5 percent from 6 percent.[71] Twenty years ago California cut off aid to illegal immigrants but in 2011, they passed laws permitting state financial aid, in-state tuition, and acceptance of privately funded college grants.[72]

The real threat to American culture is this "ideology that wants to write into law…that there shall be a resident subclass of laborers constrained by government to work for wages so low no American would accept them. This ideology is a form of materialism that puts the pursuit of profit above all else. It is the inordinate love of money. It would dissolve what is best about America in a culture of greed."[73]

Gangs, Drugs, and Mexican Cartels

It is very difficult to separate gangs and drugs from the operations of the Mexican cartels. President Nixon declared a war on drugs 40 years ago, but the problem has only worsened. A map of drug distribution in the US shows a presence in every state in the union with heavy concentrations in California (San Diego, Los Angeles, San Francisco, and the Sacramento valley), Oregon, Washington, Chicago, the East Coast (Washington DC to New England), the Carolinas, Atlanta, the coast all the way around Florida, and Texas. There are 21 gangs listed with this distribution map with their cartel affiliations. Some of the names are quite familiar: Bloods, Crips, Hells Angels, Mara Salvatrucha (MS 13), Mexican Mafia, and Vagos.[74]

We are part of the problem. "The U.S. helped create this beast. According to the White House Office of National Drug Control Policy, Americans consume $65 billion worth of illegal drugs annually, roughly what they spend on higher education, and most of those drugs are either produced in Mexico or transit through it."[75] **US drug consumption is a threat to US national security.**

The U.S. helped create this beast. Americans consume $65 billion worth of illegal drugs annually, roughly what they spend on higher education, and most of those drugs are either produced in Mexico or transit through it.

This is big business worldwide. In addition to marijuana, cocaine, and opium, there has been the boom in synthetic drugs, amphetamines. The production of amphetamines in 2009 was estimated at 160 tons, worth nearly $20 billion, with a market of 53 million consumers. It was estimated that the US consumed 37.7 tons with a wholesale value of $2.479 billion and a retail value of $4.815 billion. The worldwide figures for 2010 were about 600 thousand tons of marijuana with a world market of 190 million consumers, 800 tons of cocaine valued at $80 billion with a market of 19 million consumers, and 8,000 tons of opium valued at $65 billion and 22 million consumers. "The production and consumption of amphetamine type stimulants is not centralized, which means it happens around the world and tends to move as they apply controls on precursor chemicals."[76]

Drugs are not the only thing smuggled across our borders. While drugs may be a $10 to $29 billion business, there is also a $6.6 billion dollar business in smuggling people. People pay anywhere from $7,000 to $30,000 and X-rays have shown over 200 people jammed into a trailer truck.[77] The movement of drugs and people has led to more violence. Gangs control some of the crossings and force migrants to carry drugs and more are carrying guns. In addition to crime in the US, attacks on Border Patrol agents increased 41% from 2006 to 2010. As one sheriff said, "The guys smuggling people and narcotics now are more sinister."[78] [The 2011 National Gang Threat Assessment reported 33,000 gangs with 1.4 million members, up 40% from 2009.]

The gangs, drugs, and crime come mostly from across our southern border. Large percentages of the Hispanic gangs in the US are illegal. The MS-13 gang (Mara Salvatrucha founded in Los Angeles by El Salvadorians) has grown to over 10,000 members in 30 states.[79] MS-13 is heavily into the drug traffic and the level of violence has greatly increased including attacks on Border Patrol agents.[80] The Mexican drug cartels use Latino and Black prison and street gangs as their operational muscle and conduits for drug sales within the US. The membership of the gangs has grown as the financial and weaponry rewards have increased.[81]

Some 1,200 National Guard troops were deployed along the border in 2010, however all but about 300 were withdrawn in 2012 despite the worsening situation. The Justice Department's 2011 Drug Market Analysis for Arizona stated that Mexican drug cartels "have begun to threaten local police officers to deter their enforcement activities. Violent criminal groups often referred to as border bandits, rip crews, or bajadores, operate along trafficking corridors in remote location, preying upon law enforcement officers and smugglers who transit their territories." The cartels were expanding use of street gangs, such as Brown Pride in Tucson and the New Mexican Mafia in Phoenix.[82]

In 2008, the National Drug Intelligence Center reported that Mexican DTOs (Drug Trafficking Organizations) were operating in at least 195 cities in the US. The National Drug

Threat Assessment which was published in August 2011 states: "Mexican-based TCOs were operating in more than a thousand U.S. cities during 2009-2010." [TCO – Transnational Criminal Organization – replaced DTO "to convey that the Mexican cartels are now viewed as more threatening and capable (with transnational reach) entities.] "This would mean that Mexican cartel operational penetration into U.S. cities is now thought to be 500% higher than previously estimated in the time frame of roughly three years." This raises a major strategic decision question: should we continue focusing on al Qaeda (and its terrorist network) as the principal threat to the US or "will the Mexican cartels (and their supporting gang networks) now be recognized as replacing Al Qaeda as the number one threat to our government and safety of our citizens?" We continue to recognize the violence potential of al Qaeda and radical Islam, but "the violence associated with the criminal insurgent potentials of the Mexican cartels and their ability to corrupt and undermine governments in the Western Hemisphere must now be considered far more threatening to our nation."[83]

Mexican cartels are now operating in over 1,000 US cities, up from 195 in 3 years. These cartels are now considered a greater threat than al Qaeda.

On 25 July 2011, the National Security Staff released a document "Strategy to Combat Transnational Organized Crime: Addressing Converging Threats to National Security." It notes that this transnational organized crime is attempting "to gain influence in government, politics, and commerce through corrupt as well as legitimate means" and that it "poses a significant threat to national and international security." Robert Bunker analyzed the documents calling the cartel and gang threats "misunderstood and underestimated." He wrote that the threat perceptions were "woefully obsolete" and only perpetuate the legalistic charade of the nation-state's 'monopoly on political violence' and 'control over its sovereign borders,'…not fully recognizing the TOC threat." He added, "Criminal-insurgencies are currently raging across Mexico, in areas of Central America, and in other locales. Cities and regions have been captured by de facto politicized cartel and gang entities with criminal para-states established by the Zetas, the Sinaloans, and other criminal organizations. This is representative of the blurring of crime and war 'nightmare scenarios'."[84]

Drug-related violence killed 34,162 people in Mexico by the end of 2010, with 15,273 in 2010 alone.[85] Since President Felipe Calderón took office in December 2006 and deployed more troops and police trying to break the cartels, about 45,000 people have died making Mexico more violent than Afghanistan or Pakistan.[86] Mexico said the number was 47,500 in February 2012. It is even worse across Central America where there have been 67,000 killings.[87] The cartels have reacted with unprecedented violence, torturing, beheading, and dismembering bodies of police and soldiers as well as others, largely cartel members as the cartels fought for control of the lucrative drug routes into the US. It has become a daily occurrence for heads, body parts in bags to be left in public places, or bodies hung from bridges. They have even taken to dissolving bodies in barrels of acid. A particularly brutal new player was Los Zetas, which came from as many as 200 U.S.-trained Mexican security personnel - elite counter-narcotics teams - who defected to drug cartels.[88] They initially provided muscle for cartels but, evidently they saw so much money that they decided they should take over rather than be employees.

There was a macabre competition among the drug lords to ratchet up the gore. Some like the "Zetas are fond of posting Internet videos of the prolonged torture and murder of their enemies." There was even wage bidding for "the best butchers and surgeons to perform beheadings of murdered rivals." Slaughter was rampant with the discovery of "*fosas,* or mass graves" where some 500 corpses have been found.[89]   The brutality of the Zetas led to the formation of a new group, the "Mata Zetas" or "Zeta Killers" apparently "part of the New Generation drug cartel" in the northwestern state of Jalisco. According to their spokesman, "Our only objective is the Zetas cartel," and unlike the Zetas they did not "extort or kidnap" citizens but were "anonymous warriors, without faces, but proudly Mexican" working "clandestinely" but "always to benefit Mexico's people." Vigilante justice might get approval but it did not bode well for the rule of law.[90]

The cartels are not only involved with drugs; they will move into any area that will yield money, such as extortion and "kidnapping, a crime that's up 317% in Mexico since 2005."[91]   Secretary of State Hillary Clinton has described the cartels "as a 'criminal insurgency' that seeks not to overthrow the Mexican government but rather to keep it under its blood-soaked thumb."[92]

The drug menace continued with Mexico drifting toward becoming a narco-state. With six million Americans using cocaine (90 percent of cocaine from South America that arrives in the US funnels through Guatemala and across Mexico[93]), the southern border area of the US had become a battlefield. The amounts of marijuana and cocaine transiting the border are staggering. To make it worse, coca cultivation increased. Cultivation in Colombia increased from 78,000 hectares in 2006 to 99,000 hectares or 383 square miles, a shocking 27 percent increase despite major US efforts. Cultivation in the three main sources of coca, Colombia, Peru, and Bolivia, rose 16 percent to 181,600 hectares, or 701 square miles.[94]

With America busy in Iraq and Afghanistan, the problems in Latin America received little attention. That may come back to haunt!

Mexico should be a great country; it has a large economy with significant oil reserves, access to two oceans, and hard working citizens, but it is the most corrupt government in the western hemisphere. It is a Third World country in many ways with people living in shacks and the "colonias" or "new neighborhoods"- shanty towns along the border. With the drugs and corruption, education is low, the birth rate high, and the average Mexican makes less than $5 a day. Yet, Mexico has 22 billionaires! Instead of solving those problems, Mexico exports their poor to the US so the American taxpayers can take care of them.[95]

But Mexico is close to being a failed state and not one to emulate.[96] Some would say that Mexico has always been a failed state; a country that exports its own population to keep a lid on its internal situation really has a problem. Corruption is so ingrained into the system (La Mordida – the bite! - in all transactions) that there is no likelihood of it being removed without extreme violence.[97]   Transparency International, the corruption watchdog, "estimates that Mexicans paid $2.75 billion in bribes to police and other officials last year. Meanwhile, 95% of violent crimes go unsolved."[98] With the enormous amounts of money available to the drug cartels, corruption is brutally simple: **"plomo o plata"** – lead or silver – you are dead or paid off (handsomely).[99]

Some think that Mexican lawlessness is a legacy from the Spanish conquistadors, who were more interested in pillaging than ruling and left Mexico with the warped idea that law enforcement is a private rather than a public duty. That aided the drug mafias that appeared after World War II, restricted only by the authoritarian Institutional Revolutionary Party (PRI) which was the "cartels' tacit partner" during its 71 year rule. When the National Action Party defeated the PRI in 2000, the "cartels splintered and embarked on an orgy of violence that spawned soulless killing machines."[100] A former Mexican foreign minister wrote that to start,

Mexico needs a single national police force and a functional justice system, "with oral trials, an independent prosecutions structure and a federalization of the criminal code."[101]

With the enormous amounts of money available to the drug cartels, corruption is brutally simple: "plomo o plata" – lead or silver – you are dead or paid off (handsomely).

In addition to failing to enforce the laws, the US Government, when it did take an action, managed to kill Americans. "The Bureau of Alcohol, Tobacco, Firearms and Explosives (ATF) made a colossally dumb decision when it concocted a sting operation that let 2,020 high-powered weapons slip across the border into Mexico." It was called **Operation Fast and Furious** and it was started in 2009 with the goal of permitting the large-scale purchase of assault weapons in the US so they could supposedly be traced up the cartel chain to score major arrests. However, it was botched from the beginning with the proper people not being informed and it resulted in an American border patrol agent being killed. Two weapons were found at that scene, but there was a third weapon and a FBI cover-up trying to hide it, supposedly to protect a confidential informant who evidently was given $70,000 in "seed money" by the FBI to buy weapons.[102] Great use of taxpayers' money! "At least 122 of the guns have been recovered from crimes in Mexico; 1,430 are still unaccounted for."[103] About a dozen weapons have been found at crime scenes in the US.[104] It got worse: "In El Paso, Texas, 42 weapons were seized from two crime scenes alone."[105]

"Robert Mueller of the FBI and Ken Melson of the ATF obviously knew of these gunwalking operations." "Eric Holder had to know. Janet Napolitano,…had to know."[106] Obama surely had to know. Ten Arizona sheriffs blasted the Obama administration and called for Holder to step down or be fired and that "Fast and Furious" was a "betrayal of state law enforcement."[107] According to *The Daily Caller,* Holder's No. 2 deputy, Lanny Breuer, wrote in late 2009 that it was a "terrific idea."[108] The conspiracy theory was that Obama and Holder, both strong anti-gun advocates, set up the operation to gain gun control legislation. This stinking scandal is still playing out.

The growing gang and drug activity in the US was compounded by the Mexican drug cartel operations which were not only taking over Mexico and killing thousands of Mexicans but increasingly there have been killings on the US side of the border. Some of the killings were directly drug related and others were assassinations of people who had fled Mexico to escape from the cartels. In addition, there were over 250 incursions by suspected military forces into the US in the past decade, often apparently supporting drug operations. There was a shootout by the Zetas in Houston and they became so brazen that they were patrolling looking for Border Patrol agents a dozen miles inside the US.[109]

The threat to the US of the cartels is the possibility of anarchy or a drug republic on our border and then the strategic question of would we have to intervene to protect our country.

Cost

All this comes at a very high cost. The figures vary, but the magnitude is clear. Illegal immigrants in US: 23.6 million; money wired to Mexico since January 2006: $38.9 billion; money wired to Latin America since 2001: $316 billion; cost of social services for illegal immigrants since 1996: $397.5 billion; illegals enrolled in public schools K-12: 5.5 million; cost of illegal immigrants enrolled in K-12 since 1996: $178.5 billion; illegal immigrants incarcerated: 460,517; cost for incarceration since 2001: $28.6 billion; illegal immigrant fugitives: 784,938; anchor babies: 5,091,008; jobs lost to illegal immigrants: 12,360,248.[110]

Below is a compilation of statistics (some are a little old but the trend is clear):

1. $11 billion to $22 billion spent on welfare to illegal aliens each year.
2. $2.2 billion dollars a year spent on food assistance programs such as food stamps, WIC, and free school lunches for illegal aliens.
3. $2.5 billion dollars a year spent on Medicaid for illegal aliens.
4. $12 billion dollars a year spent on primary and secondary school education for children here illegally.
5. $17 billion dollars a year spent for education for the American-born children of illegal aliens, known as anchor babies.
6. $3 million dollars a day [$1.1 billion per year] spent to incarcerate illegal aliens.
7. 29 percent of all Federal Prison inmates are illegal aliens.
8. $90 billion dollars a year spent on illegal aliens for welfare & social services by the American taxpayers.
9. $200 billion dollars a year in lost-suppressed American wages caused by the illegal aliens.
10. Illegal aliens in the United States have a crime rate that's two and a half times that of citizen-taxpayer Americans. Their children make a huge additional crime problem in the United States.
11. During the year of 2005, there were 4 to 10 million illegal aliens that crossed our Southern Border. In addition, as many as 19,500 illegal aliens arrived from terrorist countries. Millions of pounds of drugs, cocaine, meth, heroine and marijuana, crossed into the U. S. from the Southern border.
12. In 2006 illegal aliens sent home $45 billion in remittances back to their countries of origin. Obfuscation may have hidden $35 billion more.
13. "The Dark Side of Illegal Immigration: Nearly One Million Sex Crimes Committed by Illegal Immigrants in the United States."
14. Every day (average), 12 Americans are murdered by an illegal alien. Another 13 Americans are killed by uninsured drunk illegal aliens, and eight American children are victims of a sex crime committed by an illegal alien each day! Local cops, acting in error, sometimes "forget" to annotate nationality on reports. The numbers may be worse.
15. Today, criminal aliens account for over 29 percent of prisoners in Federal Bureau of Prisons facilities and a higher share of all federal prison inmates. These prisoners represent the fastest growing segment of the federal prison population.
    Incarceration of criminal aliens cost an estimated $624 million to state prisons (1999) and $891 million to federal prisons (2002), according to the most recent available figure from the U.S. DOJ Bureau of Justice Statistics.
16. "Illegal Aliens and American Medicine," "Many illegal aliens harbor fatal diseases that American Medicine fought and vanquished long ago, such as drug-resistant tuberculosis, malaria, leprosy, plague, polio, dengue and Chagas disease." The Journal of American Physicians and Surgeons.
17. In 2002, HIV/AIDS was the third leading cause of death among Hispanic men aged 35 to 44 and the fourth leading cause of death among Hispanic women in the same age group. Most Hispanic men were exposed to HIV through sexual contact with other men. Source (U.S. CDC).
18. If enacted, the Comprehensive Immigration Reform Act (CIRA, S. 2611) would be the most dramatic change in immigration law in 80 years, granting Amnesty to 30 million illegal immigrants, and allowing an estimated 100-203 [sic 103-200] million persons to legally immigrate to the U.S. over the next 20-40 years a number equal to fully two-thirds of the current population of the United States.
19. U.S. Sen. Jeff Sessions (R-AL) today unveiled an impact analysis that shows the Senate immigration bill should it become law would permit up to **217.1 million new legal immigrants** into the United States over the next 20 years, a number equal to more than 70 percent of the total current population.

20. The number of illegal immigrants in the United States is at least 20 million, and may be as many as 30 million people, more than triple the official nine million people estimated by the Census Bureau. 03 Jan 2005.
21. Cases of Leprosy on the Rise In The U.S., The New York Times. "While there were some 900 recorded cases in the United States 40 years ago, today more than 7,000 people have leprosy." Leprosy is an airborne virus; it can also be spread by touching and coughing.[111]

The cost is over **$300 billion a year**. Are we really that stupid?

Even the cost of deporting illegal immigrants is expensive, running at least $12,500 per person. In 2010, 56% of apprehensions were people who had been caught before, up 44% from 2005. And the number of deportees who had been deported before was increasing. About 1.1 million have been deported under the Obama administration ($13.75 billion) and between October 2008 and July 2011, 180,229 were deported who had returned anyway costing $2.25 billion.[112]

> **Once the coffers of the federal government are opened to the public [including illegals!], there will be no shutting them again.**
>
> **- Grover Cleveland**

There are many additional costs: the ethnic balance of the US is changing and English is threatened as our language with everything from drivers' licenses, voting ballots, and even citizenship ceremonies being offered in dozens of foreign languages. Almost all the increase in our public schools has been due to immigrants and in some places they need to build a new school a day to keep up with the flood of immigrants. Bilingual stupidity costs $10 billion a year. Our cultural identity is under assault as America's heroes, history, and great achievements have been undermined by political correctness and depiction of the US as an oppressor nation. 400,000 foreigners collect SSI benefits from the Social Security Administration without having to work one day in the US. The SSA even opened an office in Mexico City. Most of our population growth has been from immigrants straining all areas of our economy and society.[113]

Deamericanization

This influx of illegal immigrants is not limited to the border states but has spread all across the nation.[114] "In 303 counties, nearly one in 10, the share of whites has slipped below 50 percent."[115] The governors of Arizona and New Mexico declared states of emergency and pushed Washington to act on illegal immigrants.[116] Of course, the government did not help; it attacked the states instead. The law to revoke business licenses of employer violators in Arizona had an effect. "Scores of immigrants are fleeing to other states or back to their Latin American homelands." The attraction is very clear as one woman with three US-born children said, "There's no work over there in Mexico. People there live so poorly. Here, my kids have health insurance and Medicare. Over there, there's nothing." But as State Rep. Russell Pearce said, "Why in the world do (illegal immigrants) think they have a right to break the law? And we are the bad guys for insisting that the law be enforced? The public doesn't agree with that."[117]

> **The ACLU's position is that illegal aliens have a right to enter our border and stay in this country as long as they want.**

"Interstate 20 has become a major corridor for immigrant smugglers. It runs across the South, passing through Atlanta and linking up with other major highways that lead to Miami to the south and Baltimore, Philadelphia, New York and Boston to the north."[118] The problem of illegal immigration has swept all around the country. "In the blue-collar town of Danbury, Connecticut, about 20 percent of the town's population (75,000) is estimated to be illegal. The situation is so out of control that town officials found thirty cots in the basement of one home, each being rented for five dollars a night."[119]

Calls for amnesty, building a wall along the border, and demonstrations by Hispanics stirred emotions all around. The Minutemen, which Bush called "vigilantes," started monitoring the border and the ACLU shadowed them and alerted the illegals to their presence, but the numbers dropped significantly wherever the Minutemen were. Probably because the US Border Patrol notified the Mexican government of the Minutemen locations!! The Mexican army sent troops to those areas and diverted the illegals and drug smugglers away from the Minutemen. "The ACLU's position is that illegal aliens have a right to enter our border and stay in this country as long as they want."[120] Citizens wanted to build a fence since the US government was too slow! As one agent said, "as fast as they put it up, on the southern side they take plasma torches and cut holes." Even where there is a vehicle barrier, "drug smugglers use hydraulic ramps to boost cars over for a quick dash into town." In the Nogales area where they have the Normandy barrier, crisscrossed railroads iron, "smugglers like to cut this fence with torches, then carefully put everything back in place so the border patrol won't notice." There is big money involved in smuggling – people and drugs – so they don't want any fence to stop them![121]

It seems unbelievable that the US government betrays Minuteman patrols to Mexico. "While Minuteman civilian patrols are keeping an eye out for illegal border crosser, the U.S. Border Patrol is keeping an eye out for Minutemen – and telling the Mexican government where they are. According to three documents on the Mexican Secretary of Foreign Relations web site, the U.S. Border Patrol is to notify the Mexican government as to the location of Minutemen and other civilian border patrol groups when they participate in apprehending illegal immigrants. A U.S. Customs and Border Protection spokesman confirmed the notification process, describing it as a standard procedure meant to **reassure the Mexican government** that migrants' rights are being observed."

We have to reassure the Mexican government about their criminals!

Chris Simcox, founder of the Minutemen, said, "It's unbelievable that our own government agency is sending intelligence to another country. They are sending intelligence to a nation where corruption runs rampant, and that could be getting into the hands of criminal cartels. They basically endangered the lives of American people."

To add to the stupidity, "Once an illegal alien is apprehended, they can request counsel. We have to give their counsel the information about their apprehension, and that includes where they are apprehended, whether a Minuteman volunteer spotted them or a citizen." A paradise for shady lawyers!

Also, the union, which represents the Border Patrol agents, "said agents have complained for years about the Mexican consulate's influence over the agency. 'It worries me (that the Mexican government) seems to be unduly influencing our enforcement policies. That's not a legitimate role for any foreign nation,'" according to the union president. To emphasize the poor relationship between the Border Patrol and the Minutemen, one agent stated, "Last year an internal memo notified all agents not to give credit to Minuteman volunteers or others who call in sightings of illegal aliens."[122]

The Mexican government took out "ads urging Mexican workers to denounce rights violations in the United States." Vincente Fox called the wall "shameful," his foreign secretary

Luis Ernesto Derbez let loose with his usual tirade, and they "hired Allyn & Company, a Dallas-based public relations company to help improve Mexico's image and stem the immigration backlash."[123]

"Mexico counts on sending almost a million illegal aliens into the United States each year to ensure billions of dollars in remittance from expatriates, a sympathetic Hispanic lobbying presence in the United States, and easy exits for potential dissidents unhappy with Mexico City's failure to provide basic services for its own indigenous people. [Remittances are second only to oil as a source of income in Mexico.[124]]

"To facilitate such massive illegal immigration, Mexican officials hector their American counterparts about our supposed illiberality in not letting millions more stream in unchecked. They have even gone so far as to publish a **government comic book** instructing their own citizens how to cross the American border safely – and in flagrant violation of our laws." [Emphasis added] The Mexican government also provides people who advise the illegals near the border.[125]

> **Mexico is not going to bear, it is not going to permit, and it will not allow a stupid thing like this wall.**
> **- Luis Ernesto Derbez, Mexican foreign secretary**

Numerous anti-immigration groups appeared around the country where people were tired of the lack of law enforcement. Southern states had seen a boom in their Hispanic populations in the 1990s: Arkansas up 337 percent, Georgia 300 percent, Tennessee up 278 percent, and South Carolina up 211 percent and the growth has only continued.[126] Not all the illegals coming here have to look for a job; some companies work with smugglers to deliver the number of workers they need. That usually includes arranging fake IDs, which are readily available in places like Los Angeles.[127]

A growing concern was the threat of terrorists crossing undetected into the US. Officially there is a category OTM (other than Mexicans) which may be as large as 200,000 slipping in each year. According to a congressional report, hundreds of illegals from the Middle East and South Asia had been apprehended. Oliver North also reported that Hugo Chavez from Venezuela was providing documents to foreigners that could be used to obtain Venezuelan passports and American visas.[128] In addition to people from Latin America, including Venezuela, illegals have crossed from Afghanistan, Bulgaria, Russia, China, Egypt, Iran, and Iraq.[129] In addition to Venezuela, the government found that terrorists had obtained South African passports and one woman who was thought to be an al Qaeda operative crossed into the US as many as 250 times.[130]

The first decade of the 21st century saw a different America with the transformation into a "post-European-dominated society" with over 50 million Hispanics. That was up 43%, or over half the growth from 2000, while the non-Hispanic population grew only 5%. Hispanics are now 16% of our 309 million population with rapid growth in the South: doubled in Alabama, Arkansas, Kentucky, Mississippi, and the Carolinas. Almost half of all children are other than non-Hispanic white. Minorities are now 36% of the population.[131] America has changed forever.

Multiculturalism

In the days of the Melting Pot, new immigrants took pride in learning English to become productive citizens. But now the "immigrants' rights" activists and multiculturalists insist that foreigners do not have to learn English and that they are "victims" who need our "protection." "Assimilation is the key to any successful immigration policy, and no country has succeeded in assimilating immigrants as well as the US. Turning immigrants into Americans didn't happen by accident but was the result of a comprehensive national effort called Americanization. Sadly Americanization has given way to an insidious multiculturalism."[132]

> Multiculturalism's goal is not to teach about other cultures, but to promote – by means of distortions and half-truths – the notion that non-Western cultures are as good as, if not better than, Western culture. Far from "broadening" the curriculum, what multiculturalism seeks is to diminish the value of Western culture in the minds of students. But given all the facts, the objective superiority of Western culture is apparent, so the multiculturalists must artificially elevate other cultures and depreciate the West."[133]

There is nothing wrong with looking for value in other cultures and accepting people of other cultures. "One of the reasons democracies are so much more enjoyable countries to live in than non-democratic countries is because we are so tolerant of each other."[134] The problem is when it becomes self-destructive, a blind dumbed-down, oversimplified multicultural ethos that could be our downfall. Can we continue with a questionable sustainable population of 312 million with people from 150 countries speaking 100 languages? With too many hyphenated-Americans and illiteracy rates exceeding 50% ("42 million Americans cannot read or write. Another 50 million read at the fourth grade level."), 50-60% dropout/flunkout rates (76% in Detroit), about "1.2 million teens hit the streets every spring unable to read or write." That is one of the defining terms of Third World countries: **illiteracy**. "At what point will Americans stand up for being Americans? On every level – unrelenting and accelerating immigration cannot be sustained environmentally, educationally, linguistically or culturally – if America hopes to survive the 21st century."[135]

Any man who carries a hyphen about with him carries a dagger that he is ready to plunge into the vitals of this Republic whenever he gets ready.

- Woodrow Wilson

A person from India wrote about multiculturalism, "that idiotic concept which only serves to divide a nation and add or aggravate communal strife." Multiculturalism is the opposite of nationalism because it highlights the differences between peoples rather than the similarities. Nationalism highlights the similarities among peoples while obscuring the differences. "It seeks to 'melt' everybody into one unit, which, as a whole, reveres the nation, even as single members of the unit sustain cultural differences – on an individual basis." Referring to the CAIR and American Muslim Council push for the addition of "Islamic" to "Judeo-Christian" values of American heritage, he wrote, "Point to ponder: Which American values can, even remotely, be called Islamic? Democracy? Freedom? Equality? Secularism? Gender equity? Freedom of thought? The right to free expression? The right to critique any holy cow? Does even one of these values exist in a single Islamic state…? Is even one of these values extended to all Muslim citizens of an Islamic state?" He criticized the lack of debate among so-called moderate Muslims and asked, "Can everybody else be wrong, and only Muslims, right…?"[136]

Multiculturalism is the opposite of nationalism because it highlights the differences between peoples rather than the similarities.

The welfare state seems to be another result of multiculturalism. Laredo, Texas is 96% Hispanic, the kids are poor, 98% of the children are eligible for free lunches from the federal government, but they do not seem to have the same enthusiasm as kids building a high school in Kenya. They have a wonderful new school but they did not do anything. It raised the question, "does that sense of entitlement take away their drive?" They seem to have lost their old Hispanic values and traditions. Liberal groups, such as LULAC (League of United Latin American Citizens) in Laredo, always want more: "more government funding, more affirmative action, more new programs."[137]

Victor Davis Hanson wrote a very critical book, *Mexifornia,* in which he explained how immigration was destroying California and that it would continue across the country and destroy the American Dream. He stated it bluntly: "The really perilous course lies in preserving the status quo and institutionalizing our past failed policies: open borders, unlimited immigration, dependence on cheap and illegal labor, obsequious deference to Mexico City, erosion of legal statutes, multiculturalism in our schools, and a general breakdown in the old assimilationist model." Since Hanson is a military historian, he follows Karl von Clausewitz' concept of the center of gravity of the enemy. Hanson sees the center of gravity as the de facto alliance of the Corporate/Libertarian Right and the Multicultural Left which protects and promotes this system.[138]

This divisive multicultural ideology pervades the media, the education system, and politics.

In July 2004, Hanson talked about his book at an immigration-overpopulation conference in Washington DC. Afterwards, former Colorado Governor Richard D. Lamm gave a stunning speech on how to destroy America. Quoting Toynbee that all great nations commit suicide, he listed eight steps. First, "Turn America into a bilingual or multi-lingual and bicultural country. History shows that no nation can survive the tensions, conflict, and antagonism of two or more competing languages and cultures. It is a blessing for an individual to be bilingual; however, it is a curse for a society to be bilingual." Second, "Invent 'multiculturalism' and encourage immigrants to maintain their culture." Third, "The key is to celebrate diversity rather than unity. I would encourage all immigrants to keep their own language and culture. I would replace the melting pot metaphor with the salad bowl metaphor."

"Fourth, I would make our fastest growing demographic group the least educated. I would add a second underclass, unassimilated, undereducated, and antagonistic to our population. I would have this second underclass have a 50% dropout rate from high school." His fifth point was to "get big foundations and business to give these efforts lots of money. I would invest in ethnic identity, and I would establish the cult of 'Victimology.' I would get all minorities to think their lack of success was the fault of the majority. I would start a grievance industry blaming all minority failure on the majority population." His sixth step for America's downfall was "include dual citizenship and promote divided loyalties. I would stress differences rather than similarities."

Next to last, "I would place all subjects off limits – make it taboo to talk about anything against the cult of 'diversity.' I would find a word similar to 'heretic' in the 16th century – that stopped discussion and paralyzed thinking. Words like 'racist' or 'xenophobe' halt discussion and debate." He then said "Having made America a bilingual/bicultural country, having established multiculturalism, having the large foundations fund the doctrine of 'Victimology,' I would next make it impossible to enforce our immigration laws. I would develop a mantra: That because immigration has been good for America, it must always be good. I would make every individual symmetric and ignore the cumulative impact of millions of them." His audience was silent. Finally he said, "Lastly, I would censor Victor Davis Hanson's book Mexifornia. His book is dangerous. It exposes the plan to destroy America. If you feel America deserves to be destroyed, don't read that book." There was no applause, but the group recognized that the immigration monster must be stopped or America will be destroyed.

This divisive multicultural ideology pervades the media, the education system, and politics. "The attitude of the open-borders crowd seems to be that as long as the lawns are groomed, the crops are picked, the dishes are washed, and their kids get their diapers changed, who cares?"[139] He left out the votes!

There will be no special bilingual program in the schools, no special ballots for elections, all government business will be conducted in our language.

Foreigners will NOT have the right to vote no matter how long they are here.

Foreigners will NEVER be able to hold political office.

Foreigners will not be a burden to the taxpayers. No welfare, no food stamps, no health care, or other government assistance programs.

Foreigners can invest in this country, but it must be an amount equal to 40,000 times the daily minimum wage.

If foreigners do come and want to buy land that will be okay, BUT options will be restricted. You are not allowed waterfront property. That is reserved for citizens naturally born into this country. (Actually not within 30 miles of coast or 60 miles of border)

Foreigners may not protest; no demonstrations, no waving a foreign flag, no political organizing, no bad-mouthing our president or his policies, if you do you will be sent home.

If you do come to this country illegally, you will be hunted down and sent straight to jail.

Harsh? Possibly what the US should have? The above laws happen to be the immigration laws of MEXICO![140]

People who are ashamed of their own culture will not defend it.

- Robert Spencer[141]

As Pat Buchanan noted, "That cultural unity, that sense that we were one people, is gone." The Melting Pot has broken and the concept was rejected by our élites. Identity politics is in and minorities are urged to maintain their own traditions, customs, and languages. Multiethnic, multicultural countries have broken apart: the Soviet Union into 15 countries and Yugoslavia into a half dozen. Americans have repeatedly stated they do not want to go down this road, why do our élites?[142]

There is so much nonsense written about illegal immigration and so many myths.[143] One example is the columnist Ruben Navarrette, who seems to be the spokesman for illegal

Mexicans. To him, all complaints are anti-Latino. He refuses to understand facts and wrote that they are myths that are aimed to feed resentment and fears and to create anti-immigrant hysteria. "Among the most common myths: that illegal immigrants commit more than their share of crime, drain social services and conspire to retake the Southwest and return it to Mexico."[144] His heart seems to be in Mexico but his wallet here!

The worst myth is that we cannot send them all back. That is a horrendous excuse for not enforcing the law. We would not have to deport them: just announce that by a certain date (say 6 months from now) any illegal immigrant in the US will be arrested, identified positively, including eye scans, placed in a data bank, would not be eligible for any amnesty or guest worker programs, and would never be allowed in the US again even as a tourist. The roads would be clogged to the border as they left. Corporate America would join up if a few of the company presidents were sent to jail. Also, the idiocy of anchor babies should be terminated immediately and retroactively. One lady described our situation better than most politicians do:

> Let's say I break into your house. Let's say that when you discover me in your house, you insist that I leave. But I say, "I've made all the beds and washed the dishes and did the laundry and swept the floors; I've done all the things you don't like to do. I'm hardworking and honest (except for when I broke into your house).
>
> According to the protesters, not only must you let me stay, you must add me to your family's insurance plan, educate my kids, and provide other benefits to me and to my family (my husband will do your yard work because he too is hardworking and honest, except for that breaking in part).
>
> If you try to call the police or force me out, I will call my friends who will picket your house carrying signs that proclaim my right to be there.
>
> It's only fair, after all, because you have a nicer house than I do, and I'm just trying to better myself. I'm hardworking and honest, um except, for well, you know.
>
> And what a deal it is for me! I live in your house, contributing only a fraction of the cost of my keep, and there is nothing you can do about it without being accused of selfishness, prejudice and being an anti-housebreaker. Oh yeah, and I want you to learn my language so you can communicate with me!

A nation that cannot and will not defend its own borders will not forever remain a sovereign nation.

- Fred Thompson, presidential candidate, 2007

The leadership of Australia put it well in June 2006. Muslims who want to live under sharia were told to get out. "Immigrants, not Australians, must adapt. Take it or leave it….This is OUR COUNTRY, OUR LAND, and OUR LIFESTYLE, and we will allow you every opportunity to enjoy all this." But there is also "THE RIGHT TO LEAVE. If you aren't happy here then LEAVE." Oh, if we only had leaders with the courage of the Aussies! Perhaps we should add: To hell with multiculturalism and political correctness!

When we ignore the law, we breed contempt and weaken the very foundations of our society. That is why amnesty is irresponsible, because granting amnesty to people who have already broken the law communicates a serious lack of respect for the rule of law and only encourages more people to flaunt US laws. Illegal immigration is a major threat to deamericanize this great nation and turn it into a Third World country.

Notes

1. "U.S. Immigrant Population at All-Time High: 40 Million," Newsmax.com, 13 November 2011.
2. Chuck Shepherd, Universal Press Syndicate, "Foreign expectant mothers use 14thAmendment," *Reno Gazette-Journal,* 1 August 2010, p. 5B.   Raquel Maria Dillon and Christina Hoag, AP, "Alleged homes for 'maternity tourists' found," *Reno Gazette-Journal,* 27 March 2011, p. 8C.
3. See also Ann Coulter, "Look Who's 'Nativist' Now!" Human Events, 18 August 2010.
4. Alan Gomez, USA TODAY, "8% of U.S. births are to illegal migrants," *Reno Gazette-Journal,* 12 August 2010, p. 1B.
5. Elizabeth Weise, USA Today, ""Nation's ERs not providing adequate translations," *Reno Gazette-Journal,* 20 July 2006, p. 7B.
6. Donald L. Bartlett and James B. Steele, "Who Left the Door Open?" *Time,* 20 September 2004, p. 55.
7. *Nevada News & Review,* 18 August 2010.
8. Chuck Muth, publisher, DumpHarry.com, 13 August 2010.
9. Haya El Nasser, USA TODAY, "Minority infants almost the majority," *Reno Gazette-Journal,* 25 August 2011, p. 1C.
10. For many, if not most, the trip to the US is to make money to send back to Mexico. "A lot of Mexicans go to the United States dreaming that they will one day return to their beloved Mexico." Ivan Funes, general director of Conficasa, which offers mortgages in Mexico. Quoted in Ivan Moreno, AP, "Mortgages allow immigrants to buy homes in Mexico," *Reno Gazette-Journal,* 8 March 2008, p. 4B.

    As one man said, he decided to come to the US "'to work and make a little bit of money.' His dream is to return to Mexico and build a house." Geralda Miller, *Reno Gazette-Journal,* 7 December 2005, p. 3A. See also Ioan Grillo, AP, "American dream reaches past the border," *Reno Gazette-Journal,* 18 June 2006, p, 10C, about building a big house for about $10,000 with money from remittances.
11. A good example of the depth of our stupidity is the Equal Employment Opportunity Commission (EEOC) suing the Salvation Army. The Salvation Army has a policy of requiring employees to speak English on the job and a Boston federal judge approved it. The Salvation Army store in Framingham, Mass. told two employees they had one year to improve their English proficiency. Not having done so, they were fired after that one year. But they had worked there for 5 years for a total of 6 years, but the US government sued for discrimination in that they were inflicting "emotional pain, suffering, loss of enjoyment of life, embarrassment, humiliation and inconvenience." That raises two good questions: "Why is the government undermining the efforts of charities to encourage people to learn English? And doesn't it have better things to do with our tax dollars?" Newt Gingrich, *Winning the Future,* 30 April 2007.
12. Charles Krauthammer, "In Plain English: Let's Make It Official," *Time,* 12 June 2006, p. 112. See the Point/Counterpoint about making English the national language with George Will, "It is reasonable to require immigrants to learn English," and Ruben Navarrette, "Declaring English 'national language' insulting, divisive." Will wrote of expectations: "One is that you can read the nation's founding documents and laws, and can comprehend the political discourse that precedes the casting of ballots." Navarrette saw it as "anti-Latino and anti-Mexican, and that the immigration debate has become a proxy for an assault on the language and culture of a minority that is, in parts of the country, on its way to becoming a majority." Navarrette evidently sees California with a Mexican majority, but he does not say whether he then wants that Mexifornia to secede and join Mexico.
13. "Apparently nobody insists that American citizens voting in American elections should do so in the language of American civic life." Boston Globe columnist Jeff Jacoby, "English Ballots," Muth's News & Views, 16 July 2007. "More evidence that the immigration crisis is really an assimilation crisis: the current flap in Boston over whether the names of candidates on Chinese-language ballots should be printed in English or transliterated into Chinese. Because such transliteration can have ludicrous unintended meanings – Mayor Thomas Menino's name, for instance, could be read as 'Barbarian Mud No Mind of His Own' – the state's top election official is insisting that the names remain in English. The US Justice Department and the Chinese community activists insist that they be rendered in Chinese."
14. "Will English Survive Immigrant Flood?" Human Events, 21 August 2006, p. 1.
15. Then California Governor Arnold Schwarzenegger at the National Association of Hispanic Journalists convention in San Jose on 13 June, Muth's News & Views, 15 June 2007.

    Even George Bush finally got it partially right as he kept pushing for amnesty. Jennifer Loven, AP, "New immigrants must learn English, adopt American values, Bush says," *Reno Gazette-Journal,* 8 June 2006, p. 6C.

    A California court suspended California's high school exit exam so that failed students could graduate. The reason why they failed was "due to their lack of English skills, as established by their own admissions." Juliet Williams, AP, "Preliminary injunction granted against high school exit exam," *Reno Gazette-Journal,* 13 May 2006, p. 7A.
16. Thomas Sowell, "Call Them Gate Crashers," Human Events, 3 April 2006, p. 8. Deborah Baker, AP, "Illegal immigrant's removal from school brings about furor in New Mexico town," *Reno Gazette-Journal,* 5 March 2008, p. 4B. This 18 year old high school student was pregnant and fortunately sent back to Mexico.

    In an E-mail from southern California, a man wrote about his wife who was in charge of ESL at a Title 1 (low income level) high school. "My wife tells me that 100% of the students in her school and other Title 1 schools are on the free breakfast, free lunch program. When I say free breakfast I'm not talking a glass of milk and roll...but a full breakfast and cereal bar with fruits and juices that would make a Marriott proud. The waste of food is monumental, with trays and trays of it being dumped in the trash uneaten. She estimates that well over 50% of these students are obese or at least moderately overweight. About 75% or more DO have cell phones.

    The school also provides day care centers for the unwed teenage pregnant girls (some as young as 13) so they can attend class without the inconvenience of having to arrange for babysitters or having family watch their kids."

    She was ordered to spend $700,000 in her department even though she did not need anything, so she bought new computers, "half of which, one month later, have been carved with graffiti by the appreciative students who obviously feel humbled and grateful to have free education in America.

"She has had to intervene several times for young and substitute teachers whose classes consist of many illegal immigrant students here in the country less than 3 months who raised so much hell with the female teachers, calling them 'Putas' – whores – and throwing things that the teachers were in tears."

He ended with it's all about culture. "A third-world culture that does not value education, that accepts children getting pregnant and dropping out of school by 15 and that refuses to assimilate...and an Americana culture that has become so weak and politically correct that we don't have the will to do anything about it."

Another teacher, who had taught in LA, said, "All of this is true" and added, "No mention was made of the gold jewelry many students wear, the graffiti clean up expense, the expensive label clothing or low rider and late model cars in addition to the cell phones and waste of resources (food, supplies, etc.), but I've witnessed that also."

17. Julie Watson, AP, "Booing of Miss USA reflects political relations," *Reno Gazette-Journal,* 30 May 2007, p. 3B. Michelle Malkin, "Doing the Booing Americans Won't Do," Human Events, 4 January 2007, p. 12.

18. Below is a great example of circular logic, but it shows a total indifference to America. On the streets of downtown Houston, 1 May 2006. Jim Moore reporting for a Houston TV station:

Jim: Juan, I see that you and thousands of other protesters are marching in the streets to demonstrate for your cause. Exactly what is your cause and what do you expect to accomplish by this protest?

Juan: We want our rights. We will show you how powerful we are. We will bring Houston to its knees!

Jim: What rights?

Juan: Our right to live here...legally. Our right to get all the benefits you get.

Jim: When did you come to the United States?

Juan: Six years ago. I crossed over the border at night with seven other friends.

Jim: Why did you come?

Juan: For work. I can earn as much in a month as I could in a year in Mexico. Besides, I get free health care, our Mexican children can go to school free, if I lose my job I will get Welfare, and someday I will have the Social Security. Nothing like that in Mexico!

Jim: Did you feel badly about breaking our immigration laws when you came?

Juan: No! Why should I feel bad? I have a right to be here. I have a right to amnesty. I paid lots of money for my Social Security and Green Cards.

Jim: How did you acquire those documents?

Juan: From a guy in Dallas. He charged me a lot of money too.

Jim: Did you know that those documents were forged?

Juan: It is of no matter. I have a right to be here and work.

Jim: What is the "right" you speak of?

Juan: The right of all Aliens. It is found in your Constitution. Read it!

Jim: I have read it, but I do not remember it saying anything about rights for Aliens.

Juan: It is in that part where it says that all men have Alien rights, like the right to pursue happiness. I wasn't happy in Mexico, so I came here.

Jim: I think you are referring to the declaration of Independence and that document speaks to unalienable rights... Not Alien rights.

Juan: Whatever.

Jim: Since you are demanding to become an American citizen, why then are you carrying a Mexican Flag?

Juan: Because I am Mexican.

Jim: But you said you want to be given amnesty ... to become a US citizen.

Juan: No. This is not what we want. This is our country, a part of Mexico that you Gringos stole from us. We want it returned to its rightful owner.

Jim: Juan, you are standing in Texas. After wining the war with Mexico, Texas became a Republic, and later Texans voted to join the USA. It was not stolen from Mexico.

Juan: That is a Gringo lie. Texas was stolen. So was California, New Mexico and Arizona. It is just like all the other stuff you Gringos steal, like oil and babies. You are a country of thieves.

Jim: Babies? You think we steal babies?

Juan: Sure. Like from Korea and Vietnam and China. I see them all over the place. You let all these foreigners in, but try to keep us Mexicans out. How is this fair?

Jim: So, you really don't want to become an American citizen then.

Juan: I just want my rights! Everyone has a right to live, work, and speak their native language wherever and whenever they please. That's another thing we demand. All signs and official documents should be in Spanish. Teachers must teach in Spanish. Soon, more people here in Houston will speak Spanish than English. It is our right!

Jim: If I were to cross over the border into Mexico without proper documentation, what rights would I have there?

Juan: None. You would probably go to jail, but that's different.

Jim: How is it different? You said everyone has the right to live wherever they please.

Juan: You Gringos are a bunch of land grabbing thieves. Now you want Mexico too? Mexico has its rights. You Gringos have no rights in Mexico. Why would you want to go there anyway? There is no free medical service, schools, or welfare there for foreigners such as you. You cannot even own land in my country. Stay in the country of your birth.

Jim: I can see that there is no way that we can agree on this issue. Thank you for your comments.

Juan: Viva Mexico!

19. Quoted in David Horowitz, "Top 10 Most Dangerous Professors in America," Based on the new book, *The Professors: The 101 Most Dangerous Academics in America.* Gutierrez was #6. Gutierrez was a former judge for Zavala County, Texas and established the militant La Raza Unida ("The Unified Race"), an association dedicated to the belief that the Southwest does not rightfully belong to the US. He was a political science professor and former head of the Mexican-American Studies

Center at the University of Texas, Arlington. #5 on the list was Armando Navarro who taught ethnic studies at the University of California, Riverside, who advocated the overthrow of the US government by Latinos and Mexico's reclaiming the Southwestern US. In 2002 he was sworn in as a member of the State Central Committee for the Party of Democratic Revolution, a Socialist party in Mexico.

Jerome R. Corsi and Jim Gilchrist, "The *Reconquista* Movement: Mexico's Plan for the American Southwest," HumanEventsOnline, posted 27 July 2006, third in a series of excerpts from the book *Minutemen: The Battle to Secure America's Borders*. They quoted from a tape of Gutierrez: "We remain a hunted people. Now, you think you have a destiny to fulfill in this land that historically has been ours for forty thousand years. We are a new Mestizo Nation. This is our homeland. We cannot, we will not, and we must not be made 'illegal' in our homeland. We are not 'immigrants' that came from another country to another country. We are migrants free to travel the length and breadth of the Americas because we belong here."

20. Photo in Human Events, 3 April 2006, p. 7.
21. Corsi and Gilchrist, "The *Reconquista* Movement."
22. Ibid.
23. In a speech on 2 September 2007, "Welcome to the United States of Mexico," Muth's News & Views, 6 September 2007.
24. Corsi and Gilchrist, "The *Reconquista* Movement." See also Human Events, 3 April 2006, p. 4. The head of the Mexica Movement was Olin Tezcatlipoca. It is pronounced Meh-SHEE-kah after the Nahuatl word to identify indigenous people from Mexico. Tezcatlipoca wrote on the web site: "This is our land and our continent, this is not property of the Europeans or their descendants. Not one inch of this continent belongs to Europeans, no matter what lies or distortions of ownership they may present.... Remember that we have **only temporarily** (and illegally) been deprived of the rights to our continent and our heritage. This occupation of our continent is **not a permanent condition**." [Emphasis added]
25. Human Events, 3 April 2006, p. 8.
26. "Well Known Group 'MEChA' – With Chapters on Every U.S. College Campus – Says Western U.S.A. Belongs to Them and They Started the Fires to Burn White People Out!!!" Breaking News CNN, 27 October 2007.
27. Jacques Billeaud and Bob Christie, AP, "McCain blasted for blaming blazes on illegal immigrants," *Reno Gazette-Journal,* 22 June 2011, p. 2C.
28.   An example of a school that teaches children to hate the US is Academia Semillos del Pueblo, a charter school partially funded by the Los Angeles Unified School District. "The school's principal, Marcos Aguilar, is a Mexican revolutionary radical who allegedly led a group of Latino students to seize a faculty lounge at UCLA in 1993 and set it on fire, causing $50,000-$100,000 in damages. In 2003, he told an interviewer with UCLA, 'Ultimately, the White way, the American way, the neo liberal, capitalist way of life will eventually lead to our own destruction.'"

The 8th Grade US History class is called, "A People's history of Expansionism and Conflict" including "A thematic survey of American politics, society, culture and political economy; Emphasis throughout on the nations the U.S. usurped, invaded and dominated; Connections between historical rise of capitalism and imperialism with modern political economy and global social relations."

A founding grant to the school came from the National Council of La Raza, a radical organization which supports Reconquista and Aztlan. When Doug McIntyre for KABC Radio tried to interview Aguilar, he was assaulted. Tom Fitton, "A Mexican 'Separatist' School in L.A.?" HumanEventsOnline, 24 August 2006.

Reconquista organizations regularly sponsor forums on TV calling for return of Aztlan, open borders, and insisting on redistricting in order to double the voting strength needed to pass legislation to reach that objective. Their frankness is astounding and would only be permitted in this free country.
29. Immigration Watch, August/September 2011, p. 3.
30. Mike Picione, "Outrage! US Government Funding La Raza with Your Tax Dollars," Guns & Patriots, 11 March 2011.
31. Corsi and Gilchrist, "The *Reconquista* Movement." They have 100 smaller groups in addition to 50 on David Horowitz's DiscoverTheNetworks.org.
32. "Reconquista Shows Its Might," www.lonsberry.com/writings.cfm?story=1871, 26 April 2006. "A Bunch of Illegals. An invading army of people who have flooded our borders and insinuated themselves into our society and economy. An army of people who drain America's prosperity through their disproportionate use of government services and their wholesale export of American currency. They are the bird flu of demographic change. They are the end of American sovereignty as we know it. Since the Manchus breached the Great Wall and the Vandals sacked Rome there has not been such an example of a mighty people being pillaged by a weaker neighbor."

"And now a half million clog the streets of Los Angeles. People who largely have no right to be here. People who any other nation on earth would unflinchingly deport. People whose words betray a strong antipathy for the United States. People who said over and over that the United States would be nothing without them. People who have no gratitude for this nation, but resentment."

"The Mexican national anthem declares that 'heaven gave you a soldier in each son.' And so it is that an army of Mexicans sons and daughters has come to occupy America."
33. Corsi and Gilchrist, "The *Reconquista* Movement."
34. The reversal from Europeans dictated that 85 percent of immigrants hail from the Third World and Asia, which will just help reduce us to Third World status. A moratorium on immigration is needed. "End immigration now, before it ends us." Selwyn Duke, "The Only Way To Win the Immigration Battle," posted 28 September 2007, letters@canadafreepress.com.
35. Quoted in Bartlett and Steele, "Who Left the Door Open?" *Time,* 20 September 2004, p. 53.
36. Human Events, 11 June 2007, p. 6.
37. Rep. Tom Tancredo, "'Sanctuaries' show contempt for our immigration laws," and Wayne Madsen "GOP immigration proposals smack of racism, xenophobia," *Reno Gazette-Journal,* 9 April 2006, p. 19A. Madsen evidently saw no need to enforce US laws.

38. Liz Chandler, Knight Ridder, "Federal agencies control data on illegal immigration," *Reno Gazette-Journal,* 23 April 2006, p. 1A.

39. "2 illegal immigrants win Arizona ranch in court," *Reno Gazette-Journal,* 20 August 2005, p. 3C.

40. Olgar Rodriguez, "U.S. border crackdown has Mexican illegal migrants giving up sooner," *Reno Gazette-Journal,* 2 May 2008, p. 2B. Cinnamon Stillwell, "San Francisco: Sanctuary City Gone Awry," http://www.sfgate.com/cgi-bin/article.cgi?f=/g/a/2008/07/16/cstillwell. DTL, 16 July 2008.

41. USA Today-Gallup poll, *Pittsburgh Tribune-Review,* 22 April 2006.

    Ron Maxwell, a film writer, director, and producer, wrote an open letter to President Bush. He pleaded with the president not to go forward with his amnesty plan. "This is invasion masquerading as immigration." He wrote about reconquista and then, "Many pundits claim you will be remembered in history as the president who won (or lost) the war in Iraq. I see it differently. I believe you will come to be seen, in the years and decades to come, as the president who saved (or lost) the Southwest of the United States.

    "Mr. President, this is a time for candor. Your immigration policy is viewed as captive to the cheap-labor, big-business lobby and inimical to the survival of our country.... Dear Mr. President, this is a utopian creed, which must be discarded before it is too late." He wrote about watching the Senate debate with none "speaking on behalf of the American people," and "you'd think the senators were elected in Mexico."

    Referring to movies he had made about the Civil War and slavery, he wrote, "it troubles me that we appear today to be importing a second virtual slave class, of low-wage workers who are hired to replace or displace less-educated or privileged Americans – including the very descendants of American slaves....

    "The American people have been made the victims of monumental social engineering perpetuated upon them without their consent and against their will by an arrogant governing elite....

    "To do the right thing, to take the safe course for protecting our country you will have to endure even more vilification from the Left, you will have to watch large and increasingly violent rallies by those who don't want to abide by our laws or the will of the American people; who think they are entitled; who believe this country already belongs to them; who believe the rest of us should just move aside, shut-up and smile. To pretend this problem will go away by pandering to the illegal population, or to leave it for the next generation to solve is national suicide." Ronald F. Maxwell, WorldNetDaily.com, 10 May 2006.

42. Human Events, 22 May 2006, p. 5. Marina Montemayor, AP, "Mexico Vows To Sue If Guard Detains," *Washington Times,* 17 May 2006, p. 12. "Mexico to Protest US Border Plan," *The New York Times,* 19 May 2006. Bush even posted his immigration statements and speeches in both English and Spanish. Frosty Wooldridge, "America Will Become America Again," NewsWithViews.com, 16 January 2006. "Fox installed Mexican consulates in 56 American cities to aid and abet his drones."

    Fox told BBC, "I dare say that in 10 years, the U.S. will be begging, will be pleading with Mexico to send it workers." Larry Elder, "How Does Mexico Treat Its Illegals?" Human Events, 10 April 2006, p. 17.

43. Michelle Mittelstadt, *Dallas Morning News,* "Immigration officials given orders for spinning story," *Reno Gazette-Journal,* 29 June 2005, p. 3C.

44. Julieta Nunez Gonzalez, Mexico's National Immigration Institute representative in Ciudad Juarez, Montemayor, "Mexico Vows To Sue If Guard Detains." She quoted one Mexican who had come from the south, "My family is hungry and there is no work in my land. I have to risk it."

45. Alicia A. Caldwell, AP, "Data shows 98 percent of illegal border-crossers are never prosecuted," *Reno Gazette-Journal,* 7 April 2007, p. 6B.

46. "Top 10 Reasons to Oppose Senate Amnesty Bill," Human Events, 17 July 2006, p. 10.

47. Critics tried to attack the figures but their arguments were weak. William Douglas, Knight Ridder, "Think tank's immigration study challenged by critics," *Reno Gazette-Journal,* 24 May 2006, p. 8C.

48. George Will, "Immigration bill has fundamental problems," *Reno Gazette-Journal,* 16 June 2007, p. 8C. See also Mac Johnson, "Of Course, America Has Right to Limit Immigration," Human Events, 18 June 2007, p. 17.

49. "Top 10 Worst Amnesty Provision of the Senate Immigration Bill," compiled by Kris W. Kobach and Matthew Spalding of the Heritage Foundation, Human Events, 4 June 2007, p. 10.

50. Rep. Sam Graves (R-MO) in Muth's News & Views, 15 June 2007.

51. Robert Rector of the Heritage Foundation, Muth's News & Views, 7 June 2007.

52. Alex Alexiev, "Continental Amnesties," National Review Online, 1 May 2006.

53. "Legalizing millions means raising taxes," *Reno Gazette-Journal,* 27 June 2007, p. 12C.

54. Former Sen. Fred Thompson, Muth's News & Views, 6 June 2007.

55. Development, Relief and Education for Alien Minors (DREAM) Act. Audrey Hudson, "Senate Spectacle Thumbs Nose at Immigration Law," HumanEvents.com 1 July 2011.

56. Immigration Watch, August/September 2011.

57. **Purpose**...This memorandum offers administrative relief options to promote family unity, foster economic growth, achieve significant process improvements and reduce the threat of removal for certain individuals present in the United States without authorization. It includes recommendation regarding implementation timeframes and required resources...

    Summary...In the absence of Comprehensive Immigration Reform, USCIS can extend benefits and/or protections to many individuals and groups by issuing new guidance and regulations, exercising discretion with regard to parole-in place, deferred action and the issuance of Notice to Appear (NTA), and adopting significant process improvements...

    ...This would enable thousands of individuals in TPS status to become lawful permanent residents. Similarly where non-TPS applicants have been deemed inadmissible under section 212(a)(6)(A)(i) of the Immigration and Nationality Act ("the Act") for having entered without inspection, USCIS could grant "parole-in-place" (PIP) in the exercise of discretion to create a basis for adjustment in the U.S....

...For example, USCIS could allow employment authorization for H-4 dependent spouses of H-1B principals where the principals are also applicants for lawful permanent residence <u>and have extended their non-immigrant</u> status under the provisions of AC21...

...where no relief appears available based on an applicant's employment and/or family circumstances, but removal is not in the public interest, USCIS could grant deferred action. This would permit individuals for whom relief may become available in the future to live and work in the U.S. without fear of removal...

...Finally, for applicants who have requested relief from USCIS, whether in-country or abroad, and whose application require a waiver of inadmissibility, USCIS could issue guidance or a regulation lessening the "extreme hardship" standard.

This would encourage many more spouses, sons and daughters of U.S. citizens and lawful permanent residents to seek relief without fear of removal. It would also increase the likelihood that such relief would be granted.... Sent out by Judicial Watch.

58. Judicial Watch, August 2011.
59. Letter from Edwin J. Feulner, President, The Heritage Foundation. A *New York Times* Editorial supported Obama's edict not to deport illegals who pose no threat and to focus on criminals. "Toward Immigration Sanity," 19 August 2011.
60. "Parts of Ala. Immigration law cleared," *Reno Gazette-Journal,* 29 September 2011, p. 1C. The Alabama law permits police to arrest people suspected of being illegal, businesses must check the legal status of new workers, and schools have to check student status. It supposedly makes it a crime to give a ride to an illegal immigrant or to knowingly rent to one. Editorial Board, "Congress, administration must tackle immigration," *Reno Gazette-Journal,* 10 July 2011, p. 6D.
    One result of the Alabama law was children withdrawing from schools and Hispanic families considering moving to other states. Jay Reeves, AP, "Hispanic students leaving Alabama public schools," *Reno Gazette-Journal,* 1 October 2011, p. 3C.
61. Thomas Sowell, "The amnesty fraud, Part II," Jewish World Review, 22 May 2007. "There are jobs that just simply aren't getting done because American won't do them." President George W. Bush, Cleveland, Ohio, 20 March 2006.
62. Human Events, 3 April 2006, p. 1.
63. Jim Gilchrist and Jerome R. Corsi, "21st Century Slave Trade: The 'Guest Worker' Amnesty," HumanEventsOnline, 25 July 2006. This was the first in a series of excerpts from the new book, *Minutemen: The Battle to Secure America's Borders.*
    During the Bracero program after 1942, illegal border crossings dropped, supposedly plummeting by 95 percent between 1953 and 1959. *Wall Street Journal* editorial, 13 June 2007.
    That may have been a result of Operation Wetback in 1954 during the Eisenhower presidency. He put Gen. Joseph Swing in charge of the Immigration and Naturalization Service and he deported Mexicans, often including their American-born children. Many Mexicans grew fearful and fled back across the border. His agents found 1 million illegal immigrants in the US. Political correct pressure forced the operation to be abandoned.
    Also, during the Great Depression, President Herbert Hoover ordered deportation of all illegal aliens in order to make jobs available to US citizens who desperately needed work.
64. Columnist Bruce Bartlett, "Political Reality Check," Muth's News & Views, 13 June 2007. Referring to the defeat of amnesty immigration reform, Columnist Dick Yarbrough wrote, "Our political leaders failed to grasp that we consider citizenship a privilege, not a political chip to curry favor with Hispanic voters." Muth's News & Views, 14 July 2007.
65. Bob Lonsberry summed it up: "both parties have been treasonably impotent on this issue. The interests of America were dismissed to serve the interests of the parties." www.lonsberry.com/writings.cfm?story=1871, 26 April 2006.
    If you don't think the people were getting mad, try these comments from Charlie Daniels: "Where are you, you bunch of lily livered, pantywaist, forked tongue, sorry excuses for defenders of The Constitution? Have you been drinking the water out of the Potomac again?" "Mexican Standoff," www.charliedaniels.com, 3 April 2006. The next week was "And the truth is that the gutless, gonad less, milksop politicians are just about to sell out the United States of America because they don't have the intestinal fortitude to stand up to face reality." "Out Of My Face," 10 April 2006.
66. James H. Reza, "Asleep At The Wheel," 26 April 2006.
67. Julie Hirschfeld Davis, AP, "Diminished immigration issue remains politically volatile," *Reno Gazette-Journal,* 9 June 2008, p. 5B.
68. Take as an example, an illegal Mexican sneaked in with his wife and five children and takes a job for $5-6 an hour. With six dependents, he pays no income tax and if he files a tax return, he would get "earned income credit" of up to $3,200 free. He qualifies for Section 8 housing and subsidized rent, food stamps, and free (no deductible, no co-pay) health care. His children get free breakfasts and lunches at school. They require bilingual teachers and books. He qualifies for relief from high energy bills. If they become aged, blind, or disabled, they qualify for SSI. Once qualified for SSI, they can qualify for Medicare. All of this is at taxpayers' expense. He doesn't have to worry about car insurance, life insurance, or homeowner's insurance. Taxpayers provide Spanish language signs, bulletins, and printed material. He cannot be fired, sued, or harassed. Working Americans are lucky to have $5 or $6 an hour after paying their bills and his. Yes, cheap labor!
69. Mac Johnson, "Buchanan's *State of Emergency* Offers One Last Chance on Immigration," Human Events, 28 August 2006, p. 21. "10 Questions for Pat Buchanan," *Time,* 28 August 2006, p. 6. Interview, "Americans Want Their Border Secured Now," Human Events, 25 September 2006, p. 7.
70. Pat Buchanan, "State of Emergency: The Third World Invasion and Conquest of America," Human Events Book Service, 3 August 2006.
71. "Crowded California's population projected to reach nearly 60 million residents by 2050," *Reno Gazette-Journal,* 10 July 2007, p. 2B.
72. Alan Gomez, USA TODAY, "Calif. Bill: A shift on immigration?" *Reno Gazette-Journal,* 13 September 2011, p. 1B.
73. Terence P. Jeffrey, "Yes, Immigration Is About Culture," Human Events, 11 June 2007, p. 5.
74. "Narcos extienden red en EU," *El Universal,* 6 January 2011.
75. Tim Padgett, "Day of the Dead. The drug war is Mexico's tragedy," *Time,* 11 July 2011, p. 27.
76. "Market for Synthetic Drugs Expands," *Milenio* (Mexico), 1 May 2011. http://www.milenio.com/node/707330.

77. Katherine Corcoran, AP, "Truckloads of immigrants a billion-dollar business," Reno *Gazette-Journal,* 20 May 2011, p. 2B. Even Mexican discount airlines jumped on the gravy train by offering "rock-bottom fares to cater to legal and illegal emigrants heading for the U.S." Chris Hawley, USA Today, "Mexican carriers cater to emigrants with low fares," *Reno Gazette-Journal,* 12 October 2007, p. 1B.

78. Damien Cave, "Coming Over, and Over," *The New York Times,* 2 October 2011.

79. Pete Yost, AP, "Latin American gang menacing U.S., FBI says," *Reno Gazette-Journal,* 18 August 2005, p. 1C. Drug busts often are dominated by Hispanic names. See for example: Martha Bellisle, "Drug bust nets 10 arrests," *Reno Gazette-Journal,* 21 May 2008, p. 9A. All 10 were Hispanic.

     MS-13 is operating in 42 US cities according to the *Washington Times,* 29 April 2011.

80. Sam A. Carter and Kenneth Todd Ruiz, "Gang plots border attack," Inland Valley Daily Bulletin, 28 January 2006. Fred Burton, "Mexico's Cartel Wars: The Threat Beyond the U.S. Border," Stratfor: Terrorism Intelligence Report, 25 October 2006. Eileen Sullivan, "Violence in Mexico spills across U.S. border," Associated Press, 14 May 2008.

81. Thanks to Lawrence Martines who is an expert on these gangs. An engineer who spent considerable time in Mexico claimed that 15-25 percent of the illegal Mexicans crossing into the US were criminals and 20-40 percent of the illegals were using or dealing in drugs. He wrote, "If there was a way for people across the world to walk into the USA as Mexicans do, there would be fully 4 billion people coming our way." Dr. Todd. D. Stong, Leola, PA.

82.   Dave Gibson, "DOJ reports cartels targeting local cops in Arizona as National Guard leaves," *Examiner,* 13 January 2012. One lady commented on the article with her vehicle having been hit by an illegal with all fake ID and she had to pay all damages. She said there were "shootouts on our main streets" and her community had been taken over by Mexicans and she had "to have an interpreter in several of our stores here in town, including Walmart." She took her daughter out of school because "90% of the kids were illegals and she was being forced to learn Spanish." She noted 2 Mexican families applying for food stamps and free medical care. When they went out into the parking lot, "one family with 5 kids got into a huge Mercedes SUV, and the other, into a Lincoln SUV."

     Another person commented that "my Great-aunt was forced to sell her house practically on the border way below market value to one of the cartels (probably as a 'safe house') almost literally at the point of one of their guns here in Texas."

83.   Robert Bunker, "Mexican Cartel Strategic Note," 25 September 2011, http://smallwarsjournal.com/blog/mexican-cartel-strategic-note. The August 2011 Threat Assessment is at http://www.justice.gov/ndic/topics/ndtas.htm#y2011.

84.   The document is at http://www.whitehouse.gov/administration/eop/nsc/transnational-crime. Robert Bunker, "Mexican Cartel Strategic Note No. 3," http://smallwarsjournal.com/print/11580, 5 October 2011.

85. "El Saldo de la Gruerra," ElUniversal.com.mx, 13 January 2011.

86. Tim Padgett, "Day of the Dead. The drug war is Mexico's tragedy," *Time,* 11 July 2011, p. 28.

87. Mimi Whitfield, "Drug thugs called greatest security threat in the Americas," *Miami Herald,* 6 May 2011.

88. Stewart M. Powell, "U.S.-Trained Forces Reportedly Helping Mexican Cartels," *Houston Chronicle,* 15 May 2008.

89. Tim Padgett, "Day of the Dead. The drug war is Mexico's tragedy," *Time,* 11 July 2011, p. 28.

90. Jose de Córdoba, "Mexico Fears Rise of Vigilante Justice," *The Wall Street Journal,* 29 September 2011.

91. Tim Padgett, "Day of the Dead. The drug war is Mexico's tragedy," *Time,* 11 July 2011, p. 26.

92. Ibid., p. 27.

93. Nick Miroff and William Booth, "In southern Mexico, a neglected frontier," *Washington Post,* 22 June 2011.

94. Tony Muse, AP, "UN reports 'shocking' 27 percent rise in coca cultivation in Colombia," *Reno Gazette-Journal,* 19 June 2008, p. 2B. It may have gone even higher by now.

95. Frosty Wooldridge, "America Will Become America Again," NewsWithViews.com 16 January 2006.

     "The President of Mexico actively encourages its citizens to illegally emigrate to the U.S. and in fact frequently refers to those who do so as 'heroes.'

     "I can give you the names of eight high-level Mexican politicians who have left office in the last decade with a minimum of $700 million each." Testimony of David J. Stoddard, submitted to the US Subcommittee on Criminal Justice, Drug Policy and Human Resources, Representative Mark Souder, Chairman, 22 February 2002.

96. See George Friedman, "Mexico: On the Road to a Failed State?" Strategic Forecasting, Inc., 13 May 2008. . Stressing how critical this drug war is, see Robert J. Caldwell, "A War We Cannot Afford To Lose," *San Diego Union-Tribune,* 25 May 2008.

97.   See Sergio Solache, *Arizona Republic,* "Bribes take a bite out of Mexican economy," *Reno Gazette-Journal,* 4 September 2006, p. 1C. "Payoffs, kickbacks are way of life in Mexico." Here are the top 10 reasons Mexican pay bribes:

     1. To keep traffic police from towing cars.
     2. As 'rent' to someone who has claimed control of public parking spaces.
     3. To avoid being ticketed or detained by a traffic cop.
     4. To get goods past a customs agent, police roadblock, etc.
     5. To recover a stolen car from the police.
     6. To file a complaint, get authorities to continue investigating a case, or to avoid arrest.
     7. To work or sell in a public right-of-way, such as a sidewalk.
     8. To get city garbage collectors to collect trash.
     9. To get a judge to hear a legal case.
     10. To obtain construction, zoning or demolition permits, or a postal address.

98. Tim Padgett, "Day of the Dead. The drug war is Mexico's tragedy," *Time,* 11 July 2011, p. 28.

99. Thanks to Lawrence Martines for his extra insights to Mexican history. See Mark Stevenson, AP, "Mexican drug cartels threaten cops' lives," *Reno Gazette-Journal,* 19 May 2008, p. 2B, for the cartels sending a brutal message to Mexican police and soldiers: "Join us or die." Also, Andrea Canning and Christina Ng, "Jailed U.S. Border Agent Scary Inside Look at Drug Cartels," http://abcnews.go.com/US/corrupt-guard-offers-inside-mexican-drug-cartels/story?id=14519807, 20 September 2011.

100. Tim Padgett, "Day of the Dead. The drug war is Mexico's tragedy," *Time,* 11 July 2011, p. 30.
101. Jorge G. Castaneda, "The Way Forward," *Time,* 11 July 2011, p. 31.
102. William Lajeunesse, "Exclusive: Third Gun Linked to 'Fast and Furious' Identified at Border Agent's Murder Scene," FoxNews.com, 9 September 2011.
103. "No Excusing the A.T. F., or Congress," *The New York Times,* 28 July 2011.
104. Reuters, "Guns from botched US operation found at Mexican crime scenes," guardian.co.uk, 26 July 2011.
105. Alexander Belensky, "Kenneth Melson Resigns As ATF Chief Over 'Fast And Furious' Gun Trafficking Operation," *The Huffington Post,* 30 August 2011.
106. William Lajeunesse, "Exclusive: Third Gun Linked to 'Fast and Furious' Identified at Border Agent's Murder Scene," FoxNews.com, 9 September 2011.
107. Amanda Lee Myers, AP, "Sheriffs blast botched gun-smuggling operation," *Reno Gazette-Journal,* 8 October 2011, p. 4B.
108. Matthew Boyle, "Holder's No. 2 in 2009: Gunwalking, Fast and Furious a 'terrific idea'," 2 February 2012.
109. http://www.mysanantonio.com/news/articles/Zetas-blamed-for-shootout-in-Houston-2283252.php, 23 November 2011. "Armed illegals stalked Border Patrol," *Washington Times,* 22 November 2011.
110. Figures from http://www.immigrationcounters.com/ as of 26 September 2011.
111. Frosty Wooldridge, "How Much Further Into This Nightmare?" rense.com, 22 January 2007.
     Frosty Woodridge wrote an interesting piece, "What If 20 Million Illegal Aliens Vacated America? NewsWithViews.com, 29 October 2007. He noted huge savings in California, Colorado, Florida, and Chicago, and that the US economy would return to the rule of law. "Employers would hire legal American citizens at a living wage. Everyone would pay their fair share of taxes because they wouldn't be working off the books. That would result in an additional $401 billion in IRS income taxes collected annually, and an equal amount for local, state and city coffers.
     "No more push '1' for Spanish or '2' for English….Our overcrowded schools would lose more than two million illegal alien kids at a cost of billions in ESL and free breakfasts and lunches." We would lose 500,000 inmates, 15,000 MS-13 gang members (and the $130 billion in drugs annually), and 20,000 from LA's 18th Street Gang. It would reduce traffic on our highways, those remittances would not leave our economy, and we would not have all those additional anchor babies.
     An interesting idea. We should try it!
112. Damien Cave, "Crossing Over, and Over," *The New York Times,* 2 October 2011.
113. See Michelle Oddis, "Rising Tide, Rising Burden," HumandEventsOnline, Posted 30 November 2007. Hobbs, *You and the New World Order,* pp. 200-201. The goody-goody social engineers have wreaked havoc in this country. The disastrous bilingualism school programs which started out with the Bilingual Education Act of 1968 with a $7.5 million budget grew to a typical Washington monster that now eats $10 billion a year. And it is a **total failure**.
     New York City reported that the immigrant children in its bilingual program ($300 million a year) did less well at every grade level than similar students who took their classes in English. A 1990 study found that transitional bilingual education was basically no different from doing nothing at all for non-English speaking students.
114. Haya El Nasser and Brad Heath, USA Today, "Hispanic boom extends east," *Reno Gazette-Journal,* 9 August 2007, p. 1B.
115. Andrew Ryan, AP, "2,100 illegal immigrants caught in move against violent criminals," *Reno Gazette-Journal,* 15 January 2006, p. 4C. That was in Boston, part of Operation Return to Sender. Across the country, there were "more than 500,000 'fugitive aliens" who have been deported by judges and either slipped back into the country or never left."
     Erin Texeira, AP, "Immigration from Mexico grows in Northeast," *Reno Gazette-Journal,* 1 August 2005, p. 1B. Nathan Thornburgh, "Inside the Life of the Migrants Next Door," *Time,* 6 February 2006, p. 34. That was in the wealthy Hamptons in New York. The Pew Hispanic Center in Washington noted an irony: "Many towns [Mexican] have lost the best of their labor force. There's money coming in [from the US] but not job creation back home. **It just shows that migration does not solve migration."** p. 41. Denver had to agree not to try to execute a cop killer captured in Mexico so he could be extradited. "Illegal Alien Murderer Cheats the Chair," *Washington Times,* 11 June 2005. Rukmini Callimachi, AP, "Study examines work conditions of immigrants in New Orleans," *Reno Gazette-Journal,* 7 July 2006, p. 5C. Tomas Alextizon, Los Angeles Times, "Sheriff takes own tack on immigration policy," *Reno Gazette-Journal,* 13 May 2006, p. 10A. That was in Oregon.
     Nathan Thornburgh, "How Not to Treat the Guests," *Time,* 4 June 2007, p. 42. North Carolina had a guest worker program that was orderly, rational, and legal – yet it was completely unworkable.
     Robert Tanner, AP, "Governors want action on illegal immigration," *Reno Gazette-Journal,* 27 February 2006, p.1C.
116. Donald L Bartlett and James B. Steele, "Who Left the Door Open?" *Time,* 20 September 2004, p. 51.
117. Jacques Billeaud, AP, "Law pressures immigrants to move," *Reno Gazette-Journal,* 1 March 2008, p. 1B.
118. Alicia A. Caldwell, AP, "Border strategy shift inland," *Reno Gazette-Journal,* 25 January 2008, p. 1B.
119. Rep. J.D. Hayworth in *Whatever It Takes,* quoted in Muth's News & Views, 2 August 2006.
     Three young college students were executed by an illegal immigrant in Newark, New Jersey, thanks to irresponsible politicians and a stupid judge who let him go free on bail from a child rape charge. Newt Gingrich, "Enough is Enough!" "Winning the Future," 14 August 2007. Bill O'Reilly, "Action needed to stop crimes by immigrants," *Reno Gazette-Journal,* 20 August 2007, p. 10E.
120. According to Grey Deacon. "That's what one of the leaders of the group told me personally." Deacon told Joseph Farah on his WorldNetDaily Radio Active program. 15 April 2005.
121. WorldNetDaily.com, 26 April 2006. See David Von Dregle, "A New Line In the Sand," *Time,* 30 June 2008, p. 28.
122. Sara A. Carter, "U.S. tipping Mexico to Minuteman patrols," www.dailybulletin.com/news/ci_3799653, 9 May 2006.
123. Mark Stevenson, AP, "Mexicans attack plan for wall along border," *Reno Gazette-Journal,* 21 December 2005, p. 1C. One might ask, "If a fence doesn't work, why is there one around the White House?"
124. Individual money remittances sent to Mexico from abroad, with US the largest source, rose 1.8% in July 2010 to $1.867 billion. Despite recession, Mexico received $12.495 billion January-July. "Current data of monetary remittances," El Imparcial/Hemosillo, Sonora, 1 September 2010.

125. Victor Davis Hanson, "Hypocrisy That Undermines Civilization," posted, 19 June 2007.

126. Duncan Mansfield, AP, "Anti-illegal immigration movement spreads," *Reno Gazette-Journal,* 18 July 2005. p. 1C. Bill Povey, "Hate crimes against Hispanics in South on rise, say officials." *Reno Gazette-Journal,* 30 July 2005, p. 11C. Jeffrey Ressner, "Rousing the Zealots," *Time,* 5 June 2006, p. 36. Judy Keen, USA Today, "Immigration marches draw backlash in U.S." *Reno Gazette-Journal,* 19 April 2006, p. 1C.

127. See Bartlett and Steele, "Who Left the Door Open?" p. 58, including taped conversations with a chicken plant manager. Peter Prengaman, AP, "Fake ID sellers unconcerned about immigration reform," *Reno Gazette-Journal,* 3 June 2006, p. 1C.

128. Oliver North, "Back Door to Terror," townhall.com, The Conservative Review, 20 October 2006. He referred to a staff report from the House Committee on Homeland Security, "A Line in the Sand: Confronting the Threat at the Southwest Border," which indicated that the border is a sieve.

   Of 445,000 people detained at the southwest border in 2010, 59,000 were OTM and 663 from "special-interest countries" like Afghanistan, Libya, Pakistan, Somalia, and Yemen plus state-terrorist countries Cuba, Iran, Syria, and Sudan. Edwin Moore, "663 Illegal Aliens From Countries With Ties to Terrorism Arrested Along Southwest Border in 201, Senator Says," http://cnsnews.com/sources/74028, 18 March 2011.

129. Bartlett and Steele, "Who Left the Door Open?" p. 52. As we have seen, government enforcement of the laws was pathetic. Two of the men involved in the first World Trade Center attack, had requested asylum in this country and were never discovered. p. 65.

130. J.J. Green, "Al-Qaida Suspect Arrested in Texas," FederalNewsRadio.com, 28 July 2004.

131. Haya El Nasser, USA TODAY, "New face of America: Hispanics surpass 50M," *Reno Gazette-Journal,* 25 March 2011, p. 1B. Non-Hispanic whites now 196.6 million, 64% versus 69% in 2000. Fastest growing was Asians at 14.5 million; now 37.7 million black.

   The good news, if it pans out, is that the influx from Mexico is slowing as life in Mexico improves. Michael Barone, "New Reality Emerging on Illegal Immigration," Human Events, 14 July 2011.

132. Rep. J. D. Hayworh (R-AZ), "Insidious Multiculturalism," *The Arizona Republic,* 29 January 2006.

133. Elan Journo of the Ayn Rand Institute, Muth's News & Views, 20 August 2007.

134. "How a Tolerant Country Can Avoid Being a Doormat for Intolerant Countries," Citizen Warrior, 18 November 2011.

135. Frosty Wooldridge, "What Happens When Diversity Displaces the Host Country's Language and Culture?" *Denver Post,* 24 August 2010.

136. Varsha Bhosle, "The perils of 'multiculturalism'," Rediff India, 2 June 2003, Jihad Watch, 20 January 2010.

137. Joe Klein, "The View from the Border," *Time,* 26 September 2011, p. 26.

138. Quoted in John Fonte, "Victor Davis Hanson's Second Thought on Immigration: A Review-Essay on Mexifornia," Hudson Institute, www.hudson.org, 15 August 2003. Hanson's book is *Mexifornia: A State of Becoming,* (San Francisco, Encounter Books, 2003).

139. Rep. J.D. Hayworth, Muth's News & Views, 14 August 2006.

140. Rush Limbaugh described them "No Mas" on his web site, www.RushLimbaugh.com 6 April 2006.

   Hypocritical? The Mexican police are brutal with illegal immigrants, beating and extorting them. Illegals traveling from Central America are extorted in every stop in Mexico. Mark Stevenson, AP, "Double standard on migrants found in Mexico," *Reno Gazette-Journal,* 19 April 2006, p. 1C.

   A UN report stated, "Mexico is one of the countries where illegal immigrants are highly vulnerable to human rights violations and become victims of degrading sexual exploitation and slavery-like practices, and are denied access to education and health care." In a poll, 73% of Mexicans called Americans racist and 62% said Americans became wealthy by exploiting others. "Mexicans think of Americans as racist, intolerant and not very hard-working." Larry Elder, "How Does Mexico Treat Its Illegals?" Human Events, 10 April 2006, p. 17.

   See also Victor Davis Hanson, "Hypocrisy That Undermines Civilization," posted 19 June 2007, about the brutal Mexican treatment of the Guatemalans.

141. Quoted in "Multiculturalism and the Defense of Liberty," Citizen Warrior, 12 November 2010.

142. Pat Buchanan, "Path to national suicide,"WorldNetDaily.com, 22 May 2007. See Marc Cooper, "Exodus," *The Atlantic Monthly,* May 2006, p. 123, for a review of the illegal immigration problem.

143. One example is Joe Klein, complaining about "cynically exploiting fears born of economic anxiety, ignorance or plain old 'European American' racism." "The Hottest Issue," *Time,* 10 December 2007, p. 33.

144. Ruben Navarrette, "Pundits perpetuate Latino myths, fears," *Reno Gazette-Journal,* 30 May 2008, p. 8E.

145. "The Border," *The Atlantic Monthly,* January/February 2006, p. 54.

One out of every nine Mexicans, Mexican citizens, people born in Mexico, live in the United States today. [Note that he called them Mexican citizens.]

-Jorge Castañeda, Mexico's foreign minister 2000-2003,
Now professor of politics at New York University

Immigration pressure from Mexico is unlikely to abate anytime soon. Nearly half of all Mexicans asked by Pew [Hispanic Center] said they would come to the United States immediately if they had "the means and opportunity." Twenty-one percent said they would do so even if they had to come illegally. Indeed, many Mexicans seem to have a sense of entitlement regarding the United States: 58 percent surveyed in a 2002 Zogby poll believe that "the territory of the United States' Southwest rightfully belongs to Mexico."[145]

Chapter 11

The New World Order

Now we can see a new world coming into view. A world in which there is the very real prospect of a new world order… in which the principle of justice and fair play protect the weak against the strong.

- George H. W. Bush

When China awakens, the world will tremble.

- Napoleon

With the end of World War III, the Cold War, and the advent of World War IV, the Third Great Jihad, a new order began to evolve among nations in the world. Despite the breakup of the Soviet Union, Russia is still a major power and the upsurge in the price of oil has only enhanced the Russian economy and power and renewed its fervor to offset American power. When I first started writing about World War IV, I considered it to be about China but that had to be postponed to World War V.[1] China and India are the two most populous countries with over one billion people each, one third of the total world population, and both are already major players on the world scene and both will be great powers in this century.[2] If India maintains its democratic path, it will not likely become a world threat but can be a major factor in the protection of the sea routes of the Indian Ocean and into Southeast Asia. On the other hand, China, as a Communist country and a major nuclear power with a booming economy, is one of the Big Five on the UN Security Council and has developed interests all over the world, and we have clashed with China directly in Korea, indirectly in Viet-Nam, and spar over Taiwan and their maritime disputes as they search for oil.

The US has clearly turned its attention to Asia and what Secretary of State Hillary Clinton called "America's Pacific Century." The shift to the Asia-Pacific region would displace Europe of the 20th century as the center of gravity for US economic, political, and security interests. Over half the world's economic activity is in countries on the Pacific Ocean and over 60% of US exports go to the APEC (Asia-Pacific Economic Cooperation) economies. Even though this would likely be more of a maritime strategy with less need for Army and Marine Corps troops, Obama made a deal with Australia to base 2,500 Marines in northwest Australia.[3]

The world order has been based on the nation state since the Treaty of Westphalia in 1648, but we now have some non-state actors on the world stage. As we moved into World War IV, we had one rogue major state actor, Iran, and a new non-state actor, al Qaeda, which we have already discussed. Al Qaeda made alliances with other terrorist organizations or developed franchises in other parts of the world. Al Qaeda in Iraq was fairly well decimated. The effort to establish in Saudi Arabia was smashed by the Saudis so it moved to Yemen and established Al Qaeda in the Arabian Peninsula (AQAP). The Jasmine Revolution and the resulting Arab turmoil provided an opening for AQAP to expand in Yemen. The other area where al Qaeda was active was in Africa.

Al Qaeda in Africa

Osama bin Laden lived in the Sudan from 1992 until 1996 after being kicked out of Saudi Arabia. Washington pressured for his removal from Sudan and he went to Afghanistan where he established al Qaeda. Sudan offered to turn bin Laden over to the US but the Saudis objected. Even after he departed Khartoum, Sudan offered in 1997 and 1998 to provide their intelligence on bin Laden but the Clinton administration rejected it. After the US embassies in Nairobi and Dar es Salaam were bombed in 1998, Sudan arrested two of bin Laden's men who were involved and offered them but Clinton's Secretary of State, Madeleine Albright, blocked it. The two men were deported to Pakistan and vanished.[4]

One of the newer areas of al Qaeda's expanded operations was in North Africa. Officials had been tracking the Algeria-based Salafist Group for Preaching and Combat, (known as GSPC for its initials in French) which had long fought in Algeria but had also funneled fighters to Iraq and was involved in attacks across North Africa and in Europe.[5] On the fifth anniversary of 9/11, al Qaeda chose GSPC as its representative in North Africa. In January 2007, the group joined forces with Osama bin Laden and changed its name to **Al Qaeda in the Islamic Maghreb (AQIM)**. The objective was to combine the efforts of various groups: Morocco's Islamic Combatant Group, Libya's Islamic Fighting Group, and the Tunisian Combatant Group. There was further activity across the Sahel, south of the Sahara, including Mauritania, Mali, Niger, Chad, and Nigeria. The new name brought added prestige, better fund raising, and a boost in morale. This base in North Africa is close to Europe and many North Africans have ties to communities in Europe and North America. The problem for the US is that people with European passports can come to the US without visas. There have already been attacks by AQIM and there will be more.[6]

Horn of Africa

Somalia had been in anarchy since the warlords overthrew Mohamed Siad Barre in 1991 and then fought among themselves. The UN and the US tried to help resulting in "Blackhawk down" in 1993 and the US withdrawal. Radical groups like *al-Itihaad al-Islamiya*, supported by Osama bin Laden, had operated in Somalia for years. Ras Kamboni on Somalia's southern border was al Qaeda's oldest training camp in Africa. Three of the suspects in the 1998 embassy bombings were based in Somalia and were part of bin Laden's network according to the FBI. They were also evidently involved in the 2002 attack on the Israeli-owned Paradise Hotel near Mombasa, Kenya and the unsuccessful launching of two missiles against an Israeli airliner. There had also been a plot to attack the US base in Djibouti in 2006 which had opened in 2002 for the Combined Joint Task Force – Horn of Africa. The US Sixth Fleet, based in Gaeta, Italy, periodically patrols the coasts of Africa and works with other navies in operations against the Somali pirates. In 2007, a new headquarters, AFRICOM (US Africa Command), was established in Stuttgart, Germany to deal with Africa. US military teams were active working with local forces in numerous African countries.[7]

> **Somalia had been in anarchy since the warlords overthrew Mohamed Siad Barre in 1991.**

Peace talks in Kenya in 2004 resulted in a transitional federal government being formed in Baidoa but it could not move to Mogadishu due to the growing influence of al-Itihaad, which had imported large amounts of munitions despite an arms embargo. The UN named 17 specific military training camps set up by the group.[8]

After heavy fighting with the warlords (evidently backed by the US), the Union of Islamic Courts was in control of Mogadishu by June 2006.   The UIC claimed to be a popular, indigenous group; however, it was more like the Taliban.   The UIC consisted of at least three major jihadi groups in addition to al-Itihaad and was reinforced by foreign jihadis.   The first objective was obviously Somalia, but Ethiopia and Kenya would not be far behind as they both had large populations of ethnic Somalis and pockets of jihadis.[9]

Taliban-style rule became evident quickly as sharia was imposed.   A wedding party was broken up because of music and men and women socializing together and two people were killed while watching a World Cup soccer broadcast.[10]   There have been repeated incidents since with public amputations, executions for blasphemy and apostasy, and brutal attacks on any non-Muslims.   Ethiopia, which had sent its troops into Somalia in 1993 and 1996 to put down Islamic militants, sent its troops in to support the government in Baidoa.   Hassan Dahir Aweys, the head of the UIC, which had absorbed al-Itihaad, called for "a holy war against Ethiopians in Baidoa," and expanded its control and the US accused it of harboring al Qaeda bombers.[11]

While the UIC was in control they even sent a force of 720 to fight alongside HezbAllah in the 2006 War with Israel.   In return HezbAllah arranged for Iran and Syria to provide arms and supplies to the UIC.   The UN reported that 200 UIC fighters were flown "to Syria to undergo military training in guerrilla warfare" and that Syria delivered large quantities of arms, including surface-to-air missiles.   Iran supplied thousands of machine guns, grenade launchers, and 45 man-portable surface-to-air missiles (MANPADS) on one occasion and 80 on another.   Interestingly, Iranians were looking for uranium.[12]

The Ethiopians invaded at the end of 2006 and quickly routed the UIC and installed the transitional federal government in Mogadishu.   Many of the UIC fled to Ras Kamboni and Kenya and the leadership went to Eritrea.   The US made several air strikes against the al Qaeda forces in the South and a US warship fired on jihadis in the North.[13]   **Al-Shabaab al-Mujahedin** (Jihadist Youth or Mujahedin Youth Movement), originally the militant wing of the Islamic Courts Union, waged an insurgency since 2006 against Somalia's transitional government and its Ethiopian supporters.   It was supplied from Eritrea with large amounts of arms including SA-18 (Russian) MANPADS and one was used to shoot down a Belarus cargo plane.   Al-Shabaab leaders have claimed since 2007 that they were affiliated with al Qaeda.[14]   There were numerous reports of American citizens in Somalia with al-Shabaab, with one report listing a total of 40.[15]   Al-Shabaab claimed responsibility for two bombings in Kampala, Uganda on 11 July 2010 that killed 70 people and in numerous attacks against the African Union peacekeeping forces, they have killed AU soldiers.[16]   They also conducted attacks in Kenya including one in which they captured two Spanish aid workers.[17]

Al Qaeda long supported al-Shabaab in its efforts to prevent stability in Somalia and the leaders of al-Shabaab claimed affiliation with al Qaeda since 2007.

The transitional government split along clan loyalties again and the threat arose of a regional war with Eritrea providing a base for Somali rebels, the UIC, and Eritrean-backed Ethiopian rebels fighting the Ethiopian army in the Ogaden in eastern Ethiopia.   The UN was concerned about "a military buildup along the Eritrea-Ethiopia border, where the U.N. has had peacekeepers since 2001."   The head of the UIC militia "issued a proclamation hailing bin Laden and calling on Somalis to target peacekeepers."   The UIC announced that Somalia was open to the mujahedin from around the world, "We're saying our country is open to Muslims worldwide.   Let them fight in Somalia and wage jihad, and God willing, attack Addis Ababa."

As a senior US special operations commander said, if we drive al Qaeda out of its sanctuary in Pakistan, where will they go? Africa.[18]

Even before the death of Osama bin Laden in May 2011, there had been talk of al Qaeda operatives moving from Pakistan to Yemen or Somalia. There were even rumors that Ayman al-Zawahiri, the new leader of al Qaeda, had left Pakistan for the Horn of Africa or that region.

In addition to the fallout from Somalia into Kenya, Uganda, Ethiopia, and Eritrea, there was a different player in Nigeria. **Boko Haram** is a radical Muslim group in Nigeria's Muslim north. Boko Haram, which means roughly "Western education is sin," was formed in 2002 by Muhammad Yusuf, a radical salafist cleric with the goal of overthrowing the Nigerian government and establishing an Islamic state and imposing sharia. After some early activity, the group went underground from 2005 until 2008. There have been many attacks since, particularly against Christians, with thousands killed. There was a major battle with the government on 26 July 2009 in which 800 were killed (mostly Boko Haram) and Yusuf was executed. Nigeria is the largest country in Africa and quite diverse with 150 million people, 50% Muslim, 40% Christian (mostly in the south), and 10 local sects, with 350 ethnic groups speaking 250 languages. US officials claimed that Boko Haram was coordinating with both AQIM and al-Shabaab.[19]

China – Rival or Partner?

The Chinese civilization is one of the oldest and richest in history and both historically and culturally, it is the civilization of the Far East. China was an empire until the revolution of 1911, but that is somewhat misleading because China was the superior member of a Confucian family of nations rather than a geographical area in a political sense. China has some 56 ethnic groups with Han being 92% (they are not homogenous). The world to the Chinese consisted of The Middle Kingdom – China proper – at the center, with various tributary states or political satellites around it which accepted Chinese culture or some variation of it, usually in direct proportion to the distance from the center. The rest of mankind, the outside world, consisted of barbarians who were far below the cultural level of the Chinese and therefore of little interest or importance. So impressed were the Chinese with the grandeur of their way of life that they were contemptuous of all other peoples; even the Chinese language evokes this image: the word for foreigner is barbarian.

> **Every Chinese is born at least thirty-five hundred years old.**
>
> - K. S. Latourette

Trade has always been considered a means of controlling tributary states not as a source of income for the government. China's isolation was shattered by the expanding West, mainly England and the US. At the same time they were being pressured by the outsiders, there was the T'ai-p'ing and other rebellions and unrest internally. With the Opium War and the various treaties they were forced to accept in the 19th century, China suffered severe humiliation which left scars no doubt to this day. The instability indicated the Manchu dynasty was losing the Mandate of Heaven, a key axiom of Confucianism which is probably in the backs of the minds of current Communist leaders.

> **The disaster that hit China in the 19th Century is one of the most comprehensive any people ever experienced.**
>
> **- John K. Fairbank**

After Mao Tse-tung came to power in 1949, he instituted central planning and the country continued as drab as the Mao uniforms. Deng Xiaoping was able to rationalize scrapping Mao's disastrous economic policies by saying, "It doesn't matter if a cat is black or white, as long as it catches mice." He delighted the masses by saying "To become rich is glorious."[20] Deng said "Reform and openness are China's only way out," and established an "open door" policy for investment and trade and the Chinese economy took off. He called it "socialism with Chinese characteristics," but it was more realistically "capitalism with Chinese characteristics." The country was no longer totalitarian, just authoritarian. As a Tiananmen Square survivor said, "There has been a compromise between the government and the Chinese people. They're concentrating on the economy and we're minding our own business."[21] This was a largely accepted "post-1989 social contract in which the Party provided rising living standards in return for not questioning its monopoly on power."[22]

Most are aware of the booming Chinese economy and its exports, particularly to the US; but many are unaware of the extent of Chinese activities around the world. Because of its foreign investments and its voracious appetite for raw materials, China is helping economies across Africa, the Middle East, and Latin America. This is due partly, of course, to the search for oil since China has to import 47 percent of its oil. China was a net oil exporter in the 1970s and 1980s but shifted to a net importer in 1993 as its economy boomed. China owns 40 percent of the oil concession in southern Sudan and operated there throughout the civil war (there were supposedly some 4,000 Chinese troops protecting their interests), has a major operation in Nigeria, was drilling in Angola, and in the Ogaden in Ethiopia (Ogaden National Liberation Front rebels attacked the Chinese company on 24 April 2007 killing 68 Ethiopians and nine Chinese). China has made deals in South America and signed a $16 billion contract with Iran for natural gas and will help develop some of their oil fields. In contrast with Chinese help in dealing with North Korea's nuclear program, China has sided with Russia in blocking strong sanctions against Iran.[23]

> **China does not give away money as gifts; those infrastructure jobs are deals paid for by mining concessions, oil, or some other commodities.**

China was looking for food, oil, and minerals in Africa while building roads, railroads, and opening textile factories. They were buying beef and soy from Brazil, phosphates from Morocco (even though some were in the disputed Western Sahara); they own a manganese smelter in Zambia; they blasted open the Mekong River so large boats could carry Chinese goods to markets in Southeast Asia. China has 20 percent of the world's population and exports labor to many countries with many going to the Middle East. Nearly half the 18,000 foreign workers in an unsafe place like Algeria are Chinese. President Hu Jintao spent two weeks in South America in 2004 pledging billions of dollars in investment in Argentina, Brazil, Chile, and Cuba. Premier Wen Jiabao visited 15 countries in 2006. In 2006 Hu visited Kenya, Morocco, Nigeria, Russia, Saudi Arabia, and the US, and he hosted leaders from 48 African countries promising "to double aid to Africa by 2009, train 15,000 professionals and provide scholarships to 4,000 students and help Africa's health-care and farming sectors. He also found time to visit Viet-Nam (they fought in 1979), Laos, India (they fought in 1962), and Pakistan.

Hu reached out to India to double their trade and bid jointly on oil projects. He also tried to improve relations with longtime rival Japan.[24]

China does not give away money as gifts; those infrastructure jobs are deals paid for by mining concessions, oil, or some other commodities. Chinese investment in Africa now exceeds $100 billion, much more than foreign aid. One advantage is that while it takes years for loan talks with the World Bank or the International Monetary Fund, it only takes weeks with China.[25] All this was good business for Chinese companies which found doing business in Africa less competitive than back home. Africans have noted the economic instability in the West and see "a better model in Asia, which has achieved more growth by combining state capitalism and illiberal politics." Chinese practices, particularly the number of Chinese workers on projects, have provoked opposition. "Chinese companies bring to Africa the poor labor relations, low wages, inadequate safety standards, and weak environmental protections they are used to at home."[26] It may or may not be neocolonialism, but some criticism of Chinese practices appeared which may dampen their successes in the future.

> **Other countries say, This country has huge problems. We say, This country has huge potential. In 50 years, we will still be here. So will Congo and the mines. Short term, sure, problems. Long tern, not much risk.**
> **- Wu Zexian, Ambassador to the Democratic Republic of Congo**

Doubts about Chinese intentions remained and the leaders addressed them. For example, Premier Wen Jiabao tried to assure critics at a news conference in Cairo at the start of his tour of seven African countries. He stated that China's efforts to expand trade and energy ties in Africa and Latin America posed no threat to US interests. Chinese foreign policy was based on mutual benefits and would not interfere in domestic politics.[27] Those living in the shadow of the Middle Kingdom wanted the US to be far more active in the area. "You have many friends in this region," said Singapore's Prime Minister, Lee Hsien Loong. "But the attitude of many Asian nations is that China will be here for 2,000 years. America is here today but may go away. And if you stop paying attention to us, we have only one suitor and only one option."[28]

Yet some still feared confrontation between China and the West because of the massive modernization of the Chinese military and a possible war over Taiwan.[29] Since China seems to have everything going for it now, it would be stupid to risk it all over Taiwan. Huang Jing of Brookings said, "China is now basically on the same page as the U.S. when it comes to Taiwan. Neither wants independence for Taiwan. Both want peace and stability." Let's hope that wise minds prevail. It would be good for China and the US to work together, such as trying to solve the energy problem.[30]

China's Domestic Situation

But China is still a poor country with a growing gap between rich and poor. The enormous population still exceeds the number of jobs that can be created. What would happen if the Chinese boom collapsed? The economic problem would become a socio-political problem. Many non-viable enterprises are kept afloat by cash and cheap exporting. If exports slow, that could lead to failure in some of those enterprises which would lead to unemployment which could lead to instability. China does not need that and was making every effort to prevent it. Adding to the exposure of the economy, nonperforming and troubled loans are a very large part of the GDP. The political arrangements between the richer coastal provinces and the poorer interior would be strained which could weaken Beijing's authority and lead to instability and regionalism.   Then it would no longer be an economic crisis, but a political crisis.[31]   There may be something like 100,000 serious riots each year and the Chinese leadership is very sensitive about stability and moves quickly to suppress any protests.[32]

> **In China's thousands of years of civilization, the conflict between humanity and nature has never been as serious as it is today.**
> **- Minister of Environment Zhou Shengxian, February 2011**

A population of 1.34 billion requires an enormous amount of resources. They require plenty now but by 2035, China's income per person should equal the current US level. If they were to spend like Americans, an interesting picture evolves. China would need 1.5 billion tons of grain to feed 1.38 billion people. That is 70% of current world production. Would that remaining 30% be enough for the other 7.1 billion people? They would use 80% of the amount of paper produced in the world today, leaving 20% for the other 84% of the population. It is estimated that China will have 1.1 billion cars, the current world total. They will require highways, roads, and parking lots equal to 66% of the land used to grow rice. That pavement will impact on food production. China will need 85 million barrels of oil per day, current world production. The outlook is for only about that same amount in 2035. It shows that the "western economic model – the fossil-fuel-based, automobile-centric, throwaway economy – will not work for the world." It will not work for China and not for India which is projected to have an even larger population than China.[33]

China requires a great deal of food and as diets change with a higher standard of living, there is an increase in meat consumption which requires grain for feed. China already buys a quarter of all US soybeans and recently bought a large amount of corn.   The Chinese "Communist Party worries in particular about food inflation, which could put social stability at risk." If China consumed meat like the US, it would require "an additional 24 billion bushels of corn, or about twice what the U.S. produces in a year." There is not enough in the world for that.[34]

All that agriculture requires water and China has only about one fourth of the world average in per capita water resources and it is unevenly distributed. Northern China produces over 50% of GDP with over half the agricultural land and 40% of the population, but it receives only 12% of the precipitation.   Southern China receives 80% of the precipitation but has skyrocketing pollution. Industry is another large water consumer using about 25%, "from four to 10 times more water per unit of GDP as other competitive economies." There is heavy use for energy with coal processing alone using 20% of all water. China is already the world's largest producer of hydropower and they plan to triple it by 2020. Agriculture consumes 62% of the water and irrigation is very inefficient in the dry north which has most of the arable land with less than half actually reaching crops. China plans to urbanize 400 million people by 2030 which will only further stress the water supply since urban middle class dwellers use three times as much water as rural users.[35]

> **China has only about one fourth of the world average in per capita water resources and it is unevenly distributed.**

China is not blessed with farm land as it has only 15% arable land. In the south, 90% of their water comes from surface water which is now so polluted that 25% is not even usable for industry and half is undrinkable. The situation is only growing worse as "from 2000 to 2009, the amount of accessible water in China decreased by 13 percent....In rural China, 320 million people –one-quarter of China's total population – don't have access to safe drinking water." As if those problems were not enough, desertification in the north near the Gobi Desert is removing 1,060 square miles annually. These problems translate into crop loss, poisoned fish and livestock, water shortages for factories, and serious public health issues leading to social unrest which is the major policy concern. The number of environmental protests has increased reaching 180,000 in 2010. Another result of the information revolution is that the Internet and cell phone texting have aided the protesters in presenting their cases.[36]

There is a global impact to China's need for water that has brought them into conflict with their neighbors. Some of the large rivers have headwaters in China, particularly the Mekong and the Brahmaputra. China built a dam on the Mekong which is critical to Southeast Asia and has adversely affected Viet-Nam, Cambodia, and Thailand. Without telling India, China started building a $1.2 billion dam on the Brahmaputra (Yarlung Tsangpo River in China) which supplies 30% of India's water and 40% of its hydropower. The South-North Water Transfer project is of further concern to India. It is an audacious $60-80 billion project to channel water from the south to the north via three tunnels, each over 700 miles long. It would divert 5% of the Yangtze River's flow to the Yellow, Hai, and Huai Rivers with accompanying disruption of farmers like what happened with the Three Gorges Dam. China expects to spend $615 billion on water projects in the next decade. Population growth is estimated to require 25% more agricultural production yet that production is projected to drop by 23% by 2050. The shortage of water and arable land has led China to buy land abroad with large-scale Chinese farms in Argentina, Australia, Brazil, Kenya, Russia, and Zimbabwe. As noted above, Chinese actions have produced some opposition: "the Chinese proclivity to export its farmers along with its capital has been a source of ongoing popular concern in some of these countries, some of which view China as the next colonizing power."[37]

China already consumes a large amount of coal and hydropower for power generation. Currently 5.3 Chinese live on the electricity the average American consumes in a year (China consumes 20% of the US electrical supply on a per capita basis). Incidentally, in India, 30 live on the electricity of a single American. Daily Wealth, 12 August 2010. Obviously, as these economies grow, there will be an increased demand for resources for power generation.

While China has searched abroad for minerals to feed its industrial boom, one strategic area has become a problem: rare earths which are key to high technology production. Environmental regulations shut down most US production and China has a near monopoly producing 97% of the world's rare earths, half of which come from a single mine in Inner Mongolia. They are needed for TVs, hybrid vehicles, fiber optics, wind turbines, energy-efficient lightbulbs, iPods, and military electronics (which makes it a national security problem). China used its position in the recent clash with Japan over a sea incident by cutting off sales of rare earths to Japan. The problem has generated the reopening of US mines to expand access.[38]

> **In addition to the conflicts generated by the search for oil in the South China Sea, a potential new conflict area has arisen in the Indian Ocean.**

In addition to the conflicts generated by the search for oil in the South China Sea and the East China Sea, a potential new conflict area has arisen in the Indian Ocean. In July 2011, China "secured approval from the International Seabed Authority (ISA) to explore the southwestern Indian Ocean ridge for polymetallic sulphide nodules." This was not well received in India which sees this as paving the way for a Chinese naval presence in the Indian Ocean. China has been using a manned submersible program while India has used unmanned submersibles. As an apparent result, India has stood firm with its exploration interests with the Vietnamese in their area of the South China Sea. It is clear a new "arms" race is underway between the world's two most populous countries.[39]

While the world focused on Europe and the US in their economic recoveries, concerns have grown about the Chinese economy. Infrastructure has been overbuilt, partially because it provided jobs for low-skilled workers. Along with inflation and bad bank loans, there is a widening gap between rich and poor, which again threatens stability. There are vacant shopping centers, office buildings, and apartment towers. "The Chinese government is deliberately bringing down real estate prices to improve the affordability of housing and prevent the housing bubble from becoming worse."[40] The Mall of China is one of the largest in the world, but it sits empty. The building frenzy led to questionable financial practices. "Local governments, borrowing heavily against land slated for construction – their major revenue producer – will need increased central government funding (official debts have reached $1.6 trillion with defaults estimated at 20 percent to 30 percent)." China's economic growth has been truly phenomenal but it may be a victim of its own success. "Without a true middle class revolution, China's economic foundations will increasingly rest on shifting sands."[41]

When all the debts are totaled, "the country's gross public debt would be somewhere in the vicinity of 70 percent of GDP, making its public finances appear much worse than official announcements would indicate" much having been incurred in the past two years and the debt accumulation is continuing.[42] In addition to the state-owned enterprises which are inefficient and corrupt and employ from 25 to 40% of the urban labor force which is not likely to be reduced due to the threat of instability, Doug Casey believes "that most of the banks in China are soon going to be bankrupt." He added, "I think the odds of a financial debacle in China are high, and its consequences could include political, social, and military turmoil."[43]

> **While the world focused on Europe and the US in their economic recoveries, concerns have grown about the Chinese economy.**

One result of that growth is the end of cheap labor in China. Real wages for manufacturing workers have grown about 12% annually (now projected that "wage and benefit costs will increase 15% to 20% annually in China as it becomes a consumer-oriented economy"[44]). Adjusted for productivity, the Chinese wage is now about half the US wage and projected to be about two-thirds by 2015. This has helped Viet-Nam, Laos, Cambodia, and India as well as western China where wages are still lower. Also, many multinationals are now focused on the Chinese market rather than exports.[45] As for holding such a large portion of their reserves in dollars, $1.5 trillion, one writer said, all they can do is "continue to buy, hold and grumble." There really is no other place to put their money. As one analyst described the situation, "the fiscal cold war means 'China is increasingly integrated with the future of the U.S. But that could be a good thing, for both sides.'"

Those large reserve holdings fit in with another stated Chinese goal – to create a new world currency to replace the dollar and to recover as much as possible of that $1.5 trillion. To accomplish that, China is buying up gold. China is already the largest gold producer and is buying up gold companies and gold itself to evidently make the Chinese currency (the yuan or renminbi) the new world reserve currency. Accompanying this plan would be the opening of a new gold exchange to compete with the London Metals Exchange and the COMEX in New York.[46]

The commerce minister made an interesting proposal: He said that China "would like to convert some of its US government debt into investment opportunities." He said that "China could help the United States in its infrastructure, clean energy and technology build-up." Renovating US roads and railway infrastructure "would tie China in with the overall US economy" and help allay "fears that Beijing would use its massive foreign reserves as a political weapon against the US."[47]

One dissident wrote, "that without reform of the economic system – and especially if they fail to insert democracy within their domestic politics – they will not be able to avoid social unrest and the collapse of the one-party dictatorship." He claimed that transnational capital was the exploiter and that "Global free trade has been transformed into a tool of transnational capital for excess profits." He wrote that this "will force the West to speed up its process of protectionism and simultaneously speed up the outbreak of social conflict in China, thus speeding up the collapse of communist regime." The Chinese Communist Party (CCP) "is controlled by the big capitalists, for whom it is impossible to give up excess profits and impossible to truly initiate the reform process. Thus, capital and the CCP can only take China into the abyss, and cause a new round of global economic turmoil."[48]

The CCP which was once a revolutionary party is now firmly the establishment. As is typical of any one-party system, everything becomes subordinate to keeping the Party in power. As a senior official said, China's "number one core interest is to maintain its fundamental system and state security." The Party now has some 76 million members, but the country is run by a tight-knit group of about 300. The Party "keeps a lock-hold on the state and three pillars of its survival strategy: control of personnel, propaganda and the People's Liberation Army." It, in that sense, is still very much still a communist party. A small number of these major executives are tied together by a "red phone" on their desks, the ultimate status symbol.[49] The Party is a dictatorship with capitalist trappings.

All is not well in China even though the economy should grow more than 9% in 2011. Criticism of the government is exploding (despite censorship) and a poll showed 40% unhappy with their lives. Another poll reflected 70% of farmers unhappy and 60% of the rich are emigrating or thinking about it. Upward mobility is limited unless one is a member of the party. Tightened credit measures to slow inflation and efforts to raise taxes are increasing discontent. With economic problems in Europe and the US, all is not rosy in China either.[50]

China contributed 19% of world economic growth in 2010 and was expected to add 24% in 2011. A crash would be devastating to the global economy. The Chinese miracle of 30 years was based on cheap labor, cheap land, and cheap capital. However, that model was breaking down. Wen Jiabao called the economy "unbalanced, uncoordinated and unsustainable." The real estate bubble is still threatening. "Local government debt grew about 30% in 2010 from the previous year." In the first six months of 2011, Chinese investment in real estate was up 33% from the same period in 2010. Part of the problem in changing the model is "local and provincial government's addiction to revenue from land sales." Land sales doubled from 2009 to $500 billion in 2010. "Because provincial officials are promoted on the basis of their GDP growth figures and because land sales are an important part of local revenue, it's difficult to curb enthusiasm of local officials for project development."[51]

Many companies are expanding their business in China. Gap, the US jeans company, announced it was closing 20% of its US stores but tripling the number in China. This makes for irony: "wobbly Western economies are depending on the Chinese Communist Party to save their capitalist bacon. Likewise, the Chinese government's grand scheme to rebalance its economy hinges on Western-style materialism."[52]

Unrest is strong in three areas of the country: Tibet, Inner Mongolia, and Xinjiang, which are not ethnically Chinese. The Chinese government has reacted brutally at times and has pursued a policy of encouraging Han immigration to change the ethnic make-up. Tibet has been under Chinese domination since the Dali Lama was forced to flee. Inner Mongolia is the fastest growing province but the environmental costs of mining in a resource-rich area have stirred ethnic strife. Unrestrained mining is destroying local lands and Mongolian culture with Mongolians reduced to under 20% of the population.[53] Xinjiang in the far west has a Turkic Muslim majority, Uighurs, which are of concern to Beijing due to the activities of militant Islam in other countries. The Chinese military claimed (with no explanation) that "Separatist forces working for 'East Turkistan independence' and 'Tibet independence' have inflicted serious damage on national security and social stability."[54]

One of the controversial policies was the one-child policy which did slow population growth by half but has left an older and more urbanized population. India is now expected to surpass China in 2026 with about 1.5 billion people.[55] Now China is loosening the policy with a pilot project in five provinces. Some 400 million births were prevented but with the traditional preference for boys and a large number of abortions of girls, there are tens of million of men who cannot marry and there are less children to take care of parents who live longer.[56]

With all those millions of bachelors and a dearth of arable land and water, China may decide it needs some place to expand. The only open space is to the north – Siberia. With a declining Russia and an ascendant China, there may well be a Chinese push into Siberia in coming decades.

> **One of the controversial policies was the one-child policy which did slow population growth by half but has left an older and more urbanized population.**

China has decided that it needs to move into higher-quality goods and services, so it decided to invest in human capital. It has made a massive investment in education since 1998 by tripling the GDP share for it. The number of colleges has doubled and the number of students has increased five-fold from 1 million in 1997 to 5.5 million in 2007.[57] Chinese emphasis is clear with about twice as many undergraduates in science and engineering as in the US. They are well positioned to absorb new technology and their technological sophistication is growing.[58] One indicator is the number of scientific papers published: 25,474 in 1996 (US 292,513) and 184,080 in 2008 (US 316,317). China may overtake the US in scientific output in 2013.[59] An accomplishment which was a particular sense of pride was in 2010 when China built the fastest supercomputer ever made, the Tianhe-1A which is 1.4 times faster than the next fastest.[60]

China moved past Japan and became the world's second largest economy and some predicted that China's GDP might be almost double that of the US by 2030.[61] Depending how one weighed the three key factors of GDP, trade, and net creditor status, "China was already ahead of the United States in 2010." Internal stability may well be their greatest threat. Regardless, "a strong rival has emerged. China may not quite be an adversary, but it is not an ally, either."[62]

China's Military

The People's Liberation Army (PLA) had been modernizing with double digit budget growth annually over the past two decades. The PLA moved away from the human wave tactics of Korea and had slimmed down to 2.3 million members, still the largest in the world, with infantry now a much lower proportion with increases in the air force, navy, and Second Artillery Corps which contains their nuclear missiles. Their goal was a slimmer, more mobile force with advanced weaponry and the latest technology.[63] Again, Premier Wen Jiabao tried to allay fears of Chinese growing military power. China tested its anti-satellite weapon in January 2007 by shooting down one of its weather satellites.   Wen said China did not want an arms race in space and called for an international convention to ban weapons in outer space.[64]

Emphasizing the significance of their ICBM capability, China moved into space launching lunar probes in 2007 with the intent of putting a man on the moon after 2017. (India launched a probe in 2008.)[65] In 2010, China matched the US number of rocket launches into space with 15.   Further demonstrating their ambition to be a major space power, China launched a box-car-size Tiangong-1 module on a Long March 2FT1 rocket from the Jiuquan center on the edge of the Gobi Desert.   They announced plans to launch an unmanned Shenzhou 8 spacecraft very soon to practice remote controlled docking maneuvers with the module.[66]

We must transform the Chinese coastal defense force into a blue water navy.
                                                                    - Chou En-lai

---

The People's Liberation Army Navy (PLAN) continued its buildup with some 562 ships, 65 submarines, including five new nuclear-powered strategic missile submarines (SSBNs) called the Type 094 each equipped with 12 new JL-2 missiles with a range of 5,000 miles.   Those would join 60 land-based DF-31 missiles to provide long range nuclear capability. The missiles could have multiple warheads "since China is known to have acquired all the needed technology from the U.S. during the 1990s." They also had a cruise missile similar to the Tomahawk and were upgrading and increasing their large fleet of attack submarines and surface ships. They now have more classes of submarines than any other navy. The Type 052C Luyang IIs are guided-missile destroyers and the "small craft like the stealthy, missile-armed Type 022 Houbei fast attack craft" are suitable for swarm attacks as we noted with the Iranian fleet in the Persian Gulf.[67]

Their J-10 aircraft entered service in 2004. It looks like the Israeli Lavi jet that the US wasted $1.3 billion on before getting it cancelled in 1987. The J-10 has no US-made parts (its engine is Russian); however, "after Israel discontinued the largely U.S.-funded project, it sold China the plans for the Lavi and the associated secret U.S. technology."[68] They have SU-27 jet fighters and the new J-20 stealth jet which may not be operational until 2018.

The 2011 Military Assessment highlighted two new systems which had been flaunted during Defense Secretary Gates' visit to China in January 2011. The first was the Anti-Ship Ballistic Missile (ASBM) DF-21D which had been developed faster than expected and was clearly a threat to our aircraft carriers. It is a truck-launched system capable of striking ships hundreds of miles at sea. The second was the J-20, a new fighter with stealth capability. Their military budget is always difficult to calculate but was estimated at $100 billion. Chinese intentions are always unclear due to no transparency which could "contribute to regional tensions and anxieties."

By perhaps 2015, the PLA will be entirely funded by US taxpayers paying the interest payments on US debt held by China.[69]

Their next goal is aircraft carriers,[70] which are symbols of great power status, clearly a Chinese aspiration; but they are very complex and not cheap and require a support group of escort and logistic ships. They had talked about it for 25 years and they bought one old Russian hulk from Ukraine in 1998, the Varyag, which is their first carrier. There are several reasons in addition to the international prestige to be a world power. The most pressing may be to defend sea lines of communication particularly with their dependence on imported oil. The Strait of Malacca is a dangerous bottleneck that they might deem necessary to protect. It would provide power projection, useful in disputes as a forward mobile airfield in the South China Sea and would help in their rivalries with India (which has carriers) and Japan. A last reason is relief operations, since they were embarrassed when they were unable to do anything to help after the tsunami in 2004. Carriers would not be necessary for an attack on Taiwan, but operations east of the island would further complicate Taiwan's defense which is already difficult by forcing them to defend to the east as well as to the west. The Varyag, now evidently called the Shi Lang, has an upswept deck for assisting aircraft takeoff and is now in sea trials. Carrier operations are not easy and it will take the Chinese years to develop their skills and tactics. With rotation and maintenance time, one carrier will not suffice so there will be several more eventually. The political impact is key in that "China has emerged, that China really is no longer just a second-tier country, but economically, politically and militarily, China is one of the big boys now."[71]

> **The political impact of China having an aircraft carrier is that China really is no longer just a second-tier country, but China is one of the big boys now.**

China's new naval base at Sanya on the southern end of Hainan Island far from the Taiwan Strait indicates power projection, particularly over disputed territories in the South China Sea and closer to vital sea lanes and the critical Strait of Malacca. The base has large piers capable of hosting a large fleet of surface ships and a large underground submarine base for both nuclear and non-nuclear subs. The size is not known but it appears it could hold from 8 to 20 subs. Their first SSBN was at the Bohai Gulf in the north, but that area is too shallow, while nuclear deterrent patrols would be safer in the 5,000 meter deep areas south of Hainan. It could be expected that the Type 094s would be based at Sanya. With their interest in protecting sea lanes, "Sanya can be expected to host future Chinese aircraft carrier battle groups and naval amphibious projection groups. Some Chinese sources suggest that the PLA could eventually build four to six aircraft carriers." China took Vietnamese and Philippine islands or reefs in recent years, so there will likely be more confrontations. The US will be watching closely because of various treaties with affected countries.[72]

China was obviously looking at new strategies and improving its offensive capability. The Indian Ocean and the choke points – Straits of Hormuz and Malacca and the Bab el Mandeb – were susceptible to terrorism. China gave Pakistan $200 million for a port at Gwadar,[73] only 390 nautical miles from the Strait of Hormuz and worked with Myanmar for a port on the Bay of Bengal. Gwadar would also be the terminus of a proposed China-Pakistan natural gas pipeline to Tashkurgan in Xinjiang province. The upside is that security in the Persian Gulf is now as important to China and India as to the US, and they have more influence in Iran than the US and they are less tolerant of a disruptive war. China was modernizing its nuclear weapons capability, but it continued to maintain that it would not be the first to use nuclear weapons despite threats by a couple of their generals to use nukes against the US in a conflict over Taiwan.[74]

Upon acceding to the throne, Saudi King Abdullah's first trip outside the Middle East was to China where he signed five agreements including closer cooperation in oil, natural gas, and minerals. Since the Saudis bought Chinese CSS-2 ballistic missiles in the 1980s which are now obsolescent, we should expect to see newer models in Saudi Arabia.[75] Saudi Arabia is in the buying mode again with the increased threat from Iran.

One of the less acceptable aspects of China's foreign policy is its willingness to sell to almost anyone. They sold large quantities of weapons to Saddam Hussein's Iraq and the Taliban in Afghanistan via Iran. Also Chinese HN-5 anti-aircraft missiles were reported being used by the Taliban.[76]

The Director of the CIA, Michael V. Hayden, felt that "China's rise is posing serious challenges and its military buildup and international behavior could produce an 'adversarial' relationship with the world." He called the buildup "troubling" and said that India and China will affect strategic planning. "But China, a communist-led nuclear state that aspires to and will likely achieve great power status during this century, will be the focus of American attention in that region of the world." He saw China as an economic competitor and increasingly a "geopolitical" competitor. The PLA has studied the lessons from both Persian Gulf wars and "They've developed an integrated advanced weaponry into a modern military force." He expressed concern that Chinese military power posed a threat to US forces and interests in the region.[77]

From all appearances, China was striving for military parity with the US.

From Harmonious World to New Assertiveness

China's president, Hu Jintao, had touted a "harmonious world," but by 2011, Sino-American relations had deteriorated. President Obama was treated rudely during his 2009 visit and then they flaunted a new missile and a stealth fighter just before Defense Secretary Gates' visit in January 2011. They also increased tensions with their neighbors in the South China Sea, with Japan over a trawler incident, with India over Kashmir and working with Viet-Nam in oil exploration, and refused to condemn the North Korean sinking of a South Korean ship and shelling a South Korean island. Evidently this new assertiveness was a result of a debate inside China over the use of their new power. The internationalist wing has lost out to the nationalist group, "fanned by the internet, which mistrusts an American-led international order." *The Economist* called this a miscalculation about US decline which "could slide into competition and confrontation and bring about a cold-war stand-off or rivalry" and "This does not serve China's interests."[78]

Disputes over the South China Sea have raged for decades. China has claimed "indisputable sovereignty" over the entire sea calling it a "core interest" (a term used only for Taiwan and Tibet before) which clashes with the claims of Viet-Nam, the Philippines, Brunei, Malaysia, and Taiwan. Potential oil and gas deposits around two outcroppings of reefs and small islands at the Paracels and the Spratlys are the centers of disputes. The Paracels are to the north near Viet-Nam. The Spratlys are 100 miles off the Philippines (which they call Kalayaan, or freedom) but over 1,000 miles from China. In 2010, China consumed 10.4% of total world oil production and 20.1% of all energy consumed on the planet. As already noted, China is desperate for energy sources and has become pugnacious about claiming them.[79]

China: We have "indisputable sovereignty" over the entire South China Sea as a "core interest."

Viet-Nam: Our claims in the South China Sea are "incontestable." Giving up the region of the offshore oil in the South China Sea is "non-negotiable."

The definition of a world class dispute!

China and Viet-Nam were in a fight over a Chinese ship cutting a Vietnamese cable. Viet-Nam announced that Chinese boats "seriously violated Vietnam's sovereign rights." China accused Viet-Nam of "seriously infringing" Chinese sovereignty. Beijing: "as everyone knows, China possesses indisputable sovereignty" over the Spratlys which they call the Nansha Group. Hanoi announced its claims in the South China Sea were "incontestable" within the 200 mile exclusive economic zone according to international law. As a result, Viet-Nam decided to buy six Kilo-class submarines from Russia.[80]

Wikileaks exposure of cables showed a long list of protests by China against international oil firms working with Viet-Nam and pressure on those companies resulting in some pulling out or delaying their plans. China warned India: "India should bear in mind that its actions in the South China Sea will push China to the limit. China cherishes the Sino-Indian friendship, but this does not mean China values it above all else….China has been peaceful for so long that some countries doubt whether it will stick to its stated bottom line. China should remind them of how clear this line really is."[81]   One envoy stated, "It is not so much a campaign as the need to assert sovereignty whenever and wherever that sovereignty is challenged,…And Vietnam's attempts to internationalise this dispute with foreign oil exploration are a clear challenge… we have made it very clear that it is unacceptable." US companies were pressured and Exxon Mobil was threatened that its actions were "a breach of China's sovereignty" but decided to stay on.[82]   Chevron pulled out of a $2 billion joint venture at a loss of $200 million. However, they were evidently paid off by China with a deal with PetroChina in Sichuan province which gave it a significant opening in China. This was clearly a part of China's campaign to assert its supposed maritime rights and firms wanting a role in China's energy market had to face the difficult choice of going ahead with work in the South China Sea or risk falling out of favor with China.

Political power grows out of the barrel of a gun.

- Mao Tse-tung

Another area of conflict is the Senkaku/Diaoyu Islands which are known to have significant oil and gas deposits in the area. A Chinese fishing boat rammed a Japanese vessel in disputed waters and Japan arrested the fishing boat captain. China suspended diplomatic relations, halted the sale of rare earths, and demanded an apology. The Chinese have long memories of the mistreatment and atrocities they endured during the Japanese invasion in the 1930s. These islands are inside the Japanese "exclusive economic zone" under international law. China is developing the Chunxiao gas field nearby which is just outside the Japanese zone. The 200 mile exclusive zone is very significant because from the center, even if it is only a little reef, the 200 mile radius circle provides 125,664 square miles of potential exploitation area for oil and natural gas.[83]

Concern for China's power was evident in the US decision not to sell Taiwan new F-16 fighters. It was a compromise decision "to help Taiwan – but not too much" by agreeing to upgrade their F-16A/B models. At the same time, the US upgraded its defense pact with Australia providing greater access to Australian bases and ports. "The trend line suggests that China will annex Taiwan by, in effect, going around it; by adjusting the correlation of forces in its favor so that China will never have to fight for what it will soon possess." [That is straight from Sun Tzu.] Some 1,500 Chinese missiles are aimed at Taiwan but there are 270 weekly commercial flights between the mainland and Taiwan and about one third of Taiwan's exports go to China so independence is fading. The power shift comes from China needing to spend less time concentrating on capturing Taiwan leaving them free to focus on the East and South China Seas and then the Indian Ocean.[84]

America's slow responses to China's actions in the South China Sea prompted Sen. James Webb, a former secretary of the Navy, to claim that the US is "approaching a Munich moment with China" in the South China Sea. That, of course, means "appeasement" as thought of in 1938 with Neville Chamberlain and the acceding to Hitler over Czechoslovakia. The US has repeatedly declared a US national interest in the Sea and the US Maritime Strategy states that the US will "remain the leading sea power in the Western Pacific and the Indian Ocean for the foreseeable future." These disputes are in "China's historic periphery, where China believes it must get its way." The problem is "Would concessions egg China on, encouraging it to aggrandize itself further at its neighbors' expense?"[85]

> **Asia is the most explosively unstable part of the world. Though far away from us, fires in Asia could lead to greater conflagrations elsewhere.**
>
> **- Edwin O. Reischauer**

One writer blamed China's "rudeness" on greater military power, leadership weakness, and xenophobic nationalism. Its maritime strength was "meant to cow weaker neighbors." When Viet-Nam stood up to China, "the official Chinese press warned South East Asian nations not to become too close to the United States." To get Viet-Nam back in line, the PLA moved a brigade of its short range missiles to the frontier. He considered the leadership weak because they could not keep the politburo in line with the policy of Deng Xiaoping of "biding time and hiding capabilities." With weak leadership, the PLA has gained power for its more hawkish foreign policy. "Since the Tiananmen massacre of 1989, the Party has engaged in a massive 'patriotic education' campaign stressing both China's civilizational supremacy as well as its humiliation at the hands of great powers such as Japan and the United States."[86]

An example of the hawkish nature of the PLA is an essay written by General Liu Yuan in which he called for China to return to its "military culture" and that party leaders had betrayed the revolutionary heritage. Liu is one of the "princelings" – whose parents founded the PRC; he is the son of Liu Shaoqi, who was to have been Mao's successor until he was purged by the Red Guards. A few quotes indicate the increasing assertiveness appearing in Chinese foreign policy: "Military culture is the oldest and most important wisdom of humanity. Without war, where would grand unity come from? Without force, how could fusion of the nation, the race, the culture, the south and the north be achieved?" Since war is a natural extension of politics and economics, "man cannot survive without killing," and the nation state is "a power machine made of violence."[87]

> **Military culture is the oldest and most important wisdom of humanity. Without war, where would grand unity come from?**
>
> **- General Liu Shaoqi, PLA**

The US has viewed Chinese policy as "access denial" or an effort to keep the US out of the region. In addition to the ASBM, which is supposedly aimed at US aircraft carriers, the PLA has improved its spy satellite capability to near parity with the US and much improved its drone and missile technologies. In July 2011, they deployed the Silver Eagle, a new drone. Their advances in spy satellites are impressive – "with at least 12 Yaogan advanced electro-optical and synthetic aperture radar (SAR) remote sensing satellites launched in the last 4 years." The PLA does not use the term access denial, but they call their strategy "active defense" and they are building on "space deterrence." So is the US reading the strategy correctly? One study lists the PLA strategy as based on three warfares: "psychological warfare, public opinion warfare, and legal warfare, with the first proving the most important for space operations."

> PLA descriptions of how space deterrence can be effected are consistent with this definition of psychological warfare [aimed at the broader population]. For example, Chinese analysts note that space systems are very expensive. It is possible, then, to hold an opponent's space infrastructure hostage by posing a question of cost-benefit analysis: is the focus of deterrence (e. g, Taiwan) worth the likely cost of repairing or replacing a badly damaged or even destroyed space infrastructure?[88]

In *A Contest for Supremacy: China, America, and the Struggle for Mastery in Asia*, Aaron Friedberg discusses China's view of its strategic situation. Instead of being a status quo power, Chinese leadership sees the US as revisionist with the goal of removing China's one-party rule. He sees a difficult challenge for US policy makers in that Chinese leaders are tough and calls for a firm US approach to prevent Chinese miscalculation due to US vacillation. He, like Robert Kaplan, sees Chinese tactics emphasizing patience and in the way of Sun Tzu, "to win without fighting" by creating alternative alliances and networks.[89]

One critical point to remember in the deterrence game is that it works both ways; the US can also take out China's space infrastructure.

Some have claimed that China has taken a free ride by not providing troops to the wars in Iraq and Afghanistan. However, although they have excluded a military commitment, they have had Chinese companies invest in developing those countries' natural resources and infrastructure required for transport. In Afghanistan, they invested $3 billion in the Aynak copper mine south of Kabul and another half to one billion dollars in road construction. They have also trained hundreds of Afghan officials in various fields. By providing employment and helping the Afghan and Iraqi economies, Chinese investments support those governments and that is in the US interest.[90]

In addition to the economic relationship, the US has a military relationship which is very important to develop strategic trust. There are differences of course but there are also common concerns so it is imperative to keep talking. Despite differences over the South China Sea and transparency, the two countries are both dependent on unhindered trade and are concerned about piracy, movement of weapons of mass destruction, and drug trafficking as well as stability in the Korean Peninsula and Pakistan. An agreement was signed for joint counter-piracy operations in the Gulf of Aden.[91]

A pessimistic view was presented by a former state department official who wrote that US attempts to establish military ties with China had "utterly failed" and "have served to strengthen the" PLA. He would suspend or cut back on such relations until there is "a mutually beneficial relationship" with US conditions such as renouncing the use of force against Taiwan and free navigation in the South China Sea.[92]

An interesting development which may add to stability in the Middle East was the announcement of closer ties with Saudi Arabia and the UAE during Premier Wen Jiabao's January 2012 visits. The Saudis have worked with China since the first Gulf War. Wen and King Abdullah announced strengthening cooperation in several areas including security.[93] In the UAE, the two governments "announced their intention to form a strategic partnership in various fields, including the military and energy sector." "A recent analysis concluded that Arab states friendly to the US now perceive that the will to use US influence in the Middle East is waning and thus have begun looking for other partners to help ensure their long term security."[94] That may or may not be true, but Chinese influence could be helpful, particularly in Iran, which has major investments in the Iranian oil sector and buys 11% of its oil from Iran.

Treasury Secretary Tim Geithner met with Wen Jiabao in January 2012 urging China to support further sanctions on Iran. However, China objects to the imposition of sanctions on Iran about its nuclear program. The new US law denies access to the US financial system for institutions that do business with Iran's Central Bank.[95]

China is expected to have a major leadership turnover in 2012 with Xi Jinping designated to become president. He is one of the princelings, but he is purported to be approachable and pragmatic.[96]   With so much at stake and with our economies so interconnected, hopefully cooperation will increase and continue into the future which would serve the interests of both countries.

Cyber Warfare

Nations planned for fighting on land, at sea, in the air, and even in space, but now there was a fifth dimension – cyberspace. Cyber warfare was not even known 20 years ago but with modern societies greatly dependent on data networking in telecommunications, transportation, finance, power and almost everything in modern life, disruption of computer systems would cripple a government. There were calls for international accords for global cyber control, mainly from authoritarian governments. Part of the problem was some governments justifying expanded control over the Internet. A fundamental question was at issue: "Which view of 'cyber peace' will prevail? Does it mean protection against the destruction of civilian infrastructure that would result from an all-out cyber war? Or might it mean increased governmental control of Internet communication to ensure that politically problematic content is kept to a minimum or removed entirely?" The attack was on the US control of the Internet Corporation for Assigned Names and Numbers (ICANN). International law is unclear and any new accord will be difficult to reach, but it is clear that peacemaking and warfighting will never be the same again.[97]

Chinese proverb: "There are always ears on the other side of the wall." Modern version: "Chinese are on the other end of your Internet connection."[98]

Cyberthieves, such as LuluSec, Zeus, and Anonymous, are very active. "Hacktivists, pranktivists, idealists and malware coders are oozing past the circa-2000 network-security gates of corporations and governments with ease." The cyberattack which shut down Sony's PlayStation Network on 20 April 2011 is estimated to have cost Sony $173 million. The "amount stolen using the Zeus malware program" is estimated at $1 billion. "There is also a real cyberwar being waged by nations. Reports of cybersecurity incidents from federal agencies have increased 660% over the past five years, to 41,776 in 2010." The DOD networks "are probed millions of times every day. More than 100 foreign intelligence agencies have attempted to penetrate DOD networks or those of military contractors – attacks characterized as APTs, or advanced persistent threats."[99]   Springfield, Illinois reported that an attack on 8 November 2011 on the city water utility kept turning on and off the control system burning out a water pump. The hackers were evidently from Russia.

GhostNet, an electronic network mainly based in China, infiltrated 1,300 government computers in 103 countries in March 2009. In April 2010, 15% of the Internet's routes were hijacked for 18 minutes when "the state-controlled telecommunications company China

Telecom Corp., redirected some of the world's Internet traffic, including data from U.S. military." While the US, Russia, and Israel have significant cyber capabilities, China has "the fastest-growing and most active cyber-attack program of all nations." China is trying to become a cyber superpower, which is a US national security threat. Their offensive doctrine states: "seizing control of an adversary's information flow [is] a prerequisite to air and naval superiority." On the defense, they are concerned that "the development of the Internet in China created 'unprecedented challenges' in 'social control and stability maintenance.'" Fortunately, China is as vulnerable as any other nation to cyber attack.[100]

China's aggressive spying, computer attacks, and theft of technology became the major threat to US national security. One congressman stated, "China has now become the No. 1 espionage threat to the United States." A great concern was the "illegal foreign acquisition of restricted U.S. military technology.[101] There were a number of arrests of people selling secrets to China and "the FBI believes that China may have set up more than three thousand front companies in the United States to acquire military or industrial technology illegally."[102]

There was an estimate that China could knock out US military satellites by 2010, which with our reliance on GPS could blind our forces. Also China trained a large number of computer hackers for cyber warfare on US computer networks.[103] Evidently they had even hit some computers in congressional offices looking for names of dissidents.[104] China placed a great deal of emphasis on asymmetric warfare. I suggest you read *Unrestricted Warfare: China's Master Plan to Destroy America* by two PLA colonels.[105]

The PLA studied and replicated the US computer network operations in the Balkans and the two Iraq wars and established its first cyber warfare unit in 2003 which became operational in 2004. The PLA set a "strategic goal of building informationalized armed forces and being capable of winning informationalized wars by the mid-21st century." To do that, they reduced troop strength by 200,000 and invested $50-100 billion on development and new cyber militia units [Another reason why it is so difficult to determine Chinese defense spending which is claimed to be only $78 billion!]. As one general noted, "some penetrations of Pentagon systems were efforts to map out U.S. government networks and learn how to cripple America's command-and-control systems as part of a future attack." Defense recorded some 44,000 malicious cyber attacks in the first six months of 2009. Remediation cost was over $100 million and it is estimated that cyber espionage costs the US up to $200 billion annually.[106] General Keith Alexander, head of NSA and also Cyber Command, said that the Department of Defense "computer network is so disordered and chaotic that it cannot be defended from cyberattacks."[107]

> **The PLA set a "strategic goal of building informationalized armed forces and being capable of winning informationalized wars by the mid-21st century."**

Defense companies are prime targets trying to get details on new weapon systems, but other private companies are also targets. Microsoft had to give China the source codes for Office software to be permitted to do business in China and there have been regular attacks on Google. The goal of China's cyber efforts is quite clear: "boost the ability to attack an adversary's satellite communications and sensor systems, critical transportation and energy infrastructure, ports of embarkation, and command systems."[108] That is why we now have a US Cyber Command.

This is non-kinetic combat – "capabilities to dominate in the electromagnetic spectrum." The Stuxnet attack in Iran showed that a cyber attack can destroy or misorient pieces of equipment so the threat is real. It became current with the report that a computer virus infected the networks at Creech Air Force Base in Nevada which controls the drones being flown on the warfronts.[109] It even reached the presidential campaign when Mitt Romney said that in addition to restoring the navy, "I will order the formulation of a national cybersecurity strategy, to deter and defend against the growing threats of militarized cyber-attacks, cyber-terrorism, and cyber-espionage."[110]

The Navy's chief officer in this area said, "the technology I'm most concerned about is China's focus and attention on trying to develop capabilities to dominate in the electromagnetic spectrum, to conduct counter-space capabilities, and clearly to conduct cyber activities." He added that, "Chinese planners have developed a strategy that directs their engineering talent at U.S. vulnerabilities and in a way that both avoids and negates U.S. strengths."[111]

The US government "pinpointed many of the Chinese groups responsible for cyberspying in the U. S., and most are sponsored by the Chinese military." US officials "warned China about the diplomatic consequences of economic spying." The US counterintelligence chief reported that China is the world's "most active and persistent" perpetrator of economic spying.[112] Even the Editorial Board of the generally liberal *Washington Post* (15 December 2011) noted the "massive cyberwar" the Chinese are waging against the US "aimed at stealing it most sensitive military and economic secrets and obtaining the ability to sabotage vital infrastructure." They wrote that the US "should demand that Beijing shut down the military-backed groups." They called for countermeasures including sanctions and possible new legislation. The Board ended with "the Chinese offensive – and the economic and national security threat it poses – is simply too important to ignore."

Leftist Surge in Latin America

There was an upsurge in democratic governments in Latin America during the last decades of the 20th century as old dictators were overthrown, but the new governments did not produce all they promised and, unable to overcome their tradition of graft, a slide back to the left occurred in numerous countries. The most glaring was the rise of Hugo Chavez in Venezuela. Now the US was faced with not just a virulently anti-American in Caracas who wanted to unite all Latin America against the "imperial giant," but an authoritarian Marxist with lots of oil money.

Hugo Chavez – Background

The man who was jailed for leading a failed coup against his government in 1992 was a product of the interior plains of Venezuela and did not go to Caracas until he was 17, hoping to be a baseball star. He entered the military academy and, disappointed that he was not to be a big baseball player, entered the army. He had been raised in an atmosphere of Karl Marx and Simon Bolivar. Just as Bolivar fought Spanish colonialism, Chavez saw himself with an historic mission to assume the mantle of Bolivar and to liberate Latin America from the influence of the imperial US. His hero was Simon Bolivar.

While fighting leftist guerrillas in his early years, he changed sides and volunteered his services to the guerrillas through his older brother, a Marxist university professor. He served that double life as a revolutionary conspirator for 10 years while rising in the military, meanwhile plotting a coup with his group, Movimiento Bolivariano Revolucionario 200 (the "200" was 200 years since Bolivar's birth). They struck on 3 February 1992, but military intelligence had learned of his intentions and the coup failed. The army made a fatal mistake in that instead of killing Chavez, they gave him one minute to address the nation on television hoping to get other battalion commanders to surrender. That one minute, wearing his red beret, made him a national hero. The next president freed him, and wearing that same red beret, five years later he won the presidency.

Chavez had not suddenly become a democrat; he ran for the presidency only because he believed he would win. He changed the official name of Venezuela to the Bolivarian Republic of Venezuela in 1999 and immediately started restructuring the government in his "socialism of the twenty-first century" with a new constitution. (He distributed little blue books with the text of the constitution and the Chavistas carry them, like Mao Tse-tung's little Red Book and Muammar al Qaddafi's Green Book.) The point, however, was to concentrate power in the presidency. It reduced the legislature to a one-chamber National Assembly and eliminated congressional oversight of the military (so he could stack it with friendly generals), and it removed the restriction on consecutive terms. He added 12 seats to the 20-seat supreme court and stacked it with cronies. He restricted radio and television and gradually and shrewdly imposed authoritarian measures and issued an intelligence decree which basically created an informant system among the people.[113]

He arranged to have a third term, but it was rather clear that he wanted to stay for life. He will likely be in power for the next 30 years if he is not stopped or if cancer does not finish him.

Hugo Chavez – Socialist Dictator and Demagogue

He was an admirer of Fidel Castro and was in regular contact with him and provided oil to Cuba in return for doctors; he went to Havana for his cancer treatment. Caracas became a "refugee camp" for socialists from various countries and a Mecca for American leftists who wanted to spout their anti-Americanism. Those providing support or making the pilgrimage included Cindy Sheehan (the anti-Iraq War activist who hounded President Bush - she preferred Chavez to Bush and urged the world to bring down the US empire – all she needed was an anti-aircraft gun and helmet to complete her image!), Danny Glover (Chavez provided $20 or $30 million to finance his films), Harry Belafonte (Bush is the greatest terrorist in the world and millions of Americans support your revolution), Sean Penn (your constitution is "a very beautiful document"), Kevin Spacey, Ed Asner, and supermodel Naomi Campbell. One who did not support Chavez was Cuban-born actress Maria Conchita Alonso, who said Chavez is "a totalitarian dictator" who wants to be president for life.[114]

There was a coup against him in 2002 but it fizzled quickly and he remained in firm control. He purged the military and increased patronage to the rest, and he poured money into the slums, where he had support because of his dark skin and folksy manner like an evangelical preacher. But there was "little evidence of any coherent social policy." It resembled the populism of Juan Peron of Argentina. "It is an incoherent mess, dependent on constant infusions of oil money, and is highly unlikely to lead to sustainable development for Venezuela. It is governed primarily by an age-old autocratic goal: the maintenance of personal power." He seemed more interested in liberating Latin America's underclass than concerning himself with what sort of society might evolve – he yearned to be a hero, not a technocrat. Along with that he wanted Venezuela to be a regional power to balance the US.

Chavez's "new political appointments in the early days of January [2012] confirm his regime's descent into militant narcoterrorism." He named a very wealthy old Chavista as president of the unicameral National Assembly who will be in a position to appoint Supreme Court justices as well as members of the National Electoral Commission. The latter group "will oversee and count the votes in the three upcoming elections: for the presidency on October 7, for the governorships in December and for mayors in April 2013." He also named a new defense minister who was "sanctioned by the US Treasury Department in September 2008 as a drug-trafficker aiding the FARC [Revolutionary Armed Forces of Colombia]."[115]

The Threat to the USA

If Hugo Chavez were just another tinhorn dictator of a poor country, he could be written off as a buffoon, but he leads a country with significant oil revenues (even though he was depleting the capacity by incompetence) allowing him great flexibility in spreading around his largesse. He was actively working for leadership in Latin America and striving to reduce US influence. Venezuela provided about one-seventh of the oil to the US and there were 14,000 CITGO stations in the US. CITGO, a US corporation, had been completely taken over by Venezuela and all US officials removed and replaced by Chavez loyalists.[116]

Chavez has used his oil money in many ways in addition to supplying heating oil for poor Americans in Massachusetts. In 2005, he agreed to provide cheap financing for oil imports for 13 Caribbean countries. He bought $1 billion of Argentinean debt and offered to buy $300 million of Ecuador's debt and gave aid and financial assistance to Bolivia. This was not altruism; he was assembling a bloc of nations against the US.[117] Yet there were food shortages and the infrastructure was in bad need of repair with a main bridge that collapsed and the oil fields suffering from a lack of reinvestment.[118]

He was much less than helpful in the war on drugs. He would not permit any US forces to operate in Venezuela and blocked US efforts to aid Colombia in its fight against the FARC and to build a US base there. He publicly lauded FARC and called the Colombian government illegitimate. Files on a captured computer hard drive linked high level Venezuelans to helping FARC obtain weapons.[119]

Chavez attacked President Bush directly on the floor of the UN General Assembly by calling him "the devil." He called the US a "false democracy," and told Time's Tim Padgett, "Capitalism is the way of the devil and exploitation, of the kind of misery and inequality that destroys social values…only socialism can really create a genuine society."[120] Chavez shadowed Bush as he travelled through Latin America holding rallies with cheers of "Gringo, go home."[121]

Hugo Chavez cut a wide swath as he visited many countries and made deals, usually aimed at the US. He met with Putin in Russia and bought $3 billion in arms, including jet fighters, military helicopters, and 100,000 Kalashnikov rifles (supposedly for home defense but some may have been "smuggled to leftist South American terrorist organizations in neighboring countries, such as FARC in Colombia"). He was back in Moscow in July 2008 for his sixth visit increasing his purchases to $5-6 billion. He added tanks, coastal surveillance aircraft, air defense systems and non-atomic submarines, plus he signed energy exploration agreements giving the Russians an expanded role in the energy field. Chavez spoke of a "strategic alliance" to meet "the threat of the United States" and asked the Russians to establish a base in Venezuela. All of this was fuelling a regional arms race with Chile, Brazil, and Colombia greatly increasing their defense budgets. He became big buddies with Mahmoud Ahmadinejad in Iran and they have met several times and he announced support for both Iran and HezbAllah. He visited Viet-Nam and his old friend Castro in Cuba. He struck deals with the Chinese and received a hero's welcome in Syria. He even visited Belarus and called for an alliance.[122]

> **Hugo Chavez cut a wide swath as he visited many countries and made deals, usually aimed at the US.**

In Syria, he said the two countries would "build a new world" free of domination by the US and vowed to "dig the grave of US imperialism." He was pushing for a rotating seat on the UN Security Council. Bashar al-Assad talked of "rejection of international hegemony," and the two met for 2 ½ hours and signed 13 political and economic agreements and he offered to help Syria build a 200,000 barrels per day oil refinery.[123]

Chavez unsuccessfully attempted to move to rule by presidential decree in early 2007 but he continues his one-man rule.[124]   He continued working on his anti-American coalition. He urged the leftist governments in Bolivia, Ecuador, Nicaragua, plus the island nations of Antigua, St. Vincent, and Dominica to join an alliance, the Bolivarian Alternative for the Americas, to challenge free trade agreements negotiated by the US. He urged investors to withdraw their funds from US banks and he moved to curtail oil supplies to the US.[125]

Is there a threat to US interests in the region? "Chavez speaks incessantly about the coming military confrontation with the gringos, a war that he predicts will last a hundred years." He followed the Iraq War closely and told his military to study guerrilla warfare. Those 100,000 Kalashnikovs were for citizen militias. The head of the National Assembly replied about relations with the US as "Conflict, in all likelihood war, is the future."[126]   In Caracas, Hugo Chavez said, "perpetual conflict with the United States is inevitable."[127]

Those who serve the revolution plow the sea.

- Simon Bolivar

Perhaps Hugo Chavez should look back to his great hero; Simon Bolivar's grand plan failed and he found the continent ungovernable and the Venezuelans turned against him. He ended up a depressed man who died and was buried in Colombia.[128]   Dictators rarely leave a great legacy.

Trends in Latin America

Castro's Cuba still labors along even though the old one is gone. It is difficult to argue that Cuba was better off because of Castro. Much was written about the deadly dictatorships in South America, but little about Castro's death toll of supposedly 102,000.[129]   The Shining Path guerrillas were again active in Peru backed by drug money with an estimated strength of about 800.[130]   The new president of Argentina, Cristina Fernandez, was accused that an intercepted suitcase full of money from Hugo Chavez was destined for her election campaign.[131]   And in Nicaragua, Daniel Ortega and the Sandinistas returned to power.[132]

Iran has been active in the region, particularly in Venezuela with $70 billion in joint ventures, but also in Bolivia ($1 billion) and Nicaragua. Also Iran has opened numerous "embassies" in Latin America.[133]

The drug menace continued with Mexico drifting toward becoming a narco-state. With millions of Americans feeding the drug market, most of which comes in from Mexico, the southern border area of the US had become a battlefield. The amounts of marijuana and cocaine transiting the border are staggering. Since President Felipe Calderon came to office and started his crackdown, nearly 48,000 people have died in drug-related crimes. To make it worse, as noted in the last chapter, coca cultivation increased. Cultivation in Colombia increased from 78,000 hectares in 2006 to 99,000 hectares or 383 square miles, a shocking 27 percent increase despite major US efforts. Cultivation in the three main sources of coca, Colombia, Peru, and Bolivia, rose 16 percent to 181,600 hectares, or 701 square miles.[134]

There was a reduction to 159,000 hectares, mainly in Colombia but with an increase in Peru, but progress was obviously slow.[135]

With America busy in Iraq and Afghanistan, the problems in Latin America received little attention. That may come back to haunt!

USCRIB

There are many problems in the world, particularly with the Islamic world and the Arab turmoil. These are not likely to be resolved soon as Iran, Turkey, and Egypt vie for their positions in the new order. Africa will continue to fester and Europe will be busy with its economic problems and it drift toward Eurabia, which we will review in the next chapter.

Regardless of all the turmoil created by the Muslims and others, the major players in the world, besides the US, will be China, Russia, India, and Brazil. Many use the term **BRIC** for these players, but I elect to use **USCRIB** in order to put them in a relative order as to their power role as we proceed into the 21st Century. Despite the premature reports of America's demise, the US will continue to be the superpower for years to come. We have already dealt with China. Russia will keep trying to recoup its position in the sun and high oil prices will assist and give them increasing influence over their neighbors and Europe. India will join or oppose China on the world scene. It is important to note that in addition to the maritime disputes with China, these two countries have long standing border disputes and they fought one small war in the high mountains.[136] Brazil has developed a strong economy with per capita income rising from $3,700 in 2000 to $8,536 in 2008.[137]

The new world order is still evolving but it will shape the remaining years of the 21st Century.

One of modern China's most difficult problems: coping with the intensifying urbanization of the country. China already has 12 cities with a population above 5 million – more than any other country in the world. There are roughly 600 million urban residents in the nation today, a figure that will rise to 1 billion by 2030.

- **Bill Powell,** "Taming Shanghai's Sprawl," *Time,* 14 February 2011, p. 46.

Notes

1. I actually wrote two versions in 1994: *World War IV: China's Quest for Power in the 21st Century* and *World War IV: Chinese Nationalism and Their Drive for Power in the 21st Century*

2. Both China and India (as well as Japan) are concerned about the shipping lanes for oil in the Indian Ocean – 80 percent of China's oil and 65 percent of India's use those lanes. There is potential rivalry as both are trying to gain control with friendship pacts and ports. See Gavin Rabinowitz, "China, India face off in Indian Ocean," *Reno Gazette-Journal,* 8 June 2008, p. 11B.

3. Richard Wolf, USA TODAY, "Obama turns attention to Asia," *Reno Gazette-Journal,* 11 November 2011, p. 1B. "Hard Choices for Ground Forces, *Defense News,* 17 October 2011.

4. "Sudan offered deal in 1996," *Jane's Intelligence Digest,* 15 January 2005. In 1994, Sudan had allowed a French intelligence team to fly into Khartoum and snatch Ilich Ramirez Sanchez, known as Carlos the Jackal.

5. See Kevin Whitelaw, "The Mutating Threat: Why U.S. official worry about a group you've never heard of," *U.S. News & World Report,* 26 December 2005.

6. See Fred Burton, "Al Qaeda's Pan-Maghreb Gambit," Stratfor: Terrorism Intelligence Report, 21 November 2006; Craig S. Smith, "North Africa Feared As Staging Ground For Terror," *The New York Times,* 20 February 2007, p. 1; Craig Whitlock. "From Iraq to Algeria, Al-Qaeda's Long Reach," *Washington Post,* 30 May 2007, p. 7; Craig Whitlock, "Group In Algeria Turned To Al-Qaeda For Assistance, *Washington Post,* 30 May 2007, p. 9; and Katherine Shrader, AP, "U.S. counterterror authorities watch African alliance," *Reno Gazette-Journal,* 10 June 2007, p. 4C.

7. Alex Perry, "Remember Somalia," *Time,* 10 December 2007, p. 50. "U.S. Holds Al-Qaida At Bay In Somalia," *Baltimore Sun,* 3 January 2006. US counterterrorism forces were operating in East Africa.

8. Rodrique Ngowi, AP, "Al-Qaida-linked group gains foothold in Somalia," *Reno Gazette-Journal,* 12 July 2005, p. 3C.

9. J. Peter Pham, "The New Taliban," *The Wall Street Journal,* 19 June 2006, p. 14. The other three groups in the UIC were: *al-Takfir wal-Hijra* (Excommunication and Exodus), so extreme that it tried to kill Osama bin Laden in Sudan in 1996 because they considered him too moderate; *al-Islah* (Reconciliation), Islamists striving for an Islamic state in Somalia; and *al-Tabligh* (Making Known), Islamist missionaries with ties to the same madrassas in Pakistan which provided the Taliban. The reinforcements came from at least Arabs, Afghans, Kashmiris, Pakistanis, Palestinians, and Syrians and received supplies from the Arabian Peninsula.

    For the US involvement, see Craig Timberg, "Mistaken Entry Into Clan Dispute Led to U.S. Black Eye in Somalia," *Washington Post,* 2 July 2006, reprinted in Other Voices, *Washington Report on Middle East Affairs (WRMEA),* September/October 2006, p. OV-15.

10. Mohamed Olad Hassan, AP, "Somali militiamen break up wedding in increasingly radical crackdown," *Reno Gazette-Journal,* 9 July 2006, p. 8C.

11. Mohamed Olad Hassasn, "Islamic leader pits Ethiopians against Somalis in holy war," *Reno Gazette-Journal,* 22 July 2006, p. 5C. Elizabeth Kennedy, AP, "Islamic militia expands in Somalia." *Reno Gazette-Journal,* 26 August 2006, p. 10C.

12. Sam Dealey, "Terror's Playground," *Time,* 27 November 2006, p. 50.

13. Alex Perry, "Remember Somalia?" *Time,* 10 December 2007, p. 50. Mohamed Olad Hassan, AP, "Missiles kill reputed al-Qaida chief," *Reno Gazette-Journal,* 2 May 2008, p. 2B. The strike evidently killed the top al Qaeda commander in Somalia.

    Surprisingly there was support for the sharia regime in Minneapolis where 1,500 Somalis demonstrated against the US support for the Ethiopians. One might ask what they are doing in the US. Robert Spencer, "Sharia in Minneapolis," Human Events, 8 January 2007, p. 14.

14. Chris Tomlinson, AP, "U.N.: Eritrea has sent secret arms shipments to Islamic insurgents battling Somalis," *Reno Gazette-Journal,* 27 July 2007. Stephanie Hanson, "Al-Shabaab," Council on Foreign Relations, 10 August 2011.

15. "Lawmakers: 40 Americans Joined Somali Al-Qaida Linked terror group," Associated Press, 26 July 2011.

16. Stephanie Hanson, "Al-Shabaab," cfr.org, 10 August 2011. 53 AU peacekeepers were killed. Abdinasir Mohamed, "In Riven Somalia, Islamists Dig In," *The Wall Street Journal,* 5-6 March 2011, p. A9.

17. "Kenya: Al Shabaab raids refugee camp, kidnaps Spanish aid workers in Kenya," Afrique en ligne, 14 October 2011.

18. Perry, "Remember Somalia?" Spencer, "Sharia in Minneapolis." I have traveled into the Ogaden from Addis Ababa, and it is one desolate area.

19. Toni Johnson, "Boko Haram," Council on Foreign Relations, 31 August 2011.

20. Doug Casey, "A Chinese Conundrum," The Daily Crux, 14 May 2011.

21. Sichuan Governor Ziao Yang said, "There is no other way, because we are not willing to go back to the planned economy. If we do, we will just throw everybody back into poverty."

22. "Why China Is Unhappy," *The Wall Street Journal,* 12 November 2011.

23. Michael Elliott, "The Chinese Century," *Time,* 22 January 2007. John Gee, "Middle East-Chinese Trade Ties Renew Old Links," *WRMEA,* July 2007, p. 25.

24. Ibid.

25. Alex Perry, "China's New Continent," *Time,* 5 July 2010, p. Global 3.

26. Deborah Bräutigam, "China in Africa: Think again," The European Financial Review, 16 August 2010.

27. "Premier Says China Is No Threat to Africa," *Washington Post,* 19 June 2006, p. 19.

28. Fareed Zakaria, "Losing Another War…in Asia," *Newsweek,* 30 April 2007, p. 49.

29. There were large celebrations in both China and Taiwan on the 100th anniversary of the 1911 uprising which ended the Qing dynasty. Some in Taiwan claim it is "the legitimate ruler of all of China because it is they who have fulfilled Sun's [Sun Yat-sen] Xinhai Revolution and his famous Three Principles of the People: nationalism, democracy and the people's livelihood." Calum MacLeod, USA TODAY, "China, Taiwan mark century since uprising," *Reno Gazette-Journal,* 10 October 2011, p. 1B.

30. Elliott, "The Chinese Century." See also Annie Huang, AP, "Taiwan counts on Chinese for tourist industry boost," *Reno Gazette-Journal,* 18 May 2008, p. 7B.

31. George Friedman, "Crisis and Implications," Stratfor, 20 June 2006. Friedman wrote another analysis, "Geopolitics of $130 Oil," 27 May 2008. He noted that Asia is the big loser and Russia the big winner. The Arabian Peninsula is awash with cash and they do not want the Strait of Hormuz closed by Iran or Iran blockaded by the US. They are making strong efforts to stabilize the region.

Some comparisons for perspective [*Time,* 22 January 2007.] out of date but good for comparison:

	China (pop. 1,314,480,000)	US (pop. 301,325,000)
GDP	$2.7 trillion ($2,054 per person)	$13.1 trillion ($43,950 per person)
Taxes collected	$486 billion ($370 per person)	$2.5 trillion ($8,297 per person)
Balance of trade	$177.5 billion surplus	$225 billion deficit
Cell phone users	461 million (35 per 100 people)	219 million (73 per 100 people)
Cable TV subscribers	139 million (11 per 100 people)	110 million (37 per 100 people)
Airline passengers	160 million	658 million
Foreign visitors	22 million (9% from the US)	51 million (1% from China)
Private cars	11.5 million (9 per 1,000 people)	136.4million (450/1,000 people)
Deaths in traffic accidents	89,455	48,433
Practicing doctors	1.97 million (15 per 10,000 people)	745,000 (25 per 10,000 people)
Feature films produced	330	699

32. Doug Casey, "A Chinese Conundrum," The Daily Crux, 14 May 2011.
33. Nick Hodge, "The Chinese are Coming," Energy & Capital, 23 September 2011.
       A similar prediction but earlier was "If the Chinese economy was to continue to expand at 8 per cent a year in the future, its income per head would reach the current US level in 2031, at which point it would consume the equivalent of two-thirds of the current world grain harvest and its demand for paper would double the world's current production. If it were to enjoy the same level of per capita car ownership as the US does today, it would have 1.1 billion cars compared with the present 800 million; and it would use 99 million barrels of oil a day compared with a worldwide total production of 84 million barrels in 2006." Martin Jacques, *When China Rules the World,* (New York: The Penguin Press, 2009), p. 169.
34. Scott Kilman and Brian Spegele, "Chinese Hunger for Corn Stretches Farm Belt," *The Wall Street Journal,* 17 August 2011.
35. Elizabeth Economy, "China's Growing Water Crisis," *World Politics Review,* 9 August 2011.
36. Ibid. Since China has jumped from the 18th century to the 21st century in just over 30 years, "The result is a huge ecological deficit of two centuries accumulated in just a few decades: growing water shortages, over three-quarters of river water that is unsuitable either for drinking or fishing, 300 million people lacking access to clean drinking water, rampant deforestation, sixteen of the world's twenty worst-polluted cities, acid rain affecting a third of Chinese territory, desert covering a quarter of the country, and 58 per cent of land classified as arid or semi-arid." Jacques, *When China Rules the World,* p. 170.
37. Elizabeth Economy, Ibid.
38. Bryan Walsh, "Got Yttrium?" *Time,* 28 March 2011. p. Business 8.
39. Saurav Jha, "India, China in Race for the Bottom in Indian Ocean," *World Politics Review,* 5 October 2011.
40. Keith Bradsher, "Government Policies Cool China's Real Estate Boom," *The New York Times,* 10 November 2011.
41. Brian P. Klein, "The Danger to China's Economy," The Diplomat, 9 August 2011. Stratfor reported local government debt as $1.7 trillion.
42. "China's Growing Debts," Stratfor, 27 June 2011.
43. Doug Casey, "A Chinese Conundrum," The Daily Crux, 14 May 2011.
44. Bill Saporito, "Made (Again) in the U.S.A.," *Time,* 10 October 2011, p. 20. This may return manufacturing jobs to the US.
45. Bill Powell, "The End of Cheap Labor in China," *Time,* 27 June 2011, p. Business 4.
46. David Barboza, "China's Treasury Holdings Make U.S. Woes Its Own," *The New York Times,* 18 July 2011. Porter Stansberry, "China's Secret Plan to Take Over the World's Gold Market," Stansberry's Investment Advisory, January 2012.
47. *China National News,* 3 December 2011.
48. Wei Jingsheng, "The West is a Chinese colony. But this will collapse," AsiaNews, 8 August 2011.
49. Richard McGregor, "China's Private Party," *The Wall Street Journal,* 15 May 2011.
50. "Why China Is Unhappy," *The Wall Street Journal,* 12 November 2011.
51. Ken Miller, "Be Very Afraid of The China Bubble," *Time,* 31 October 2011, p. 30.
52. Bill Saporito, "A Great Leap Forward: Can China's famously thrifty worker become the world's big spenders?" *Time,* 31 October 2011, p. 36. See Rana Foroohar, "The Senate's China Misstep," *Time,* 24 October 2011, p. 17, for the mistake by Sen. Chuck Schumer trying to pressure Beijing to revalue its currency. Efforts should not be made in public since "loss of face is anathema in the Middle Kingdom." Hinting at tariffs on Chinese goods only creates defiance.
53. Brinan Spegele, "China Makes Effort to Cool Unrest in Inner Mongolia," *Reno Gazette-Journal,* 31 May 2011, p. A11.
54. Phillip C. Saunders and Ross Rustici, "Chinese Military Transparency: Evaluating the 2010 Defense White Paper," Strategic Forum, National Defense University, July 2011, p.4.
55. "Still No. 1 – but Not for Much Longer," *Time,* 16 May 2011, p. 13.
56. Calum MacLeod, USA TODAY, "China considers loosening its one-child policy," *Reno Gazette-Journal,* 9 September 2010, p. 1B.
57. Fareed Zakaria, "The New Challenge From China," *Time,* p. 54.
58. Arvind Subramanian, "The Inevitable Superpower," *Foreign Affairs,* September/October 2011.
59. "Another Way China May Beat the U.S.," *Time,* 11 April 2011, p. 15.
60. Ashlee Vance, "China Wrest Supercomputer Title From U.S.," *The New York Times,* 28 October 2010. That is 29 million times faster than the early supercomputers in 1976. It performs 2.5 times 10 to the 15th power mathematical operations per second.
61. "Now No. 2, Could China Become No. 1?" *Time,* 28 February 2011, p. 15.
62. Arvind Subramanian, "The Inevitable Superpower," *Foreign Affairs,* September/October 2011.

63. Mark Magnir, "China's Vast Military Cuts Fat, Adds Muscle," *Los Angeles Times,* 10 January 2006. "China Plans 15% Boost in Military Spending," *The Wall e Street Journal,* 6 March 2006. The increase was to $35.1 billion, but it could really be four times larger or over $140 billion. The boost was 17.8 percent in 2007. The military voice in government was clear in that active duty members of the PLA make up 10 percent of the National People's Congress. Christopher Bodeen, AP, "Chinese military gets boost with defense funds increase," *Reno Gazette-Journal,* 10 March 2007, p. 9C.

64. Charles Hutzler, AP, "Premier says world should not fear China's military rise," *Reno Gazette-Journal,* 17 March 2007, p. 6C.

65. "China Moon Shoot," *New York Post,* 23 October 2007.

66. "China launches space station module," Reno *Gazette-Journal,* 30 September 2011, p. 1B.

67. James Holmes & Toshi Yoshihara, "Underestimating China," The Diplomat, 17 January 2011.

68. John Gee, "Has Israel's U.S.-Funded Lavi Jet Been Reborn as China's J-10 Warplane?" *WRMEA,* April 2007, p. 42.

69. Mark Steyn, *After America: Get Ready for Armageddon.*

70. Bill Gertz, "China Expands Sub Fleet," *Washington Times,* 2 March 2007, p. 1.

71. Tyler Durden, "Presenting The First Chinese Aircraft Carrier," Zero Hedge, 7 April 2011. James Holmes, "Blue Water Dreams: Why China wants an aircraft carrier," *Foreign Policy,* 27 June 2011.

72. Richard D. Fisher Jr., "China's Naval Secrets," *Asian Wall Street Journal,* 5 May 2008, p. 13.

73. See CDR Muhammed Azam Khan, Pakistan Navy Ret, "The United States, The North Arabia Sea and Pakistan," US Naval Institute *Proceedings,* May 2007, p. 36.

74. Robert Spencer, "China To Modernize Nuclear Weapons Capability," *London Daily Telegraph,* 9 May 2008. "Chinese Gen. Zhu Chenghu told reporters in 2005 that China would attack U.S. cities with nuclear weapons in response to any conventionally armed U.S. missile strikes against China during a conflict over Taiwan. Years earlier, Gen. Xiong Guangkai threatened to use nuclear weapons against Los Angeles if the U.S. helped Taiwan defend against a Chinese invasion of the island." Gertz, "China Expands Sub Fleet."

75. Richard L. Russell, "Oil-For-Missiles," *The Wall Street Journal,* 25 January 2006, p. 12.

76. Bill Gertz, "China arming terrorists," Inside the Ring, 15 June 2007. *Washington Times,* 5 June 2007.

77. "CIA: China's Military Could Get 'Adversarial,'" World Tribune, 9 May 2008.

78. "Discord," *The Economist,* 15 January 2011.

79. Andrew Higgins, "In South China Sea," *Washington Post,* 18 September 2011.

80. James Hookway, "Vietnam Plans Live-Fire Drill After China Spat," *The Wall Street Journal,* 10 June 2011. See also "Beijing accuses Hanoi escalating sea tensions," Reuters, 10 June 2011 and James Hookway, "Tensions Flare in South China Sea," *The Wall Street Journal,* 9 June 2011.

81. State-run Global Times, September 2011.

82. *South China Morning Post,* July 2008.

83. For the location of the islands and the exclusive zones, see Jacques, *When China Rules the World,* map on p. 311.

84. Robert D. Kaplan, "A power shift in Asia," *Washington Post,* 23 September 2011.

85. James R. Holmes, "America's 'Munich Moment'?" *The Diplomat,* 17 July 2011.

86. Daniel Blumenthal, "Riding a tiger: China's resurging foreign policy aggression," *Foreign Policy,* 15 April 2011. Now Red songs are used again to praise the Party and the party members. (idiotic to some!), Edward Wong, "Repackaging the Revolutionary Classics of China, New York Times, 29 June 2011. See also, Fareed Zakaria, "China's New Parochialism," *Time,* 25 July 2011. p. 26, about the restriction on foreign movies imported and revival of Maoism. He ends with "A new generation of Chinese leaders might decide they have learned enough and that it is time to turn inward and celebrate China's unique ways."

87. John Garnaut, "Chinese general rattles saber," *Sydney Morning Herald,* 23 May 2011.

88. Craig Guthrie, "US in 'denial' over China's Pacific strategy," *Asia Times,* 28 July 2011.

89. Reviewed in Robert Haddick, "This Week at War: Let's Talk About China," *Small Wars Journal,* 23 September 2011.

90. Richard Weitz, "Why China's Free-Riding OK," *The Diplomat,* 12 August 2011.

91. Mike Mullen (Chairman of the Joint Chiefs of Staff), "A Step Toward Trust With China," *New York Times,* 26 July 2011.

92. Randy Schriver, "Bound to fail, U.S. military ties with China work only to PLA's advantage." The Washington Times, 25 July 2011.

93. "China, Saudi Arabia vow to enhance ties," China National News, 16 January 2012 (IANS).

94. NightWatch, 17 January 2012.

95. Michael Wines, "China Balks on Geithner's Pressure for Iran Curbs," *The New York Times,* 11 January 2012.

96. Keith B. Richardson, "Xi Jinping, likely China's next leader, called pragmatic, low-key," Reuters, 15 August 2011.

97. Tom Gjelten, "Behind the Cyber 'Disarmament' Debate," *Army,* March 2011, p. 30.

98. Dr. J. P. "Jack" London, "Made in China," *Proceedings* (US Naval Institute), April 2011.

99. Bill Saporito, "Hack Attack," *Time,* 4 July 2011, p. 50.

100. London, op. cit.

101. Bill Gertz, "Beijing Espionage Poses 'No. 1' Threat," *Washington Times,* 30 January 2008, p. 5.

102. Lara Jakes Jordan, AP, "4 in U.S. are charged with selling secrets to Chinese," *Reno Gazette-Journal,* 12 February 2008, p. 1B. Richard Bush and Michael O'Hanlon, *A War Like No Other: The Truth About China's Challenge to America,* quoted in Maj. Gen. Edward B. Atkinson, "China: The Stirring Dragon," *Army,* January 2008, p. 14.

103. "Pentagon: China improving its ability to launch surprise attacks," *Reno Gazette-Journal,* 26 May 2007, p. 2B. Robert D. Kaplan, "Lost At Sea," *The New York Times,* 21 September 2007. Bill Gertz, "Pentagon Details China's New Military Strategies," *Washington Times,* 25 May 2007, p. 1.

104. Pete Yost and Lara Jakes Jordan, AP, "Officials allege Chinese hacking," *Reno Gazette-Journal,* 12 June 2008, p. 1C.

105. Col. Qiao Liang and Col. Wang Xiangsui, (Panama City, Panama, Pan American Publishing Company, 2002) Presented in summary translation. Originally published in 1999 by the People's Liberation Army, Beijing. They predicted the attack on

the World Trade Center and "Chinese military planners believe that terrorism is just one of the many tools at the hands of nations and their terrorist allies to wage total war against the United States."

Also, see Robert D. Kaplan, "How We Would Fight China," *The Atlantic Monthly*, June 2005, p. 49.

106.   London, op. cit.

107.   Joseph Fitsanakis, "US Pentagon computers cannot be protected, says NSA head," intelnews.org, 13 January 2012.

108.   London, Ibid.   For the effect on civilian companies, see Rep. Ted Poe, "POE: Time to deal with China's high-tech mafia, American businesses, consumers hurt by government cover for fake products," *The Washington Times*, 23 August 2011.

109.   Lolita C. Baldor, "Report: Computer virus hits military drone program," Associated Press, 8 October 2011.

110.   Speech, 7 October 2011 at The Citadel, South Carolina.

111.   Robert Haddick, "Forget about China's missiles and stealth fighter: worry instead about 'non-kinetic' combat," *Small Wars Journal*, 19 January 2011.

112.   Siobhan Forman, "U.S. Probe Ties Chinese Cyberspying to Military," *The Wall Street Journal*, 12 December 2011.

113.   See Franklin Foer, "The Talented Mr. Chavez," *The Atlantic Monthly*, May 2006, p. 94, for an extensive review of Chavez. Also see "Defending Hugo Chavez," by a number of academics and Foer's reply in the July/August issue, p. 27. Christopher Toothaker, AP, "New law resembles Cuba-style spy system." *Reno Gazette-Journal*, 4 June 2008, p. 2B.

114.   Ana Maria Ortiz and Matthew Vadum, "Marxist Hugo Chavez Calls on Friends in America," Human Events, 17 March 2008, p. 9.

115.   Vanessa Neumann, "Venezuela Heads Deeper Into Militant Narcoterrorism," Foreign Policy Research Institute, 9 January 2012.

116.   See Foer, "The Talented Mr. Chavez," Ortiz and Vadum, "Marxist Hugo Chavez Call on Friends in America," and Mac Johnson, "Chavez's CITGO Is No Friend of America," Human Events, 9 October 2006, p. 15, for details on CITGO and the heating oil program provided through former Rep. Joseph P. Kennedy II of Massachusetts.

117.   Foer, "The Talented Mr. Chavez."

118.   See Mary Anastasia O'Grady, "The Neo Tehran-Caracas Axis," *The Wall Street Journal*, 13 January 2006, p. 13.

119.   Juan Forego, "Venezuela Offered Aid To Colombian Rebels," *Washington Post*, 15 May 2008, p. 1.   Venezuela offered to help FARC obtain surface-to-air missiles.   Frank Bajak, AP, "Files in rebel's laptop show Chavez's ties in Colombia," *Reno Gazette-Journal*, 6 March 2008, p. 7C.   Christopher Toothaker, AP, "Chavez Tells Colombia Not To Build Base For US," MiamiHerald.com, 15 May 2008.   Bajak had a later article, "Files show tight Venezuelan ties to Colombian rebels," *Reno Gazette-Journal*, 12 May 2008. p. 2B, in which he wrote, "Most importantly, they outline a joint strategic project between Venezuela and the Colombian rebels, with Venezuela even seeking rebel training in 'asymmetrical warfare' in preparation for a feared U.S. invasion."   The only US base in South America was at Manta in Ecuador for which President Rafael Correa, a close ally of Chavez, did not renew the lease in 2009.

Chavez threatened his neighbor Guyana and claimed ¾ of its territory.   He would not allow US drug surveillance flights in Venezuelan airspace, but he allowed HezbAllah and Hamas to open offices in Caracas. Ortiz and Vadum, "Marxist Hugo Chavez Calls on Friends in America."

120.   David Jackson, "Chavez refers to Bush as 'the devil' at the U.N.," *USA Today*, 21 September 2006, p. 10A. *Time*, 2 October 2006, p. 18.   Tim Padgett, "Crazy Like A Fox," *Time*, 2 October 2006, p. 40.   Bush gained company when Chavez accused German Chancellor Angel Merkel's party of having the same ideals as Adolf Hitler.   "Chavez lashes out at Germany's Merkel," *Reno Gazette-Journal*, 13 May 2008, p. 2B.

121.   Deb Riechmann, AP, "Chavez tries to bait Bush," *Reno Gazette-Journal*, 11 March 2007, p. 1C.

122.   Ortiz and Vadum, "Marxist Hugo Chavez Calls on Friends in America."   Stephen Brown, "Comrades In Arms," FrontPageMagazine.com, 31 July 2008.   "Russia regards its support for Chavez as a countermove to the much disliked missile defence system the United States intends to set up in Czechoslovakia and Poland."   Also, "Moscow announced as another countermeasure its intention to have long-range bombers refuel in Cuba, six years after it had closed its last base there."   A "Latin American newspaper reported that Mexican drug cartel criminals are being sent to Iran via Venezuela for advanced training in building car bombs."

123.   "Venezuelan Seeks Another Anti-U.S. Ally In Syria," *The New York Times*, 31 August 2006.

124.   See Ian James, AP, "Chavez decree to usher in new era," *Reno Gazette-Journal*, 30 January 2007, p. 3C, for the details of the proposal.

125.   Ortiz and Vadum, "Marxist Hugo Chavez Calls on Friends in America."

126.   Foer, "The Talented Mr. Chavez," p. 97.

127.   Ian James, AP, "Venezuelan president: Conflict with U.S. inevitable," *Reno Gazette-Journal*, 6 March 2008, p. 7C.

128.   Foer, "The Talented Mr. Chavez," p. 105.

129.   See George Will, "Castroism remains despite departure," *Reno Gazette-Journal*, 8 March 2008, p. 6D and Humberto Fontova, "Historians Try to Absolve Fidel Castro," Human Events, 21 August 2006, p. 9.

130.   "Shining Path ambushes police patrol in Peru," *Reno Gazette-Journal*, 25 March 2008, p. 2B.   Monte Hayes, AP, "Peru rebels return with drug funding," *Reno Gazette-Journal*, 1 June 2008, p. 2C.

131.   "President rebukes claims that Venezuelan cash was for her campaign," *Reno Gazette-Journal*. 14 December 2007, p. 3B.

132.   Robert D. Novak, "Nicaraguan tragedy," Townhall.com, The Conservative Review, 31 October 2006.

133.   Martin Arestegui, "Iran Tries to Gain Sway in Latin America, " *The Wall Street Journal*, 6 December 2011.

134.   Tony Muse, AP, "UN reports 'shocking' 27 percent rise in coca cultivation in Colombia," *Reno Gazette-Journal*, 19 June 2008, p. 2B.

135.   "Coca cultivation declining in Colombia but on the rise in Peru, UN agency reports," UN News Centre, 22 June 2010.

136.   The border east of Bhutan to Myanmar is disputed as well as the border west of Nepal to Jammu and Kashmir with one area held by China. In Kashmir, the area ceded by Pakistan to China is claimed by India. See Map 13 in Jacques, *When China Rules the World*, p. 341.

137.   *Time*, 6 December 2010, p. 20.

Chapter 12

Eurabia – Muslim Europe

Who says you own Britain, anyway?
Britain belongs to Allah.
The whole world belongs to Allah.

- Anjem Choudary

Multiculturalism is an absolute failure.

- Angela Merkel

A 23-year old Tunisian-born French woman was stoned to death after she refused the advances of a teenage boy; a film maker in Holland was shot and had his throat slit because of a movie he made about how Muslims treat women; an Albanian boy bled to death on the ground after being stabbed by an Arab because the ambulance was waiting for a police escort because parts of Malmö, Sweden are ruled by violent gangs of Muslim immigrants; the Nordgårdsskolen in Aarhus, Denmark became the first Danish school with no Danish children since all the students came from Muslim immigrants; 70 percent of the inmates in French prisons are Muslim; four out of five residents at Oslo's main women's shelter are non-Norwegian women seeking protection from male family members; Muslims make up 5 percent of the Danish population but receive 40 percent of welfare outlays. As the OECD concluded, Europe is in deep trouble.

Now there are women on the streets in burqas and veils, Muslims rioting and burning cars, bombings and killings, blocking streets with their Friday prayers, separate seats in theaters for men and women, separate hours at swimming pools for men and women, sharia courts, polygamy (and governments paying welfare to more than one wife), halal meals, female genital mutilation, Muslim lawyers are not required to stand when a judge enters a court, a Dutch member of parliament (Geert Wilders) hauled into court for hate speech for describing Islam as a totalitarian ideology, a Danish journalist (Lars Hedegaard) fined for criticizing the way women are treated in Islam in a private conversation he did not know was recorded, an Austrian human rights activist (Elisabeth Sabaditsch-Wolff) fined for criticizing Muhammad, fathers and brothers killing daughters and sisters for violating their "honor," paying "protection money" to Muslim "security guards" (Arhus, Denmark), Muslims attacking guards in the Roman Catholic cathedral in Cordoba, Spain with knives claiming the cathedral was theirs, and no-go zones which are sharia governments within a government and where local governments fear to tread.

No-Go Zones

That is not the Europe of fond memories most of us have. Whether you had your pocket picked on the Metro by Algerian brats, as I did, or encountered thugs in Londonistan or other parts of Europe, it is not the same place anymore. The Champs Elysee is still delightful, but to get to the Charles DeGaulle Airport, you have to pass through some areas that are more Muslim than French. You do not want to go into them and the French police do not either. These are "no-go" zones or Zones Urbaines Sensibles (ZUS), Sensitive Urban Zones; there are

751 ZUS where the French state has lost control containing 5 million Muslims. A full list of the ZUS is available on a government website, including satellite maps and exact street demarcations. It is not just in Paris but also in Lyon, Marseilles, and Toulouse. You have probably seen the videos of Muslims closing off streets and sidewalks (closing down local businesses and trapping non-Muslims in their homes or offices) to have their Friday prayers. Local authorities have refused to intervene in this "occupation without tanks or soldiers" because of fear of sparking riots – you probably have memories of the burning cars and rioting in Paris.

There are now Muslim no-go zones in England described as "areas dominated by radical Islamic ideology where people of different faiths reportedly face physical attacks." This was "**voluntary apartheid** – shutting themselves in closed society, demanding immunity from criticism." [Emphasis added][1] These "no-go" zones are microstates governed by sharia, and with the governments having lost control, they often are unable to provide basic services of police, firemen, and ambulances. Unfortunately, this is the result of decades of policies of multiculturalism which led Muslims to remain segregated and create parallel societies.

A British group, **Muslims Against the Crusades**, campaigned to turn 12 British cities, including Londonistan, into Islamic Emirates, autonomous enclaves under sharia and totally outside British jurisprudence.[2] In the "Islamic Republic of Tower Hamlets," extremist imams, the "Tower Hamlets Taliban," regularly make death threats to women refusing to wear veils. Streets are plastered with signs "You are entering a Sharia controlled zone: Islamic rules enforced."

London sign: "You are entering a Sharia controlled zone: Islamic rules enforced."
Extremist Abu Izzadeen to former Home Secretary John Reid: "How dare you come to a Muslim area."

This goes on across Europe. In Germany, despite official denials, the police know where they can go with a patrol car and where it is better to have a personnel carrier (armored vehicle). Crimes are not reported; the "power of the state is completely out of the picture." Brussels, the capital of Belgium, is 20% Muslim and there are numerous "no-go" zones. Showing concessions and being "politically correct," police in the Molenbeek district of Brussels were ordered not to eat a sandwich or drink coffee or tea during Ramadan. Muslims have taken over the Piazza Venezia in Rome for prayers and have repeatedly threatened to bomb San Petronio cathedral since is has a 600-year-old fresco showing Muhammad being tormented in hell which was inspired by Dante's Inferno.

A Dutch court ordered the Netherlands government to release a list of 40 "no-go" zones in Holland. The top five problem areas are in Amsterdam, Rotterdam (3), and Utrecht. Sweden has some of the most liberal immigration laws in Europe and large sections of Malmö (25% Muslim) are "no-go" zones. In the largely Muslim district of Rosengaard, fire and emergency workers will not enter without police escort. When they attempted to put out a fire at the main mosque, they were attacked by stones. Unemployment in that district is over 80%. Muslim youths have been throwing gas bombs at police cars in Gothenburg and in the appropriately named Angered district, over 15 police cars have been destroyed and young punks have pointed lasers at police officers' eyes temporarily blinding some of them. In what should be the ultimate insult, Malmö Imam Adly Abu Hajar pronounced: "Sweden is the best Islamic state."[3]

Bat Ye'or, the writer about dhimmitude, the institutionalized oppression on non-Muslims in Muslim societies, observed, Europe is reaping what it has long sown. She said

Europe began some thirty years ago down a path of appeasement, accommodation, and cultural abdication to Islam in pursuit of short-sighted political and economic benefits. "Europe has evolved from a Judeo-Christian civilization, with important post-Enlightenment/secular elements, to a 'civilization of dhimmitude,' i.e. Eurabia: a secular-Muslim transitional society with its traditional Judeo-Christian mores rapidly disappearing." Bernard Lewis told the German newspaper *Die Welt* that "Europe will be Islamic by the end of the century."[4]

Demographics

Estimates about the number of Muslims in Europe vary with some sources estimating as high as 50 million.[5] "The number of Muslims in contemporary Europe is estimated to be 50 million. It is expected to double in twenty years. By 2025, one third of all European children will be born to Muslim families. Today Mohammed is already the most popular name for newborn boys in Brussels, Amsterdam, Rotterdam, and other major European cities."[6] There are several factors at work here. Birth rates in several European countries have fallen below replacement level meaning that Europe's population will likely drop by 100 million by 2050. On the other hand, the Muslim population is much younger and has a birth rate three times higher with the result that while the European population was projected to fall by 3.5 percent by 2015, the Muslim population will have doubled.[7]

> **The number of Muslims in contemporary Europe is estimated to be 50 million. It is expected to double in twenty years. Europe is in a "demographic death spiral."**

Europe is in a "demographic death spiral" - the worst is in the former Communist countries: "the five lowest birth rates in the world are Latvia, Bulgaria, Slovenia, Russia, and Ukraine." Europe is dying: "nineteen of the lowest twenty birth rates in the world are on the Continent (the twentieth is Japan)."[8] This complicates the labor and welfare problems as there are not enough people projected for the labor force and not enough people to pay for the care of the elderly.

Adding to the fertility problem, about 900,000 people immigrate to Europe each year with a large proportion coming from North Africa and the Middle East plus a likely surge after the Jasmine Revolution in 2011. Part of this was due to their colonial past: Algeria was considered part of France; Pakistanis and Indians were part of the British Empire; likewise Indonesia with the Netherlands. In addition, there was a need for workers. Germany imported millions of Turks as "guest workers" after the war as did some of the other EU countries, but they had no immigration plan for the long term. They "pursued policies that encourage massive illegal immigration and then compound the problem by legalizing it. They do so by providing generous public assistance to illegal immigrants, tolerating large-scale abuse of asylum laws, failing to deport those apprehended, and granting periodic amnesties which trigger ever larger inflows."[9] **Take note America!**

It was Algeria's Houari Boumédienne who said at the UN in 1974: "One day, millions of men will leave the Southern Hemisphere to go to the Northern Hemisphere. And they will not go there as friends. Because they will go there to conquer it. And they will conquer it with their sons. The wombs of our women will give us victory." Abd Al-Rahman Al-'Arifi, imam of the mosque of the King Fahd Defense Academy, said that Muslims "will control the land of the Vatican and will control Rome and introduce Islam in it." It was Al-Jazeera's Yusuf al-Qaradawi who said, "Islam will return to Europe as a conqueror and victor" and that "the conquest this time will not be by the sword but by preaching and ideology."[10]

The need for workers is likely to only grow worse as the European population grows older and increasingly strains its welfare-state economies.[11] The UN projected in 2000 that the EU would need 949,000 each year to maintain their 1995 population, but 1,588,000 to maintain the working age population of 1995, and even more astounding 13,480,000 to keep the ratio in 1995 of working age to retired people. Demographic projections are notoriously inaccurate, but regardless of the actual numbers, the trend is ominous.[12] The problem with importing Muslims to do their work is that Europeans will have to sell their souls to get those welfare payments.

The problem with importing Muslims to do their work is that Europeans will have to sell their souls to get those welfare payments.

One of the products of these foreign workers is an underground economy because employers and employees do not want to pay payroll taxes which for the EU average 36 percent. With these high levies, those illegal immigrants, often unskilled and uneducated, become unemployable in the regular workforce. This leads to a shadow economy which "ranges from 8.4 percent of GDP in the U.S. to 14.5 percent in France, 16.8 percent in Germany, and nearly one-third of GDP in high immigration countries like Italy."[13]

The number of Muslims may not appear exceedingly large in the overall population of Europe but they are concentrated in a few countries and they tend to congregate around large cities. One third of France's Muslims are in the Paris area, mainly in the northern suburbs, while 40 percent of Britain's Muslims are in the London area. They tend to live in neighborhoods or large housing projects that become ghettos, isolated culturally and economically from society. These ghettos suffer from the typical ghetto problems of high crime rates, poor education, and high unemployment, which can make some susceptible to radical Islam.[14]

As is true throughout the Muslim world, only a small percentage is radical, but they are, what one Frenchman called "EuroIslam," enough of a threat to make Europe a major "training and staging ground for terrorism" (several of the World Trade Center bombers came from a cell in Hamburg and European jihadis have gone to Iraq and Afghanistan) as well as a target – major bombings in London and Madrid. Of course this led to a backlash against Muslims and immigration policies. One State Department official reported that "younger Muslims are resisting assimilation into secular European societies even more steadfastly than the older generation did." Europe never had the "melting pot" approach to immigration that the US did and thus has a major problem with assimilation. We are fighting a world war against Islamic radicals while our European allies have growing Muslim populations that support those radicals. As Giles Kepel observed, "The most important battle in the war for the Muslim minds during the next decade will be fought not in Palestine or Iraq, but on the outskirts of London, Paris, and other European cities, where Islam is already a growing part of the West."[15]

Move to Australia or New Zealand. That is the only option they [young people] have if they want to avoid the plagues that will turn the old continent uninhabitable."

The radical imams in Europe do not change: "The real weapons of mass destruction are the desire for martyrdom... Half a million martyrdom shadeed is enough for Muslims to control the whole of earth forever. In the end of the day, Islam must control earth, whether we like it or not." (Imam Abu Hamza al-Masri, Imam in Britain). "We don't make a distinction between civilians and non-civilians... Only between Muslims and unbelievers. And the life of an unbeliever has no value." (Sheikh Omar Bakri Mohammed, Syrian-born British Muslim cleric).[16]

Henryk M. Broder, the German author, told the Dutch newspaper *De Volksrant* (12 October 2006) that young Europeans who love freedom should emigrate. "Europe as we know it will no longer exist 20 years from now." While enjoying the passers-by and the scenery from a terrace in Berlin, he noted, "We are watching the world of yesterday." Although he said he was too old to emigrate, he urged young people to "move to Australia or New Zealand. That is the only option they have if they want to avoid the plagues that will turn the old continent uninhabitable."

Broder was convinced that Europeans were unwilling to oppose Islam. "The dominant ethos is perfectly voiced by the stupid blonde woman author with whom I recently debated. She said that it is sometimes better to let yourself be raped than to risk serious injuries while resisting. She said it is sometimes better to avoid fighting than run the risk of death."

> **Like the days when many said "better Red than dead," it appears that now many Europeans would rather submit than die, rather be Islamic than dead.**

Dutch author Oscar Van den Boogaard referred to Broder's interview in an op-ed in the Brussels newspaper *De Standaard* (23 October 2006) and wrote that coping with the Islamization of Europe was like "a process of mourning" and he was overwhelmed by a "feeling of sadness." He wrote, "I am not a warrior, but who is? I have never learned to fight for my freedom. I was only good at enjoying it." One is left with the feeling like Broder that they have chosen submission, like in earlier days when "they preferred to be Red rather than dead." Now it is that perhaps they would rather submit than die or rather be Islamic than dead. Fortunately, we still have some Americans who are willing to fight for liberty!

Multiculturalism -- Non-assimilation

Multiculturalism is a concept whereby communities with separate identities can live together peacefully united by some semblance of national ideology. As Mark Steyn subtly put it, "contemporary multiculturalism absolves one from knowing anything about other cultures as long as one feels warm and fluffy toward them. After all, if it's grossly judgmental to say one culture's better than another, why bother learning about the differences? 'Celebrate diversity' with a uniformity of ignorance." One of the rude awakenings of the London 7/7 bombings was that "ordinary boys" - "such lovely lads" - could carry out such attacks in their own country. But that was precisely the problem: these young men of Pakistani origin did not see Britain as "their country" but as the enemy or part of Dar al-Harb.[17]

This human rights charade, supported by the EU and the UN, is manipulated to use multiculturalism to support Islam. The Parliamentary Assembly of the Council of Europe stated in 2008 that member states must "condemn and combat Islamophobia" and ensure "that school textbooks do not portray Islam as a hostile or threatening religion." The UN Human Rights Council passed a resolution in March 2010 criminalizing "defamation of religions." It was authored by Pakistan and the only religion mentioned is Islam. The Organization of the Islamic Conference, as we have already noted, uses its voting power in the UN to subvert human rights and freedom. The OIC rejected the 1948 Universal Declaration of Human Rights in 1990 replacing it with the Cairo Declaration on Human Rights in Islam, its article 24 states: "All the rights and freedoms stipulated in this Declaration are subject to the Islamic Sharia."[18]

Geert Wilders noted that Westerners have criticized Islam and Muhammad for 1,400 years "because they recognized evil when they saw it. But then, suddenly, in the last decades of the past century, especially from the 1970s onwards, Western intellectuals stopped doing so." He saw the Marxist cultural and moral relativism as leading Western intellectual and political elites "to adopt a utopian belief in a universal brotherhood of mankind." He said "Multiculturalism is a culture of repudiation of Europe's heritage and freedoms."[19]

> **This failure to defend our own culture has turned immigration into the most dangerous threat that can be used against the West. Multiculturalism has made us so tolerant that we tolerate the intolerable.**
>
> **- Geert Wilders**[20]

In a similar speech, Wilders said: "Our Judeo-Christian Western culture is far better and far superior to the Islamic culture. We must be proud to say so!" He added "Multiculturalism is a disaster. Almost everyone acknowledges this today, but few dare say why. Let me tell you why: Multiculturalism made us tolerate the intolerant, and now intolerance is annihilating tolerance." "A moderate Islam does not exist and will never exist. And because there is no such thing as a moderate Islam, the Islamization of our free Western societies is an enormous danger."[21]

Ghettos have already been mentioned. There is one other word, race, which applies: "there's one taboo issue that the officially colorblind France has been unable to confront: race." The riots in France exposed the division along color lines with Arabs and blacks trapped in ghettos. The French have tried to soft pedal the situation by referring to the rioters as "youths" from "sensitive urban zones" rather than ghettos. The French have so idealized the melting pot in the name of equality that they have made their minorities invisible, at least on paper. "The country does not compile statistics on the foreign-born or their French-born children." The result is that France does not really know how many Muslims live in France [It might be 6 million or it might be 8 million.], and this colorblind approach has limited their ability to recognize and treat the problems of the minorities.[22] "In fact, if the birth rate continues as projected, France will have a Muslim majority in less than 25 years." It is "a cautionary tale of immigration run amok" and with just a few decades of immigration of a high fertility group, and due to the "constant appeasement attitude of officials," France may be the first European country to introduce sharia. Muslims outnumbered all other minorities in France and their lack of assimilation was a major problem. "Decades of immigration had produced a large class of young men who claim Islam, not France, as their identity and consider crime as an acceptable life style."[23]

> **Decades of immigration had produced a large class of young men who claim Islam, not France, as their identity and consider crime as an acceptable life style.**

There was discussion in British newspapers about the worsening segregation and some areas turning into "fully-fledged ghettos." According to one writer, Britain was playing with fire "in not recognizing the scale of the change that needs to be undertaken by whites, non whites but also Muslims to secure the alternative and imperative process of integration." An editorial in *The Guardian* (24 September 2005) noted, "Mr. Phillips [Trevor Phillips, head of the Commission for Racial Equality] has sometimes been too sweeping a critic of multiculturalism. Nevertheless, there is some truth in his view the policy has concentrated too much on celebrating diversity and not enough of emphasizing our commonality."[24] Britain has long been a haven for Islamic radicals due to its generous asylum policy and its history of admitting large numbers of poor, uneducated Pakistanis and Bangladeshis from the empire. Politicians have lauded their multiculturalism without looking too deeply at the segregation and divisiveness beneath. "Assimilation was never policy…They accepted as natural what you may call cultural and religious tribalism, and now it's turning against them. They confuse tolerance with negligence."[25]

> **Assimilation was never policy…They accepted as natural what you may call cultural and religious tribalism, and now it's turning against them. They confuse tolerance with negligence.**

Theo van Gogh was murdered in Amsterdam for the film he made about Muslim women. He was shot eight times and his throat was slit repeatedly trying to behead him, and then a five-page manifesto was stuck in his chest with a fillet knife stating he deserved to die for insulting Islam and calling for Muslims to rise up against the "infidel enemies" in the West. The Dutch Moroccan fanatic who killed him said it was not anything "personal;" it was only that Islamic law compelled him "to chop off the head of anyone who insults Allah and the Prophet." Ayaan Hirsi Ali, who wrote that film ("Submission"), was a member of the Dutch parliament and was under a death threat. Hirsi Ali fled from Somalia and became an outspoken critic of women's rights in Islam and unrestricted Muslim immigration into Europe. "She wasn't a multiculturalist, and she had nothing but contempt for the Dutch model. She thought Dutch 'tolerance' was a kind of Western weakness. She said that Muslims who wouldn't attempt to assimilate didn't belong in Holland….radical Islam would always be the enemy" and that "the oppression of women is built into Islam." She was forced to resign from parliament in May 2006 after the Dutch Immigration Minster Rita Verdonk pressed the fact that Hirsi Ali lied in her request for asylum and could be stripped of her Dutch citizenship. She went to the US.[26]

> **The Dutch Moroccan fanatic who murdered Theo van Gogh in Amsterdam said it was not anything "personal;" it was only that Islamic law compelled him "to chop off the head of anyone who insults Allah and the Prophet."**

The Dutch started importing laborers as early as 1964 and one prime minister was "not much interested in making Dutchmen out of Muslim immigrants." He said, "My job then was modernizing the Dutch economy." They were provided the benefits of a welfare state and as he said, "Our theory was that people in a multicultural society needed space to preserve their own culture and their own language." Holland had already divided itself into pillars: "a Catholic pillar, a Protestant pillar, and a 'humanist' pillar" to "live 'separately' together." That arrangement had actually started to crumble even before the Turks and Moroccan Berbers arrived. Official policy (1983) "assured the immigrants' right to 'socioeconomic equality,' to 'inclusion and participation in the political domain,' and finally, to 'equity in the domains of culture and religion' – which is to say, the right to be 'authentically' themselves. Authenticity was a nice folklore fiction – 'integration, not assimilation.'" It became a country that had "let its immigrants rot in their own privacy…because they are going back." But they did not go back! So with illiterate Berbers who "hardly knew there was such a thing as Dutch culture or Dutch law," and the imam of Amsterdam's most radical mosque who would not meet with the mayor and who does not speak Dutch, the Dutch had a problem with over 1 million immigrants. "The left was mugged by reality," as Hirsi Ali put it. It was difficult to determine the politically correct position to take toward people who live among you but feel free to kill you. It seemed that their "multicultural success" their "model of tolerance" that "peculiarly Dutch myth of a democracy integrated but not assimilated might be not only a contradiction in terms but a dangerous fiction."[27]

The cartoon stupidity awakened the Dutch; now their borders are virtually shut. Dutch has to be spoken in public in Rotterdam and the burqa was banned. A High Court Judge in The Hague said: "We no longer accept that people don't learn our language, we require that they send their daughters to school, and we demand they stop bringing in young brides from the desert and locking them up in third-floor apartments." So much for multiculturalism! Nicolas Sarkozy, before he became president of France, already recognized, "The French way of integration no longer works." He introduced new measures similar to the Dutch requiring learning French, looking for a job, failure meant deportation, and "In the case of a woman kept hostage in her home without learning French, the whole family will be obliged to leave." Rita Verdonk, Dutch Integration Minister, who was under death threat, told that imam who refused to shake her hand that he better learn Western customs and "Next year I expect to talk to you in Dutch."[28]

The notion of multiculturalism has fallen apart. It is an absolute failure. Anyone coming here must respect our constitution and tolerate our Western and Christian roots.
- Angela Merkel, German Chancellor

However, the Dutch government lost a court case when the court of appeal ruled that Turkish nationals do not have to attend integration courses. The court ruled that "because Turkey has an association agreement with the European Union, Turkish nationals living in the Netherlands may not be forced to attend language and civic studies courses." The clear implication is that EU citizens do not have to integrate.[29]

The problem is the same all over Europe, particularly with its open borders which permitted easy movement once inside the EU. From Spain and Sicily to Norway, governments, politicians, and the media were giving up on diversity and deciding that Islamism, what the French call the fundamentalism in the ghettos, was not compatible with Europe's liberal values. The political parties in Italy were looking for votes (sounds like the US) and showing their "tolerance" as immigrants continued to flood in, but a clash of civilizations was underway.

Spain found that Moroccans who lived among them were the ones who blew up their trains. An imam in Berlin was caught on hidden TV in his mosque telling his flock "Germans can only expect to rot in the fires of hell because they are nonbelievers." Scandinavia, which had always been very tolerant, found that the immigrants did not accept their ways. Rape had increased, particularly after a mufti, Shahid Mehdi, said on Copenhagen TV that women who go out without a hijab are "asking for rape." One young legislator said, "I believe integrating a large number of Muslims can't be done. It's an illusion." He continued, "They don't have the desire to blend in with other people. We've been a Christian country for 1,000 years and we are the oldest monarchy in the world. I want to get married and have a lot of kids who can walk around in a society not influenced by Muslims." When radio hosts call for Muslims to be expelled from Western Europe or exterminating fanatical Muslims, it was getting serious. If integration cannot succeed in Denmark, one of the most liberal nations, could it survive in more conservative ones?[30]

The jihad is a functioning version of everything multiculturalists have promoted for years.

In some ways multiculturalism is perfect for Islam when it is in the minority. When leaders talk of their country being a "nation of nations" or the one world concept, Islamists are left free to pursue their own idea of one world. "The jihad is a functioning version of everything multiculturalists have promoted for years."[31] The Netherlands was a good example of the new liberal Europe, trying to break from its racist or colonial past, which was perfect for Muslim immigrants. "Thus, it was far safer for radical Islamic fascists to damn the West openly from a mosque in Rotterdam than for a moderate Christian to quietly worship in a church in Saudi Arabia, Iran, or Algeria. And yet we learn not just that the Netherlands has fostered a radical sect of Muslims who will kill and bomb, but, far more importantly, that they will do so after years of residency among, and indeed in utter contempt of, their Western hosts." The Europeans preached "a postmodern gospel of multiculturalism and the end of oppressive Western values" and thousands of unassimilated Muslims mocked French, British, Dutch, German, and other societies. Millions of Muslims flocked to Europe for its freedom and tolerance but the Europeans, perhaps too late, discovered that radical Islamic extremism wanted to destroy that tolerant society. Europe was trapped in its own utopian rhetoric.

> But gut-check time is coming for Europe, with its own rising unassimilated immigrant populations, rogue mosques entirely bent on destroying the West, declining birth rate and rising entitlements, the Turkish question, and a foreign policy whose appeasement of Arab regimes won it only a brief lull and plenty of humiliation. The radical Muslim world of the madrassas hates the United States because it is liberal and powerful; but it utterly despises Europe because it is even more liberal and far weaker, earning the continent not fear, but contempt.[32]

Governments, including the US, have bent over backwards to not offend Muslims from banning profiling, tolerating radical imams, amnesties, and not enforcing laws. Sheikh Omar Bakri Mohammed was free to say he expected to see the banner of Islam flying over Downing Street. The question of flags became interesting. "In 2005, Anne Owens, Her Majesty's chief inspector of prisons, banned the flying of the English national flag in English prisons on the grounds that it shows the cross of St. George, which was used by the Crusaders and so is offensive to Muslims. The Drivers and Vehicles Licensing Agency has also banned the English flag from its offices. So has Heathrow Airport."[33] Flags may not seem important but gradual surrendering one's culture may result in the loss of that culture. **Bigamy** is a crime in England, but the government has approved welfare benefits for multiple wives.[34] Small concessions can aggregate over time into major cultural changes that may be almost irreversible.

Sarkozy, Merkel and British Prime Minister Davis Cameron have all spoken about the end of the European dream of multiculturalism.[35]

One should not surrender one's culture and some practices are unacceptable: female mutilation, stoning to death, and some restrictions that are totally out of date from problems of long ago (not eating pork, for example, might have made sense thousands of years ago due to trichinosis but not now since pork is one of the best sources of food per pound available). Suttee – the tradition of burning widows on the funeral pyres of their husbands – is another. The British encountered that when they controlled India. General Sir Charles Napier dealt with it multiculturally: "You say that it is your custom to burn widows. Very well. We also have a custom: when men burn a woman alive, we tie a rope around their necks and we hang them. Build your funeral pyre; beside it, my carpenters will build a gallows. You follow your custom. And then we will follow ours." It is difficult to deny that India is better off without suttee even though they still burn some brides. "Non-judgmental multiculturalism is an obvious fraud, and was subliminally accepted on that basis." Almost all who consider all cultures equal really do not wish to live any place other than an advanced Western society. "It is a quintessential piece of progressive humbug." What if a large percentage of the people around you believed in suttee or the prohibition of music, alcohol, or women going out without being veiled or covered? "Multiculturalism was conceived by the Western elites not to celebrate all cultures but to deny their own: it is, thus, the real suicide bomb."[36]

Multiculturalism was conceived by the Western elites not to celebrate all cultures but to deny their own: it is, thus, the real suicide bomb.

The Danish cartoon controversy is a good example of the extreme differences in cultures. When major Western newspapers refused to print them, that was not being "prudent;" that sent the message to the Muslim world that the West is weak and is ripe for the picking.[37] There is an Arab proverb: **"A falling camel attracts many knives."**

The problem is that Europe is not so much multicultural as it is bicultural. Some cities in Scandinavia have in just a few decades become almost majority Muslim. The examples of Fiji and Rwanda are not encouraging. "Bicultural societies are among the least stable in the world, especially once it's no longer quite clear who's the majority and who's the minority – a situation that much of Europe is fast approaching." With "post-Christian secular gay potheads and anti-whoring anti-sodomite anti-everything-you-dig Islamists," these two cultures are not compatible. One man observed that those French "youths" look like LA gangsters.

> But that's the point. The theoretical virtue of "multiculturalism" is that it's a form of mellifluous cultural cross-pollination: the best of all worlds. But just as often it gives us the worst of all worlds: the worst attributes of Muslim culture – the subjugations of women [and anti-almost everything] – combined with the worst of Western culture – license and self-gratification. Tattooed, pierced Pakistani skinhead gangs swaggering down the streets of northern England are as much a product of multiculturalism as the turban-wearing Sikh Mountie in the royal escort. Islamofascism itself is what it says: a fusion of Islamic identity with old-school European totalitarianism.[38]

Clearly, a civilization that feels guilty for everything it is and does will lack the energy and conviction to defend itself.
                                    - French philosopher Jean-François Revel[39]

We are faced with a 7th-century Islam that wants the conveniences of the 21st century. Will these Muslims live by the laws of England, France, etc.? "Or is their primary identity a new worldwide Islamic identity?" Multiculturalism turns nations into holding pens where, without cultural confidence, demography will decide the future. As James C. Bennett noted: "Democracy, immigration, multiculturalism. Pick any two." "At the heart of multiculturalism is a lie: that all cultures are equally 'valid.' To accept that proposition means denying reality – the reality of any objective measure of human freedom, societal health, and global population movement." Multiculturalism means just feeling good, "making bliss out of ignorance. If the guy's rich vibrant cultural tradition involves standing over you with a scimitar shouting 'Allahu Akbar!' well, you can't complain you're not getting your share of cultural diversity. Given the growing Muslim populations in Europe and the remarkable success hitherto obscure Muslim lobby groups have had in constraining certain aspects of the war on terror, it seems almost certain that Islamist political parties will arise on the Continent within the next decade."[40]

At the heart of multiculturalism is a lie: that all cultures are equally "valid."

The question becomes identity, allegiance, the whole basis of the nation state system. That is called into question when you have a Muslim leader like **Anjem Choudary** in England, who thinks 9/11 was "magnificent" conducted by "heroes" and calls for sharia for the UK. Of course, he and his wife are both on welfare even though he jets around to other countries to meet with like-minded Muslims. When asked on BBC why didn't he just move to a country that has sharia, he replied, "Who says you own Britain, anyway? Britain belongs to Allah. The whole world belongs to Allah."[41]

If that represents culture, then we are in for a very long war!

Organizations

Muslims are involved in a multitude of organizations starting with their mosques, Islamic centers, charities, and student organizations. These were initially local, then countrywide organizations and eventually across Europe and include publications such as magazines and books. Some of the major organizations which eventually appeared in Europe were formed in the 1920s. The very secretive **Tablighi Jamaat** (Proselytizing Group) was formed in 1927 in Mewat, India, near Delhi, by a Deobandi cleric Maulana Muhammad Ilyas Kandhalawi. Another was the **Muslim Brotherhood** (Hizb al-Ikhwan al-Muslimum) founded in Egypt in 1928 by Hassan al-Banna.

The Tablighi Jamaat are trained missionaries who dedicate much of their lives to spreading Islam around the world. "They rejected modernity as antithetical to Islam, excluded women, and preached that Islam must subsume all other religions." Marc Gaborieau, a French Tablighi expert, said their ultimate objective is a "planned conquest of the world" in the spirit of jihad. The Muslim Brotherhood's creed is: "Allah is our objective. The Prophet is our leader. The Qur'an is our law. Jihad is our way. Dying in the way of Allah is our highest hope." Although the Brotherhood lost some of its appeal and power in the Middle East, it gained power in Europe where it strives to impose Islamic law in Europe and the US.[42]

Thousands of students left the Middle East in the 1950s and 1960s to study at German universities, not only because of the good technical schools but also to escape repression at home. After Gamal Abdel Nasser had clamped down on the Brotherhood starting in 1954, some members fled Egypt. West Germany had decided to cut relations with countries that recognized East Germany, so when Egypt and Syria recognized East Germany, West Germany elected to welcome political refugees from those countries. Often those admitted were Islamists. One of the first was **Sa'id Ramadan**, who had been the personal secretary to Hassan al-Banna, who moved to Geneva in 1958 and went to law school in Cologne. He founded the **Islamische Gemeinschaft Deutschland** (Islamic Society of Germany, **IGD**) and presided over it until 1968. He also co-founded the **Muslim World League**, funded by the Saudis, and accused by the US of financing terrorism. With that Saudi money, he also founded the **Islamic Center of Geneva**, run by his son **Hani** with another son, **Tariq**, on the board, whose visa to teach at Notre Dame was revoked by the US.

Ghaleb Himmat, a Syrian with Italian citizenship, ran the IGD from 1973-2002. He helped found the **Bank al-Taqwa**, which Italian intelligence calls, the "Bank of the Muslim Brotherhood" for financing terrorist groups. He helped Youssef Nada run al-Taqwa and to set up companies in Switzerland, Liechtenstein, and the Bahamas, noted for their lack of financial regulations. The US Treasury Department designated both Himmat and Nada as terrorism financiers in 2001. Al-Taqwa financed numerous Islamic centers around Europe and Islamist publications, such as *Risalatul Ikhwan*, the official magazine of the Brotherhood. The Egyptian branch of the Brotherhood established its base in Munich, with the large **Islamic Center of Munich** financed by Saudis. The center's magazine, *Al-Islam*, has explicitly rejected a secular state. The Syrian branch built its headquarters in Aachen at the Syrian al-Attar family's Bilal mosque and the **Aachen Islamic Center**.

IGD grew and incorporated dozens of Islamic organizations and Islamic centers in more than thirty German cities are under its umbrella. Ibrahim el-Zayat, an Egyptian who led numerous student groups, took over from Himmat and focused on the next generation by sponsoring many student and youth organizations throughout Germany. He is linked to the **World Assembly of Muslim Youth (WAMY)** which is a Saudi NGO seeking to spread Wahhabism. WAMY, the largest Muslim youth organization in the world, is under the umbrella of the **Muslim World League**. WAMY published a book, *Tawjihat Islamiya* (Islamic Views) which tells the children to love taking revenge on the Jews and the oppressors... and make jihad for the sake of Allah." Zayat was linked to the **Institut Européen des Sciences Humaines** in France where European imams are prepared.

Zayat was also linked to **Milli Görüş** (National Vision in Turkish) which had 30,000 members and perhaps 100,000 sympathizers, and although it publicly supported Western-style democracy, its hidden agenda was the formation of an Islamic state. The organization's official journal, *Milli Gazete*, stated, "Milli Görüş is a shield protecting our fellow citizens from assimilation into barbaric Europe."

> **Milli Görüş [National Vision in Turkish] is a shield protecting our fellow citizens from assimilation into barbaric Europe.**

The Saudis created in 1989 the **Islamische Konzil Deutschland** (Islamic Council of Germany) under the auspices of Abdullah at-Turki, dean of Bin Saud University in Riyadh. Zayat and officials from Milli Görüş and the Islamic Center of Munich held other top positions. In 1994 an umbrella organization, the **Zentralrat der Muslime** was formed by 19 organizations, including IGD and the Islamic Centers of Munich and Aachen, nine of which were part of the Muslim Brotherhood. The significance is that "Politicians seek the Zentralrat's endorsement when they want to reach out to the Muslim community. Many German politicians are uninformed about Islam and do not understand that the view and the interpretation of Islam that the Zentralrat expresses, as does the IGD and Milli Görüş, is that of the Muslim Brotherhood and not that of traditional Islam."

The Muslim Brotherhood, with Saudi financing, has increased its power beyond Germany. The **Union des Organisations Islamiques de France** (Union of Islamic Organizations of France) became the dominant organization in the **French Islamic Council** set up by then Interior Minister Nicolas Sarkozy. Italy's main partner regarding Islamic issues was the extremist **Unione delle Comunita' ed Organizzazioni Islamiche in Italia** (Union of the Islamic Communities and Organizations in Italy). The Brotherhood also established pan-European organizations to parallel the European Union such as the **Federation of Islamic Organizations in Europe**. Just as they had success with youth in Germany, they joined with other groups to form the **Forum of European Muslim Youth and Student Organizations (FEMYSO)** which is "a network of 42 national and international organizations bringing together youth from over 26 different countries." FEMYSO became the de facto voice of

Muslim youth in Europe and was regularly consulted by the Council of Europe, the European Parliament, the UN, the European Youth Forum, and numerous European NGOs. The politicians having met with these radical groups gave them legitimacy and implied endorsement which the moderate voices without the generous Saudi funding could not match. Thus the Muslim Brotherhood had more opportunity "to influence and radicalize various European Muslim communities."[43]

Tablighi Jamaat became "a major recruiting agency for terrorist causes worldwide."

The Tablighi Jamaat expanded into Europe a little later, in the 1970s, particularly after the Saudi Wahhabis accepted the South Asian Deobandis and started financing them. The World Muslim League, from Saudi Arabia, financed the Tablighi mosque in Dewsbury, England, which became the European headquarters of Tablighi Jamaat. Tablighi was active in North Africa, in both Algeria and Morocco, and the Dutch were investigating links to the Moroccan cells in the murder of Theo van Gogh. Tablighi recruited for terrorist organizations and sent recruits to Pakistan and Algeria for training. Over 2,000 British Muslims were sent to Pakistan for training and it is estimated that about 100 French Muslims fought for al Qaeda. Tablighi became "a major recruiting agency for terrorist causes worldwide." For most young Muslim extremists, joining the Tablighi was the first step to extremism. "Perhaps 80 percent of the Islamist extremists in France come from Tablighi ranks, prompting French intelligence officers to call Tablighi Jamaat the 'antechamber of fundamentalism.'"[44]

In 1951, al-Hay'at al-Tahrir al-Islami (The Islamic Society of Liberation) was founded in East Jerusalem. From it evolved **Hizb ut-Tahrir al-Islami** (The Islamic Party of Liberation) which grew to tens of thousands of secret members throughout the Muslim world and in about 40 countries and called for the return of the caliphate in a global Islamic state under sharia. Hizb ut-Tahrir rejects democracy and capitalism as well as assimilation. It was the "finishing school" for several top al Qaeda members, including Abu Musab al-Zarqawi, who was finally killed in Iraq, and could be considered "a 'gateway drug' that seduces young Muslims away from assimilation, then softens their brains and hardens their ideological dogma to forge them into True Believers in the utopian vision of a future Islamo-fascist Third Reich's global domination."[45]

One researcher described Hizb ut-Tahrir as a totalitarian organization, the marriage of Leninist strategy and tactics to Orthodox Islamist ideology.

One researcher described it as a totalitarian organization, the marriage of Leninist strategy and tactics to Orthodox Islamist ideology. It took two years of indoctrination to become a member and then members were grouped in compartmentalized cells. **Omar Bakri Mohammed** took Hizb ut-Tahrir to London after he was expelled from Saudi Arabia in 1986. He had created another organization calling for a global caliphate, **Al Muhajiroun** (The Emigrants), in Saudi Arabia in 1983 and he also activated it in the fertile British soil. In 1999, he sponsored the **International Islamic Front (IIF)** which recruited British Muslims to undergo combat training and then go fight jihad in the Balkans and Chechnya. Omar said he headed the "political wing" of IIF with no link to Osama bin Laden but he later admitted that bin Laden ran the "military wing." Al Muhajiroun's web site said the foreign policy of the new Caliph "is to conquer the whole world by Jihad" thus bringing a new world order under Islamic domination. One of their tactics will be:

To formulate a fifth column as a community pressure group which is well equipped with the Islamic culture e.g. ruling, social, economic, judicial, penal and ritual systems in order to become capable of implementing Islam fully and comprehensively in society,

The weapons to be used to establish global Islamic political power range from debate, media appearances and the law to the funding of Jihadists and recruiting of suicide bombers.[46]

Omar Bakri was replaced by **Abu Hamza Al Masri** and he celebrated the first anniversary of 9/11 with a conference to launch a new organization the **Islamic Council of Britain (ICB)** with a stated goal to "implement sharia law in Britain." The poster for the event at Al Masri's Finsbury Park mosque in North London showed a large photograph of the World Trade Center with the caption **"September the 11th 2001: A TOWERING DAY IN HISTORY."** Hizb ut-Tahrir was eventually banned in several European countries.[47]

Al Muhajiroun's web site said the foreign policy of the new Caliph "is to conquer the whole world by Jihad" thus bringing a new world order under Islamic domination.

Lorenzo Vidino described the growth of radical Islam in Europe as a tripartite threat which can be visualized as a **pyramid.** "At the **top** of it are the **violent jihadists**, a few thousand individuals scattered throughout the continent who openly challenge the societies they live in, and are willing to spill blood to achieve their goals…. In Britain alone, MI5 believes that there are around 4,000 terror suspects and 200 jihadist networks spread throughout the country." The **second** level is **"peaceful revolutionaries,"** networks and groups that want to impose sharia but have not resorted to violence. The best organized of this group is Hizb ut-Tahrir. The large **base** of the pyramid is "groups that **publicly** purport to **support democracy and the integration of Muslim communities with the European mainstream, but quietly work to radicalize Europe's Muslim population.**" Among these are the Muslim Brotherhood, the Pakistani Jamaat-e-Islami, and the Turkish Milli Görüş plus the various organizations listed earlier. Each of these levels poses a different challenge to Europe and must be addressed.[48]

British security agencies circulated a document in 2007 which stated that al Qaeda had "established a foothold in most countries across North Africa and the Middle East and poses a far greater threat to Britain than previously thought." It also predicted that Afghanistan would replace Iraq as the center for "terrorists planning violent acts against the West." It warned of increased attacks in Britain including suicide bombers.[49]

Some British cultural habits in politics, the media, and the courts played a role in the establishment of "a well-rooted Islamist micro-environment in Britain." The mayor of London for years was "Red" Ken Livingstone, who was rather sympathetic to the radical Arab view. The British courts provided "legalistic protections to terrorists" resulting in what became known as **"Londonistan."** They often refused to extradite Muslims accused or convicted in foreign countries. Mohammed Al-Guerbuzi had lived in London for decades but he was sentenced to 20 years in prison by Morocco. He was considered to be a leader of the **Moroccan Islamic Combatant Group (MICG)** which was responsible for the Casablanca and Madrid attacks. Some of the lords on the High Court were more concerned about human rights and discrimination; as one put it: "I do not underestimate the ability of fanatical groups to kill or destroy, but they do not threaten the life of the nation." Many of the terrorist organizations kept a low profile in London but operated recruiting centers from there sending people to Afghanistan, Chechnya, Israel, etc. Omar Bakri was finally barred from reentering England and Al Muhajiroun was disbanded but remained influential. Abu Hamza headed the Supporters of Sharia in North London and was wanted for murder in Yemen and in the US for planning an Oregon training site. Yasser al-Sirri headed the Islamic Observation Center in London and was sentenced to death in absentia in Cairo for trying to kill an Egyptian prime minister. Seven of Egypt's most wanted terrorists were based in England. Another fiery preacher was Abu Qatada al-Philisteeni (the Palestinian) who entered the UK in 1993 on a forged UAE passport and was granted asylum. His real name was Omar Mahmoud Othman, a Palestinian from Jordan. He had "an intercontinental network of recruits and terrorist protegees." He influenced Muhammad Atta, Abu Musab al-Zarqawi, Zacarias Moussaoui, and shoe-bomber Richard Reid. Like most of these thugs, he received welfare and housing from the country he denounced. He was convicted in Jordan, indicted in Spain, and arrested in England. A Spanish judge called him Osama bin Laden's "spiritual ambassador to Europe." Numerous terrorist actions in recent years involved Muslim British citizens or those based in Britain, including attacks on US embassies and the murder of Daniel Pearl in Pakistan. As Tony Blair said, "There is a tendency, I think, to compromise too much with their arguments."[50]

Violence and Terror

It is absolutely irrelevant that most Muslims are good law-abiding citizens. As we have seen, it only takes a small number to conduct guerrilla or terrorist operations. Britain thought it had about 10,000 al Qaeda supporters in the UK in 2004 and "less than 1 percent" of their Muslims were involved in terrorist activities, but that would still be 16,000. Yet after the 7 July 2005 London bombings, six percent of British Muslims polled thought they were justified; that is about 100,000 people. Another 24 percent had some sympathy with the bombers' motives; that comes to almost half a million people who were not strongly against the bombings. One of the major changes is that young terrorists no longer need to go to other countries for training. The new generation is "learning without leaving" – "training to become jihadists right at home, through videos and the Internet. Some radical propaganda videos are now even shot or subtitled in English so Western Muslims who don't speak Arabic can understand them."[51]

With people like Anwar al-Awlaki and Samir Khan, who were killed in Yemen, but sent out much information in English via the Internet and their *Inspire* web magazine, the information technology has brought social networking worldwide via Facebook, Myspace, Twitter, as well as the Internet.[52] Arid Uka, who killed two US servicemen in March 2011 at Frankfurt Airport, was a Facebook friend of Pierre Vogel (Abu Hamza), a German Salafist, whose sermons and internet videos were popular with young people.[53] During the British riots in 2011, online forums called for Muslims in Britain to support the rioters with Internet campaigns urging them to bring down the government. One wrote that an Internet attack is very important and that "chaos is useful to militants in London."[54]

The 11 March 2004 attacks on the trains in Madrid which killed 191 people were conducted by a group of Moroccans who had lived in Spain for years and were a clear demonstration of the political power of terror. It was timed just prior to the elections and there had been a call for the withdrawal of the Spanish troops from Iraq. The incumbent prime minister was defeated and the new government promptly withdrew the Spanish troops. The **Islamic Commission of Spain**, representing about 200 of the 285 mosques in Spain finally issued a fatwa condemning Osama bin Laden as an apostate and stated that he should not be considered a Muslim.[55]

The bombings in London by four British citizens which killed 56 people were different in that they were suicides not remotely detonated bombs. Three of the four had been granted political asylum and lived on welfare while the fourth came from a comfortable family. Having expressed delight with 9/11, his father sent him back to Pakistan for some "discipline" but it evidently only enhanced his suicidal fanaticism.   The Brigades Abu Hafs as-Masri - Qaida/Jihad - Europe Division claimed credit for both the London and Madrid bombings.[56]

Islam has an identity crisis that it must combat. A virulent strain that mixes testosterone and a nihilistic theology has afflicted a small minority of young Muslims.
- London *Times* editorial, 11 August 2006[57]

In August 2006, The British uncovered a plot to blow up as many as 10 US bound passenger planes with liquid explosives and arrested 23 British-born Muslim Pakistanis. This was the result of good intelligence cooperation among various agencies in the UK, the US, and Pakistan. This plot was very similar to the **plan Bojinka** in 1994 when Pakistani terrorist **Ramzi Yousef** and **Khalid Sheikh Mohammed**, 9/11 mastermind, planned to bomb 12 planes over the Pacific using liquid explosives carried on board in carry-on bags and then assembled on board.[58]   This was another example of people growing up in comfortable England becoming radicals willing to kill in the name of ideology.[59] An unusual episode was the British priest who was told by an al Qaeda leader in Jordan, "Those who cure you are going to kill you." "Then came the news that six physicians were among the eight suspects detained in the failed attacks in Britain."[60]

Countries with freedom of speech and freedom of religion do not like to impose on people, but when they do it can be shocking. Britain's Channel Four took a hidden camera into several **mosques** and heard preaching about hatred of Jews and Christians, subjugation of women, and Islamic supremacism. Examples were: "**Allah has created the woman – even if she gets a Ph.D. – deficient. Her intellect is incomplete, deficient.** She may be suffering from hormones that will make her emotional." "By the age of 10, it becomes an obligation on us to **force her to wear hijab**, and if she doesn't wear hijab, **we hit her**." [Emphasis added] "Men are in charge of women. Wherever he goes, she should follow him and she shouldn't be allowed to leave the house without his permission." Right out of the Qur'an! "You have to live like a state within a state until you take over." "We want the laws of Islam to be practiced. We want to do away with the man-made laws."[61]

We noted in Chapter 3 the increase in rapes and that 100% of the rapes in Oslo, Norway's capital, were committed by "non-Western immigrants." "The latest news is that in Stavanger, Norway's 4th largest city, nine out of ten rapes are committed by 'men from minority groups'."[62] In Denmark, a Danish cop finally broke the taboo and admitted that "Immigrant criminals target Danes to make them move out of (Muslim) areas." Translations were provided from a Christian priest, a Danish police officer, and a council chairman. The police officer talked about police being shot at, racism, and "an extreme hatred towards authority." The council chairman said "Ethnic conflict is about to be started." He said that "It's gangs of mainly Palestinian and Somali background who are behind the attacks."[63] The pot is starting to boil in parts of Europe.

Members of what was Al Muhajiroun were still active protesting outside the Danish embassy in London on the anniversary of the cartoon nonsense with "bomb Denmark, nuke Germany, nuke France, nuke the USA" and "we want blood on the streets of England."[64] Gary Smith was just teaching a world religions course, not proselytizing, but four Muslims attacked him for teaching other religions to girls. Akmol Hussein, Sheikh Rashid, Azad Hussain, and Simon Alam did not kill him; they just slashed his face and fractured his skull.[65]

We have already noted the killing of Theo van Gogh in the Netherlands. The suspect was a Dutch Moroccan with ties to al Qaeda. There were tit-for-tat attacks on mosques and then churches. Then two young men were arrested for trying to get someone to "behead" a politician. The previous year a young Moroccan was arrested before he could carry out planned attacks on the Dutch parliament, Schiphol airport, and the Borsselle nuclear reactor.[66] Radicals singled out individuals for assassination including lawmakers and several attempts at bombings and assassinations were uncovered by Dutch security. Gunmen fired on the office of Immigration Minister Rita Verdonk and numerous officials had bodyguards after receiving death threats.[67] After the Norway shootings of young people, the Left tried to blame Geert Wilders for his anti-Islam stance. He responded: "I would say to Cohen and the rest of the left in the Netherlands; it is not my words, but your silence about the dangers of Islam which has the negative influences."[68] Feliz Muhammad, born in Sydney, Australia but based in Malaysia, referred to Wilders as "this Satan, this devil, this politician in Holland" – anyone who talks about Islam like Wilders should be beheaded.[69]

Germany became more active in dealing with its terrorists after finding that three of the 9/11 pilots came from Hamburg. Still there was concern about returning to the Nazi or Stasi (East German secret police) eras of "security." They were lucky when two trains were bombed on 31 July 2006 by two Lebanese students; the detonators went off but failed to trigger the devices.[70] Islam Bassam Tibi predicted in the summer of 2004 that within 10 years Germany would see "large running battles between police and gangs of marginalized Muslim youth, bringing cities like Berlin, Cologne and Frankfurt to the brink of chaos." This was because they were not interested in integration and that by 2014 the "Muslim population would have doubled to 10 million, sharia would have been gradually introduced in Germany and the Islam preached there would be even more radical and resemble Nazi totalitarianism." Less than four years later, a German interior ministry study of young Muslims showed 44 percent had fundamentalist beliefs, 50 percent believed that you went to paradise if you died in jihad, and 25 percent were ready to use violence against non-Muslims.[71]

The German Interior Minister, Han-Peter Friedrich, met with Muslim leaders "to discuss how they can prevent youth radicalization. Muslim leaders countered that the responsibility lies with the government." They complained about lack of integration and that the government needs to make Muslims feel at home and to work against Islamophobia. With 2,500 mosques, they claimed there were only a few fringe groups.[72] They failed to mention the efforts not to integrate and the calls for Sharia.

The number of radicals continued to grow in Germany, rising to 37,470 in 2010 with 31,370 connected to Turkish groups, almost all in **Milli Görüş** (the founder called for an Islamic state in Turkey). According to the intelligence head, most worrying was the increased numbers in **"Salafi"** groups which were "especially successful at recruiting young people, such as the Frankfurt airport killings. He said, "Not every Salafi is a terrorist but almost every terrorist that we are aware of has had contact with a Salafi."[73] At a meeting of German state interior ministers, one noted, Salafism was a "centre and pivot for those who want to participate in so-called holy war. Salafism can in this way lay the path to Islamist terrorism." He added they need to change the law so that "hate preachers" can be more easily deported and that Salafists wanted "a return to a stone-age Islam and want to turn Germany into a theocracy."[74]

A disturbing report from England about Salafis impacts on the US. A report from the Quilliam Foundation revealed some bad activities at the City University in London.

- Promotion of Salafi jihadist ideologues like Abu Muhammad al Maqdisi and Anwar al-Awlaki by the University Islamic Society
- Islamic society forcing Muslim girls to cover up on campus
- Islamic society intimidating and threatening jews, homosexuals and other Muslims who didn't agree with them (including Shiites)
- Calls during Friday prayers on campus to kill adulterers and apostates.

It was a London University graduate, Abdulmutallab, who was radicalized there and tried to kill Americans in a plane over Detroit on Christmas Day.[75]

We all saw the pictures of Muslim youths rioting and burning cars in France starting in Paris but it spread to many other French cities. The latest even had the rioters using fire arms and throwing Molotov cocktails. A difference in France was that the rioting was partly religious but more out of anger. Even though French-born, these youths were excluded from mainstream society and most could not break out of poverty. They had no real roots; they were considered foreigners in North Africa and foreigners in France. However, there was still a jihadist side to activities in France. Attacks on Jews and synagogues had dramatically increased and over 23,000 inmates in French prisons were Muslims, over six times their proportion in the population. Al Qaeda was recruiting in France and there were estimated to be military style units of between 35 and 45 thousand men. The families of ten Arab men convicted of raping a teenage girl left the court calling for revenge. The court was burned down eight days later and the girl and her family had to flee.[76]

Another example of their contempt for the system was the trial of a young French man from the Ivory Coast, leader of a self-proclaimed "gang of barbarians" who kidnapped a young Jewish man, tortured him for 24 days, and then killed him. At the trial, he smirked at the victim's family and shouted "Allahu Akbar" at them. He identified himself to the judge as "Arabs African revolt barbarian salafist army."[77]

Another country with a heavy radical Islamic presence is Italy with enormous numbers of illegal immigrants entering daily. Milan has one of the largest and most active mosques in Europe and has become a center for European jihadis. There is even an illegal population from Bolivia in Milan running the cocaine trade. There are heavily armed gangs operating in the country and the public is still indifferent and the government takes little action.[78]

Islam is a religion of "peace" and Muslims will kill you to prove it.

- Paris Dispersico[79]

The Iraq War led to an increase in recruiting in Europe for jihadis to go fight in Iraq. Abu Mousab al-Zarqawi was probably the biggest recruiter in Europe while he was alive.[80] In addition to al Qaeda in Iraq, **Ansar al-Islam**, originally a small Kurdish group that was smashed early in the war, had regrouped and grown into a major radical group and also had an extensive underground recruiting network in Europe to bring hundreds if not thousands of "new anti-U.S. jihadists" to the fight. Ansar was active in at least Norway, Sweden, Germany, Britain, and Italy.[81]

Throw in Chechnya, the attacks in Moscow, the terrible tragedy of the children in Ossetia, the problems in the Balkans, without including the Islamic violence in the rest of the world from the Middle East to India to Indonesia, and we have a clearly global threat to the international community.

The Muslim world still blamed the West for its "self-inflicted miseries." It was still unfair to Islam to criticize Islamic fascism so mullahs and madrassas were allowed in our countries to spread hate and intolerance so we would not offend Islam. Their goal is to bring back the caliphate, create another al Andalus. As George Habash, the Marxist leader of the Popular Front for the Liberation of Palestine told Oriana Fallaci in 1972, "Our revolution is a part of the world revolution. It is not confined to the reconquest of Palestine."

Palestinians are part of the Arab nation. Therefore, the entire Arab nation must go to war against the West. And it will. America and Europe don't know that we Arabs are just at the beginning of the beginning. That the best is yet to come. That from now on there will be no peace for the West... To advance step by step. Decade after decade. Determined, stubborn, patient. This is our strategy. A strategy that we shall expand throughout the whole planet."

She wrote that the Mediterranean could become an Islamic lake before the end of the century and she decried the "shortsighted Europeans who are more concerned about violating multiculturalist sensibilities than fighting for their own survival."[82]

Sharia and Dhimmitude

Sharia is slipping into the European legal system and the people are drifting into dhimmitude. This is the stealth jihad. There are now over 85 Sharia courts in Britain, some advising illegal actions and transgressing human rights standards.[83]   The Archbishop of Canterbury did not help with his prediction that Sharia law was inevitable. There is an EU plan for family courts across Europe to use the laws of whichever country the involved couple is from which means judges could be forced to bow to Sharia in some divorce cases.[84] Some 61% of British Muslims (18% in Denmark) want Sharia law.[85] The problem is that Sharia courts take appalling and illegal behavior for granted, not even considering reporting to civil authorities such crimes as polygamy and domestic violence. For a woman who was beaten and left at home because her husband spent most of his time with his second wife, the Sharia court said "The burden is on the wife to 'keep up the façade of cordial relations.'"   It is an inconsistent and inefficient system. One of the judges, "Dr Suhaib Hasan, wants Britain to introduce the penal law where women are stoned for committing adultery, and robbers have their hands amputated."[86]

A leaked government document indicated that Sharia-style multiple marriages could be officially recorded. This is, of course, against British law and only adds to the welfare burden; but it would recognize Sharia and open a duel legal system.[87]   Chancellor Angela Merkel claimed that Sharia was not practiced in Germany, but she was contradicted by a leading law professor "saying a variety of Sharia-based rulings were being made all the time." There are family and inheritance rulings and women in polygamous marriages have been in courts, for example, to share in a dead husband's pension benefits and a second wife who was not deported because "it would not be fair to send her to Iraq alone."[88] As previously noted, a study found that immigrants in Denmark, mostly Muslim, "constitute five percent of the population but consume upwards of 40 percent of the welfare spending." Many of the "single" women on welfare are actually wives of polygamous Muslim men.[89]

Sharia is coming with various small cuts at a time. In "moderate" Islamist Turkey, new rules "ban alcohol from sports advertising and events for young people, and sales are limited to licensed shops and restaurants." While protecting "young adults from alcoholism," of course there will be no harm to the food and entertainment industries![90] We have already noted that there is no fun in Islam; no humor either! UK comedienne Sharon Horgan who has a political satire show, Have I Got News For You, told a joke: "The Independent described the Dostoevsky metro station... as the Mecca for suicides. Not to be confused with the Mecca of suicides – which is Mecca." The Muslims went ballistic. The Muslim Public Affairs Committee announced: "By making such a comment she is giving the message that the holiest site in Islam is the centre of all terrorism and that Islam is inherently linked with violence." [Maybe he knows more than he admits!] They demanded that viewers E-mail BBC and demand an apology.[91]

As we noted in Concessions in Chapter 4, there are endless examples. In France, Quick, the No. 2 burger chain after McDonald's, serves halal-only food in 22 of its outlets, of course targeting Muslims. Halal means cows slaughtered according to Islamic law, that is killing a cow by cutting its jugular vein and draining all the blood. It does not change the taste of the meat at all![92] Some might call this an inhumane way to kill an animal. A British air stewardess was fired for refusing to fly to Saudi Arabia after she had been ordered to wear the traditional Islamic black robe, an abaya, and walk behind her male colleagues. The airline had given the female employees abayas and required them to put them on when leaving the aircraft and told them to "walk behind their male counterparts in public areas such as airports no matter what rank." She refused to be treated as a second-class citizen and was sacked.[93]

There was the ruckus over the Swiss ban on minarets and clashes over veils and burqas. In 2004, France banned head scarves and other "ostentatious" religious symbols such as large Christian crosses and Jewish skullcaps in state offices and schools. In 2009, President Sarkozy called for the parliament to ban wearing full veils in public, the burqa and niqab, (which cover completely leaving only the eyes exposed). He said "The burqa is not a religious sign, it's a sign of subservience, a sign of debasement. It will not be welcome on the territory of the French Republic." He said it turns women into "prisoners behind a screen."[94] A member of parliament called the burqa and niqab "a moving prison" for women. The Housing Minister Fadela Amara (Algerian background) was alarmed at the number of women "who are being put in this kind of tomb."[95] The law was passed in 2010 and went into effect in 2011 "to increase security but claimed it would liberate Muslim women from the oppression of their veil." Posters went up all over France reminding such women that "The Republic lives with its face uncovered." [They might have recalled that the "Lady of France," symbol of the French Revolution, was topless as she held the Tricolor.] Failure to lift her veil could cost a woman 150 euros ($205) and be required to attend re-education classes. If anyone was guilty of forcing a woman to wear a veil in public or private faced "a fine of 30,000 euros and a year in jail." But some women defied the law (a few were converts to Islam). One said, "I will not obey it, I will only respect laws of the French Republic which are not in contradiction with me, my religion and my faith." [She won't be a good citizen any where since she is above the law.][96] The situation turned into farce when police arrested two women but when one went to court, she was refused entry, because she would not remove her face covering or even give her complete name. (The other woman stayed home because she knew she would be stopped from entering.) But that is why they were arrested. "Police are under strict orders not to remove face coverings themselves," so the woman was told to leave. The French were regrouping trying to solve their dilemma.[97]

It was not only France; the top court in Belgium upheld the ban on headscarves. In the Netherlands, many companies banned headscarves at work. Turkey tried to lift a ban on headscarves for female students at university but it was blocked by the constitutional court.[98]

As usual under Islam, it turned violent. Talibanesque thugs in the Tower Hamlets of London threatened a woman to dress more modestly or they would kill her. She was not a practicing Muslim and feared losing her job.[99]

The Muslim Council of Britain (MCB) took a hard line and announced that "not covering the face is a 'shortcoming' and suggested that any Muslims who advocate being uncovered could be guilty of rejecting Islam." [That is a capital offense!] One of the signatories of this proclamation was from Hizb ut-Tahrir.[100]

The notorious group **Muslims Against the Crusades (MAC)** has called for three emirates (Bradford and Dewsbury in Yorkshire and Tower Hamlets in London) to be independent states and live by Sharia. Their demands included ending CCTV cameras near mosques, the release of all Muslim prisoners, a ban on Muslims joining the police or armed forces, and a rejection of British democracy. It ended with "We can conclude that measures by the UK government are nothing more than an attempt by them to strip the Muslim community of their Islamic identity and to integrate them into the non-Islamic way of life."[101]

Similar to the US, they permit such nonsense to be taught in schools. A BBC investigation found that some 5,000 pupils, age 6-18, are being taught Sharia punishments in "weekend-school" textbooks and that whoever does not believe Islam will go to hell. Textbooks covered cutting off the right hand for stealing (cut off a foot for a second offense) and cauterizing the arm and that the "main goal" of Jews is to "have control over the world and its resources." The schools belong to the "Saudi Students Clubs and Schools in the UK and Ireland" and the BBC said one school in London is owned by the Saudi government.[102]

The **double standards** in the West about Islam reached a low with the trial of Geert Wilders, a member of parliament in the Netherlands, for "sowing hatred" because of his criticism of Islam. Freedom of speech was on trial. He was harassed for seven years starting in 2004 until finally acquitted in 2011. His party greatly increased its numbers with his platform to stop the Islamization of the Netherlands. He made a distinction between Islam the ideology and Muslims. "Islam is not a religion, it's an ideology, the ideology of a retarded culture. I have a problem with Islamic traditions, culture, ideology. Not with Muslim people." He wants to ban the Qur'an: "The Koran is a fascist book which incites violence. That is why this book, just like Mein Kampf, must be banned. The book incites hatred and killing and therefore has no place in our [Dutch] legal order."[103]

In his final remarks to the court, Wilders quoted Frederick Douglass, "To suppress free speech is a double wrong. It violates the rights of the hearer as well as those of the speaker." He ended with a quote from George Washington: "If the freedom of speech is taken away then dumb and silent we may be led, like sheep to the slaughter."[104] Even the prosecutors, who had been ordered to hold the trial by a higher court, wanted Wilders acquitted.[105]

Geert Wilders, the champion of free speech, was barred from Britain but the chief imam of the Grand Mosque in Mecca, Sheikh Abdul Rahman al Sudais, was welcomed to preach at the East London mosque. Sudais, who called Jews "scum, rats, pigs, and monkeys," Christians "cross worshippers," and Hindus "idol worshippers," had been banned from Canada. The East London mosque had received $1 million from the Saudis.[106]

The concessions to Muslims reached the ridiculous when a café owner was forced to tear down an extractor fan, which had been in place for three years, because the smell of frying bacon "offends" Muslims. The hard working café owner is a Turkish Muslim; he cooks the bacon himself and his Turkish friends regularly come in for a sandwich.[107]

Extreme political correctness and the **dhimmi** attitude of "don't offend Muslims" were demonstrated when a UK foreign officer minister claimed "that an alternative symbol is needed for the Red Cross because of the logo's supposed links to the Crusades." They were debating "the adoption of the 'red crystal' – a diamond-shaped body – to avoid the religious connotations of the cross and crescent symbols currently used by the international body."[108]

Another very sad case of **willful dhimmitude** appeared in the UK *Daily Telegraph.* The Church of England Bishop of Bradford, the Right Reverend Nick Baines, wrote that some of his parishes were 95% Muslim but that was not a problem. "This is a fantastic opportunity. It is a challenge, yes, but it's an opportunity to rethink what it means to be a Christian community. We often ask Muslims to learn what it is to be a Muslim as a minority culture. Maybe we could benefit from learning some of the same lessons in some of our cities." As Babs Barron wrote, "Really? The poor mystified fool!" He obviously does not understand the threat from Islamic supremacism. As Paul Weston wrote:

> But at the top of the pile sits Islam. Imported and appeased by politicians of all parties, Islam is the real winner here and is promoted as <u>the religion of peace</u> when it is clearly no such thing. Polygamy laws are ignored in order that Muslims may demographically destroy us, laws are introduced to curtail any criticism on pain of exhibiting "Islamophobia", and money is directed

toward them in order that they need not work to house their multiple wives and children even as they plan to overthrow us.

The rest of us, however – the war veterans, the elderly, the young, the new-born, the indigenous population, the non-Islamic immigrants, the middle-class, the working-class and the Christians – have been betrayed in our entirety.

"And the Rt Rev Nick Baines is complicit in that betrayal."[109]

Russian law guarantees women the freedom to dress as they choose, but in Chechnya women who refuse to wear headscarves are prohibited from working in the public sector and female students are required to wear them in schools and universities. The Kremlin has taken no action to stop this unwritten and unlawful practice.[110]

Usama Hasan led prayers at his mosque in London for 20 years but was forced out over his views on evolution which resulted in Muslims calling him an apostate and infidel and seeking fatwas to kill him. Clerics in Kuwait, Pakistan, and Saudi Arabia issued such fatwas. He wrote of the "appalling state of science in the Muslim consciousness" and described the belief from the Qur'an that Adam was made of clay and then became a human when Allah breathed life into him as a "children's madrassa-level understanding" of the origins of man. Hasan is not just a lay person; he is a scientist having studied theoretical physics at Cambridge and is a senior engineering lecturer at Middlesex University.[111]

We noted earlier the hundreds of millions of dollars poured into universities in Europe and the US from Arab countries to influence the intellectual climate and push Islam. These Islamic centers generally are pro-jihad and anti-freedom, almost exclusively anti-Western.[112]

One little known initiative to bring Europe and some of the Islamic countries together is the **Euro-Mediterranean Partnership** which came into effect on 1 January 2010. It started as the Barcelona Process in 1995 to create a Greater European Union of both Europe and North Africa "with the Mediterranean Sea becoming a domestic Eurabian Sea." The goal is "comprehensive political partnership," with a "free trade area and economic integration", "considerably more money for the partners", and "cultural partnership" – ["that is, importation of Islamic culture into post-Christian Europe."] Stop the Islamization of Europe (SIOE), the European human rights group, has been working to expose the mass immigration of Muslims in this plan. According to SIOE, "Europe is to be Islamized. Democracy, Christianity, European culture and Europeans are to be driven out of Europe. Fifty million North Africans from Muslim countries are to be imported into the EU." This is in line with "Brussels economists claim Britain and other EU states will 'need' 56 million immigrant workers between them by 2050 to make up for the 'demographic decline' due to falling birthrates and rising death rates across Europe. To offset this decline, a 'blue card' system is to be created that will allow card holders to travel freely within the European Union and have full rights to work – as well as the full right to collect welfare benefits." [That is a problem for the US such as the Christmas Day bomber who flew from Amsterdam to Detroit without a passport.] There are now 44 states in the Euro-Med Partnership, 27 from the EU and extending from the Eastern Mediterranean across North Africa.[113]

Bat Ye'or, the pioneering historian of dhimmitude, wrote after Geert Wilder's acquittal that Eurabia was still advancing. The EU, which she calls "a mastodon Kafkaesque structure, consuming astronomical sums," has a "globalist Islamophile ideology." She wrote that "the foundation stone of the Eurabian mind consist of two principles stated in article 22 of the 1990 Cairo Declaration on Human Rights in Islam:

"a. Everyone shall have the right to express his opinion freely in such a manner as would **not be contrary to the principles of the Shari'a**.

"b. Everyone shall have the right to advocate what is right, and propagate what is good, and warn against what is wrong and evil **according to the norms of Islamic Shari'a."** [Emphasis added]

Even though they claim to defend human rights, Europe has "adopted these principles and obeys a fundamental law of dhimmitude: dhimmis are forbidden on pain of death to propagate ideas considered hostile to Islam."[114]

Europe's Rising Islamophobia

The attacks in London and Madrid and the rioting in France have generated reactions against Muslims. "At the heart of Europe's rising Islamophobia is the debate between integration and multiculturalism." Liz Fekete, deputy director of the London-based Institute of Race Relations, said that Western Europe's idea of multiculturalism was in jeopardy and that there "is definitely a rise in Islamophobia across Europe." The supposed unilateralism and parochialism of the US is contrasted with the internationalism, moderation, and social progressiveness of Western Europe with its "affluent, eco-conscious citizens."[115]

The British seem to be waking up. Baroness Cox introduced a bill in the House of Lords that Islamic courts would be forced to acknowledge the primacy of English law. She was concerned that Muslim women were suffering discrimination under Sharia.[116] There was evidently a bitter cabinet battle over multiculturalism which PM David Cameron won. He had stated earlier that "state multiculturalism" had failed. The Labour Party had worked for a decade to change Britain into a "truly multicultural society." The new counter-terrorism strategy has a broader definition of extremism going beyond groups condoning violence but to non-violent views, such as advocating Sharia, do not "reflect British mainstream values." As Cameron said, those who espoused an ideology of Islamic extremism alongside those who supported violence "Move along the spectrum, and you find people who may reject violence, but who accept various parts of the extremist world view, including real hostility towards western democracy and liberal values."[117]

For Europe, the enemy is within. Young Muslims living all over Europe, many born and raised in the openness and affluence of the West they want to destroy, provide a pool for jihadist networks. This could be called the **"Generation Jihad"** – restive, rootless young Muslims who have spent their lives in Europe but now find themselves alienated from their societies and the policies of their governments.[118] According to Eric Denécé, director of the French Center of Intelligence Research in Paris, "These are young men who were born and grew up in Europe. They look like normal Europeans; they sound like normal Europeans; and they harness this seething anger and sense of righteous outrage in a manner adapted to what they see as jihad in Europe." These second-generation European Muslims, most are EU citizens, are a security risk to the US because they are eligible for US visa waivers, "which means they can represent a direct threat" to the US.[119]

A Spanish newspaper article put it bluntly: "Europe died in Auschwitz." "We killed six million Jews and replaced them with 20 million Muslims." Then under the pretense of tolerance and to prove we were cured of racism, "we opened our gates to 20 million Muslims, who brought us stupidity and ignorance, religious extremism and lack of tolerance, crime and poverty due to an unwillingness to work and support their families with pride." Beautiful Spanish cities had been turned into the third world, "drowning in filth and crime." They plot the murder and destruction of their naïve hosts while shut up in apartments provided free by the government. "And thus, in our misery, we have exchanged culture for fanatical hatred, creative skill for destructive skill, intelligence for backwardness and superstition."[120]

Mathias Dapfner, Chief Executive of the huge German publisher Axel Springer AG, wrote a blistering attack in *Die Welt,* Germany's largest daily newspaper, against the timid reaction of Europe in the face of the Islamic threat titled "Europe – Thy Name Is Cowardice." He blasted Europe for appeasement and dithering about Kosovo until the US came in and did their work for them. Europeans know the truth. "Ronald Reagan ended the Cold War, freeing half of the German people from nearly 50 years of terror and virtual slavery." And Bush "recognized the danger in the Islamic War against Democracy" in Iraq. While the US acted, Europe sat back "with charismatic self-confidence in the multicultural corner instead of defending liberal society's values and being an attractive center of power.... On the contrary – we Europeans present ourselves, in contrast to those 'arrogant Americans,' as the World Champions of 'tolerance.'" "While we criticize the 'capitalistic robber barons' of America because they seem too sure of their priorities, we timidly defend our Social Welfare systems." "Appeasement? Europe – thy name is Cowardice. – God Bless America –"

Both Denmark and the Netherlands have tightened immigration requirements. Denmark, once proudly open-minded, now has the strictest immigration laws in Europe. There is growing hostility toward Muslims and Islam in Germany. Some 58% want to restrict religious freedom for Muslims and 37% feel Germany would be better off without Islam. In France, 80% of voters supported the ban on burqas.[121] In Norway, 54% wanted no more immigrants, 80% felt that language skill had to be proved before becoming a citizen, and over 80% said no to hijabs in police uniform.[122]

Herbert E. Meyer wrote an open letter to Europe, 11 November 2004, after the reelection of President Bush. He decried their nasty comments about Bush, pointed out the greatness that had made Europe the glory of Western civilization, and noted that Europe was dying.

> But before you write us off as just a bunch of sweaty, hair-chested, Bible-thumping morons who are more likely to break their fast by dipping a Krispy Kreme into a diet cola than a biscotti into an espresso – and who inexplicably have won more Nobel prizes than all other countries combined, host 25 or 30 of the world's finest universities and five or six of the world's best symphonies, produce wines that win prizes at your own tasting competitions, have built the world's most vibrant economy, are the world's only military superpower and, so to speak in our spare time, have landed on the moon and sent our robots to Mars – may I suggest you stop frothing at the mouth long enough to consider just what are these ideas we hold that you find so silly and repugnant.?...
>
> What worries me even more than all this is your willful blindness. You refuse to see that it is you, not we Americans, who have abandoned Western Civilization. It's worrisome because, to tell you the truth, we need each other. Western Civilization is under siege, from radical Islam on the outside and from our own selfish hedonism within. It's going to take all of our effort, our talent, our creativity and, above all, our will to pull through. So take a good, hard look at yourselves and see what your own future will be if you don't change course. And please, stop sneering at America long enough to understand it. After all, Western Civilization was your gift to us, and you ought to be proud of what we Americans have made of it.[123]

Bat Ye'or, who has written much about Eurabia, said, "The policy of collusion and support for terrorists in order to gain self-protection is a delusion." She defined it: "This is the threat of a global jihad, with its ideology, strategy and tactics, coordinated with its cells worldwide. The difference between Europe and America is that Europe denies it because it cannot nor does it wish to fight for certain values already forfeited. We see here the collision of two radically opposed strategies." Trying to be optimistic, she said, "The war will be won if we name it, if we face it, if we recognize that it obeys specific rules of Islamic war that are not ours; and if democracies and Muslim modernists stop justifying these acts against other countries." "The war against a global jihadist terrorism can be won if the civilized world is united against barbarity."[124]

Victor Davis Hanson reviewed the causes, the propaganda, the methods, and the aims involved in the clash with radical Islam and concluded with: "It is our task, each of us according to our station, to speak the truth to all these falsehoods, and remember that we did not inherit a wonderful civilization just to lose it to the Dark Ages.[125] It is in the US national interest that Europe not degenerate into Eurabia for both the strategic necessity of not having a radical Islamic empire or caliphate and because of the global economy which is critical to the American economy.

Perhaps Dalil Boubakeur, who is the director of the largest mosque in Paris, put it best when he commented on President Sarkozy's push to ban the burqa. He hoped [inshAllah of course] there would be no ill-feeling, controversies, or incidents "in this confrontation between an Eastern idea and Western life, **or then eastern Muslims will have to return to the Orient**...completely unable to assimilate and uncomfortable in a Western system."[126] [Emphasis added] He may have hit on the solution!

What can be done? Geert Wilders and others have presented some actions to be taken. Freedom of speech must be defended. Political correctness and multiculturalism when there is no mutuality must be ended. Tolerating the intolerant acts of Muslims must stop. Make no concessions that conflict with Western values. Since Islam is an ideology with only a façade of a religion, it should not be treated as a religion but as an ideology like communism or fascism. Islamization must be stopped, immigration halted or reduced, criminal immigrants deported, the building of mosques and Islamic schools stopped and both monitored. Close all mosques and schools that present seditious or anti-Western views. Deport seditious imams. Muslims must assimilate or leave. The nation state and pride in country must be restored. Finally, wise and courageous leaders must be elected who will face the threat of Islam and stand up for Western civilization.

It may take a bloody fight but Europe has to take it on both to save Europe and to save Western civilization.

Hizb ut-Tahrir despises democracy and believes shari'a law must be imposed over the whole world, by force if necessary.
> **- Shiraz Maher, a former HT regional director in England, who left the group and produced a documentary for BBC about it**[127]

Notes

1. Alex Alexiev, "Stumbling toward Eurabia," Posted 30 April 2008.
2. They are Birmingham, Bradford, Derby, Dewsbury, Leeds, Leicester, Liverpool, Luton, Manchester, Sheffield, Waltham Forest in northeast London, and Tower Hamlets in East London.
3. For information on "no-go" zones, see Soeren Kern, "European 'No-Go' Zones for Non-Muslims Proliferating," Hudson New York, 22 August 2011, Jihad Watch, 24 August 2011. See the Thomas Moore Law Center, "The First 'No Go Zone' on American Soil?" 3 May 2011, about Dearborn, Michigan.
4. Quoted in Robert Spencer, "The Mullah's Europe," FrontPageMagazine, 22 September 2004. Carlo Romano, Knight Ridder, "What will radical Islam bring Europe?" *Reno Gazette-Journal,* 26 February 2006, p. 4B.
5. "There are signs that Allah will grant Islam victory in Europe – without swords, without guns, without conquests. The 50 million Muslims of Europe will turn it into a Muslim continent within a few decades." Quoted in Robert Spencer, "Canada Bans Truth-Telling," Human Events, 24 December 2007, p. 11. The Canadian Human Rights Commission was suing Mark Steyn, author of *America Alone,* but the statement really was made by Libya's Colonel Qaddafi, Steyn, *America Alone,* pp. 35-36.

    Part of the confusion may be the definition of Europe. Many think of Europe as the countries in Western Europe. Even the EU has expanded eastward. There are more countries to the East as far as Russia. Regardless, the number of Muslims is significant and growing rapidly.

    There were 6,845,000 Muslims in Europe (question Western Europe) in 1982 which increased to 15,231,000 in 2003, which was then four percent, but the European population of non-Muslims is declining. Ross Douthat, "A Muslim Europe?" *The Atlantic Monthly,* January/February 2005, p. 58.
6. Paul Belien, "The Rape of Europe," *The Brussels Journal,* 25 October 2006.
7. Douthat, "A Muslim Europe?" Fortunately, there were modest improvements in birth rates in 16 European countries but not in Spain, Portugal, Netherlands, Norway, and Austria. Jeffrey Stinson, USA Today, "Birth rates increase in Europe," *Reno Gazette-Journal,* 17 August 2007, p. 2C.
8. Mark Steyn, *America Alone,* (Washington, DC, Regnery Publishing, Inc., 2006), p. 56.
9. Alex Alexiev, "Continental Amnesties," National Review Online, 1 May 2006.
10. Quoted in Robert Spencer, "Canada Bans Truth-Telling," Human Events, 24 December 2007, p. 11.
11. "In 25 years the number of working-age Europeans will decline by 7 percent, while those older than 65 will increase by 50 percent." Efforts to let older people work have met with resistance. Fareed Zakaria, "The Decline And Fall Of Europe," *The New York Times,* 14 February 2006, p. A15. He was writing about a 160 page OECD study, "Going for Growth," which pointed out the trend toward economic decline in Europe.
12. Douthat, "A Muslim Europe?" "The EU figures it needs another fifty million immigrants in the next few years just to maintain a big enough working population to fund the lavish social programs its vast retired army of baby boomers expects to enjoy. And the only available sources of immigrants are North Africa and the Middle East." Steyn, *America Alone,* p. 189.
13. Alexiev, "Continental Amnesties."
14. Douthat, "A Muslim Europe?"
15. Douthat, "A Muslim Europe?" The State Department official was Timothy Savage, head of the Northern Europe and Regional Analysis Division. Gilles Kepel is a French scholar of radical Islam.
16. "D.C. Watson: Letter To Congress: Islamic Radicals? Or Fundamentalists?" 12 June 2011. Jihad Watch.
17. Michael Radu, "London 7/7 and Its Impact," Watch On the West, Volume 6, Number 5, July 2005. Steyn, *America Alone,* p. 71. "A recent Pew study found that 15% of British Muslims identify themselves with fundamentalists. And among those British Muslims surveyed, a remarkable 81% - a percentage higher than that for Muslims not just in France and Germany but also in Egypt and Jordan – said they thought of themselves as Muslims first and citizens of their native country second." Michael Elliott, "Such Lovely Lads," *Time,* 21 August 2006, p. 29.
18. "Geert Wilders: The Failure of Multiculturalism and How to Turn the Tide," speech at the Annual Lecture at the Magna Carta Foundation in Rome, 25 March 2011, Jihad Watch, 26 March 2011. This is an excellent review of multiculturalism. He reviews the gradual fall of Rome where they "scarcely noticed what was happening. They did not perceive the immigration of the Barbarians as a threat until it was too late." He referred to current thinking about Rome. "The whole of Europe will become Islamic. We will conquer Rome." – former Turkish Prime Minister Erbakan. "Very soon Rome will be conquered." – Hamas cleric Yuni al-Astal. "Islam will conquer Rome." – Ali Al-Faqir, former Jordanian Minister of Religion. "We will control Rome and introduce Islam in it." – Sheikh Muhammad al-Arifi, imam of the Saudi Defense Academy mosque.

    "The problem with multiculturalism is a refusal to see reality. The reality that our civilization is superior, and the reality that Islam is a dangerous ideology." "We need to confront reality and we need to speak the truth. The truth is that Islam is evil, and the reality is that Islam is a threat to us."
19. Ibid. Wilders. He added, multiculturalism "weakens the West day by day. It leads to the self-censorship of the media and academia, the collapse of the education system, the emasculation of the churches, the subversion of the nation-state, the break-down of our free society."
21. Geert Wilders, speech in Nashville, Tennessee on 12 May 2011, Citizen Warrior, 16 May 2011. For a somewhat different take on multiculturalism, see Kenan Malik, "Assimilation's Failure, Terrorism's Rise," *The New York Times,* 6 July 2011.
22. Jenny Barchfield and John Leicester, AP, "Riots point to racial divisions in France," *Reno Gazette-Journal,* 1 December 2007, p. 6B. There are problems with discrimination and equal opportunity in France and many immigrants get in trouble with the authorities. "It is no surprise the 60 percent of prisoners in France are of a foreign origin." "In fact, however, although it does not perceive itself as a multicultural nation, France is a land of immigrants – with more than 20 percent of its residents being immigrants or born in France to immigrant parents. Instead, its national identity is founded on the demand for unconditional assimilation and cultural uniformity, rendering immigrant cultures almost invisible." Samah Jabr, "The Rebellion of France's Poor: An Act of Anger, Not of Hatred," *Washington Report on Middle East Affairs (WRMEA),* January/February 2006, p. 35.

23. Thomas D. Segel, "Muslim Problems In France," Paragon Foundation News Service, 5 May 2004.
24. Will Hutton in *The Guardian,* 25 September 2005. Quoted in "Britain Said to Be 'Playing With Fire' Over Growing Segregation," *WRMEA,* December 2005, p. 41.
25. Ken Dilanian, Knight Ridder, "Experts contend Islamic radicalism growing in England," *Reno Gazette-Journal,* 10 July 2005, p. 10B. Actually it evidently was policy at one time. "In October 2009, Andrew Neather, the former advisor of British Prime Minister Tony Blair, confirmed that the British Government had deliberately organized mass immigration as part of a social engineering project. The Blair Government wanted to 'make the UK truly multicultural.' To achieve this end, 2.3 million foreigners were allowed to enter Britain between 2000 and 2009. Neather says this policy has 'enriched' Britain." Wilders, Rome speech.
26. Jane Kramer, "The Dutch Model: Multiculturalism and Muslim immigration," *The New Yorker,* 3 April 2006, p. 60. Robert Spencer, "Holland Hounds Hirsi Ali," Human Events, 22 May 2006, p. 19.
27. Jane Kramer, "The Dutch Model."
28. Stefan Theil, "Farewell, multiculturalism. A cartoon backlash is pushing Europe to insist upon its values," *Newsweek International,* 6 March 2006. Yet there were still some who did not see the problem and just wanted plotters treated as common criminals rather than soldiers of jihad. Also, the European Court of Justice overturned Britain's anti-terrorism laws. "Plotters Should Be Treated as Common Criminals, *Times* Columnist Says," *WRMEA,* November 2006, p. 47.
29. "Turks need not integrate," Dutch News, 16 August 2011, Jihad Watch, 17 August 2011.
30. Robert Spencer, "Uncovered Women Are Like Uncovered Meat," Human Events, 6 November 2006, p. 12. Jeffrey Fleishman, Los Angeles Times, "Denmark illustrates Muslim plight," *Reno Gazette-Journal,* 13 November 2005, p. 2C. Charles Bremer, "Stoned to death… why Europe is starting to lose its faith in Islam," 4 December 2004. Stefania Lapenna, "Italy's Open Border Problem," posted 27 November 2007.
31. Steyn, *America Alone, p.* 90.
32. Victor Davis Hanson, "The Ents of Europe: Strange rumblings on the continent," victorhanson.com, 10 December 2004.
33. Steyn, *America Alone,* p. 197.
34. *Sunday Telegraph,* February 2008.
35. Rana Foroohar, "The End of Europe," *Time,* 22 August 2011, p. 27.
36. Steyn, *America Alone,* pp. 193-194.
37. *The New York Times* pompously explained that it had a duty to "refrain from gratuitous assaults on religious symbols." The next day they showed some New York "art" - the Virgin Mary covered in elephant dung. "Multiculturalism seems to operate on the same even-handedness as the old Cold War joke in which the American tells the Soviet guy that 'in my country everyone is free to criticize the president,' and the Soviet guy replies, 'Same here. In my country everyone is free to criticize your president.'" It would appear that the loathing of our own culture may be the more damaging. Steyn, *America Alone,* p. 201.
38. Steyn, *America Alone,* pp. 118-120.
39. Quoted in Steyn, *America Alone,* p. 200.
40. Steyn, *America Alone,* pp. 202-204.
41. Quoted in Steyn, *America Alone,* p. 90.
42. Alex Alexiev, "Tablighi Jamaat: Jihad's Stealthy Legions," *Middle East Quarterly,* Vol. XII, No. 1, Winter 2005. Lorenzo Vidino, "The Muslim Brotherhood's Conquest of Europe," *Middle East Quarterly,* Winter 2005.
43. Lorenzo Vidino, "The Muslim Brotherhood's Conquest of Europe."
44. Alex Alexiev, "Tablighi Jamaat."
45. Lowell Ponte, "Islamists Down Under," FrontPageMagazine.com, 24 April 2006.
46. Ibid.
47. Ibid. "Radical Muslim clerics to meet on Sept. 11," *Reno Gazette-Journal,* 8 September 2002, p. 3A. "The conference will discuss the 'positive outcomes' of Sept. 11, which delegates perceived as a battle against an 'evil superpower.'"
48. Lorenzo Vidino, "The Tripartite Threat of Radical Islam to Europe," *Journal of Counterterrorism & Homeland Security International,* Vol. 14, No. 2, p. 44.
49. Sean Rayment, London Sunday Telegraph, "Intelligence Report Reassesses Threat Of Al Qaeda," *Washington Times,* 26 February 2007, p. 13.
50. Michael Radu, "London 7/7 and Its Impact," Watch on the West, Volume 6, Number 5, July 2005. Vanora McWalters and Sebastian Rotella, Los Angeles Times, "British crack down on Islamic ideologues," *Reno Gazette-Journal,* 12 August 2005, p.1C.
51. Michael Radu, "London 7/7 and Its Impact." John Cloud, "3 Lessons from London," *Time,* 18 July 2005, p. 38. The government figure was 10,000 to 15,000 British Muslim supporters for al Qaeda according to the *Sunday Times.*
52. See Paisley Dodds, AP, "Extremists of all ideologies flock to Facebook for recruits." *Reno Gazette-Journal,* 30 July 2011, p. 7C. There are thousands of web sites.
53. "Salafist threat growing, interior ministers say," *The Local,* 21 June 2011.
54. "In online forums, Islamic militants urge rioters in Britain to topple government," Associated Press, 10 August 2011.
55. Daniel Woolls, "Spain Muslims Issue Fatwa Against Bin Laden," AP, 10 March 2005. According to the Qur'an, "the terrorist acts of Osama bin Laden and his organization al-Qaida… are totally banned and must be roundly condemned as part of Islam." It added: "Inasmuch as Osama bin Laden and his organization defend terrorism as legal and try to base it on the Quran … they are committing the crime of 'istihlal' [the act of making up one's own laws] and thus become apostates that should not be considered Muslims or treated as such."
56. Michael Radu, "London 7/7 and Its Impact."
57. Quoted in "Plotters Should Be Treated as Common Criminals, *Times* Columnist Says," *WRMEA,* November 2006, p. 47.
58. Amanda Ripley, "How Much Are We Willing to Take?" *Time,* 21 August 2006, p. 23.
59. Terence P. Jeffrey, "Democracy didn't Stop British Terrorists," Human Events, 21 August 2006, p. 5.

60. Paisley Dodds, AP, "Al-Qaida warns British priest of attacks," *Reno Gazette-Journal,* 5 July 2007, p. 2B.

61. Robert Spencer, "Islamic Supremacism in Britain," Human Events, 29 January 2007, p. 11.

62. Nicolai Sennels, "Stavanger, Norway: Nine out of ten rapists are 'men from minority groups'," Jihad Watch, 23 January 2012.

63. Nicolai Sennels, "Denmark: More Muslim Violence against non-Muslims," Jihad Watch, 30 January 2012.

64. Alex Alexiev, "Stumbling toward Eurabia," Posted 30 April 2008.

65. "Four men slashed teacher's face and left him with fractured skull 'for teaching other religions to Muslim girls.'" *Daily Mail,* 21 February 2011.

66. Arnaud de Borchgrave, "Mini clash of civilizations," UPI, 15 November 2004.

67. Craig Whitlock, *Washington Post,* "For public figures in Netherlands, terror becomes a personal concern," *Reno Gazette-Journal,* 12 November 2005, p. 4C.

68. "Wilders accuses left of demonizing him over Norway shootings," *Dutch News,* 1 August 2011, Jihad Watch.

69. "Muslim cleric calls for beheading of Dutch politician," Reuters, 3 September 2010.

70. David Rising, AP, "Germany's anti-terrorism measures eyed," *Reno Gazette-Journal,* 31 August 2006, p. 3C.

71. Alex Alexiev, "Stumbling toward Eurabia," Posted 30 April 2008.

72. German interior minister urges Muslims to combat militancy," *Deutsche Welle,* 25 June 2011, Jihad Watch.

73. David Rising, "Germany says Islamic terrorism still a threat," Associated Press, 1 July 2011.

74. "Salafist threat growing, interior ministers say," The Local, 2 June 2011.

75. http://www.quilliamfoundation.org/images/stories/pdfs/radicalization-on-british-university-campuses.pdf?dm_i=JI3,9VVO, 2Q60WK,QMSG,1.

76. Thomas D. Segel, "Muslim Problems In France," Paragon Foundation News Service, 5 May 2004. Robert Spencer, "Jihad in France," Human Events, 21 November 2008, p. 22. Samah Jabr, "The Rebellion of France's Poor: An Act of Anger, Not of Hatred," *WRMEA,* January/February 2006, p. 34. Elaine Ganley, AP, "Some French TV stations scale back riot coverage," *Reno Gazette-Journal,* 13 November 2005, p. 2C. Jocelyn, AP, "Youths attack police in Lyon." *Reno Gazette-Journal,* 13 November 2005, p.1C. Scheherezade Faramarzi, AP, "Parents in riot-hit French neighborhoods say they're losing control of their kids," *Reno Gazette-Journal,* 12 November 2005, p. 2C. "Many parents are not French citizens and never learn to speak French, while their children don't learn the language of their ancestors." Many of the parents are illiterate. When one woman was asked why she had not learned French after living in France for 27 years, she answered, "I don't go out, I'm home all the time. I don't meet anyone." She is a prisoner!

77. "Gang on Trial For Torturing French Jew to Death," Reuters, 29 April 2009.

78. From a personal report by a US counterterrorism expert who attend a counterterrorism conference in Milan in the summer of 2007.

79. Ian Robertson, "'Anti-Muslim' author beaten," *Ottawa Sun,* 26 August 2011, Jihad Watch, 27 August 2011. Paris Dispersico, 24, born Muslim, wrote a book, *Wake Up Call.* He was beaten and received a death threat from the Middle East. Having been raised in Canada, he said, "'I'm not saying every Muslim is violent or every Muslim is a bad person.' Fully realizing 'for a Muslim to go against Islam, the punishment is death,' he said violent ones are often 'ignorant,' brainwashed with twisted religion-based messages."

80. Sarah Baxter, "Iraq Terror Chief Recruits Britons," *London Sunday Times,* 12 December 2004. Katrin Bennhold, "French Court Convicts 7 For Helping To Send Youths To Join Jihadist Fight In Iraq," *The New York Times,* 15 May 2008.

81. Craig Whitlock, "In Europe, New Force For Recruiting Radicals," *Washington Post,* 18 February 2005. p. 1. On 9 November 2005 the first Western female suicide bomber was a Belgian citizen who had been recruited by a Belgian-Moroccan. There were evidently more available. "Belgium, hotbed for Islamist terrorism," http:///counterterror.typepad.com/, 5 January 2006.

82. A book review of *The Force of Reason* by Oriana Fallaci (Rizzoli, 2006) by Robert Spencer, "The Force of Reason Against Jihad Ideology," Human Events, 28 August 2006, p. 15.

83. Press Association, 29 June 2009.

84. "EU judges want Sharia law applied in British courts," *Daily Mail,* 26 April 2009.

85. "Denmark: 18% of Muslims want to see Sharia law implemented," *Islam in Europe,* 30 April 2009.

86. For a good description, see Jonathan Wynn-Jones, "Sharia: a law unto itself," *The Telegraph,* 7 August 2011.

87. Tom McTague, "Sharia-style marriages could be officially recorded by the government," *Daily Mirror,* 22 July 2011.

88. "Sharia law being used in Germany in Muslims' domestic disputes," *The Local,* 9 October 2010. Jihad Watch, 10 October 2010.

89. Kathy Shaidle, "Islamists on Welfare: Paid to Plot the West's Demise," Pajamas Media, 4 April 2011. Jihad Watch, 5 April 2011. She wrote that the cost to Sweden was about $7 billion a year and contributed to bringing the state to the "brink of bankruptcy." One Iranian immigrant said: "In Sweden my family encountered a political system that seemed very strange. The interpreter told us that Sweden is a country where the government will put a check into your mailbox each month if you don't work. She explained that there was no reason to get a job."

90. "Turkey alcohol curbs raise secular fears," BBC, 12 January 2011, Jihad Watch.

91. "Anger at HIGNFY's Mecca joke," Chortle, 6 June 2011, Jihad Watch, 7 June 2011.

92. Angela Doland, AP, "French debate: First it was burqas, now it's burgers," *Reno Gazette-Journal* 8 September 2010, p. 4E.

93. Jon Ungoed-Thomas, "BMI told stewardess to wear Muslim robe," Times Online, 26 April 2008.

94. Jamey Keaten, AP, "Burqas 'are not welcome' in France, Sarkozy says," *Reno Gazette-Journal,* 23 June 2009, p. 3B.

95. Chris Bremmer, "French MPs in call to unveil Islamic dress code," *The Times,* 21 June 2009.

96. Dheepthi Namasivayam, "For life, liberty and the burqa: Muslim women defy France's ban on full-face veils," *Herald Sun,* 11 April 2011, Jihad Watch.

97. Peter Allen, "French burka ban descends into farce," *The Telegraph,* 17 June 2011, Jihad Watch.

98. "Belgium: Top court upholds headscarf ban in schools," Adnkronos International, 7 April 2011.

99. "'Wear a headscarf or we will kill you': How the 'London Taliban' is targeting women and gays in bid to impose sharia law," *Daily Mail,* 17 April 2011, Jihad Watch.

100. Andrew Gilligan, "Muslim Council: women cannot debate wearing veil," *The Telegraph,* 16 April 2011, Jihad Watch, 17 April 2011.
101. "Dewsbury, Bradford and Tower Hamlets... where Islamic extremists want to establish independent states with sharia law, *Daily Mail,* 5 July 2011, Jihad Watch.
102. "British pupils taught how to carry out Sharia punishments at Islamic schools, AFP, 22 November 2010.
103. Babs Barron, "The Show Trial of Geert Wilders – Part 1," Citizen Warrior, 9 June 2011.
104. "Final remarks by Geert Wilders at his Sharia trial in Amsterdam today," Jihad Watch, 2 May 2011.
105. "Find Wilders not guilty of inciting hatred, says prosecution," Dutch News, 25 May 2011, Jihad Watch, 26 May 2011.
106. "Anti-Semitic Saudi chief imam feted in London: Senior cleric of Mecca's Grand Mosque speaks at East London Mosque," from Peter Tatchell, Green Party parliamentary candidate for Oxford East, 4 August 2009.
107. "Cafe owner ordered to remove extractor fan because neighbour claimed 'smell of frying bacon offends Muslims,'" *Daily Mail,* 21 October 2010.
108. Michael Lea, "Calls for Red Cross symbol to be axed over links to the Crusades," *Daily Mail,* 10 June 2009, Jihad Watch, 12 June 2009.
109. Babs Barron, "The Betrayal of the Christians of Bradford UK," FaithFreedom.org, republished by Citizen Warrior, 16 July 2011.
110. "Enforcement of Islamic Dress Code for Women in Chechnya," Human Rights Watch, 19 November 2010, Jihad Watch, 21 November 2010.
111. Andrew Carey, "UK cleric leaves mosque over evolution," CNN, 22 March 2011. Hasan described "this gulf, this impasse, and at some point people may have to address this issue." As he said, "What I would like to point out now is that religious scholars, in the main, are opposed to evolution, they believe it is blasphemy, it is against the Quran, whereas scientists say that evolution is a scientific fact, or a scientific theory with overwhelming evidence."
112. Stephen Pollard "Libya and the LSE: Large Arab gifts to universities lead to 'hostile teaching,'" *The Telegraph,* 3 March 2011, Jihad Watch, 6 March 2011.
113. Pamela Geller, "Europe's looming demise," *Washington Times,* 30 December 2009.
114. Bat Ye'or, "On Geert Wilders's Acquittal," Hudson New York, 5 July 2011, Jihad Watch.
115. "Is Islam Endangering 'Europeanness'?" ABCNews.com, 7 December 2004.
116. "Bill limiting sharia law is motivated by 'concern for Muslim women'," *The Guardian,* 8 June 2011.
117. "PM wins row with Nick Clegg over crackdown on Muslim extremists," The *Guardian,* 4 June 2011, Jihad Watch, 5 June 2011.
118. Bill Powell, "Generation Jihad," *Time,* 3 October 2005, p. 56.
119. John Cloud, "3 Lessons from London," *Time,* 18 July 2005, p. 38.
120. Sebastian Vilar Rodriguez, "All European Life Died in Auschwitz," February 2007.
121. "Europe's Rising Islamophobia," Citizen Warrior, 16 May 2011.
122. Nicolai Sennels, "Norway: 54% want no more immigrants," Jihad Watch, 7 July 2011.
123. Meyer served during the Reagan Administration as Special Assistant to the Director of Central Intelligence and Vice Chairman of the CIA's National Intelligence Council.
124. Jamie Glazov, "Eurabia," Interview with Bat Ye'or, FrontPageMagazine.com, 21 September 2004.
125. "The Same Old, Same Old...An anatomy of the London bombing," 8 July 2005.
126. Jamey Keaten, AP, "Burqa 'are not welcome' in France, Sarkozy says," *Reno Gazette-Journal,* 23 June 2009, p. 3B.
127. Lorenzo Vidino, "The Tripartite Threat of Radical Islam to Europe," p. 46.
128. Sandro Magister, "Eurabia Has A Capital: Rotterdam," Chisea, 19 May 2009.
129. Graeme Wilson, "Don't call extremists 'extremists'." *The Sun,* 4 December 2009.
130. Bat Ye'or, "From Europe to Eurabia," Talk at Antisemitism, multiculturalism, and ethnic identity International conference, Hebrew University, Jerusalem, posted on Pamela Geller, Atlas Shrugged and Jihad Watch, 3 February 2010.

Eurabia's Capital: Rotterdam – Holland's second largest city by population, and the largest port in Europe by cargo volume. Here, entire neighborhoods look as if they have been lifted from the Middle East, here stand the **largest mosques** in Europe, here parts of **sharia law** are applied in the courts and theaters, here many of the **women go around veiled**, here the **mayor is a Muslim**, the son of an imam.[128]

An eight-page **Whitehall guide** [for UK government ministers] lists **words they should not use when talking about terrorism in public** and gives **politically correct alternatives**.

They are told **not to refer** to **Muslim extremism** as it links Islam to violence. Instead they are urged to talk about terrorism or violent extremis.

Fundamentalist and Jihadi are also **banned** because they make an "explicit link" between Muslims and terror.

Ministers should say criminals, murderers or thugs instead. **Radicalisation** must be called brainwashing and talking about **moderate or radical Muslims** is to be avoided as it "splits the community".

Islamophobia is also out as it is received as "a slur that singles out Muslims".[129]

Allow me to go a little further into the themes of this **cultural jihad** and **multiculturalism**. Through the **myth of Andalusia**, Islam tries to prove its historical, cultural and demographical **legitimacy in Europe**. Several European leaders have affirmed that Islam is at home in Europe and that it is at the root of European culture. Thus, it can legitimately impose itself, invoking **multiculturalism** in the education system – as the Obin Report pointed out for France (2004) – and it the European legal and cultural spheres with the introduction of **shari'a** principles, as well as of Islamic customs and political ethics, under the mantle of **multiculturalism**.

For Muslim leaders, **multiculturalism** in Europe was a fundamental requirement in the Euro-Arab agreements governing immigration, for it allows Muslim immigrants to **not integrate** and to protect them "from the aberrations, the mores and thinking of non-Muslims" – as called for by Mohammed al-Tohami at the second Islamic Conference, at Lahore in February 1974. **Multiculturalism** encourages the coexistence of **parallel communities** that will **never integrate**, thus replicating the **Ottoman millets** or the conditions of **Islamic colonization** after its conquest of non-Muslim peoples. **Multiculturalism and nationalism are polar concepts.** The modern fight against European nationalism within the inter-European scenes – for the integration of Europe – allowed millions of Muslim immigrants to import their culture to Europe and establish it on an equal footing, using **two fundamental arguments:** the **Andalusian myth and an Islamic origin of European culture.**

- Bat Ye'or[130]

Chapter 13

Hostage to Black Gold

It is the apparent inability of nations to avoid dependence on fossil fuels that gives energy supplies such importance, in geopolitical realignments or in the plaintive cries of people in the world's poorest countries. Energy politics has sparked wars and toppled governments in the past, and will reliably fuel domestic and international concerns for as long as oil and gas make the world go around.

- Will Swarts[1]

The U.S. leads the world in corn and soybean production, but even if 100% of both crops were turned into fuel, it would be enough to offset just 20% of on-road fuel consumption.

- Michael Grunwald[2]

Oil in History

Oil has been known to mankind and been an item of commerce for a very long time.[3] In the Middle East, a semisolid oozy substance called bitumen seeped to the surface in Mesopotamia 3,000 BC. The most famous location was Hit on the Euphrates River near Babylon (and Baghdad). At Baba Gurfur, six miles northwest of Kirkuk, two dozen holes had been venting natural gas – always alight – for thousands of years. They are thought to be the "burning fiery furnace" into which King Nebuchadnezzar of Babylon had cast the Jews. Local inhabitants – so Plutarch wrote – set afire a street sprinkled with oil seepage to impress Alexander the Great.[4]

Refining technology was transmitted to Europe via the Arabs. Collecting oil from seepage sites or digging proved inadequate – some form of drilling was required. Salt boring, which had been developed in China 1,500 years earlier where they had drilled to depths of 3,000 feet, provided the solution.[5]

A Yale chemistry professor, Benjamin Silliman Jr., needed extra money and contracted with a group to do an outside research project to determine if "rock oil" found around Oil Creek in northwest Pennsylvania was suitable to be an illuminant. It was called "Seneca oil" for the Indians and was used mostly for medicinal purposes. After finally being paid his exorbitant fee of $562.08 (about $5,000 today), the group received his excellent report and established the Pennsylvania Rock Oil company. It was a Canadian who developed kerosene – he made up the word from *Keros* – Greek for wax – and *elaion* – Greek for oil, but he changed the latter to "ene" to make it like camphene (which was made from turpentine).[6]

In Titusville, Pennsylvania, population 125, oil was discovered on 27 August 1859 at 69 feet. Land prices shot up. The problem was what to do with it? Every whiskey barrel they could find was used and whiskey barrels soon cost almost twice the cost of the oil inside. In 1865, oil was found at Pithole, 15 miles from Titusville, and as one visitor observed, the whole place "smells like a corps of soldiers when they have the diarrhoea." The boom collapsed in 1866 and a parcel of land which had sold for $2,000,000 in 1865 was auctioned in 1878 for $4.37. The supply of Camphene from the South was cut off during the Civil War giving a boost to kerosene both in the US and as an export.[7]

John D. Rockefeller and four others founded Standard Oil Company in 1870. Cutthroat competition ensued in an oil war with oil at 48¢ per barrel, which was cheaper than water in the oil region. By 1879, the oil war was over and Standard Oil controlled 90% of US refining capacity.[8] The harnessing of electricity in 1882 presaged the demise of kerosene but a new market was arriving – the horseless carriage – the great automobile boom.[9] (It was in 1919 when a young Captain Dwight Eisenhower led a force of Army vehicles across the country departing Washington on 7 July and not arriving in San Francisco until 6 September. The lessons learned from that trip led President Eisenhower to create the interstate highway system.[10]) John D. Rockefeller was the richest man in the world by the end of the 19th Century. (He gave away $550 million dollars and his descendants are still donating money. New products were developed: gasoline, lubricants, and petroleum jelly – trademark Vaseline.)[11]

The harnessing of electricity in 1882 presaged the demise of kerosene but a new market was arriving – the horseless carriage – the great automobile boom.

In 1901, the Lucas 1 well at the Spindletop salt dome gave us a new word "gusher" producing 75,000 barrels per day and the Texas oil boom.[12] Other company names arrived: Gulf Oil (the Mellons), Sun Oil, and Texaco. By 1899, Standard Oil of New Jersey was the main holding company for Rockefeller's empire which he controlled by a series of trusts.[13] After a long battle with Teddy Roosevelt, the "Trust Buster," Standard Oil of New Jersey became eventually Exxon, Standard Oil of New York became Mobil, Standard Oil of California became Chevron, Standard Oil of Indiana became Amoco, Continental Oil became Conoco, Atlantic became part of ARCO and then eventually Sun.[14]

The boom continued and, with many wildcat operations, competition grew. In 1926, oil was $1.85 per barrel; by 1930, it was down to $1 per barrel in the depression and by May 1931 it was 15¢ with some at 6¢ and even as low as 2¢ per barrel. By June 1,000 wells had been completed and East Texas was producing 500,000 barrels per day.[15] There was anarchy in the oil fields which was not ended until the National Industrial Relations Act and other programs of the New Deal were imposed.

The first oil well in the Persian Gulf, "Bahrain No. 1," came in on 1 June 1932 at a depth of 2,008 feet. Frank Holmes was a mining engineer from New Zealand and became known as Abu Naft, the father of oil.[16] One of the great stories of oil exploration lore is the effort by Socal (Standard Oil of California) in Saudi Arabia. Under unbelievable difficulties in operating in the desert where everything they needed had to be brought from California and then transported by camels to the interior. Socal's management in San Francisco was growing discouraged with almost three years of dry holes and money spent including paying the penniless Saudis. In November 1937 they directed that no new projects be started. In true Hollywood fashion, in March 1938 with the team itself discouraged at Well No. 7, they decided to go just a little deeper and then give it up. At 4,727 feet, they hit large quantities of oil, and despite a hiatus during World War II, Ibn Saud, Saudi Arabia, and ARAMCO (Arabian American Oil Company) were on the road to riches.[17]

The rest of the world was also searching for oil. In the 1870s, a Swedish chemist from Russia arrived in Baku. His son, Ludwig, built an oil empire. Another son, Alfred, built a dynamite empire. Upon Ludwig's death, his obituary erroneously referred to him as the "Dynamite King" and "Merchant of Death." Alfred brooded over that and then rewrote his will to establish the prize in his name. The Rothschilds, who were driven out of Russia to Paris, provided competition for the Nobels.[18]

Meanwhile, Marcus Samuels, the Jewish son of a London shell merchant, engineered the Coup of 1892 – he introduced bulk tankers and storage to lower transportation costs. He got Lloyds of London to approve his new design and he shipped kerosene by "tankers" via Suez to the Far East. He called his company Shell Transport and Trading.[19]

The British were also active in Persia (Iran after 1935) where in May 1901 they obtained a concession covering three fourths of the country. It took seven years but oil was found in 1908 and the Anglo-Persian Oil Company was formed.[20] The British were in Basra during World War I to protect the oil pipeline.

In 1901, Admiral John Arbothnot Fisher, "God Father of Oil," wrote that "oil will absolutely revolutionize naval strategy" – "Wake up England." Naval supremacy was critical to the British Empire. Fisher became First Sea Lord in 1904. Fisher was calling for changing the Royal Navy from coal, which was plentiful in Wales, to oil, which was not readily available. Winston Churchill was against the changeover until Kaiser Wilhelm sent the German gunboat *Panther* into Agadir in July 1911. Churchill saw war with Germany as inevitable and changed his mind and determined the Royal Navy must convert to oil. In September, he became First Lord of the Admiralty and brought Fisher out of retirement as his adviser. The British-German naval race was on and Churchill wanted British control of the Anglo-Persian Oil Company (which he pushed through Parliament and they obtained 51%).[21]

In 1901, Admiral John Arbothnot Fisher, "God Father of Oil," wrote that "oil will absolutely revolutionize naval strategy" – "Wake up England."

But World War I came too soon and Anglo-Persian was not ready and Churchill recognized "We shall have to buy our oil from elsewhere."[22] The British became concerned about oil shortages particularly during the German submarine campaign which was sinking merchant ships and tankers in the Atlantic. By 1917, two-thirds of world oil production came from America which supplied 80% of the Allies' oil. Oil was key and Colonel John Norton-Griffiths "Empire Jack" was sent to destroy the Rumanian oil fields as the Germans approached. The last field – Ploesti – was burned in December 1916. It was down for five months and the fields did not regain full production during the war.[23]

Concern about oil grew after the war. By 1919, the US demanded an Open Door policy for access. The San Remo Agreement (by which France gave up its claim to Mosul to the British in return for 25% of the oil) was called "imperialism" by the US. Congress passed the Mineral Leasing Act of 1920 which demanded equal access and was aimed at the Dutch in Indonesia and the British in Mesopotamia (Iraq).[24]

Churchill was again on the scene, now as head of the Colonial Office, and wanted an Arab government under British control so he installed Faisal (who had been kicked out of Syria) as King of Iraq in 1921. He made Faisal's brother, Abdullah, King "of the vacant lot which the British christened Amirate of Transjordan." Interestingly, Yergin states that the Jews were the largest group in Baghdad.[25]

Drilling began in Kirkuk in April 1927 and at 3 AM on 15 October, Baba Gurgur #1 at 1,500 feet blew its derrick. It took over 8 days to control it and it was producing 95,000 barrels per day. Negotiations were needed for a final settlement which was reached on 31 July 1928 with Royal Dutch/Shell, Anglo-Persian, and the French plus Near East Development Company (to hold American company interests since the British had relented and permitted the Americans to take part) receiving 23.75% each with the remaining going to Calouste Gulkenhian, the Armenian "Mr. Five Percent."[26]

Oil was again critical in World War II. The Japanese, without oil, built their "Greater East Asia Co-Prosperity Sphere" partially to gain control of the Dutch East Indies and its oil. The Germans successfully produced much synthetic oil but Hitler still needed oil and compromised his Russia campaign by splitting his forces to attack the oil fields in the Caucasus. The wells in Kuwait were plugged with cement in 1941 for fear the Germans would capture them and operations in Saudi Arabia were closed down except for a skeleton crew.[27] A good example of the significance of oil was when General Patton ran out of gas in his race across France.

Oil was critical in World War II as the Japanese built their "Greater East Asia Co-Prosperity Sphere" partially to gain control of oil in the Dutch East Indies and Hitler split his attack on Moscow to attack the Caucasus oil fields.

The Middle East played an increasing role with the repeated wars between Israel and the Arabs and concern over the security of the Gulf oil fields. Americans got their first real taste of oil shortages when oil prices quadrupled during the 1973 embargo resulting from Nixon's and Kissinger's blatant support of Israel by taking equipment from US troops in Germany and flying it directly into the Sinai for the Israelis.

The CIA produced a memorandum "The Impending Soviet Oil Crisis" in 1977. When the Soviets invaded Afghanistan, Jimmy Carter concluded they were headed for the Middle East oil fields. Ronald Reagan took up the same position and Caspar Weinberger announced it was essential that the US establish bases in the Persian Gulf "to act as a deterrent to any Soviet hopes of seizing the oil fields." The US backed Osama bin Laden against the Soviets (with unintended consequences for the future) and backed Saddam Hussein in his war against Khomeini's Iran. The Soviets were not running out of oil. They were the world's number two producer exporting 3 million barrels per day – in 2006, they passed Saudi Arabia as the world's leading oil producer.[28]

In 1990, Saddam Hussein invaded Kuwait in a dispute over oil wealth resulting in the Gulf War. In the aftermath of that war, 9/11 brought an invasion of Iraq which finally wound down at the end of 2011 and some claimed it was all about oil. Access to Middle Eastern oil falls under vital national interests for a number of countries. "Fossil fuel deposits under the Earth's surface recognize no borders. But quirks of geology and geography have made some nations energy producers, and others perpetual customers. Industrial nations and their largest corporations court the leaders of countries where poverty stalks millions, but streams of oil and gas mean rivers of cash for otherwise friendless governments."[29]

As the price of oil exceeded $140 per barrel in 2008, it was ironic that some of the main backers of terrorists were receiving an enormous windfall in billions of extra dollars through no technological breakthroughs or industrial efforts on their part. Thus the industrial world was financing the very people who were trying to destroy it!

The 1973 Oil Embargo

Having been the world leader in oil production, America was slow to adapt to its declining position and failed to adjust by developing alternatives; besides oil was cheap. The US was not too concerned about Middle East oil in the years when there was adequate, even surplus, American oil production capacity and only limited use of imports. That gradually changed from only about 8 percent imported in 1947 to over 36 percent by 1973. American oil companies were active overseas so we did not see much of a problem. But Lyndon Johnson's total shift of US support behind Israel's illegal seizure of land from Egypt, Jordan, and Syria in 1967 changed our relations with Arab countries. The Arab humiliation led to a need for regaining honor and further Soviet influence in the area. The situation remained tense in the years after 1967 with constant skirmishing and raiding.

> **The US only imported about 8 percent of its oil in 1947 but that increased to over 36 percent by 1973. In 1973, oil was still cheap, about $3.00 a barrel.**

In 1973, oil was still about $3.00 a barrel. Even though Henry Kissinger claimed he was surprised by the embargo, he should not have been since he had received many messages before the war. King Faisal ibn Abdul Aziz of Saudi Arabia "had been warning the Nixon administration with increasing urgency that he would employ the oil weapon unless Washington forced Israel to return Arab lands it had been occupying since 1967."[30] Kissinger had been Assistant to the President for National Security Affairs since 1969 and on 22 September 1973, he also became Secretary of State. Nixon was deeply mired in Watergate and then Vice President Agnew's resignation, so Kissinger was pretty much in charge of US foreign policy and relations with what he considered "our de facto ally Israel." Kissinger admitted: "At that time I had no experience with Saudi Arabia at all or of the indirect, adaptable, and subtle method by which Saudi policy is conducted."[31]

Faisal had decided that, with his large oil reserves, he could use his oil as a political weapon in the Arab-Israel conflict. Faisal had not gotten along well with Nasser but he liked Anwar Sadat, and was even more impressed by him when he expelled the Soviets. But the US did not respond to Sadat's bold move and then when Nixon was re-elected, there was a large increase of arms to Israel, so "Sadat confided to the King that he had finally concluded only war could get back Arab lands." For all Arabs, but particularly Faisal as the spiritual head of Islam and keeper of the holy places, with Jerusalem being the third most holy city in Islam, that continued occupation was unacceptable. "He responded to Sadat's confidence by promising to finance the war and, more significantly, to employ the oil weapon if the United States did not modify its pro-Israel policy." He assembled about $1 billion from other Arab leaders to help Egypt and to purchase arms.[32] Kissinger had received a message from Sadat on the second day of the war, 7 October. "Until this message, I had not taken Sadat seriously….The expulsion of the Soviet advisers from Egypt in 1972 suddenly took on a new significance…. Sadat's ability from the very first hours of the war never to lose sight of the heart of his problem convinced me that we were dealing with a statesman of the first order."[33]

> **Sadat confided to the King that he had finally concluded only war could get back Arab lands.**

Saudi Arabia was producing 7.2 million barrels a day bringing in more money than they knew what to do with and yet they were being pressed to increase that to 20 million barrels daily by 1980. Faisal did not intend to do that unless he could return Jerusalem to Muslim control, so he sent his Oil Minister, Sheikh Ahmad Zaki Yamani, to Washington in April 1973 to warn them that he was serious about an oil embargo. Yamani met with Kissinger who urged him to keep the threat a secret because it would make them appear threatening and extreme. Yamani felt that Kissinger's being Jewish kept him from being impartial about the Middle East and that he was more interested in keeping from the American people the price they might have to pay for supporting Israel's conquests. Yamani responded with an interview in *The Washington Post,* in which he warned the US that it needed to be more evenhanded in the Middle East. "We'll go out of our way to help you. We expect you to reciprocate."

The *Post* did recognize the link between oil and US policy but it also was unimpressed. It ran an editorial the next day criticizing Yamani's threat adding, "it is to yield to hysteria to take such threats as Saudi Arabia's seriously." The Nixon administration's rejection of his message irritated the King so much that he granted his first ever interview to American TV, in which he said: "America's complete support of Zionism against the Arabs makes it extremely difficult for us to continue to supply U.S. petroleum needs and even to maintain friendly relations with America."

> **America's complete support of Zionism against the Arabs makes it extremely difficult for us to continue to supply U.S. petroleum needs and even to maintain friendly relations with America.**
>
> **- Saudi King Faisal ibn Abdul Aziz**

The general feeling was that Faisal was bluffing or that he was just supporting Sadat. Of course, we bought the Israeli line which encouraged ignoring Faisal – Foreign Minister Abba Eban: "there isn't the slightest possibility" of an oil embargo, and "The Arab states have no alternative but to sell their oil because they have no other resources at all." But the old King was serious; in May, he summoned Frank Jungers, chairman of Arabian American Oil Company to his palace and warned him about a possible oil embargo. Jungers knew Faisal as a man of his word, so he reported his visit to the White House and the State Department, but "It was ignored." Latter that month Faisal warned four other leading oil men that Arab passions about US support for Israel were rising and told them, "You may lose everything. Time is running out." They tried to alert Washington, but no one in the White House, the State Department, or the Pentagon took the threat seriously, and Kissinger would not meet with them.

Other oil men also tried to alert the public. Otta N. Miller, chairman of Standard Oil Co. of California, sent a letter to 300,000 shareholders warning about US policy ignoring the Arabs without mentioning Israel. The Israel Firsters attacked, as usual, even threatening a boycott of Standard Oil, and he had to issue a letter supporting the legitimate interests of Israel. Maurice F. Granville, chairman of Texaco, appealed to Americans "to review the actions of their government in regard to the Arab-Israeli dispute and to compare those actions with its stated position of support for peaceful settlement responsive to the concerns of all the countries involved." He was also unsuccessful.

Warnings continued throughout the summer from oil men, King Faisal, and other Arab leaders that an explosion was near and that the oil weapon could be used. The King gave an interview to *Newsweek* in September stating that, "logic requires that our oil production does not exceed the limits that can be absorbed by our economy." He was telling the US that he had enough money and to increase production as the US wanted would be a favor. Therefore, to return the favor, Washington should disavow "Zionist expansionist ambitions." Nixon and Kissinger continued to parrot the Israeli line that the Saudis were not serious. "George Shultz, who later as secretary of state proved completely incompetent in dealing with the Middle East, dismissed Faisal's warnings as Arab 'swaggering.'" Nixon was asked if he would change policy toward Israel because of the Arab threat. He said he would not. Nixon also repeated the Israeli mantra that "oil without a market…does not do a country much good." No one in Washington "seemed to be willing to consider that America and the rest of the industrialized world were so dependent on oil that even its potential denial would be devastating."[34]

> **Kissinger was not listening even though his professionals gave him good advice.**

Denial continued right up to the outbreak of the war on 6 October 1973. Kissinger was not listening even though his professionals gave him good advice. "When the war began, there was vague talk in our government about a possible oil embargo. Remembering the experience of 1967, few believed that it could have any lasting impact. Deputy Assistant Secretary of State Roy Atherton, however, predicted an embargo as early as the WSAG meeting on the morning of October 6, and Deputy Secretary Kenneth Rush worried that we had no contingency plans for it."[35] Kissinger, like everyone else, thought it would be another lightning war and be over in a few days.[36]

Showing his bias, he told Alexander Haig, Nixon's chief of staff, the US should let Israel "beat them up for a day or two and that will quiet them down." But the war was not going well. Ambassador Simcha Dinitz frantically called Kissinger in the middle of the night and they met early on 9 October with Dinitz reporting they had lost 49 aircraft, including 14 F-4 Phantoms, and 500 tanks. The Israelis requested intelligence information. "I instructed Scowcroft 'to give them every bit of intelligence we have.' I never doubted that a defeat of Israel by Soviet arms would be a geopolitical disaster for the United States."[37] It must be noted that Kissinger usually kept his focus on the Cold War and the global rivalry between the US and the Soviets.

Moshe Dayan, who had been "swaggering" and "arrogant" in his contempt for the Arab armies earlier, panicked on 8 October: "The situation is desperate. Everything is lost. We must withdraw." "It was Israel's darkest hour, but no withdrawal was ordered. Instead, Israel called its first nuclear alert and began arming its nuclear arsenal. And it used that alert to blackmail Washington into a major policy change."[38] Kissinger did not mention the nuclear alert in his memoirs.

> **Israel called its first nuclear alert and began arming its nuclear arsenal. And it used that alert to blackmail Washington into a major policy change.**

Golda Meir and her advisers met all night 8 October to review Dayan's gloomy assessment. They reached three decisions: counterattack, arm and target their nuclear weapons in case of collapse, and inform Washington about the nuclear action and demand an emergency airlift of replacement arms and munitions. At that urgent meeting Dinitz had spoken with Kissinger privately and told him Golda Meir was willing to come to Washington to plead with Nixon for the arms. He rejected it without consulting Nixon and wrote, "Such a proposal could reflect only either hysteria or blackmail." That is the only time he used the word blackmail.[39] It worked because Kissinger immediately assured Dinitz that all war losses would be replaced and he went to work on expedited resupply.

The CIA, Defense, and State felt that Israel was just asking for more military aid before victory and many concurred with Secretary of Defense James Schlesinger's view that he saw no problem with sending some auxiliary equipment, "But his concern was that meeting Israel's requests and thus turning around a battle that the Arabs were winning might blight our relations with the Arabs. Schlesinger pointed out the distinction between defending Israel's survival within its pre-1967 borders and helping Israel maintain its conquests from the 1967 war."[40] It should be emphasized that in all the wars from 1948 on, Israel has never fought on what could be even remotely considered its own territory, but always on areas outside Israel proper, in Egypt, Jordan, or Syria.

Stalling was one of Kissinger's favorite tactics. It started on the second day when Golda Meir wanted a delay on any ceasefire vote in the UN and continued throughout the war as Kissinger bought Israel time to recoup and then to smash the Egyptians and the Syrians.[41]

US conducted a massive airlift to the Israelis, including taking equipment from our troops in Europe.

The Soviets were airlifting supplies to Egypt and Syria; and, only ostensibly in response, the US conducted a massive airlift to the Israelis, including taking equipment from our troops in Europe. Oil men were concerned that the Saudis would carry out their threat of an oil embargo because of the US total support of Israel. On 12 October, the chairmen of "Aramco's four parent companies - J.K. Jamieson of Esso, Rawleigh Warner of Mobil, M.F. Granville of Texaco and Otto N. Miller of Socal – sent a joint memorandum to President Nixon expressing their alarm at the possibility of an oil boycott and price rise if the United States continued its coddling of Israel." It read in part: "We are convinced of the seriousness of the intentions of the Saudis and Kuwaitis and that any actions of the U.S. Government at this time in terms of increased military aid to Israel will have a critical and adverse effect on our relations with the moderate Arab oil-producing countries."[42] At a news conference that day, Kissinger was asked whether Arab threats to cut off oil would affect our decision to resupply Israel. He replied: "We have made a serious effort, in this crisis, to take seriously into account Arab concerns and Arab views. On the other hand, we have to pursue what we consider to be the right course; we will take the consequences."[43]

There isn't the slightest possibility of an oil embargo.
- Israeli Foreign Minister Abba Eban

The US support bolstered the Israelis and they pushed the Syrians and the Egyptians back and crossed the Suez Canal on 16 October. On that day, the oil countries met in Kuwait and raised the price from $3.01 to $5.12 a barrel, a 70 percent increase, and announced a production cutback of 5 percent, "to be followed by successive monthly cutbacks of 5 percent until Israel withdrew to the 1967 frontiers." The next day, Kissinger met with the foreign ministers of Algeria, Kuwait, Morocco, and Saudi Arabia and still thought "there would be no immediate oil embargo."[44]

On 18 October, King Faisal warned Washington that the war was helping the Soviets and that Israel needed to withdraw to the 1967 borders and threatened to cut off all oil to the US. The Saudis that day cut back production 10 percent instead of the 5 percent like the other countries. Kissinger was not deterred; he was watching the Israel successes and decided they needed "to gain a little more time for Israel's offensive." Brezhnev sent an urgent message to Nixon that the situation was dangerous and threatening US-Soviet relations and that Kissinger should come to Moscow. That was perfect for Kissinger because it meant a delay of several more days for the Israelis to continue their counterattack.[45]

Brezhnev's request for Kissinger to come to Moscow was perfect for Kissinger because it meant a delay of several more days for the Israelis to continue their counterattack.

Libya cut off all oil to the US and raised its price from $4.90 to $8.25 a barrel. Then, at the worst possible timing, Nixon requested a huge amount of $2.2 billion in emergency aid for Israel, which was the last straw for Faisal. That request told the Arabs that the US "would finance Israel's fight to retain its illegal occupation of their land." After having issued warnings for six months, Saudi Arabia imposed a **total oil embargo** on the US on 20 October. The other Arab oil states quickly joined and international commerce was violently disrupted.[46]

Kissinger, Mr. Israel in the US as Secretary of State and National Security Adviser, carefully made sure that any ceasefire was kept separate from any peace negotiations which the Arabs and the Soviets called for. Nixon, even though he was beset with other problems, was quite lucid when Kissinger brought him into the discussions. Kissinger wanted a peace process and Nixon was quite clear on it also. Brezhnev had brought it up repeatedly and again to Kissinger in Moscow. Nixon sent a message to Kissinger in Moscow:

> The Israelis and Arabs will never be able to approach this subject by themselves in a rational manner.   That is why Nixon and Brezhnev, looking at the problem more dispassionately, must step in, determine the proper course of action to a just settlement, and then bring the necessary pressure on our respective friends for a settlement which will at last bring peace to this troubled area.[47]

Kissinger blocked Nixon's initiative. What a different world it might have been if Nixon's message had been given to Brezhnev!
The boycott was not lifted until March 1974. "Kissinger admitted: 'I made a mistake.' Skeptics might wonder whether it was a mistake, or wanton disregard of U.S. interests during a passionate effort to help Israel."[48] The cost was high: $750 billion to **$1 trillion** - $300 billon to $600 billion in GDP loss and $450 billion in increased oil import costs. One additional cost often overlooked was the creation of the Strategic Petroleum Reserve (SPR) to protect Israel and the US from a future oil embargo. It was designed to hold one billion barrels of oil and had cost $134 billion by 2003. "Thus the 1973 oil crisis, all in all, cost the U.S. economy no less than $900 billion, and probably as much as $1,200 billion,"[49] long gas lines, lost jobs, enormous amounts of wealth in oil-producing countries which disrupted world financial markets, and the continued rise in oil prices. The peace negotiations that were to follow a ceasefire are still as distant four decades later as then. **Nixon was right.**

Peak Oil or Plenty of Oil?

The world produces over 80 million barrels of oil per day (mbd) and the US consumes about one fourth of all that oil (20-21 mbd), and we produce only about one fourth of that (5+ mbd), having to import the rest. Ever since oil was first discovered, there have been people predicting that it would soon run out. One of the most famous was the late M. King Hubbert, a geophysicist at Shell Oil and later at the US Geological Survey. He predicted in 1956 that US production would peak in the early 1970s, called "Hubbert's Peak," which it evidently did in 1970 at about 9.5 mbd. Debate on "peak oil" continued with predictions of the halfway mark of total world oil production being reached in 2005 and then 2006. Others predicted that global demand would exceed supply by 2010 while many oil analysts believed production would continue to grow for at least the next 30 years. Some feel the world supply will not be exhausted before 2056 and, when the vast tar sands and oil shale deposits are included, there could be "500 years of oil supply at the 2000 production rates" and that "the world contains enough oil to last well beyond 2100."[50]

The question of peak oil continued with *Time* addressing the subject in December 2007. World oil production was 85.5 mbd in 2006 and but fell to 83.9 mbd in late 2007. As opposed to the peak oil predictions of the turning point in that decade, many officials expected production to peak at over 110 mbd around 2030. The leaders of OPEC (Organization of Petroleum Exporting Countries), which produces about 41% of world oil, state "that high prices are the fault of speculators and the falling dollar, not low production." One economist agreed: "there's more than enough oil for sale right now. The price pressure, he explains, 'is coming from financial participants in futures markets.'"[51]

The discussions over peak oil have brought out a new definition. Oil from "conventional" sources evidently peaked in 2006 and existing oilfields are declining at about 6.7% annually. Demand is expected to continue to rise reaching 99 mbd by 2035 according to the International Energy Agency. The era of cheap oil is over and future oil will be much more difficult to produce having to come from "unconventional" sources and therefore more expensive.[52] Disagreements continue over reserves because many are not accessible and thus not available for production. The US Geological Survey estimates 4-5 billion barrels in the Bakken [North Dakota], but the CEO of a company that pioneered those shale fields says 24 billion barrels. Likewise, other CEOs estimate 20 billion barrels in the Eagle Ford [Texas], 20 billion barrels in the Marcellus [NE US], and another 20 billion barrels among the other shale plays. Each of these is over double the official US reserves.[53]

Regardless, high oil prices are impacting all aspects of our economy. Daniel Yergin succinctly described our massive dependence on oil:

> Today, we are so dependent on oil, and oil is so embedded in our daily doings, that we hardly stop to comprehend its pervasive significance. It is oil that makes possible where we live, how we live, how we commute to work, how we travel – even where we conduct our courtships. It is the lifeblood of suburban communities. Oil (and natural gas) are the essential components in the fertilizer on which agriculture depends; oil makes it possible to transport food to the totally non-self-sufficient megacities of the world. Oil also provides the plastics and chemicals that are the bricks and mortar of contemporary civilization.[54]

The pervasive influence of oil reaches into every corner of the world. This influence is most conspicuous, however, in the largest consumer nation: the United States of America.
- Charles A. Kimball[55]

But man is a resilient beast as demonstrated by finding ways to improve agricultural yields to feed a growing world population despite dire predictions. Oil production predictions were probably accurate based on the known science at the time, but science and technology have bailed us out again. New techniques for extracting oil from tar sands and rock plus discovery of enormous amounts of natural gas mean there should be ample fuel for this century. There have also been some major new discoveries, particularly in the Western Hemisphere.

It has long been known that there were plentiful hydrocarbons in the Americas but they were trapped in shale rock, oil sands, heavy oil formations, and offshore deposits, all of which were difficult to recover economically. These "unconventional" oil reserves are over 2 trillion barrels in the US, 2.4 trillion in Canada, and over 2 trillion in South America – well exceeding the 1.2 trillion in the Middle East and North Africa.[56]

The new technologies include 3-D seismic mapping, horizontal drilling, and hydraulic fracturing (fracking). The oil sands in Canada, also know as tar sands, are very heavy oil mixed with sand and clay like molasses and won't flow until separated and treated. Production has grown to 1.5 mbd and should reach 3 mbd by 2020. Environmentalists opposed the proposed 1,700 mile Keystone XL pipeline to move oil from Alberta to Texas refineries, concerned about the Ogallala aquifer. Obama delayed approval (hopefully until after the 2012 elections) even though it held the prospect of thousands of jobs. However, the Republicans brought it up again in January 2012, but Obama blocked it again. Not surprisingly, the Canadian Prime Minister Stephen Harper was disappointed in his American "friends" and flew off to China to talk with Chinese officials about oil.[57]   Brazil thought it had no oil so it concentrated on developing ethanol from sugar.   But with improvements in reading seismic signals, they found huge oil reserves off the southern coast under a belt of salt that is over a mile thick. It will be difficult and expensive, but Brazil could be producing 5 mbd by 2020. By applying shale-gas technology –fracking – "tight oil," which is oil in dense rock which is so hard the oil will not flow, has become accessible. The Bakken formation in North Dakota has moved from almost no production to about 0.5 mbd, and together with fields in Texas, output could reach 3 mbd by 2020.[58]

Horizontal drilling and hydraulic fracturing have opened up enormous new reserves.

According to the US Energy Information Administration (EIA), the world was producing 86.8 mbd of oil in 2010 and world crude oil proven reserves were 1,341.6 billion barrels, so at current production that would last 42.35 years. World natural gas consumption increased by over 25% since 1990 reaching over 115 trillion cubic feet (tcf) in 2010. With proven reserves of 6,289 tcf, that would last 54.5 years at current consumption. However, according to a map in *Time*, there are enormous areas of shale gas potential around the world.[59] The technically recoverable shale gas reserves appear to be at least several times the proven reserves.   Gas from shale is the fastest growing energy reserve in the world and we are already seeing a natural gas glut. The US is shifting from being an importer to an exporter. One US company, Cheniere Energy, unwisely spent nearly $1 billion to build a huge LNG (liquefied natural gas) import terminal in Louisiana. Now the company has applied for approval to build an export facility on the site.

Fracking, which has been used since the 1940s, starts with drilling thousands of feet of a concrete encased well and gradually bending and then going horizontally for as much as a mile in a layer of shale. A perforating gun is lowered down to the end and it fires off explosives that open microfractures in the shale. Then millions of gallons of water, mixed with sand and additives (fracking chemicals), are pumped down under high pressure which widens the fractures in the shale. The grains of sand keep the cracks open and gas or oil is forced by natural pressure back up the well for years. Of course, nothing comes without a cost. There was concern by environmentalists that the chemicals would contaminate groundwater. However, these wells are often over 7,000 feet down and are well below aquifers.   The chemicals are another concern even though they are only about 0.5-2% of the fluid. A typical hydrofracked well in the Marcellus Shale, which runs thousands of feet under Pennsylvania and New York, uses as much as 5 million gallons of water. Much of that water comes back up and is contaminated and must be disposed of or decontaminated. Leaks or spills can cause problems. It is a problem but it is something that has to be dealt with as in any other industrial process.[60]

Booming economies, such as in China and India, will require increased imports of oil.

Demand may have peaked in the US but booming double-digit growth economies in China and India add new demand[61] which require greatly increased imports of oil. Politics impinge on the supply of oil with problems in the Middle East, Iraq and Libya went offline for a while, and Iran is a threat to the region, unrest in Nigeria, Sudan trying to come out from a civil war, and poor management has reduced yields in Mexico and Venezuela, all of which make the markets nervous. Yet, we still have oil beneath the Arctic National Wildlife Refuge and offshore which the politicians continue to block due to the naïve, selfish, and disastrous efforts of the conservationists. Such devastating restrictions have kept us from building a new refinery for 35 years.[62]

Regardless of arguments over peak oil, it is still prudent to find alternatives for the future. The alternative fuel technologies are not yet a solution: hydrogen power is probably a decade or more away; solar, fuel cells, and wind power are more advanced but they could only provide a fraction of our needs; and nuclear power is expensive and the politicians have kept it shackled for over 20 years but we are finally starting building new plants. Electric cars are starting to appear but, along with cars running on natural gas, a complete infrastructure is needed and little progress has been made. Oil has the unique feature of being portable and energy rich which leads to the sad conclusion that there is no portable alternative to oil now that is commercially feasible in this decade.

The cost of gasoline, which is the benchmark that we feel the fastest in the pocketbook, is quite interesting. We hear of the gouging by the oil companies. But they make only about 13 cents on each gallon of gas.[63] The government really rakes it in because they get the great windfall in the taxes that the oil companies pay which run into the hundreds of billions (trillions) of dollars (over $2.2 trillion over the past 25 years according to the Bureau of Economic Analysis and the US Department of Energy). On average, oil companies pay about $3 in taxes for every $1 of profit. From 1992 to 2006, according to Ernst and Young, oil companies made $900 billion in profits but spent $1.25 trillion on long-term investment (exploration, development, etc.)

The real gouging is in some of the producer countries that do nothing but collect their enormous revenue checks. The breakdown for where your gas dollar goes is roughly: 60% to the crude supplier, 10% for refining, 10% for distribution and marketing, and 20% taxes.[64] The federal tax is 18.4¢ while state and county taxes add up to a national average of 46¢ with New York being the highest at 60.8¢.[65]

The new technologies have bought us more time, but only a "breathing space," and the rest of the world is busy searching for more oil in the Caspian Sea area, China's Tarim Basin, the South China Sea, Eastern Siberia, Saudi Arabia and around the Persian Gulf, and in Africa. Oil is a strategic resource in modern economies and will continue to play a major world role in this century.

Energy Independence

Why are we so dependent on imported oil? After the 1973 oil embargo, President Carter called for a major effort for alternative fuels. That fizzled after the collapse of oil prices resulted in lost interest and low economic viability. President George W. Bush in his 2006 State of the Union address called for technology to reduce oil imports from the Middle East by 75% by 2025. Yet there is no visible effort. We are making more ethanol which has driven up the price of meat and milk due to the diversion of corn, but there is still debate over whether it takes more energy to produce ethanol (from corn or other sources) than is gained in the product and whether it actually increases global warming. Brazil has made the most effort with ethanol and flex-fuel technology.[66]

Ethanol has become very much in vogue as the "vanguard of the green-tech revolution" with all the environmentalists and now the politicians jumping on the bandwagon, much of which comes from the pressure of the farm lobby. The US has increased its ethanol production fivefold in the past decade and Washington has mandated that renewable fuels be quintupled in the next decade. The energy bill of December 2007 mandated 36 billion gallons of biofuels by 2022. (The US produced 7 billion gallons in 2007 (13 billion gallons in 2010) at a cost of $8 billion in subsidies to taxpayers - $1.14/gallon.) It was small business, only $5 billion worldwide in 1995, but increased to $38 billion by 2005 and has moved to over $100 billion. The impact on other sectors was not significant when it was small scale (and corn was often in surplus), but now that it has gone global, the law of unintended consequences sets in. High oil prices drove people to accept that biofuels would reduce global warming and were greener than gasoline even though ethanol produces less energy than gasoline. The improvement was only about 20 percent for corn ethanol because so much energy is consumed in its production. Deforestation, which is taking place in Indonesia, Malaysia, and Brazil, was not considered and is having devastating effects. Forests are great storehouses of carbon and their destruction has long range effects: "it will take more than 400 years of biodiesel use to 'pay back' the carbon emitted by directly clearing peat lands to grow palm oil; clearing grasslands to grow corn for ethanol has a payback period of 93 years… overall, corn ethanol has a payback period of about 167 years because of the deforestation it triggers." Deforestation currently accounts for 20 percent of carbon emissions.

> **There has been controversy over ethanol as to whether it takes more energy to make than it yields, its effect on global warming, and whether it inflates food prices.**

There has been considerable debate about ethanol with controversy over whether it does or does not take more energy to produce than it yields, its greenhouse improvements, and its effect on food consumption. US farmers sell one-fifth of their corn for ethanol production; so soybean farmers switch over to corn, the price of those commodities goes up, food costs thereby rise, and even the price of ethanol goes up. "The grain it takes to fill an SUV tank with ethanol could feed a person for a year." Taking grain and turning it into fuel instead of food is endangering the hungry in what the UN calls a "global emergency" and a "crime against humanity." As one man described it, "biofuels pit the 800 million people with cars against the 800 million people with hunger problems." There were great hopes for ethanol. "But several new studies show the biofuels boom is doing exactly the opposite of what its proponents intended: it's dramatically accelerating global warming, imperiling the planet in the name of saving it. Corn ethanol, always environmentally suspect, turns out to be environmentally disastrous. Even cellulosic ethanol made from switchgrass, which has been promoted by eco-activists and eco-investors as well as by President Bush as the fuel of the future, looks less green than oil-derived gasoline."[67]

Scientists are trying to make another source commercially viable – algae, some varieties of which are up to 50% oil that can be converted into biodiesel or jet fuel. The problem so far is cost which is perhaps $20 per gallon. Washington stopped its algae research over 10 years ago, but the Department of Energy recently joined with Chevron to pursue the subject. The Department of Defense, the largest energy consumer in the world, needs new sources of jet fuel. The Defense Advanced Research Projects Agency is working on the problem. If any group can do it, DARPA is the most likely; they have a great history, including developing the internet (No, not Al Gore!). An advantage is that an "acre of corn can produce about 20 gallons of oil per year… compared with a possible 15,000 gallons of oil per acre of algae." Unfortunately, algae oil under $5 per gallon, or preferably under $2-3, is many years away.[68]

The US Air Force is testing synthetic fuel in a B-52 bomber. This would be extremely valuable since the Air Force uses 2.6 billion gallons of jet fuel each year and commercial airlines use almost eight times as much, 53 million gallons per day.[69] During World War II, 92% of German aviation fuel and one-half of total production was synthetic fuel. South Africa has used it for over 50 years producing something like 2,000 barrels per day. Synthetic fuels burn more cleanly and can run in existing engines. The Defense Department wants synthetic fuels (costing supposedly $35 per barrel!) but big oil has not been supportive (having blocked such efforts in the 1930s and 1940s). Montana has 120 billion tons of coal which is over one third of US reserves and the liquid fuel equivalent of one fourth of the oil in the Middle East.[70]

What is to be done? If we could build an atomic bomb in four years and go to the moon in less than a decade with technologies that had not even been invented, we could develop alternative energy sources if only we had the will to do it! With the high world demand and the volatile world political situation, we are not likely to ever see $10 a barrel oil again; thus it will make economic sense to develop alternatives.

> **Regardless of the amount of new oil found, it is in the US national interest to develop alternative energy sources for transportation to assure our independence.**

Thomas Friedman wrote a blistering article attacking Bush and Cheney for not "focusing the nation on greater energy efficiency and conservation…Sticking with oil, and basically saying that a country that can double the speed of microchips every 18 months is somehow incapable of innovating its way to energy independence – that is for sissies, defeatists and people who are ready to see American values eroded at home and abroad." He said it is "a national security imperative." He wrote that our biggest threat is not from Islamism or any of the "isms," but from petrolism – the politics of using oil income to buy off one's citizens and enemies and stay in power. We cannot stop "violent Islamism in the Middle East without drying up our consumption of oil." "We need a president and a Congress with the guts… [to impose] a real energy policy…rather than the welfare-for-oil-companies-and-special-interests that masqueraded last year as an energy bill."[71]

Oil plays an important role in almost every part of our economy, not only in transportation but in manufacturing and agriculture from fertilizer to tractors. We need to be independent so that we are not beholden to any foreign government which may act contrary to our national interests.

Vulnerability

In addition to a terrible balance of payments deficit, total dependence on importing foreign oil has two other major threats to the US. The enormous amount of dollars collected by various oil-exporting states leaves them with the need to place that money. It can be placed in banks, buy US Treasury notes, build things, or buy up real estate and companies (including US). This glut has seen the weakening of the dollar, a major recession, and calls for changing the commerce of oil away from dollars.[72]   Some countries, including China, are already bartering oil rather than dealing in dollars. The decline of the dollar is critical and if the dollar were no longer the world reserve currency, it would have a major impact on the US economy.

The second threat is that our economy and our way of life are at the mercy of what has been called The Guerrilla Oil Cartel. That is that global guerrillas now have control over the price of oil by reducing the flow of oil by means of rather easy low technology attacks on oil facilities in any of a number of producing countries. This is totally different from a 9/11 attack, a single large attack; this is a threat of "sustainable disruption" – we have seen some of this in Iraq – pipeline attacks, sabotage, kidnapping employees, attacking tankers or refineries or storage facilities. It appears that they could control over five mbd, well over the 2 mbd of swing production in Saudi Arabia. The success of guerrillas in Iraq and Nigeria will only lead them to other areas, such as Russia and the Caspian Sea producers.[73] After the overthrow of the

Mubarak government in Egypt, we saw repeated attacks on the natural gas pipeline in the Sinai to Israel.

The critical Abqaiq oil processing complex in Saudi Arabia was attacked by al Qaeda in Saudi Arabia on 24 February 2006 by three cars loaded with explosives. It was supposed to be a strategic attack to massively affect world oil supplies, but it turned into a fiasco. The first car blew a hole in the fence but the guards took out the rest and they never got any farther. That pointed out that either the Saudis had penetrated al Qaeda or their security was very good, or both. Al Qaeda claimed that they carried out the attack "based on the instructions of our leader Osama bin Laden," and that they will target more oil facilities.[74]

OPEC could be considered another aspect of the Guerrilla Oil Cartel since it still controls a significant percentage of world oil production. Since oil is fungible, even if new sources are brought online, OPEC could cut production which increases prices negating any price reduction hoped for from the new sources. Since some of the OPEC countries fund terrorism, this is added argument for alternative fuels for transportation to reduce the power of OPEC.

Iran has threatened to pull its 2.5 mbd off the market if attacked and even to close the Strait of Hormuz thereby shutting off the Persian Gulf from which 20% of world oil (40% of the seaborne oil) or 16.5-17 mbd flows. Such actions would certainly spook the international oil market which "is already psyched up because of Mideast tensions," but it would also have a devastating effect on Iran itself. The mullahs have not shown themselves to be totally insane yet, so it is unlikely they will change now.[75] All of the LNG from Qatar flows through the Strait. However, the UAE was nearing completion of a 370 km pipeline to move 1.5 mbd of crude to their Fujairah terminal which is on the Gulf of Oman, outside the Strait.

Oil is great if you have it. Russia sits on over "a quarter of the world's proven reserves of natural gas, 17% of its coal and 6% of its oil." That makes for pending problems for us as "Russia is the only major power that has an interest in high energy prices. It is therefore the only major power with no interest in Middle Eastern stability." That brings us into confrontation over Iran's nuclear weapons program.[76] Russia has rebuilt its power particularly with relation to the former Soviet republics and with Europe which is growing more dependent on its oil and gas.

> **Russia is the only major power that has an interest in high energy prices. It is therefore the only major power with no interest in Middle Eastern stability.**

Dr. John Scire prepared some interesting statistics on our dependencies, national security impacts, and economic costs of our oil dependency. By 2006, our imports of oil were 66 percent of our consumption, and of the 20 mbd consumed, 65 percent or 13 mbd, went for gasoline and diesel fuel. He said the annual costs to maintain the forces to be available to intervene in the Persian Gulf were $49.1 billion before the Iraq War and have escalated to $137 billion per year. We are experiencing net capital outflows of about $150 billion per year with predatory capital inflows as those countries flush with oil money buy up our assets. Supply disruptions in 1973, 1979 and 1990 cost our economy about **$2.3 trillion**. Regardless of the timing of any "peak oil," "the reality today is that worldwide demand growth is already outpacing supply growth. The DOE predicts our use of motor fuels will increase by 28 % by the year 2030 while the world demand is supposed to grow by over 30%." Dependence on importing oil also results in political and diplomatic impacts: it requires us to support repressive regimes; it strengthens worldwide Islamist terrorism, particularly due to funding from the

Middle East; it strengthens other states who oppose our foreign policy, such as Venezuela and Russia; and it reduces our diplomatic options when China or Russia can block us in the UN.[77]

China is now the largest energy consumer in the world. There were 17 million new cars sold in the US in 2000 and about 2 million in China. In 2010, there were 17 million cars sold in China and 11 million in the US.[78] China puts over 1,000 new cars on the streets of Beijing alone each day and with the increased energy demands by China and India in particular, at some point for any one of various reasons (production, delays, disruptions, wars), we are going to see demand outstrip supply. That always means prices go up. For the oil consuming countries, the result will be crippling inflation, unemployment, and economic instability. Kenneth S. Deffeyes, a geologist at Princeton, predicts "a permanent state of oil shortage." The experts think it will take over a decade for conservation measures and new technologies to close the supply and demand gap.[79]

The key question is: if demand does exceed supply, will there be wars to gain access to oil? At some point, $200, $300, $400 per barrel might have such a drastic impact on a country's economy that it could decide it was better to seize some oil fields rather than pay what might be considered blackmail.

> **China is now the world's largest energy consumer and will likely be the world's largest oil consumer by 2020.**

The new discoveries will likely shift the center of the world oil map to the Western Hemisphere, but we will still need supplies from the rest of the world, just not to the same degree. That oil will be going to Asia. China consumes half as much oil as the US now but could become the world's largest oil consumer by 2020. This has a major geopolitical impact in that Asian economies, particularly China and India, will have a growing interest in stability of supplies from the Middle East. The Persian Gulf will continue to be strategically important, which raises the question: "How will responsibility be shared among the great powers for the stability of the Persian Gulf?"[80]

Think back to the 1973 crisis which impacted on nearly every sector of American life and it only lasted six months. Not only did the price of gas go up, but there were long lines at gas stations. The speed limit was cut back from 65 to 55 mph; airlines, buses and train travel was affected; there were brownouts; we were told to cut back on our air conditioning and heating; and businesses and jobs were affected. Next time will be worse because there is no source to bail us out.

New sources cannot be brought on line quickly. It takes time to drill, build new refineries, pipelines, or new nuclear power plants. The Arctic National Wildlife Refuge production would probably be only six months of our current consumption. Nuclear still appears to have a future despite the Fukushima disaster in Japan. The World Nuclear Association reported that there are 52 reactors under construction, 135 planned, and 295 proposed. Later figures listed 433 nuclear reactors in operation with 62 being built with plans for 156 by 2020 and 343 by 2025 (with China and India having 260). Looking out to 2018, we are about 400 million pounds short of uranium. The 433 reactors needed 65,000 tons of uranium but only 53,663 tons were mined worldwide. The shortage was made up from reprocessing nuclear warheads. About 122 million pounds are produced annually, but the top ten producers make up about 90% of the market. Our nuclear dependency is highlighted by the fact that 84% of our uranium is imported or downblended from our uranium and plutonium stocks. Worldwide production of yellowcake was 102 million pounds in 2004 but 173 million pounds were consumed. The difference was met by downblending to mixed-oxide fuel (MOX).

We have plans for 31 new nuclear power plants but only one facility to enrich yellowcake.[81] We have large amounts of depleted uranium that, now that the price of uranium has greatly increased, could be worth over $7 billion.[82]

Another part of the nuclear future is nuclear fusion – fusing two atomic nuclei. It is attractive because of no greenhouse gases and no chance of catastrophic failure. It would use deuterium which is available from seawater. However, it is an extremely difficult science and engineering challenge because it requires a hot gas – plasma – at a temperature of about 100 million degrees Celsius. It has been done and progress is being made with numerous countries working on it, while the US has not committed to the program.[83]

One of the long range possible alternative energy sources is osmotic power which Norway has been pursuing. It is based on "salt water's osmotic tug on freshwater" – the by-product of that action is energy. "It's a promising carbon-free renewable energy that could one day help marginalize fossil fuels."[84]

The alternative energy sources are years (if not decades) away because we have not been serious about developing them. The politicians must start thinking about our country and not just their next election. The oil industry is not going to lose any money, but it is not their business to develop alternative energy sources which might reduce their own business. We need a "Manhattan Project" for energy independence **NOW**. We need to drastically cut back the uses of imported petroleum for non-vehicular uses, such as plastics, chemicals, and power generation. Unfortunately, oil is still the only major source we have for the foreseeable future to power vehicles.

We need to conserve and be more efficient. Just as there may well be wars over water in this century, there will likely be wars over oil (some say that already started with Iraq). Sudan has been in civil war for decades. The Republic of South Sudan declared its independence on 9 July 2011, making it the 54th African state and at the bottom of the developing world. The South has oil but it is dependent on a pipeline through the North to move it to market, and the North charged an exorbitant $32 per barrel (one-third of value) for transit. The South was looking at an alternative route through Kenya to the Indian Ocean (naturally the Chinese were interested in financing it). Fighting has continued, particularly around Abyei, an oil rich area claimed by both sides but seized by the North. Current fighting is all about oil.[85]

Black Gold made the 20th Century but it has taken us prisoner and is the Achilles' heel of the 21st as our economy is under extreme pressure, partially from the enormous balance of payment deficits including the trillions of dollars exported importing oil, which also filled the coffers of those countries who do not wish us well. Washington still does not appear to be willing to address our energy problem which is a major cause of our economic destruction. We need to get deadly serious about rapidly developing the sources we have as well as developing alternative fuels for the security of our country.

Notes

1. *World Press Review*, October 2000, p. 6.
2. "The Clean Energy Scam," *Time*, 7 April 2008, p. 44.
3. Much has been written about the history of oil. An exhaustive coverage is *THE PRIZE The Epic Quest for Oil, Money & Power*, the Pulitzer Prize winning book by Daniel Yergin, (New York, A Touchstone Book, Simon & Schuster, 1993). Yergin had three themes: the rise of capitalism and modern business, oil intertwined with national strategies and power, and the "Hydrocarbon Society" – the 20th Century became the "Century of Oil." pp. 13-16.
4. Ibid., pp. 23, 204.
5. Ibid., pp. 24-25.
6. Ibid., pp. 19-23.
7. Ibid., pp. 26-31.
8. Ibid., pp. 40-43.
9. Ibid., p. 79.
10. Ibid., pp. 207-208.
11. Ibid., pp. 49, 51.
12. Ibid., p. 85.
13. Ibid., pp. 88-98.
14. Ibid., p. 110.
15. Ibid., p. 247.
16. John Bulloch, *The Persian Gulf Unveiled*, (New York, Congdon & Weed, Inc., 1984), pp. 73, 79.
17. Yergin, *The Prize*, p. 300.
18. Ibid., pp. 58-60.
19. Ibid., pp. 65-67, 86.
20. Ibid., pp. 134-137.
21. Ibid., pp. 151-154, 161.
22. Ibid., p. 173.
23. Ibid., pp. 180-181.
24. Ibid., pp. 189, 195.
25. Ibid., p. 201.
26. Ibid., p. 204.
27. Ibid., p. 301.
28. *British Financial Times*, 23 August 2006.
29. "Power Plays: How Energy Fuels World Politics," *World Press Review*, October 2000, p. 6.
30. Donald Neff, "Nixon Administration Ignores Saudi Warnings, Bringing On Oil Boycott," *The Washington Report on Middle East Affairs (WRMEA)*, October/November 1997, p. 70.
31. Henry Kissinger, *Years of Upheaval*, (Boston, Little, Brown and Company, 1982), pp. 467, 523.
32. Donald Neff, *Warriors Against Israel: How Israel Won the Battle to Become America's Ally 1973*, (Brattleboro, Vermont, Amana Books, 1988), pp. 110-112.
33. Kissinger, *Years of Upheaval*, p. 482.
34. Donald Neff, "Nixon Administration Ignores Saudi Warnings," *WRMEA*, pp. 71-71. Donald Neff. *Warriors Against Israel*, pp. 112-114. Kissinger, *Years of Upheaval*, p. 508.
35. Kissinger, *Years of Upheaval*, p. 871. I served in Atherton's Bureau for 3 years and then met with him regularly while he was ambassador in Cairo. He was a true professional and a great gentleman.
36. Among the effects of the total Israeli victory in 1967 was that Israeli intelligence was considered the world's best and not to be questioned. "This became especially true in the Nixon administration; Nixon and Henry A. Kissinger, his national security adviser, became renowned inside the CIA for preferring Mossad's intelligence assessments on the Middle East to those supplied by the Agency." Seymour M. Hersh, *The Samson Option*, (New York, Random House, 1991), p. 168. That is how you set yourself up for disinformation. Also, our ambassador in Israel, Wally Barbour, announced after the 1967 War, "Israel is going to be our main ally…Arab oil is not as important as Israel is to us."
37. Kissinger, *Years of Upheaval*, pp. 491-493.
38. Hersh, *The Samson Option*, pp. 222-223. Dayan also said, "This is the end of the Third Temple." Hersh confirmed the nuclear alert from several sources including Ambassador Hermann Eilts and that "Israel was prepared to use nuclear weapons against the Syrians if they'd broken through." Also, Kissinger told Sadat after the war. See Hersh's Chapter 17 Nuclear Blackmail, pp. 226-240. According to Hersh, Israel had 25 nuclear warheads in 1973. p. 179.
    Kissinger knew in the fall of 1967 when he was teaching a course at the Israeli Defense College that Israel was making nuclear warheads. pp. 168-169.
39. Hersh, Ibid., p. 225. Kissinger, *Years of Upheaval*, p. 493. "To be sure that Israel could quickly communicate with him, Kissinger ordered installed in Ambassador Dinitz's office at the Israeli Embassy a private, secure telephone line that directly linked the secretary of state with the ambassador, a unique privilege for a foreign country." Neff, "Nixon Administration Ignores Saudi Warnings," p. 71.
40. Kissinger, Ibid.
41. See for example, Kissinger, Ibid., pp. 476, 477, 501, 502, 519, 539-544.
42. Neff, "Nixon Administration Ignores Saudi Warnings," p. 71.
43. Kissinger, *Years of Upheaval*, p. 508. Kissinger did understand the problem for the Arabs. Raymond H. Close, who was in the CIA at the time, wrote, "I have preserved the text of a private and secret message from Secretary of State Kissinger that I delivered on 25 October 1973 to Fahd bin Abd-al-Aziz, now King of Saudi Arabia, but then only a deputy prime minister,

just after the imposition of the Arab oil embargo on the United States. In his message, Henry Kissinger said this to Fahd: 'We recognize that conditions that produced the current [1973] war were intolerable to the Arab side, and must be eliminated.' Now it is almost 40 years later, and the United States has still not publicly acknowledged that Israeli seizure of Arab land is an intolerable state of affairs that deserves to be 'eliminated.'

"Double standard? Of course, without question. How do we expect an Arab to feel? And yet we wonder why deep bitterness and disillusion are still breeding terrorism?" "The Only Effective Defense Against Terrorism Is To Rebuild America's Reputation For Fairness," *WRMEA,* October/November 1998, p. 15.

44. Kissinger, Ibid., pp. 534-537.
45. Kissinger, Ibid., pp. 539, 541-544.
46. Neff, "Nixon Administration Ignores Saudi Warnings," p. 71.
47. Kissinger, *Years of Upheaval,* pp. 468 and 551. Kissinger was able to ignore Nixon's message because, when he called Al Haig, he received no sympathy but a testy reply: "The President has just fired Cox. Richardson and Ruckelshaus have resigned and all hell has broken loose." p. 552.
48. Neff, "Nixon Administration Ignores Saudi Warnings," p. 72. Kissinger was a brilliant operator in world politics dealing with Viet-Nam, China, Chile, the Soviet Union, and the rest of the world. But he was Jewish and that put internal pressure on him. He told Golda Meir during the shuttle diplomacy: "First, I am an American; second I am the Secretary of State of the United States of America; third, I am a Jew." Golda Meir replied without missing a beat: "That's all right, sonny, we read from right to left." Hersh, *The Samson Option,* p. 230.
49. Thomas C. Stauffer, "The Cost to American Taxpayers of the Israeli Palestinian Conflict: $3 Trillion," *WRMEA,* June 2003, p. 22. John L. Mearsheimer and Stephen M. Walt, *The Israel Lobby,* (New York, Farrar, Strauss and Giroux, 2007), p. 54, state the cost as $48.5 billion in 1974 alone (about $140 billion in 2000 dollars) and a 2 percent reduction in GDP.
50. See for example "Group: Oil to peak in 2010," *Reno Gazette-Journal,* 25 May 2002, p. 1A; Llewellyn King "Drilling, economic growth sucking old oil reserves dry" and H. Sterling Burnett "World's current reserves will last well past 2100," *Reno Gazette-Journal,* 30 May 2004 p. 11C; Kenneth Deffeyes "It's the End of Oil" and Peter Huber "Oil is Here to Stay," *Time,* 31 October 2005, p. 66 (Deffeyes predicted the "halfway mark" in 2005; Huber claimed we had trillions of barrels of oil sands, etc., we just need the political will to extract them.); and Matt Crenson "Is the end of the road coming for oil?" *Reno Gazette-Journal,* 29 May 2005, p. 7C. See also "Why Gas Won't Get Cheaper," *Time,* 9 May 2005, p. 40.
51. Justin Fox, "Peak Possibilities," *Time,* 3 December 2007, p. 52.

World natural gas consumption has increased by over 25 percent since 1990 to about 100 trillion cubic feet (tcf). It is expected to more than double by 2030 with a projected consumption of about 180 tcf. The top five exporters are Algeria, Qatar, Iran, Russia, and Venezuela, *Time,* 16 April 2007, p. 16.

For a five-part series on shale, see Sandy Shore, AP. "Shale gets a new look from energy industry," *Reno Gazette-Journal,* 16 October 2005, p. 2E, "Cooking oil: Shale is tough nut to crack for industry," p. 3E, "Canada's tar sands industry 'smells like money,'" p. 7E, "Industry scrounging for labor even without shale boom," p. 7E, "Wildlife effects of natural energy boom still unknown," p. 8E. The US has an "estimated 2.1 trillion barrels of oil – in the form of oil shale – buried deep in the western United States."
52. Nick Hodge, "Peak Oil is Past Tense," Energy & Capital, 15 November 2011.
53. "America's Oil Boom," Stansberry's Investment Advisory, 18 November 2011.
54. *The Prize,* pp. 14-15.
55. *Religion, Politics, and Oil: The Volatile Mix in the Middle East,* (Nashville, Abingdon Press, 1992), p. 78.
56. "Adios OPEC: The Americas, Not the Middle East, Will Be the World Capital of Energy in the Future," Carpe Diem, Professor Mark J. Perry's blog for Economics and Finance, 17 August 2011.
57. Matthew Brown, AP, "Change in pipeline plan could present new problems," *Reno Gazette-Journal,,* 12 November 2011, p. 2B. "Canadian PM in oil talks with China," *Reno Gazette-Journal,* 4 February 2012, p. 2B.
58. Daniel Yergin, "Oil's new world order," *Washington Post,"* 30 October 2011. There is also a major discovery off the coast of French Guyana.
59. Bryan Walsh, "The Gas Dilemma," *Time,* 11 April 2011, pp. 44-45.
60. Ibid., p. 40.
61. *The Washington Times,* 8 April 2005, p.1. "An increasingly assertive China competing for energy supplies," *Washington Post,* 26 December 1997, p. 2E.
62. Charles Krauthammer wrote about getting serious about oil in his column of 12 November 2005. "Let's get serious. We live at the edge of oil shortages and in perpetual vulnerability to oil blackmail. We have soldiers dying in the oil fields of the Middle East, yet we leave untouched the largest untapped oil field in North America so that Lower-48ers can enjoy an image of pristine Arctic purity. This is an indulgence bordering on decadence.

"As is our refusal to drill on the continental shelf. Offshore drilling technology is far safer and more efficient than it was decades ago, when this prohibition was passed. We're starving ourselves.

"The same logic applies to refineries. We have not built one since 1976. Gasoline doesn't grow on trees. The U.S. refining industry operates at 96 percent capacity. That is unsustainable. We need the equivalent of the military base closing commission, whereby outside experts decide which bases should be closed in the national interest. A refinery commission that would situate 15 new refineries scattered throughout the United States (some perhaps on Army bases scheduled for closing) would spread the pain, depoliticize the process and arm us against future shortages."
63. George Will, "Media coverage of 'soaring' gas prices belie the truth," *Reno Gazette-Journal,* 7 April 2007, p. 8C.
64. Department of Energy used the figures : 50% for crude oil, 17% refining, 15% taxes, 9% distribution and retail, and 1% store income for a tank of gas in 2007. "Slim profits for stations," *Reno Gazette-Journal,* 7 April 2008, p. 7A.
65. "Casino profits hinge on gas prices," *Reno Gazette-Journal,* 25 May 2007, p.1A. Some other states: Hawaii 60.4¢, California 58.6¢, Connecticut 55.4¢, Washington 52.4¢, Illinois 52¢, Wisconsin 51.3¢, Florida 51¢, Nevada 50.9¢, and Pennsylvania 50.7¢.

If you think a gallon of gas is expensive – it is a matter of perspective.

Diet Snapple	16oz. $1.29	$10.32/gallon
Lipton Ice Tea	16oz. $1.19	$9.52/gal
Gatorade	20oz. $1.59	$10.17/gal
Ocean Spray	16oz. $1.25	$10.00/gal
Brake Fluid	12oz. $3.15	$33.60/gal
Vick's Nyquil	6oz. $8.35	$178.13/gal
Pepto Bismal	4oz. $3.85	$123.20/gal
Whiteout	7oz. $1.39	$25.42/gal
Scope	1.5oz.$0.99	$84.48/gal
The real kicker		
Evian Water	9oz. $1.49	$21.19/gal for water where you do not even know the source (x 42 = $889.98/barrel)

Remember Evian spelled backwards is **NAÏVE**.

The price of gas in Europe is about $10 per gallon.

66.   Volkswagen Brazil stopped production of gas only models in Brazil on 6 June 2006. All now have flex-fuel capability. Over 75% of all new vehicles in Brazil are flex-fuel. Brazil offers 100% ethanol at gas stations as well as E-25 (25% ethanol and 75% gas) and no longer offers plain gasoline. About 25% of Brazil's transport fuel market is ethanol compared to about 1% worldwide. *Green Car Congress,* 22 August 2006.

Two articles addressed ethanol. One was in favor and said it was cheaper. The second said that subsidies were negative claiming that "every $1 spent subsidizing ethanol costs consumers more than $4." He pointed out that using corn for ethanol meant less for food with resulting higher prices, and that since it contains water, ethanol cannot be shipped through pipelines.

"Worse, most studies show that it takes more energy to produce and deliver a gallon of ethanol than the energy it produces – a net loss of energy. Imported fossil fuels are used to produce, distill and transport ethanol." Ethanol supposedly produces less CO, but "it increase the emissions of volatile organic compounds (VOC) which are a prime component of smog." Bob Stallman, "Increased ethanol use would benefit consumers," H. Sterling Burnett, "Ethanol would require huge taxpayer subsidies," *Reno Gazette-Journal,* 5 June 2005, p. 11A.

A pair of competing articles looked at oil exploration. H. Sterling Burnett (National Center for Policy Analysis), "Off-shore oil drilling necessary for nation," and Amy F. Issacs (Americans for Democratic Action), "Expanding exploration foolish, too expensive," *Reno Gazette-Journal,* 6 August 2006, p. 15A.

Another pair of articles addressed gas prices. A congresswoman wanted to stop price gouging. The law professor said that in 1973, we controlled gas prices resulting in 2-3-hour gas lines, and that Congress is the problem for blocking new production with all their restrictions. US Rep Carolyn B. Maloney, "Stronger laws against price-gouging first-step," Robert Hardaway, "Politicians misleading public about gas prices," *Reno Gazette-Journal,* 10 June 2007, p. 7B. Another pair commented on Sen. Obama's call for an oil-free America this century. Wayne Madsen, "Freedom from oil use is realistic, imperative," Andrew P. Morris, "Energy policy must not ignore history's lessons," *Reno Gazette-Journal,* 27 May 2007, p. 17C.

A 1,724-page energy bill was passed in 2005 but it has not yet had any significant impact. It did, however, permit some new drilling without environmental studies. John Heilprin, AP, "Studies waived in push for new drilling," *Reno Gazette-Journal,* 19 October 2005, p. 2D.

The price of gas is hard on everyone. Our country is based on vehicles now; most everything we buy is moved by trucks and the high prices hit them hard even before they pass on the costs. "Truck firms fuming about high gas prices: Owners say they're spending more on fuel than employees," *Reno Gazette-Journal,* 15 March 2008, p. 1A.

67.   Michael Grunwald, "The Clean Energy Scam: Hyped as an eco-friendly fuel, ethanol increases global warming, destroys forests and inflates food prices. So why are we subsidizing it?" *Time,* 7 April 2008, p. 40.

The farm lobby is "the most powerful force behind biofuels on Capitol Hill. Ethanol isn't about just Iowa or even the Midwest anymore. Plants are under construction in New York, Georgia, Oregon and Texas."

It is a long cycle but US farmers contribute to deforestation in Brazil. US corn is diverted to more than 100 ethanol refineries. Corn prices shoot up. Soybean growers want to cash in, so they switch to corn; soybean prices rise. Global demand for soybeans draws farmers in Brazil to expand into fields previously used as pasture for cattle. Displaced ranchers clear new grazing land in the Amazon rain forest or the Cerrado savanna (south of the Amazon about three times the size of Texas), releasing carbon. In the last 6 months of 2007, 750,000 acres of Brazilian rain forest were lost, equal to the area of Rhode Island. "The basic problem is that the Amazon is worth more deforested than it is intact." The market is the driving force, "so without incentives to prevent deforestation, the Amazon is doomed."

One study concluded that when "this deforestation effect is taken into account, corn ethanol and soy biodiesel produce about twice the emissions of gasoline. Sugarcane ethanol is much cleaner, and biofuels created from waste products that don't gobble up land have real potential, but even cellulosic ethanol increases overall emissions when its plant source is grown on good cropland." Grunwald ended his article with "biofuels aren't part of the solution at all. They're part of the problem."

68.   Steve Karnowski, AP, "Algae fuel new renewable energy research increase," *Reno Gazette-Journal*, 2 December 2007, p. 15C.

69.   "Military tests 1st synthetic fuel for jets," *USA Today,* 21 September 2006, p. 3A.

70.   "The Other Black Gold" by Brian Schweitzer, Governor of Montana, *The New York Times,* 3 October 2005.

71.   Thomas L. Friedman, "The New Red, White and Blue," *The New York Times,* 7 January 2006.

72.   Sen. Richard G. Lugar (R-Indiana) gave a speech at the Lugar-Purdue Summit on Energy Security on 29 August 2006. He listed six threats: 1) oil supplies are vulnerable to natural disasters, wars, and terrorist attacks, 2) large industrializing nations like China and India seek new supplies which makes oil and natural gas more expensive, 3) adversarial regimes, from

Venezuela to Iran to Russia, use supply as leverage, 4) billions of dollars are going to authoritarian regimes which are some of the least accountable in the world, 5) the threat of climate change is made worse by the inefficient and unclean use of non-renewable energy, and 6) without diversification of energy supplies, national economies of energy poor nations will remain depressed with negative effects on stability, development, disease, and terrorism.

He pointed out that the US, with 5 percent of the world's population, uses 25 percent of the world's oil; and that within 25 years, the world will need 50 percent more energy. We spent $300 billion on oil imports which equaled the cost of the first three years of the Iraq War. State-owned companies control 79 percent of world oil. He complained that US oil companies and car companies were not moving fast enough. He said we need E85 and flex fuel cars. There are 897 E85 stations in the US but only 1 in California. He called for ethanol production of 100 billion gallons per year by 2025 and that all new cars be flex fuel capable. That would replace 6.5 mbd which would equal one third of all US oil and one half of our imports.

73. "The Guerrilla Oil Cartel," John Robb, http://www.typepad.com/t/trackback/4094197, 22 January 2006. See also Joe Katzman, "Oil Infrastructure: The Next Terror Target?" http:////www.windsofchange.net/archives /005983.php, 7 December 2004. About two-thirds of Saudi oil moves through Abqaiq, and one tenth of the world's oil supply flows daily through its large terminal at Ras Tanura. Also Yanbu on the Red Sea is connected by a 750-mile pipeline. SITE Institute, "Targets for Jihad Operation Focus upon Oil Pipelines, Refineries, and Pumping Stations in Iraq, Afghanistan, and Within the United States," SITE Publications, 30 December 2005.

Responding to bin Laden and Zawahiri, a 12-page presentation of targets for jihad operations was posted on a protected al Qaeda site. The US targets were in Alaska, Texas, Louisiana, Californian, and Oklahoma. Also, the Trans-Alaska pipeline, noting that "four bullet holes placed in the pipe" or properly placed IEDs (improvised explosive devices) would do the greatest damage. John C. Daly, "Saudi Oil Facilities" Al-Qaeda's Next Target?" The Jamestown Foundation, Global Terrorism Analysis, 23 February 2006. There are 10,000 miles of pipelines, 30 pumping stations, and six generators. Half of Saudi oil is in eight massive fields, covering 2,600 square miles. Over 60 percent of global oil is carried on 3,500 tankers which pass through a small number of chokepoints, such as the Strait of Hormuz.

74. Donna Abu-Nasr, AP, "Al-Qaida vows more attacks," *Reno Gazette-Journal,* 26 February 2006, p. 17C. George Friedman, "Of Mosques, Oil Fields and Ports," Stratfor, 28 February 2006.

75. George Jahn, AP, "Iran would hurt self in choking oil flow," *Reno Gazette-Journal*, 2 December 2007, p. 14C.

76. Niall Ferguson, "The Godfather," *Time,* 26 February 2007, p. 40.

77. Dr. John A. Scire, "Energy and National Security Background Fact Sheet," University of Nevada Reno, 11 December 2007.

78. Daniel Yergin, "10 Questions," *Time,* 13 October 2011, p. 70.

79. Matt Crenson, AP, "Is the end of the road coming for oil?" *Reno Gazette-Journal,* 29 May 2005, p. 7C.

80. Daniel Yergin, "Oil's new world order," *Washington Post,* 30 October 2011.

81. Scire, op. cit.

82. James R. Carroll, "Used uranium could be worth billions," *Reno Gazette-Journal,* 8 April 2008, p. 1B.

83. Stewart C Prager, "How Seawater Can Power the World," *The New York Times,* 11 July 2011, p. A19.

84. Mark Hallper, "Norway's Power Push," *Time,* 13 December 2010, p. Global 1.

85. See Alex Perry and Alan Boswell, "Born in Blood," *Time,* 18 July 2011, p. 38. "Sudan bombs S. Sudan refugee camp," *Reno Gazette-Journal,* 11 November 2011, p. 1B.

Iran threatened to close the Strait of Hormuz. The economic sanctions were hurting the Iranian economy.

Iran will assist any nation or group that confronts Israel.

We will retaliate – especially against the U.S. – for tough new oil sanctions and Western military threats.

These kinds of threats are detrimental to the U.S. The war itself will be 10 times as detrimental to the U.S.

- Ayatollah Ali Khamenei, Supreme Leader of Iran

Chapter 14

White Gold

It's inevitable that we'll solve our water problems. The trick is how much pain we can avoid on the path to where we want to be.

Peter Gleick, President, Pacific Institute

It's counterintuitive, but water is just too important to go to war over.

- Chuck Lawson[1]

Water, water everywhere, but not a drop to drink. We all recited that as children. Water is essential for life and there is no substitute. We start out in a watery fluid and about two-thirds of our bodies are water, but who owns water? Ecuador is the first to put the rights of Nature in its constitution – that rivers and forests are not supply property but have a right to flourish.[2] It is a major part of nature and critical to almost everything we do. Some call it "blue gold" and many consider it "the world's most precious commodity." About 70% of the earth's surface is covered by water, but 97.5% is undrinkable seawater. Most of that 2.5% remaining is inaccessible leaving only 0.1% readily available for human use and consumption. Yet demand for water continues to grow due to the ever increasing world population and more development since water used for energy production and meat consumption increases as countries become more developed. Even though population growth has slowed, if it grows by just 1% annually, there will be another 1 billion people on the planet by 2025.[3]

The world population tripled during the 20th century but use of water increased six fold. Population growth has slowed, but world population may still increase 40-50% in the next 50 years which will make for an enormous demand for already stressed water supplies. There are 1.1 billion people who do not have access to clean drinking water and 2.6 billion people lack adequate sanitation. Many people have access only to dirty water and cannot afford to purify it so that some 1.8 million people die annually from diarrheal diseases; 3,900 children die every day (1,423,500 annually) from waterborne diseases.[4]

Water demand doubles every 21 years according to the World Bank and that pace will only accelerate as emerging economies develop. However, the world water supply is tenuous with droughts, pollution, crumbling infrastructure, low water recycle rates, and depleting aquifers. As usual, it is the poor who suffer most. Per capita daily water usage is 350 liters (93 gallons) in North America and Japan, about 200 liters (53 gallons) in Europe, but only 10-20 liters (2.6-5.3 gallons) in Sub-Saharan Africa.[5] In very poor areas, such as southern Ethiopia, where water is difficult to obtain and is usually dirty, the people cannot afford to waste water washing their hands (also they cannot afford to buy soap) and wash their clothes only once a year. What little money they do have is spent taking their children to a clinic to treat diarrhea. The clinics even use dirty water and the staff did not wash their hands.[6] As the middle class expands, particularly in Asia, they shift to a more meat-centric diet and water demand skyrockets. It takes 1,000 liters of water to produce one kilogram of wheat, 1,400 liters to produce 1 kg of rice, but 13,000 liters to produce 1 kg of beef.[7] The contrast is that it takes only 100 liters of water to grow 1 kg of potatoes.[8]

There are over 260 river basins that are shared by two or more countries, mostly without adequate legal or institutional arrangements.[9] Changes in these basins lead to tensions across international boundaries and can lead to conflicts.

World Situation

The enormous growth in world population plus urbanization and industrialization place great stress on the world water supply and also affect the environment. We have seen the effects of droughts from Africa to Texas. The estimates are that by 2030, there will be only enough water to meet 60% of global demand and $50-60 billion will be spent annually trying to bridge that gap. The problem is that we have the same amount of water we had a century ago but we have two or three times as many people using it and climate change has resulted in water "moving around to different places," giving us a mismatch between where water is needed and where it is. People were wasteful of water in the past because it was relatively easy to find another source, "But those days are over."[10]

> The amount of moisture on Earth has not changed. The water the dinosaurs drank millions of years ago is the same water that falls as rain today. But will there be enough for a more crowded world?[11]

According to a UN report, at least 80 countries have shortages of water now and it is estimated that 2/3 of the world population will be "water stressed" by 2025.[12] A world map of Water Stress Indicator shows areas of "Very High Stress" in the middle to southwest of the US; a ban across the Andes in South America; a wide swath from the Atlantic across North Africa, the Middle East, South Asia to northern China; plus part of South Africa; and southeastern Australia. Advances in agriculture have made food availability fairly secure over recent years, but water for agriculture still takes 66% of world water (up to 90% in arid regions). The remaining 34% is used by industry (20%) and domestic households (10%), with 4% evaporated from reservoirs. As lifestyles change, particularly eating more meat, and changing water availability, there is growing pressure on the supply of water for industry and agriculture. This also results in a "profound effect on aquatic ecosystems and their dependent species."[13]

The Himalayas – China, India

The melting snows of the Himalayas feed some of the great rivers: Yangtze, Yellow, Mekong, Ganges, and Indus. Some two billion people depend on that water. The vast Tibetan Plateau averages two miles high and the glaciers feed some of those great rivers. There are 37,000 glaciers on the Chinese side but the area is very vulnerable to climate change and it is heating up twice as fast as the global average. As a result, the glaciers are receding and perhaps 40% could disappear by 2050. Thousands of lakes have dried up and 1/6 of the plateau is now desert. There have been floods, landslides, loss of topsoil, and dangerous new lakes have formed which if breached could wipe out villages. There is concern about eventual depletion of Asia's greatest rivers in the next 40-50 years which would cause acute water and electricity shortages and a plunge in food production and perhaps migration or even conflict.

China has less water than Canada but 40 times the number of people. In Xinjiang, China has plans to build 59 reservoirs. China is planning to dam the Mekong which causes problems in Southeast Asia.[14] Pollution is a major threat to the world's water supply and is especially bad in China and India. It is so bad in China that a 2006 inspection found that 28% of rivers and 48% of major lakes and reservoirs in China had such poor quality that they were unsafe for any use.[15] We discussed China's water problems in Chapter 11.

Farther west in Central Asia, Tajikistan and Kyrgyzstan have glacier water but they may restrict flow to their parched but oil-rich neighbors: Uzbekistan, Kazakhstan, and Turkmenistan. On the south side of the mountains, India and Pakistan have to share the Indus River which is the lifeline of Pakistan. In addition to water, rivers can also be a source of power by building dams for generating electricity which is badly needed in developing countries. Hydroelectric dams are critical to India in order to reduce their energy shortfall which restricts their economy. Some 40% of Indians are not on the power grid, so they are building a dam on the Kishenganga River (which flows into the Indus) on the India-controlled side of Kashmir. Pakistan, which has "the world's largest contiguous irrigation system," is understandably concerned that its large neighbor "would have the power to manipulate the water flowing to its agriculture industry – a quarter of its economy and employer of half its population."

A treaty was signed in 1960 after a decade of tough negotiations which gave Pakistan 80% of the water from the Indus River system. India is permitted to use some of the water for drinking, farming, and power generation, but it is not to store too much. The Kishenganga dam is permitted under the treaty, but the dispute is over how it is built and when water is released since if India chose to fill the dam at a crucial time, it could destroy a crop. If India builds all the projects it has planned, it could hold a month's worth of water and wipe out an entire planting season.[16] We will discuss this possible conflict further below.

India's largest hydroelectric project is the Tehri Dam on one of the key tributaries of the Ganges coming from the Himalayas. The springs that once fed the villages nearby have dried up and the people have had to give up farming. There are many of these disputes all over India. The Upper Ganga Canal (Ganga is what Indians call the Ganges) carries clean drinking water 121 miles to New Delhi (on the Yamuna River), which is a bit pampered with an availability of 66 gallons (250 liters) per person per day. But the water is not evenly distributed: the richer parts of the city get as much as 132 gallons (500 liters) per person per day while other sections receive as little as 8 gallons (30 liters). So like the people in Tehri, "the poor line up at municipal water tankers and hand pumps."[17]

Despite this, water demand in New Delhi exceeds supply by 300 million gallons per day (there is supposedly 40% leakage in their system plus another 10% lost to theft). There is fear that there may be an exodus from the city within 5-10 years due to lack of water.[18]

The population of the city has exploded by 60% since 1995 and sanitation is another gap between rich and poor. Over 6 million people are not connected to any sewer line (many in unauthorized housing areas) and some 475.5 million gallons (1.8 billion liters) of untreated waste water flows into the Yamuna River daily. The Yamuna is almost dead downstream. Over on the parallel Ganges, the river is severely depleted by the time it reaches Kanpur, which has 400 tanneries which add 8 million gallons (30 million liters) of water daily contaminated with chemicals. The Ganges and Yamuna meet at Allahabad and there are stretches where the river disappears completely. Tributaries provide some replenishment but the water level is very low when the Ganges reaches Varanasi, India's holiest city. With its rivers and springs being depleted, India has turned to groundwater and it is "the largest user of groundwater in the world, consuming more than 25% of the global total."[19]

The amount of available water supply cannot keep up with the demands for agriculture, industry, and human consumption. China, India, and Pakistan all have growing populations but, at the same time, they have declining food production.[20]

Africa

When we think of droughts, we often recall the recurring, seemingly almost endless, droughts in parts of Africa such as the Sahel and Somalia. Deserts advance partially by nature and partially by man's actions. The people living near the deserts often cut down whatever vegetation they can find for firewood which only exacerbates the loss and shows why reforestation has proved to be so successful. In parts of Sub-Saharan Africa, women walk 8 hours daily to collect water. Some 40% of households are more than ½ hour from water and it is getting worse.[21]

> **If the millions of women who haul water long distances had a faucet by their door, whole societies could be transformed.[22]**

Most of the water they take from rivers is dirty, whether from animals walking in it or because the people defecate in open fields near the same rivers they draw their drinking water from. Due to custom, it is women's work to fetch the water, otherwise they would be considered lazy. Of course, the men are sitting in the shade. If there were less time expended in getting water and if they had good water, there would be more time for growing food, raising animals, or even starting income-producing businesses. There would be less sickness and girls could go to school. Few women in these villages even know how old they are. This is not only in the rural areas, but in the slums of cities, women wait in long lines at pumps or for water trucks to get water.[23]

The Sahara has continued to grow with an area the size of Somalia becoming desert over the past 50 years. The UN says that 14 countries in Africa currently suffer from water scarcity or stress and that number is expected to rise to 25 by 2025. Also, 46% of Africa faces land degradation and desertification is "the greatest environmental challenge of our times." Even though countries like Niger still lose 195,000 to 250,000 acres annually to desert, the desert can be stopped. Two steps have helped turn the tide. First, the building of barriers to catch the drifting soil which when held stationary for a while could then be planted with tough desert trees and second the planting of millions of trees. These Sahel Re-Greening Initiatives in Niger, Mali, Burkina Faso, Tanzania, and Ethiopia have been successful so far in that rainfall has increased and hunger has declined due to improved food production and the reclaimed land actually produced badly needed income for people working the regreened land. Over 200 million trees were planted on over 13 million acres in Niger. One of the problems is cultural: persuading the people to give up herding cattle to work the land. But as the chief of one village said, "We stopped the desert and everything changed."[24]

United States

The American South had a record-breaking drought in the summer of 2011 and it may only get worse. By the end of July, 12% of the continental US was in "exceptional drought" state and by November, 33% was in a drought and the cost was already $10 billion. The cause was La Niña, cooling of central Pacific Ocean water, and it was expected to continue through the winter. There were massive wildfires in Arizona and over 2 million acres of Texas farmland was abandoned. Cattle had to be sold early (so beef prices should rise in 2012) and wheat harvests in Kansas, Oklahoma, and Texas fell 25-50%. Computer climate models indicate that the region was to become more arid, "perpetual drought" or "perpetual desert."

Like other countries around the world, the US loses water via aging infrastructure – 7 billion gallons of drinking water lost annually through leaky pipes.[25]

Water infrastructure includes sewer lines, water distribution lines, water treatment plants, and water storage sites. Many of these date to before the 1960s and some back to the Great Depression. About 30% of the pipes that serve over 100,000 people are from 40 to 80 years old, with 10% over 80. Just like other developed and developing economies, a great deal of money needs to be spent on infrastructure - $150 billion over the next 10 years for drinking water infrastructure and an additional $180 billion for clean water over the next 15 years.[26]

A heroic system of dams, pumps, and canals can't stave off a water crisis.

In addition to the drought in the southern part of the country, California after three years of drought was badly stressed – despite having "one of the most elaborate water-delivery systems on the planet." The major problem was that 70% of the rain falls in the North of the state while 80% of the demand is in the southern two-thirds of the state. This was not accidental in that there had been a concerted effort over the years to attract people to the South and the population of Southern California still goes up 200,000 per year. The 223 mile Los Angeles Aqueduct, completed in 1913, diverted the entire Owens River to the South and Owens Lake became a dust bowl. Built in the 1930s, the Central Valley Project pumped much of the Sacramento and San Joaquin Rivers south and with 500 miles of canals provided water to over 10% of the entire irrigated farmland in the US. This permitted California to produce one-half of the vegetables, fruits, and nuts in the US. The State Water Project developed in the 1960s with the 444 mile California Aqueduct serves some 23 million people from north of the Bay Area to the Mexican border and irrigates 755,000 acres of farmland.

The Peripheral Canal, which was supposed to be the final link but was defeated in the 1982 referendum, is back on the table. What has slowed the area now is the Endangered Species Act which has been enforced to protect a small smelt and Chinook salmon. This has hurt farmers, particularly in the Fresno area where 250,000 acres have been cut off with no water since 2009. The town of Mendota which was the "Cantaloupe Center of the World," now has 40% unemployed. There are several problems. In Southern California, 70% of residential water is used outside homes for lawns, pool, and other niceties. The largest and weakest link is the Sacramento-San Joaquin Delta, "a former 700,000-acre marsh that has been drained, diked into islands, and farmed for more than a century," and many islands are now more than 20 feet below sea level. Added to that is that the area sits on the Hayward Fault, one of the most dangerous in the US, and chances are 2 out of 3 for a major earthquake in the next 30 years. The levees and canals are vulnerable and it could take years to repair damage from a major quake.

San Diego pipes in 90% of its water. The largest desalination plant in the US broke ground in 2009 in Carlsbad to produce 50 million gallons/day from 100 million gallons of seawater. There are 19 more plants on the drawing board.[27] There has been friction over allocation of the water from the Colorado River for years among the states and Mexico and between farmers and cities. One effort is working with Mexico on plans for two large desalination plants in Mexico about 15 miles south of San Diego.[28] While disputes continue over the Colorado River allocations, the Salton Sea is drying up.[29] Obviously, Southern California needs to urgently address water recycling and conservation.

US groundwater provides 31% of the water for agriculture and is being depleted 160% faster than it is being recharged. The Ogallala Aquifer, which is under Nebraska, Oklahoma, and Texas, is the center of controversy over the Keystone XL pipeline to carry tar sands oil from Canada to Texas,

In addition to the growing tensions over shared water between farmers and cities, there are the growing disputes about water among the countries.

Tensions – Conflicts

We live on a planet where neighbors have been fighting over rivers for thousands of years. Even the word "rival," which comes from the Latin *rivalis,* originally referred to competitors for a stream or river. As noted earlier, there are over 260 river basins that are shared by two or more countries. Water diverted from rivers in countries of the headwaters reduces availability in downstream countries which can have critical results.

Some of these transboundary disputes are in areas that are already tense such as between China and India, India and Pakistan, and Israel and its Arab neighbors. We mentioned China's need for water in Chapter 11. Their dam on the Brahmaputra increased tensions with India with whom they fought a war in 1962.

As noted above, India has tremendous need for more electricity and has a major program of building dams for hydroelectric power. The Kishenganga project in Kashmir exacerbates an already very tense area between Indian and Pakistan. The dam is "a matter of national prestige" in India but the potential to restrict the flow makes Pakistan very vulnerable. Pakistan already has a water shortage and only limited means to store large quantities of water make it very anxious. Also, "the design of the dam requires that much of the water in the Kishenganga River be diverted for much of the year. That will kill off fish and harm the livelihoods of the people living in the Pakistan-administered side of Kashmir." Water only adds to the 60 years of antagonism and three wars between these nuclear states and detracts from the US efforts in Afghanistan.[30]

> **We may not get all the water we want. But we can have the water we need.**[31]

There are many potential clashes over watersheds worldwide, such as between India and Pakistan over the Indus, Egypt and Ethiopia over the Nile, Syria and Turkey over the Euphrates, and Namibia and Botswana over the Okavango. According to one study, there were 37 shooting conflicts over water since 1950 and 32 took place in the Middle East, 30 of which involved Israel and its Arab neighbors. Most of those involved the Jordan River and its tributaries. The conflicts over the Jordan demonstrate the worldwide potential for clashes over water.[32]

Israel has strived for additional water sources and fought for them since its founding in 1948. The Jordan, with its headwaters in Lebanon and Syria, and the water stored in the Sea of Galilee, are critical to Israel, but also critical for its neighbors. After Syria attempted to divert the Baniyas River (one of the Jordan's headwaters in the Golan Heights) in the 1960s, Israel attacked Syria. Arabs attacked the National Water Carrier system which Israel built to send water from the Sea of Galilee to the south of Israel. These were precursors to the 1967 War. Relations between Israel and Jordan became very tense in 1979 over a sandbar in the Yarmuk River. Israel had wanted to extend its northern border to the Litani River in Lebanon and that was part of the reason for Ariel Sharon's 1982 invasion of Lebanon. Israel threatened in 2002 to shell agricultural pumping stations on the Hasbani (headwaters of the Jordan in southern Lebanon). The good part is that these conflicts have led to negotiations, even in time of war.

The Jordan is now depleted due to drought, pollution, and overuse. Israel continued its search for water drilling 42 deep wells in the Occupied West Bank and transporting that water to Israel. Israelis use four times as much water per person as Palestinians according to the World Bank. Now Palestinians have to buy back water that Israel took.[33] Gaza is another hot spot. Israel's Christmas 2008 bombardment of Gaza left 90% of Gaza's water undrinkable. "Israel purposely bombed sewage plants, so 60 million liters of sewage now are pumped daily into the Mediterranean."[34]

When rivers cross boundaries, there are bound to be disputes. Great rivers like the Euphrates are very important to Iraq and Syria, so when Turkey builds a dam on the river, it is surely going to influence the other two countries. Rather than fight over it, they need to work out acceptable solutions.

Solutions

So much of the world is under water stress that it is clear that our water supply is limited and needs to be protected in both quality and quantity. There are two ways to go according to Peter Geick, President of the Pacific Institute. The hard way is to develop new supplies including big dams, aqueducts, and pipelines to move water great distances. He prefers a softer comprehensive approach that "includes conservation and efficiency, community-scale infrastructure, protection of aquatic ecosystems, management at the level of watersheds instead of political boundaries, and smart economics." Albuquerque, New Mexico thought it had plenty of water but when it found out that it was dwindling, the city went to work and reduced consumption from 140 gallons per day per person to 80 gallons.[35] One novel idea for additional supply is to tow icebergs, which are floating reservoirs of pure water, to water short regions.[36]

> **There is a water crisis today. But the crisis is not about having too little water to satisfy our needs. It is a crisis of managing water so badly that billions of people – and the environment – suffer badly.[37]**

There is no golden solution to our water problem, but there are measures that can be taken to reduce water scarcity. One of the most reliable and inexpensive supplies is by recycling or reclaiming sewage water. Technology has brought the filtering process to the point where it can reclaim clean drinking water much cheaper than piping in water from distant reservoirs.

Since our planet is covered with salt water, that is an obvious source. Desalination has developed technically as well so that there are now over 15,000 desalination plants turning out 17 billion gallons (64 billion liters) of fresh water daily. But it comes with a price: up to five times the cost of recycling. However, work progresses on new techniques and how to reduce the energy costs needed to power the plants as well as how to reduce the ecological impact.

Even cities with abundant rainfall can have water shortages, such as in Bangalore, India. When their wells went dry and running water was available for only two or three hours a day, they went to mandatory rainfall collection. It only takes a relatively small investment for setup. The city hopes that rainwater collection will provide 40% of the city's supply in the near future.

Governments can provide incentives via subsidies, tax reductions, rebates, and fines. Xeriscaping is a natural solution by replacing lawns, which take so much water, with native plants or rocks. Rebates can be given for low-flow toilets and high-efficiency washing machines. Watering times can be established and homeowners can be fined for letting their sprinklers run so long that water runs off into the street.[38]

Water is not a dwindling asset like oil; it is always here; it just moves around in different forms. We need to recycle it and use it wisely. Water has national security implications because of its impact on world economies and its potential for conflict.

Notes

1. Former US official who worked on Israeli-Palestinian water issues in the 1990s, Quoted in Don Belt, "Parting the Waters, *National Geographic,* April 2010.
2. Barbara Kingsolver, "Fresh Water," *National Geographic,* April 2010.
3. Chris Wood, "Water Investing 101," Casey Research, 24 August 2011.
4. World Water Council, 2010. Tina Rosenberg wrote that "Dirty water and lack of a toilet and proper hygiene kill 3.3 million people around the world annually, most of them children under age five." "The Burden of Thirst," *National Geographic,* April 2010.
5. World Water Council, 2010.
6. Rosenberg, "The Burden of Thirst."
7. World Water Council, 2010. It takes 7 to 13 lbs. of grain to finish and produce 1 lb. of beef and 3 to 6 lbs. of grain for 1 lb. of pork. Chris Wood, "Water Investing 101, Casey Research, 24 August 2011.
8. "Water Crisis," World Water Council, 2010.
9. World Water Council, 2010.
10. Anita Hamilton, "Droughtbusters," *Time,* 3 October 2011. p. Business 2.
11. Barbara Kingsolver, "Fresh Water," *National Geographic,* April 2010.
12. Chris Wood, "Water Investing 101."
13. "Water Crisis," World Water Council, 2010.
14. Brook Larmer, "The Big Melt," *National Geographic,* April 2010.
15. Chris Wood, "Water Investment 101."
16. Lydia Polgreen and Sabrina Tavernise, "Water Dispute Increases India-Pakistan Tension," *The New York Times,* 20 July 2010.
17. Jyoti Thottam, "How India's Success Is Killing Its Holy River," *Time,* 19 July 2010, p. 28
18. Brook Larmer, "The Big Melt," *National Geographic,* April 2010.
19. Thottam, op. cit.
20. Brook Larmer, "The Big Melt," *National Geographic,* April 2010.
21. Barbara Kingsolver, "Fresh Water," *National Geographic,* April 2010.
22. Rosenberg, "The Burden of Thirst."
23. Rosenberg, "The Burden of Thirst."
24. Alex Perry, "Land of Hope," *Time,* 13 December 2010, pp. 70-72.
25. Doyle Rice, USA TODAY, "Drought costs in '11 exceed $10B so far," *Reno Gazette-Journal,* 11 November 2011, p. 1B. Bryan Walsh, "Parched Earth," *Time,* 22 August 2011, p. 40.
26. Chris Wood, "Water Investing 10."
27. Joel Bourne, "California's Pipe Dream," *National Geographic,* April 2010.
28. Elliot Spagat, AP, "U.S. might tap Mexico water," *Reno Gazette-Journal,* 16 October 2011, p. 2B.
29. Elliot Spagat, AP, "Dying lake strains river deal," *Reno Gazette-Journal,* 16 January 2011, p. 2B.
30. Lydia Polgreen and Sabrina Tavernise, "Water Dispute Increases India-Pakistan Tension," *New York Times,* 20 July 2010.
31. Elizabeth Royte, "The Last Drop," *National Geographic,* April 2010.
32. Don Belt, "Parting the Waters," *National Geographic,* April 2010.
33. Ibid.
34. Pat and Samir Twair, "John Ging Headlines KinderUSA Program, Corries, Richard Falk at Rebuilding Alliance," WRMEA, July 2010, p. 42.
35. Elizabeth Royte, "The Last Drop," *National Geographic,* April 2010.
36. Thomas K. Grose, "Just Thaw And Serve," *Time,* 23 May 2011, p. Business 1.
37. "Water Crisis," World Water Council, 2010.
38. See Anita Hamilton, "Droughtbuster," *Time,* 3 October 2011, p. Business 1.

Chapter 15

Dumbing Down and a Flood of People

*Education is a profound national
security problem strategically.*

- Newt Gingrich

*Population tends to grow faster
than the means of subsistence.*

- Thomas Malthus, 1798

*Failure to address the population problem
may be the ultimate global blunder.*

- Werner Fornos, President, Population Institute

It has been said that more knowledge was generated in the 20th century than in all of past history yet our education system has let us down by not teaching our children the basics much less the history that got us here. High school students cannot pass the graduation exam in math and English even though they are geared at the eighth grade level in math and ninth or tenth grade levels in English. Not only are they not taught history, they are not taught to reason. They would not recognize Jefferson's "A person once surrendering reason, has no remaining guard against absurdities the most monstrous." The emphasis has been on it is OK to fail rather than to excel. We have unpatriotic women in PTAs who don't want any US military recruiters in schools because only poor kids fight wars. They develop girls who referring to Viet-Nam can say I would run away to Canada too, not even knowing that the draft was for males only.

The US has gone "soft." The World Economic Forum (WEF) ranked the US No. 5 in global competitiveness, "behind Sweden, Singapore, Finland and Switzerland." A tougher rating system was used by the Information Technology and Innovation Foundation which rated 44 countries and found the US next to last. The US used to lead the world in percentage of college graduates, but we are now ninth and falling. "The WEF report ranks the U.S. a stunning 51st in science and math education." We have become more interested in psychology and fitness studies instead of the physical sciences. In the 1970s, California spent 10% of its general revenue on higher education and the result was the exceptional University of California system. They only spent 3% on prisons. "Today, 11 % goes to prisons and 8% to higher education, a number that is dropping fast. There are now about as many Americans who work in the prison business as in auto manufacturing."[1]

> There is no one institution that has contributed more to the deterioration of America than our system of government schools.
> **- Talk show host Neal Boortz**

"You could have a Ph.D. in Astrophysics, a Nobel prize in literature, have held an Ambassadorship to a prominent nation, have managed the largest privately held company in the world, and held the office of U.S. President, and not be able to teach 3rd grade because you didn't have an 'Education Degree.' There are plenty of competent professionals who would gladly volunteer or switch professions to teach but are discouraged by the pedantic requirements of the education elites. It seems the teacher unions have a lock on mediocrity"[2] Up to a third of freshmen in college have to undergo remedial courses because they are not prepared from high school. Social science textbooks are so set in political correctness and multiculturalism that they fail to give students an honest account of American history.[3]

The battle in Wisconsin that Governor Scott Walker fought with the Teacher's unions was to remove their collective bargaining rights. The result was that the union had a sweetheart deal with their own insurance company which charged exorbitant rates. When removed and competitive insurance companies were allowed to bid, some school districts went from a deficit to a large surplus. This is a racket that has permeated our government services sectors and has badly damaged our country.[4] The unions need to prove that they are interested in educating our children rather than feathering their nests and using union dues to elect officials who will keep them in power.

The US government is right in there with the unions ripping off the taxpayers. Part of the great Department of Education is to handle student loans. Over $20 billion go to for-profit schools getting 26% but making up 43% of the defaults. They give out loans just like the sub-prime mortgages to people who can never afford them. Then they cook the books: "borrowers who default after the first two years of repayment aren't counted." You cannot find out how much money is really being lost because "The Department of Education won't make that data public." Our government – you the taxpayers - takes all the risk while the investors and executives keep all the profits. "The for-profit education 'business' is one of the most obvious frauds ever foisted on the American people."[5]

Technology has advanced so rapidly that we now talk about "singularity" – a term borrowed from astrophysics referring to a point in space time when the rules of ordinary physics no longer apply such as in a black hole. It refers to artificial intelligence. Computing power has grown so rapidly that "Maybe the computer will turn on humanity and annihilate us." As one of the gurus of this theory said, "within 30 years, we will have the technological means to create superhuman intelligence. Shortly after, the human era will be ended." Technological progress expands exponentially, not linearly. They expect to reverse engineer the human brain by the mid 2020s and "by the end of that decade, computers will be capable of human-level intelligence." Singularity may arrive by 2045, "the quantity of artificial intelligence created will be about a billion times the sum of all the human intelligence that exists today."[6] Are we preparing our youth for this future?

> **In 1983…A Nation at Risk reported that our schools were so bad that if a foreign power did to our children what we are doing to them it would be considered an act of war.**

Former House Majority Leader Newt Gingrich did an analysis of US security. Facing the threats from China, Russia, radical Islam, and WMDs in the hands of rogue states, he observed that we were failing to modernize our education system which is a key component in US strategic power. "In 1983, 25 years ago, A Nation at Risk reported that our schools were so bad that if a foreign power did to our children what we are doing to them it would be considered an act of war." As he put it, "Education is a profound national security problem strategically." Also, we have lost our economic edge. "Economic strength cannot be sustained in a system of litigation, regulation, taxation, bureaucracy, and health costs that are simply unsustainable." He noted that it took three years and eight months to defeat the Germans and the Japanese, but "it takes 23 years to add a runway to the Atlanta airport." We are prohibited from drilling for oil in our own areas; we cannot build clean coal plants on time; we are restricted in building refineries and nuclear power plants. "The decay of our economy and our education system make it harder and harder for us to compete with China and Russia." He addressed our "irrational and dangerous" oil policy. "Very expensive oil makes dictators more secure, more powerful, and more aggressive….weakens the economies of the democracies and strengthens the economies of dictators and autocrats….gives Russia and Iran a lot more resources with which to invest in competing with the United States…. gives the Saudis much more money with which to subsidize Wahhabist extremist propagandizing on a worldwide basis. The absence of an effective American energy policy is a strategic failure second only to the collapse of education in its long term implications for weakening America and making us more vulnerable."[7]

> **If one does not know the history of this country, one cannot appreciate its greatness. If one does not know history and geography, one cannot comprehend international relations.**

In addition to the failure to teach our citizens the history of this great country and the threat from Islamic jihadis, there are several other threats to the USA and the rest of the world. The burgeoning population, mainly in the Third World, places enormous pressure on countries to create jobs and provide services for more people than they can already handle.

Overpopulation

The community of nations faces the problem of overpopulation and the related problems of global aging, food – famine, unemployment, disease, and migration. They tend to be closely linked and it will be difficult to keep them separated. We may well see riots or wars over food and water in coming years.

There are too many people in the world. The US passed 300 million in 2002, has already passed 312 million, should reach 322 million by 2015, and is expected to pass 400 million well before 2050.[8] The world population passed 7 billion in late 2011 and may increase to over 9 billion by mid-century.[9] In developed countries, the birth rate declines which means the populations of most of the industrialized countries are declining creating the disaster that 99 percent of world growth will be in the poorest countries since they are growing three times faster than developed countries. How will Africa cope with another billion people with Congo tripling to 181 million and Nigeria doubling to 307 million? India is estimated to grow to 1.6 billion passing China by 2025 and Pakistan may grow to 349 million by 2050. Women in Yemen have seven children each on average; with over 20 million now, Yemen could pass Russia as one of the most populous nations in the world. But Russia's population is projected to fall by 21% by mid-century and Ethiopia's may triple. Some of the oil producing countries will double in population in 25 years. Yes, they can afford them, but that may mean they will need more oil at home and less to export adding to our energy woes.[10] All of these will potentially have serious impacts on economic and security polices.

> **Man's greatest pollution of Earth is the flood of additional human beings.**

One of the more interesting, or unusual, proposals was a thesis written by Audrey Tomason, Obama's Director for Counterterrorism, entitled "Apocalypse Equation." She claimed that the world population has been "artificially inflated" over the past century by a global economy based on petrochemicals and fossil fuels that was "non-sustainable" and if left "unchecked" could possibly destroy all life on Earth. She felt the "sustainable population" of our planet could only be 1.5 billion human beings. She wrote that a population suffering an economic collapse and reverting to "Basic Needs" would be "ungovernable" and pose "tremendous risks" to the state leading to "wholesale breakdown of law and order." Thus the collapse of civilization would be "inevitable" and world leaders should consider the possibility of "mass genocide" to reduce our world's population to a more "sustainable level commensurate with our Earth's resources." That would be done by limited nuclear war and the use of chemical and biological agents. As chilling as this proposal is, it does recognize that perhaps there are too many people on Earth and that it is a critical subject that needs to be addressed.

Over two centuries ago Thomas Malthus inspired society to think about the problems of unbridled population growth, but our understanding of this problem has been minimal. In 1944 before the end of World War II, the *Encyclopedia Britannica* estimated the world population to be 1.9 billion and projected that it would increase to 4 billion by 2031. But the figures are quite different. At the time of the Black Death, 1350, there were about 370 million people. It took until 1804 to reach 1 billion and another 123 years to reach 2 billion in 1927. Then it started accelerating: 33 years to 1960 for 3 billion, 14 years to 1974 for 4 billion (the above estimate was off by 57 years!), 13 years to 1987 for 5 billion, 12 years to 1999 for 6 billion, and 12 years to 2011 for 7 billion. One estimate is for 8 billion by 2027 and 9 billion by 2046. But it is difficult to be optimistic about the projection of 9 billion by mid-century and the unbelievable demands that will ensue for food, water, infrastructure, energy, jobs, and services.

The largest growing sector of the population is the poor. Poverty is still extensive: 1 billion people live on less than $1 per day and 2 billion on less than $2 a day. That is why the doubling of food prices is a disaster for them. What is required is elimination of poverty, increased access to schooling and jobs, and population control policies. Yet domestic politics by anti-abortion advocates blocked US support for such needed policies. Under President George W. Bush, $34 million was withheld from the UN Population Fund and then the US withdrew from the 1994 Program of Action which had been adopted in Cairo by 179 nations because the terms "reproductive services" and "reproductive health care" implied a right to abortion.[11]

Population control must be an integral part of any development strategy. Unfortunately, the abortion issue has been taken over by radicals on both sides; yet polls have repeatedly shown that a majority of Americans support a woman's right to choose. Birth control is a major requirement in the world and the US must support it. It is a vital issue for the West as well as for the Third World. The monumental change, at least in perception, is that the women in the Third World want to practice birth control. There have been significant birth-rate declines in a number of countries due to great efforts by the UN and other agencies.

The Catholic Church, unfortunately, has never been helpful in this need with its prohibition on contraception. The Hispanic world is heavily Catholic so it has only aggravated the problem. A lower birth rate in the Third World would yield dramatic results. It was not a "white man's plot" to reduce the number of "coloreds," but the only way they were going to be able to make it in this century. The enormous strain on resources which adds to political and social chaos would be lessened. Poverty would be reduced and living standards should rise.

Consequently, the Third World would likely be more stable and less dangerous for its people and for the rest of the world.

One of the strictest population control programs in the world is in China with its over 1.34 billion people, but even with its authoritarian government which can impose edicts, it has had troubles. Despite much opposition, particularly in the rural areas, the government renewed its program of only one child per family in an effort to hold the growth rate to 1 percent and yet births still exceeded deaths.   We noted in Chapter 11 problems with this policy and a pilot program to relax it due to their aging population.

Does every person have the *"right"* to have as many children as he or she wishes?

The Chinese Government position of permitting only one child per family raises some interesting questions. In the hunting, nomadic, and agrarian phases of man's evolution, there was never any consideration of limiting the number of children. But now in the post-Industrial Age, perhaps the question should be asked. Does every person have the **right** to have as many children as he or she wishes?

There has been mention of restricting the insane and carriers of certain diseases or genetic defects from reproducing. Fortunately, we did not reach the age of Big Brother in *1984*. But almost every aspect of our lives is controlled now: we have to have a Social Security card (even a baby), we have to have certain shots to go to school, we have to have a license to drive a car or fly an airplane, we need a license to get married, we cannot drink or vote until a certain age, we may even have to pass a drug test to get a job.

Yet a teenage girl can have a baby if she wants to and a poor woman can keep having babies and there is no license required! There is no test to determine if she is mentally capable, whether she is on drugs or has AIDS, whether there will be a father for this child, whether she has the money to have the baby, the money to raise the baby for the next 20 years. In other words, she does not have to have anyone's permission to bring a new person onto this planet who will cost several hundred thousand dollars to support, require a complete infrastructure including hospitals, day care if she ever works, schools, food service, clothing, housing, utilities, entertainment, courts, jails, transportation, roads, and hopefully a job for this new soul who may live 80 or 90 years.

There is no "right" to pollute the world with unneeded, and often unwanted, babies.

Should we subsidize children or poor women having babies? If the government can force bikers to wear a helmet because it might be a liability to taxpayers, should there be a ban on single motherhood which is potentially a much greater societal cost? This is a monumental decision that impacts on every taxpayer. Perhaps it is time to reconsider whether she has that **right.** This is certainly more significant than driving a car. Yes, she could kill someone with a car, so we make her get a license. But offspring from poor mothers have a high probability of killing someone too. These are some of the punks who will go into a life of crime or join a gang and kill people.

We treat animals with more logic. We cull herds of wildlife so they do not exceed their habitat and starve to death. We have programs to neuter our cats and dogs, but we still have too many and put millions to sleep each year. We cannot start putting our excess humans to sleep, so we had better get to work now to stop having too many born before we destroy our own world due to our stupidity and lack of discipline!

Freedom and individual rights have always needed to be balanced by responsibilities and their impact on other people's rights. We agree on freedom of speech but still agree that one cannot falsely yell "Fire" in a crowded theater.

The question is does the government have to protect you from yourself? The people of the world in general and the US in particular seem to think they have a god-given right to act like idiots. The problem comes when that act affects you or me. I contend that we are all vested in the population issue, both in our country and around the world, and therefore it dramatically impinges my freedom and your freedom. There is no "right" to pollute the world with unneeded, and often unwanted, babies.

Many studies over the years have shown that improvements in the level of education in a country result in lower birth rates. A World Bank study showed that educating girls as well as boys may be the best investment for the future for developing countries. Providing women with even an elementary education raises the living standard in poor countries. The changes are that they have fewer children, take better care of the ones they have, work better at home, and earn more on jobs or when they market their crops.

> **If you want to change the world, invest in girls. Investment in girls' education may well be the highest return investment available in the developing world.**[12]

There are many obstacles to educating girls in many countries, such as we saw with the Taliban. Some have to go to extremely poor quality schools with little or no facilities. Some cultures think that school encourages promiscuity because they see it as Western liberal education which encourages sexuality. Cost is a problem for some and in other countries even the smallest girls are expected to help their mothers. There is a very strong conclusion that investment in education of girls may well yield the highest return available in the developing world.

A large percentage of the world's population is young. For example, the median age in Yemen is 17.89 with 35% jobless and 45.2% below the poverty line. In the West Bank and Gaza, the media age is 20.9 with 16.5% jobless and 46% below the poverty line.[13] As these billions of young people enter their reproductive years, there will the threat of worsening economic distress in developing countries, the threat of more immigration, and the threat of them turning to radicals. According to Werner Fornos, president of the Population Institute, "Failure to address the population problem may be the ultimate global blunder."

Historically, the population of mankind has been kept in check by disease, war, and famine. Modern medicine has put a brake on disease except that AIDS has set us back a bit. We have tried to reduce war and the breadbasket of the US has slowed famine, but the biofuels nonsense may soon remove that buffer. But the consequences of overpopulation are more than famine and possibly migration. The economic pressures can lead to political upheaval and potentially to violence either internally or spilling over internationally.

As Georgie Anne Geyer wrote, "There is no question that overpopulation is the major factor in creating young and deliberately suicidal terrorists – yet we refuse to embrace the long-range policy of helping the world contain its population….There is no question that no country can rise beyond endless poverty and develop without, at the very least, controlling its population so it will not outstrip its economic capacity and so it can be correlated to economic changes."[14]

The increasing pressures of population in less developed countries will leave us with few options, particularly if their effects spread over into our spheres of economic interest or draw us into wars. We will be forced to abandon our pious policies and lead a world effort to reduce population, starting with our own.

Global Aging

Democratic trends have been important in many political upheavals, migrations, invasions, and environmental catastrophes in history. A new trend which can cause disruption and affect living standards, economic growth, and the future world order is global aging. Aging, population decline, and falling birth rates are hitting the developed nations. The median ages of Japan and Western Europe were 33 and 34 in 1980 but will rise to 52 and 47 by 2030 according to the UN Population Division (their figures will be used in this section). Italy, Japan, and Spain will have half their adults older than the retirement age and "there will be more people in their 70s than in their 20s." The working-age population is already contracting in some countries, Germany and Japan, and will in all developed countries except the US. At present rates, Japan and some countries in Europe will lose half their population by 2100. Japan is projected to lose 30% of its population by 2060 dropping from 128 million to 90 million with two-fifths over age 65.[15]

> **Two-thirds of all people who ever lived past 65 are alive today!**

This threatens to impact on the developed nations' ability to maintain world security. With working-age populations contracting by 0.5 to 1.5% annually, growth in GDP could stagnate or decline. The increase in pensions and health care costs could add 7% of GDP to government budgets by 2030. Russia's population will implode and China will have a massive age wave. China's one-child policy served them well but by the 2020s, the generation before the fertility decline will retire putting great pressure on their children and the state. Russia, and Eastern Europe, will be in a steep population decline and with Russia falling from 4th place to 16th in world population.

The Muslim world is projected to grow from 1.6 billion to 2.2 billion by 2030 with a world "youth bulge" of 29% of those ages 15 to 29 and their aspirations are not likely to be met. As Indonesia has prospered, its birth rate has fallen but South Asia's is still high. Pakistan is expected to add 80 million people to 256 million in less than 20 years, surpassing Indonesia at 239 million. India's Muslim minority will grow to 236 million while Nigeria's Muslims will increase from 76 million to 117 million. Referring back to the education of girls, illiteracy is 71.9% among Nigerian women of child-bearing age; they average six to seven children and two-thirds lack any formal education. The US Muslim population is slated to increase from 2.6 million to 6.2 million.[16] We have already noted the problems of Eurabia. By 2030, the percentages of Muslims will double in France and triple in Germany and some major cities may have Muslim majorities. We noted in Chapter 5 how Muslim minorities move toward Islamization as their percentages increase. Ethnic tensions are likely to grow which can lead to increased extremism. Chronic unrest is likely in countries like Afghanistan, Palestine, Somalia, Sudan, and Yemen. Pakistan and Iran are both slated to see a leap in the 15 to 24 age group which should stress an already strained social fabric. One is unstable and is already a nuclear power and the other seeks regional hegemony and seems well on the nuclear path.

> **All told, population trends point inexorably toward a more dominant US role in a world that will need America more, not less.**

Demography is the geopolitical cartography of the 21st century. Even though GDP of the developed countries will drop as part of the world total, the US will fare better than the others. Six of the top twelve most populous countries in 1950 were developed countries; by 2000 only three. By 2050, there will be only one – the US still in third place – and "it will be the only country among the top twelve committed since its founding to democracy, free markets, and civil liberties."[17]

Perhaps the greatest disservice ever done to much of the world was to provide advanced medicine without tying it to the cultural problems it generated. Agricultural societies have traditionally had large families to add hands for the fields and because many of the babies never survived to adulthood, and in most societies children were looked to for caring for parents in old age. As societies became more urban, industrialized, and educated, their birth rates declined.

> **Demographic change may be even more menacing to the security prospects of the Western alliance than was the cold war for the past generation.**
>
> **- Nicholas Eberstadt**

In that humanitarian zeal to do good through better nutrition and healthcare, many diseases were reduced and babies were helped to survive resulting in the extension of lives of many millions of people, yet unwittingly creating a new problem of burgeoning population that governments were unable to support. This extension of the human life span is best exemplified by the statistic that "One million people cross the 60-year mark every month, and of them, 80 percent live in the developing world." The fastest growing segment is those over 80, some 70 million projected to rise to 350 million by mid-century, which will be about 20 percent of the aged. Before the turn of the last century the number of aged exceeded the number of children (up to age 14). "The potential support ratio (PSR) is the number of persons between the age of 15 and 64 to one older person aged 65 years or above." This reflects the dependency burden for the future. In the last half of the 20th century it fell from 12 to 9. By mid-century, it is expected to fall to four working age people to one 65 or older.[18] Life spans are now nearly 30 years longer than at the beginning of the last century.

Food - Famine

At the same time that the world is faced with ever growing population, the sad truth is that we are finding that there is less food. The supply of fish, meat, and grain is lower than it was in the early 1990s which signaled that population growth was outpacing the food available for humans.[19] Back in 1998, a study reported that a third of the world's resources had been lost in the past 25 years. "The number of creatures in the seas and oceans over the 25-year period studied dropped by an estimated 30 percent, while about 10 percent of the world's natural forest cover was lost."[20] Despite the technological advances in crop yields, a Stanford report states "half the world's population faces major food crisis by 2100." On top of that, there is less land: "about 5 million to 8 million hectares of the world's total of 1.5 billion (3.7 billion acres) of farmland goes fallow each year because of deteriorating quality."[21] We have already mentioned the water problem.

Food supplies had increased for decades but have slowed down. The main sources of food, which are farms, livestock ranches, and oceanic fisheries, have reached their maximum per-capita output. World meat production per person has fallen and the peak harvest of 100 million tons of fish taken from the sea in 1989 has not been seen since. Grain production has not kept pace with growing demand. Growth in cropland area, water supplies, and fertilizer use are also not keeping up. The world is losing almost 18 million acres of cultivable land annually according to the FAO – that is about the size of Ireland. According to a study at Cornell, erosion is destroying about 29 million acres of farm land annually. Topsoil cannot be replaced quickly and it is being lost about 17 times faster than nature replaces it. They estimated that it takes about 1.2 acres to feed one person a varied diet for one year. However, with 7 billion people, there is only 0.53 acre per person available now worldwide. If we get to 9 billion people, the available land will be down to 0.41 acre per person.

Are we going to have enough good land to feed the extra 2.6 billion people who will be on this planet by the year 2025?

Edouard Saouma, Director General FAO

Some land is being lost due to man's actions as areas are turned into blacktop by urbanization. In China alone in the last 10 years, 3 million hectares of rice land have been lost to concrete. The Sahara Desert continues to advance relentlessly forward. Part of the reason is that the people along the edges cut the bushes and trees for firewood for cooking. Without the ground cover, the desert quickly advances. Even in the early 1990s, the director of the FAO said, "Land degradation is now proceeding so rapidly that few African countries can hope to achieve sustainable agriculture in the near future, while serious food consequences could eventually be felt as well in Latin America and Asia….This raises a fundamental question: Are we going to have enough good land to feed the extra 2.6 billion people who will be on this planet by the year 2025?"[22]

Poppy farmers in Afghanistan need to shift to wheat farming or other crops instead of supporting the drug world. China is buying corn from the US and is buying farmland in Africa and building railroads and infrastructure to move grains to market. The prices of the three world food staples (corn, rice, and wheat) are shooting up with one report saying they may rise 120% to 180% by 2030. The estimated increases without climate change (with climate change in parentheses) are: paddy rice 72% (107%), wheat 53% (82%), maize 71% (126%), and processed rice 34% (48%). This affects some 926 million undernourished people, about one in seven in the world.[23]

This global food crisis, which Niels Jensen called "a silent tsunami," threatens to undermine global political and economic stability. People in the poorest countries spend 80 percent of their income on food, which makes for a vast difference compared to people with adequate incomes.[24] Even in China, they spend 33% of their income on food and 35% in India. Some of the figures are quite high: Tunisia 36%, Egypt 38%, Nigeria 40%, Indonesia 43%, Belarus 43%, Kenya 45%, Pakistan 46%.[25] Food prices continued to rise and there were food riots in some 30 countries. Rice tripled in price in six months during oil price surges. The cost of oil impacts food prices from plowing fields to pesticides and fertilizers, to harvesting to hauling food to market. Food is a relatively inelastic commodity in terms of demand; people still must eat no matter how bad the economy is, thus it is basically a function of population. Food shortages are likely to continue to worsen and eventually become a global food crisis.[26]

Food shortages are likely to continue to worsen and eventually become a global food crisis.

How did we arrive at this global food crisis? The major cause, which we could see coming, was the continued growth in population, to which should be added increased income, resulting in increased demand for food and feed grains. But there are other culprits. In the poorest countries, lack of means to pay for seeds, fertilizers, and irrigation caused chronic low productivity. Higher yields require more fertilizer, but since fertilizer production is petro-chemical dependent, the fivefold increase of the cost of oil closed out that option for many. In many places, less acreage was planted, down 12 percent in the former Soviet Union for example. In many of those large producers, productivity was not high: grain yields in Kazakhstan were 1.1 tons per hectare, 1.8 tons in Russia, and 2.4 tons in Ukraine, compared to 6.4 tons in the US.

Next is the misguided (some say stupid) policy in both Europe and the US of diverting food crops to make biofuels, particularly ethanol made from corn. It takes 232 kg of corn to produce the ethanol to fill an average 50 liter car gas tank – that is enough corn to feed a child for an entire year.

Water is critical. According to the UN, water use globally has increased six fold over the last century, twice the population growth rate, with inefficient agricultural systems the biggest drain. Climate change, water or lack thereof, such as the droughts in Australia and Europe, cut grain production in 2005 and 2006 and in the US in 2011. Severe drought in Australia, one of the world's largest grain producers, cut production by 50 percent from the previous year. China has a serious problem with water depletion, land erosion, and poor fertility. Having been one of the world's major grain exporters, China is now a major importer. China abandoned its biofuel program due to water shortage and it was not cost effective. Saudi Arabia was running out of water and was closing down its domestic agriculture industry and would soon be a total food importer.

One third of the world population is in China and India and with their dynamic economies, they are able to buy more pricey foods such as meat. Meat consumption in China has more than doubled since 1980 and the consumption of milk has tripled with the expected result that more grain was diverted to feeding livestock reducing that available for feeding people. Japan has also moved to more of a meat based diet. The change is significant because "it takes over 3 kg of corn to produce 1 kg of pork and over 8 kg of corn to produce just 1 kg of beef!"

Governments grew complacent and permitted food stocks to dwindle. In the US, wheat inventories were the lowest since the late 1940s when the population was only half the current level. Rice stocks were at the lowest level since 1976 and 3 billion people in Asia rely on rice as their staple food. With reduced stocks, some countries felt compelled to reduce exports to protect their own supplies, further driving up prices. Asian countries are large importers of both food and oil. The problem reached the level of concern that the World Bank was predicting food riots in over 30 countries worldwide.[27]

What could be done to deal with this global food shortage? First would be to stop subsidizing the conversion of food grains, mainly corn, into fuel. We are taking food from people to fill gas tanks. Second, make fertilizer and high yield seeds available to the farmers in poor countries. The example of Malawi could be used where they established a special fund to assist farmers obtain high yield seeds and fertilizer and their harvest doubled in one year. Such an international fund could be established at a cost of perhaps only $10 billion, small compared to the crisis. Farmers need help for protection against drought; farm ponds to collect rainwater being one solution. A Climate Adaptation Fund has been offered but not implemented.[28]

The **"green revolution"** of the 1950s greatly increased food productivity, but it does not appear that we will be able to repeat that miracle. One promising but controversial area is genetically modified crops. Genetically modified rice, corn, cotton, soybeans, etc. to provide better yields or protect against infestations offer great hope but many people are scared of them and some governments oppose their import.[29] This is probably the best hope for the future.

If we are all going to survive and thrive in this world of 7 billion people, we will need to cultivate the seas just as we do the land.

One of the more optimistic areas is fish farming, called **aquaculture**. It is not new in that the Chinese have had fishponds for over 4,000 years but only in the past 50 years has it become a true industry with production growing from under 1 million tons in 1950 to over 52 million tons in 2008. Now about half the seafood consumed comes from farms. The annual world catch has plateaued at about 90 million tons while annual per capita consumption has gone from 22 pounds to 38 pounds (133 million tons). There just is not enough seafood in the seas. According to the UN, 32% of world stocks are overexploited or depleted with 90% of some large fish like tuna and marlin fished out. The UN projected that world food production needs to double by 2050 to meet demand. Since seafood is a good source of protein, fish farming appears unavoidable. China is the world leader with 61% of aquaculture. The US has a trade deficit for seafood of $9 billion, second only to oil. About 84% of US seafood consumption is imported, half from aquaculture. Efforts are underway to improve efficiency, develop better fish, and reduce pollution. One of the new fish is the barramundi, which is a vegetarian so it does not consume fish meal, is high in omega-3 oil, and tastes good![30] Since we are told to eat more fish, it seems that aquaculture will surely be part of our future.

This food crisis will likely lead to famine in some countries. Mankind has known famine across the centuries. In the 1930s, it was the poor, starving children in China. In recent years, it has been famine in the Sahel in Africa. There were repeated famines in the Sudan due to both the long civil war and the lack of infrastructure whereby crops regularly rot in one part of the country because of the lack of transportation to move them to another part. Thousands starved in Angola during that war. Similarly, the Bosnian Muslims were cut off from food and the US even parachuted food to them. Somalia has been in anarchy for over 20 years and the US committed troops in 1992 when the warlords were stealing, extorting, or blocking the shipments of food. Now it is Somalia again and the clans fight over food. The US withheld food aid to the al-Shabaab area because of its ties to al Qaeda and for fighting the official Transitional Federal Government.[31]

A columnist had some perceptive comments about Somalia at the time of Blackhawk Down. After seeing the photo of a dead US soldier being dragged through the streets of Mogadishu, her angry reaction, like most Americans, was:

"The hell with all of them. Let's pull our troops out and let 'em starve." However, she had pangs of guilt since she recalled other photos that showed "stick-figure women with stick-figure babies at their dry breasts and more starving stick-figure children at their bony feet. **Damn! If you can't feed the children you have, why have more? If we're going to send flour and milk, toss in some birth control pills, for Pete's sake.**"[32]

We have been called upon repeatedly to send relief to famines in Africa. Even recently we have seen poor people forced to eat dirt pancakes.[33] Some famines were caused by poor governments such as in Ethiopia, Sudan, Somalia, and North Korea. Starvation is a terrible fate. Who can forget the horrible photograph in *Time* (23 August 1993) of a naked Sudanese man walking on all fours with a totally emaciated body reminiscent of the pictures of the survivors of Auschwitz? We do not treat animals like that. No human being should suffer like fate.

Our politicians need to show some responsibility for a change and deal with the problems of energy and water. World leaders must address the problems of overpopulation and the inability to feed their peoples. There are only limited options: migration out of the areas, population reduction, or agricultural improvements. All cost money, require education, and are difficult to implement.

Unemployment

Another product of overpopulation is unemployment. We have observed around the globe that the world cannot provide productive work for its young as well as much of the older population. Unemployment figures stay in double digits throughout the Third World. Much of the Third World has not industrialized. It has not been able to create jobs for its millions of new people. In many ways, the major crop of some of these countries has been people, but as more of them have left the land and moved to cities, there is nothing for them to do.[34] We have even seen industrialized countries in Europe run unemployment over 10 percent. Employment in the US is over 9% (more like 15% when the people who have given up are counted) and Nevada is at 14%. There are well over one billion people who cannot find a job or find enough work to make ends meet. The pressure on society will only increase as we add billions more to our Earth. The figures are staggering. According to a World Bank study, the nations of the Middle East and North Africa alone will need to create 100 million jobs by 2020; that is double their current employment level and less than 10 years away.[35]

Teenage boys and young men stand idly on street corners from Cairo to Colombo, from Oslo to Capetown, from London to Tashkent, from Havana to Buenos Aires, and from New York to Los Angeles. They are candidates for the gangs and radical movements of the world who will have them if no one else will. As young disasters waiting to happen, they become key to the questions of war or peace.

In search of employment to support families, many people go to other countries to work and send money back home. These remittances, about $240 billion, are extremely important in some economies. For several countries, remittances as a part of GDP exceeded 25 percent: for 2006 both Tajikistan and Moldova the figure was 36.2 percent, 27.4 percent for Kyrgyzstan, 32.3 percent for Tonga, and 25.6 percent for Honduras. In Mexico, remittances are second only to oil sales in the national economy.[36]

There were riots in South Africa against foreigners, many of whom were refugees from the economic collapse in Zimbabwe. South Africans were already struggling with high food prices and high unemployment. They were frustrated at the government's inaction but took it out on foreigners who they felt took scarce jobs and housing. Competition for scarce resources will only get worse and blaming crime and unemployment on immigrants has been a common practice around the world.[37]

Social values have been weakening on every level. The threat is that wars of the future may not be so much soldiers' wars on borders, but people's wars involving migration or internal ethnic conflicts. There does not appear to be any likelihood that enough jobs can be created to keep pace with the flood of population.

Disease

Disease was a constant threat to early man and it served as a brake on runaway population growth. There were many different diseases that were chronic keeping the average life span rather short. There were also devastating plagues that struck from time to time such as the Black Death, or bubonic plague, which swept eastward across Europe starting in 1347, lasting about 50 years and killing more than half the population in some places in just a few months.

In addition to the rather common diseases that were around, we remember from the history books the outbreaks of cholera, yellow fever, and tuberculosis. Advances in medicine slowly put an end to them to the point where now cases of such diseases are news. However, there is a new flu virus every couple years and about every 20 years a super-virus appears such as ebola in Zaire. The flu epidemic of 1918 killed 30 million people, several times as many as World War I.

Perhaps half the world's people are sick at any one time and many die from easily preventable diseases. "Poverty is the world's deadliest disease." Poverty, poor sanitation, and lack of medical facilities in the Third World still leave many people exposed to diseases but not to the extent of population control.

Is it moral to save a person from AIDS so that he can starve to death?   Maybe contraception measures should be as important as those against AIDS.

However, we have one disease which may kill millions – AIDS (Acquired Immune Deficiency Syndrome). AIDS first appeared in Africa in the 1970s, spread across that continent and with the modern mobile world of aviation, it soon spread around the world. It was bad in Uganda but worse in Botswana where about 40 percent of people from 15 to 49 were infected and the population was projected to decline by 43 percent by 2050 to under 1 million.[38] AIDS was a major problem in South Africa with about 1,000 dying daily, with some 5.4 million infected out of a population of 48 million. However, they finally were making progress with a major treatment program.[39]

It appeared that AIDS would remain with us for some time; however progress had been made to control it. It had raised moral questions as to whether it was "God's punishment for immoral behavior" or just another cycle of nature. Should medical cures be provided without complementary policies to reduce population growth?[40]

Migration

Another product of overpopulation or a result of its pressure is migration. We have seen the mass migrations from the rural to the urban areas. Some were accelerated by civil wars, such as in Uganda. There was the sad case of a 9 year old boy who had been chipping rocks into gravel 12 hours daily to make 18 cents.[41] It is estimated that between 1820 and 1925, over 33,000,000 people left Europe and settled in the United States. People can migrate voluntarily due to lack of job opportunities, persecution, or just searching for a better life; or they can be forced as refugees as we saw millions displaced as a result of World War II and most other wars, including the Palestinians after the creation of Israel.

In the early years of the US, immigrants were welcomed to build and expand the country. Now they are not as welcome, particularly many of the illegal immigrants who do not intend to assimilate. The subject of illegal immigration has become white hot in the US as we have seen.

We have already discussed immigration in Europe, but there was still more migration westward as more nations joined the EU. The largest numbers were from Poland to Germany and from Romania to Italy and Spain.[42] Even Israel was facing illegal immigrants from Africa, mostly from Eritrea, and planned to deport them.[43] Not all of Latin America's emigrants go to the US. Perhaps half of the Brazilians in the US are illegal, but many also go to Europe for work. Their goal is not to live in Europe but to make enough money to return home and build a home and business.[44] Both Argentina and Brazil have thousands of illegal immigrants, many who left Bolivia, South America's poorest country, to find work. Argentina had 750,000 illegals from Bolivia as well as Paraguay and Peru.[45]

Canada's liberal immigration policies led to a Muslim community of 750,000, with about 40 percent Shiite. Relations grew more tense after arrests of some Muslims for suspected terrorist activities.[46] In many of the African countries, unemployment is so high that many working age men try to go to Europe, particularly Italy, for work. In some villages of Senegal, the men are only home for a couple months around August leaving their wives and children behind while they work in Europe. Senegal is fairly typical of Africa: over half its people live below the poverty line and about half the population is unemployed."[47]

As should be expected, one country's solution may become another country's problem. Thus, when millions of people leave a country, that government may be relieved of the burden of housing, feeding, clothing, educating, caring for, and providing jobs for them. But those requirements devolve on the receiving country and if its economy is weak, then it may not look favorably on all those immigrants, particularly if they are poor, illiterate, or unskilled and do not assimilate easily due to cultural, racial, religious, or language differences.

Small numbers can almost always be absorbed easily and quickly, but an influx of very large numbers strains all the infrastructure and facilities of an economy. If that economy is already fragile, then there is the possibility of serious backlash against the newcomers leading to xenophobia.

An additional problem is the emigration of the educated or skilled, often called "brain drain." This often results from those who go to other countries for education and then decide that there is little future or life is not too good at home so they emigrate to that country. Of course, that robs the home country of one of the key ingredients it needs for progress, more educated people.

The sad situation is that because of the size of the world population now, there is no suitable place for refugees or migrants to go. Once again, the concept of freedom can be overstretched. The "right" of one person to move and live where he desires is possible to accommodate. However, movement of millions of people can destabilize governments. Infrastructure, food, schools, hospitals, housing, and jobs cannot be instantly created.

Migration will not end but it is not a solution to overpopulation. There are no more great empty spaces for people to go to for a new life. Any large movement of people only shifts the problem from one government to another and may result in conflict.

The question of the overpopulation of the world is very sensitive yet it may be the most crucial problem of the century. The significance is that population problems can become security problems leading to tensions or even wars. For that reason alone, we need to address these problems.

If the population of China walked past you in single file, the line would never end because of the rate of reproduction.

Notes

1. Fareed Zakaria, "The Hard Truth About Going 'Soft'," *Time,* 17 October 2011, p. 26.
2. Paul Klocko, Wausau, WI, Muth's Truths, 6 July 2004.
3. *Washington Times,* 28 March 2004.
4. http://washingtonexaminer.com/politics/2011/07/Wisconsin-schools-buck-union-cut-health-costs.
5. Porter Stansberry, "New American Socialism," Stansberry's Investment Advisory, June 2011.
6. Lev Grossman, "sin·gu·lar·i·ty." *Time,* 21 February 2011, p. 43.
7. "United States Security and the Strategic Landscape," Business Executives for National Security, Washington, D.C, 15 May 2008.
8. The projection is for 438 million by 2050 driven by the Hispanic population which will double. Haya El Nasser, USA Today, "Hispanic population surge to drive U.S. growth," *Reno Gazette-Journal,* 12 February 2008, p. 1B.
9. The world projections for 2050 are: Africa 1.9 B, Asia 5.2 B, Europe 674 M, Latin America & Caribbean 765 M, and North America 448 M.
10. Harry Dunphy, AP, "World population growth ensured for many decades," *Reno Gazette-Journal,* 24 August 2005, p. 6C. "Global   population could swell to 9 billion by 2050, report says," *Reno Gazette-Journal,* 23 July 2003, p. 1A. David R. Francis, "The Mideast 'Bomb' No One Talks About," *Christian Science Monitor,* 4 November 2004. "The world in 2050: Expect Big Population Shifts," *Time,* 11 July 2011.

    Stephen Ohlemacher, AP, "U.S. population swells as other nations thin out," *Reno Gazette-Journal,* 6 July 2006, p. 4C. Haya El Nasser and Paul Overg, "Fertility rate in USA on upswing," *USA Today,* 20 December 2007, p. 1A. Mike Stobbe, AP, "Baby boomlet sees largest number of births in 45 years," *Reno Gazette-Journal,* 16 January 2008, p.7C.

    Chinese are older and more urbanized than Indians. The median age in China is 35.5, India 26.2; urban population 47% in China, 30% in India; life expectancy in China 73, India 64. "Still No. 1 – but Not for Much Longer," *Time,* 16 May 2011, p. 13.
11. Knight Ridder, "U.S. to withhold $34M from family planning program," *Reno Gazette-Journal,* 20 July 2002, p. 5A. David Broder, "U.S. move to withhold money costs lives," *Reno Gazette-Journal,* 5 August 2002, p. 9A. Jodi Enda, Knight Ridder, "Bush administration backs away from reproductive health pact," *Reno Gazette-Journal,* 2 November 2002, p. 4A.
12. Nancy Gibbs, "The Best Investment," *Time,* 14 February 2011, p. 64. "An extra year of primary school boosts girls' eventual wages by 10% to 20%. An extra year of secondary school adds 15% to 25%. Girls who stay in school for seven or more years typically marry four years later and have two fewer children than girls who drop out."
13. Middle East social indicators, CIA World Factbook, 27 January 2011.
14. Georgie Geyer, "Powell comment on condoms highlights schism in administration," *Reno Gazette-Journal,* 24 February 2002, p. 13C.
15. Neil Howe and Richard Jackson, "Global Aging and the Crisis of the 2020s," *Current History,* January 2011. *Time,* 13 February 2012, p. 14.
16. Pew Research Center, "The Future of the Global Muslim Population," in Print Edition, 27 January 2011.
17. Neil Howe and Richard Jackson, "Global Aging and the Crisis of the 2020s," *Current History,* January 2011.
18. Parvathi Menon, "Growing Old – Staying Young," *Frontline* (Independent biweekly), Chennai, India, 10 May 2002, reprinted in *World Press Review,* August 2002, p. 20.
19. See Joshua Schneyer, "Brazil's Answer to Global Hunger," *Business Week,* 2 June 2008, p. 72. They are rapidly expanding soy bean production but at a cost to the rain forest of the Amazon.
20. "Study: A third of world's resources lost in 25 years," *Reno Gazette-Journal,* 2 October 1998, p. 5A.

    Another major loss is in the big cats – lions, leopards, tigers, and cheetahs. "Biologists have documented that removal of top predators from wild settings almost inevitably leads to prey numbers to explode…Without top predators, booming prey populations soon strip vegetation and later collapse from illnesses and starvation." This also applies to wolves, tiger sharks, and sea otters. Dan Vergano, USA TODAY, "Efforts urged to save the big cats," *Reno Gazette-Journal,* 28 October 2011, p. 1C.
21. Nick Hodge, "Moo, Says the Bull," Energy & Capital, 28 September 2011.
22. See Richard Hobbs, *You and the New World Order,* (Sparks, Nevada, ColDoc Publishing, 1995), pp. 145-146. Another potential source is bugs. See Bryan Walsh, "Eating Bugs: They're packed with protein and environmentally friendlier than other meat. But can greenies kick the ick factor?" *Time,* 9 June 2008, p. 47.
23. "World Faces Epic Food Crisis," *Time,* 13 June 2011, p. 15 The 926 million undernourished are: developed countries 19 M, Near East and North Africa 37 M, Latin America and Caribbean 53 M, Sub-Saharan Africa 239 M, and Asia 578 M.
24. Niels Jensen, "Food for Thought," InvestorsInsight, John Mauldin's "Outside The Box," 14 May 2008.
25. "A Hungry World," *Time,* 28 February 2011, p. 19.
26. "7 Reasons Food Shortages Will Become a Global Crisis," Activist Post, 7 January 2011.
27. Jackson Dykman, "Why the World Can't Afford Food," *Time,* 19 May 2008, p. 34. With oil cost up five times, the global food price index more than doubled so far in this century. AP, "Global population could swell to 9 billion by 2050, report says," *Reno Gazette-Journal,* 23 July 2003, p. 1A. Jensen, "Food for Thought." "Governments in India, Thailand, Vietnam, Argentina, Cambodia, China and Egypt have all imposed export controls in order to secure domestic needs." Jensen pointed out that making ethanol from corn particularly since US producers rely heavily on fertilizers was quite inefficient. "33,000 cubic feet of natural gas are required to produce just 1 ton of ammonia!... According to Goldman Sachs, the cost of ethanol from corn is now over $80 per barrel, it is about $145 from wheat and over $230 from soybeans. Other countries recognized this problem a long time ago and use crops with higher carbon hydrate content. In the Philippines they use coconut oil and the Brazilians use sugar cane. Goldman reckons that the cost of one barrel of ethanol based on sugar cane is about $35. So why not import sugar cane from Brazil instead of using corn? One simple answer: Brazilian farmers do not vote at American elections. Idaho farmers do."

28. Jeffrey D. Sachs, "Act Now, Eat Later." *Time,* 5 May 2008, p. 44.
29. J. Madeleine Nash, "Grains of Hope," *Time,* 31 January 2000, p. 39.
30. Bryan Walsh, "The End of the Line," *Time*, 18 July 2011, p. 29.
31. Alex Perry, "A Famine We Made," *Time,* 5 September 2011, p. 40.
32. See Hobbs, *You and the New World Order,* p. 147.
33. See Anita Powell, AP, "Hunger in Ethiopian spreading to adults," *Reno Gazette-Journal,* 10 June 2008, p. 2B. Jonathan M. Katz, AP, "Haiti's poor resort to eating dirt," *Reno Gazette-Journal,* 20 June 2008, p. 7C.
34. There has been "explosive growth of cities worldwide" with about 50 percent of the world's population living in urban areas, about 75 percent in advanced countries. Richard Florida, "The World Is Spiky," *The Atlantic Monthly,* October 2006, p. 48.
35. David R. Francis, "The Mideast 'Bomb' No One Talks About," *Christian Science Monitor,* 4 November 2004.
36. "Work In, Cash Out," Time, *19 May 2008,* p. 14.
37. Celean Jacobson, AP, "Riots against foreigners kill 12," *Reno Gazette-Journal,* 19 May 2008, p. 2B. Donna Bryson, AP, "Slums erupt over immigration," *Reno Gazette-Journal,* 20 May 2008, p. 1B. "Groups help attacked migrants," *Reno Gazette-Journal,* 21 May 2008, p. 2C.
38. AP, "Global population could swell to 9 billion by 2050, report says," *Reno Gazette-Journal,* 23 July 2003, p. 1A.
39. Clare Nullis, AP, "South Africa wages intensified war on AIDS," *Reno Gazette-Journal,* 25 May 2008, p. 10C.
40. See Hobbs, *You and the New World Order,* pp. 150-151.
41. Katy Pownall, AP, "Ugandan children work on rock pile," *Reno Gazette-Journal,* 2 June 2008, p. 2B.
42. Aron Heller, AP, "Israel struggles to deal with influx of African refugees," *Reno Gazette-Journal,* 27 February 2008, p. 2C.
43. Alan Clendenning, AP, "Seeking better life at home, Brazilians head abroad," *Reno Gazette-Journal,* 31 July 2005, p. 16B.
44. Shayna Chabner, AP, "South America tackles migrant worker issues," *Reno Gazette-Journal,* 6 May 2006, p. 3C.
45. Beth Duff-Brown, AP, "Shiite leader issues fatwa barring violence against innocent Canadians," *Reno Gazette-Journal,* 15 June 2006, p 4C.
46. Heidi Vogt and Marta Falconi, AP, "Migrants struggle with split families, hard living," *Reno Gazette-Journal,* 2 July 2006, p. 14C.

> **If advanced countries make no serious efforts to reduce the unsustainable short work weeks and early retirement, they will have to import workers to maintain the current levels of health benefits and pensions. Such immigration will be Muslims in Europe and Hispanics in the US. Will it be possible for a society to become more Islamic or Hispanic in its demographic character without becoming more Islamic or Hispanic in its political character?**
>
> **If the tax burden on Americans to pay for the spendthrift government in Washington becomes too heavy, the fertility rate will surely fall causing that requirement for imported labor. It is the problem now in Europe and is just a matter of time for the US.**

Conclusion

*Civilization begins with order, grows
with liberty, and dies with chaos.*

\- Will Durant, US Historian (1885-1981)

*I do not love the bright sword for its sharpness,
nor the arrow for its swiftness,
nor the warrior for his glory.
I love only that which they defend.*

\- J. R. Tolkien

      The three most divisive elements in human relations are race, language, and religion. We have dealt with our difficult race relations fairly well over the years. We were doing fairly well on language in this country until recent years when we descended into multiculturalism and felt that it was politically correct for everyone to speak their own languages rather than English. We are now inundated with foreign language TV, radio, and publications plus the endless press 2 for Spanish. As a vast and one time united country, we are weak in foreign languages, especially Arabic. Religion is more difficult in that we tend to be very tolerant but it can be the most brutal. Some of the worst crimes in history have been conducted in the name of religion. Christianity and Judaism reconciled with the evolving modern world in the 16th century separating church from state resulting in the scientific revolution and the greatest advances in human history. Our founders were quite religious but wisely also separated church and state, but it is the crux of our major world threat. When religion enters a political dispute – my God versus your God – logical discourse becomes impossible.

> **The biggest world challenge in the coming decades will be to separate church and state.**

      Islam has been at war with all kafirs since its very beginning with the guidance and actions of Muhammad. Since the end of the Second Jihad on that fateful 9/11 in 1683 at the gates of Vienna, the West has gone forward while Islam has gone backward. Islam has been unable to reconcile with the modern world. Muslims are now almost one fourth of the world's population and they like to claim that Islam is a religion of peace, but there is a fundamental and activist part of Islam based on the actual Islamic texts that uses the façade of "religion" for the Third Jihad with the intention of reestablishing the Caliphate and ruling the world under sharia. Islam was born by the sword and there are certainly enough passages in the Qur'an that they can use to justify their actions in following the example of Muhammad. And there are enough radical imams around the world, including in the US, who preach hatred against all kafirs, including Israel and the United States, and piously rationalize barbarity. This sort of civil war between the orthodox and those trying to become modern within Islam is critical not only to the ideology but to the world. First the Muslims must admit that their totalitarian ideology is motivating the terrorists and then they must have a Reformation of Islam.[1] As Prince Turki Al-Faisal said, "we are not engaged in a clash of civilizations; we are instead engaged in a war for civilization. It is a war that pits all peace-loving people, regardless of their culture or faith, against the forces of darkness."[2]

Perhaps the sword is indicative of basic philosophical and ethical differences between Islam and Christianity. For Muhammad, "The sword is the key to heaven and hell," while Christ said, "He who lives by the sword shall perish by the sword." While many (or some) Muslims think of jihad as the struggle in the heart, there are also many who see jihad as "essentially a permanent state of hostility that Islam maintains against the rest of the world." Do not forget the **Dar al-Islam** (Land of Submission) and **Dar al-Harb** (Land of War). We cannot forget Ayatollah Khomeini, who started World War IV with his overthrow of the Shah of Iran and is a saint to millions of Muslims, stating that "The sword is the key to paradise" and that this is a war of conquest – "the domination of Koranic law from one end of the earth to the other." Muslims, including American, "are faced with a profound spiritual decision. Can they break with sacramental ties to a religion that is based upon an unending Jihad against all other religions? Other major religions have evolved over the centuries. Only Islam appears resistant to any change." We saw the irrational reaction to the cartoon fiasco which sparked outrage from Muslims. "Islam must reject its intolerance." The vast majority of good Muslims must reclaim their Islam and they must reform it or discard it. The future of Western values and all human progress are at stake.[3] This raises the sad situation wherein if Islam refuses or is unable to reform and join the civilized world, that since it was born by the sword, it may have to die by the sword.

If a nation expects to be ignorant and free, it expects what never was and never will be.
- Thomas Jefferson

Multiculturalism is not bad; it is just that the doctrine is incomplete without **mutuality**. "One of the reasons democracies are so much more enjoyable countries to live in than non-democratic countries is because we are so tolerant of each other." But mutuality is key; the doctrine should be amended to: "We respect all religions and cultures who do us the honor of respecting ours as well. All others will be treated with less generosity." The problem is that "Islamic supremacism is religiously-sanctioned intolerance, and many in the West tolerate the intolerance out of blind multiculturalism." **We must stop tolerating their intolerance.**[4]

Multiculturalism leads to a moral equivalence of white guilt and a "born in a Western country guilt." Victor Davis Hanson made some interesting observations: we have a need for "cultural neutrality" – for seeing ourselves as no better than anybody else. That is not so bad but it becomes so well-ingrained that it causes a kind of willful blindness that overrides common sense and the basic instinct of self-preservation. He wrote that "so strong is the tug of cultural neutrality that it trumps even the revulsion of Western progressives at the…jihadist agenda, with its homophobia, sexism, religious intolerance, and racism." This leads to "the compulsive, undiscriminating reflex to defend Islam and criticize Western countries."[5]

When Jimmy Carter was running for president in 1976, he said America needed "a government as good as its people." Perhaps he was right but not in the way he meant. "The threat to U.S. power comes not principally from Chinese innovation or Indian engineering graduates but from America's own cultural indolence, just as the sack of Rome was a symptom of the fall of the empire rather than the cause."[6] The American people are indifferent and the US Government has lost its way. "The New American Socialism retains the profit motive for the rich and the well connected….It's capitalism for the rich, without any risks. And socialism for the poor, without any rights." "The government takes all of the risk while investors and executives keep all of the profits."[7] Special interest groups take bites out of total national wealth with tax breaks, special appropriations, earmarks, favors, etc. No single one is too much, but over decades, they threaten to convert any stable democracy into a big, inefficient, favor-ridden, corrupt state.   Jonathan Rauch coined the term **"demosclerosis"** – "a government's progressive loss of ability to adapt."

There is growing discontent with the institution of democracy and there is talk now of whether the US is becoming a police state with oppressive break-ins of peoples' homes and strict court decisions,[8] and whether we are facing the end of democracy. There is disillusion with the political pandering of the government, especially the Congress, and concern as to whether there might be a military coup to change the government. It is discouraging to go back and read the 1920 (February 24) Nazi Party platform. Some of it sounds like where we are headed.

Kenneth Minoque, professor at the London School of Economics, wrote in the *Liberal Mind* 50 years ago, that government was obliged to provide the good life, but ended with a warning: "A populace which hands its moral order over to governments, no matter how impeccable its reasons, will become dependent and slavish." In his recent sequel, *The Servile Mind: How Democracy Erodes the Moral Life,* he documents how democracy "requires strict obedience to the state." He was ambivalent about democracy: "We would certainly tolerate no other system in our own country. Yet most people are disenchanted with the way it works. One reason is that our rulers manage so much of our lives that they cannot help but do it badly." He wrote that "governments have no business telling us how to live. They are tiresome enough in the exercise of authority. They are intolerable when they mount the pulpit. Nor should we be in any doubt that nationalizing the moral life of the people is the first step toward totalitarianism."[9]

Now there is argument over the US Constitution and whether it allows certain current practices. The Constitution is not a document delivered from God, but the fought over compromised work of real men who were not even sure it would work. Chief Justice John Marshall wrote that the Constitution was "intended to endure for ages to come, and consequently to be adapted to the various crises of human affairs." This is not a crisis, but a conflict and "Conflict is at the core of our politics, and the Constitution is designed to manage it."[10] Yes, California has 69 times the population of Wyoming and each has 2 votes in the Senate, so does Rhode Island, and half of Americans live in the 10 most populous states, only 20 votes.   And yes we have senators and representatives who stay in Congress forever and become wealthy professional politicians rather than being citizen legislators.   There are arguments over the 14th Amendment and Anchor Babies (The US is the only advanced country left that provides birth citizenship) and perhaps the 17th Amendment should be revisited as to the election of senators by direct vote instead of by state legislatures. There are things that are out of date, but that should be expected after two centuries. The Constitution should be considered a masterful guideline and a work in progress.

A disturbing poll indicated that 69% of Americans believe the US is in "decline" and 83% indicated they were "worried about America's future." This country "was built on self-reliance and personal achievement" and keep government out of the way. Tradition faded with the Viet-Nam War and as the family structure collapsed, entitlements became more common, leading to massive debt. We have lost that economic base of power and only the people can regain it.[11]

The US is no longer No. 1 in spending on research, patents, and venture funding and in measures for innovation (government funding for basic research, education and corporate-tax policies), of 40 countries analyzed, "the U.S. came in dead last." Other countries are putting more money into nurturing new industries, and even though the US government does spend billions, it has become politicized such as going to agribusiness. Apple, the largest company, employs 50,000 people, but Foxconn in Taiwan, which is about the same size and makes many of the Apple products, employs 1,000,000. "We need innovation urgently. But if we are to get the U.S. back to work, we need perhaps even more urgently to rebuild American education, reform our training system, revive high-end manufacturing, focus on new growth industries and rebuild our infrastructure."[12]

Ralph Peters wrote a brilliant article about the American "effete view of warfare" and that none of our enemies can "defeat us in direct confrontation, but we appear determined to defeat ourselves." He listed a number of reasons why Americans had forgotten the cost of victory. We have had safety for so long, "unthinkable" horrors have been erased, the end of the draft gave us a wonderful military but a detached population, "an unholy alliance between defense industry and academic theorists seduced decisionmakers with a false-messiah catechism of bloodless war," a white-collar suburban society that is more litigious than tough, and history is no longer a serious subject in our schools with the result that "politicians lack perspective; journalists lack meaningful touchstones; and the average person's sense of warfare has been redefined by media entertainment."

> **The tree of liberty must be refreshed from time to time with the blood of patriots and tyrants.**
>
> **- Thomas Jefferson**

He contends that we are scared to talk about religion but our Islamic enemy is inspired by it. We are in denial about their objective but they state publicly they want to destroy us. Islam is in a "long descent into cultural darkness and civilizational impotence. Behind all its entertaining bravado, Islam is fighting for its life, for validation." Muslims feel humiliated and are "furiously jealous," not competitive, and barbaric. Peters notes that "our fiercest enemies are in love with death" while we "pretend that war can be made innocently." Instead of agonizing over bloodshed, we need to recognize that "the greatest 'war crime' the United States can commit is to lose." He lambasts the media as "a hostile third party in the fight." They attack our civilization and our troops and portray barbaric enemies as innocent. "Indeed, the passionate belief of so much of the intelligentsia that our civilization is evil and only the savage is noble looks rather like an anemic version of the self-delusions of the terrorists themselves." Peters ended with "Of all the enemies we face today and may face tomorrow, the most dangerous is our own wishful thinking."[13]

How did we reach this state? Are we like the Roman Empire? Victor Davis Hanson wrote an article explaining the Roman decline. He wrote that the great wealth "undermined the old republican virtues of small farmers and merchants" and "created a dependent class on the dole and corruption among the elite." Global standardization and Romanization subsidized Rome – for us it is Americanization, globalization, and the dollar as the world's reserve currency. American culture boomed through much of the 19th and 20th centuries due to "traditional American values like the Protestant work ethic, family thrift, limited and stable government, equality of opportunity rather than result, lower taxes, personal freedom, opportunity for advancement and profit, and faith in American exceptionalism." We have lost our values and now the "emphasis in our schools is more on race/class/gender engineering, regulation, redistribution, etc, all of which in classical terms is not necessarily wealth creation."

We are borrowing $2 trillion annually, half from the Chinese, spending $45,000 a year to keep a felon in prison in California, and feel we are owed a standard of living. What ruined Rome? – "affluence and laxity warped Roman sensibility and created a culture of entitlement that was not justified by revenues or the creation of actual commensurate wealth – and the resulting debits, inflation, debased currency, and gradual state impoverishment." Hanson wrote that these "wild swings in civilization are at their base psychological: decline is one of choice rather than necessity." We could balance our budget tomorrow, we could cut government spending, we could create our own energy – "but too many feel such medicine is worse than the malady, and so we probably won't and can't. An enjoyable slow decline is apparently preferable to a short, but painful rethinking and rebirth."[14]

American's indifference and tuning out of politics and politicians play directly into the hands of the Stealth Jihad which uses our tolerance of other viewpoints against us. The Muslim Brotherhood, and its multitude of affiliates in the US like CAIR and the Muslim Students Association, "has become highly skilled in exploiting the civil liberties and multicultural proclivities of Western societies for the purpose of destroying the latter from within."[15] The American public and its official representatives must realize that these organizations, despite their smooth talk to mislead all, do not wish to operate within our very free system but to destroy that system; that is the definition of **treason**.

It is impossible to know how many Muslims support the jihadis and how many do not. Islam gives poor oppressed people something to feel pride in - perhaps a continuation of former theology student Joseph Stalin's **"religion is the opiate of the masses."** The problem for the rest of the world is that even if there were a large percentage of moderate Muslims, it would make no difference because they are irrelevant. As we have noted in the Arab Turmoil after the Jasmine Revolution, many more Islamists have begun to appear on the scene.

"Regardless of the color of our skin, the color of the blood running through all of our veins is the same. Unfortunately, there are those who believe that a higher spirit has commanded them to kill, convert, or subjugate those who don't follow the same beliefs that they do. This ideology is bigotry and racism in its purest form."[16]

The cost of freedom is always high…and Americans have always paid it. And one path we shall never choose…is the path of surrender or submission.

- John F. Kennedy

Modern communications, particularly including the Internet, but now with Twitter and Facebook, have brought the global situation to almost everyone making it impossible for any regime to keep its people in the dark. The people, particularly the young, can see that their governments have not brought them the prosperity that the West enjoys. Antagonism started toward their governments but then their frustration, or envy, shifted to foreign countries, often the United States. The US Central Command (CENTCOM) and the State Department have both created teams that monitor foreign blogs and respond in their languages. They seem to be effective in establishing dialogue and rebutting some of the wild nonsense that is on the internet.[17]

Despite the many good things Americans have done, the festering sore irritating many, perceived as hypocrisy, is America's blatant and uncritical support for Israel which is viewed as a direct attack on Muslims. The atrocious treatment of the Palestinians by the Israelis openly and clearly supported by the US was endorsed in April 2004 when President Bush announced that Israel would not have to return to the Green Line or give up the colonies, now euphemistically called "major population centers." The Congress responded as always in lockstep (House 407-9 and the Senate 95-3) to Bush's unilateral abrogation of international law and the Israelis immediately accelerated the expansion of their colonies to carve Palestine into cantons. "Apartheid might well emerge in Israel-Palestine, but progressive civil society resistance will render it untenable."[18] In the meantime, the US will remain a target of Muslim hatred.

Israel cannot continue indefinitely as a European enclave of 4 million Jews in the Arab Middle East with no intention of assimilating into the area but only intending to dominate. The idiocy of military superiority with a very large nuclear arsenal, supported by the US, guarantees that Arab/Muslim states will deem they must have nuclear weapons. Israel claims it is threatened by a sea of Arabs, but the truth is that it is the Arab states that are threatened by a nuclear Israel. Israel is the threat that helps destabilize the Middle East. It is Israel that has attacked its neighbors and threatens to attack Iran. There is no logical way to talk Iran out of developing nuclear weapons as long as Israel has its large arsenal. The only way to stop a nuclear arms race in the Middle East will be to remove the Israeli arsenal and that would require a nuclear-free zone, often proposed but always rejected.

The Israelis live in a fantasy world of myths and self-deception. They refuse to acknowledge the results of their own actions and their dreams of expansion. Israeli society is badly divided yet it has some of the best brains in the world, offset by diehard radical colonists, and an ultraorthodox group comparable to their Islamofascist enemies living centuries in the past. Israeli governments have been willing to accept living with an indefinite low level insurgency rather than making peace and giving up their expansionist dreams. They thrive on conspiracy theories, always blaming but not accepting responsibility; it is always someone else's fault (just like their Arab protagonists). The country is in dire need of introspection, settlement of its borders, making peace, and integration into its region.

Israel cannot continue indefinitely as a European enclave of 4 million Jews in the Arab Middle East with no intention of assimilating into the area but only intending to dominate.

The threat of nuclear weapons in the hands of the mullahs in Iran is the Damocles' sword hanging over the world community, even though it might not actually be that great a threat. World War I resulted from a blank check given to Austria by Germany. World War II erupted after Britain gave a blank check to Poland. "No great power should ever give to a small ally or client state a blank check to drag it into a war. This raises the question: Has President Bush given Israel a blank check?"[19] In the current context, even though President Obama has been less supportive of Israel, he cannot give up on them due to the major Jewish role in Democratic politics, but the question is whether the US Congress has given Israel a blank check to attack Iran?

Prime Minister Ehud Olmert finally admitted, after he resigned of course, that Israel needed to withdraw from the colonies and East Jerusalem to attain peace. Noting that defense thinking had not changed since 1948, he said, "Who thinks seriously that if we sit on another hilltop, on another hundred meters, that this will make the difference for the state of Israel's basic security?"[20] There was even talk in Israel that the Saudi Plan had some merit even though they had ignored it for almost a decade. That did not remove the political reality of the requirement to include some of the radical religious parties to form a government.

That introspection is made difficult, if not impossible, by the unthinking US support led by the neocons, the Israel Firsters, the Israel Lobby, and the Christian Zionists. These people work not only against the long term interests of Israel but also against the US national interest which calls for a stable Middle East. Changing the regime in Iraq "while leaving the Palestinians to face Israeli tanks and helicopter gunships is a virtual guarantee of unending Islamic wrath against the United States." Some form of settlement meeting at least some of the Palestinian aspirations, perhaps with UN support and guarantees, is required – even a UN Mandate perhaps. "This is an awesomely tall order, but if America cannot find the will to enforce this minimum of justice, neither it nor Israel will have any safety from terror.... A successful American political strategy against terror depends on providing enough peace for both Israelis and Palestinians that extremists on either side begin to lose the support that keeps violence alive."[21]

Michael Scheuer, in his book *Imperial Hubris,* posed the questions that need debating:

> Does unvarying military, economic, and political support for Israel serve substantive – *vice* emotional – U.S. interests, those that by definition affect America's survival? Do we totally support Israel because it is essential to our security, or because of habit, the prowess of Israel's American lobbyists and spies, the half-truth mantra that Israel is a democracy, the fear of having no control over a state we allowed to become armed with WMD, the bewildering pro-Israeli alliances of the liberal democrats and Christian fundamentalists, and a misplaced sense of guilt over the Holocaust?

Scheuer then defined the main point: "The question is whether U.S. interests require Americans to be Israel's protectors and endure the endless blood-and-treasure cost of that role." The logical answer to that is No. He warned that the "Status quo U.S. policy toward Israel will result in unending war with Islam."[22] As Ronald Reagan said: "status quo" is Latin for "the mess we're in."

There are other major territorial disputes whose resolution would greatly aid world peace. One that seriously impinges on our operations in Afghanistan is Kashmir. The US or any major power or the UN should offer its good offices to remove this festering sore between two nuclear powers. Another is the South China Sea where China and the neighboring countries dispute the territorial waters because of the potential for oil and gas. The UN or an international commission is needed to resolves these disputes to preclude military actions. It would be helpful if an international body created global guidelines for waterways traversing international boundaries.

Despite having the greatest military force in history, American power is slowing drifting away. The New World Order will evolve with China and India, with well over one third of the world's population, as new centers of power. Russia is recovering, despite its projected population loss, due to its oil/natural gas wealth, and is rebuilding its military. An economic interdependence has evolved with China. Their economy is fragile with a real estate slump and any reduction in their exports threatens political instability. We are subsidizing their economic development and they are feeding our demand economy and carrying our debt. With hundreds of millions of Chinese moving to the cities, they need jobs; therefore, it will remain in the interest of both countries to continue strong economic and military ties and not let them be disrupted.

A business and trade corridor is growing between the Middle East and Asia, dubbed the "new Silk Road" which is "largely the result of the confluence of China's and India's economic growth and high oil prices." Dubai is the unofficial capital in the Middle East of the new Silk Road while the GCC (Gulf Cooperation Council) countries have been investing strongly in banking, real estate, and infrastructure across Asia. Since a great deal of that money came from the US, we should try to attract some of that GCC money to our hemisphere.[23] Some of it does in the military purchases of billions of dollars projected due to their concern about Iran.

A great civilization cannot be destroyed from outside if it has not already destroyed itself from within.

- Will Durant

Through our totally inept energy policy, we have permitted a massive shift of wealth to the oil producing countries, some of whom are financing our enemies. We have an ever more intrusive government trying to regulate everything, led by Democrats and the socialistic ideas of Obama. The world economy fell into turmoil, sparked by the mortgage crisis in the US which had been created by Congress (investment institutions were forced to lend money to unqualified people under Presidents Carter and Clinton), the same people who were going to fix it. The price of oil came down, not due to the rantings of Congress at oil company presidents, but due to a reaffirmation that the law of supply and demand is still more significant than talking heads in Congress.

The new religion is environmentalism – the unlimited "license to intrude." "Ecofundamentalism, the quasi-religion of green alarmism" promises "global salvation,"[24] while they are destroying our economy. Despite the "breathing spell" provided by new shale oil and natural gas discoveries, the country desperately needs an energy policy that will develop alternative fuels to free us from the internal combustion engine. Since the government has refused to act, they should consider tasking and funding DARPA (Defense Department's research arm - they created the Internet, not Al Gore) with the mission. In the meantime, the stupidity of no drilling offshore or in ANWR, no new nuclear power plants (finally moving slowly), and no new refineries, must be reversed. The lack of political leadership in energy borders on treason.

Americans have never been good at empire. Edward Gibbon noted in *The Decline and Fall of the Roman Empire* in 1776 that "empires endure so long as their rulers take care not to overextend their borders." But "vanity or ignorance" led them astray. "This characteristic delusion of imperial power is to confuse global power with global domination." Michael Ignatieff wrote that America is becoming an empire even if in a "state of deep denial." But "even the overwhelmingly powerful need friends and allies." He reminded us that "Empires survive when they understand that diplomacy backed by force, is always to be preferred to force alone." Empire is no match in the long term for nationalism. "The age of empire ought to have been succeeded by an age of independent, equal, and self-governing nation-states. But that has not come to pass. America has inherited a world scarred not just by the failure of empires past but also by the failure of nationalist movements to create and secure free states – and now suddenly, by the desire of Islamists to build theocratic tyrannies on the ruins of failed nationalist dreams." He ended with the US cannot control the struggle and that "empires survive only by knowing their limits."[25]

Experience has taught us that no one nation has the power or the wisdom to solve all the problems of the world or manage its revolutionary tides; that extending our commitments does not always increase our security.

- John F. Kennedy, 25 May 1961

A wise military officer put our problem in Iraq in perspective as the collision of logics. He said that General David Petraeus and Ambassador Ryan Crocker are on the protracted warfare/nation building logic which accepts small gains and advocates endless patience. He said the Senate, particularly in a long election period, is on a public policy/domestic politics logic set. That creates timelines and abandons non-productive courses of action. Public policies have rollouts, mid-points, and end dates; protracted conflicts do not. He said that the Senate is unschooled in war and is unwilling to accept a realistic, but tortuous, process of winning a protracted war. He ended on a pessimistic note in that we have made progress following Sun Tsu in knowing your enemy, but we are not sure who we are. We are the people of plenty and the people of "right now." We may be organically unable to fight and win the wars that civilization and its faults have put in our paths. The last best hope of mankind may just not be good enough.[26]

When we find ourselves starting to believe all the anti-American sentiment and negativity about our government and its policies, we might remember what England's Prime Minister Tony Blair said. During an interview, he was asked by one of his parliament members why he believed so much in America. His reply: "A simple way to take measure of a country is to look at how many want in ... And how many want out."

In 1940, we knew who we were, we knew who the enemy was, we knew the dangers and the issues,...It is different today. We don't know who we are, we don't know the issues, and we still do not understand the nature of the enemy.

- Bernard Lewis[27]

We are fighting a worldwide Islamic insurgency, not terrorism or criminality. We are fighting a mindset, an ideology. General John Abizaid compared it to the 1920s when Communism and Nazism had not really taken hold in Russia and Germany. We must prevent it from taking hold, but that will be a long course with a long commitment. There is no geographical center; it is a virtual organization connected by the Internet. We need to openly discuss it and we need the will of the American people to be sustained for the long haul.[28]

Bat Ye'or said, "The war against a global jihadist terrorism can be won only if the civilized world is united against barbarity." She summed it up with, "America has the choice of forgoing its liberty and adopting the European line of dhimmitude and supplication, or maintaining its resolve to fight the war against terrorism for freedom and for universal human rights values."[29] Herbert Meyer put the cost in perspective. "The culture war is the whole ballgame. If we lose it, there isn't another America to pull us out."[30]

Remember: You are the target of a massive psychological program to take over the USA.

Europe and Japan are dying due to decline of their populations. Japan will not import workers so it is just shutting down having closed some 2,000 schools and closing about 300 annually. Europe brought in millions of Muslims but they did not integrate into the culture and so they have a political disaster. Europe will either soon become Eurabia or else dictators will arise who will drive out the non-Europeans; either case will be ruinous. The US is facing a similar threat from a large illegal immigrant population that refuses to integrate and some of whom have revanchist dreams of reuniting with Mexico. This group threatens the future of the USA. If they are granted amnesty, only millions more will rapidly follow like the last amnesty. Will a man on a White Horse appear to save the country or will the US devolve into a Third World country? Neither is good; we are on a path to national suicide. "That cultural unity, that sense that we were one people, is gone. Today's immigrants exceed in number anything any nation has ever known. They now come from cultures and countries whose people have never before been assimilated by any First World country. Not only is the Melting Pot broken, it is rejected by our elites. Minorities are urged to hold onto their own language, customs, traditions. Identity politics is in."

The one absolutely certain way of bringing this nation to ruin, of preventing all possibility of its continuing to be a nation at all, would be to permit it to become a tangle of squabbling nationalities.

- Theodore Roosevelt addressing the Knights of Columbus in 1915[31]

The question is sometimes asked whether Israel would live to 100 and the answer is doubtful. The next question is whether the USA will live to 300 and again it appears doubtful. The type of people we have in the Congress and the narcissistic types who run for president show no evidence of the ability required to lead this country through this century. Alexander Tyler, a Scottish history professor at the University of Edinburgh wrote in 1787, about the time our country was formed, concerning the fall of the Athenian Republic:

> **A democracy is always temporary in nature; it simply cannot exist as a permanent form of government. A democracy will continue to exist up until the time that voters discover that they can vote themselves generous gifts from the public treasury. From that moment on, the majority always votes for candidates who promise the most benefits from the public treasury, with the result that every democracy will finally collapse due to loose fiscal policy, which is always followed by a dictatorship.**
>
> **The average age of the world's greatest civilizations from the beginning of history, has been about 200 years. During those 200 years, those nations always progressed through the following sequence:**
> 1. **from bondage to spiritual faith;**
> 2. **from spiritual faith to great courage;**
> 3. **from courage to liberty;**
> 4. **from liberty to abundance**
> 5. **from abundance to complacency;**
> 6. **from complacency to apathy;**
> 7. **from apathy to dependence;**
> 8. **from dependence back into bondage.**

It would appear that the US is now somewhere between "complacency" and "apathy," with about half of the population already in the government dependency phase.

> **Remember, democracy never lasts long. It soon wastes, exhausts, and murders itself. There never was a democracy yet that did not commit suicide.**
> **- John Adams**

We are in a Long War and we need to get off our short attention span and recognize it. We must teach our children more history. We, as a people, are grossly ignorant of history. If you do not know history, you cannot understand the present or prepare for the future! Many of our citizens lack pride in our country because academia has refused to teach them the history of this great country and the sacrifices of our forefathers, and in many cases have actually denigrated it! Europe was occupied during the first half of the 19th century fighting Napoleon and from 1870 to 1945 fighting Germany. World War II did not start at Pearl Harbor, but in 1928 with the Japanese invasion of China. It was officially over in 1945 – 17 years - but there was a ten-year occupation making it a 27 year war. Its adjusted cost was almost a full year's world GDP – about $12 trillion with between 50 and 100 million killed. World War III, the Cold War, lasted 42 years – from about 1947 until the Berlin Wall came down in 1989. World War IV has already gone on for 33 years with no end in sight. It portends to dominate the 21st century.

History is replete with clashes of cultures about ideas and power, ideas about what civilization and society should be and who should rule. Now we face a breed of militant

Muslims, who like to call themselves Jihadis, but Raymond Kraft and others prefer to call them Nazis in Kaffiyehs. They believe that their radical form of Wahhabism should control the world and anyone who does not agree should be killed, enslaved, or subjugated. Unless we want an Islamic America, something like Iran, we have to deal with these barbarians until we defeat them, because they will not go away just by ignoring them. The stakes are high: a world of representative legal governments with civil and human rights and personal freedom or a world dominated by radical Muslim mullahs and sharia.

Egypt: Women Herded and Tied Like Camels[32]

Note the rope around the women, herding them like camels; note the man to the right holding the leash, walking them. Some say this is a common "precautionary measure" to keep women form mixing with men during protests. Is that what you want for the women of America? Look again at the photos in Appendix B.

This is truly a world war because it has already extended from the Americas to Europe to Africa to Asia. The Shia already have their territorial base in Iran but the Wahhabi Sunnis do not, (not completely that is since they share power in Saudi Arabia) since they lost Afghanistan under the Taliban; however, they have partially reestablished a base in the tribal areas of Pakistan along the Afghan border. Fortunately, there is still the schism between Shia and Sunnis. Recall that Abu Mousad al-Zarqawi was reprimanded by Ayman al-Zawahiri for killing Shia in Iraq. Despite that division, both are still a threat to modern Western life. It is not merely a matter of defeating Western civilization, they seek to destroy it and turn it into history.

Islam/Sharia – Communism with a God.

- Frank Gaffney

We have already noted many possible actions that should be taken. The major one is we must defend freedom of speech. We must rebuild our economy. We must say NO to Imperial Islam. We must stop granting Islam a free pass as a religion and treat it for what it is: a totalitarian ideology like communism or fascism. For radical Islamists there are only two ways: as Ralph Peters said "the leading rebels or terrorists must be killed"[33] or we must pressure them to the point where they renounce their quest for world domination. We must end our suicidal trend toward cultural relativism, multiculturalism, and political correctness when there is no mutuality and we are being duped. We must stop Islamization and Deamericanization, control immigration (including Muslim and Hispanic) if they do not wish to assimilate, expel criminal immigrants and prosecute any who preach sedition or treason. We must restrict the building of mosques and Muslim schools and monitor both now. We must restrict foreign language media and firmly establish that English is the language of this country. We must restore pride in this great country as a nation state. Finally, we must elect wise and courageous leaders who will face the threat to our economy, the threat from Islam, the threat from illegal immigration, denounce unthinking multiculturalism, and place the interests and security of the USA foremost.

There are some who see the Long War as "a monumental flop" and that rather than trying to change the world, we should change America. They see a different choice:

> We can either persist in our efforts to change the way they live – in which case the war of no exits will surely lead to bankruptcy and exhaustion. Or we can recognize the folly of generational war and choose instead to put our house in order: curbing our appetites, paying our bills and ending our self-destructive dependency on foreign oil and foreign credit.[34]

I agree with the professor on some of his points, but I do not think we have that luxury. This is not a fight one can walk away from; they will just bring it to us; they already have!

The world needs a reduction in egos. We are still in the age of ignorance. Even in 1982, the influential chief mufti in Saudi Arabia could write a book that Earth is the center of the universe and the sun moves around it. He also claimed that the 1969 landing on the moon was a TV fake.[35] Bill Anders (former CEO of General Dynamics and pilot for the lunar module on the Apollo 8 mission) emphasized how we are small and insignificant. There are over 100 billion galaxies, most with billions of stars and Earth is a tiny planet in an obscure galaxy. The distance to the moon is only 1.5 light seconds, yet the Hubble Space Telescope has now seen out to 13 billion light years – that is 880,000,000,000,000,000,000,000,000 (880 sextillion) miles. Yes, we are insignificant![36]

World War II was two different wars at the same time. World War III was a struggle between two radically different ideologies and it ended with the failure of communism. With the war over the Third Jihad, an unstable world, our fiscal irresponsibility, illegal immigration (which may prove to be a greater threat to the US than the Islamists), an evolving new world order with the rise of China and the leftist surge in Latin America, the threat of Eurabia, growing shortages of oil and water, burgeoning and aging world population, World War IV may prove to be the Complex War. The major threat is our economy which can destroy the fabric of our society. The US Government refuses to adequately address our dependence on foreign oil which is a major cause of the damage to our economy accompanied by the profligacy of elected officials. Islam is a more insidious threat because of our kindness: we need first to recognize the seriousness of the threat and its total incompatibility with democracy and liberty, then expose it for the farce that it is, and finally purge it from our country. Individually these threats might be manageable, but taken together they could produce the thousand cuts that could bleed our great country. These are problems that cannot be ignored. They must be faced and resolved or there will be no United States of America. **Wake up America!**

> War is an ugly thing, but not the ugliest. The decayed and degraded state of moral and patriotic feeling which thinks nothing is worth a war is worse. A man who has nothing which he cares about more than his personal safety is a miserable creature and has no chance of being free, unless made and kept so by the exertions of better men than himself.
>
> - John Stuart Mill

Postscript

As a reminder about our economic crisis and how democracies commit suicide, we should look back at Argentina. In 1902, Argentina was one of the richest countries in the world. Great Britain's maritime power and its wide empire made it dominant among the world's industrialized nations, only the United States challenged Argentina for the second spot. Like the US, Argentina has abundant agriculture with rich farmland, navigable rivers, and accessible ports. Its level of industrialization exceeded many European countries. But in 1916, they elected a new president, Hipólito Irigoyen, of The Radical party with a banner of "Fundamental Change" - an appeal to the middle class. The changes were mandatory pension insurance, mandatory health insurance, and support for low-income housing construction to stimulate the economy. In short, the state assumed economic control of a large part of the country's operations and began assessing new payroll taxes to fund its efforts. With this income flow into the entitlement programs, the government payouts soon became overly generous. Before long, outlays surpassed the income – the government was underfunded – similar to Social Security and Medicare in the US.

The death knell came with the election of Juan Perón (and his wife Eva) and his fascist background. His populist agenda was to tax the rich. The size of the government bureaucracy exploded with government jobs which attracted the peons from the countryside, which caused a decline in beef and wheat production. By 1970, there were meatless days and Argentina was importing wheat. By 1989, there was hyperinflation, imposition of more taxes, and by 2002 the comparison was with the Great Depression.

A man from Argentina wrote "We pay only cash here for homes, cars, etc (credit does not exist, for all practical purposes), and when I say cash, I mean bills with Ben's face on them (no, Franklin's). It's not uncommon for 400 grand to change hands in a private room in a bank. After 2 centuries of cronyism in government and blatant abuse of the system, it falls apart. Nobody believes in anything except 'things' and cash (read Greenbacks, and now even those won't be worth the paper they are printed on). **Welcome to our World...the third one!"**

Notes

1. Irshad Manji, "When Denial Can Kill: We Muslims must admit that our religion might be motivating the bombers," *Time,* 25 July 2005. Manji is the author of *The Trouble with Islam Today: A Wake-Up Call for Honesty and Change.*
2. "Prince Turki Al-Faisal Addresses 59th MEI Conference," *Washington Report on Middle East Affairs (WRMEA),* January/February 2006, p. 73. Prince Turki was Saudi Ambassador to the US and spoke at the National Press Club on 8 November 2005.
3. Alan Caruba, "Islam: The Endless Jihad," Daily Mail Reporter, 1 July 2008.
4. "How a Tolerant Country Can Avoid Being a Doormat for Intolerant Countries," Citizen Warrior, 18 November 2011.
5. "The Key to Your Listener's Inability to Confront the Disturbing Truth About Islam," Citizen Warrior, 7 May 2011.
6. Mark Steyn, *America Alone,* (Washington, DC, Regnery Publishing, Inc., 2006), p. 207.
7. Porter Stansberry, "New American Socialism," Stansberry's Investment Advisory, June 2011.
8. See for example, Doug Hornig, "This Is America?" Casey Research, 10 June 2011.
9. Neil Reynolds, "Nationalizing the moral life of the people is the first step toward totalitarianism," *Globe and Mail* (Canada), 4 October 2010.
10. *Time* did a cover article by Richard Stengel, "Does It Still Matter?" 4 July 2011, p. 32. Se also, James Fallows, "How America Can Rise Again," *The Atlantic,* January/February 2010.
11. Bill O'Reilly, "Hard working folks built the world's greatest country," *Reno Gazette-Journal,* 30 October 2011, p. 7D. See also his column, "All aboard the federal spending gravy train," 31 October 2010, p. 9D. He notes that "far-left billionaire George Soros donated $1.8 million to NPR so they could hire some reporters." O'Reillly was writing about the heavy left tilt of NPR and PBS. George Soros was born György Schwartz in Hungary 12 August 1930 in a non-practicing Jewish family. In 1944, he worked for a man who was confiscating Jewish property – which he called the "best year of his life."
12. Fareed Zakaria, "Innovate Better" *Time,* 13 June 2011, p. 30.
13. Ralph Peters, "Wishful Thinking and Indecisive Wars," *The Journal of International Security Affairs,"* Spring 2009 – No. 16.
14. Victor Davis Hanson, "Why Did Rome Fall – And Why Does It Matter Now?" Pajamas Media, February 2010.
15. "Shariah: The Threat to America," The Center for Security Policy, 2010, p. 10.
16. D.C. Watson – 9 August 2006 interview at Frontpagemag.com.
17. Thom Shanker and Eric Schmitt, "U.S. Military Goes Online To Rebut Extremists' Message," *The New York Times,* 18 November 2011. CENTCOM established its Digital Engagement Team in 2008 with 20 native speakers and State has its Digital Outreach Team with Arabic and Urdu speakers.
18. Jeff Halper, "The Narrow Gate to Peace," *WRMEA,* September/October 2005, p. 20.
19. Patrick J. Buchanan, "No More Blank Checks for War," HumanEventsOnline.com, 11 July 2008. "After the assassination of the archduke in Sarajevo on June 28, 1914, Austria got from Kaiser Wilhelm a 'blank cheque' to punish Serbia. Germany would follow whatever course its ally chose to take. Austria chose war on Serbia. And World War I resulted.

    "On March 31, 1939, Britain gave a blank check to Poland in its dispute with Germany over Danzig, a town of 350,000 Germans. Should war come, Britain would fight on Poland's side. Poland refused to negotiate, Adolf Hitler attacked, and Britain declared war. After six years, the British Empire collapsed. Germany was burnt to ashes. Poland entered the slave quarters of Joseph Stalin's empire."
20. Ethan Bronner, "Olmert says Israel should pull out of West Bank," http://www.iht.com/articles/2008/09/29/mideast/israel.php.
21. Michael Ignatieff, "The Burden," *The New York Times Magazine,* 5 January 2003, p. 22.
22. *Imperial Hubris: Why the West is Losing the War on Terror,* (Washington, D.C., Brassey's, Inc., 2004), p. 257.
23. Afshin Molavi, "The New Silk Road," *The Washington Post,* 9 April 2007, reprinted in Other Voices, *WRMEA,* July 2007, p. OV-14.
24. See George Will, "Polar bears launch war over warming," *Reno Gazette-Journal,* 24 May 2008, p.4D.
25. Ignatieff, "The Burden."
26. Personal correspondence, 17 April 2008.
27. Quoted from *The Wall Street Journal,* in Steyn, *America Alone,* p. 208.
28. General Abizaid Comments to Naval War College Students, 23 November 2005.
29. Jamie Glazov, "Eurabia," FrontPageMagazine.com, 21 September 2004, interview with Bat Ye'or.
30. "Four Major World Transformations Shaping Political, Economic & World Events," A Global Intelligence Briefing for CEOs.
31. Pat Buchanan, "Path to national suicide," WorldNetDaily.com, 22 May 2007.
32. The photograph was taken at a Salafi demonstration in Cairo on 29 April 2011 and made the rounds on various Arabic websites. Considering that certain Islamic texts describe females as "she-camels in heat," or that it is traditional for some men to divorce their wives by saying "you are given free rein and unloosed like that camel," or that Muslims are thought to have a mind-frame rooted in sand, camels, and ropes – this measure must surely seem natural.

    The signs say "They slaughtered Salwa Adel, because she converted to Islam, killed her child and husband. We call for the release of Muslim females who are detained in the churches before they kill them." The problem with that is that it was Muslims who were forcibly converting Coptic Christian women and killing Copts and burning their churches.

    At any rate, to those who think that history must always progress, take note: fifty years ago, the overwhelming majority of women in Egypt wore dresses, hair uncovered, and would never have condescended to being walked on a leash. Such is "progress" – "Arab Spring" style. Raymond Fitzgerald, Jihad Watch, 10 November 2011.
33. Ralph Peters, "Wishful Thinking and Indecisive Wars."
34. Andrew J. Bacevich, "The 'Long War' Fallacy," *Los Angeles Times,* 13 May 2008, p. 17. Bacevich teaches at Boston University.
35. Malise Ruthven, *A Fury For God,* (London, Granta Books, 2004), p. 148.
36. http://www.flixxy.com/hubble-ultra-deelp-field-3d.htm.

GLOSSARY

ACLU: American Civil Liberties Union.

ACORN: Association of Community Organizations for Reform Now.

AFL-CIO: American Federation of Labor – Congress of Industrial Organizations.

ANWR: Alaska National Wildlife Reserve.

AQAP: Al Qaeda in the Arabian Peninsula.

AQIM: Al Qaeda in the Islamic Maghreb.

AMC: American Muslim Council.

ASBM: Anti-Ship Ballistic Missile.

ATF: Bureau of Alcohol, Tobacco, Firearms and Explosives.

CAIR: Council on American-Islamic Relations.

CASA: Group in Maryland to support Central American refugees.

CBO: Congressional Budget Office.

CCTV: Closed Circuit TV.

CEO: Chief Executive Officer.

CIA: Central Intelligence Agency.

CNN: Cable News Network.

COLA: Cost of Living Allowance.

DARPA: Defense Advanced Research Projects Agency.

DHS: Department of Homeland Security.

DOD: Department of Defense.

DOE: Department of Energy

DOJ: Department of Justice

DREAM Act: Development, Relief and Education for Alien Minors Act.

ESL: English as a Second Language.

EU: European Union.

FAO: Food and Agriculture Organization (UN).

FATA: Federally Administered Tribal Areas (in Pakistan next to Afghanistan).

FBI: Federal Bureau of Investigation.

FBIS: Foreign Broadcast Information Service (provided by the CIA).

GCC: Gulf Cooperation Council (Bahrain, Kuwait, Oman, Qatar, Saudi Arabia, and the United Arab Emirates).

GDP: Gross Domestic Product.

GPS: Global Positioning System.

HLF: Holy Land Foundation.

ICBM: Intercontinental Ballistic Missile.

ICE: US Immigration and Custom Enforcement.

ICNA: Islamic Circle of North America.

IED: Improvised Explosive Device.

IIIT: Islamic Institute of Islamic Thought.

ISAF: International Security Assistance Force (Afghanistan).

IRS: Internal Revenue Service.

ISI: Inter-Services Intelligence (Pakistan).

ISNA: Islamic Society of North America.

MANPADS: Man Portable Air Defense System (like STINGER).

MAS: Muslim American Society.

MEChA: Moviemento Estudiantil, Chicano de Atzlán (Chicano Student Movement of Atzlan).

MEMRI: Middle East Media Research Institute.

Mossad: Israeli intelligence service.

MPAC: Muslim Public Affairs Council.

MSA: Muslim Students Association.

Mujahedin: Muslim freedom fighters

NAIT: North American Islamic Trust.

NATO: North Atlantic Treaty Organization.

NGOs: Non-Governmental Organizations.

NIE: National Intelligence Estimate.

NPR: National Public Radio.

NSA: National Security Agency.

NSC: National Security Council.

NYPD: New York Police Department.

OECD: Organization for Economic Cooperation and Development (Europe).

OIC: Organization of Islamic Conference, changed to Cooperation.

OPEC: Organization of Petroleum Exporting Countries.

PA: Palestinian Authority.

PBS: Public Broadcasting System.

PLA: People's Liberation Army (China).

PLAN: People's Liberation Army Navy.

PLO: Palestine Liberation Organization.

PM: Prime Minister.

PRC: People's Republic of China.

ROTC: Reserve Officers Training Course.

SSBNs: Nuclear powered strategic ballistic missile submarines.

SU: Soviet Union (broke up into 15 states).

TCO: Transnation Criminal Organizations.

TOC: Transnational Organized Crime.

UAE: United Arab Emirates.

UIC: Union of Islamic Courts (in Somalia).

UK: United Kingdom, Great Britain.

UN: United Nations.

UNGA: United Nations General Assembly.

UNRWA: United Nations Relief and Works Agency.

UNSC: United Nations Security Council.

USCIS: US Citizenship and Immigration Services.

WMD: Weapons of Mass Destruction.

WRMEA: The Washington Report on Middle East Affairs.

WSAG: Washington Special Action Group.

Index

RESOURCE DIRECTORY

The following books by Richard Hobbs are available from ColDoc Publishing. There is an order form on the next page.

WORLD WAR IV AND BEYOND Islamofascism, the Third Jihad, and other threats to the USA
We have been engaged in World War IV for almost 30 years, yet many still refuse to recognize it. This critical war against radical Muslims is also a civil war within Islam. We must deal with this major threat plus the problems of oil, weapons of mass destruction, as well as the threat of a detoriating Europe going Muslim. To compound the threats to the USA, we are faced with overpopulation in the world, illegal immigration and Deamericanization of the USA, a leftist surge in Latin America, movement of al Qaeda into Africa, the looming uncertainty of China, and fiscal irresponsibility.

ISBN: 978-0-9647788-5-6 Softcover, 7 x 10, 476 pages (including 125 pages of notes), index, $29.95

YOU AND THE NEW WORLD ORDER How You Can Influence the Alarming and Growing Domestic and International Problems
This book took The New World Order below and made it into a citizens' handbook by determining some of the options available and possible actions that could be taken to address some of these enormous problems. After a brief review of how we got into this mess, it addresses tribalism, nationalism, religion, the nation state, the United Nations, war crimes, overpopulation, famine, disease, unemployment, migration, terrorism, war, and the mess in America, including guns, drugs, crime, welfare, and minorities. It asks where are we going? where do we want to go? and asks you, the citizen, to take part in determining that future.

ISBN: 0-9647788-6-6 Softcover, 5.5 x 8.5, 256 pages, index, $19.95.

THE MYTH OF VICTORY What Is Victory In War?
Foreword by Admiral Arleigh Burke, former Chief of Naval Operations and founder of The Center for Strategic and International Studies in Washington. This book examines the need for reconciliation between the democratic dislike of war and the appropriate use of the military instrument in world politics. It questions whether the results obtained in war are worth the expenditures made and contends that victory gained from total war is illusory and not commensurate with the terrible cost. (Originally published by Frederick Praeger at Westview Press)

ISBN: 0-89158-388-2, Hardcover, 6 x 9, 566 pages, index, $29.95.

For orders or information, contact:

ColDoc Publishing
P. O. Box 50682-S, Sparks, Nevada 89435-0682 USA
Tel. (775) 424-6333 Fax: (775) 424-6334
E-Mail: coldoc@coldoc.com
Or visit our web site at
http://coldoc.com

ORDER FORM

Fax orders: (775) 424-6334

Telephone orders: (775) 424-6333 (9 to 5 Pacific time)

Postal orders: ColDoc Publishing
P. O. Box 50682-S
Sparks, Nevada 89435-0682 USA

E-Mail: coldoc@coldoc.com

On line: http://coldoc.com

Please send _____ copy (ies) of **Death by a Thousand Cuts**
(ISBN 978-0-9647788-8-7) $29.95 each.

I understand that I may return any books for a full refund -- for any reason, no questions asked.

Other books or paintings:

_____

_____

Company name: _____

Name:_____

Address:_____

City: _____State:_____Zip:_____ - _____

Telephone:(____)_____Fax:(____)_____

E-mail:_____

Sales tax:

Please add 7.725% for books shipped to Nevada addresses.

Shipping:

Book rate: $4.50 for the first book and $1.75 for each additional book.
Contact ColDoc Publishing for International Rates and Shipping and Handling for Paintings.

Payment:

❑ Check   ❑ Money Order   Make payable to Richard Hobbs/ColDoc Publishing

To order using a credit card, go to the E-store on http://coldoc.com

Total Amount: _____

CPSIA information can be obtained at www.ICGtesting.com
Printed in the USA
LVOW010155140912

298754LV00004BA/51/P

9 780964 778887